Lecture Notes in Computer Science 13341

More information about this series at https://link.springer.com/bookseries/558

Klaus Miesenberger ·
Georgios Kouroupetroglou · Katerina Mavrou ·
Roberto Manduchi ·
Mario Covarrubias Rodriguez · Petr Penáz (Eds.)

Computers Helping People with Special Needs

18th International Conference, ICCHP-AAATE 2022
Lecco, Italy, July 11–15, 2022
Proceedings, Part I

Springer

Editors
Klaus Miesenberger
Johannes Kepler University
Linz, Austria

Katerina Mavrou
European University Cyprus
Engomi, Cyprus

Mario Covarrubias Rodriguez
Politecnico di Milano
Milan, Italy

Georgios Kouroupetroglou
National and Kapodistrian University of Athens
Athens, Greece

Roberto Manduchi
University of California at Santa Cruz
Santa Cruz, CA, USA

Petr Penáz
Masaryk University
Brno, Czech Republic

ISSN 0302-9743 ISSN 1611-3349 (electronic)
Lecture Notes in Computer Science
ISBN 978-3-031-08647-2 ISBN 978-3-031-08648-9 (eBook)
https://doi.org/10.1007/978-3-031-08648-9

This Springer imprint is published by the registered company Springer Nature Switzerland AG
The registered company address is: Gewerbestrasse 11, 6330 Cham, Switzerland

Preface

Welcome to the proceedings of ICCHP-AAATE 2022! We are delighted to present to you the proceedings of the Joint International Conference on Digital Inclusion, Assistive Technology, and Accessibility, a conference jointly organized by the International Conference on Computers Helping People with Special Needs (ICCHP) and the Association for the Advancement of Assistive Technology in Europe (AAATE).

Rapid technological deployments are showing the way to a world with no barriers and more flexibility, with personalized and adaptable technologies that will allow full participation of people with disabilities of all ages. We are in a position to hold high-level discussions on the topics of eHealth and eCare, eLearning and eInclusion, eDemocracy and eGovernment, eServices and social innovation, ambient and assisted active living, accessible traveling and tourism, user centered design for all, and many others.

Within this framework, and after the COVID-19 pandemic forced us to cancel AAATE 2021 and move ICCHP 2020 online, we decided to join efforts and propose a new venue for researchers and practitioners in assistive and access technologies, to showcase their work and mingle together. By merging our bi-annual meetings into a single event, we endeavored to provide a single platform for exchanging ideas, stimulating conversation, and facilitating networking. The result is a success in terms of the number of answers to the Call for Contributions and the broader and richer thematic scope: we received a total of 37 proposals for Special Thematic Sessions (STS). A total of 285 abstracts were submitted from which 112 were accepted for publication in these proceedings. More than 25 proposals for workshops, tutorials, seminars, posters, policy sessions, and a product/demonstrator presentation framed a rich and interesting program for discussion and exchange.

The ICCHP-AAATE joint conference was hosted during July 11–15, 2022, by the Politecnico di Milano at its campus in Lecco, by the picturesque Lake Como. Following the tradition of the ICCHP and AAATE biannual meetings, it was an event open to everyone and anyone interested in new and original ways to put technology at the service of people living with a disability. ICCHP-AAATE 2022 hosted presentations, panels, and forums devoted to the creation of tools, systems, and services that are accessible by design and that can level the playing field for a world where everyone can enjoy equal opportunities. By bringing the AAATE and ICCHP communities together, this joint conference explored the common threads linking policy, practice, research, and advocacy for people living with disabilities, working together towards a more equitable, just, and participatory future.

Participants contributed to the conference in multiple ways. The scientific contributions, which underwent a rigorous peer review process, are now available in two different publications:

- these Springer Lecture Notes in Computer Science (LNCS) volumes, which focus more on the development, engineering, and computer science perspective of assistive technology and accessibility, and

- the open access compendium Assistive Technology, Accessibility and (e)Inclusion, which focuses more on the policy, education, implementation, and social services perspective of the field.

Both publications are structured into 22 Special Thematic Sessions. The review process involved 137 experts from around the globe. Three to five independent reviews of each submitted abstract were assessed by one of the program chairs to allow a fair final decision on acceptance during a two-day decision meeting and to provide professional advice for the submissions of the camera-ready versions of papers for publication.

This three step review process sought to guarantee the high-quality of the ICCHP-AAATE publications. Additionally, ICCHP-AAATE invited selected sessions on topics of high interest to publish new and extended work in their domain in a Special Issue of AAATE's Technology and Disability Journal.

Contributions to the Inclusion Forum, which provided a space for discussion, collaborations, and participation of multiple stakeholders, were reviewed by the Program Committee and presented in the conference in different programs including workshops, tutorials, seminars, poster sessions, and policy sessions with panel discussions. It also included a space where participants showcased projects, products, and services. Inclusion Forum contributions are published in the Book of Abstracts, which collects short descriptions and abstracts of all contributions to the conference. In addition, students presented their ongoing research in the Young Researchers' Consortium.

We would like to thank all the members of the Scientific Committee, the Young Researchers Committee, the Inclusion Forum Committee, the Organization Committee, the additional paper reviewers, and the student volunteers who dedicated precious time and effort to the organization of this event.

Moreover, we want to thank all of the participants at the conference for furthering the mission of AAATE and ICCHP, based on the belief that technology can contribute to breaking barriers, empowering people, and enhancing equity and inclusion for people with all abilities.

July 2022

Klaus Miesenberger
Georgios Kouroupetroglou
Katerina Mavrou
Roberto Manduchi
Mario Covarrubias Rodriguez
Petr Penáz

Organization

Conference Chair

Mavrou, K.	European University Cyprus, Cyprus

Scientific Chair

Manduchi, R.	University of California, Santa Cruz, USA

Publication Committee

Covarrubias Rodriguez, M.	Politecnico di Milano, Italy
Kouroupetroglou, G.	University of Athens, Greece
Miesenberger, K.	University of Linz, Austria
Penáz, P.	University of Brno, Czech Republic

Scientific Committee Chairs

Archambault, D.	University of Paris 8, France
Buehler, C.	TU Dortmund, Germany
Coughlan. J.	Smith-Kettlewell Eye Research Institute, USA
Debevc, M.	University of Maribor, Slovenia
Fels, D.	Ryerson University, Canada
Graziosi, S	Politecnico di Milano, Italy
Kobayashi, M.	Tsukuba University of Technology, Japan
Suzuki, M.	Kyushu University, Japan
Weber, G.	TU Dresden, Germany
Zagler, W.	TETRAGON Braille Systems GmbH, Austria

Young Researchers Committee

Archambault, D.	University of Paris 8, France
Chen, W.	University of Bergen, Norway
Caruso, G.	Politecnico di Milano, Italy
Fels, D.	Ryerson University, Canada
Fitzpatrick, D.	National Disability Authority, Ireland
Kobayashi, M.	Tsukuba University of Technology, Japan
Morandell, M.	Smart In Life and Health University of Applied Sciences Tyrol, Austria

Pontelli, E.	New Mexico State University, USA
Prazak-Aram, B.	University of Vienna, Austria
Ruh, D.	Ruh Global IMPACT, USA
Weber, G.	TU Dresden, Germany
Zimmermann, G.	Stuttgart Media University, Germany

Inclusion Forum Committee

Ferrise, F.	Politecnico di Milano, Italy
Hoogerwerf, E. J.	AIAS Bologna Onlus, Italy
Puehretmair, F.	KI-I, Austria
Petz, A.	University of Linz, Austria
Tarabini M.	Politecnico di Milano, Italy

Scientific Committee

Abascal, J.	University of the Basque Country, Spain
Abbott, C.	King's College London, UK
Abu Doush, I.	American University of Kuwait, Kuwait
Andrich, R.	The Global Assistive Technology Information Network (EASTIN), Italy
Atkinson, M. T.	TPGi, USA
Augstein, M.	University of Applied Sciences Upper Austria, Austria
Azevedo, L.	Instituto Superior Tecnico, Portugal
Banes, D.	Dave Banes Access, UK
Bernareggi, C.	Universita degli Studi di Milano, Italy
Besio, S.	Università degli Studi di Bergamo, Italy
Boland, S.	Saint John of God Liffey Services, Ireland
Bonarini, A.	Politecnico di Milano, Italy
Bosse, I.	Technische Universitaet Dortmund, Germany
Bu, J.	Zhejiang University, China
Burger, D.	Inserm, France
Chamberlain, H.	Helen Chamberlain Consulting, USA
Chen, W.	Oslo Metropolitan University, Norway
Christensen, L. B.	Sensus, Denmark
Chutimaskul, W.	King Mongkut's University of Technology Thonburi, Thailand
Craddock, G.	Centre for Excellence in Universal Design, Ireland
Crombie, D.	Utrecht School of the Arts, The Netherlands
Dantas, P.	Universidade Federal do Rio Grande do Norte, Brazil
Darvishy, A.	ZHAW Zurich, Switzerland

Debeljak, M.	University of Ljubljana, Slovenia
DeRuyter, F.	Duke University Medical Centre, USA
Desideri, L.	AIAS Bologna Onlus, Italy
De Witte, L.	University of Sheffield, UK
Diaz del Campo, R.	Antarq Tecnosoluciones, Mexico
Draffan, E. A.	University of Southampton, UK
Dupire, J.	Cnam, France
Ebling, S.	University of Zurich, Switzerland
Encarnação, P.	Catolica Lisbon School of Business & Economics, Portugal
Engelen, J.	Katholieke Universiteit Leuven, Belgium
Fanucci, L.	University of Pisa, Italy
Ferrando, M.	K-veloce I+D+i, Spain
Gherardini, A	AIAS Bologna Onlus, Italy
Galinski, Ch.	InfoTerm, Austria
Gardner, J.	Oregon State University, USA
Gowran, R. J.	University of Limerick, Ireland
Hakkinen, M. T.	Educational Testing Service, USA
Haselwandter, T.	University of Applied Sciences Upper Austria, Austria
Hemmingsson, H.	Stockholm University, Sweden
Hill, K.	University of Pittsburgh, USA
Hoeckner, K.	Hilfgemeinschaft der Blinden und Sehschwachen, Austria
Holloway, C.	University College London, UK
Inoue, T.	National Rehabilitation Center for Persons with Disabilities, Japan
Iversen, C. M.	U.S. Department of State (retired), USA
Jaskova, L.	Comenius University of Bratislava, Slovak Republic
Jitngernmadan, P.	Burapha University, Thailand
Kacorri, H.	University of Maryland, USA
Kanto-Ronkanen, A.	Kuopio University Hospital, Finland
Kiswarday, V.	University of Primorska, Slovenia
Koumpis, A.	University of Passau, Germany
Kozuh, I.	University of Maribor, Slovenia
Kueng, J.	Johannes Kepler University Linz, Austria
Kunz, A.	ETH Zurich, Switzerland
Layton, N.	ARATA, Australia
Leader, G.	National University of Ireland Galway, Ireland
Leblois, A.	G3ict, USA
Lee, S.	W3C WAI, UK

Leporini, B.	Italian National Research Council (CNR), Italy
Lewis, C.	University of Colorado at Boulder, USA
Lhotska, L.	Czech Technical University in Prague, Czech Republic
Malavasi, M.	AIAS Bologna Onlus, Italy
Mattia, D.	Fondazione Santa Lucia, Italy
McDonald, J.	DePaul University, USA
Mirri, S.	University of Bologna, Italy
Mohamad, Y.	Fraunhofer Institute for Applied Information Technology, Germany
Mrochen, I.	University of Silesia in Katowice, Poland
Muratet, M.	INSHEA, France
Nussbaum, G.	KI-I, Austria
Ono, T.	Tsukuba University of Technology, Japan
Oswal, S.	University of Washington, USA
Paciello, M.	WebAble, USA
Panek, P.	Vienna University of Technology, Austria
Paredes, H.	University of Tras-os-Montes e Alto Douro, Portugal
Petrie, H.	University of York, UK
Pissaloux, E.	University of Rouen Normandy, France
Rassmus-Groehn, K.	Lund University, Sweden
Raynal, M.	University of Toulouse, France
Rea, F.	Italian Institute of Technology, Italy
Scherer, M.	The Institute for Matching Person & Technology, Inc., USA
Seeman, L.	Athena ICT, Israel
Sik Lányi, C.	University of Pannonia, Hungary
Simsik, D.	University of Kosice, Slovakia
Slavik, P.	Czech Technical University in Prague, Czech Republic
Sloan, D.	TPGi, UK
Starcic, A.	University of Ljubljana, Slovenia
Stephanidis, C.	University of Crete and FORTH-ICS, Greece
Stiefelhagen, R.	Karlsruhe Institute of Technology, Germany
Stoeger, B.	University of Linz, Austria
Takahashi, Y.	Toyo University, Japan
Teixeira, A.	Universidade de Aveiro, Portugal
Teshima, Y.	Chiba Institute of Technology, Japan
Tjoa, A. M.	Technical University of Vienna, Austria
Truck, I.	University of Paris 8, France
Velleman, E.	The Accessibility Foundation, The Netherlands

Vigo, M.	University of Manchester, UK
Vigouroux, N.	IRIT Toulouse, France
Wagner, G.	University of Applied Sciences Upper Austria, Austria
Wada, C.	Kyushu Institute of Technology, Japan
Waszkielwicz, A.	Foundation for Persons with Disabilities (FRONia), Poland
Watanabe, T.	University of Niigata, Japan
Weber, H.	University of Kaiserslautern, Germany
White, Jason J.	Educational Testing Service, USA
Wolfe, R.	DePaul University, USA
Yamaguchi, K.	Nihon University, Japan
Yeliz, Y.	Middle East Technical University, Cyprus
Zapf, S.	Rocky Mountain University, USA

Organization Committee

Ayala Castillo, C.	Politecnico di Milano, Campo Territoriale di Lecco, Italy
Bieber, R.	Austrian Computer Society, Austria
Brunetti, V.	Politecnico di Milano, Campo Territoriale di Lecco, Italy
Bukovský, T.	Masaryk University, Czech Republic
Caruso, G.	Politecnico di Milano, Campo Territoriale di Lecco, Italy
Cincibus, Z.	Masaryk University, Czech Republic
Covarrubias Rodriguez, M.	Politecnico di Milano, Campo Territoriale di Lecco, Italy
Feichtenschlager, P.	Johannes Kepler University Linz, Austria
Ferrise, F.	Politecnico di Milano, Campo Territoriale di Lecco, Italy
Graziosi, S.	Politecnico di Milano, Campo Territoriale di Lecco, Italy
Hoogerwerf, E.	AAATE, Italy
Letocha, J.	Masaryk University, Czech Republic
Lobnig, S.	AAATE, Italy
Miesenberger, K.	Johannes Kepler University Linz, Austria
Murillo Morales, T.	Johannes Kepler University Linz, Austria
Ondra, S.	Masaryk University, Czech Republic
Pavlíček, R.	Masaryk University, Czech Republic
Peňáz, P.	Masaryk University, Czech Republic
Perego, P.	Politecnico di Milano, Campo Territoriale di Lecco, Italy

Petz, A.	Johannes Kepler University Linz, Austria
Schult, C.	Johannes Kepler University Linz, Austria
Seyruck, W.	Austrian Computer Society, Austria
Stöger, B.	Johannes Kepler University Linz, Austria

ICCHP Roland Wagner Award Committee

Dominique Burger	BrailleNet, France
Christian Buehler	TU Dortmund and FTB Vollmarstein, Germany
E. A. Draffan	University of Southampton, UK
Deborah Fels	Ryerson University, Canada
Klaus Höckner	Hilfsgemeinschaft der Blinden und Sehschwachen, Austria
Klaus Miesenberger	Johnannes Kepler University Linz, Austria
Wolfgang Zagler	Vienna University of Technology, Austria

Acknowledgements. Once again we thank all those who helped in putting ICCHP-AAATE in place and thereby supporting the AT field and a better quality of life for people with disabilities. Special thanks go to all our supporters and sponsors, displayed at https://www.icchp.org/sponsors-22.

/

Contents – Part I

Interactions for Text Input and Alternative Pointing

Cognitive Disabilities and Accessibility

Contents – Part II

Digital Accessibility: Readability and Understandability

Serious and Fun Games

Robotic and Virtual Reality Technologies for Children with Disabilities and Older Adults

ICT to Support Inclusive Education - Universal Learning Design (ULD)

Design for Assistive Technologies and Rehabilitation

Art Karshmer Lectures in Access to Mathematics, Science and Engineering

Art Karshmer Lectures in Access to Mathematics, Science and Engineering
Introduction to the Special Thematic Session

Dominique Archambault[1](✉), Katsuhito Yamaguchi[2], Georgios Kouroupetroglou[3], and Klaus Miesenberger[4]

[1] CHArt/THIM, Université Paris 8-Vincennes-Saint-Denis, Saint-Denis, France
dominique.archambault@univ-paris8.fr

[2] Junior College Funabashi Campus, Nihon University, Tokyo, Japan
eugene@sciaccess.net

[3] National and Kapodistrian University of Athens, Athens, Greece
koupe@di.uoa.gr

[4] Johannes Kepler University, Linz, Austria
klaus.miesenberger@jku.at

Abstract. Pr Art Karshmer started this series of sessions about access to STEM by people with visual impairment 20 years ago, aiming at presenting the state of the art of researches dedicated to non visual access to scientific content and calculation. This year we will read ten papers presenting research works using machine learning, but also computer algebra systems and natural language processing, to help blind and partially sighted users to access to scientific content, to understand them and finally to learn mathematics and to do calculations. Also, four of these papers concern access to graphical content.

Keywords: Accessibility to mathematics · Science · Engineering and technology

In memoriam of Pr Arthur I. Karshmer (1945–2015), the founder and long serving chair of this STS

Twenty years ago, our dear colleague, mentor and Computer Science guru Professor Arthur I. Karshmer, organised a thematic session, which became a series, about access to Mathematics and Science at ICCHP in 2002 in Linz. In his introduction [3], he described the aim of this session papers as *"new approaches to offer blind students a better access to math, to provide tools for doing math as well as to support teachers in teaching math."*. It has been observed many times that people with visual impairment are under-represented in STEM studies (STEM stands for Science, Technology, Engineering, and Mathematics), and we agreed that there is no specific reason in the nature of scientific content in itself. Most often STEM topics require mathematical calculation and the difficulty comes from the access to the content itself and not in the content itself [1].

K. Miesenberger et al. (Eds.): ICCHP-AAATE 2022, LNCS 13341, pp. 3–6, 2022.
https://doi.org/10.1007/978-3-031-08648-9_1

This is why many research works have been carried out in the last 35 years on this domain and this series of session aims at presenting them.

Art left us in 2015 and it needed no less than 4 colleagues to take over the chair of new sessions in this series, that we entitled after Art's name from the ICCHP 2016 conference. We try to keep up according to his inspiration. It's now the 11th thematic session on this subject, making it one of the longest lasting STS of ICCHP, with a total of 106 papers published within the proceedings, and 10 more in the current volume. We believe that it constitutes a fair knowledge base about the topic of access to STEM content.

We are happy to see that many papers from our session this year were proposed by teams that contribute to this series since a long time (some since the very first [2]). But we are as happy to see that new researchers also join at every session of the series.

Since a few sessions, we have more and more papers about access to STEM graphical content, which was considered – twenty years ago – as more or less impossible. Indeed this type of content is very important to understand scientific topics. Recent technologies, including devices allowing for tactile visualisation but also computer vision and machine learning, allow to imagine more and more assistive tools. This year we will have 4 papers about this kind of subjects.

As for the access to mathematical equations content we had identified [1] three main areas : Accessing, Understanding and Doing calculations. These three areas are all represented in this year's session.

1 Accessing

This was the topic of the first research works of our domain: to work on mathematical formulas, one needs to access to actual content in a format that he or she can handle. Mathematical formats such as LaTeX and MathML can be used. Many Braille specific codes for mathematics are available, while many users use speech synthesis. This implied works about conversion of format but also, lately, works on accessibility of mainstream Mathematical formats.

Currently, two formats – namely PDF and PPT/PPTx – are widely spread for distributing documents to students, but their accessibility is usually not optimal, especially when they contain mathematical content. The 2 first papers, from colleagues of the Science Accessibility Net non profit organisation in Japan, are proposing solutions for these two formats, respectively [A-1] and [A-2].

Two other papers use different techniques including machine learning to help improving the accessibility of scientific documents, especially in the case of equations [A-3], and chemical formulas [A-4].

A-1 Katsuhito Yamaguchi and Masakazu Suzuki, from Nihon and Kyushu Universities: *"Conversion of Multi-Lingual STEM Documents in E-Born PDF into Various Accessible E-Formats"*

A-2 Toshihiko Komada, Katsuhito Yamaguchi and Masakazu Suzuki, from Nihon and Kyushu Universities: *"An Efficient Method to Produce Accessible Contents for Online STEM Education"*

A-3 Sanjeev Kumar Sharma, Shivansh Juyal, Neha Jadhav, Volker Sorge and M Balakrishnan, from Indian Institute of Technology and University of Birmingham: *"Making Equations Accessible in Scientific Documents"*

A-4 Merlin Knaeble, Zihan Chen, Thorsten Schwarz, Gabriel Sailer, Kailun Yang, Rainer Stiefelhagen and Alexander Maedche, from Karlsruhe Institute of Technology: *"Accessible Chemical Structural Formulas through Interactive Document Labeling"*

2 Understanding

When a user have a document in an accessible format, the next issue is to understand it. The complex structure of mathematical content make it difficult to handle it using a linear modality. Therefore tools allowing to enhance the way it is said by a speech synthesizer or to navigate within the formulas are necessary to improve their understanding. [U-1] present a system, also using machine learning, to enhance the audio rendering of equations.

U-1 Akashdeep Bansal, Volker Sorge, M Balakrishnan and Aayush Aggarwal, from Indian Institute of Technology and University of Birmingham: *"Towards Semantically Enhanced Audio Rendering of Equations"*

3 Doing

Finally understanding an equation is necessary but it is also needed to perform calculations, to actually do maths ! This means we need to have editors allowing to work with the content. Many projects have been presented in the past during this series of sessions. [D-1] use a well known theorem prover to give some hints to the user in order to help her or him on each step of the calculation.

D-1 Bernhard Stöger, Walther Neuper, Klaus Miesenberger and Makarius Wenzel, from Johannes Kepler Universität Linz: *"Designing an Inclusive and Accessible Mathematical Learning Environment Based on a Theorem Prover"*

4 Graphical Content

As mentioned earlier, we have several papers addressing the question of graphical representations, which are very important in science understanding.

In a very pragmatic way, [G-1] propose to create a corpus of images taken from a selection of schoolbooks and to classify them. [G-2] and [G-3] focus ways to interact with graphical data. In [G-2] the user interacts with Natural Language. Summaries are processed and presented to the user, and then the interface will allow the user to submit queries to the system. In a totally different perspective, [G-3] propose an interface using a Computer Algebra System to enable the user to create tactile representations of data. Finally [G-4] present a audio-tactile system, where tactile overlays are placed on the touch screen of a device allowing to play audio descriptions. The particularities of this system is that it is mobile, and able to adapt the level of content to the level of the user. Additionally it can be used to test the level of knowledge of user.

G-1 Theodora Antonakopoulou, Paraskevi Riga and Georgios Kouroupetroglou, from National and Kapodistrian University of Athens: *"Developing a corpus of hierarchically classified STEM images for accessibility purposes"*

G-2 Tomas Murillo-Morales and Klaus Miesenberger, from Johannes Kepler Universität Linz: *"Accessible Non-visual Diagrams through Natural Language"*

G-3 Thorsten Schwarz, Giuseppe Melfi, Stefan Scheiffele, and Rainer Stiefelhagen from from Study Centre for the Visually Impaired in Karlsruhe Institute of Technology: *"Interface for automatic tactile display of data plots"*

G-4 Michał Maćkowski, Piotr Brzoza, Mateusz Kawulok and Tomasz Knura, from Silesian University of Technology in Gliwice: *"Mobile e-Learning Platform for Audio-Tactile Graphics Presentation"*

This set of 10 papers, written by 31 authors and co-authors, gives a good overview of the current trends that are actively explored by researchers of this domain. It is remarkable that this year several works are using high level techniques such as machine learning, computer algebra systems, or natural language processing. We already look forward the next steps that these exciting papers will stimulate in the near future.

References

1. Archambault, D.: Non visual access to mathematical contents: state of the art and prospective. In: Proceedings of the WEIMS Conference 2009 (The Workshop on E-Inclusion in Mathematics and Science), pp. 43–52 (2009)
2. Kanahori, T., Suzuki, M.: Infty alpha test site. In: Miesenberger, K., Klaus, J., Zagler, W. (eds.) ICCHP 2002. LNCS, vol. 2398, pp. 512–513. Springer, Heidelberg (2002). https://doi.org/10.1007/3-540-45491-8_97
3. Karshmer, A.I., Bledsoe, C.: Access to mathematics by blind students. In: Miesenberger, K., Klaus, J., Zagler, W. (eds.) ICCHP 2002. LNCS, vol. 2398, pp. 471–476. Springer, Heidelberg (2002). https://doi.org/10.1007/3-540-45491-8_90

Conversion of Multi-lingual STEM Documents in E-Born PDF into Various Accessible E-Formats

Masakazu Suzuki[1] and Katsuhito Yamaguchi[2](✉)

[1] Institute of Mathematics for Industry, Kyushu University, Fukuoka, Japan
msuzuki@sciaccess.net

[2] Junior College Funabashi Campus, Nihon University, Tokyo, Japan
eugene@sciaccess.net
http://www.sciaccess.net/en/

Abstract. A new method of mathematical OCR to improve remarkably recognition accuracy for e-born PDF by making use of SVG information generated from the PDF is shown. Even if a local language is used to represent texts in the PDF, without a special OCR engine for that language, it can be converted into various accessible e-formats. The software GUI is improved so that end users can customize it easily for their language. Its French and Vietnamese versions are actually released by using this new feature. Some evaluations done in Vietnam are also reported.

Keywords: Multi-lingual e-born PDF · Automatic conversion · STEM

1 Introduction

One of the most serious problems in digitized STEM (science, technology, engineering and mathematics) contents, which are provided in PDF in most cases, is their poor accessibility. Print-disabled people usually use OCR (optical character recognition) software to read those PDF. However, the ordinary software cannot recognize technical parts such as mathematical formulas properly, and it is hard for them to read such PDF. To solve this problem, we have been working on the development of OCR software for STEM contents, "InftyReader" [1].

It is said that 90% of visually disabled people live in developing countries. Recently, accessible e-books have been becoming gradually available even in those countries [2]. However, for the present, ordinary conversion tools usually cannot treat STEM contents in their local language, and it still requires a lot of manual works for them to convert inaccessible STEM contents in their own language into an accessible form.

There are essentially two different types in PDF. The first one, "e-born PDF" is PDF produced from a digital file such as a document in Microsoft Word, LaTeX, Adobe InDesign, etc. We refer to the other type as "image PDF," which is usually made by scanning or copying.

K. Miesenberger et al. (Eds.): ICCHP-AAATE 2022, LNCS 13341, pp. 7–14, 2022.
https://doi.org/10.1007/978-3-031-08648-9_2

We have released the English and the Japanese versions of InftyReader for almost twenty years. Through user supports for the software, we have realized that in recent years, most of the (individual) end users use InftyReader to read STEM contents in e-born PDF, and the importance of e-born PDF accessibility is definitely increasing.

From the viewpoint of computerized processing to convert e-born PDF into accessible form, its most significant advantage is that the accurate information on each character/symbol such as the character code, the font name, the coordinate on a page is embedded in it. In ICCHP2016, we reported the new method of mathematical OCR to improve recognition accuracy for e-born PDF, by combining analysis technologies in our mathematical OCR with character/symbol information extracted from the PDF by a PDF parser [3]. At that time, the ambiguity of the character coordinate obtained by the PDF parser was our main problem, which is solved in this paper by making use of a new method developed by Fujiyoshi [4].

If a character set for a local language is included in Unicode, character information in e-born PDF is usually represented in Unicode. As is well known, to recognize a local language correctly, image-based OCR software does need a special OCR engine well-customized for that language. However, our new method for e-born PDF no longer uses image-based OCR in the recognition of local-language texts. Thus, without a special OCR engine, it is possible to develop a system to convert e-born STEM contents in other local languages into accessible format. Here, we show our recent work in this course of action. We have improved InftyReader so that it can treat e-born PDF in any Unicode-based language. Those e-born STEM contents can be converted automatically into various accessible e-formats: LaTeX, human-readable (HR) TeX, Microsoft Word, xHTML with MathML, accessible EPUB3, Multimedia Daisy [5], ChattyBook (audio-embedded HTML5 with JAVA script) [6]. We also develop a scheme to allow end users to customize the software GUI (graphic user interface) so that it is represented in their local language.

2 Background

As was mentioned, we reported our first approach to improve recognition quality for e-born PDF in ICCHP2016 [3]. Sorge, et al. have also studied a method to recognize e-born PDF for STEM by making use of embedded character information and image-based OCR [7,8]. However, as far as a mathematical part is concerned, a font rect-area (rectangular area) extracted from e-born PDF by a PDF parser often differs significantly from the graphical rect-area of the original character image. Consequently, in the previous works, it was impossible to realize mathematical recognition based only on character information extracted from PDF. To solve this problem, we as well as Sorge et al. estimated the correct graphical rect-area of characters/symbols in a mathematical part, by combining the extracted data with image-based OCR.

In the DEIMS2021 conference, Fujiyoshi, et al. reported a completely new approach to extract character information from PDF [4]. They developed an application named "PDFContentExtracter" that makes the vector information of drawing each character/symbol in scalable vector graphics (SVG) by trapping a function for printing PDF. This application allows us to get a correct graphical rect-area even in a mathematical part. Actually, by making use of his application, we have improved InftyReader so that its structure analysis of mathematical formulas is less dependent on the image-based OCR result of characters/symbols.

3 Method

Our new recognition method for e-born PDF is carried out in the following workflow.

(1) Converting e-born PDF into SVG with PDFContentExtracter. PDFContentExtracter, which is a utility using a PDF parser named "PDFBOX" (developed in JAVA), converts e-born PDF into SVG. The SVG consists of three types of elements: characters, images and path elements; where the path is a set of point sequences to draw lines, arcs and Bezier curves with color information to fill up the inside of closed path elements. Concerning a character element, not only its vector image (the path command in SVG) but also its font name and character code are output.

(2) Analyzing the SVG. To make the SVG include only texts in black for recognition, three tasks: removing background images, extracting image areas and changing all character colors to black are performed. In addition, while large mathematical symbols such as fraction bars, big parentheses, radical signs, integral signs, etc. are often represented as graphics, they should be detected and changed to mathematical symbols with character information.

(3) Checking the character code of each mathematical symbol to treat user-defined character fonts. Although most of mathematical symbols can be represented in Unicode, user-defined character fonts are often used in STEM contents. The user-character-code area of Unicode is usually assigned to them, but sometimes, ASCII character codes are irregularly assigned.
To avoid the misrecognition caused by this type of special user-defined fonts, InftyReader checks the character codes of each font used in a target PDF by making use of image-based OCR. To make this process efficient, the check is done for each font of ASCII code or code in the user-character-code area of the Unicode table when they appear firstly in a document; the result is used to construct a character-code map special for the fonts used in the target PDF.

(4) Judging a font category. In STEM, various font styles are used to represent different notions: math Italic, Roman, script, Fraktur, bold, Blackboard bold, calligraphic, etc. Here, we call them font categories. Even if the category is different, in Unicode representation, a same ASCII code is assigned to all those different-category fonts. Certainly, their font names are different from each other. However, it is difficult to get the category just from

the font names since there is no standard table of the font names which is commonly used all over the world.
In InftyReader, at first, some typical code characters are chosen, which should have clearly different shapes among the different categories. For instance, to distinguish two categories: Italic and calligraphic, D, E, F etc. can be chosen while C and S should be excluded. The shapes of selected code characters in Italic and calligraphic are clearly different from each other while the excluded characters such as C and S have similar shapes (see Fig. 1). Using image-based OCR, InftyReader recognizes the code characters selected for the distinction and judges the category of each font name. All categories appearing in a document are judged in this manner.

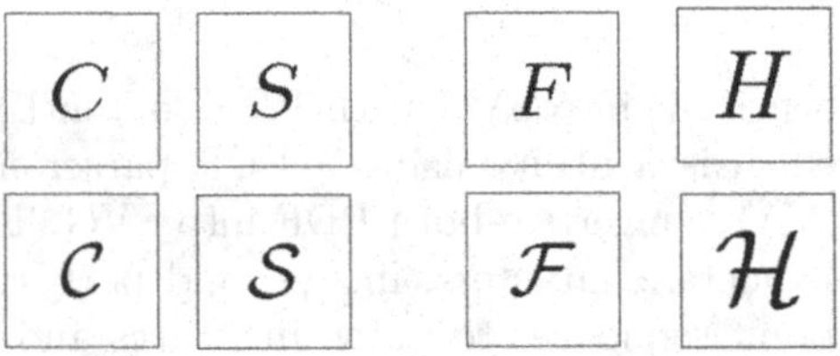

Fig. 1. Distinguishable and undistinguishable characters between Italic and calligraphic.

(5) Structure analysis of mathematical expressions. The method to analyze mathematical structures is essentially the same as our conventional one [9]. However, there is an important advantage in e-born PDF case since no misrecognition occurs in distinguishing between upper- and lowercase letters for the characters that have similar shapes such as "C" and "c" or "S" and "s," etc. (Usually, the character size of "c" and "s" (lowercase) on a baseline is almost same as the character "C" and "S" (uppercase) at a subscript position, and sometimes, that gives rise to the misrecognition.) As the result, the accuracy of the mathematical structure analysis is improved in comparison with image-based OCR.

(6) Segmentation of text and math elements. In a language using Roman/Latin characters such as European languages, Vietnamese, Malayan, Indonesian, etc., some literal words are often misrecognized as a math object or vice versa. Function names such as log or other technical elements should be distinguished correctly from short-length words appearing in that local text. Certainly, an element having a math structure is automatically judged as a math part; however, even for other elements (a character sequence) having no math structure, this judgement also plays an important role in the use of recognition results; for instance, aloud reading, Braille translation, etc. This classification is a strongly language-dependent job. For this purpose, we do need an appropriate dictionary for each local language. For the new version, we collected STEM contents in WIKI to construct the dictionary

for several local languages. Although the size of the collected source texts is not so large, the obtained short-word dictionaries seem to work well surprisingly, and in the latest version, we actually incorporate such dictionaries for 20 languages: English, Czech, Danish, Dutch, Finish, French, German, Hungarian, Italian, Indonesian, Malay, Norwegian, Polish, Portuguese, Russian, Slovak, Spanish, Swedish, Turkish and Vietnamese.

After completing these steps, the recognition result can be converted into various accessible e-formats: LaTeX, human-readable (HR) TeX, Microsoft Word, xHTML with MathML, accessible EPUB3, Multimedia Daisy, ChattyBook.

4 Multilingual Support in GUI

In our accessible STEM-document editor, "ChattyInfty3," we have introduced a localization scheme to allow end users to customize easily its graphical user interface (GUI) and aloud reading of mathematical formulas so that they are represented in a local language [10]. This time, we have also developed a localization scheme in the InftyReader GUI.

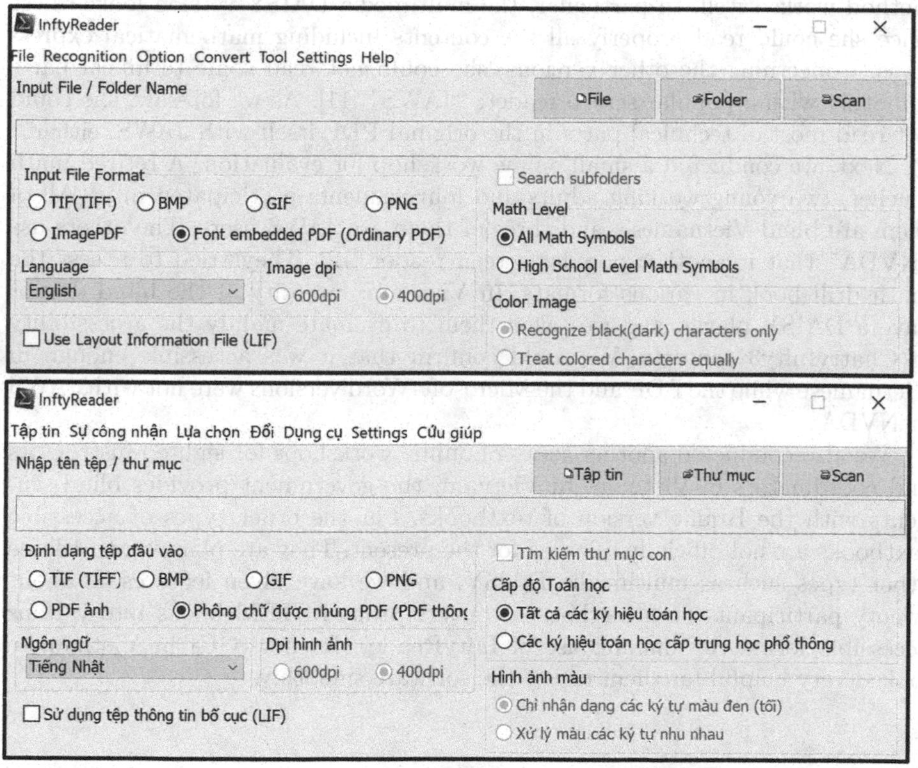

Fig. 2. The GUI in English and Vietnamese

We prepare a definition table for GUI as an xml file separate from its main program. All menu items, button names, etc. are loaded from this definition table, in which any Unicode characters can be used to represent those GUI items. By simply placing a local-language version of the definition table in a specified folder, end users become able to select that language to represent the InftyReader GUI. Thus, they can translate the GUI into their local language without modifying the main program. Actually, French and Vietnamese teams have prepared the definition table for their language, and for the present, English, French, Japanese and Vietnamese can be chosen as the GUI language. Here, we show the GUI in English and Vietnamese (see Fig. 2). As will be discussed later, the Vietnamese GUI has been actually used in workshops for sighted Vietnamese instructors and coordinators.

5 Evaluation

As the first test, using the new mathematical-OCR method, we converted an e-born-PDF math drill book in Vietnamese into some accessible formats such as LaTeX, xHTML with MathML, multimedia DAISY. A blind end user in Hanoi evaluated them to check their accessibility. She said, the new mathematical-OCR method worked well. In particular, the multimedia DAISY version looked best since she could read properly all the contents including mathematical expressions. Concerning the other versions, she could not read some technical parts smoothly with a popular screen reader: "JAWS" [11]. As we foresaw, she could not read most of technical parts in the original PDF itself with JAWS, either.

Next, we conducted a small online workshop for evaluation. A retired math teacher, two young working adults and four students participated in it. All of them are blind Vietnamese, and three of them are JAWS users. The others use "NVDA" that is another popular screen reader [12]. They tried to access the math drill book in various formats. In Vietnam, majority of the blind do not have a DAISY player, and we asked them to evaluate mainly the accessibility of ChattyInfty3 contents. We could confirm that it was accessible enough in Vietnamese while the PDF and the Microsoft-Word versions were not with JAWS or NVDA.

We also conducted another series of online workshops for sighted instructors and coordinators in Vietnam. In Vietnam, the government provides blind students with the Braille version of textbooks, but the other types of accessible textbooks are not officially released for the present. They are planning to release other types such as multimedia DAISY, and we have given lectures to about twenty participants on a method to convert printed STEM books into various accessible format by making use of InftyReader. Its new GUI in Vietnamese looked very helpful for them to use the software smoothly.

6 Conclusion and Future Works

Here, we discuss our new mathematical OCR method implemented recently in InftyReader, which improves remarkably recognition accuracy for e-born PDF STEM contents represented in Latin characters. Even if a Unicode-based local language is used in its text part, without a special OCR engine for that language, InftyReader can convert the PDF into various accessible e-formats. In addition, the software GUI is also improved so that end users can customize it easily for their local language; its French and Vietnamese versions are actually released. In the next step, we intend to work on the following tasks.

Concerning other Asian languages represented in non-Latin characters, we have already incorporated three languages: Japanese, Korean and Thai in InftyReader. However, there still remain a lot of other such languages in Asia, which have a large speaker population - for instance, Chinese, Hindi, Arabic, etc. As for Chinese, a current problem for us is that the PDF parser, PDFBOX, does not support sufficiently the fonts used frequently in Chinese at this moment. On the other hand, in Hindi and Arabic, we need further investigation about the character and word representation system in those languages. It should be our important future task to realize proper recognition for them in InftyReader.

Another remaining important task in InftyReader is how to analyze complicated layout correctly. In school textbooks, recently, page layout becomes increasingly complicated as publishing technologies develop. For the present, we have to do many manual jobs to treat them properly. Further development of machine-learning technology to replace these jobs with automatic processing is strongly desired.

References

1. sAccessNet. http://www.sciaccess.net/en/. Accessed 31 Mar 2022
2. Accessible Books Consortium. http://www.accessiblebooksconsortium.org/portal/en/. Accessed 31 Mar 2022
3. Suzuki, M., Yamaguchi, K.: Recognition of E-Born PDF including mathematical formulas. In: Miesenberger, K., Bühler, C., Penaz, P. (eds.) ICCHP 2016. LNCS, vol. 9758, pp. 35–42. Springer, Cham (2016). https://doi.org/10.1007/978-3-319-41264-1_5
4. Nakamura, S., Kohase, K., Fujiyoshi, A.: Extracting precise coordinate information of components from E-Born PDF Files. In: Proceedings of the 4th International Workshop on "Digitization and E-Inclusion in Mathematics and Science 2021" (DEIMS2021), Nihon University, online, pp. 15–18 (2021)
5. DAISY Consortium. http://www.daisy.org/. Accessed 31 Mar 2022
6. Suzuki, M., Yamaguchi, K.: On automatic conversion from E-born PDF into accessible EPUB3 and audio-embedded HTML5. In: Miesenberger, K., Manduchi, R., Covarrubias Rodriguez, M., Peňáz, P. (eds.) ICCHP 2020. LNCS, vol. 12376, pp. 410–416. Springer, Cham (2020). https://doi.org/10.1007/978-3-030-58796-3_48
7. Baker, J., Sexton, A., Sorge, V.: Extracting precise data from PDF documents for mathematical formula recognition. In: Proceedings of the 8th IAPR International Workshop on Document Analysis Systems (2008)

8. Baker, J.B., Sexton, A.P., Sorge, V.: A linear grammar approach to mathematical formula recognition from PDF. In: Carette, J., Dixon, L., Coen, C.S., Watt, S.M. (eds.) CICM 2009. LNCS (LNAI), vol. 5625, pp. 201–216. Springer, Heidelberg (2009). https://doi.org/10.1007/978-3-642-02614-0_19
9. Suzuki, M., Tamari, F., Fukuda, R., Uchida, S., Kanahori, T.: INFTY - an integrated OCR system for mathematical documents -. In: Proceedings of the ACA Symposium on Document Engineering 2003, Grenoble, pp. 95–104 (2003)
10. Yamaguchi, K., Suzuki, M.: An accessible STEM editor customizable for various local languages. J. Enabl. Technol., Emerald Publishing Ltd. **13**(4), 240–250 (2019). https://doi.org/10.1108/JET-12-2018-0064
11. Freedom Scientific Inc.: "JAWS," https://www.freedomscientific.com/. Accessed 31 Mar 2022
12. NV Access Ltd.: "NVDA," https://www.nvaccess.org/. Accessed 31 Mar 2022

An Efficient Method to Produce Accessible Contents for Online STEM Education

Toshihiko Komada[1(✉)], Katsuhito Yamaguchi[1], and Masakazu Suzuki[2]

[1] Junior College Funabashi Campus, Nihon University, Tokyo, Japan
komada.toshihiko@nihon-u.ac.jp, eugene@sciaccess.net
[2] Institute of Mathematics for Industry, Kyushu University, Fukuoka, Japan
msuzuki@sciaccess.net
http://www.sciaccess.net/en/

Abstract. Many online educational materials for STEM are now produced with Microsoft PowerPoint (PPT); however, many of them are not necessarily accessible for print-disabled students. By making use of Infty software, our new add-on allows users to add easily alt text/aloud reading with a TTS voice to any technical part such as math expressions included in PPT slides. An accessible MP4 video for STEM education also can be produced efficiently. The video contents produced in this manner are preliminarily evaluated by comparison with another accessible content: "ChattyBook" (audio-embedded HTML5).

Keywords: Online education · PowerPoint · Add-on · STEM

1 Introduction

All of us are still in the coronavirus pandemic that is a rare crisis in modern history. Fortunately, however, digitization provides us many powerful tools to get past this serious situation. For instance, digitized content is actively used in online/distance education everywhere in the world.

Many online educational materials for sighted students are produced with Microsoft PowerPoint (PPT). They are provided as lecture videos in MP4 and/or PDF. Otherwise, the PPT slides are displayed directly on a computer screen in remote lectures. In an inclusive class, if the lecture were face-to-face, a teacher could explain directly any part of the PPT or PPT-originated educational materials as necessary even if they were not necessarily accessible. On the other hand, in case of distance education, print-disabled students should access the entire content for themselves at home.

Currently, various method to make PPT presentations accessible are suggested by Microsoft or other organizations [1]. Certainly, in terms of non-technical contents, we actually can produce accessible PPT contents in a certain level, based on those methods. However, as far as STEM (science, technology,

K. Miesenberger et al. (Eds.): ICCHP-AAATE 2022, LNCS 13341, pp. 15–21, 2022.
https://doi.org/10.1007/978-3-031-08648-9_3

engineering and math) contents are concerned, there is still a serious difficulty. In many cases, print-disabled students hardly access important elements such as math formulas, diagrams and tables included in STEM educational materials created with PPT.

Math accessibility has been remarkably improved for the past more-than-20 years. For instance, "Digital Accessible Information System" (DAISY), which is an international standard of accessible digital books, has adopted MathML to represent mathematical formulas (DAISY Consortium n.d.), and some DAISY/ accessible EPUB3 players can read out mathematical formulas in MathML with a text-to-speech (TTS) voice. In terms of web accessibility, recently, MathJax is widely used to represent MathML formulas on the web. the current version of JAWS, the most popular screen reader in Windows OS, can read out such mathematical contents to a certain extent (MathJax n.d.; Freedom Scientific, Inc. n.d.). Unfortunately, however, you do not have such a good tool to make PowerPoint or PowerPoint-originated STEM contents be accessible for the present.

As was mentioned, in terms of non-technical content, we can produce accessible educational materials with PowerPoint [1]. Print-disabled students can read them with ordinary assistive tools such as a screen reader, a Braille translator, etc. However, as far as a technical part such as a math expression is concerned, embedding an alternative text (alt text) is usually only effective countermeasures to make it accessible. Accessible math editors such as EquatIO [2] can help you with preparing an alt text for a math expression in a PPT slide, but embedding such alt texts in the slide is not easy and requires to teachers a lot of extra time and efforts. Furthermore, if the content were changed, some alt texts should be revised as well, but all the corrections process should be done manually.

Another solution to make PPT contents accessible is to add audio (aloud reading) information to them as audio objects. You could add the explanation in a recorded voice to each slide and export the result to a MP4 video. However, this process should require also a lot of extra manual work.

For more-than-twenty years, our group has been developing assistive tools for print-disabled people to access STEM contents. "ChattyInfty" [3], which is our accessible math-document editor, has a function of reading out a content including math formulas with a TTS voice. It also has a function of exporting a document in other accessible formats such as multimedia DAISY, audio-embedded EPUB3, etc. "InftyReader" [3], which is our OCR (optical character recognition) software for STEM contents, can recognize properly a document in print or PDF and convert the result into ChattyInfty document or other accessible formats. It is expected that they should be useful to make PowerPoint STEM contents accessible; however, the collaboration of PowerPoint with Infty software has not yet been realized.

Here, we show a new efficient method to make PPT or PPT-originated STEM educational content be accessible by making use of Infty software [3]. Using its functions, our new add-on for PowerPoint allows you to embed easily an alt text and aloud reading with a TTS voice to any technical part such as math expressions included in PPT slides. An accessible MP4 video for STEM education also can be produced efficiently. The video contents produced in this manner are preliminarily evaluated by comparison with another accessible content: "ChattyBook" (audio-embedded HTML5).

2 Method

As was mentioned, we have recently developed a PowerPoint add-on with VBA (Visual Basic for Application) to realize a systematic/efficient-processing mechanism for embedding alt texts or/and aloud reading in PPT contents [4]. This new add-on requires that computer OS is Microsoft Windows 8.1 or later and that PowerPoint, ChattyInfty and InftyReader are all installed and work properly.

The add-on provides you with three ways to embed the alt text or/and the MP3 audio file (aloud reading) for each math part in PPT slides.

(1) Converting a math part in an existing PPT slide into the alt text and the MP3 audio file and embedding. By copying a selected math part in the PPT slide, it is stored on the Windows clipboard as an image. The add-on uses VBA shell functions to recognize the image automatically with InftyReader, its command-line application and to paste the result into ChattyInfty in an editable form. If necessary, the result can be corrected in an intuitive manner, and then, it can be converted manually into its word description (alt text) or/and MP3 audio file (aloud reading) with a TTS voice. In the next step, the add-on converts the generated audio file into a PPT audio object and embeds it at the background of the original math part in the slide. The generated text is treated as an alt text for this audio object and also embedded. In addition, the math part in ChattyInfty format is added to the background as well.

(2) Converting a math part in PDF into the alt text or/and the MP3 audio file. If a PDF or other printed source of a PPT slide is available, you may copy a selected math part from it with a Snapshot function in Acrobat Reader. The add-on also can generate the alt text or/and the MP3 audio file in the same manner as is described (1).

(3) Newly creating a math formula together with its alt text or/and MP3 audio file. When editing a PPT slide, the add-on allows you to start up ChattyInfty to create newly a math formula. You can insert it into the slide together with its alt text or/and MP3 audio file.

In addition, the add-on also allows you to revise/correct easily the alt text or the MP3 audio file that is already inserted in the slide. By clicking the math part, at the background of which the audio object is embedded, ChattyInfty opens automatically to display its ChattyInfty form, and you can revise/correct it as you like. The previous audio object will be replaced automatically with the revised one.

In summary, using the add-on, you can make PPT STEM contents accessible systematically/efficiently in the following workflow (Fig. 1).

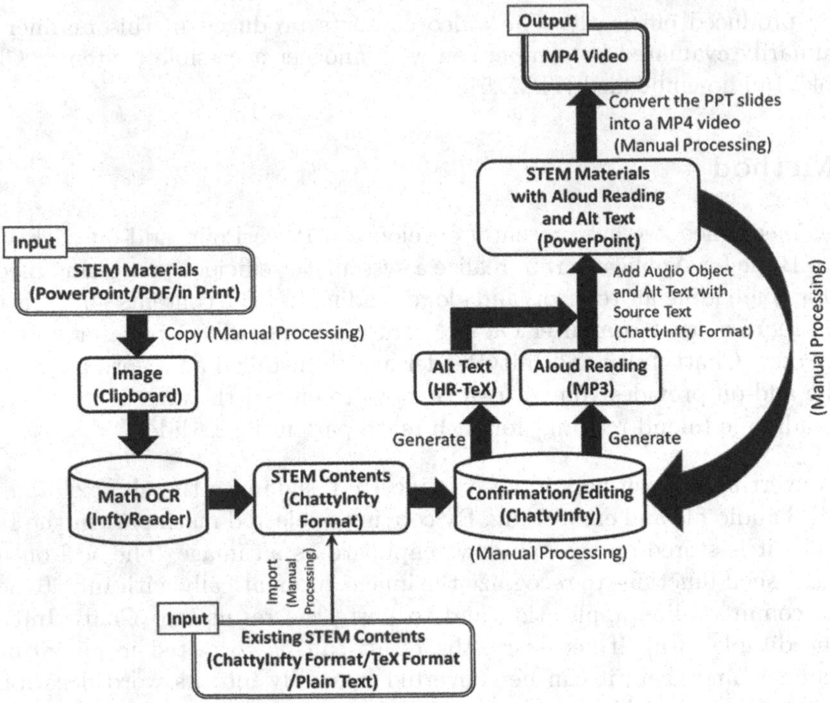

Fig. 1. An overview of a systematic/efficient-processing mechanism for adding alt text or/and audio information (aloud reading) in PPT contents.

From the viewpoint of software GUI (graphic user interface), by installing the add-on, two new items appear in the PowerPoint ribbon menu: "Add Recognized Result as" and "Add New Math Item".

Using "Add Recognized Result as", you can select a math part in a PPT slide and paste it into ChattyInfty. As was mentioned, its snapshot is automatically recognized by InftyReader, and the result is pasted into ChattyInfty in an editable form. After correcting recognition errors (if necessary), the math formula is converted into its word description (alt text) or/and aloud reading with a TTS engine. You can add that alt text and/or aloud reading at the indicated position in the original Slide.

"Add New Math Item" starts up ChattyInfty automatically. As was also mentioned, if a math formula is not written yet in the PPT slide, you may create the necessary formula directly in ChattyInfty (which is easily done in an intuitive manner) and insert it into the PPT slide together with alt text and/or aloud reading.

By making use of this method, teachers can easily/efficiently make math parts in PPT slides be accessible. Furthermore, ChattyInfty can read out entire STEM contents and convert that into a MP3 audio file. If a lecture script for PPT slides were prepared in ChattyInfty, you could add the speech presentation generated by ChattyInfty to each slide and convert PPT into a MP4 video, in which all the content including technical parts would be read out properly with a TTS voice.

3 Preliminary Evaluation Report

We actually produce accessible MP4 videos for online education in this manner at Nihon University. Due to the COVID-19 pandemic, in Nihon University, many STEM courses have been given online in 2020 and 2021. In a class entitled "Applied Information Science, Laboratory II", one of the authors, Komada taught about twenty students how to treat statistical data with the software "R."

In 2020, he prepared just PowerPoint slides for each lecture and provided students with those slides in PDF form. In addition, he added the speech presentation in recorded voice to the slides and convert that PPT into a MP4 video. Those materials were provided through a learning management system (LMS) in Nihon University. However, he realized that this method required to him a lot of extra time and efforts. Thus, our team has decided to develop the new method described in the previous section.

In 2021, by making use of the new method, Komada produced a MP4 video in the following steps.

(1) Convert the PPT slides prepared in 2020 into ChattyInfty; in addition, create/input directly new STEM contents in ChattyInfty or convert existing PDF STEM contents including math formulas into ChattyInfty (also with the math-OCR system, InftyReader).
(2) Prepare a lecture script for the PPT slides by editing the ChattyInfty content.
(3) Generate aloud reading of the lecture script in MP3 with ChattyInfty and embed the MP3 files into the slides.
(4) Convert the PPT slides into a MP4 video.

We realized that this way is certainly more efficient than the previous. In addition, if necessary, you can modify the accessible MP4 video quite easily.

To compare this video with other accessible format, we also prepared the a "ChattyBook" content [5] for the same class. ChattyBook is an accessible web content: audio-embedded HTML5 with JAVA script which has the same operability and functionality as multimedia DAISY.

We issued a questionnaire to the students to ask their impressions on those two-type accessible contents. The rate of the students who judged the content "easy to understand" or "rather easy to understand" are 84% for the MP4 video and 91% for the ChattyBook content in total, respectively.

4 Conclusion and Future Tasks

Here, we show a new efficient method to make PPT or PPT-originated STEM educational content be accessible by making use of Infty software. Using its functions, our new add-on for PowerPoint allows you to embed easily an alt text and aloud reading with a TTS voice to any technical part such as math expressions included in PPT slides. An accessible MP4 video for STEM education also can be produced efficiently.

We intend to work on tasks listed below in the near future. Some of them should be completed by the ICCHP 2022 conference.

(1) Realizing more-automatic processing in the workflow For the present, there are some manual steps such as selecting each math part in our workflow of adding alt text or/and aloud-reading. It requires you a certain skill to carry out. It should be improved so that the process is done automatically as well as possible.
(2) Making the add-on multilingual The add-on has been developed for Japanese in first stage. It is implemented by making use of ChattyInfty/InftyReader as PowerPoint VBA. Several other local languages such as English, Vietnamese, French, etc. are available in ChattyInfty/InftyReader, and it is possible to localize the add-on by writing down VBA in each local language. In ICCHP 2022, at least, we will develop its English version and demonstrate how it works.
(3) Seamless transformation between PowerPoint and ChattyInfty formats We intend to realize more-direct transformation from PPT to ChattyInfty and vice versa. If this function were realized, it would be possible to convert a PPT content (via ChattyInfty) into various other accessible formats such as multimedia DAISY, accessible EPUB3 or audio-embedded HTML5 (ChattyBook). A ChattyInfty content could be also converted into accessible PowerPoint directly. It should give a more efficient way to produce accessible materials for inclusive math education.
(4) More thorough evaluation for the PPT add-on. We intend to conduct more thorough evaluation test to understand remaining tasks in the PPT add-on, which we should work on. We will provide math teachers with its trial version to ask them to test it on their online STEM lectures. Based on its feedback, we intend to polish up it and to release its official version in the near future.

References

1. Accessible PowerPoint, for instance, https://www.csun.edu/universal-design-center/PowerPoint. Accessed 31 Mar 2022. DAISY Consortium (n.d.), "Home, DAISY Consortium", http://www.daisy.org/. Accessed 31 Mar 2022. Freedom Scientific Inc, "JAWS", https://www.freedomscientific.com/. Accessed 31 Mar 2022. MathJax "Accessibility Features MathJax v3.1", https://docs.mathjax.org/en/v3.1-latest/basic/accessibility.html. Accessed 31 Mar 2022

2. EquatIO for STEM Accessibility. https://www.csun.edu/universal-design-center/equatio-accessibility. Accessed 31 Mar 2022
3. Science Accessibility Net. http://www.sciaccess.net/en/. Accessed 31 Mar 2022
4. Komada, T.: Realization of inclusive environment in online STEM lectures using powerpoint. In: Proceedings of the 4th International Workshop on "Digitization and E-Inclusion in Mathematics and Science 2021" (DEIMS2021), online, 18 February 2021
5. Yamaguchi, K., Kanahori, T., Suzuki, M.: "ChattyBook: Making Math Accessible for Online Education. In: The 36th Annual CSUN Assistive Technology Conference, online, 10 March 2021

Making Equations Accessible in Scientific Documents

Shivansh Juyal[1], Sanjeev Sharma[1(✉)], Neha Jadhav[1], Volker Sorge[2], and M. Balakrishnan[1]

[1] Indian Institute of Technology Delhi, Delhi, India
{shivansh.juyal.mcs20,sanjeev.kumar.sharma.mcs20, neha.manik.jadhav,mbala}@cse.iitd.ac.in

[2] University of Birmingham, Birmingham, UK
v.sorge@cs.bham.ac.uk

Abstract. Unlike a standard text document, a STEM document not only consists of text information but different components such as tables, figures, captions, mathematical equations etc. This paper presents a novel technique to detect mathematical equations in PDF documents and convert those equations into a more accessible format such as LaTeX. We use visual features of the document to detect the mathematical equations using object detection and subsequently apply heuristics to the generated bounding boxes to precisely cover the complete equation. These detections are passed to a tool called Maxtract which will rewrite the equations in LaTeX.

Keywords: STEM · Object detection · Heuristics · Accessibility · Digital accessibility

1 Introduction

With the expansion of the digital footprint, physical copies of scientific documents are getting replaced by digital versions in all areas of scientific research. The implication is that to facilitate the inclusion of visually impaired readers into mainstream scientific research, the conversion of scientific documents into a more accessible format is of utmost importance.

Among many components of scientific documents, mathematical equations are absolutely essential for providing full access to scientific documents for visually impaired readers and learners. Given the variety of ways they can be embedded in a document, it poses a major challenge for making documents accessible. Current popular OCR system, for example Tesseract [12] shown in Fig. 1, fails to recognise mathematics reliably. The implication is that we need to explicitly build such systems that can detect and convert mathematics to more readable and accessible formats.

2 Previous Work

Many attempts have been made to detect mathematics in PDF documents in the past. In the initial days, researchers have proposed rule-based systems [6,7]

K. Miesenberger et al. (Eds.): ICCHP-AAATE 2022, LNCS 13341, pp. 22–29, 2022.
https://doi.org/10.1007/978-3-031-08648-9_4

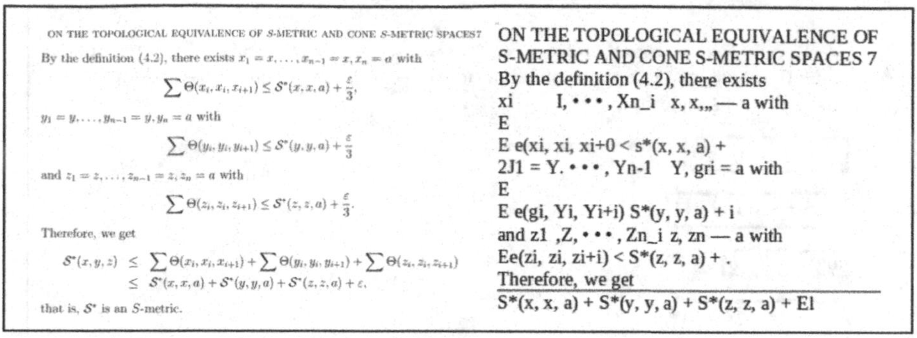

Fig. 1. Conversion of text data in the image (left) to its digital form using OCR (right)

which detected the mathematics based on the parsing of characters. Clearly, writing a comprehensive set of rules is a cumbersome task that is neither reliable nor efficient. In [11] authors have proposed Infty, where they expose the inability of traditional OCR engines to detect math expressions. The regions where OCR is unable to produce a meaningful string are likely to contain math expressions, and then those are further processed for math detection and conversion to its LaTeX equivalent. One disadvantage of Infty is that it is not an open-source tool. An alternative approach realised in [1,2] is to extract and use precise character information from digitally-born PDF documents that embed all the symbol and font information. While this technique is considerably more reliable in recognising and reproducing correct mathematical formulas, its drawback is that PDF comes in many different encodings, often depending on the particular document processor generating the PDF file, that reliably extracting all the relevant information is a non-trivial task on its own.

With the advancement of AI technology, learning-based systems have also been proposed. These solutions based on neural networks learn the features of mathematics based on the layout of the mathematics vis-a-vis the surrounding text in the documents. As in other fields, deep learning techniques are also being tried to detect mathematics [4,8,13].

The mapping of the problem of detecting mathematics in a document to object detection looks more natural, as shown in Fig. 2. Further, drawing rectangular bounding boxes around the mathematics as precisely as possible is the first step in converting these equations into LaTeX. Despite much research happening in detecting and isolating the presence of mathematics in the document, few efforts are visible on how and where to use such detected symbols and equations. While testing some of the reported works that have claimed very high F1-score, we found the quality of bounding boxes covering the mathematical terms to be inadequate. To process these equations, it is important that the bounding boxes are precise and cover the entire equation. The absence of exact bounding boxes would imply a loss of semantics in LaTeX conversion process.

Here are several mathematical equations to test the accuracy of the maths detection system. it consist of inline maths $\boxed{x + y = 10}$ equations and many display maths equations. .

$\boxed{x^2 + 2x + 6 = 0}$

$\boxed{\cos^2 \theta + \sin^2 \theta = 1}$

$\boxed{\log a = \log b}$

$\boxed{\lim_{x \to n-1} \exp(x) = 0}$

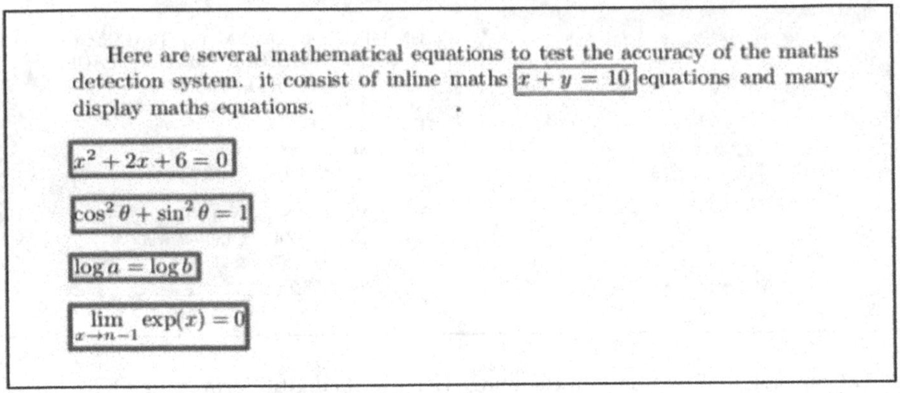

Fig. 2. Mathematics detection from the lens of object detection

3 Methodology

In our work, we propose a novel pipeline, which is a combination of object detection and heuristics, to identify and convert the mathematics in a document to LaTeX. We use the features of the document we get from the RAVI framework [10] like characters with ASCII values, font families, font sizes, the relative position of symbols and text, line bounding boxes etc. and try to use these to improve the bounding boxes we get from the object detection module. For converting the maths expression to LaTeX we use MaxTract [2] which is a tool that converts PDF files containing mathematics into multiple formats including LaTeX, HTML with embedded MathML, and plain text.

In object detection literature, the model's effectiveness is measured in terms of mean average precision (mAP). In some object detection applications, it may not be very critical that the bounding box covers the object entirely, while on the other hand, it is vital in this application. Even the slightest imperfect bounding box is of little to no use if we want to convert the mathematics into LaTeX. This is because for converting the text inside the bounding boxes to LaTeX, the text should be semantically and syntactically correct. Thus the parameters that are used for comparing multiple techniques should include the metric of how precise the bounding boxes formed around the equations or symbols are. Evidently, not only the bounding boxes should cover the entire equation, but they also should not cover the surrounding text.

3.1 Pipeline

Figure 3 shows the pipeline used to detect and convert mathematical equations into LaTeX. The module consists mainly of five parts :

– **PDFtoImage** : Takes PDF as input and gives images of each page as output.
– **RAVI**: Takes a PDF file as input and analyses symbolic and drawn content of the PDF. It extracts features such as line bounding boxes, character meta

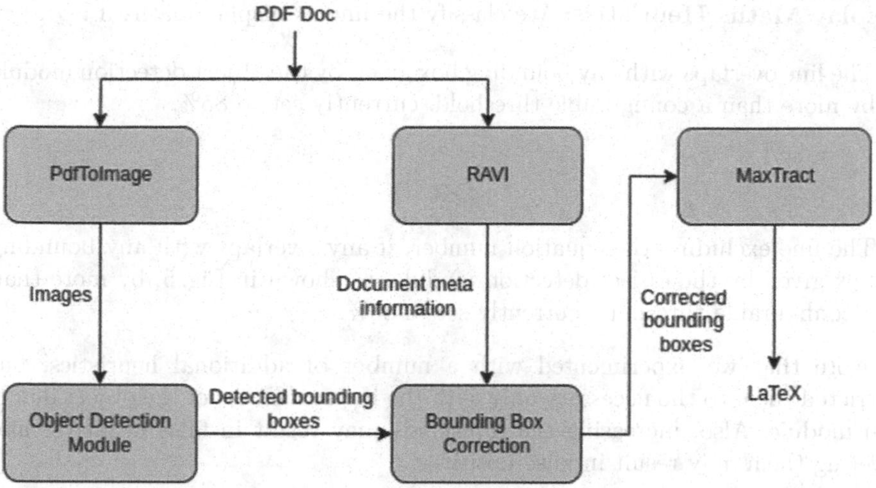

Fig. 3. Framework for maths detection and conversion

information like unicode position, font family, font size, glyph bounding boxes and relative position of text & symbols.

- **Object detection module** : Takes image as input and infer bounding boxes for mathematics.
- **Bounding box correction**: Corrects bounding boxes of mathematics based on the features from the RAVI module.
- **MaxTract** : Sends the maths inside the corrected bounding boxes to the MaxTract system to convert into LaTeX

3.2 Heuristics - Display and Inline Maths

After the object detection module has inferred the bounding boxes of a math expression, further heuristics are applied to these bounding boxes to correct to increase their quality by correction their exact dimensions. The overall idea of how the pipeline works is exemplified with a concrete math expression in Fig. 4.

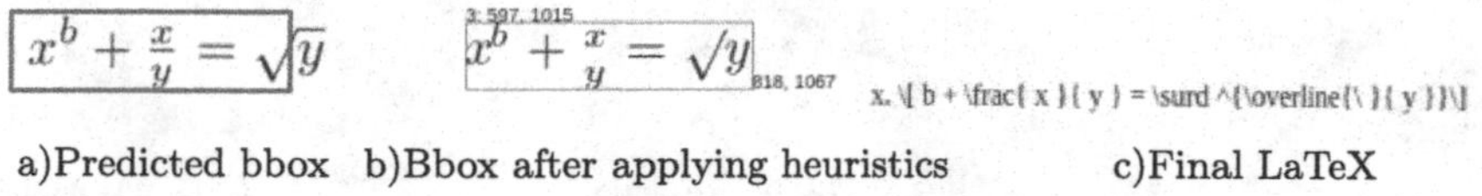

Fig. 4. Illustration of working pipeline

Display Maths Heuristics: We classify the line as display maths if :

- The line overlaps with any bounding box given by the object detection module by more than a configurable threshold, currently set to 85%.

OR

- The line excluding the equation number, if any, overlaps with any bounding box given by the object detection module, as shown in Fig. 5, by more than a configurable threshold, currently set to 85%.

Note that we experimented with a number of additional heuristics, but restricted them to the necessary only with the improvements of the object detection module. Also, increasing the thresholds may result in false negatives and lowering them may result in false positives.

Inline Maths Heuristics: We expand the bounding boxes in both directions till we find :

- Common maths symbols: +, −, $\sum$, etc.
- Numerals: 0–9
- Computer modern fonts: CMMI, CMSY, CMEX. These are hard-coded since nicely written documents in LaTeX use these font families.
- Most frequent font family in the text inside the bounding boxes detected from the object detection model. This is done because we already have information about the text, most probably mathematics.

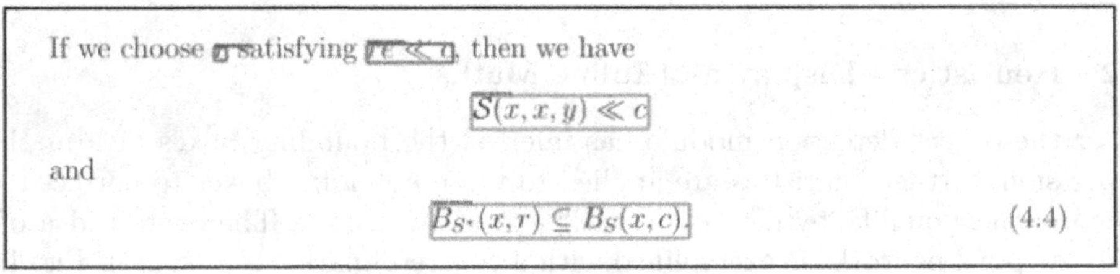

Bbox of display maths detected by model(Red)

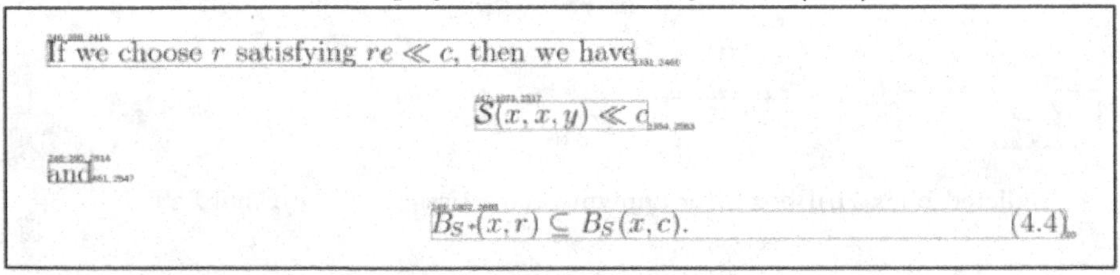

Bbox of display maths(Red) after applying heuristics

Fig. 5. Display maths detection (Color figure online)

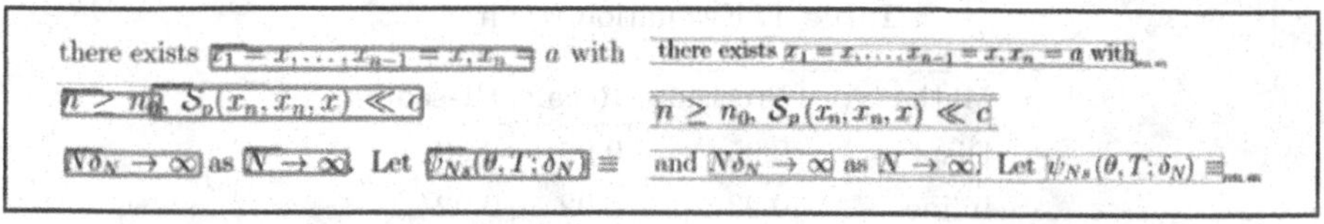

Fig. 6. Inline maths detected by model(left) and Bbox after applying heuristics(right)

- Occurrence of subscript or superscript symbols

Similarly, we shrink the bounding boxes until we find text that does not satisfy any of the above heuristics. Some examples of these heuristics are shown in Fig. 6.

4 Work Status and Results

At present, we have trained a YOLO [3] model, which is a single-stage object detection model, as well as Faster-RCNN [9] which is a two-stage object detection model on IBEM Mathematical Formula Detection Dataset [5]. The dataset consists of 8272 pages containing 29593 display and 136635 inline mathematical expressions.

We found in our experimentation that data augmentation techniques like improving the training data (image rotation, image flipping etc.) do not perform well with mathematics. This is because rotating and flipping the mathematics creates wrong images for training data which is not the case for real-world objects. The random crop was also turned off because it sometimes truncates largely isolated formulas. We also found that coloured text in training images negatively affects the model's accuracy. Thus, we also used greyscale images for training. The current YOLO model gives us an mAP value of 0.91, and Faster-RCNN gives us an mAP of 0.94.

We have also added heuristics for detecting display and inline mathematics based on the features we get from the RAVI module. This is necessary to correct the bounding boxes to their proper size and get semantically correct mathematics. The heuristics to correct the bounding boxes range from a very simple checking of the intersection area between bounding boxes from the RAVI framework and object detection module for a configurable threshold to some complex heuristics to deal with the equation numbers we often get with display mathematics which are not covered by object detection module. Evaluation of the proposed method was performed on single column documents where the detections were made using the Faster-RCNN model on more than 200 pages which consist of 640 display maths equations and 2135 inline maths equations. The results obtained are explained in Table 1. The precision, recall and F1-score are not in terms of object detection but as a classification problem, i.e. whether the maths is fully detected or not after applying the heuristics.

The object detection models are modular and can be replaced by any other object detection model. Our experimentation shows the better the object

Table 1. Evaluation result

Maths type	Precision	Recall	F1-score
Display	0.95	0.98	0.96
Inline	0.93	0.92	0.92

detection model, the less is the number of heuristics required. Thus, increasing the robustness is still a work in progress.

The challenge of precisely detecting inline mathematics is quite different, and so are the heuristics involved. As the object detection model does not take the semantics of mathematics into account, a single equation that gets split into multiple lines is detected as separate equations. Though we have achieved considerable success in accurately identifying inline maths, the heuristics for covering the complete inline math expressions are still in progress. Some of these problems arise due to poorly written scientific documents in which the text surrounding the maths is also of the same font, probably due to being surrounded by $ in case of LaTeX. This results in false expansion due to the heuristics, thus giving false positives as shown in Fig. 7.

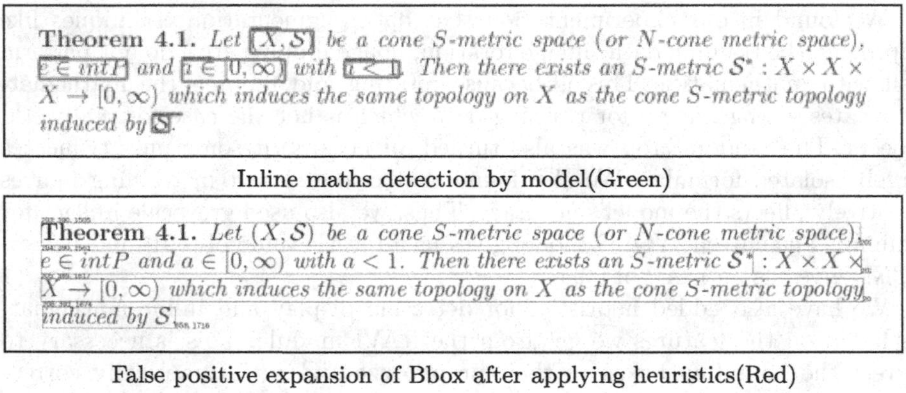
Theorem 4.1. Let (X, S) be a cone S-metric space (or N-cone metric space),
e ∈ intP and a ∈ [0, ∞) with a < 1. Then there exists an S-metric S* : X × X ×
X → [0, ∞) which induces the same topology on X as the cone S-metric topology
induced by S.
Inline maths detection by model(Green)
Theorem 4.1. Let (X, S) be a cone S-metric space (or N-cone metric space),
e ∈ intP and a ∈ [0, ∞) with a < 1. Then there exists an S-metric S* : X × X ×
X → [0, ∞) which induces the same topology on X as the cone S-metric topology
induced by S.
False positive expansion of Bbox after applying heuristics(Red)

Fig. 7. False positive expansion of inline maths (Color figure online)

5 Conclusion and Future Work

For inclusion of people with visual impairment into mainstream scientific research, analyzing and converting digital scientific documents into more readable format is essential. Detecting mathematical equations and then converting them into LaTeX is an important part in making STEM documents accessible. Different approach should be taken to detect and convert mathematical equations as traditional OCR systems fail to do so as shown in Fig. 1.

While most of the previous work aims at detecting mathematics through the lens of heuristics, regression models and object detection, there has been no work which aims to detect and convert mathematics into LaTeX. We aim to create a comprehensive framework to detect and convert, both inline and display mathematics, into LaTeX. Further, our objective is to develop heuristics to precisely cover the inline mathematics inferred by the object detection model.

Also some of the problems can be better dealt with the fusion of object detection and natural language processing techniques which can look into the semantics of the text in the PDF documents. In future work we do hope to explore this.

References

1. Baker, J.B., Sexton, A.P., Sorge, V.: A linear grammar approach to mathematical formula recognition from PDF. In: Carette, J., Dixon, L., Coen, C.S., Watt, S.M. (eds.) CICM 2009. LNCS (LNAI), vol. 5625, pp. 201–216. Springer, Heidelberg (2009). https://doi.org/10.1007/978-3-642-02614-0_19
2. Baker, J.B., Sexton, A.P., Sorge, V.: MaxTract: Converting PDF to LaTeX, MathML and Text. In: Jeuring, J., et al. (eds.) CICM 2012. LNCS (LNAI), vol. 7362, pp. 422–426. Springer, Heidelberg (2012). https://doi.org/10.1007/978-3-642-31374-5_29
3. Bochkovskiy, A., Wang, C.Y., Liao, H.Y.M.: YOLOv4: optimal speed and accuracy of object detection. arXiv preprint arXiv:2004.10934 (2020)
4. Gao, L., Yi, X., Liao, Y., Jiang, Z., Yan, Z., Tang, Z.: A deep learning-based formula detection method for PDF documents. In: 14th International Conference on Document Analysis and Recognition, vol. 1, pp. 553–558. IEEE (2017)
5. ICDAR: https://zenodo.org/record/4757865#.Yf5E0nUzZH5
6. Inoue, K., Miyazaki, R., Suzuki, M.: Optical recognition of printed mathematical documents. In: Proceedings of the Third Asian Technology Conference in Mathematics, pp. 280–289 (1998)
7. Kacem, A., Belaïd, A., Ahmed, M.B.: Automatic extraction of printed mathematical formulas using fuzzy logic and propagation of context. Int. J. Doc. Anal. Recogn. **4**(2), 97–108 (2001)
8. Mali, P., Kukkadapu, P., Mahdavi, M., Zanibbi, R.: ScanSSD: scanning single shot detector for mathematical formulas in PDF document images. arXiv preprint arXiv:2003.08005 (2020)
9. Ren, S., He, K., Girshick, R., Sun, J.: Faster R-CNN: towards real-time object detection with region proposal networks. Adv. Neural Inf. Process. Syst. **28**, 91–99 (2015)
10. Sorge, V., Bansal, A., Jadhav, N.M., Garg, H., Verma, A., Balakrishnan, M.: Towards generating web-accessible stem documents from PDF. In: Proceedings of the 17th International Web for All Conference, pp. 1–5 (2020)
11. Suzuki, M., Tamari, F., Fukuda, R., Uchida, S., Kanahori, T.: INFTY: an integrated OCR system for mathematical documents. In: Proceedings of the 2003 ACM Symposium on Document Engineering, pp. 95–104 (2003)
12. Tesseract-Ocr: https://github.com/tesseract-ocr/tesseract
13. Zhong, Y., et al.: 1st place solution for ICDAR 2021 competition on mathematical formula detection. arXiv preprint arXiv:2107.05534 (2021)

Towards Semantically Enhanced Audio Rendering of Equations

Akashdeep Bansal[1(✉)], Volker Sorge[2], M. Balakrishnan[1], and Aayush Aggarwal[1]

[1] Indian Institute of Technology Delhi, Delhi, India
{akashdeep,mbala}@cse.iitd.ac.in
[2] University of Birmingham, Birmingham, UK
v.sorge@cs.bham.ac.uk

Abstract. At present STEM education beyond middle school is largely inaccessible to visually impaired students in countries like India. Access to equations, tables, charts and figures are the key bottleneck. With the increased penetration of screen reading software, effective audio rendering of equations can significantly help in making many of the e-texts accessible. Unfortunately, linear syntactic rendering of equations can create considerable cognitive load even for relatively simple equations. In this paper we propose an architecture to extract contextual semantic of equations based on the local definitions. This will help in adapting audio rendering of equations based on their contextual semantics.

Keywords: Contextual semantic · Equation · Audio rendering

1 Introduction and Motivation

Despite significant advances in assistive technologies, a large section of visually impaired students, especially in developing countries like India, are not able to pursue STEM subjects in senior school years and college. Inaccessible STEM content including textbooks contribute in a major way to this challenge. Clearly when significant employment opportunities depend upon STEM education, this has a huge impact on their employability and integration into society.

Access to equations is a critical requirement for STEM. Audio rendering and tactile Braille are the two main modalities used by persons with visual impairment for accessing equations. Audio is the preferred modality due to ease and cost of production, possibility of digital dissemination as well as having no need for specially trained instructors to teach Braille/Tactile Graphics. MathJax [5], MathPlayer [7], ChattyInfty [20], etc. are some of the common tools used for accessing equations using audio. All these solutions provide syntactical audio rendering with optimized use of lexical and prosodic cues. None of these solutions have the capability to adapt the rendering on the basis of contextual semantics. For example, A^T can be "the transpose of the matrix A" or "A to the power T" depending on the context whether A is a matrix or a variable,

K. Miesenberger et al. (Eds.): ICCHP-AAATE 2022, LNCS 13341, pp. 30–37, 2022.
https://doi.org/10.1007/978-3-031-08648-9_5

respectively. Current systems will always read it as “A superscript T”, which is a syntactical rendering.

Lack of contextual rendering adds cognitive load and leads to the steepness in the learning curve for users using audio rendering. Another key contributor is linearization of the long and complex equations to render it through a linear interface such as audio [2]. We are already working on a solution for effective delivery of long and complex equations [3].

In this work, we are focusing on contextually improved voicing of equations by locating and interpreting mathematical definitions in documents. Mathematical definitions are those phrases that assign mathematical properties to symbols used in subsequent text. For example, “Let $F : R^n \to R^n$ be a C^1-vector field” defines F to be a C^1-vector field. Unfortunately, definitions are only rarely given in such obvious manner and meaning is often assigned to symbols in a much more subtle way. Consequently, previous research [1,13,14,21] has demonstrated that machine learning techniques are more helpful than simple pattern matching techniques. In this paper, we present an architecture and the basic principles of the analysis to extract contextual semantic from the document.

The application of this work goes beyond enhancing audio rendering of equations. It has also the potential to help in processing documents to automatically tag mathematical content, make it amenable to search and extract mathematical knowledge for further processing and handling by computational systems.

2 Contextual Semantic Analysis

The true meaning of mathematical symbols can only rarely be deduced by their occurrence in a single formula alone. Although many commonly used mathematical symbols often have widely understood semantics, their meaning in context of a particular mathematical text might differ considerably. For example, while in non-associative algebra structures like rings when they use addition and multiplication symbols, their meaning must not be confused with their counter parts in traditional arithmetic. We can roughly divide the sources from which a given symbol or expression can get its definition in a document into three scenarios:

- **Scenario 1**: The symbol is never defined within the document, but is well understood in general or in the subject domain the document belongs.
- **Scenario 2**: The symbol is defined once within the document and is expected to carry that meaning throughout the document.
- **Scenario 3**: The same symbol is defined multiple times within the document and is expected to carry that meaning only within the scope of those definitions. In this case, it is also necessary to determine the scope of each definition and thus tailor the rendering accordingly.

Scenario (1) requires the identification of subjects domains having different semantics and creation of default symbol mappings for each domain. To some extent, this exists for certain topics, e.g., Wikipage [16] provides a detailed list of definitions of mathematical symbols in some of the subjects. While reading a document dealing with probabilities, reading $P(A)$ as "Probability of event A" is critical for understanding the equation instead of "P OpenParen A CloseParen". One could naively enforce an interpretation of P as probability or allow for explicit selection of the domain. But even if the subject domain is explicitly known to be probability theory, a default interpretation for P as probability might not necessarily be correct, as P could for example also denote a polynomial or a partition. Therefore, a dynamic approach should be more robust. In our work, we are therefore focusing on the semantic information, which can be learned from the document itself; no prior domain knowledge is required. Hence, this work covers the scenarios (2) and (3) in the above list.

3 Literature Review

In the past, there have been some attempts in this area. It has been shown previously [1,10,14,18,21] that the consideration of surrounding text can relatively improve the performance of semantic disambiguation in comparison with a mere expression analysis [6,11,15].

Wolska et al. [19] tried the disambiguation based on the similarity between the linguistic context and a set of terms from a flat domain taxonomy of mathematical concepts. The taxonomy was constructed semi-automatically by combining structural and lexical information from the Cambridge Mathematics Thesaurus and the Mathematics Subject Classification. The context information taken into account in the statistical similarity calculation includes lexical features of the discourse immediately adjacent to the given expression as well as global discourse. In particular, as part of the latter they include the lexical context of structurally similar expressions throughout the document and that of the symbol's declaration statement if one can be found in the document.

Grigole et al. [9] proposed an approach based on the surrounding text of mathematical expressions. The main idea of this approach is to use the surrounding text for disambiguation which is based on word sense disambiguation and lexical similarity. First, a local context (5 nouns preceding a target mathematical expression) is found in each sentence. For each noun, the system identifies a Term Cluster TC (derived from the OpenMath Content Dictionary) with the highest semantic similarity according to a similarity metric. The similarity scores obtained were weighted, summed up, and normalized by the length of the considered context. The assigned interpretation is the TC with the highest similarity score. However, the approach addressed only those mathematical expressions which are syntactically part of a nominal group and in particular, are in an apposition relation with an immediately preceding noun phrase, i.e. the expressions addressed came from a linguistic pattern: "...noun_phrase symbolic_math_expression ...", as in the example: "...the inverse function $\omega 1$...". Only the immediate left linguistic context of a symbol was used in the disambiguation process, despite the fact that mathematical texts are known to introduce notations and concepts as they go along.

Fig. 1. Architecture to extract contextual semantic from the document.

There are also some efforts towards conversion of presentation MathML to content MathML [8,11]. However, Content MathML is not found to be adequate for semantic disambiguation of equations.

To solve this problem, we need an universal math-term disambiguator. To achieve this, we need a knowledge base which will cover all the topics related to mathematics and clearly this is not possible to develop manually. Hence, a self-learning system is required which can harvest the definitions in the document and learn with time. So, we plan to focus on scenario (2) and (3) where one can disambiguate by just harvesting definitions available in the document.

It has also been demonstrated [21] that machine learning based approaches can provide better results in comparison to simple pattern matching based methods. We therefore follow a machine learning approach for inferring mathematical definitions automatically from the document using a classifier-cum-locator. In particular we aim to extend the work from [1] to train a classifier on the basis of a large ground truth set of definitions obtained from a concordance analysis [4], following a methodology that is outlined in Fig 1.

4 Architecture

Our machine learning approach is based on a concordance analysis, that is on a enumeration of all expressions in question together with the context in which they occur. In our case, we are working with mathematical expressions and as context we consider five words or expressions before and after the principal expression. The proposed architecture for the analysis is shown in Fig. 1. Brief description of each individual module follows.

4.1 Definition Extractor

Given and XML/HTML documents, the tool first identifies the mathematical entities (maybe a symbol or expression). As in general on the web, we found documents which are not appropriately tagged. Hence, the tool searches for various tags such as MathML, bold, and italic, and also look for the LaTeX expressions. The tool searches for bold and italic because many of the times authors tagged the mathematical entities by bold/italic to give the same visual appearance. Corresponding to each identified entity, five previous and five next words are extracted. This whole extracted part, including the central mathematical entity is referred to as a concordance in this paper.

Table 1 contains a number of examples of concordances, where the principal mathematical expression is marked in red. Note, that single mathematical expressions are counted as a single element of the concordance, regardless of the number of symbols they contain. Moreover, while the principal is usually in the center, this can be broken up by paragraph making concordance pre- or postfixes shorter than five expressions/words.

Table 1. Sample concordances that do or do not represent mathematical definitions.

Concordance	Definition	Explanation
We present, in dimension $n \geq 2$, a survey of samples to:	Yes	n is a dimension
Ensuring that an equilibrium point x^* is a local attractor is	Yes	x^* is a point
Let us recall that the C^1-vector fields $F : R^n \rightarrow R^n$ satisfying that for any $x \in R^n$	No	This is not a definition of C^1
Construct polynomial maps $F = \lambda I + H : R^3 \rightarrow R^3$ with JH nilpotent, such that the WMYC	No	This is not a definition of JH

4.2 Classifier

Obviously not every concordance constitutes a definition of a mathematical expression. Table 1 contains examples along with an explanation why or why not a concordance can be seen as a definition. As a consequence, it is necessary to build a classifier, which can classify them based on whether they contain valid definition or not. Here, we have used the ground truth which we created during our previous work [4]. The ground-truth contains 892 positive samples and 4199 negative samples. We have split this collection into training and test set in 80:20 ratio.

In our previous work [4], we have considered Naive Bayes and SVM as classification models. Where, the concordance pre-processing requires removing punctuations and stopwords, using NLTK library, and replacing mathematical symbols/expressions with keyword "MATH". Table 2 shows some sample concordances after replacing mathematical symbols/expressions by the keyword "MATH". Each concordance is vectorized using term frequency and inverse document frequency, abbreviated as tf-dif. We have used uni-grams as well as bi-grams and taken logarithm of their term-frequency. The SVM, from library sickit-learn, is trained with early-stopping and uses 20% of the training data as validation set. We have used the same tf-idf based feature vector for SVM as well.

Further, we have tried Neural Network (NN) with two hidden layers, Convolutional Neural Network (CNN) with the same structure as NN but with max-pooling conv1d, and Random forest. Now, we have used GloVe embedding [12] instead of tf-idf. This time, we have also considered stopwords and found them useful. As evident from the Table 3, CNN and Random forest provides better accuracy and f1-score and makes for a better choice for classifier.

4.3 Semantic Extractor

Once we get the concordance containing valid mathematical definition, the task that remains is to extract the semantic information from it. Here, we are explor-

Table 2. Tokenized form of sample concordances after replacing mathematical symbols/expressions with the keyword "MATH".

Concordance	Tokens
We present, in dimension $n \geq 2$, a survey of samples to:	We present, in dimension MATH, a survey of samples to:
Ensuring that an equilibrium point x^* is a local attractor is	Ensuring that an equilibrium point MATH is a local attractor is

Table 3. Accuracy and f1-score of various classifiers.

	Naive Bayes	SVM	NN	CNN	Random Forest
Accuracy	0.841	0.852	0.855	0.866	0.876
f1-score	0.652	0.702	0.717	0.748	0.749

ing pattern matching based heuristics. Some of the heuristics being considered are as follows.

- Words between the keyword and principal expression – We have observed a list of keywords such as 'the', 'for', 'consider', 'define', 'exists', 'of', 'on', and many more. The words which comes between the keyword and principal expression has very high likelihood of containing the semantic.e.g., "solution of the **Dirichlet problem** MATH under appropriate assumptions on the" and "the jump of the **function** MATH across the hypersurface Γ. Here,".
- Comma for association –In case of multiple semantics within the same concordance, we found "Comma" to be helpful for association. e.g., "the density, MATH the velocity, MATH the deformation gradient, and p".
- Trim at sentence boundary – We didn't find words from the neighbouring sentences useful. Hence, concordances can be trimmed using the sentence boundary.
- Stopwords – Stopwords are removed from the surroundings. e.g., If the phrase between the keyword and primary expression is "be an open set" then after removing stopwords, it will be "open set".

We are getting good performance using this approach. We are still working on its refinement to cover more diverse scenerios. It is very important to classify concordances and make sure that the incoming concordance has a valid mathematical definition. Otherwise, there will be lot of noise as well as many of these patterns can be observed in the concordances which doesn't have any valid mathematical definition. Below are some of the example concordances which doesn't contain any valid mathematical definition.

- to denote the completion of MATH with respect to the norm
- general equations of the type MATH see Subsect. 4.5. We then

4.4 Scope Finder

Once we have the definition, now the task is to enrich the expression with appropriate definition by considering the possibility of each scenario (as described in Sect. 2). Similarly, for a complex expression that contains a number of symbols we can enrich them semantically by finding an appropriate definition corresponding to each symbol. By default, the expression/symbol would be mapped to the lexical meaning. After working on the scenario (1), it can be mapped to the default meaning associated with the subject.

If there are multiple definitions for a symbol, the question arises, which one should be taken? One that comes before the expression, would be possible. But what about "EXPRESSION, where MATH is ....". This is effectively a reverse scope. Then scoping becomes important. Do we just work backwards through the expressions? Or do we immediately define (maximal) scopes after we have found definitions. Again reverse scopes need to be handled.

Once appropriate definitions have been associated with the symbols. The last part remains is to update the speech output. To accomplish the same, we have integrated this with MathJax using wink-nlp node package [17].

5 Conclusion

The proposed architecture sounds promising for extracting semantic information from the local definitions in the document. This will enhance the audio rendering of equations and will reduce the cognitive load experienced by the users. The algorithms for semantic extraction and scoping requires multi-years efforts to make it (nearly) universal, that is, it can process any mathematical document with (nearly) 100% accuracy. Hence, for now, we are planning to provide multiple output with confidence score.

Acknowledgement. This project is supported by the Google Faculty Award for Inclusion Research. MathJax work was supported in part by Simons Foundation Grant, No. 514521.

References

1. Almomen, R.: Context classification for improved semantic understanding of mathematical formulae. PhD thesis, University of Birmingham (2018)
2. Bansal, A., Balakrishnan, M., Sorge, V.: Comprehensive accessibility of equations by visually impaired. Accessibil. Comput. **126**, 1 (2020)
3. Bansal, A., Balakrishnan, M., Sorge, V.: Evaluating cognitive complexity of algebraic equations. J. Technol. Persons Disabill. **170**, 170–200 (2021)
4. Bansal, A., Kumar, P., Sorge, V., Balakrishnan, M.: Locating mathematical definitions in a document. In: 4th International Workshop on Digitization and E-Inclusion in Mathematics and Science (2021)
5. Cervone, D., Krautzberger, P., Sorge, V.: New accessibility features in MathJax. J. Technol. Persons Disabil. **4**, 167–175 (2016)

6. Doush, I.A., Alkhateeb, F., Al Maghayreh, E.: Towards meaningful mathematical expressions in e-learning. In: Proceedings of the 1st International Conference on Intelligent Semantic Web-Services and Applications, pp. 1–5 (2010)
7. Frankel, L., Brownstein, B., Soiffer, N.: Navigable, customizable TTS for algebra. In: 28th Annual International Technology and Persons with Disabilities Conference Scientific/Research Proceedings. California State University, Northridge (2014)
8. Ginev, D., Jucovschi, C., Anca, S., Grigore, M., David, C., Kohlhase, M.: An architecture for linguistic and semantic analysis on the arxmliv corpus. Informatik 2009-Im Focus das Leben (2009)
9. Grigore, M., Wolska, M., Kohlhase, M.: Towards context-based disambiguation of mathematical expressions. In: Joint Conference of ASCM, pp. 262–271 (2009)
10. Nghiem, M.-Q., Kristianto, G.Y., Topić, G., Aizawa, A.: A hybrid approach for semantic enrichment of MathML mathematical expressions. In: Carette, J., Aspinall, D., Lange, C., Sojka, P., Windsteiger, W. (eds.) CICM 2013. LNCS (LNAI), vol. 7961, pp. 278–287. Springer, Heidelberg (2013). https://doi.org/10.1007/978-3-642-39320-4_18
11. Nghiem, M.-Q., Yoko, G., Matsubayashi, Y., Aizawa, A.: Towards mathematical expression understanding. inftyreader.org (2014)
12. Pennington, J., Socher, R., Manning, C.D.: GloVe: global vectors for word representation. In: Empirical Methods in Natural Language Processing (2014)
13. Shan, R., Youssef, A.: Towards math terms disambiguation using machine learning. In: Kamareddine, F., Sacerdoti Coen, C. (eds.) CICM 2021. LNCS (LNAI), vol. 12833, pp. 90–106. Springer, Cham (2021). https://doi.org/10.1007/978-3-030-81097-9_7
14. Stathopoulos, Y., Teufel, S.: Mathematical information retrieval based on type embeddings and query expansion. In: 26th International Conference on Computational Linguistics (2016)
15. Stuber, J., Van den Brand, M.: Extracting mathematical semantics from +LATEX documents. In: International Workshop on Principles and Practice of Semantic Web Reasoning, pp. 160–173. Springer (2003). https://doi.org/10.1007/978-3-540-24572-8_11
16. List of mathematical symbols by subject. Wikipedia (2020)
17. wink-nlp - npm. https://www.npmjs.com/package/wink-nlp (2022)
18. Wolska, M., Grigore, M.: Symbol Declarations in Mathematical Writing. Masaryk University Press (2010)
19. Wolska, M., Grigore, M., Kohlhase, M.: Using Discourse Context to Interpret Object-Denoting Mathematical Expressions. Masaryk University Press (2011)
20. Yamaguchi, K., Komada, T., Kawane, F., Suzuki, M.: New features in math accessibility with Infty software. In: Miesenberger, K., Klaus, J., Zagler, W., Karshmer, A. (eds.) ICCHP 2008. LNCS, vol. 5105, pp. 892–899. Springer, Heidelberg (2008). https://doi.org/10.1007/978-3-540-70540-6_134
21. Yokoi, K., Nghiem, M.-Q., Matsubayashi, Y., Aizawa, A.: Contextual analysis of mathematical expressions for advanced mathematical search. Polibits **43**, 81–86 (2011)

Accessible Chemical Structural Formulas Through Interactive Document Labeling

Merlin Knaeble[1(✉)], Zihan Chen[2], Thorsten Schwarz[2], Gabriel Sailer[1], Kailun Yang[2], Rainer Stiefelhagen[2], and Alexander Maedche[1]

[1] Research Group Information Systems I, Karlsruhe Institute of Technology (KIT), Karlsruhe, Germany
merlin.knaeble@kit.edu

[2] Center for Digital Accessibility and Assistive Technology, Karlsruhe Institute of Technology (KIT), Karlsruhe, Germany

Abstract. Despite a number of advances in the accessibility of STEM education, there is a lack of advanced tool support for authors and educators seeking to make corresponding documents accessible. We propose an interactive labeling method that combines an AI with user input to create accessible chemical structural formulas and incrementally improve the model. The model is a deep learning method based on a convolutional neural network and a transformer-based encoder-decoder. We implement this in a tool that enables graphical labeling of structural formulas and supports the user by performing a similarity search to suggest matches. Our approach aims to improve both the efficiency and effectiveness of labeling chemical structural formulas for accessibility purposes.

Keywords: Accessibility · STEM · Chemistry · Structural formulas · Interactive labeling

1 Introduction

Making learning materials accessible to visually impaired people is of utmost importance, especially in schools and higher education. The lack of accessible content was cited as one of the reasons why few blind students choose STEM subjects [18]. Learning chemistry, e.g., seems almost impossible, without its molecules visualized in structural formulas [7]. Thus, making such structural formulas accessible demands priority for STEM education. The issue is exacerbated when neither the authors are familiar with accessibility requirements, nor those who seek accessibility have the required STEM background.

Recently, in the research field of automatic image description generation promising deep-learning-based approaches for the recognition of mathematical formulas have been proposed [2]. However, the recognition of chemical structural formulas is more challenging. Often, it is based on low-level image processing approaches that require copious amounts of fine-tuning [9,11,16]. Further, none of the previous approaches integrate well into the established semi-automated

K. Miesenberger et al. (Eds.): ICCHP-AAATE 2022, LNCS 13341, pp. 38–46, 2022.
https://doi.org/10.1007/978-3-031-08648-9_6

approach in which STEM content is usually being made accessible. Currently either content authors themselves, or third parties like educators, try to make documents as a whole accessible. Thereby fully autonomous approaches while solving the issue of the process being time-consuming, do not tackle the challenge of quality control. Neither fully automated approaches, due to lack of oversight, nor fully manual approaches, because of the error-proneness of the linearized label input, satisfy this. As such, there is a lack of research on how to facilitate interactive labeling of structural formulas efficiently and effectively.

In this paper we propose such an interactive approach and show its feasibility with a prototype. Firstly, we generated a dataset of images of structural formulas and their linear representations. We then trained a deep learning model using this dataset. To label new structural formulas, the model prediction is being fed into an interactive labeling interface that supports the user in either deciding that the prediction was accurate and thus accepting it, or correcting the linear representation of the input image. With this user input the deep learning model can be further improved, while also forming the basis to generate suitable alternative text representations for structural formulas that can be read and further used by blind chemists. We thus demonstrate the feasibility of interactive labeling approaches for structured image contents in document accessibility.

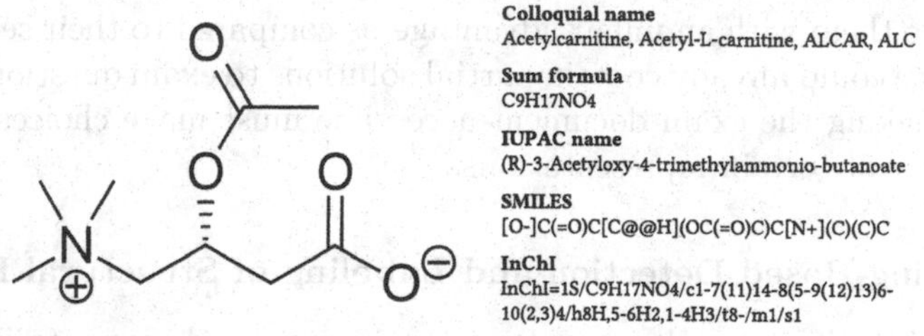

O
O
O
N
O
Colloquial name
Acetylcarnitine, Acetyl-L-carnitine, ALCAR, ALC
Sum formula
C9H17NO4
IUPAC name
(R)-3-Acetyloxy-4-trimethylammonio-butanoate
SMILES
[O-]C(=O)C[C@@H](OC(=O)C)C[N+](C)(C)C
InChI
InChI=1S/C9H17NO4/c1-7(11)14-8(5-9(12)13)6-10(2,3)4/h8H,5-6H2,1-4H3/t8-/m1/s1

Fig. 1. Acetylcarnitine as visualized in its structural formula (https://en.wikipedia.org/wiki/Acetylcarnitine and different text based (linear) representations of it.

2 Related Work

2.1 Accessibility of Structural Formulas

Research focusing on the accessibility of chemical structural formulas has undertaken several avenues. Via image segmentation and subsequent rule-based recognition, researchers have managed to make a first step towards automatic extraction of linear representations from an image [14]. Their approach initially translates the bitmap image into geometrical forms in a vector graphic. Such vector graphics are more easily accessible for the blind, especially with guidance and further labeling. However, slight errors during the translation of the image into geometric components make a rule-based detection of the underlying molecule all but unfeasible, as the resulting vector representations could be chemically impossible. Other approaches such as [11] build upon similar rules to extract geometric components. Practical applications, e.g. for teaching blind students chemistry in secondary education [18], underline how important not only vector representations, but also semantic enrichment of them are. However, such approaches require a certain domain expertise of the labeler.

Recent literature has been focusing largely on a single linearized representation called SMILES. This is a clear disadvantage because different standards may be helpful to different readers of the document. There is a variety of textual representation formats for molecule structures including SMILES, InChI, colloquial name, IUPAC name, and sum formula [6], as illustrated in Fig. 1. Among those standards, SMILES [19] and InChI [3] are compact, unique, and able to represent the entire molecule including its structure. SMILES [19] was designed to be read and written by humans, and it is therefore relatively straightforward to interpret, provided that the user knows a few basic principles of the format and thus usable for the people with visual impairments. InChI does not fulfill the human readability requirement (c.f. Figure 1). Finally, other representations such as aforementioned sum formulas, names or browseable vector graphics can be generated from this. This allows for a range of options regarding the output, such as generating a list of representations in the alt-text of a PDF, or using the multiple-rendition feature of EPUB3 to provide all alternatives simultaneously and selectable by user-choice [12]. In an educational setting, further requirements like exam fairness come to mind. Hereby giving blind students the IUPAC name would provide them with an unfair advantage as compared to their seeing peers, as such a name could already contain partial solutions to exam questions. Hereby, the person making the exam document accessible must make choices regarding the availability of certain representations.

2.2 Learning-Based Detection and Labeling of Structural Formulas

The task of identifying molecular structure images in documents is challenging due to various reasons, especially because of complexity of molecule structures and the diversity of image formats and styles. Conventionally, low-level image processing techniques (scanning, vectorization, etc.) are used in conjunction with high-level rules to organize components into their respective structures [9,11,16]. Each stage must be fine-tuned independently as well as in relation to the other parts, leading to a time-consuming process of incorporating new elements requiring high amounts of human intervention. On the other hand, deep learning approaches using sequence-to-sequence models involve training a complex learning system represented by a single artificial neural network that embodies a complete target system. This system does not include explicit intermediate stages usually present in the traditional pipeline approach. Recently, deep learning has been applied to a variety of problems ranging from image-to-text and text-to-text tasks, many of which have demonstrated strong performances with sequence-to-sequence models [17]. Therefore, it is intuitive to apply sequence-to-sequence prediction models like transformers to this problem given the suitability of the image inputs and the sequential outputs [15] presented deep learning solutions to predict SMILES encodings from bitmaps. They showed that deep learning can learn to predict images of molecules from literature at reasonably high accuracy. [10] used transformer models to predict SMILES encodings of chemical structure depictions with about 90% accuracy.

Outside of accessibility research, the domain of chemistry and specifically cheminformatics, have developed graphical labeling and search tools. A prominent example of such a tool is *kekule.js* [4]. Among other features it provides a graphical user interface supporting the entry of structural formulas. As further aids for chemists there exist a series of databases of already discovered molecules, searchable by e.g., SMILES, InChI, IUPAC or name. Existing work has already incorporated graphical editors, foremost *kekule.js*, as input for such databases, e.g., [13]. Combined with a similarity search this allows for the retrieval of either structurally related molecules or a certain haziness in the users search input.

3 Interactive Labeling of Structural Formulas

Our method and tool are designed to be used either in batch processing of a large set of pre-segmented images of structural formulas or as a component of a document accessibility platform that is being invoked when there is an image containing such formulas in a document. Thereby, we consider our work as complimentary to existing research, e.g. [14], that focus largely on automated extraction and means of comprehensibility for blind users. The encoder-decoder concept was first designed to handle machine translation tasks in which both the input and output modalities are textual sequences. However, this concept is also known to be highly flexible such that the infrastructure of the encoder or decoder can be changed according to the required modality. In our specific context, it is intuitive to use a convolutional architecture to accommodate the imagery input, and a sequential auto-regressive model to handle the sequential generation nature of the decoder. Our overall architecture is a widely-used image captioning model [20], using a CNN-based encoder for feature extraction and an attention-augmented RNN decoder for generating outputs, namely SMILES and InChI in a multi-task learning setup.

Our work investigated different architectures, from simple to sophisticated, in order to show a progressive observation over the effectiveness of these architectures. We acquired a training dataset of about 4 million images from the PubChem database with matching SMILES labels of length less than 100. In our encoder-decoder architecture, for the encoder, we leverage 8 different EfficientNet variations B0, B3, and B7 with adding a transformer encoder layer [17] as well as ResNet152 for feature extraction. From a $3 \times 256 \times 256$ input image, we extract the last convolutional feature of a CNN-based encoder, which downsamples the image yet adds extra channels, as a $1024 \times 20 \times 20$ input for the decoder. From the point of view of sequence generation with attention, this can be viewed as an input with 400 memory states for querying in attention. On the other hand, the simplest solution for the decoder is an auto-regressive (without bi-directional) LSTM recurrent network that processes the text sequences in characters while using the attention mechanism [1] to align the generated characters with the input states in the encoder. In addition to such Convolution-Recurrent architecture, we take advantage of the power of Transformers to increase the modeling capacity and thus enhance learning performance in the next step. Transformer [17] originally replaces recurrence or convolution with self-attention and is theoretically able to represent both local and global connectivities, which CNN and RNN excel at, respectively. This model is also highly parallelizable and can utilize the computational power of devices such as GPUs more efficiently than other networks. Using Transformers leads to adding self-attention layers on top of the convolutional features of the encoder and replacing the LSTM decoders with self-attentional decoders.

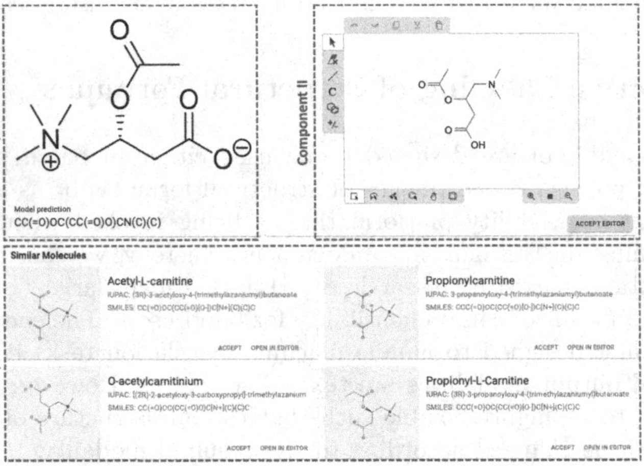

Fig. 2. User interface of our tool

Figure 2 shows the user interface (UI) of the interactive labeling tool. We have designed this interface with three main components to effectively support the creation of accessible chemical structural formulas. The focus is to automate the process as much as the state-of-the-art allows, while simultaneously using the input to collect more training data in order to further improve the model. We hereby follow established approaches concerning the development of interactive labeling systems [8]. Situated in the top left corner of the UI, **component I** depicts the original input image for reference, as well as the SMILES string that our model predicted. In **component II**, on the top right side, we integrated the established *kekule.js* molecule editor. Upon invocation of the interface, the editor is pre-loaded with an automatically generated graphical representation of the SMILES string the model predicted. The user can now compare this representation with the original input image to identify discrepancies - or to accept the current rendering in the editor. Furthermore, errors can be corrected via the graphical editor. This can be either small changes to the existing structure or a completely new one may be entered. Finally, **component III** shows similar molecules and is situated along the bottom. Specifically, it shows the structural formulas, names, IUPAC and SMILES representations of four molecules retrieved from the PubChem[1] database via a similarity search [6]. With this feature we provide advanced support for the user beyond the graphical editor. It is reasonable to assume that the molecules shown in literature are real existing molecules which are recorded in the PubChem database. This database is not only searchable via SMILES strings, but also allows for a similarity matching of structurally kindred molecules. This search is initialized with the model prediction, but updates live as the user makes changes in the graphical editor. The user has the option to open any suggestion in the editor to make changes, or to accept it as is. Our labeling interface potentially allows for incorporating users without any chemical domain knowledge in the process of making PDFs accessible. Specifically, no knowledge about the output format of SMILES, is required, as the input image can be matched by visual comparison only. For a well performing model and similarity search engine, even the amount of manual graphical input is limited to edge cases, as predictions could be correct out of the box or the matching molecule may be contained in the suggestions in component III.

4 Evaluation

The two best performing model configurations were EfficientNet B2 and B7, each with 2 transformer encoder layers, respectively. Validation set accuracies for exact identifications are similar among them at 98.22% for B2+2 and 98.87% for B7+2. However, on yet unseen test data the results differ between them. To evaluate this, we use the mean Tanimoto similarity (T), as well as mean Levenshtein distances (L). The former refers to an established measure in chemistry, comparing molecule similarity along functional groups and the molecules effects in chemical reactions. Also known as edit distance, the latter is a general-purpose string distance measure, better representing the amount of changes required in the interactive labeling procedure. Hereby we report values of $T_{B2+2} = 70.50\%$ and $L_{B2+2} = 81.69\%$, as well as $T_{B7+2} = 80.86\%$ and $L_{B7+2} = 82.66\%$.

Comparing our results to other state-of-the-art solutions also employing deep-learning methods, we find that our performance is competitive. We achieve slightly better results than the work of [5] which reported a validation accuracy (on a molecule level) of 92.80% with our model version B7+2 at 98.87%. Furthermore we do so with significantly less training data of 2 versus 10 million images. Using even more data, at 35 million images, [10] obtain Tanimoto similarities of 96.47% far surpassing our values. They do however, limit the options for input severely, by allowing only the 12 most common elements, limiting the number of bonds and the weight, disallowing stereochemistry, counterions, charged groups and isotopes, and limiting the SMILES string to a length of 40. As compared to that, we pose just a single restriction of SMILES lengths less than 100. Following suggestions from other researchers, we could improve upon

[1] https://pubchemdocs.ncbi.nlm.nih.gov.

our work by adding image augmentations like blur and noise [10] and extending the size of our dataset, especially including low-quality real-world data [5].

A currently still missing subsequent user evaluation of our tool may focus on different types of users. Firstly, to obtain a baseline comparison to the current approach to making chemical formulas accessible, an evaluation should involve educators to blind or vision impaired STEM students. With this target audience performance and user-related benefits against aforementioned baseline can be investigated. Further, it allows for studying implications of different representational formats on the users of the output of our system (i.e. blind students and chemists). Students may have different needs from seasoned chemists, as they may not need an efficient input on what information is contained in the image, e.g. as an IUPAC name, but may need to first understand how such a molecule is constructed, e.g. as a SMILES string or a vector graphic. Complementary, an evaluation may also involve users not previously involved in working on document accessibility. Hereby varying levels of chemical expertise could be represented in a stratified sample. On the top end, chemists with experience in using SMILES strings could typify power users that may not even profit from graphical entry as they proficiency with writing such strings may be too high. The other end of the spectrum is represented by chemical novices, knowing little more than the fact that the graphically labeled molecule should look the same as in the input image. Such an evaluation could provide input into the required domain expertise required to effectively contribute to making STEM documents accessible. If our tool is indeed capable in lowering the entry barrier for supporting the costly and labor-intensive process of labeling [8], it may contribute significantly to the goal of making knowledge accessible for all.

5 Conclusions

In this paper we have introduced a new interactive labeling method and tool to support making chemical structural formulas accessible. Thereby, we leverage the respective strengths of humans and computers. Creating accurate textual representations such as SMILES is achievable with state-of-the-art deep learning technology. However, precision cannot be guaranteed. Our interactive labeling approach involves a human, who is strongly supported by simultaneously accelerating input and checking its credibility. Thereby a first suggestion is being made by our deep learning model, while the subsequent correction process is supported by similarity matching. Graphical, as opposed to text-based, label input enables novices to contribute. With our approach, we do not only ensure precision, but also support continuous model improvement. There is still a lot of potential for optimization in the automated recognition of structural formulas, but our proof of concept has demonstrated its feasibility. The deep learning model is considered to be able to further improve upon a multi-task learning strategy in the future. Data acquired from using the tool will support here.

Ultimately, our next steps lie within improving our classifier, evaluating our interactive labeling tool with users, and later integrating it into broader platforms to make documents with STEM content accessible in a scalable way.

References

1. Bahdanau, D., Cho, K., Bengio, Y.: Neural machine translation by jointly learning to align and translate. arXiv preprint arXiv:1409.0473 (2014)
2. Deng, Y., Kanervisto, A., Rush, A.M.: What you get is what you see: A visual markup decompiler. arXiv preprint arXiv:1609.04938 (2016)
3. Heller, S.R., McNaught, A., Pletnev, I., Stein, S., Tchekhovskoi, D.: InChI, the IUPAC international chemical identifier. J. Cheminformatics **7**(1), 1–34 (2015)
4. Jiang, C., Jin, X., Dong, Y., Chen, M.: Kekule.js: an open source javascript chemoinformatics toolkit. J. Chem. Inf. Mod. **56**(6), 1132–1138 (2016)
5. Khokhlov, I., Krasnov, L., Fedorov, M.V., Sosnin, S.: Image2smiles: transformer-based molecular optical recognition engine. Chem.-Meth. **2**(1), e202100069 (2022)
6. Kim, S., Thiessen, P., Cheng, T., Yu, B., Bolton, E.: An update on PUG-REST: RESTful interface for programmatic access to PubChem. Nucleic Acids Res. **46**(W1), W563–W570 (2018)
7. McGrath, M., Brown, J.: Visual learning for science and engineering. IEEE Comput. Graph. Appl. **25**, 56–63 (2005)
8. Nadj, M., Knaeble, M., Li, M.X., Maedche, A.: Power to the oracle? design principles for interactive labeling systems in machine learning. KI - Künstliche Intelligenz **34**(2), 131–142 (2020). https://doi.org/10.1007/s13218-020-00634-1
9. Park, J., Rosania, G.R., Shedden, K.A., Nguyen, M., Lyu, N., Saitou, K.: Automated extraction of chemical structure information from digital raster images. Chem. Central J. **6** (2009)
10. Rajan, K., Zielesny, A., Steinbeck, C.: DECIMER 1.0: deep learning for chemical image recognition using transformers. J. Cheminformatics **13**(1), 61 (2021)
11. Sadawi, N.M., Sexton, A.P., Sorge, V.: Chemical structure recognition: a rule-based approach. In: Document Recognition and Retrieval XIX, vol. 8297, pp. 101–109. SPIE (2012)
12. Schwarz, T., Rajgopal, S., Stiefelhagen, R.: Accessible EPUB: making EPUB 3 documents universal accessible. In: Miesenberger, K., Kouroupetroglou, G. (eds.) ICCHP 2018. LNCS, vol. 10896, pp. 85–92. Springer, Cham (2018). https://doi.org/10.1007/978-3-319-94277-3_16
13. Shave, S., Auer, M.: SimilarityLab: molecular similarity for SAR exploration and target prediction on the web. Processes **9**(9) (2021)
14. Sorge, V.: Polyfilling accessible chemistry diagrams. In: Miesenberger, K., Bühler, C., Penaz, P. (eds.) ICCHP 2016. LNCS, vol. 9758, pp. 43–50. Springer, Cham (2016). https://doi.org/10.1007/978-3-319-41264-1_6
15. Staker, J., Marshall, K., Abel, R., McQuaw, C.M.: Molecular structure extraction from documents using deep learning. J. Chem. Inf. Mod. **59**(3), 1017–1029 (2019)
16. Valko, A.T., Johnson, A.P.: CLiDE Pro: the latest generation of CLiDE, a tool for optical chemical structure recognition. J. Chem. Inf. Model. **49**(4), 780–787 (2009)
17. Vaswani, A., et al.: Attention is all you need. In: NeurIPS, vol. 30. Curran Associates, Inc. (2017)

18. in't Veld, D., Sorge, V.: The Dutch Best Practice for Teaching Chemistry Diagrams to the Visually Impaired. In: Miesenberger, K., Kouroupetroglou, G. (eds.) ICCHP 2018. LNCS, vol. 10896, pp. 644–647. Springer, Cham (2018). https://doi.org/10.1007/978-3-319-94277-3_99
19. Weininger, D.: SMILES, a chemical language and information system. 1. introduction to methodology and encoding rules. J. Chem. Inf. Comput. Sci. **28**(1), 31–36 (1988)
20. Xu, K., et al.: Show, attend and tell: neural image caption generation with visual attention. In: International Conference on Machine Learning (ICML), pp. 2048–2057. PMLR (2015)

Designing an Inclusive and Accessible Mathematical Learning Environment Based on a Theorem Prover

Bernhard Stöger[1(✉)], Klaus Miesenberger[1], Walther Neuper[2], Makarius Wenzel[3], and Thomas Neumayr[4]

[1] Johannes Kepler Universität Linz, Linz, Austria
{bernhard.stoeger,klaus.miesenberger}@jku.at
[2] RISC Linz, Linz, Austria
walther.neuper@jku.at
[3] Dr. Wenzel, Augsburg, Germany
[4] University of Applied Sciences Upper Austria, Wels, Austria
thomas.neumayr@fh-hagenberg.at
https://sketis.net

Abstract. A novel approach to design an inclusive and accessible mathematical learning environment is presented: The technology of theorem proving shall be employed to support a student in solving mathematical problems by giving hints to him/her based on formal proofs of each step in a calculation. The system shall be made accessible by making use of the built-in accessibility coming with VSCode, a standard editor used as front-end for the theorem prover Isabelle.

Keywords: Mathematics · Accessibility · Education · Theorem prover

1 Introduction

Although long-year research and development efforts have been carried out to enable blind and visually impaired people to learn and do mathematics effectively through information technology, until now no system exists which would be widely used at school or university. The present paper describes current efforts to bring new energy and inspiration into the process by following a completely novel idea: A theorem prover shall be used to support a person learning and doing mathematics by assisting him/her through hints given by the prover. The prover shall analyze the student's approach to a mathematical problem and shall give information about the formal correctness of the actions performed by the student. Thus the student will remain creative in solving a problem, but he or she will get confirmation and advice on his/her mathematical activity.

The accessibility of the environment to be designed will be based on the accessibility of VSCode, a front-of-the-wave IDE with open source featured by Microsoft which is also an alternative front-end for Isabelle [5], the theorem

K. Miesenberger et al. (Eds.): ICCHP-AAATE 2022, LNCS 13341, pp. 47–55, 2022.
https://doi.org/10.1007/978-3-031-08648-9_7

prover intended as the core of the learning environment. VSCode itself is well accessible because it rests upon the Chromium library[1], which is able to furnish enough accessibility to be the basis for Google Chrome, a web browser used by many blind people worldwide.

Already now, the Isabelle theorem prover furnishes valuable support to people working in mathematics, be they blind, visually impaired, or sighted—however restricted to *reading* access. This support is due to the fact that, being a theorem proving system, Isabelle comes with a wealth of mathematical concepts with precise formal definitions, and theorems derived from them, with formally correct and well readable proofs. Therefore, with the Isabelle library we have a database of present mathematical knowledge which is already now accessible to everyone.

This paper outlines ideas, plans and preparatory work which emerge from joint efforts of three partners, where two of them were collaborating pairwise for a long time, but never all three of them. One partner is from the community of the proof assistant Isabelle [5], which is promoted by several institutions around the world; another is IIS, the institute "Integriert Studieren"[2] at Johannes Kepler University, and the third one is the *ISAC*-project[3].

The collaboration between Isabelle and *ISAC* results from the fact, that the latter uses the former as a conceptual and technological base. For some time there are plans to intensify this collaboration [3] for technical reasons. Great advances of Isabelle's front-end suggest to stop developing a proprietary front-end for *ISAC* and to advance *ISAC*'s integration into Isabelle such that it can re-use all of its front-ends (and eventually inherit accessibility).

And the collaboration between IIS and *ISAC* arises from IIS's mission to support students with special needs and to research how to make software accessible for those students. In particular, the *ISAC*-prototype shall be improved such that it becomes usable for visually impaired and blind people. This goal fits well with *ISAC*'s original idea to narrow the gap between high-school mathematics and academia. For that purpose *ISAC* reduces the complexity of proof to "structured derivations" [1], that means, to calculations solving problems as taught in academic engineering courses as well as at high-school.

Recently an *eureka moment* triggered collaboration of all three partners. A member of IIS (and co-author of this paper) is a blind person, nevertheless he holds a degree in a formal science. At his eureka moment he exclaimed "First time I can interactively read a proof on a computer!" after having installed Isabelle/VSCode[4] and investigating the proof of the well-known theorem $p \in \mathbb{N} \wedge p\ is\_prime \Rightarrow \sqrt{p} \notin \mathbb{Q}$. This important experience showed us that, when we want to make Isabelle accessible, the right way is to use its VSCode front-end.

[1] https://www.chromium.org/chromium-projects.
[2] https://www.jku.at/institut-integriert-studieren.
[3] https://isac.miraheze.org/wiki/History.
[4] https://isabelle-dev.sketis.net/source/isabelle/browse/default/src/Tools/VSCode/extension.

A detailed case study presents a concrete worked example within the learning scenario we are aiming at. This exhibits the novelties and avoids theoretical treatise.

2 A Vision for Educational Math Software

The traditional way of using paper and pencil to write down mathematical contents and much more to do mathematical calculations is still the predominant method among all people who have to do with mathematics. This is especially remarkable if we consider the tremendous changes modern information technology brought into society over the past few decades. Although computer algebra systems such as Mathematica are widely used among mathematicians, these systems cannot help a person doing a calculation by hand, since they will do the calculation for him/her. A system where the computer with its ever increasing possibilities to support the human brain would help a person to actually do a calculation is still missing, not only, as outlined here, for the group of blind or visually impaired people, but for the sighted mainstream as well—one will publish, or distribute, mathematical content in a digital format, but, as soon as a student actively constructs a solution for a given problem step by step (where each step has to be justified), it is generally paper and pencil which is used.

Of course the situation is changing step by step and faster due to the growing number of touch/pen based systems including OCR for math, digital math-ink, which will allow developing a new digital culture of interactively doing math including and integrating the interaction with tools as computer algebra, theorem provers and tutoring systems. These new and innovative systems inviting to transfer from paper/pencil to digital doing math provide a much better and much richer source for supporting navigation and in particular doing math for blind and low vision people: What was implicit to the visual procedures and workflows of doing math with pencil and paper now has to be formally and therefore explicitly described in a machine readable and processible manner. This forms a rich digital base, to which accessibility can hopefully be efficiently added and which allows to implement assisting and supportive functionalities better in accordance with the needs of blind and low vision people.

In spite of the undisputed advantages of the traditional paper-and-pencil method, it is our conviction that the computer has a strong potential to help in a calculation, be the user sighted, visually impaired, or blind. We thus envision a scenario where methods which apparently are needed by the relatively small group of blind people may as well be of great use and value *for all people* who are dealing with mathematics. We see this formal mark-up of the procedures of doing math as a first step towards a much more personalized approach to doing math problem solving which is able to much better respect the broad diversity of users in terms of physical, sensory, psycho-cognitive and social factors.

3 User Requirements

We claim that Isabelle/VSCode is the best starting point for accessibility of proof assistants. The Isabelle platform already includes the Prover IDE (PIDE) framework for various front-end editors: Isabelle/jEdit is currently the best developed one, but accessibility of its underlying Java/Swing GUI framework is lacking. In contrast, Isabelle/VSCode benefits from up-to-date components by Microsoft and Google, which are most of the time perfectly accessible—standard assistive technology for blind users is actively supported.

Subsequently we apply user requirements stated for an earlier GUI [2,4] to the current Isabelle/VSCode IDE. User requirements are abbreviated by "UR".

UR.1: Decomposition of terms into proper sub-terms A sighted person takes benefit from the highly sophisticated notation for terms elaborated during centuries: exponents, subscripts, numerator and denominator above and below a horizontal fraction bar, symbols from various languages, etc. All that can hardly be realised by a one-dimensional Braille display. However, [2] showed by experiments, that efficient navigation through sub-terms and super-terms *can* be realised via keyboard and Braille display—which supports understanding the structure of a term quite successfully. The (sub-)terms are represented as ASCII strings according to specific Braille standards.

So there is the requirement, that in parallel to the visual representation of terms (which looks nice in Isabelle's specific fonts) there is a proper term structure available for accessibility reasons—and both representations should be in parallel for the purpose of inclusive learning.

UR.2: Semantic information for term elements: Various support for requesting semantic information is well established in IDEs for a long time, in particular, getting a definition by clicking on a respective identifier in program code. Isabelle/jEdit extends this feature to mathematical terms: A click, for instance, on a plus operator in a term gets the definition of a semi-group, the simplest algebraic structure with a plus operator.

This feature has been transferred from Isabelle/jEdit to Isabelle/VSCode—and there this feature works perfectly accessible with keyboard shortcuts. High estimations of the very general tools provided by Isabelle also foster hopes, that a click on a certain element on the screen might lead to different definitions and explanations depending on a user's level of mathematics knowledge.

UR.3: Survey on structures of theories and of proofs is easily gained by a sighted person quickly scrolling up and down the screen—while the Braille display is line oriented and each line has to be touched until a survey might become satisfying.

For comprehension, arbitrary switching between detail and survey is crucial. This requirement is well met by Isabelle/jEdit with a "Sidekick" parser and by nice support for collapsing and expanding respective branches in the tree structure of theories; a mouse click on a branch immediately displays the respective detail in a theory. And proofs in Isabelle/Isar [6] are visually structured by syntax highlighting and by indentation such that the structure is presented nicely by the overall visual impression.

Visually impaired persons need an approximation to all these useful features for sighted users—an approximation that replaces vision and mouse by tactile sense, Braille and keyboard shortcuts. One concrete minimal requirement is an "Outline view" for theories and for proofs.

4 Case Study: Solving Complex Problems

Section 2 and Sect. 3 place high expectations, many of which have been accomplished by a prototype [3]. Appearance as well as students' workflow on the prototype are best illustrated by a case study. The following study focuses the most challenging phase, where human imagination triggered by text and figures has to be translated into formulas and to be related to available knowledge.

4.1 An Example from Electrical Engineering

The following text combined with a figure can be found in textbooks for electrical engineering:

The efficiency of an electrical coil depends on the mass of the kernel. Given is a kernel with cross-sectional area determined by two rectangles of same shape as shown in the figure.
Given a radius $r = 7$, determine the length u and width v of the rectangles such that the cross-sectional area A (and thus the mass of the kernel) is a maximum.

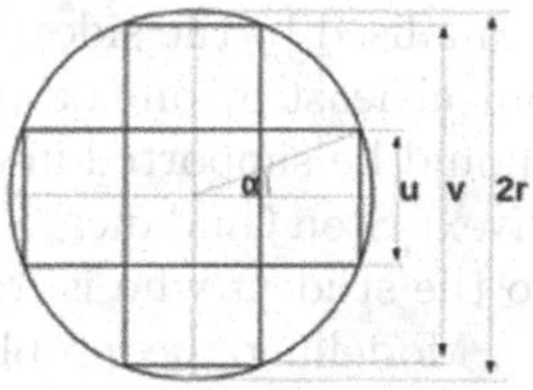

So, what kind of problem is this? The word "maximum" indicates an optimisation problem. Linear optimisation? What about approximation? Let's go deeper into details (... without being hampered by accessibility issues too early).

4.2 From Text and Figure to Formulas

The text asks for a "maximum". In order to "Find" a maximum, what do we know already, which facts are "Given"? The following template has fields to enter respective items in lines 05 and 08 respectively (where the line numbers serve for reference only on paper here):

```
01 Example <No.123 a>
02 Problem "univariate_calculus/Optimisation"
03   Specification:
04     Model:
05       Given: "Constants"  [r = 7]
06       Where: 0 < r
07       Find: "Maximum" [A], "AdditionalValues" [u, v]
```

```
08          Relate: [ A = 2·u·v − u², (u/2)² + (v/2)² = r² ]
09       References:
10             RTheory: [ "Diff_App" ]
11      [x]    RProblem: [ "univariate_calculus/Optimisation" ]
12      [o]    RMethod: [ "Optimisation/by_univariate_calculus" ]
13    Solution:
```

Above the template is filled already (frame-boxes indicate inputs) in order to shortcut explanation to the experienced reader. In the *ISAC*-project the template is offered to students in the so-called *"Specification" phase* which comprises modelling ideas into formulas and referencing available knowledge, the former labelled by "Model" (line 04) and the latter by "References" (line 09). There are three kinds of knowledge (all with the leading letter "R" for technical reasons and check-boxes "x" and "o" explained later): "RTheory" collects all the types and definitions required to get the formulas in the "Model" accepted by the system. "RProblem" is the identifier of the problem-pattern generating the specific problem at hand. And "RMethod" is able to generate the "Solution" (line 13) automatically or in interaction with the student, which is collapsed above.

4.3 "Next-Step Guidance" by a Hidden Formalisation

As already indicated just above, the general insight about right angles can be formalised by the sides' lengths in the Pythagorean triangle as $(\frac{u}{2})^2 + (\frac{v}{2})^2 = r^2$, but at least by one other equivalent formula $(\sin\alpha)^2 + (\cos\alpha)^2 = r^2$. A student should be supported in all possible ideas how to solve the problem at hand—by "Next-Step Guidance" : the system should always be able to propose a next step to the student who is free to adopt or to neglect it.

Modelling the problem at hand we already have at least two choices for the student—how to support these by the system? For that purpose *ISAC*'s prototype introduces "hidden formalisations" as follows (where the "References" are omitted, which are the same in both cases here):

$$F_I \equiv [\,[r = 7],\ [A,\ [u,\ v]],\ [A = 2\cdot u\cdot v - u^2,\ (\tfrac{u}{2})^2 + (\tfrac{v}{2})^2 = r^2],\ \{0 < .. < r\}\,]$$
$$F_{II} \equiv [\,[r = 7],\ [A,\ \alpha],\ [A = 2\cdot u\cdot v - u^2,\ \tfrac{u}{2} = r\sin\alpha,\ \tfrac{v}{2} = r\cos\alpha],\ \{0 < .. < \tfrac{\pi}{2}\}\,]$$

That knowledge[5] is hidden behind the example (p.5, line 01) as for each example, which should be capable of "Next-Step Guidance"—an additional authoring effort, small given the fact that user guidance in interactive problem solving is generated automatically afterwards.

So, the envisaged system shall be able to cope with a list of formalisations for one example under construction and to select the appropriate one, which the students seems to have in mind actually (which can change by specific input).

---

[5] The formalisations use brackets "[" and "]" denoting lists as usual in functional programming. Some inner lists, actually, are interpreted as sets.

4.4 Relate the Problem to Available Knowledge

The three kinds of knowledge mechanised in the *ISAC*-prototype have already been mentioned; now they are introduced properly—and related to accessibility first time in the case study.

1. *Theories* are inherited from Isabelle without change. Here are all the definitions required to mechanically read formulas and all theorems required to evaluate the pre-conditions in "Where" and to justify the steps in "Solution" after the specify-phase has been completed.
2. *Problems* are instantiations of a formalisation with a problem-pattern. Their representation has been introduced on p.5. Their definition is given in theories as soon as these comprise the required knowledge. And their structure is a tree—and there are lots of tools with highly elaborated accessibility, triggered by implementations of browsers for tree-structured collections of files as found in any operating system.
3. *Methods* comprise a guard and a program which supports interactive construction of a solution for the specified problem. While an optimal structure for collections of methods is still unclear, the *ISAC*-prototype collects them in a tree the same way; so the notes on accessibility apply here as well.

Searching appropriate knowledge during problem solving is probably the task which takes most advantage from software support. And most of the various tools for such search are highly accessible, as mentioned above.

Even equation solving is concern of knowledge lookup, the calculation on p.7 presents an equation on line 06: Assigning an appropriate method to solve it involves questions like "Are fractions involved?" "What is the degree?" etc.

4.5 Iterating through the Tasks

Problem solving is an iterative process between trial and error, between search and application of knowledge, between experiment and success. This iterative nature is reflected in the software-supported process as well—see a part of the "Solution" below following the completion of the "Specification", which is <*collapsed*> already):

01 Example <No.123 a>
02 Problem "univariate_calculus/Optimisation"
03 Specification: *<collapsed>*
04 Solution:
05 Problem "make/function"
06 solve_univariate $\left(\left(\frac{u}{2}\right)^2 + \left(\frac{v}{2}\right)^2 = r^2,\ v\right)$ *<collapsed>*
07 $L = \left[v = 2 \cdot \sqrt{r^2 - \left(\frac{u}{2}\right)^2},\ v = -2 \cdot \sqrt{r^2 - \left(\frac{u}{2}\right)^2}\right]$
08 $v \in \{0 < \, .. < r\}$
09 $A = 2 \cdot u \cdot v - u^2$
10 *Substitute v*
11 $A\ u = 2 \cdot u \cdot \sqrt{r^2 - \left(\frac{u}{2}\right)^2} - u^2$
12 differentiate $\left(A\ u = 2 \cdot u \cdot \sqrt{r^2 - \left(\frac{u}{2}\right)^2} - u^2,\ u\right)$
13 $A'\ u = \frac{d}{du}\left(2 \cdot u\ \sqrt{r^2 - \left(\frac{u}{2}\right)^2} - u^2\right)$

14 $\frac{d}{du}(u_1 - u_2) = \frac{d}{du}u_1 - \frac{d}{du}u_2$

15 $A'\ u = \frac{d}{du}\left(2 \cdot u\ \sqrt{r^2 - \left(\frac{u}{2}\right)^2}\right) - \frac{d}{du}u^2$

$\vdots$

29 $[u = 6.75, v = 12.25]$

The "Solution" iterates through specifying (sub-)"Problems" and interactively constructing steps towards a solution of the problems. The first encounter is Problem "make/function", immediately followed by another problem "solve_univariate" in line 06, which appears as a standard function like in algebra systems.

At the right margin there are (beyond <*collapsed*>) the justifications for the steps constructing solutions; in line 09 the negative element is dropped from the set L of solutions, because it is not element of the interval $\{0 < .. < r\}$ known from formalisation F_I; in line 10 the justification is the primitive operation "Substitute v" which in line 11 constructs the solution for Problem "make/function".

In line 12 "differentiate" is again a function known from computer algebra (so the respective "Specification" is skipped). The function creates a sequence of steps; here the justification is given by a well-known theorem. And at a certain point an engineer will be interested in concrete numbers for u and v and will decide to switch to floating point numbers in some interactive "Specification".

5 Conclusion

The research and development area dedicated to enabling blind people in mathematics, especially in learning mathematics, has been highly active but did not yet improve the central part of doing mathematics, which is still left to paper & pencil. The completely new approach of employing a theorem prover, which is outlined here, may revive this immensely important effort, leading to real-life software solutions with the ability to take away a crucial shortcoming from the community of blind and visually impaired people, but also with great potential of fertilizing mainstream mathematical teaching as well in the future.

References

1. Back, R.J.: Structured derivations as a unified proof style for teaching mathematics. TUCS Technical Report 949, TUCS - Turku Centre for Computer Science, Turku, Finland (2009)
2. Karl, N.: Developing an Inclusive Approach for Representing Mathematical Formulas. Master's thesis, Hagenberg University of Applied Sciences, Linz, Austria (2016). https://static.miraheze.org/isacwiki/0/02/Masterthesis_NatalieKarl.pdf
3. Krempler, A., Neuper, W.: Prototyping systems that explain themselves for education. In: Quaresma, P., Neuper, W. (eds.) Proceedings 6th International Workshop on Theorem proving components for Educational software, Gothenburg, Sweden, 6 Aug 2017. Electronic Proceedings in Theoretical Computer Science, vol. 267, pp. 89–107. Open Publishing Association (2018). https://doi.org/10.4204/EPTCS.267.6, https://arxiv.org/abs/1803.01470v1

4. Mahringer, M.: Formula Editors for TP-based Systems. State of the Art and Prototype Implementation in *ISAC*. Master's thesis, University of Applied Sciences, Hagenberg, Austria (2018). https://static.miraheze.org/isacwiki/d/d7/Mmahringer-master.pdf
5. Paulson, L.C., Nipkow, T., Wenzel, M.: From LCF to Isabelle/HOL. Formal Aspects Comput. **31**, 675–698 (2019). https://doi.org/10.1007/s00165-019-00492-1
6. Wenzel, M.: Isabelle/Isar – a generic framework for human-readable proof documents. In: Matuszewski, R., Zalewska, A. (eds.) From Insight to Proof – Festschrift in Honour of Andrzej Trybulec, Studies in Logic, Grammar, and Rhetoric, vol. 10, no. 23. University of Białystok (2007). https://www21.in.tum.de/~wenzelm/papers/isar-framework.pdf

Developing a Corpus of Hierarchically Classified STEM Images for Accessibility Purposes

Theodora Antonakopoulou, Paraskevi Riga, and Georgios Kouroupetroglou(✉)

Department of Informatics and Telecommunications, Speech and Accessibility Laboratory, National and Kapodistrian University of Athens, 15784 Athens, Greece
{ic1190004,p.riga,koupe}@di.uoa.gr

Abstract. Even though considerable efforts have been made to provide effective image descriptions for digital accessibility, a large portion of STEM images, especially complex STEM images, nowadays remains inaccessible to people with visual disability. The quality of alt text is much more critical for university STEM textbooks as image descriptions must be accurate and detailed but not tire out the reader. This work aims to develop a large corpus of hierarchically classified STEM images from university textbooks which later will be used for developing appropriate guidelines for meaningful non-automatic high-quality alt-text image descriptions with the purpose of accessibility in mind. We present first our approach for the creation of the corpus with the STEM images. Our corpus at the current stage includes 8.859 STEM images from 82 textbooks in the domains of Mathematics, Biology, Computer Science, Chemistry, Physics and Geology. Then, we describe the methodology we followed for the classification of the images in the corpus and in particular, the way for the creation of the five categories and twenty-four subcategories, as well as the manner of the assignment of images to categories.

Keywords: Accessibility · Alt-text · Image description · STEM

1 Introduction

The goal of this work is to develop a large corpus of hierarchically classified images in the disciplines of Science, Technology, Engineering, and Mathematics (STEM). The classification scheme of these images will later be used for developing appropriate guidelines for meaningful non-automatic high-quality alt-text image descriptions with the purpose of accessibility in mind. The reasoning behind this work is that even though considerable efforts have been made to provide effective image descriptions, a large portion of STEM images nowadays remain inaccessible to people with a visual disability, especially complex STEM images. The quality of alt-text is much more important for university STEM textbooks as alt-text image descriptions must be accurate and detailed but not tire out the reader. As the first step to our approach, we consider STEM images more thoroughly by first creating a corpus of STEM images from university textbooks, which will be hierarchically classified.

K. Miesenberger et al. (Eds.): ICCHP-AAATE 2022, LNCS 13341, pp. 56–62, 2022.
https://doi.org/10.1007/978-3-031-08648-9_8

2 Images' Selection State of the Art

Examining where, how, and what types of images have been collected in the past, we are looking into relevant domains such as the automatic generation of image descriptions [1, 2], the automatic image classification [3–9], the evaluation of alternative text descriptions quality [10], the evaluation of image description guidelines or methodology [11, 12] and the creation of image description exemplary samples [13, 14]. This can lead us to discover selections, datasets, or corpora of images that have been developed with the purpose of constructing frameworks, methodologies, and specific guidelines, of training automatic models of image descriptions, captioning, etc., but also, we can come across selections that are primarily used for evaluating and testing the aforementioned.

Regarding STEM images for automatic classification tasks, datasets are found here [4–6, 15–21]. One observes that, even though usually these corpora are large, they do not include a variety of image types, and specifically, they exclude complex diagrams and illustrations.

The common practice in manual image description for accessibility, especially for creating image guidelines, is using a small selection of images to create sample descriptions. The result is a set of guidelines and exemplary descriptions of images. In manual image descriptions compared to automatic image description tasks, we see that a variety of image types have been taken into consideration. For instance, in [14], authors have placed exemplary descriptions of STEM images under specific categories that include not only charts but also diagrams and more. However, we lack the large corpora of images that are usually provided in automatic tasks.

To our awareness, at least, there isn't an approach where authors of non-automatic alternative text first collect a large corpus of images manually, classify its images, and then exploit it to create guidelines for images. Large datasets can be found in Machine Learning and AI for creating image descriptions automatically. But in descriptions created by authors of alternative text, we see instead that the typical approach is picking a small number of images, creating sample descriptions, and then following up with user testing and surveying to figure out whether these descriptions are helpful. User-surveying and testing are very important to evaluate a description; in fact, it is necessary. However, picking only a few images to test might leave out a lot of complexities.

3 Corpus Creation Methodology

a. We first considered the task: To create approaches for meaningful, high-quality alt-text descriptions, we require a large corpus of images that covers a variety of thematic subjects and with the content of various complexity.
b. We collected the images: We tried not to exclude any significant domains of study. After we decided on the domains of study, the main thematic subjects were selected for each one of them. For each subject, several textbooks were randomly picked from university libraries. Finally, for each textbook, we digitally copied a randomly selected number of images without going through the material or choosing what seemed more relevant to us at the moment.

c. We collected additional data: For every textbook, the title, author name, and library registration number were collected. Since images are placed in the context of a textbook, it is essential that for future work, we can revisit these textbooks.

Besides the fact that we collect STEM images, the procedure can be used to collect images of any type from other scientific disciples. A possible limitation occurs from the fact that the images were selected from university textbooks, which might result in some image types appearing more frequently than others, and their complexity might be elevated. However, the latter should not be considered a negative in this case.

4 Image Classification

4.1 Creation of Categories

Following the previous methodology, our corpus at the current stage includes 8.859 STEM images from 82 textbooks in the domains of Mathematics, Biology, Computer Science, Chemistry, Physics, and Geology.

Then, we have allocated the images into categories and sub-categories. The distinction between those categories was primarily made on a structural level so that within each category, images contain a set of structural similarities. Twenty-four specific categories were created based on observation and consideration of previous image classification for accessibility (such as in [14]). We described the characteristics of each specific category in terms of structural and visual elements, logical relationships between image items, and gathered associated labels. Table 1 presents six indicative examples of images from our corpus, and Table 2 their specific type characteristics' description.

Depending on the field of study, the content of these images varies. After these images were classified into specific type categories, they were grouped into five general categories:

i. **Diagram:** Image representing information with a specific structure (for example, linear, hierarchical, or circular).
ii. **Graph:** Image used to depict numerical data.
iii. **Photograph:** Image of the real world, taken with a camera, microscope, or telescope.
iv. **Map:** Image representing an area in scale, depicting its geographical characteristics and/or relations of its sub-parts.
v. **Special image types:** Here we include images that are exclusively domain-specific.

The list of specific image categories we have developed is provided here:

i. **Diagrams:** 1. Hierarchical/tree diagrams, 2. Linear/flow diagrams, 3. Circular diagrams, 4. Nets, 5. Mixed/complex diagrams, 6. Diagrammatic illustrations (snapshots), 7. Diagrammatic illustrations (static).
ii. **Graphs:** 8. 2D Function graphs, 9. Line graphs, 10. Zone graphs, 11. Scatter plots, 12. Level graphs, 13. Bar charts, 14. Pie charts.

Table 1. Indicative image examples from the corpus.

Specific image type	Image example
Hierarchical diagrams	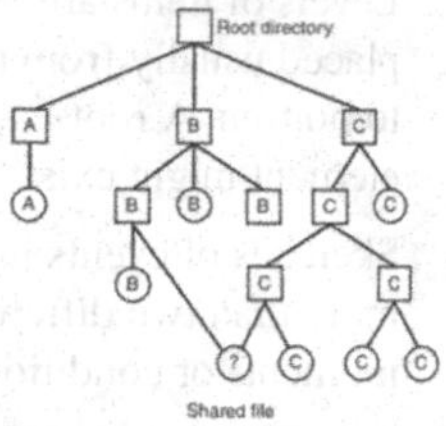
Diagrammatic illustrations (snapshots)	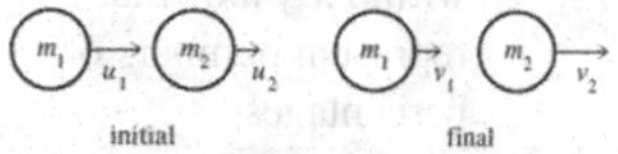
Bar charts	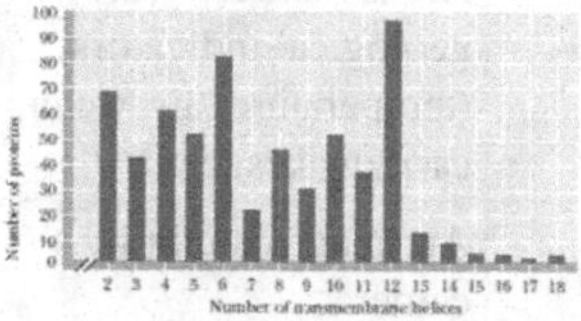
Geology map	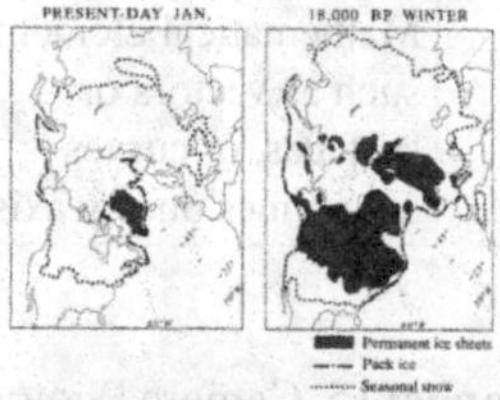
Camera Photographs	
Mathematical 2D elements	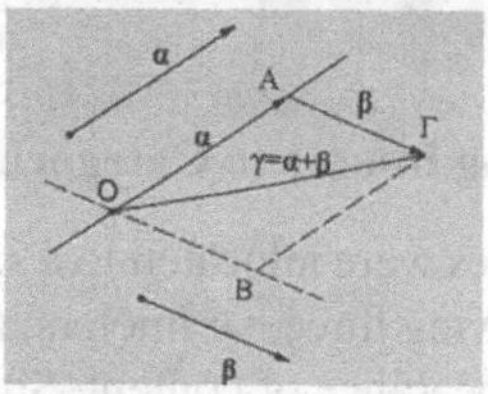

Table 2. Examples of a specific image type characteristics' description.

Specific image type	Visual/structural characteristics	Logical relationships	Associated labels
Hierarchical diagrams	Levels of items are placed usually from top to bottom. A root element might exist	Hierarchy of items	Hierarchy diagram, tree, dendrodiagram, cladogram
Diagrammatic illustrations (snapshots)	Sketches of events in more than two different moments or conditions	Sequence of items	Procedure, snapshots
Bar charts	Bars are usually placed within x-y axis that represent numbers or percentages	Quantitative relations of items	Bar graph, bar chart, bar plot
Geology map	Areas marked with geological indicators (temperature, air, water, earthquakes, etc.)	Qualitative or quantitative relations of items	Map
Camera photographs	An image caught by a camera	Not always applicable	Photograph
Mathematical 2D elements	Mathematical elements such as vectors or surfaces, or curves sometimes on x-y axis	Quantitative or qualitative relations of items	Figure

iii. **Photographs:** 15. Camera Photographs, 16. Microscope Photographs, 17.Telescope photographs.
iv. **Maps:** 18. Geology maps, 19. Other maps.
v. **Special image types:** 20. 2D Chemical compounds and equations, 21. 3D Chemical compounds and equations, 22. 2D Mathematical elements (vectors, surfaces, curves), 23. 3D Mathematical elements (vectors, surfaces, curves), 24. Periodic tables.

4.2 Assigning Images to Categories

Initially, images were allocated to a specific category on a first-glance basis. We considered the following three parameters: (a) structural similarity, (b) label of the image, and (c) overall appearance of content. Similarities to the above indicate that images belong in the same category. After this initial classification, there can still be images that, upon further analysis, might be placed in a different category. There are also images where ambiguity arises (unidentified images), and in their case, (d) specific content or (e) context of image was also considered so that their initial number was reduced. Still remain some unidentified diagrams or very domain-specific images, but they constitute a small percentage (around 10%) of the corpus.

Even after reducing unidentified images, we know that there can still be errors in classification. This is influenced by the structural similarity that can reside between different classes. There are cases where the structure of an image resembles one category, but the image might belong to another category. Some examples where we found structural similarity were in hierarchy diagrams getting mixed with linear diagrams or circular diagrams getting mixed with nets.

The final classification results some disparity between collected images. This can be influenced by the fact that some image types can be appropriately used in many scientific domains (e.g., hierarchy diagrams), while other image types are much more domain-specific (e.g., telescope photographs). There are also categories with significant variability within a class. For instance, diagrammatic illustrations contain a variety of subjects and structures, not allowing us to further break down this category into more structurally similar sub-categories. Even though this category is distinctly different from others, it does contain a lot of variability compared to other categories.

5 Conclusions

We have developed a large corpus of hierarchically classified STEM images from university textbooks. Moreover, we have described the methodology we followed for the classification of the images in the corpus and, in particular, the way for the creation of the five categories and twenty-four subcategories, as well as the manner of the assignment of images to categories. Based on the above results, we are now working towards the development of appropriate guidelines for meaningful, non-automatic, high-quality alt-text image descriptions with the purpose of accessibility in mind for university students.

Acknowledgments. This work has been partially financed by the National and Kapodistrian University of Athens, Special Account for Research Grants.

References

1. Farhadi, A., et al.: Every picture tells a story: generating sentences from images. In: Daniilidis, K., Maragos, P., Paragios, N. (eds.) ECCV 2010. LNCS, vol. 6314, pp. 15–29. Springer, Heidelberg (2010). https://doi.org/10.1007/978-3-642-15561-1_2
2. Bernardi, R., et al.: Automatic description generation from images. J. Artif. Intell. Res. **55**, 409–442 (2016). https://doi.org/10.1613/jair.4900
3. Shahira, K.C., Lijiya, A.: Document image classification: towards assisting visually impaired. In TENCON 2019 – 2019 IEEE Region 10 Conference (TENCON), pp. 852–857 (2019). https://doi.org/10.1109/TENCON.2019.8929594
4. Kavasidis, I., et al.: A saliency-based convolutional neural network for table and chart detection in digitized documents. In: International Conference on Image Analysis and Processing, 2019, pp. 292–302. Springer (2019)
5. Savva, M., Kong, N., Chhajta, A., Fei-Fei, L., Agrawala, M., Heer, J.: ReVision: automated classification, analysis and redesign of chart images. In: 24th Annual ACM Symposium on User Interface Software and Technology, pp. 393–402 (2011). https://doi.org/10.1145/2047196.2047247

6. Amara, J., Kaur, P., Owonibi, M., Bouaziz, B.: Convolutional neural network based chart image classification. In: 25th Int. Conf. Central Europe on Computer Graphics, Visualization and Computer Vision, pp. 83–88 (2017)
7. Krizhevsky, A., Sutskever, I., Hinton, G.E.: Imagenet classification with deep convolutional neural networks. In: F. Pereira, F., C.J.C. Burges, C.J.C., Bottou, L., Weinberger, K.Q. (eds.) Advances in Neural Information Processing Systems, vol. 25, pp. 1097–1105 (2012)
8. Deng, J., Dong, W., Socher, R., Li, L.J., Li, K., Fei-Fei, L.: ImageNet: a large-scale hierarchical image database. In: 2009 IEEE Conference on Computer Vision and Pattern Recognition, pp. 248–255 (2009). https://doi.org/10.1109/CVPR.2009.5206848
9. Russakovsky, O., et al.: ImageNet large scale visual recognition challenge. Int. J. Comput. Vis. **115**(3), 211–252 (2015). https://doi.org/10.1007/s11263-015-0816-y
10. Bigham, J.: Increasing web accessibility by automatically judging alternative text quality. In: 12th International Conf. Intelligent User Interfaces, pp. 349–352 (2007). https://doi.org/10.1145/1216295.1216364
11. Tang, L., Carter, J.A.: Communicating image content. In: The Human Factors and Ergonomics Society 55th Annual Meeting, 2011, pp. 495–499 (2011). https://doi.org/10.1177/1071181311551102
12. Nengroo, A.S., Kuppusamy, K.S.: Accessible images (AIMS): a model to build self-describing images for assisting screen reader users. Univ. Access Inf. Soc. **17**(3), 607–619 (2017). https://doi.org/10.1007/s10209-017-0607-z
13. NCAM: Project History and Research Methodology. http://ncamftp.wgbh.org/ncam-old-site/experience_learn/educational_media/stemdx/research.html. Accessed 1 Feb 2022
14. DIAGRAM CENTER: Accessible Images Sample Book. http://diagramcenter.org/accessible-image-sample-book.html. Accessed 18 Dec 2021
15. Shahira, K.C., Lijiya, S.: Towards assisting the visually impaired: a review on techniques for decoding the visual data from chart images. IEEE Access **9**, 52926–52943 (2021). https://doi.org/10.1109/ACCESS.2021.3069205
16. Kahou, S.E., Adam, A., Michalski, V., Kadar, A., Trischler, A., Bengio, Y.: Figureqa: an annotated figure dataset for visual reasoning. arXiv Preprint arXiv:1710.07300 (2017). https://doi.org/10.48550/arXiv.1710.07300
17. Chaudhry, R., Shekhar, S., Gupta, U., Maneriker, P., Bansal, P., Joshi, A.: Leaf-qa: locate, encode attend for figure question answering. In: The IEEE Winter Conference on Applications of Computer Vision (WACV), 2020, pp. 3501–3510 (2020). https://doi.org/10.1109/WACV45572.2020.9093269
18. Kafle, K., Price, B., Cohen, S., Kanan, C.: Dvqa: understanding data visualizations via question answering. In: IEEE/CVF Conference on Computer Vision and Pattern Recognition, 2018, pp. 5648–5656 (2018). https://doi.org/10.1109/CVPR.2018.00592
19. Methani, N., Ganguly, P., Khapra, M.M., Kumar, P.: PlotQA: reasoning over scientific plots. In: IEEE Winter Conference on Applications of Computer Vision (WACV), 2020, pp. 1516–1525 (2020). https://doi.org/10.1109/WACV45572.2020.9093523
20. Siegel, N., Horvitz, Z., Levin, R., Divvala, S., Farhadi, A.: FigureSeer: Parsing Result-Figures in Research Papers. In: Leibe, B., Matas, J., Sebe, N., Welling, M. (eds.) ECCV 2016. LNCS, vol. 9911, pp. 664–680. Springer, Cham (2016). https://doi.org/10.1007/978-3-319-46478-7_41
21. Clark, C.A., Divvala, S.: Looking beyond text: extracting figures, tables and captions from computer science papers. In: Workshops at the Twenty-Ninth AAAI Conference on Artificial Intelligence (2015). http://ai2-website.s3.amazonaws.com/publications/clark_divvala.pdf

Effective Non-visual Access to Diagrams via an Augmented Natural Language Interface

Tomas Murillo-Morales(✉) and Klaus Miesenberger

Johannes Kepler University, Altenbergerstr. 69, 4040 Linz, Austria
Tomas.Murillo_Morales@jku.at

Abstract. This paper describes the design and validation of a number of HCI techniques that enable more effective non-visual access to diagrammatically displayed data through an adapted Natural Language Interface (NLI). These techniques have been incorporated into an accessible web-based NLI to diagrams prototype and qualitatively evaluated with blind persons for solving disparate analytical and navigational tasks supported by diagrams. Each technique is described and validation results discussed.

Keywords: Natural Language Interface · Visualization · Semantic annotation · Human-computer interaction · Accessibility

1 Introduction

1.1 Diagram Accessibility

Visual representations of data (i.e. *diagrams*) exploit the human visual system thereby enabling efficient cognitive access to large amounts of data. Consequently, diagrams have become ubiquitous and the ability to access them is a necessity in many aspects of daily life.

Traditional non-visual methods for accessing diagrams include *tactile diagrams*, which are expensive to produce and must greatly simplify the original graphic, *sonified diagrams*, which are only a suitable approach for representing simple line charts, and *linear approaches*, which are far from being functionally equivalent to their graphic counterparts and often overload the working memory of the reader. Blind persons are therefore usually excluded from accessing diagrams because current alternative access methods are either too simplistic, too complex and/or expensive to use, or they require external support from a sighted expert.

1.2 AUDiaL: A Natural Language Interface to Diagrams

There exists a fourth kind of approach to non-visual access to diagrams we have not mentioned yet; namely, *Natural Language Interfaces* (NLI) allow users to

K. Miesenberger et al. (Eds.): ICCHP-AAATE 2022, LNCS 13341, pp. 63–72, 2022.
https://doi.org/10.1007/978-3-031-08648-9_9

navigate and query a graphic and the underlying dataset non-visually by means of utterances performed in natural language, such as English. As opposed to the traditional methods discussed in previous section, NLI-based approaches present many compelling properties for their application in accessibility of diagrams for blind persons.

Namely, a properly designed web-based NLI presents the following benefits over traditional non-visual diagram counterparts:

- NLIs are intuitive to use and can, for the most part, forgo the need for user training.
- Language can be employed to communicate information at any level of abstraction, from very specific information (e.g. the value of a single data point) to high-level concepts (e.g. the general trend of the displayed data). Therefore, the original diagram needs not be simplified with the resulting loss of information. Moreover, additional information can be added by the user or the system in order to improve the usability of the NLI e.g. via personalized annotations that help ligthen the working memory demands of the user.
- They do not require specific software and hardware, and can be accessed by blind persons like any other accessible web page using common assistive technology such as screen readers.

However, despite their increasing popularity, research on NLIs is rarely motivated by the goal of accessibility [3]. Consequently, we have designed and validated a software prototype for natural-language based non-visual access to diagrams. The prototype is a fully accessible web application named AUDiaL (Accessible Universal Diagrams through Language)[1]. Aspects related to the technical design of AUDiaL and an initial validation with end users are discussed in [6].

2 Accessible NLI to Diagrams

Diagrams are widely employed to communicate large amounts of data to sighted persons because they are able to exploit many perceptual, cognitive, and memorial capacities of human beings, leveraged by means of sight. An usable accessible NLI to diagrams must therefore not only allow users to execute tasks of an analytical nature (e.g. retrieving relevant statistics of the underlying dataset, see [4]), but also to benefit, insofar as possible, from the cognitive advantages of visualization itself.

2.1 HCI Techniques for NLI Accessibility

We have devised a number of HCI techniques in order to improve the efficacy of employing a NLI to diagrams by blind users. More specifically, these techniques aim to compensate for the lack of a number of cognitive benefits that diagrams

[1] AUDiaL is free software; its source code and installation instructions are available at https://github.com/tomurillo/AUDiaL.

have been demonstrated to provide to sighted persons. For further information about the specific benefits that will be mentioned throughout this document the reader is directed to [5].

These techniques, summarized in Table 1, have been added to AUDiaL and validated with blind participants in laboratory sessions. In the following, we list and briefly describe each of them.

Table 1. Summary of techniques included in AUDiaL (column headers) and the cognitive benefits (row headers) they address in the context of non-visual access to diagrams.

		Hierarchical and Sequential Navigation	Quick Jumps	Object Annotation	Home Node	High-level Summary/ Trend Description
Wayfinding	Piloting	✓		✓	✓	
	Path Integration	✓	✓		✓	
	Cognitive Map-Based Navigation	✓	✓	✓		
Resemblance Preservation	Literal			✓		✓
	Homomorphic	✓				✓
Computational Off-Loading			✓	✓	✓	✓
Breath-then-Depth Search		✓	✓		✓	✓

High-level Summaries. A short description of the diagram and its underlying data as a whole may be verbally requested by users at any time (e.g. "give me a summary"). This summary, automatically generated by AUDiaL, is necessary so that users may acquaint themselves with the diagram and the data it depicts before delving into specific analytical and navigational tasks (i.e. *breadth-then-depth search*). Moreover, readers may return at any time to consulting the summary in order to orientate themselves while navigating it, thereby facilitating *computational off-loading* by acting as an external memory.

In addition, requesting a high-level summary of the information being consumed corresponds to the first aspect of the, widely adopted in HCI research, "Visual Information-Seeking Mantra" which states "overview first, zoom and filter, then details-on-demand" [7]. This short mantra summarizes many recognized guidelines in information visualization and provides a memorable framework for the design of information visualization computer applications. By offering users an overview of the data and its visualization, AUDiaL follows well-established design practices.

Spatial Indexing and Navigation. In order to extract useful information from a newly encountered diagram, users must have the means for performing *exploration* and *quest* tasks on the graphic [1]. Therefore, the constituent elements of the diagram are automatically enhanced by AUDiaL with a transparent *navigational index* according to their logical and spatial arrangement on a graphic space. Users may issue navigational commands in natural language (e.g. "go to the next element") in order to navigate the informational nodes of the diagram in a sequential or hierarchical fashion.

Navigating the diagram hierarchically (e.g. in a scatterplot, moving from coarse-grained navigation in a cluster-by-cluster basis to fine-grained navigation within a cluster in a point-by-point basis) preserves, to some extent, the *resemblance*, both *literal* and *homomorphic*, of how data is visualized and accessed by sighted persons. Navigational indices of graphic objects in the diagram take into account their hierarchical arrangement in a domain-dependent fashion. For example, in bar charts, AUDiaL searches for stacked bars made up of a number of metric bars, and annotates them accordingly as the parent objects of their constituent bars.

Quick Jumps. Users may issue navigational commands for immediately moving to informational elements with special properties (e.g. "go to the largest bar" in a bar chart). Namely, users may jump to the informational graphic objects with associated greatest/lowest value of some variable; and to the first/last object in the automatically computed navigational sequence. Users may also issue a quick jump between the current node and any other informational node of the diagram, as shown in Fig. 2, as long as the target node can be uniquely identified from the user's input.

The ability to quick jump between elements mimics the instant accessibility of the visual form by reducing short-term memory demands, facilitating obtaining an overview of the data and external cognition. In addition, quick jumps may be performed to annotated nodes of interest to assist users in wayfinding activities, as described next.

Object Annotation. AUDiaL lets users set free-formed personal text annotations to any informational node of the diagram (e.g. "hometown last year" in Fig. 1). Users may at any time assign an annotation to the node being currently visited during a wayfinding session.

The main benefit of this technique is that it acts as an external memory, freeing up cognitive demands from the user. In addition, personal annotations are combined with other techniques when possible. For example, users may perform a quick jump to a previously annotated node to perform *cognitive map-based navigation* [1] (e.g. "jump to hometown last year").
Object annotation may also be used to prevent confusion caused by poor differentiation of similar elements and lostness during exploration activities. In addition, annotated nodes may help with preserving, to some extent, their literal

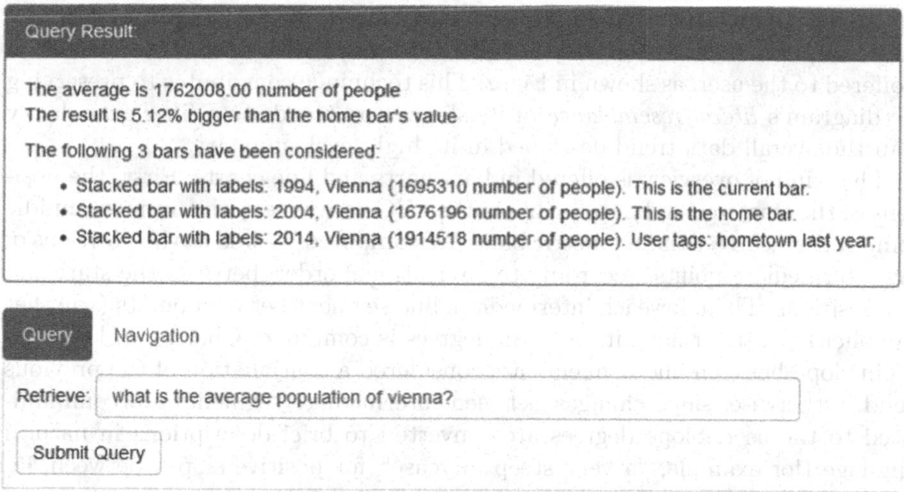

Fig. 1. The answer to an input query showing several annotation techniques in use. First, the answer to the question itself is given. Numeric answers are then compared to the associated value of the *home node*, if set. For each individual element that has been considered as part of the answer, their individual user- and system-created annotations are additionally given as part of the answer.

resemblance by e.g. describing its shape or other visually perceivable attributes of relevance.

Home Node. Stemming from their usage in non-visual exploration of link diagrams [2], AUDiaL implements the concept of *home node* to assist users in *path integration* activities. A user may choose at any time to select the current element being accessed as his or her home node, that is, a distinctive node that is used as a base for exploration and that can be easily returned to when lost [2], which from that moment onward will act as the main reference point for subsequent path integration.

Any system answer is related to the home node's associated value, if set. This includes not only the results from navigational tasks, but also answers to analytical tasks resulting on a single numerical value being output (an example is shown in Fig. 1). The value of the home node is always compared against other values in relative terms, since the aim of the home node is to serve as a reference point against which every other element of the graphic can be contrasted.

Home nodes make explicit vital information that would otherwise be lost by simply analyzing the raw tabular counterpart of a diagram. For example, comparing the sizes (as a proxy of value) of two bars in their visual form is done instinctively and almost instantly by sighted diagram readers. This cognitive benefit is explicitly recovered in AUDiaL by enabling users to choose their 'home bar' in a bar chart.

Trend Descriptions. When jumping in between distant elements, a short verbal description of the visual shape of the (inferred) line segments between them is offered to the user, as shown in Fig. 2. This technique contributes to preserving the diagram's *literal resemblance* of its slopes and trends to a finer granularity than the overall data trend described in its high-level summary.

This kind of overview is offered in bar charts and line charts. First, the positions of the start and end data points in the SVG canvas (e.g. the topmost middle point of their corresponding metric bars) are computed, as well as the positions of any intermediate points, according to navigational order, between the start and end positions. Then, for each intermediate line segment between points (whether it explicitly exists or not), its slope in degrees is computed. Changes of less than 5% in slope between line segments are considered a continuation of the previous trend. Otherwise, slope changes between intermediate segments are communicated to the user. Slope degrees are converted to brief descriptions in natural language (for example, "a very steep increase" for positive slopes between 45° and 75°).

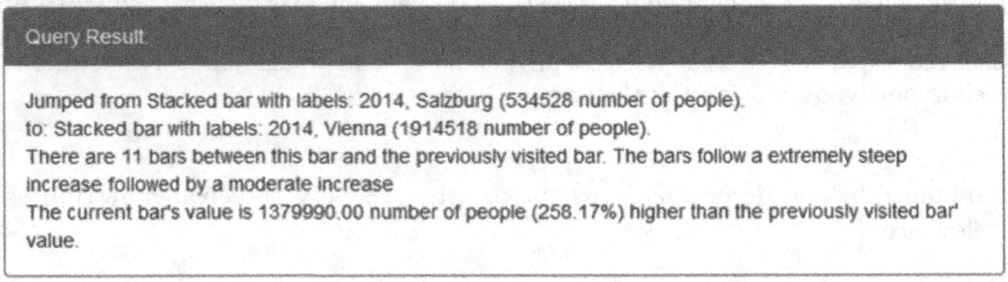

Query Result
Jumped from Stacked bar with labels: 2014, Salzburg (534528 number of people).
to: Stacked bar with labels: 2014, Vienna (1914518 number of people).
There are 11 bars between this bar and the previously visited bar. The bars follow a extremely steep increase followed by a moderate increase
The current bar's value is 1379990.00 number of people (258.17%) higher than the previously visited bar' value.

Fig. 2. System answer to a navigational jump between distant nodes. Labels and values of start and end nodes are given first, followed by a description of the visual trend between them. Lastly, values of the start and end nodes are compared in absolute and relative terms.

Note how, as summarized in Table 1, the HCI techniques listed above are reprocessed to realize more than one cognitive benefit simultaneously. In addition, these techniques are proposed as an extension of the typical capabilities of a NLI (e.g. AUDiaL, described in [6]) which include the realization of analytical tasks of a disparate nature such as clustering similar elements, computing dataset statistics, or finding anomalies in the data.

AUDiaL supports and harmonizes tasks that facilitate typical analytical activities performed on diagrammatically displayed data as well as non-visual wayfinding activities supported by the specialized HCI techniques previously discussed. In this manner, accessing a diagram non-visually can become as functionally similar as possible to doing so by means of sight.

2.2 Validation

AUDiaL has been validated in laboratory sessions with 9 blind participants with an average age of 24.11 years and a standard deviation of 12.17 years, ranging from 17 to 58 years of age. Two diagrams (a stacked bar chart and a lineup of stacked area charts) of similar complexity were selected and adapted so that they could be processed by AUDiaL. For each diagram, participants had to solve eight cognitive tasks of varying difficulty that did not require participants to have domain knowledge of the depicted data. A comparison of user satisfaction measurements between AUDiaL and traditional accessible diagram counterparts (tactile graphics, long descriptions) stemming from these validation sessions can be read in [6].

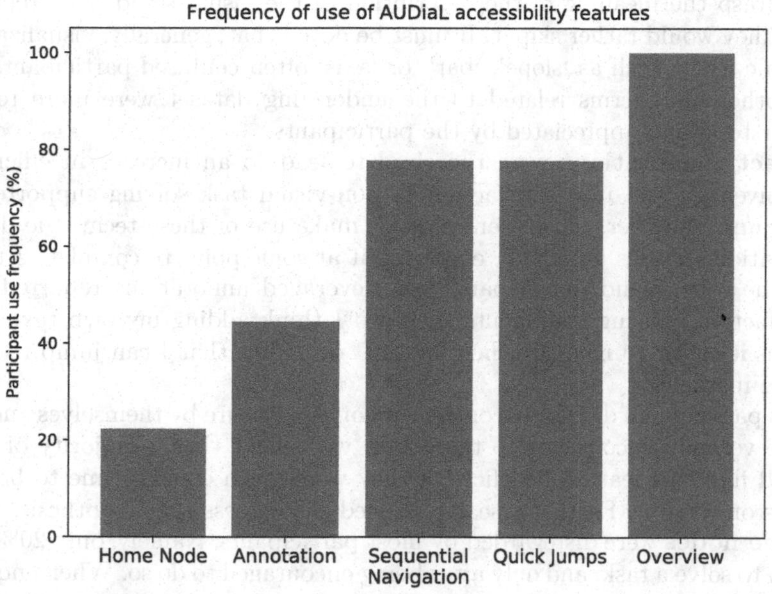

Fig. 3. Frequency with which selected accessibility features of AUDiaL were employed in at least one task solving activity by validation participants.

With regard to the HCI techniques described in Sect. 2.1, direct observation of the participants while undertaking tasks, system logs, and voluntary interviews post-session were employed to qualitatively validate their effectiveness in supporting the solving of complex cognitive tasks on diagrams. Figure 3 displays the proportion of participants that employed each technique in at least one correctly solved task.

- **High-level Summaries** were the most commonly employed technique. Every participant consulted the diagrams' summaries at some point to solve at least one task. Likewise, participants reported finding the feature useful and that it helped them in building a better mental model of the diagram and the underlying data.

- **Spatial Indexing and Navigation** features where employed by 80% of participants, sometimes even exclusively, during successful problem solving activities. All participants found this feature at least somewhat useful, especially during initial exploration of the diagram. However, most participants wished to have the possibility of jumping to the *n*th node of the navigational sequence via a single command.
- **Quick Jumps** were also commonly utilized in task solving (80% of participants). Most users reported finding this technique useful; it was routinely employed to retrieve data extrema. However, participants did not find the **trend descriptions** offered by AUDiaL as part of a quick jump command's output (c.f. Fig. 2) a convenient feature. For the most part, participants could not grasp the meaning of the description of the visual trend, who reported that they would rather skip it. It must be noted that, generally, visualization-specific terms such as 'slope', 'bar', or 'axis' often confused participants. On the other had, terms related to the underlying dataset were more readily understood and appreciated by the participants.
- **Object Annotations** were theorized to lead to an increase in efficiency, effectiveness, and user satisfaction in non-visual task solving supported by diagrams. However, most users did not make use of these technique during validation sessions (only 40% employed it at some point to complete a task). On the other hand, participants who leveraged annotations reported high satisfaction, voicing statements such as "I think adding my own text notes makes it easier to navigate the diagram" or "I like that I can jump to parts that I marked".
  Most participants did not become aware of this feature by themselves and had to be verbally encouraged to try it out; we believe that a majority of users would find this feature beneficial if they were given enough time to become accustomed to it. Further research is needed to assess this hypothesis.
- **Home nodes** were disregarded by most participants. Namely, only 20% used them to solve a task, and only after being encouraged to do so. When enquired individually, some participants reported not understating their utility with quotes such as "I don't understand what the home node does, I prefer to just type questions". However, additional research needs to be undertaken in order to determine whether users would find this feature useful given enough training time.

3 Conclusion

We have outlined a number of HCI techniques that aim to improve the usability of a Natural Language Interface (NLI) to diagrams as an advanced alternative to traditional non-visual diagram counterparts such as tactile graphics or tabular descriptions. These techniques have been devised taking into account the cognitive benefits that sighted persons benefit from as well as existing approaches in related domains (e.g. accessibility of link diagrams).

A total of six techniques have been described and qualitatively validated with target users by including them in the design of an accessible web-based NLI to diagrams. Offering a high-level verbal description of the underlying data and its visualization has been shown as being particularly effective in helping blind users form a mental model of the diagram. In addition, letting users navigate the constituent graphic objects of the diagram following their spatial or logical arrangement (as well as perform quick jumps between salient objects) has turned out to enable users to explore the diagram more effectively in order to perform some tasks. On the other hand, some more advanced techniques (object annotation, home nodes) were disregarded by most users of the NLI to diagrams prototype. Further research is needed to assess the usability of these methods given enough training time or how they ought to be improved.

Lastly, it must be noted that diagram- and visualization-specific terms such as 'bar', 'axis', and 'slope' often confused participants when given as part of the system's output, and were not employed by any user for querying the diagram. For example, one participant stated "I am not interested in the 'bars', they are a visual thing. I want to get just the data". This result suggests that natural language-based access to the underlying dataset (ignoring diagram elements) may be a more practical endeavor towards making diagrammatically-displayed data accessible to blind persons.

References

1. Allen, G.L.: Cognitive abilities in the service of wayfinding: a functional approach. Prof. Geogr. **51**(4), 555–561 (1999)
2. Brown, A., Stevens, R., Pettifer, S.: Making graph-based diagrams work in sound: the role of annotation. Hum.-Comput. Interact. **28**(3), 193–221 (2013)
3. Feng, J., Sears, A.: Speech input to support universal access. In: The Universal Access Handbook, pp. 30–1. CRC Press (2009)
4. Murillo-Morales, T., Miesenberger, K.: Non-visually performing analytical tasks on statistical charts. In: Cudd, P., de Witte, L. (eds.) Studies in Health Technology and Informatics, vol. 242, pp. 339–346. IOS Press (2017)
5. Murillo-Morales, T., Miesenberger, K.: Techniques for improved speech-based access to diagrammatic representations. In: Miesenberger, K., Kouroupetroglou, G. (eds.) ICCHP 2018. LNCS, vol. 10896, pp. 636–643. Springer, Cham (2018). https://doi.org/10.1007/978-3-319-94277-3_98
6. Murillo-Morales, T., Miesenberger, K.: AUDiaL: a natural language interface to make statistical charts accessible to blind persons. In: Miesenberger, K., Manduchi, R., Covarrubias Rodriguez, M., Peňáz, P. (eds.) ICCHP 2020. LNCS, vol. 12376, pp. 373–384. Springer, Cham (2020). https://doi.org/10.1007/978-3-030-58796-3_44
7. Shneiderman, B.: The eyes have it: a task by data type taxonomy for information visualizations. In: Bederson, B.B., Shneiderman, B. (eds.) The Craft of Information Visualization, pp. 364–371. Interactive Technologies, Morgan Kaufmann, San Francisco (2003). https://doi.org/10.1016/B978-155860915-0/50046-9

Interface for Automatic Tactile Display of Data Plots

Thorsten Schwarz(✉), Giuseppe Melfi, Stefan Scheiffele, and Rainer Stiefelhagen

Center for Digital Accessibility and Assistive Technologies, Karlsruhe Institute of Technology, Karlsruhe, Germany
{thorsten.schwarz,giuseppe.melfi,rainer.stiefelhagen}@kit.edu
https://www.access.kit.edu

Abstract. Graphical representation of mathematical functions is often inaccessible to blind people. There are methods to convert graphs into a tactile form, but this requires assistance, apart from manufacturing time and cost. In this paper, we present a system that enables blind people to independently display functions on a tactile display via a computer algebra system. Additional tools have been developed to further analyze a function (switchable axes, coordinate markers and zoom). To test the efficiency of the system, a pilot study was conducted with 5 blind participants. All participants were able to solve the tasks independently and were very positive about the system.

Keywords: Assistive technology · Tactile graphics · STEM

1 Introduction

Mathematical functions are ubiquitous in school and later at university, especially in STEM fields. Although any mathematical function can be described in words, a graphical representation is also helpful or even necessary. In school, function graphs are the first step to understanding functions. Without this foundation, it is almost impossible to get a deeper understanding of the subject. Methods already exist to make function graphs accessible to blind people. For this purpose, the diagrams are produced in a tactile way. Unfortunately, these solutions do not solve all problems: independent rework is not possible. Classes and lectures are over faster than tactile functional diagrams can be produced, so it is difficult for a blind person to follow along. In addition, the printouts are not changeable. While sighted people can change function through software and gain much better understanding, for blind people all changes must be re-embossed. Therefore, in this work, a system was developed that addresses these drawbacks and provides access to function graphs. For this purpose, an interface between a computer algebra system (CAS) and a tactile display was developed. A blind user can use it to independently input functions and immediately feel

K. Miesenberger et al. (Eds.): ICCHP-AAATE 2022, LNCS 13341, pp. 73–81, 2022.
https://doi.org/10.1007/978-3-031-08648-9_10

the matching graph on the tactile display. In addition, simple control by finger gestures is to be made possible.

The idea for this came from affected students themselves. To interactively understand mathematical graphs themselves and to use new techniques for this.

2 Related Work

Generating accessible mathematics is a widely discussed topic. An experiment [8] shows how useful graphical representation is. Subjects were asked to determine the relationship between two sets of data using different display modes. For this purpose, they were presented with a tactile graph, a tactile table, and an electronic table. While the general determination of the correlation was very high for all methods, these correlations were discovered by far the fastest for tactile graphs, followed by the tactile table and lastly the electronic table. This shows the importance of a fast and accessible method for generating the graphs. Thus, the tactile representation of graphs is essential. To make graphics accessible more quickly and interactively, a tactile display can be used. The content displayed can be changed or completely exchanged at any time. In this work the tactile display "HyperBraille" of the company Metec GmbH [6] is used. The reason for this is the fact that there are currently no other devices of this type on the market. Devices that combine tactile output and touch sensors. And it is available to our students on site, which improves implementation and everyday use. Another device of this kind in the future will be, for example, the Tactonom. With a camera to recognise gestures. Our development can be easily adapted to new output devices. Another, less direct approach is that of the Iveo Touchpad [7]. This is a device on which a printed tactile graphic is placed. The built-in touch screen then detects the finger position and can auditorily play information depending on the image element being sensed. Basic accessible software for independent work is also an important basis. For example, to make dealing with LaTeX source code somewhat easier, a special accessible editor was developed [5]. The Euromath project [1], for example, provides editors for blind and sighted people, and converts the input into a readable variant in real time for the other person. A different approach is taken in the Universal design tactile graphics production system BPLOT project [2]. This includes the Casvi project [3]. The goal is a computer algebra system (CAS) usable by blind people. This work is based on the Audio-Tactile Reader [4], which is an audio-tactile system for displaying documents with graphics. The works presented so far mostly deal with independent printing of graphs or with shared access to mathematics. There is no solution for displaying function graphs on tactile displays or a solution for independent, fast display and exploration of functions. However, this would greatly improve access to graphs and mathematics. An interactive work with graphs is the main goal of this work. This requires a system that (1) displays function graphs in a simple and understandable way, (2) can be operated independently by blind people, (3) allows the determination of coordinates, (4) provides graphs in a very short time, and (5) makes the graphs interactively adaptable.

3 Comparison of Different Computer Algebraic Systems

To select a CAS, several candidates were evaluated for accessibility and simplicity, and emphasis was placed on a symbolic approach. Another important aspect was the focus on CAS systems that are used in schools and universities in Germany and are therefore familiar to users. Finally, the CAS Maxima, Maple and Wolfram Mathematica were available for selection. Mostly a command line version is available, but smaller graphical interfaces are also offered. A particular advantage of Maxima is its close connection to LaTeX.

It was decided to develop the interface for one free and one commercial CAS. So Maxima as a free solution. Maple was chosen as the commercial variant. Maple has the significant advantage over Mathematica in that an accessible GUI variant exists. In programming the interface, the initial focus is on Maxima to provide a free program for testing as quickly as possible. Subsequently, the knowledge gained could be transferred to the interface for Maple.

4 The Tactile Plot Application

Our software provides an interface between a CAS and the HyperBraille. Inputs to the CAS are displayed as a drawing on the HyperBraille (see Fig. 1). Unimportant elements, frames or legends, are not displayed. Individual image elements (coordinate axes or markers for coordinates) can be shown or hidden. In addition, zooming and the determination of coordinates is possible on the touch-sensitive surface. Searched coordinates can also be localized.

Several approaches were investigated for generating the diagrams on the tactile display. Post-processing of the CAS graphical rendering output images resulted in inaccurate and unreliable representations. This was due to a number of combined factors, but most importantly the low resolution (10DPI) and number of display options (on or off) available on a tactile display. In addition, even when using an image in vector format (e.g. SVG), it is a challenge to derive the coordinate system to which the individual points of the functions should relate.

To solve this, we intercept the output of the CAS directly, without a graphical rendering. The various CAS are capable of writing sufficiently dense data series with X-Y coordinates to a file. Optimised to the grid of the tactile display, an optimal output can be guaranteed. The system is designed so that another tactile display can be easily implemented.

4.1 Interaction Concept

Tactile Plots runs from the command line, with the positive side effect that screen readers automatically read out the new lines on the command line. This makes it easy to write messages from the software to the terminal. Let's move on to the possibilities of application:

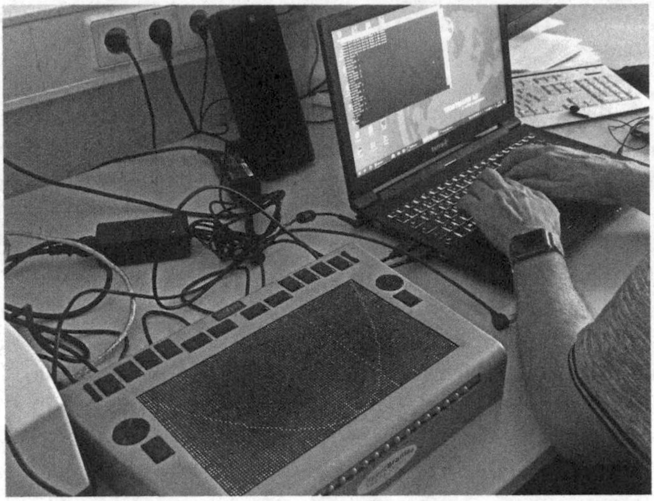

Fig. 1. One participant uses Tactile Plot with the help of a HyperBraille.

Selecting Graph Elements. Two functions can be displayed, which can be shown and hidden individually. Additionally, coordinate axes can be activated, displaying an axis cross. Coordinate markers can also be activated. For each integer coordinate, a short line is displayed at the left and bottom edges. For zero, there is a slightly longer line.

Simultaneous Work - Computer/HyperBraille. For simultaneous work, everything can also be called via the command line with additional functions.

Reading the Coordinates. If the user places a finger on a position on the display, the function coordinates can be announced by means of keys.

Finding a Coordinate. It is possible to search for coordinates via the command line. The tactile display then shows a vertical/horizontal dotted line at the specified x/y position. In addition, there is an acoustic announcement. The graphic is divided mentally into 3×3 fields and the position is assigned to these fields. For example "top left" or "middle right". By pressing any unused key, these are removed again.

Zoom. If the plot area becomes too large, it becomes confusing. Smaller changes in the slope of the function are lost due to the low resolution. The zoom function is available for this purpose. Separated in x-/y-direction or combined. Two options are available: centered and targeted zooming - only the zoom function zooms the image to the center and by placing a finger on this position. In the zoomed state, the two control crosses on the HyperBraille can be used to move the image section. Centering or deactivating the zoom is possible at any time.

5 User Study

A user study was conducted to determine how intuitive the software is to use and how helpful the presentation of function graphs on a tactile display is. Five blind persons participated in the study. Maxima was used as the CAS. After the familiarization phase, three tests were performed. The first focused on the basic understanding of the function and the use of the zoom. The second was to show whether the participants could read coordinates from the diagram. The third was to evaluate the handling of two functions simultaneously. Since the concept of interactive function graphs is very unfamiliar to most participants, no time limits were set.

5.1 Participants

The participants were all male, between 23 and 52 years old and came from the STEM field. Two were blind from birth and three were blind at a later age. Three of the participants used tactile graphics infrequently. One participant used them monthly and only one indicated that he used them weekly. Every participant had Braille skills and also used a Braille display. However, speech output was preferred when reading longer texts. Only one participant distinguished between scripts with mathematical notation and non-mathematical content. For mathematical content, he preferred the Braille display. Use of tactile displays ranged from rarely to never. A CAS were still rarely used at the time of the study. Only one participant stated that he sometimes used a CAS. Basically, everyone already had some experience with tactile mathematical function graphs. All participants received the same introduction and description of the system.

5.2 The Tasks

After first describing the input via Maxima, the function $y = x^2$ was set. Using this simple and known graph, all available functions could be tested.

Task 1 - Recognize the Function and Use the Zoom. The function $cos(x)$ was entered in Maxima in the range -8 and 8. Afterwards, the participants were given 4 sub-tasks: 1) Determine to which function category the graph belongs. Answers such as sine, cosine, angle, trigonometric function or similar were considered correct. 2) Is it more accurately a sine or cosine function? To solve this, for example, the axis cross could be inserted to determine y at the position $x = 0$. If the participant could not remember with confidence the difference between sine and cosine, he was given an alternative task. They were then simply asked what y is at the position $x = 0$. 3) How many complete periods does the function shown pass through? Thus, the incomplete periods on the left and right of the picture should be ignored. 4) The last question dealt with the zoom feature. Here, the graphic was to be zoomed in such a way that as exactly as possible two complete periods were shown on the display. For all questions, participants were given two chances each. If the first answer was wrong, then they were allowed to try again to solve the task, but then had to explain their mistake. The participants were not given any time pressure to solve the tasks.

Task 2 - Find Coordinates. The function in question was $x^2 + x - 3$ in the value range from -5 to 5 (see Figs. 2 and 3). First, they had to briefly describe the shape of the function and then determine the zeros. The axis cross in combination with the touch-sensitive surface was particularly helpful here. Finally, the y-value at the point $x = -4$ was to be determined.

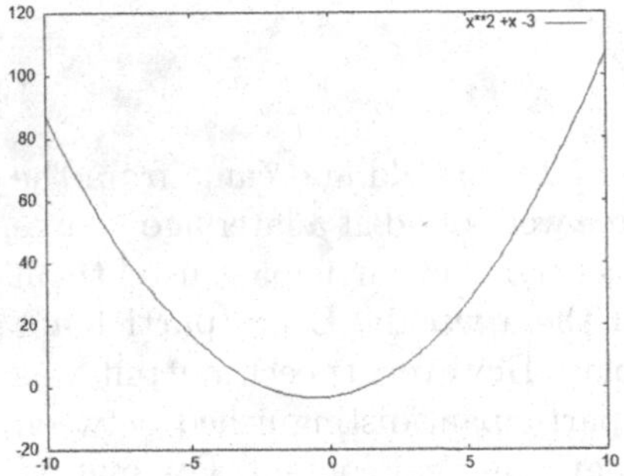

Fig. 2. The function $x^2 + x - 3$ ploted from -5 to 5 in Maxima.

Fig. 3. Output of the function on the Hyperbraille incl. axis markings.

Task 3 - Dealing with Two Functions. Finally, it was determined how intuitively the participants could handle two functions at the same time. The two functions were $2x-3$ and $-3x+5$. The x-interval was set to -5 and 5. First, participants were asked to determine the y-value at $x = 4$ for the function $-3x+5$. This was to test whether the correct fading out and fading in of the functions was mastered. In the second sub-task, the intersection of the two functions had to be determined.

6 Results

Task 1. In total, we received 20 responses. Of these, 19 questions were answered correctly directly in the first round. This resulted in a rate of 95%.

Task 2. Each participant received three questions, for a total of 15 questions. Here, 14 questions were answered correctly. This corresponds to a rate of 93.3%.

Task 3. In this task, each participant answered two questions. In total, therefore, there were ten responses. Here, the participants were able to answer 8 out of 10 questions correctly on the first attempt. This corresponds to a rate of 80%. However, both errors could be corrected on the second attempt. One participant also zoomed in with the y-zoom until the intersection point was really only a single point and was thus able to obtain a very accurate result. The second wrong answer occurred with question 2. This was a hardware error, because the HyperBraille recognized a non-existent finger in the lower left corner of the display and reported a completely wrong coordinate.

Nasa Task Load Index (TLX). The participants were asked to rate their subjectively perceived workload when solving the tasks. The average workload of the participants was very low. While four participants felt a relatively similar workload, one indicated significantly lower values. One particularly positive aspect is frustration, which was rated with the lowest possible score overall. This means that operation seems to be very intuitive and few program errors occurred. The participants are therefore confident that they have solved the tasks correctly for the most part. This is completely consistent with the test data collected.

System Usability Scale (SUS). Values of 82.5 to 100.0 were achieved. All results are thus far in the top quartile. The overall average is 90.5, which corresponds to a quality class of "excellent". The worst result was for the statement "I had to learn a lot before I could start using the system.". Out of a possible max of 20 points for this statement with the given number of participants, it scored 16. This is due to the longer introduction to the various functions of the software. For some of the participants, using the HyperBraille was completely new.

Feature Grading. In addition, participants were asked to rate some features of the software from 1 (best) to 6 (worst). All average scores are in the range of 1.0 to 1.8, with the coordinate finder receiving the highest score. The axes and coordinate markings are also rated very highly with a 1.2. Reading coordinates on the touch-sensitive surface was rated with an average of 1.4. One of the participants gave a grade of 3 to this feature, justifying it because of the too low resolution. The connection to Maxima was rated with 1.6. The complex syntax for the plotting command in Maxima as well the necessity to change the program window was criticized.

Free Text Questions. Finally, participants were asked open-ended questions. Most of the participants named the independence in learning, the speed of implementation and the interactivity as advantages compared to classic tactile graphics. They also said the system was handy for quickly entering a function and then checking its values. In this way, it was possible to specifically search for errors in the function definition that occur, for example, in exercise sheets. One participant also saw an advantage in being able to quickly change small values in the function definition and feel the difference in the graph. The most commonly mentioned disadvantage compared to traditional graphics is again the low resolution of the HyperBraille. Many braille printers offer double the resolution and can also use different dot heights.

7 Conclusions and Future Work

The goal of this work was to enable blind persons to work independently and quickly with mathematical function graphs. For this, Tactile Plots was developed to input graphs into a CAS and output them to a tactile display. This allows users to interact with graphs and better understand functions. Includes helpful tools such as axis crosses and coordinate markers. It is also possible to display two functions simultaneously. The built-in touchscreen is used to determine coordinates. Conversely, the exact position of a sought coordinate can be determined with the coordinate finder. A zoom function makes it possible to circumvent the problem of the very low resolution of the HyperBraille and to view smaller sections. In the evaluation it turned out that the system has a very intuitive operation. The users rated the features very positively and were able to handle the software without problems. All participants stated that they would like to work with the system again in the future. So we could develop a well usable tool. With a few improvements in the handling on command level it will help many users to understand mathematics and especially functions even better. If there would not be the problem of the available hardware (tactile displays). Currently, the available devices are too expensive or not interactive enough. There is still work to be done here.

References

1. Fitzpatrick, D., Nazemi, A., Terlikowski, G.: EuroMath: a web-based platform for teaching of accessible mathematics. In: Miesenberger, K., Manduchi, R., Covarrubias Rodriguez, M., Peňáz, P. (eds.) ICCHP 2020. LNCS, vol. 12376, pp. 385–392. Springer, Cham (2020). https://doi.org/10.1007/978-3-030-58796-3_45
2. Fujiyoshi, M., Fujiyoshi, A., Tanaka, H., Ishida, T.: Universal design tactile graphics production system bplot4 for blind teachers and blind staffs to produce tactile graphics and ink print graphics of high quality. In: Miesenberger, K., Kouroupetroglou, G. (eds.) ICCHP 2018. LNCS, vol. 10897, pp. 167–176. Springer, Cham (2018). https://doi.org/10.1007/978-3-319-94274-2_23
3. Mejía, P., César Martini, L., Larco, J., Grijalva, F.: CASVI: a computer algebra system aimed at visually impaired people. In: Miesenberger, K., Kouroupetroglou, G. (eds.) ICCHP 2018. LNCS, vol. 10896, pp. 573–578. Springer, Cham (2018). https://doi.org/10.1007/978-3-319-94277-3_89
4. Melfi, G., Schölch, L., Schwarz, T., Müller, K., Stiefelhagen, R.: Audio-tactile reader (atr): Interaction concepts for students with blindness to explore digital stem documents on a 2d haptic device. In: IEEE Haptics Symposium (2022)

5. Melfi, G., Schwarz, T., Stiefelhagen, R.: An inclusive and accessible LaTeX editor. In: Miesenberger, K., Kouroupetroglou, G. (eds.) ICCHP 2018. LNCS, vol. 10896, pp. 579–582. Springer, Cham (2018). https://doi.org/10.1007/978-3-319-94277-3_90
6. metec AG: Hyperbraille-website (2021). http://hyperbraille.de/
7. VIEWPLUS: Iveo 3 hands-on learning system (2021). https://viewplus.com/product/iveo-3-hands-on-learning-system/
8. Watanabe, T., Mizukami, H.: Effectiveness of tactile scatter plots: comparison of non-visual data representations. In: Miesenberger, K., Kouroupetroglou, G. (eds.) ICCHP 2018. LNCS, vol. 10896, pp. 628–635. Springer, Cham (2018). https://doi.org/10.1007/978-3-319-94277-3_97

Mobile e-Learning Platform for Audio-Tactile Graphics Presentation

Michał Maćkowski[1(✉)], Piotr Brzoza[1], Mateusz Kawulok[2], and Tomasz Knura[2]

[1] Department of Distributed Systems and Informatic Devices, Silesian University of Technology, Gliwice, Poland
michal.mackowski@polsl.pl
[2] Silesian University of Technology, Gliwice, Poland

Abstract. The use of multimedia in education means that more and more information is presented graphically. However, it limits the education of blind people, especially in science, where graphical content is the most often way of presenting the information. One of the commonly used alternative forms of graphic presentation is tactile graphics with descriptions in braille. Nonetheless, in the case of complex pictures, this form of presentation is insufficient for a blind student, and reading the tactile pictures often requires an assistant's help. In the paper, we present a developed e-learning platform for audio-tactile graphics presentation for the blinds dedicated to standard Android tablets, whose advantage is the automatic adaptation of interactive audio descriptions to the student's level of knowledge. The platform also enables the automatic assessment of the student's knowledge and exercise selection assigned to the appropriate knowledge level. The paper also presents the research results regarding the effectiveness of self-learning using our platform on two age groups of blind students while solving math exercises. The obtained research results show that the developed platform and the proposed method of verifying students' knowledge and selecting exercises positively influence the improvement of learning effectiveness. The platform can be used during the traditional lesson at school and also for self-learning which makes it especially desirable during the Coronavirus pandemic.

Keywords: Accessibility · Audio-tactile graphics · Intelligent tutoring system · Multimodal interfaces · Touch interface

1 Introduction

The use of multimedia in education means that more and more information is presented graphically. However, it limits the education of blind people, especially in science, where graphical content is the most often way of presenting the information. One of the commonly used alternative forms of graphic presentation is tactile graphics with descriptions in braille. Nonetheless, in the case of complex pictures, this form of presentation is insufficient for a blind student, and reading the tactile pictures often requires an assistant's help. The market offers dedicated devices for the interactive presentation of audio-tactile graphics along with dedicated software for PCs. As part of this paper, we present our

K. Miesenberger et al. (Eds.): ICCHP-AAATE 2022, LNCS 13341, pp. 82–91, 2022.
https://doi.org/10.1007/978-3-031-08648-9_11

e-learning platform for audio-tactile graphics presentation, whose advantage is the automatic adaptation of interactive audio descriptions to the student's level of knowledge. The platform also enables the automatic assessment of the student's knowledge and exercise selection assigned to the appropriate knowledge level. The paper also presents the research results regarding the effectiveness of self-learning using our platform on two age groups of blind students from Laski school for the blinds.

2 The State of the Art

In the professional literature, there are many research works on alternative methods of presenting graphic information to blind people, mainly in an interactive audio-tactile form. The analysis of the reviewed papers indicates a few methods for elements identification of a picture that a blind user touches and then reads their verbal description aloud. For many years schools for the blind have been using touch tablets, such as Talking Tactile Tablet produced by Touch Graphis and the IVEO by ViewPlus2, supporting the interactive presentation of audio-tactile graphics. By touching individual elements of the tactile picture, the student at the same time receives an appropriate audio description. However, sometimes the audio descriptions may be insufficient or inappropriate to the student's level of knowledge. A possible inconvenience may also be the inability to assess the student's knowledge using these systems. In order to solve the exercises, the student has to use another test-taking application or use a Braille notetaker. The mentioned devices were used in many scientific works where the authors focused on applying them in the educational process [1, 2].

Another approach towards presenting audio-tactile graphics created in a dynamic way is devices such as DotView from KGS Corporation, the Graphic Window by Handytech, or Graphiti Interactive Tactile Graphic Display by ORBIT Research. Unfortunately, due to the very high price of 5 to 20 thousand euros, such devices are rarely used. Not to mention the fact that the small working space often makes it difficult to interpret the image because it presents only a selected part of the picture. However, their undoubted advantage is converting graphical information from a computer screen into touchable images in real-time.

Research related to the presentation of tactile graphics using mobile phones and tablets is also carried out. Such devices are cheap, and students use them every day. In this solution tactile pictures are placed on a tablet screen, which is additionally supported by a dedicated mobile application to detect the elements of a picture being touched. This attitude of applying mobile tablets to the interactive presentation of audio-tactile graphics is presented in the works [3–5].

The solutions presented in the literature inspired the authors to develop their method of interactive presentation of audio-tactile graphics designed to the needs and knowledge of blind students. The platform also aims to provide the automatic assessment of the student's knowledge during the exercise solving, and the selection of subsequent exercises adapted to the student's knowledge and needs. The platform is not only used to present audio-tactile graphics but also allows the student to solve exercises on his own or during remote work with the teacher.

3 Our Research

3.1 Developed Platform

We assumed while designing the platform that the system consisted of a server application with a web interface coupled with the corresponding mobile application for a student used for presenting audio-tactile pictures (Fig. 1a and b). The server application is responsible for preparing the exercises consisting of instructions, tactile pictures with audio descriptions, and tests of various difficulty levels (Fig. 1b). The second element of the system is a mobile application that communicates with the server. When the mobile application is launched, it is possible to select an exercise to be solved. Tablet displays a digital image corresponding to a tactile picture and reads aloud the text description of touched elements. Using a dedicated interface consisting of 6 buttons at the bottom of the screen (Fig. 1a), the user can run a test and select answers to questions. The details of the implementation of the platform prototype were presented in the authors' previous work [6, 7]. Our platform also uses the knowledge vector technique [8, 9], which helps organize all necessary terms into a directed graph. This technique allows us to gradually introduce the new terms in the following exercise and assess students' level of knowledge.

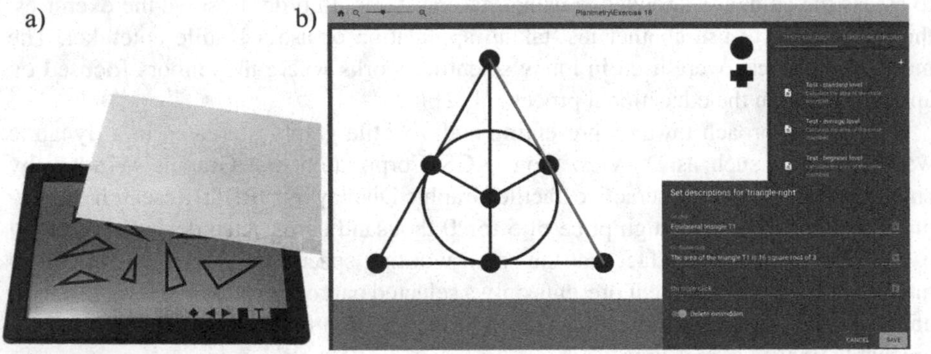

Fig. 1. a) A tactile picture containing a sample tactile image for learning to recognize the properties of triangles, b) the interface of the web application while preparing audio descriptions for the selected picture element.

After completing the test, the platform assesses the student's knowledge and suggests further exercises to be solved according to their level of knowledge. A student can receive an exercise on one of three difficulty levels, which are differentiated in terms of details included in alternative descriptions. A less skilled student will receive much more detailed information about the elements of the picture until he has mastered the material sufficiently by solving tests on various difficulty levels. The method of preparing the exercises and assessing the student's knowledge is presented in the further part of the paper.

3.2 Research Group

We conducted the research in two groups of primary students. The participants in the research group were chosen after consultations with their math teachers. None of them had other disabilities, especially motor, hearing, and mental. The participants in the research were students with a similar level of perception skills and mathematical knowledge.

- In the first group were students in grades 3–4. The group consisted of 22 students, where 17 were blind and 5 with low vision. The group consisted of 14 boys and 8 girls.
- In the second group were students in grades 5–6. The group consisted of 18 students, where 15 were blind and 3 with low vision. In terms of gender, the group consisted of 10 boys and 8 girls.

3.3 Materials

As part of the research, we prepared a set of 20 exercises for group 1, and 30 exercises for group 2. Each exercise consists of instructions, a tactile picture, an audio descriptions, and a multiple-choice test. Moreover, each exercise has been prepared in three versions, according to the level of difficulty. Each element of the picture was supported by a verbal description, read after tapping on it. Depending on the number of tapping, there are 3 various descriptions for each touched element. They were read as follows:

- 1 tap (*) – simple description, e.g., an element name,
- 2 taps (**) – detailed description, e.g., includes information about the object features such as size, angle, field,
- 3 taps (***) – advanced description – includes the definition of a term, hints, or more examples.

Depending on the level of test complexity, students received more or less detailed information adjusted to their knowledge. In the case of standard tests, the amount of information provided in a contextual manner was limited, i.e., sufficient to solve the exercise. In the case of students who had problems with mastering a given material, tests were prepared at the average and beginner level, where the exercise was divided into several or a dozen phases. Similarly, the amount of information provided after tapping elements in a tactile drawing is greater; for example the student after tapping 2–3 times on an element, may hear additional information, tips, and definitions allowing him to understand the basic concepts better. Table 1 shows the audio descriptions for the elements in the example tactile picture.

The division of the exercise into smaller phases allows the platform to identify and log information about student's faults. Our system then uses this information to assess the level of knowledge of the student and select subsequent exercises dedicated to a specific student to explain him the problematic issues.

In group 1 we prepared a set of 20 pictures covering geometric figures such as triangles quadrilaterals. Each picture included 10 figures of various sizes and shapes.

These materials were used to evaluate the effectiveness of recognizing shapes, sizes, and properties of geometric figures. In group 2 we prepared a set of 20 different pictures, covering triangles, quadrilaterals, circles. Each picture contained 1–3 figures of various sizes. Besides the exercises conveying figure properties, the students were to solve problems related to calculating areas and perimeters of figures in tactile pictures (Table 1).

Table 1. Alternative description of the elements in the picture of three types of level details.

Element description		
Standard level test	Average level test	Beginner level test
1. * Equilateral triangle T1 ** The area of the triangle T1 is 16 square root of 3 2. * Altitude h of the equilateral triangle T1 3. * A circle inscribed in an equilateral triangle	1. * Equilateral triangle T1 ** The area of the triangle T1 is 16 square root of 3 *** The formula for the area of an equilateral triangle is (1/4) * $\surd 3$ * a^2, where a is the length of triangle side 2. * Altitude h of the equilateral triangle T1 ** The formula for the altitude of the equilateral triangle is (1/2) * $\surd 3$ * a, where a is the length of triangle side 3. * A circle inscribed in an equilateral triangle ** The formula for the area of a circle is pi * r^2, where r is the radius length of the circle	1. * Equilateral triangle T1 ** The area of the triangle T1 is 16 square root of 3 *** The formula for the area of an equilateral triangle is (1/4) * $\surd 3$ * a^2, where a is the length of triangle side 2. * Altitude h of the equilateral triangle T1 ** The formula for the altitude of the equilateral triangle is (1/2) * $\surd 3$ * a, where a is the length of triangle side *** The radius length of the circle inscribed in the equilateral triangle is 1/3 of the altitude length 3. * A circle inscribed in an equilateral triangle ** The formula for the area of a circle is pi * r^2, where r is the radius length of the circle *** The approximate value of Pi is 3.14, which is the ratio of the circumference of the circle to its diameter

3.4 Research Methodology

The research was divided into three stages:

- Stage 1 – verification of the student's current knowledge. During this stage, students from group 1 solved 20 exercises and from group 2–24 exercises at the standard level, i.e., the most difficult level, where the number of clues and contextual information is minimal (but necessary to solve the exercise). During this stage, the platform registers faults made by research participants.

- Group 1 – students are likely to make the following types of mistakes while solving exercises: F1 – right triangle, F2 – equilateral triangle, F3 – isosceles triangle, F4 – acute triangle, F5 – obtuse triangle. As part of the exercise solving, students can make a maximum of 4 mistakes of each type. The maximum number of mistakes is 20.
- Group 2 – students can make the following types of mistakes while solving exercises: F1 – the area of a triangle, F2 – the perimeter of a triangle, F3 – the area of a circle inscribed in a triangle, F4 – the perimeter of a circle inscribed in a triangle, F5 – the area of a circle described on a triangle F6 – the perimeter of a circle described on a triangle. As part of the exercise solving, students can make a maximum of 4 mistakes of each type. The maximum number of mistakes is 24.

Based on the information collected on the number and type of mistakes and the time of solving exercises (decision-making time), the developed platform determines the level of student's knowledge. It classifies them into three groups: advanced, average, and beginner. If the student made more than one mistake from the selected category during the first stage, it is assumed that the student needs help mastering the material and is classified into stage 2. Otherwise, it is assumed that the student has mastered the material sufficiently, and one mistake made while solving the exercise could have been accidental.

Such classification makes the platform offers intermediate students or beginners a set of consecutive exercises adapted to their level of knowledge, i.e., the number of questions within the test is increased, and the student receives more audio descriptions related to the picture elements. This process is to help the student master the material and provide him with the necessary information to solve the following steps of the exercises, which were problematic for the student.

- Stage 2 – learning with the platform. This stage is for students with problems solving exercises at the standard level. The amount of time spent at this stage and the number of exercises solved depend on how quickly they master the material. The platform constantly monitors faults made by the student in exercises at the average or beginner level. If the student does not make mistakes in the next series of exercises, then the developed system assumes that the student has mastered the given material. From that moment on, the student is again given exercises at the standard level, i.e., he moves to stage 3 of the research.
- Stage 3 – Verify the student's knowledge while solving exercises at the standard level within a given category after learning the platform during stage 2.

4 The Research Results

Table 2 shows the data obtained during the conducted experiments. The table presents the number of mistakes made in individual categories at the standard level exercises for group 1 in stages 1 and 3. As can be seen, the most problematic for the students were solving exercises concerning the recognition of equilateral and isosceles triangles (types of faults described in Sect. 3.4). It was respectively 50% and 54.5% of the students. The exercises on recognizing right triangles were the least problematic, and only 2 out of 22 students required additional practice using the platform. In the category of recognizing acute and obtuse triangles, approximately 30% of students needed learning with the platform in stage 2.

Table 2. The number of mistakes made in individual fault categories at the standard level exercise during stages 1 & 3.

	STAGE 1 OF EXPERIMENTS					STAGE 3 OF EXPERIMENTS				
	F1	F2	F3	F4	F5	F1	F2	F3	F4	F5
S1	0	3	2	0	0	0	1	0	0	0
S1	1	3	0	0	2	1	1	0	0	0
S3	0	1	3	0	1	0	1	2	0	1
S4	1	0	0	2	1	1	0	0	0	1
S5	2	3	4	2	2	1	1	3	0	1
S6	0	2	1	1	1	0	1	1	1	1
S7	0	0	1	2	2	0	0	1	0	0
S8	1	2	2	0	2	1	1	0	0	0
S9	0	0	3	0	0	0	0	1	0	0
S10	1	2	3	2	1	0	3	3	2	1
S11	1	2	1	2	0	1	2	1	0	0
S12	1	1	3	0	1	1	1	2	0	1
S13	2	1	0	2	0	0	1	0	2	0
S14	0	1	4	0	0	0	1	3	0	0
S15	0	1	0	0	1	0	1	0	0	1
S16	0	0	1	1	0	0	0	1	1	0
S17	0	3	1	0	2	0	2	1	0	1
S18	0	2	4	0	0	0	3	2	0	0
S19	1	0	0	0	2	1	0	0	0	1
S20	0	0	2	2	0	0	0	3	1	0
S21	1	4	3	3	1	1	3	4	3	1
S22	0	3	2	0	1	0	1	1	0	1

After learning with the platform, the students were asked to solve the exercises at the standard level again (stage 3). Here, having looked at the results in each fault category, the following conclusions can be drawn. Depending on the category of faults made, learning with the platform contributed to the improvement of most students' knowledge in the range from 33 to 100%. For example, in the F1 category, 2 students had problems solving the exercises in the first stage. Still, after learning with the platform and solving the exercises again at the standard level, they did not make this type of mistake - so the learning effectiveness is 100%. In category F2, as many as 50% of students (11 out of 22) required learning with the platform, and after stage 3 it was shown that more than half of them (6 out of 11) had mastered the material and had been positively assessed. The rest of the group made more than 1 mistake and required repeating stage 2 of learning with the platform or individual consultation with the teacher.

In category F3, 12 out of 22 students broadened their knowledge while working with the platform. As can be seen in Table 2, 8 students still have not mastered the material sufficiently and make other mistakes - the effectiveness of learning with the platform can be assessed here at 33%.

The worse level of effectiveness of learning with the platform, especially in categories F2 and F3 (54% and 33%, respectively), may be caused by the tactile perception of research participants. The categories of these mistakes concerned recognizing features of equilateral and isosceles triangles. In the case of such figures, slight variations in the length of the sides may be difficult for some people to feel and interpret.

The results obtained in the second group also show an improvement during the learning process. At the beginning of the research, students were solving simple exercises related to calculating the areas and perimeters of various geometric figures. In these exercises, students had to be familiarized with the basic mathematical formulas for calculating the areas and perimeters of geometric figures such as triangles, quadrilaterals, and circles.

During the first research phase, 33% of students made, on average more than 2 mistakes for various geometric figures, and they started learning using the developed platform (stage 2). After this phase, students' level of knowledge who solved a series of exercise at the standard level was re-verified. By learning with the platform, 4 out of 6 students mastered the material, and two required further study and consultation with the teacher. The next set of exercises included problems related to calculating perimeters and areas of figures such as circles described or inscribed in triangles. These exercises are more complicated and require additional knowledge of the properties of geometric figures. Sample audio descriptions for such exercise is shown in Table 1. While solving these exercises at the standard level, 72% of students made more than 2 mistakes and required learning on the platform at the average or beginner level. In stage 3, after solving the series of exercises at the standard level again, 7 students mastered the material sufficiently (less than 2 mistakes made), and 6 still made mistakes and required further study.

The presented research results for both groups show that adapting the audio descriptions to the level of students' knowledge and the adaptive learning model based on the assessment of the student's knowledge and selection of exercises according to their level of knowledge significantly improves the effectiveness of learning with the use of the developed platform.

5 Discussion and Conclusion

The collected research results help us conclude that the developed platform and the proposed method of verifying students' knowledge and selecting exercises positively influence the improvement of learning effectiveness. The most important advantages of the presented solution include:

- Interactive presentation of audio-tactile pictures using tablets with the Android system.
- Possibility of solving exercises with tactile pictures through solving multiple-choice tests on the same tablet (the student has access to the tactile picture during solving the test on the same device).

– Possibility of self-study and automatic identification of student's problems while solving exercises. Information about mistakes made by the student is logged by the server application, which also gives the opportunity to the teacher to provide the student with appropriate consultations.
– Providing information to the student about the material they need to learn.
– Possibility of distance education or in the classroom.
– Possibility to prepare audio-tactile educational materials for various subjects.

Undoubtedly, the developed platform supports remote work with students during the Coronavirus pandemic. In the future, we plan to prepare exercises in other science subjects and carry out learning effectiveness on a broader group of students from different grades of primary or secondary school.

During and after the research, we conducted interviews with students and teachers to assess the quality of work with the platform and the ergonomics and usability of the proposed tactile-audio interface. Most of the people assessed the platform very positively. In addition to improving the learning process, the teachers also emphasized that the platform also develops tactile perceptions skills of blind students. In the opinion of users, the proposed interface is easy to use and corresponds to other accessibility tools. For some students, it was problematic to choose the right tactile pictures for solving exercises and put them on the tablet. In the future, we plan to improve this process by identifying the pictures placed on the tablet using proximity technologies, e.g., NFC tags stuck on the tactile pictures.

References

1. Hashim, R., Kazem, H., Farman, J.: (ViewPlus IVEO) device effectiveness on improving visual disabilities students skill. Indian J. Public Heal. Res. Dev. **10**, 671 (2019). https://doi.org/10.5958/0976-5506.2019.00132.3
2. Minhat, M., Abdullah, N.L., Idrus, R., Keikhosrokiani, P.: TacTalk: talking tactile map for the visually impaired. In: ICIT 2017 – 8th Int. Conf. Inf. Technol. Proc., pp. 475–481 (2017). https://doi.org/10.1109/ICITECH.2017.8080045
3. Klingenberg, O.G., Holkesvik, A.H., Augestad, L.B.: Digital learning in mathematics for students with severe visual impairment: a systematic review. Br. J. Vis. Impair. **38**, 38–57 (2020). https://doi.org/10.1177/0264619619876975
4. Melfi, G., Müller, K., Schwarz, T., Jaworek, G., Stiefelhagen, R.: Understanding what you feel: a mobile audio-tactile system for graphics used at schools with students with visual impairment. In: Conf. Hum. Factors Comput. Syst. - Proc. (2020). https://doi.org/10.1145/3313831.3376508
5. Mikułowski, D., Brzostek-Pawłowska, J.: Multi-sensual augmented reality in interactive accessible math tutoring system for flipped classroom. In: Kumar, V., Troussas, C. (eds.) ITS 2020. LNCS, vol. 12149, pp. 1–10. Springer, Cham (2020). https://doi.org/10.1007/978-3-030-49663-0_1
6. Maćkowski, M., Brzoza, P., Spinczyk, D., Meisel, R., Bas, M.: Platform for math learning with audio-tactile graphics for visually impaired students. In: Future Perspectives of AT, eAccessibility and eInclusion, pp. 75–82 (2020)
7. Maćkowski, M., Brzoza, P., Żabka, M., Spinczyk, D.: Multimedia platform for mathematics' interactive learning accessible to blind people. Multimedia Tools Appl. **77**(5), 6191–6208 (2017). https://doi.org/10.1007/s11042-017-4526-z

8. Lynch, D., Howlin, C.P.: Real world usage of an adaptive testing algorithm to uncover latent knowledge. In: Proc. ICERI 2014 Conf., pp. 504–511 (2014)
9. Maćkowski, M., Żabka, M., Kempa, W., Rojewska, K., Spinczyk, D.: Computer aided math learning as a tool to assess and increase motivation in learning math by visually impaired students. Disabil. Rehabil. Assist. Technol. (2020). https://doi.org/10.1080/17483107.2020.1800116

Digital Solutions for Inclusive Mobility: Solutions and Accessible Maps for Indoor and Outdoor Mobility

Digital Solutions for Inclusive Mobility: Solutions and Accessible Maps for Indoor and Outdoor Mobility

Introduction to the Special Thematic Session

Claudia Loitsch[1(✉)], Karin Müller[2(✉)], Gerhard Weber[1], Helen Petrie[3], and Rainer Stiefelhagen[2]

[1] Technische Universität Dresden, Dresden, Germany
{claudia.loitsch,gerhard.weber}@tu-dresden.de
[2] Karlsruhe Institute of Technology, Karlsruhe, Germany
{karin.e.mueller,rainer.stiefelhagen}@kit.edu
[3] University of York, York, UK
helen.petrie@york.ac.uk

Abstract. The current paper is an introduction to the Special Thematic Session *Digital Solutions for Inclusive Mobility: Solutions and Accessible Maps for Indoor and Outdoor Mobility.* Mobility is a valuable asset that should be equally available to all people. This chapter addresses the following problems which need to be solved so that people with disabilities can also enjoy greater mobility: getting the relevant information about buildings, orientating oneself in buildings, accessing tactile indoor maps, providing navigation in indoor and outdoor environments, tailoring the route to the users, creating accessible navigation apps, and making them adaptable to the users' needs.

Keywords: Mobile solutions · Indoor maps · Navigation · Accessibility · Disability

1 Introduction

Mobility is considered a prerequisite for participation in life in modern society. However, up till now, people with impairments face many barriers while travelling. In particular, unfamiliar environments pose challenges for many people with severe disabilities and chronic diseases due to the lack of information about accessibility and a building's infrastructure [16]. It can significantly diminish job prospects if an individual cannot meet the requirements for spatial mobility, particularly for planning and conducting work-related travel when this is difficult to accomplish and involves various barriers.

Mobile computing has allowed the development of novel assistive technologies to support people with mobility and visual impairments in their everyday needs to travel and orient themselves more independently. Mobile and wearable

K. Miesenberger et al. (Eds.): ICCHP-AAATE 2022, LNCS 13341, pp. 95–101, 2022.
https://doi.org/10.1007/978-3-031-08648-9_12

devices have become commodities for car drivers and pedestrians to increase individual mobility. In contrast to the wide availability of mobile devices, designers must understand the needs of an even wider range of users to address the needs of disabled users. Mobility services supporting universal designs should integrate both egocentric and allocentric approaches. Navigation apps guide the user on a certain route (e.g. "take 10 steps forward", "go 200 m straight"), egocentric descriptions give an overview of the immediate surrounding (e.g. "main entrance in 5 m at 2 o'clock, elevator in 2 m at 12 o'clock etc.") whereas allocentric approaches orient the user to landmarks and points of interest (e.g. "the church is beyond the post office"). These three approaches form a design space which can be explored to create accessible and useful solutions for disabled and older users. Therefore, addressing the specific needs of various user groups is essential for designing mobile solutions. The STS Digital Solutions for Inclusive Mobility dedicates equal opportunities for people with disabilities and chronic illnesses in education and everyday work by critically evaluating current measures to promote mobility, developing requirements for innovative digital solutions for various contexts, and identifying new perspectives.

2 Current Solutions to Improve Mobility

People with a disability have high adaptability to technology, and it has been empirically shown that this also increases the intention to use new assistive technologies [10]. However, to provide comprehensive support for people with mobility impairments, the technology must meet several requirements. For instance, solutions to improve mobility must be capable to adapt to individual needs and preferences, must address different wayfinding and orientation strategies and should provide accessible support for all phases of a trip, in particular planning and implementing [6]. At this point, no solution can meet all the requirements, the diversity of the target groups and the complete route for travelling from door to door. However, there is manifold ongoing research on improving the mobility of people with impairments through emerging technologies, innovative user interfaces, interaction design, and empirical research. This chapter presents the most recent developments in the universal design of mobile services and electronic travel aids, mapping services, and indoor navigation.

2.1 Information Needs

Many approaches point to the importance of general and specific information for people with disabilities about the travel route and destination [5,18,19]. However, there is no overview of the information that might be relevant for people with visual and mobility impairments in buildings. [2] presents a literature review that is useful for projects such as OpenStreetMap to suggest additional accessibility features that are missing from these databases.

2.2 Orientation and Wayfinding

People with visual and mobility impairments orientate differently in buildings and face many and diverse challenges, as recently investigated in depth by Müller et al. [16]. For these target groups, it is crucial to tailor orientation systems to their specific needs, prepare for unfamiliar environments, and build up a mental map. Mental maps increase confidence in one's mobility and can improve the safety and efficiency of travel. People with visual impairments use various techniques such as tactile maps, descriptions, or remembering from real physical experiences to form a picture of an environment and to remember tactile, verbal, or audio information or spatial cognition [16]. However, these sources of information are not always available or sufficient. New orientation systems or assistive technologies are necessary to support the independent mobility of people with visual impairments. One approach described in this chapter proposes to preview routes through buildings [22]. Upadhyay et al. developed IncluMap, which generates route previews and orientation information such as landmarks. Another contribution to this topic, in particular, to support planning a trip to an unknown building, is presented by Anken et al. [1]. They developed a system to generate structured, allocentric information about buildings and building parts such as floors or corridors.

Other research areas in this problem space address that people with visual impairments cannot obtain information from their environment, or can only obtain visual information. Image recognition can yield promising answers in this area, enabling artificial vision and looking around. In addition to technical feasibility, however, numerous hurdles must be overcome. One challenge consists in the difficulty for blind people to actively take pictures of their surroundings. Iwamura et al. investigate this problem in more depth and propose a new framework called Passive Information Acquisition (PIA) which can be updated by constantly photographing the user's surroundings and recognizing all the photos [9]. Another problem is how to assist people with blindness in finding their way around unfamiliar buildings. A possible solution are egocentric textual descriptions, which are addressed by [3]. The study investigates, how these descriptions should be structured by taking into account the user's location and orientation on a building.

Navigation systems are solutions that support wayfinding in indoor and outdoor environments. [13] present an accessible navigation map for indoor environments. This app was specifically developed for the campus of the University of Bielefeld in Germany.

2.3 Tactile Maps

For people with blindness, tactile maps are one approach to familiarizing themselves with an unfamiliar environment. The creation of such maps and their exploration is the subject of current research. One contribution to this topic deals with the problem of creating a tactile symbol set for printing methods with different resolutions [15]. They define criteria how to transfer the symbols to a different printing method and mapped them to accessibility features. A second approach investigates the use of textures in indoor maps, in particular, if they can be used and under which conditions [7]. The Authors also compare two different printing methods.

Other research focuses on the interaction with tactile graphics. People with visual impairments may overcome the disadvantages of limited space and resolution on a tactile map by incorporating audio information. One approach described herein proposes the automatic generation of audio-tactile maps from OSM data for indoor maps [8]. They use a smartphone application to get information about the interior of a building by using a digital pen. A second approach incorporates an A4 tablet with an attached tactile graphic and a digital file with audio information to give access to indoor maps [14]. They investigate in a user study if participants with and without sight can build a mental model of an indoor environment using a system for audio-tactile maps.

2.4 Location-Based Services and Adaptive Routing

Location-based services are used almost unlimited in outdoor areas, in particular, because GPS offers wide coverage for localization and positioning. This is still not the case for indoor areas where it is necessary to augment the physical environment (e.g. using beacons for RFID, NFC, Bluetooth etc.) with an infrastructure for localization that implies considerable implementation and maintenance effort and thus lacks scalability. Solutions are also being researched to enable reliable location-based indoor navigation systems without the additional setup of high-maintenance hardware. One approach presented in this chapter proposes an image-based positioning system using a monocular camera and pre-recorded videos with route information [21]. Route features are generated based on crowdsourced video data and stored in a graph object. Route finding is enabled by matching real-time images with point features to find the position. Another approach presented in this paper attempts to detect dynamic obstacles and provide auditory feedback to users with visual limitations about the position and velocity of these objects. For this purpose, RGB-D sensors are used to detect dynamic information using panoptic segmentation [17]

In addition to real-time feedback on barriers or obstacles in the environment and the positioning of users, the generation of personalized routes is an important research topic. To address the diverse requirements of the target group, intelligent and adaptive user interfaces and services can be a suitable solution in this regard [11,12]. Personalized accessible routing is based, for example, on a user profile in which characteristics of the user or the assistive device can be specified, such as wheelchair width, the maximum possible slope of a path, maximum step height, etc. [4]. However, much more information is required to address the diverse information need of people with disabilities. One paper in this chapter proposes an innovative indoor routing algorithm that takes the special needs of people with disabilities into account, following a POI-based approach. For this purpose, they enrich routing graphs with tags describing uniquely identifiable landmarks [20]. In particular, for people with blindness and low vision, information about indoor landmarks (e.g. location of main entrances and stairs) are necessary for orientation and wayfinding in unknown buildings [6].

3 Conclusions

In summary, inclusive mobility has become a reality at certain points, but no general solutions are yet available. There are still a lot of unanswered questions about how systems need to be designed so that they optimally support the needs of users. This chapter presents several promising approaches that make valuable contributions to improving independent and barrier-free mobility through new technologies. To conclude, all contributions help to achieve a common goal: the implementation of a fully accessible route for travelling, taking into account individual requirements and preferences.

Acknowledgements. The work is partially funded by the German Federal Ministry of Labour and Social Affairs (BMAS), grant number 01KM151112 and by the German Federal Ministry of Education and Research (BMBF), grant number 16SV7609.

References

1. Anken, J., Rosenthal, D., Mueller, K., Jaworek, G., Stiefelhagen, R.: Split it up: allocentric descriptions of indoor maps for people with visual impairment. In: Miesenberger, K., Manduchi, R., Covarrubias Rodriguez, M., Peňáz, P. (eds.) ICCHP-AATE 2022, LNCS, vol. 13341, pp. 102–109. Springer, Cham (2022)
2. Constantinescu, A., Müller, K., Loitsch, C., Zappe, S., Stiefelhagen, R.: Traveling to unknown buildings: accessibility features for indoor maps. In: Miesenberger, K., Manduchi, R., Covarrubias Rodriguez, M., Peňáz, P. (eds.) ICCHP-AATE 2022, LNCS, vol. 13341, pp. 221–228. Springer, Cham (2022)
3. Constantinescu, A., Neumann, E.M., Müller, K., Jaworek, G., Stiefelhagen, R.: Listening first: egocentric textual descriptions of indoor spaces for people with blindness. In: Miesenberger, K., Manduchi, R., Covarrubias Rodriguez, M., Peňáz, P. (eds.) ICCHP-AATE 2022, LNCS, vol. 13341, pp. 241–249. Springer, Cham (2022)
4. Darwishi, A.: Towards personalized accessible routing for people with mobility impairments. In: Miesenberger, K., Manduchi, R., Covarrubias Rodriguez, M., Peňáz, P. (eds.) ICCHP-AATE 2022, LNCS, vol. 13341, pp. 215–220. Springer, Cham (2022)
5. De Pascale, A., Meleddu, M., Abbate, T.: Exploring the propensity to travel of people with disabilities: a literature review. SSRN 3832082 (2021)
6. Engel, C., et al.: Travelling more independently: a requirements analysis for accessible journeys to unknown buildings for people with visual impairments. In: ASSETS 2020, New York, NY, USA, pp. 1–11. ACM (2020)
7. Engel, C., Weber, G.: Expert study: design and use of textures in tactile indoor maps. In: Miesenberger, K., Manduchi, R., Covarrubias Rodriguez, M., Peňáz, P. (eds.) ICCHP-AATE 2022, LNCS, vol. 13341, pp. 110–122. Springer, Cham (2022)

8. Engel, C., Weber, G.: Generate audio-tactile indoor maps by means with a digital pen. In: Miesenberger, K., Manduchi, R., Covarrubias Rodriguez, M., Peňáz, P. (eds.) ICCHP-AAATE 2022, LNCS, vol. 13341, pp. 123–133. Springer, Cham (2022)
9. Iwamura, M., Kawai, T., Takashima, K., Minatani, K., Kise, K.: Acquiring surrounding visual information without taking photo actively for people with visual impairment. In: Miesenberger, K., Manduchi, R., Covarrubias Rodriguez, M., Peňáz, P. (eds.) ICCHP-AAATE 2022, LNCS, vol. 13341, pp. 229–240. Springer, Cham (2022)
10. König, A.: The impact of subjective technology adaptivity on the willingness of persons with disabilities to use emerging assistive technologies. In: Miesenberger, K., Manduchi, R., Covarrubias Rodriguez, M., Peňáz, P. (eds.) ICCHP-AAATE 2022, LNCS, vol. 13341, pp. 207–214. Springer, Cham (2022)
11. Loitsch, C.: Designing accessible user interfaces for all by means of adaptive systems. dissertation, Technische Universität Dresden (2018). https://d-nb.info/1226813860/34
12. Loitsch, C., Weber, G., Kaklanis, N., Votis, K., Tzovaras, D.: A knowledge-based approach to user interface adaptation from preferences and for special needs. User Model. User-Adap. Inter. **27**(3), 445–491 (2017)
13. Dustin, M.: Unimaps - an accessible mobile indoor navigation app (OAC). In: Petz, A., Hoogerwerf, E.-J., Mavrou, K. (ed.) Assistive Technology, Accessibility and (e)Inclusion, ICCHP-AAATE 2022 Open Access Compendium. Johannes Kepler University Linz, Austria. Accepted for publication online: https://www.icchp-aaate.org
14. Melfi, G., Baumgarten, J., Müller, K., Stiefelhagen, R.: An audio-tactile system for visually impaired people to explore indoor maps. In: Miesenberger, K., Manduchi, R., Covarrubias Rodriguez, M., Peňáz, P. (eds.) ICCHP-AAATE 2022, LNCS, vol. 13341, pp. 134–142. Springer, Cham (2022)
15. Melfi, G., Müller, K., Jaworek, G., Stiefelhagen, R.: The accessible tactile indoor maps (atim) symbol set: a common symbol set for different printing methods. In: Miesenberger, K., Manduchi, R., Covarrubias Rodriguez, M., Peňáz, P. (eds.) ICCHP-AAATE 2022, LNCS, vol. 13341, pp. 153–159. Springer, Cham (2022)
16. Müller, K., Engel, C., Loitsch, C., Stiefelhagen, R., Weber, G.: Traveling more independently: A study on the diverse needs and challenges of people with visual or mobility impairments in unfamiliar indoor environments. ACM Trans. Access. Comput. (2022). https://doi.org/10.1145/3514255. just accepted
17. Ou, W., Zhang, J., Peng, K., Yang, K., Jaworek, G., Müller, K., Stiefelhagen, R.: Indoor navigation assistance for visually impaired people via dynamic slam and panoptic segmentation with an rgb-d sensor. In: Miesenberger, K., Manduchi, R., Covarrubias Rodriguez, M., Peňáz, P. (eds.) ICCHP-AAATE 2022, LNCS, vol. 13341, pp. 160–168. Springer, Cham (2022)
18. Passini, R., Proulx, G.: Wayfinding without vision: an experiment with congenitally totally blind people. Environ. Behav. **20**(2), 227–252 (1988)
19. Spindler, Martin, Weber, Michael, Prescher, Denise, Miao, Mei, Weber, Gerhard, Ioannidis, Georgios: Translating floor plans into directions. In: Miesenberger, Klaus, Karshmer, Arthur, Penaz, Petr, Zagler, Wolfgang (eds.) ICCHP 2012. LNCS, vol. 7383, pp. 59–66. Springer, Heidelberg (2012). https://doi.org/10.1007/978-3-642-31534-3_10
20. Striegl, J.: Accessible adaptable indoor routing for people with disabilities. In: Miesenberger, K., Manduchi, R., Covarrubias Rodriguez, M., Peňáz, P. (eds.) ICCHP-AAATE 2022, LNCS, vol. 13341, pp. 169–177. Springer, Cham (2022)

21. Upadhyay, V.: Indoor positioning using invariant image feature matching to assist navigation. In: Miesenberger, K., Manduchi, R., Covarrubias Rodriguez, M., Peňáz, P. (eds.) ICCHP-AAATE 2022, LNCS, vol. 13341, pp. 178–186. Springer, Cham (2022)
22. Upadhyay, V., Bhatnagar, T., Holloway, C., Rao, P., Balakrishnan, M.: Can route previews amplify building orientation for people with visual impairment? In: Miesenberger, K., Manduchi, R., Covarrubias Rodriguez, M., Peňáz, P. (eds.) ICCHP-AAATE 2022, LNCS, vol. 13341, pp. 187–196. Springer, Cham (2022)

Split it Up: Allocentric Descriptions of Indoor Maps for People with Visual Impairments

Julia Anken(✉), Danilo Rosenthal, Karin Müller, Gerhard Jaworek, and Rainer Stiefelhagen

Karlsruhe Institute of Technology, Karlsruhe, Germany
{julia.anken,karin.e.mueller,gerhard.jaworek,rainer.stiefelhagen}@kit.edu

Abstract. Planning a trip to unfamiliar public buildings is challenging for people with visual impairments as much visual information such as floor plans is not accessible. Textual descriptions of an indoor map would therefore be very useful to prepare a trip. In particular, an allocentric description independent from the current location of the user which could be used at home would support the preparation phase. However, descriptions of buildings are rarely available. So the main question is how to tailor the descriptions to the needs of people with visual impairments in order to not overwhelm them with too much information at a time. We propose a system for the generation of allocentric textual descriptions for public buildings. In a user study, we tested the usefulness of our system and found that a modular design is regarded helpful to clearly structure descriptions by splitting the description into meaningful modules and avoiding information overload.

Keywords: Allocentric description · Indoor environments · Visual impairments

1 Introduction

Traveling to unknown places is taken for granted in many societies and is associated with freedom and independence. According to the Convention on the Rights of Persons with Disabilites [10], all people should have equal opportunities to participate in a society. However, there are groups of people whose mobility is restricted by various factors. People with blindness are one group that have restricted access to many information sources such as floor plans or other visual data. Therefore, it is especially important for this target group to be able to prepare a trip with the appropriate materials. [11]. They usually make use of all different kind of information sources such as calling people at the destination, searching official websites or in crowd-source review forums. [7] found that many people with disabilities have the impression that these collected information is not sufficient or even incorrect. One of the problems is that the available information sources do not meet the needs of people with disabilities. [11] showed

K. Miesenberger et al. (Eds.): ICCHP-AAATE 2022, LNCS 13341, pp. 102–109, 2022.
https://doi.org/10.1007/978-3-031-08648-9_13

that there is a need for accessible information about indoor environments which include information about the accessibility of a building. In particular, people with visual impairments (VI) wish to use textual descriptions if they were available. They also found that people with VI require different information when planning a trip compared to usage on site. Especially when planning a trip to a public building, which is often very complex, it would be helpful to have systems that support preparation at home by providing a description adapted to the user group. Unlike egocentric information, which can be used on site, allocentric descriptions of buildings are independent of location by using an external reference system.

The question underlying this research is how to design allocentric textual descriptions tailored to the needs of people with VI when preparing a trip to unfamiliar public buildings. Thereby information must be structured in a way that it is useful to develop an idea of a building and at the same time avoiding information overload. In our approach, we collected requirements from literature and existing navigation applications to design a system that generates allocentric descriptions. We implemented a web-based system and evaluated its usefulness in a user study. We found that participants appreciate textual descriptions if they are clearly structured and available in a modular way.

The paper is structured as follows: in Sect. 2, we discuss related work. Then, we describe our system in Sect. 3. Section 4 is dedicated to the conducted user study and the results. Last, we draw our final conclusions in Sect. 5.

2 Related Work

Especially in the field of navigation for people with low vision (LV) and blindness (BL), many approaches exist that investigate information needs (e.g. [12]). In addition, a (German) grammar was developed by [2] with language instructions for a navigation system for people with blindness. However, most approaches focus on outdoor environments. [1] also includes the transition between outdoor and indoor environments, but still focuses on sidewalk-based navigation.

A variety of approaches deal with the description of floor plans. This usually occurs in the context of a system with automatic recognition of visual features from images. Here, like [4,9,13], whole sentences are generated to describe a floor plan in total. Current approaches like [6] learn textual features directly in addition to visual features. However, their focus is more on learning sentences to produce them as naturally as possible.

Overall, these approaches give the user a lot of information at once by providing one description for the whole floor plan. Especially public buildings can be very large and thus a lot of information would be presented at once. Therefore, approaches like [5] and [8] use the idea of splitting information. In [5] a system is proposed to generate a description of a floor plan image for people with visual impairments. They split the information into a general description of the floor plan with spatial relations, and a navigation description to avoid obstacles. By focusing on a floor plan, the general description includes only a single floor and in this case buildings with up to five rooms. No further subdivision of the general description is intended. [8] divide open plan areas into logical sub-areas according to the purpose of use. However, the main goal there is to generate an accessible graphical representation of a floor plan without describing individual sub-areas.

3 A System for Modular Allocentric Descriptions

For people with LV or BL, it is essential to receive only information they need and want, and not to be overwhelmed by too much information at once. In an interview, a person with BL expresses this requirement: *"Well, I usually don't feel like listening to a complete novel, only if it's about a short description."* It highlights the need for a system providing brief descriptions tailored to the current information needs of a user. Instead of generating a coherent description of the whole building, the information about the building is logically divided into sections.

3.1 Design of the System

In this section, we describe our system consisting of three modules: (1) general information about the building followed by more details about (2) floors and (3) corridors. Rooms are not considered as they usually contain movables with continuous change which should be provided on site. Moreover, we show how information is structured and the resulting output of the system.

General Building Information. When informing about an unknown building, general information about the building is necessary first, e.g. the name of the building, its shape, and how to enter it. Here, in addition to information such as the position of the (main) entrance, other details are helpful for the target group. These include, for example, warnings about obstacles in the area of the entrance or tactile guidance systems [3].

Floors and Corridors. More detailed information about floors and corridors can be obtained in a next step. Thereby users can decide for themselves if and when this information is relevant. In situations where a building is already known, a user can also skip the general building description and search directly for information of a specific floor or corridor. In this way, the information required in each case can be found as quickly as possible.

Structuring Information Using a Simple Grammar. In addition to dividing the description into modules, structuring the information can also make it easier to find it more quickly. Therefore, information is always output in the same format and in the same order. Information that is not required can be skipped. The information is formatted by key points. Each key point is expressed by the following regular expression:

```
element[:] information (,information)*.
```

An `element` is a feature of a building that is to be described in more detail. `Information` contains the concrete characteristic of the `element` as it is present in the building. At least one piece of `information` is required per `element`. In case an `element` is not present in a building, i.e. no `Information` is available, the corresponding `element` is not listed in the resulting description.

Output of the System. Starting the description as well as selecting the module description is actively done by the user. The allocentric description is generated independent of the location of a user using an external reference system. Directional information is given using the clock system (i.e. 12 o'clock as north) to describe the spatial relationships similar as in BlindSquare[1].

The system generates one general description (shown in Fig. 1), at least one floor description and any number of corridor descriptions. Open areas such as foyers are described analogously to corridors.

```
Basic shape of the building: rectangular, horizontal
Main entrance: double doors, glass
Position main entrance: Main Street 5, longer edge, centered
Warning: Bicycle rack next to main entrance
Number of floors: 10
Floors: -2 to 7
Number of toilets: 5 mens toilets (wheelchair accessible), 5 ladies
toilets (wheelchair accessible)
Accessibility: 1 tactile floor plan on floor 1, tactile guidance system
on floor 0, floor 3, floor 4, floor 7, 10 wheelchair accessible toilets
```

Fig. 1. Example of a general building description for the fictional building 1

3.2 User Interface (UI)

The user interface was developed in a user-centered design process. A blind accessibility expert tested the UI on various stages of the development and suggested improvements. The proposed system is implemented as a responsive web page and is optimized for screen reader usage. On the first page, a short explanation on how to use the system is given. The users can choose if they want general information about the building and further modular descriptions. For each of the three modular descriptions, further information can be selected by a drop-down menu (see Fig. 2) for the building, the floor and the corridor or foyer. The textual description is generated and read by the screen reader as soon as the "Start Description" button is clicked.

[1] BlindSquare. http://www.blindsquare.com/, Retrieved January 27, 2022.

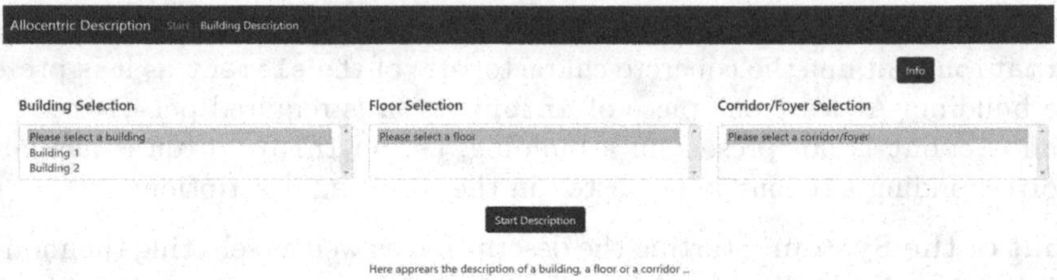

Fig. 2. User Interface showing the selection options for the modular descriptions

4 User Study

In a next step, we created an online questionnaire to test our system in a user study. The questionnaire was developed together with three accessibility experts, one of whom with blindness. We sent an invitation with a link to the online study via e-mail to a list of persons who participated in earlier studies. Five participants consisting of one person with severe VI and four persons with BL took part in the online study. Table 1 shows the demographic data of the five participants. Their age ranged from 20 to 59 years. Three of them were male, and two female. Four of them travel often alone.

Table 1. Demographic data of participants P1-P5 of the user study

Participants	Age range	Gender	Type of VI	Onset of VI	Traveling alone
P1	20–29	Male	Blindness	Birth	Often
P2	50–59	Female	Blindness		Often
P3	50–59	Male	Blindness	Birth	Sometimes
P4	20–29	Male	Blindness	10 ys	Often
P5	30–39	Female	Blindness		Often

4.1 Questionnaire and Procedure

The aim of the questionnaire was to investigate the comprehensibility of the modular building descriptions, the usability of the overall system, and whether the system provides added value to everyday life. Within the online questionnaire, a link was given to the web-interface of the system. Before answering a set of questions, a specific module description had to be read.

Comprehension questions had to be answered for each of the modular descriptions. These questions should reveal whether the descriptions were correctly understood by the participants. They differed depending on which building and which parts were selected. We also asked selection questions such as *"How many toilets are available in building 1 on floor 2?"* with several possible answers.

Moreover, questions with free text answers were asked, e.g. to describe the layout of the corridors of a floor. Additionally, for each modular description, the following two questions were posed: (1) *Is the information in the description clearly understandable?* (2) *Is the information in the description sufficient?*

4.2 Results

We analyzed the answers of the participants in more detail regarding the modules and the overall system as well as the usage of the system.

Results: General Building Descriptions. Most questions about the general building were answered correctly, only one answer was incorrect. One respondent complaint that the general building description was unclear which was due to an error in the number and name of floors. Two subjects indicated that they needed more information about a building such as the number of stairs and accessibility of the (main) entrances.

Results: Floor Descriptions. Most of the answers about floor descriptions were correct. However, the two floor descriptions differed. While all answers from all participants were correct for the first one, there were misunderstandings about the layout of the floor, the room and corridor positions in the second one. The reason was that giving descriptions using a clock system in combination with an external reference system was confusing, since in most contexts they are used in relation to the user's location (e.g. 12 o'clock to indicate in front of the user). Two of the participants stated that the floor descriptions were not understandable enough. More information about the layout of the corridors was requested in order to get a better overview.

Results: Corridor Descriptions. There were more incorrect answers in the descriptions of the corridors compared to the other two module descriptions. Nevertheless, the majority of questions were answered correctly. For three subjects, all questions were answered correctly. Two subjects stated that the information given was insufficient because of the complex layout.

Results: Overall System. The overall system was rated as very easy to understand by three participants, while two participants rated it as moderately comprehensible. Only one respondent felt that he only partially understood the structure of the floors and the building. All others indicated that they understood the structure.

Results: Usage of System. All participants could imagine using such a modular system with descriptions of indoor maps when planning a trip. One participant particularly liked the general building description to get information without having to choose a floor or corridor. P2 clearly noticed that the splitting into modules (building, floor, corridor) worked well, and complimented: "*clear division (level building, floor, corridor), clear reference point, mentioning of special features*".[2] Another participant liked the clear and structured way of the modular descriptions.

To improve the system, one participant suggested to provide more information in the general description. Another participant (P4) suggested a more detailed description of corridor crossings or even a separate module for that. He provided the following statement: "*Not enough structuring of the description, for example, it would be preferable to separate the [corridor] crossing (e.g., heading)*" (See footnote 2).

4.3 Discussion

Overall, the results of the user study show that the selection of the three individual modules of the description were chosen appropriately and therefore could be understood intuitively. The system itself, in which individual module descriptions are selected by the user, also works well and was highlighted as positive by participants. The current length of the module descriptions seems appropriate and does not overwhelm the user. On the contrary, participants requested more information, especially for the general building description. The main complaint about the system concerns the use of a clock system in combination with an external allocentric reference system. Thus, the layout of floors and corridors was not clearly understood by all participants. To address this issue, customization could be used so that users can choose the type of directional information themselves, e.g. clock system or cardinal directions.

Nevertheless, the majority of participants believe that even this way of describing a building would improve their understanding compared to their current methods.

5 Conclusions

The underlying question of this work was how to design allocentric descriptions tailored to the needs of people with VI when preparing a trip to unfamiliar public buildings. The main focus was to structure the information in a way that allows the development of a mental map of a building while avoiding information overload. Therefore we developed a system to assist people with LV and BL in planning a trip to an unknown public building. It provides allocentric information of a building independent of the specific location of the user and on the basis of an external reference system. Information is structured, and presented only on demand, to meet the main requirement of avoiding information overload. The modular system generates a general building description, as well as a description of each floor and corridor on a floor. The descriptions can be accessed independently from each other. Our initial user evaluation suggests that the presented

[2] Translation from German to English by author.

concept of modular descriptions is intuitively understandable and can support the overall understanding of a building structure. Users also stated that they can imagine using such a system and that it adds value to their everyday life by supporting them preparing a visit to an unfamiliar public building.

References

1. Balata, J., Berka, J., Mikovec, Z.: Indoor-outdoor intermodal sidewalk-based navigation instructions for pedestrians with visual impairments. In: Miesenberger, K., Kouroupetroglou, G. (eds.) ICCHP 2018. LNCS, vol. 10897, pp. 292–301. Springer, Cham (2018). https://doi.org/10.1007/978-3-319-94274-2_41
2. Constantinescu, A., Petrausch, V., Müller, K., Stiefelhagen, R.: Towards a standardized grammar for navigation systems for persons with visual impairments. In: The 21st International ACM SIGACCESS Conference on Computers and Accessibility, pp. 539–541. ACM (2019)
3. Engel, C., et al.: Travelling more independently: a requirements analysis for accessible journeys to unknown buildings for people with visual impairments. In: The 22nd International ACM SIGACCESS Conference on Computers and Accessibility, pp. 1–11. ACM (2020)
4. Goncu, C., Madugalla, A., Marinai, S., Marriott, K.: Accessible on-line floor plans. In: Proceedings of the 24th International Conference on World Wide Web, pp. 388–398. International World Wide Web Conferences Steering Committee (2015)
5. Goyal, S., Bhavsar, S., Patel, S., Chattopadhyay, C., Bhatnagar, G.: Sugaman: describing floor plans for visually impaired by annotation learning and proximity-based grammar. IET Image Process. **13**(13), 2623–2635 (2019)
6. Goyal, S., Chattopadhyay, C., Bhatnagar, G.: Knowledge-driven description synthesis for floor plan interpretation. Int. J. Doc. Anal. Recogn. (IJDAR) **24**(1), 19–32 (2021)
7. Gupta, M., et al.: Towards more universal wayfinding technologies: navigation preferences across disabilities. In: Proceedings of the 2020 CHI Conference on Human Factors in Computing Systems, pp. 1–13. ACM (2020)
8. Madugalla, A., Marriott, K., Marinai, S.: Partitioning open plan areas in floor plans. In: 2017 14th IAPR International Conference on Document Analysis and Recognition, pp. 47–52 (2017)
9. Madugalla, A., Marriott, K., Marinai, S., Capobianco, S., Goncu, C.: Creating accessible online floor plans for visually impaired readers. ACM TACCESS **13**(4), 1–37 (2020)
10. Márton, S.M., Polk, G., Fiala, D.R.C.: Convention on the rights of persons with disabilities. United Nations, USA (2013)
11. Müller, K., Engel, C., Loitsch, C., Stiefelhagen, R., Weber, G.: Traveling more independently: a study on the diverse needs and challenges of people with visual or mobility impairments in unfamiliar indoor environments. ACM Trans. Access. Comput. (2022). https://doi.org/10.1145/3514255. just Accepted
12. Nicolau, H., Jorge, J., Guerreiro, T.: Blobby: how to guide a blind person. In: CHI 2009 Extended Abstracts on Human Factors in Computing Systems, pp. 3601–3606. ACM (2009)
13. Paladugu, D.A., Tian, Q., Maguluri, H.B., Li, B.: Towards building an automated system for describing indoor floor maps for individuals with visual impairment. Cyber-Phys. Syst. **1**(2–4), 132–159 (2015)

Expert Study: Design and Use of Textures for Tactile Indoor Maps with Varying Elevation Levels

Christin Engel(✉) and Gerhard Weber

Institute for Applied Computer Science, Human-Computer-Interaction, Technische Universität Dresden, Dresden, Germany
{christin.engel,gerhard.weber}@tu-dresden.de

Abstract. Tactile maps could increase the mobility of people with blindness and visual impairments. Most research on the design and development of tactile maps focuses on outdoor environments, whereby indoor environments greatly differ in terms of represented objects, structure, information, and purpose of use. Studies on the design and use of tactile indoor maps are missing, so it is still unclear how textures can be used effectively in tactile maps and which are suitable for which areas and contexts. As a first step, we therefore conducted an expert user study with four blind participants to determine the challenges and benefits of textures in tactile indoor maps. Afterward, we initiated a follow-up study with two experts from the initial study to evaluate the influence of different elevation levels and production methods (swell paper and embossed maps) on the recognition of different textures, symbols, Braille labels, and structure of the building. We observed an influence of the elevation level of the texture on the recognition of map elements. Furthermore, the perceived structure of the texture influences the recognizability of the map elements. As a result, we identified suitable types of textures for rooms and floors in tactile indoor maps.

Keywords: Tactile indoor maps · Tactile graphic design · Textures · Elevation level · Tactile building maps

1 Introduction

Travelling independently is an important consideration in many areas - not only for participation in social life, but also in the professional field, e.g. to take part in workshops, training sessions or meetings. A necessary condition to be able to travel independently is to be able to orientate and navigate oneself during the journey but also at the destination. This is especially challenging for people with blindness in unknown environments, as they do not have a mental model of the environment. tactile maps (TM) are able to support independent travelling and orientation [8] for people with blindness by providing different types of knowledge (landmarks, routes, configurations) in an accessible way [4]. The creation of TM

K. Miesenberger et al. (Eds.): ICCHP-AATE 2022, LNCS 13341, pp. 110–122, 2022.
https://doi.org/10.1007/978-3-031-08648-9_14

requires the adaption of the design (e.g. enlargement of symbols and distances, use of textures and Braille) with respect to the tactile sense and the graphic type, because that the design of TM highly influence their readability. While the usefulness of TM has been shown in previous studies, few studies investigated the design of tactile maps (e.g. [8,9,16]). Thereby, primarily the design of symbols in maps, mostly for outdoor environments, were considered. However, maps for buildings differ significantly from outdoor maps - indoor maps usually show much more details, have a larger, detailed scale, and often represent small as well as large, open as well as closed areas [9,10]. Indoor maps represent other symbols than outdoor maps and face different requirements, so studies on design and use of indoor maps are missing. Therefore, we investigated the production, use, and design of tactile indoor maps (TIM) to improve their readability. In this paper, we will present the first step of our investigations, focusing on the use of textures on different formats and elevation levels in TIM, which has not been investigated until now. We will then evaluate various design aspects of TIM with a larger user group, while the present study aims to find important aspects for textures in TIM by conducting an expert pilot study.

2 Related Work

Many aspects influence the design of TIM, e.g. the production method [4], the function of the maps, the context of use, the purpose of the map [8] or the experiences and abilities of the user. Most of the previous research on the design of TM has focused on spatial maps with streets and buildings [3], so their results can usually be applied specifically to outdoor environments, requiring specific research for indoor environments [11]. For the design of tactile graphics general guidelines (e.g. [2,15]) can be applied to TIM (e.g. minimum sizes and distances). For specific design elements (e.g., textures, symbols) in the context of TIM, on the other hand, it is still uncertain how and whether they can be used and read effectively for different purposes. Engel et al. [7] analyzed existing, primarily large-print TIM in terms of the use of textures, symbols, labels, doors, and the objects shown. They found that symbols were used much more frequently to encode information in TIM than textures. The maps using textures represent in average three different textures, while filled areas were the most common. However, the study cannot make any judgment about the quality and readability of the analyzed maps.

In contrast, many studies examine the use and distinguishability of textures in general. Numerous previous investigations addressed the development of a highly distinguishable texture set (e.g. [6,14]). Prescher et al. [14] investigated textures in terms of their suitability for different output media, which is also important for the production and distribution of maps. They identified a texture set that is useful among swell paper, embossed graphics and pin-matrix devices (see [13]).

Berla et al. [1] conducted a study to investigate the influence of texture on performance in symbol localisation tasks. They concluded that textures could significantly decrease the performance for point symbol localisation tasks. In addition, line tracing tasks took significantly longer on a textured map. In contrast, textures could support the recognition of areas. The authors state that performance in tracing tasks is less affected when the texture is less raised than the track. For which texture pattern, contexts and elevation levels that applies was not investigated. In addition, only textured and non-textured pseudo maps were compared, and differences between textures and their suitability for indoor maps were not considered.

Nolan and Morris [12] investigated different elevation levels for point symbols, textures and line symbols with school students with blindness. They showed that elevation level could be used effectively to encode information. In addition, general guidelines (e.g. [2]) indicate that reducing the elevation level of textures may reduce cluttering. In contrast, no study has yet investigated the influence of different elevation levels of textures for different output formats on the perceived content of the map.

In summary, previous research has shown the influence of texture on the recognition of surrounding elements within the context of use. So far, no study has investigated the specific use of different elevation levels for different texture types.

3 Use of Textures for Tactile Indoor Maps

Textures are commonly used to indicate the meaning of areas (as a replacement for colored areas in visual graphics) which meaning could be referenced in the legend. They usually consist of an uniform pattern of basic symbols (e.g. circles, rectangles, lines) with which an area is filled. General guidelines provide recommendations for the minimum size of areas for textures, ranging between 2.54 cm × 1.27 cm [2] to 3.00 cm × 1.50 cm [13]. In TIM textures could be used to distinguish between rooms and floors, to indicate non-walkable or dangerous areas, to distinguish between indoor and outdoor or between different types of rooms (e.g. public and non-public rooms in public buildings). However, Braille labels or symbols can be used instead of textures to distinguish different area types. On the other hand, textures can also support the recognition of areas, as shown in previous studies. For example, in the case of open, irregular or angled surfaces, such as floors, large rooms or halls, it can be difficult to determine whether an area is part of the entire area without a texture. Therefore, it is worth investigating how and which textures can be used effectively in TIM. Furthermore, textures should be equally suitable for different output methods to be widely usable. The following requirements for the use of textures in TIM could be identified: (1) Support the recognition of areas; (2) Suitability for small, medium or large areas; (3) Suitability for irregular, angled areas; (4) Distinguishability of textures from each other when used together on a map; (5) Minimal similarity of textures to surrounding walls, symbols and Braille labels; (6) Causing minimal distraction. The challenge is to design textures that convey the meaning of specific areas while supporting area recognition with as little interference as possible with the recognition of surrounding objects. The latter may be achieved by using lower elevation levels for textures. Therefore, we investigated the influence of different elevation levels on the recognition of TIM in a first expert study. We also compared different elevation levels between swell paper and embossed TIM using the same gray values.

4 Initial User Study on Tactile Indoor Map Design

We conducted an expert study with experts with blindness in two steps. First, we investigated several design aspects and concepts of TIM with four experts, where we focus in this paper on the results regarding textures. In a second step, we evaluated a pretested texture set with different elevation levels with two experts who had already participated in the initial study. The goal was to find out whether reducing the height of the textures in contrast to the surrounding elements affects the recognizability of the like. A second research question addresses the comparison between swell paper and embossed TIM as well as different types of textures. As a result, statements on suitable elevation levels for different textures can also be expected, which will then be evaluated in a more extensive study.

4.1 Participants and Procedure

Four experts with blindness participated in our first pilot study (see Table 1). All participants were blind and have above-average experience with tactile maps and good to very good orientation skills. In addition, all participants have frequently participated in evaluations and user studies.

In this step, we first aimed to find out whether textures are appropriate for TIM in general with a semi-structured interview protocol. This study began with a training phase, where the map design was explained for the participants using an example. Afterward, the participants had to complete configurational and searching tasks with a map on swell paper (A3). We used a pre-evaluated symbol set by selecting meaningful symbols for indoor environments that were created and evaluated in the ATMAPS project [5] for elevators, stairs, target room, toilet rooms and main entrances. The design follows meaningful guidelines where rooms are represented with solid lines, outer walls of the building are thicker than inner walls and doors are represented with a gap in a wall. Furthermore, distances between textures, symbols, Braille labels and the environment have been added to support distinguishability between different elements on the maps. In addition, rooms and floors are filled with different textures. We used a dashed texture with two dashes side by side for floors and diagonal lines for rooms (taking from [13]).

First, participants should indicate floor areas on a map with narrow floorways where the dashed texture cannot be fully represented in some places and is only partially shown (see Fig. 1). Second, participants should compare a tactile map with and without textures (see Fig. 2 as well as an embossed map with textures. Map elements could be referenced in a separated legend. First, we asked the participants to identify areas for rooms and floors on the swell paper map.

4.2 Results of the Initial User Study

Since the results on textures represent only part of a more extensive user study, only the primarily qualitative results of the initial study regarding the textures are presented here in summarized form. All experts could understand the presented maps and its content well. The first task was to identify narrow floor areas with dashed texture on a map where the texture was cut off in some places and thus only partially represented (e.g., only half of the texture pattern is shown). All participants had challenges to identify all areas of the floor correctly (see Fig. 1). The area highlighted in Fig. 1 was not correctly recognized by any of the participants. In contrast, areas representing the whole texture could be identified by all subjects. The upper narrow floor, where the dashes were cut off at the top, caused uncertainty for two experts. P1 and P3 suggested referencing all of the texture variants that appear in the graphic, including partial representations of the texture, in the legend as well. P2 noted that she/he thought it had a different meaning because the texture at this location appeared different than those for

Table 1. Characteristics of the four experts who participated in the first pilot study. Information on age, gender, impairment, Braille reading skills, orientation skills and experiences with tactile indoor and outdoor maps are presented.

Characteristic/ ID	P1	P2	P3	P4
Age in years	20–30	50–60	40–50	30–40
Gender	Male	Female	Male	Female
Impairment	Blind	Blind	Blind	Blind
Braille	Very good	Very good	Very good	Very good
Orientation	Good (indoor), very good (outdoor)	Very good	Rather less (outdoor), good (indoor)	Good
Tactile maps outdoor	High	Very high	Very high	High
Tactile maps indoor	Rather less	High	Very high	High

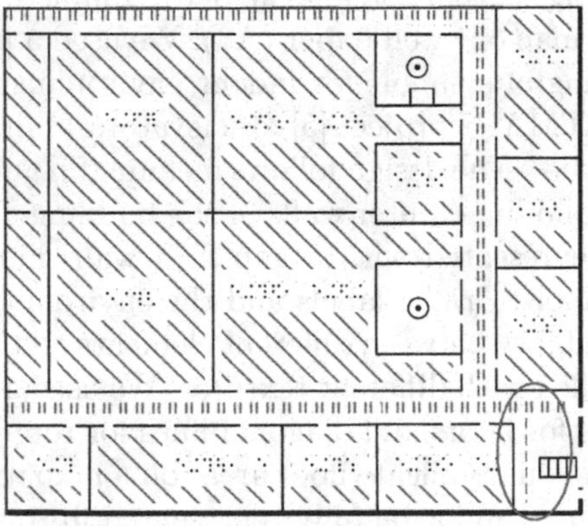

Fig. 1. Tactile indoor map used for the study: participants should identify areas with the dashed floor texture. Areas that are difficult to recognize highlighted.

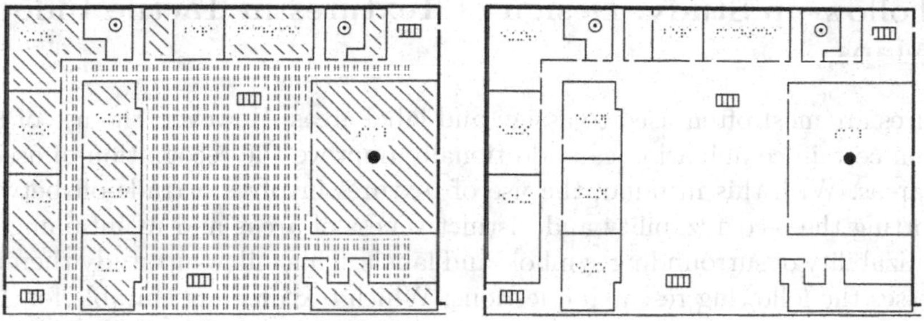

Fig. 2. Tactile indoor maps used for the initial study. Left: Part of a building with textures for floors and rooms. Right: Same map without textures.

floors. P2 stated that although the texture was not clearly identifiable, it can be concluded from context that the area must be a floor.

Next, the experts were given an indoor map with and without textures for floors and rooms on swell paper (see Fig. 2). They were asked whether they preferred the representation with textures. The answers of the experts were quite different: While P1 and P4 answered the question with "yes" or "rather yes", the other two participants (rather) preferred the presentation without textures. P3 is the only person who would generally avoid the use of textures. In contrast, the other three experts stated that large floors in particular were more difficult to recognize without textures. P4 suggested adding textures only to the floors and leaving the rooms empty, while P2 suggests the opposite. Furthermore, the experts noticed that the texture filled the entire sheet with raised elements, which makes it appear confusing. P1 and P2 therefore suggested embossing the textures less significant by either using finer textures or choosing a lower elevation level.

Finally, the subjects received the same part of the building with textures printed on swell paper and an embossed one. Once again, the experts had different preferences. P1 and P3 generally preferred the embossed indoor map, while P2 and P4 tend to prefer maps on swell paper. Two participants (P1 and P3) were able to recognize textures better on the embossed print, one person on the swell paper print (P2), and P4 recognized textures equally well on both representations. It was added that textures appear more distracting on swell paper. P1, P2 and P4 moreover suggested the need for embossed indoor maps to have larger distances between objects, e.g., for doors or dashed lines. P3, on the other hand, considered swell paper to be unpleasant and sticky.

Overall, the expert study showed that textures in TIM can be challenging and differences between production methods can also be identified. Subjects also indicated that the presentation of different elevation levels can improve the recognition of areas. That is why, we investigated the design of textures and the use of different elevation levels for textures in TIM in a follow-up study, again with P2 and P4 from our initial study.

5 Follow-up Study: Design of Textures in Tactile Indoor Maps

Textures are most often used to assign and label areas. However, the use of textures in certain combination can additionally improve the recognition of associated areas. With this in mind, the use of textures involves a trade-off between supporting the recognizability and distinctiveness of areas and maintaining the recognizability of surrounding symbols and labels. This follow-up study therefore addresses the following research questions: Which textures are suitable for TIM for which type of areas (small vs. large areas)? Does reducing the print height of textures reduce the distraction caused by textures? What is the appropriate elevation level for different textures and production methods? The aim of the study is not to provide a complete answer to these research questions. The aim of this study is to get first insights into the use of textures in indoor maps as a preparation for a larger study involving a large number of users, in order to be able to identify a small selection of suitable textures and elevation levels. These findings will then be used in a larger study as a basis for map design. Therefore, only two subjects (P2 and P4) were included in this study, each of whom evaluated the textures intensively.

5.1 Materials and Procedure

First, we selected and slightly adapted seven pre-evaluated textures (from [13] [14]) for our evaluation. The following textures were evaluated (see Fig. 3: T1. Dots Small Narrow (size: 1.2 mm; distance: 1.4 mm); T2. Dots Small Wide (size: 1.2 mm; distance: 3.8 mm); T3. Dashed; T4. Diagonal lines; T5. Large Dots (size: 2.1 mm; distance horizontal: 2.8 mm; distance vertical: 4.1 mm); T6. Grid; T7. Filled . The gray values for the different elevation levels were obtained empirically (see Fig. 3 G1–G7). The criteria for the selection of gray values were to ensure that the texture is perceptible both on swell paper and with the embossed print. A total of 6 gray values and additionally black were examined. Thus, three conditions per texture (A4 and A3 swell paper, A4 embossed print) were evaluated, each with seven different elevation levels. For all conditions, the same indoor map example were used (see Fig. 4). Each subject also received a legend with all elevation levels and textures for direct comparison (see Fig. 3). For each of the three conditions, participants were also given an indoor map without textures. We randomized the order of conditions and textures for every participant.

For every test case (condition swell paper A3 and A4/embossed maps x seven textures), we asked the following questions: Can you perceive any difference compared to the previous elevation level? How well could you recognize the texture? Could you recognize any difference in elevation compared to the surrounded elements? Does the texture support the perception of structures and areas? Are symbols and Braille letters easily recognizable? We further asked after each condition for the preferred elevation level, for what kind of rooms the texture is suitable overall, and whether the texture could be easily distinguished from the other textures.

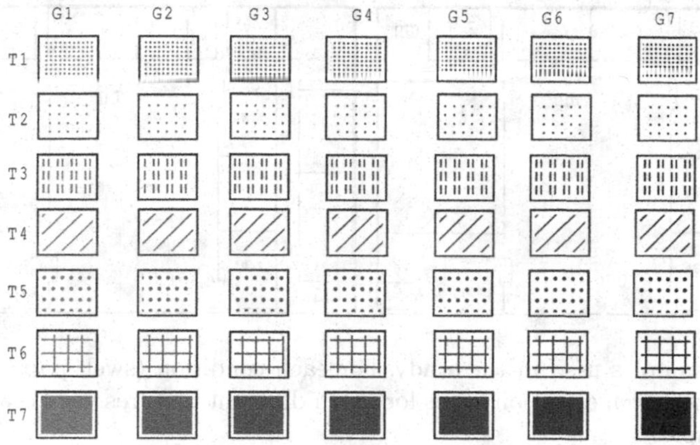

Fig. 3. Legend with all different elevation levels and textures used for this study.

The study was conducted in face-to-face interviews with both subjects individually. The study session with each participant took about 4 h.

5.2 Results and Observations of the Follow-Up Study

Due to the chosen methodology and the related small number of participants, the results presented here are primarily qualitative data and provide first indications for further studies and improvements of the design.

In general, the results of the study support the assumption that the recognizability of map elements is highly influenced by the applied elevation level of the textures. Thus, in some cases, a clear difference in the recognizability of the symbols, Braille, rooms, walls and doors could be identified. We also noticed during production that it is more difficult to control the height of the prints on swell paper, as the paper and the temperature of the Fuser have a large influence on the resulting swell height. In addition, different elevation levels were identified as optimal for the different textures, whereby the two participants preferred other heights in some cases. We also observed a great difference between the resulting elevation levels based on the same gray value for swell paper and embossed prints. There is the tendency that differences in elevation between the texture and the surrounding area are clearly better recognizable in embossed maps. Textures tend to appear less dominant with the selected gray values in embossed printings. Additionally, textures printed higher on swell paper were often perceived as unpleasant. In contrast, textures with a high density of elements were embossed irregularly, especially those with low elevation level. However, fewer differences were found in the recognizability of the textures and their surrounding elements between the A4 and A3 formats with swell paper, although the tactile impression (e.g., the perceived roughness of the textures) also differed depending on the format with same elevation level.

In the following we will provide the results for each of the seven textures.

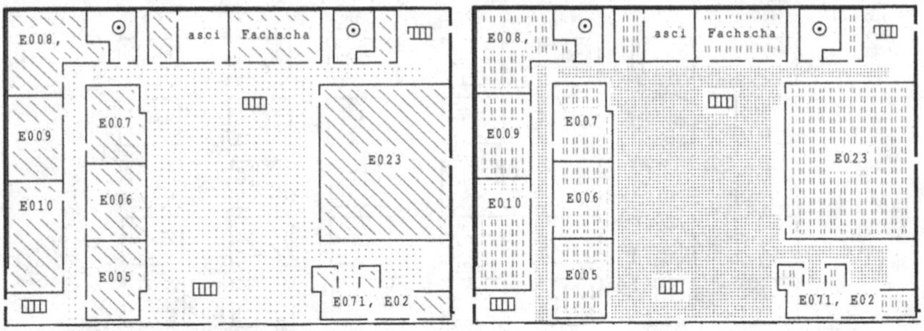

Fig. 4. Two examples used in the study. For each condition (swell paper A3/A4 and embossed prints) seven elevation levels for seven different textures were evaluated using this map example.

Dots Small Narrow (T1). The dot texture was represented to the subjects with small (T1) and larger distances between dots (Dots Small Wide T2). The participants noted that small distances lead to the texture being perceived as more planar than large distances between dots. Only minor differences were found between A3 and A4 swell paper. A clear difference to the surroundings can also be identified, whereby room walls can be better perceived with embossed map. Lower gray values were preferred for this texture, since the texture becomes unpleasant with increasing print height, especially on swell paper. In embossing, on the other hand, higher gray values or black were preferred. The participants consider the texture to be suitable for small and medium areas in indoor maps. The use on very large areas would make the texture appear very dominant. One participant noted that this texture was better suited for floors than filled textures (T7).

Dots Small Wide (T2). Both participants prefer this texture, especially for large areas and floors, because it is very fine. The lower elevation level also has a positive effect on the recognizability of the surrounding elements with this texture. Again, rather lower gray values were preferred for swell paper and slightly higher gray values for embossed printing. However, according to the subjects, the texture should only be used for floors and not for rooms, because the texture should never be used together with Braille in order to avoid confusion.

Dashed (T3). This texture provides a dominant impression according to the participants, which is why it is less suitable for large areas. In general, it can be easily distinguished from Braille letters. However, uncertainties occur at those locations where the texture is only partially represented. This occurred, for example, in room E009 and E010 above the Braille labels (see Fig. 4 right). These textures are cut-off in such a way that only the ends of the strokes are visible like dots. These dots can easily be confused with Braille. Printed with lower gray values, the texture could be recognized more poorly than with higher values, although slightly darker gray values were preferred for embossed maps. In addition, the participants noted that rooms can be recognized less effectively due to the parallelism of the texture to the room walls. While one participant does not recommend the use of this texture for indoor maps, the second participant points out the limited use of this texture. To reduce confusion with Braille, it was also suggested that Braille labels, especially in rooms, should always be placed at the same position, e.g., always in the upper left corner of the room.

Diagonal Lines (T4). This texture was identified as suitable overall, as Braille labels and symbols can be easily distinguished. According to the participants, the texture is suitable primarily for medium sized rooms, less for very small ones, as the texture requires a lot of space. The texture is suitable for medium sized rooms, less for very small ones, as the texture takes up a lot of space. Again, a lower gray value is preferred for swell paper than for embossed printing. One participant also recommends the texture for large areas, but with lower elevation level or thinner lines.

Large Dots (T5). This texture corresponds to texture T2 with larger point size. Therefore, we only asked the participants to compare it to T2. It is important to be careful not to confuse this texture with Braille letters. Both participants prefer the use of T1 over the large dots in TIM. They also recommend not to use T1 and T5 together on the same map, especially for people with less experience with tactile materials.

Grid (T6). This texture could be recognized better with a lower print height in all conditions. In embossed printing, however, it is rather weakly recognizable with lower elevation level. Overall, the statements of the participants regarding the suitability of this texture were contrary: While one person prefers the embossed representation for large areas, the second participant considers the representation on swell paper rather for small and medium areas to be better recognizable. One of the main problem of this texture is its structural similarity to room walls. It is particularly difficult to recognize doors with the texture, as they can easily be confused with the indentations of the texture. One participant therefore recommends rotating the texture by 45°C for orthogonal rooms.

Filled (T7). The filled areas were described by the participants as very dominant. This effect was perceived to be stronger on A3 swell paper than on A4 format. This texture should be printed as low as possible when used for TIM. At lower heights, Braille labels and symbols within the texture can be easily distinguished and identified. The higher the texture is printed, the rougher the surface feels, which was perceived as unpleasant with increasing height. On swell paper, bubbling occurred within the filled areas at gray values greater than #808080, which is why participants recommend the texture only with very low print heights and only for small areas on swell paper. However, care should be taken to avoid the majority of the sheet area being raised. According to one participant, it would also be feasible to use this texture for larger areas for embossed maps, but not for swell paper.

5.3 Summary of the Results

The results suggest that applying textures in TIM depends on the context, especially the represented symbols and Braille, as well as which textures are used together on a map. Using different elevation levels for textures can significantly improve recognition of surrounding elements with some limitations. However, the recognizability and suitability of the textures depends on the type of texture and also on the output medium. The use of the same gray values to define the elevation levels does not result in the same printed elevation level on swell paper and embossed printing. The elevation level also affects the perceived roughness of the area, while this effect tends to increase with increasing elevation. The structure of the texture (e.g. parallel lines) and its similarity to the building structure, also influences for which type of areas the textures are suitable. The similarity should be as low as possible. For example, the grid texture was rated as inappropriate for TIM because it has parallel lines to walls, making it very difficult to distinguish them from each other. While dominant textures (e.g., filled areas), should not be used for large areas because they are too distracting, textures that are perceived more as an area (e.g., dots narrow) seem to support the recognizability of symbols and Braille labels better, because edges and irregularities within the texture, such as symbols, can be recognized more quickly. In our study, the dashed texture (T3) and the grid pattern (T6) were identified as not suitable for TIM. This could be accommodated for the latter by rotating the texture by 45 °C. The participants recommend the use of T1 without Braille for large areas in indoor maps. Dots small narrow (T1), Diagonal lines (T4), or Grid (T6) were preferred for rooms. We further identified constraints under which the different texture types should be used in indoor maps.

6 Conclusion

We investigated the design and use of textures in TIM and evaluated the influence of different elevation levels for swell paper and embossed prints. The results of our study with four experts and the follow-up study with two experts indicate the usefulness of textures in TIM with several limitations. We found that lower elevation levels of textures could increase the recognition of surrounding map elements. The structure of the texture compared to the surrounding objects is an additional factor influencing the recognition of map elements.

In general, the results show that textures should always be evaluated in the context of the specific graphic type and its elements. For these evaluations, non-optimal representations of the textures should also be evaluated, e.g. clipped or incomplete representations of the texture.

We will redesign the texture set using the suggestions and results of this study and then evaluate it in a more extensive user study with people with blindness. This will result in an evaluated texture set for tactile building maps with guidelines for their use, taking differences between swell paper and embossed printings into account. The present study thus represents the first step towards generating well-designed and usable TIM also automatically to improve the independent mobility of people with blindness.

Acknowledgment. The project is funded by the Federal Ministry of Labour and Social Affairs (BMAS) under the grant number 01KM151112. Many thanks to all subjects for their participation in this study.

References

1. Berla, E.P., Murr, M.J.: The effects of noise on the location of point symbols and tracking a line on a tactile pseudomap. J. Special Educ. **9**(2), 183–190 (1975)
2. Braille Authority of North America and Canadian Braille Authority: Guidelines and standards for tactile graphics (2010). http://www.brailleauthority.org/tg
3. Brock, A.M.: Touch the map! designing interactive maps for visually impaired people. SIGACCESS Access. Comput. (105), 9–14 (2013). https://doi.org/10.1145/2444800.2444802
4. Brock, A.M., Truillet, P., Oriola, B., Picard, D., Jouffrais, C.: Interactivity improves usability of geographic maps for visually impaired people. Hum.-Comput. Interact. **30**(2), 156–194 (2015)
5. Charitakis, K.: Specification of symbols used on audio-tactile maps for individuals with blindness. testing results (2017). https://www.atmaps.eu/deliverables/ATMAPS-D_2_5-Testing_results_report.pdf
6. Culbert, S.S., Stellwagen, W.T.: Tactual discrimination of textures. Percept. Mot. Skills **16**(2), 545–552 (1963)
7. Engel, C., Weber, G.: Analyzing the design of tactile indoor maps. In: Ardito, C., Lanzilotti, R., Malizia, A., Petrie, H., Piccinno, A., Desolda, G., Inkpen, K. (eds.) INTERACT 2021. LNCS, vol. 12932, pp. 434–443. Springer, Cham (2021). https://doi.org/10.1007/978-3-030-85623-6_26
8. Lambert, L., Lederman, S.: An evaluation of the legibility and meaningfulness of potential map symbols. J. Vis. Impairment Blindness **83**(8), 397–403 (1989)
9. Lee, C.L.: An evaluation of tactile symbols in public environment for the visually impaired. Appl. Ergon. **75**, 193–200 (2019)
10. Lobben, A., Lawrence, M.: The use of environmental features on tactile maps by navigators who are blind. Prof. Geogr. **64**(1), 95–108 (2012)
11. Loitsch, C., Müller, K., Engel, C., Weber, G., Stiefelhagen, R.: AccessibleMaps: addressing gaps in maps for people with visual and mobility impairments. In: Miesenberger, K., Manduchi, R., Covarrubias Rodriguez, M., Peňáz, P. (eds.) ICCHP 2020. LNCS, vol. 12377, pp. 286–296. Springer, Cham (2020). https://doi.org/10.1007/978-3-030-58805-2_34
12. Nolan, C.Y., Morris, J.E.: Improvement of tactual symbols for blind children. Final report (1971)
13. Prescher, D., Bornschein, J.: Richtlinien zur umsetzung taktiler grafiken (2016). https://nbn-resolving.org/urn:nbn:de:bsz:14-qucosa-196167
14. Prescher, D., Bornschein, J., Weber, G.: Consistency of a tactile pattern set. ACM Trans. Accessible Comput. (TACCESS) **10**(2), 1–29 (2017)

15. Round Table on Information Access for People with Print Disabilities Inc.: Guidelines on conveying visual information (2005). http://printdisability.org/guidelines/guidelines-on-conveying-visual-information-2005
16. Rowell, J., Ongar, S.: The world of touch: an international survey of tactile maps. Part 2: design. Brit. J. Vis. Impair. **21**(3), 105–110 (2003)

ATIM: Automated Generation of Interactive, Audio-Tactile Indoor Maps by Means of a Digital Pen

Christin Engel(✉) and Gerhard Weber

Institute for Applied Computer Science, Human-Computer-Interaction, Technische Universität Dresden, Dresden, Germany
{christin.engel,gerhard.weber}@tu-dresden.de

Abstract. Mobile independence requires knowledge about the environment and environmental features. In particular, the location and structure of objects in the environment must be known in order to navigate independently. Tactile maps often require Braille skills as well as tactile graphic reading skills, and also contain less details or need to be divided into many sheets. Audio-tactile maps can overcome these disadvantages and can be used effectively with tactile indoor maps. In this paper, we first classify user tasks of tactile indoor maps. We further present an initial prototype that enables the automated generation of audio-tactile indoor maps on the basis of OSM data that could be used with a digital pen and a smartphone application to get detailed information about the building. It further provides search mode that supports finding a target in a building with sonification. We implemented multiple gestures to interact with the graphic and investigate an initial pilot study with one person with blindness to get first qualitative feedback in terms of our concept. The implemented workflow enables the accessible creation of low-cost, mobile and interactive audio-tactile indoor maps by means with a digital pen.

Keywords: Audio-tactile indoor maps · Accessible maps · Interactive maps · Digital pen

1 Introduction

Mobile independence requires knowledge about the environment and environmental features. In particular, the location and structure of objects of the environment must be known in order to navigate independently. Tactile maps (TM) enable independent orientation for people with blindness [6] by supporting the creation of a mental model of the environment. As an advantage, they convey different types of knowledge (landmarks, routes, configurations) [2]. Nevertheless, because of the low resolution and the need to maintain minimum sizes and distances between elements, the amount of information that can be represented with TM is highly limited. As a result, orientation maps [6], which only provide

K. Miesenberger et al. (Eds.): ICCHP-AATE 2022, LNCS 13341, pp. 123–133, 2022.
https://doi.org/10.1007/978-3-031-08648-9_15

an overview of the environment, can be presented effectively on a tactile map. However, in order to be able to orientate oneself safely on site, further information is necessary, e.g. on the location of certain features. For this purpose, TM can be printed on multiple sheets, which limits mobile use and usability, especially for inexperienced users. Furthermore, Braille knowledge is required in order to understand tactile maps. Several approaches show the advantages of interactive maps (e.g. [2]). Existing approaches primarily addressed outdoor environments, while maps for buildings significantly differ from outdoor maps. Indoor maps represent a large scale, showing rooms with different sizes (small, medium, large), several types of doors, floors, stairs and different levels and elevations. Promising audio-tactile solutions for maps (e.g. [2,7]) support necessitate the use of tablets, which are rarely used by people with blindness [4] - especially on the move. In contrast, Engel et al. [3] presented an approach to enable rich interaction with a digital pen, provided on the example of tactile charts. This approach could be effective for audio-tactile indoor maps (ATIM) as well, as it can support all phases of planning and execution of a trip to buildings (see [4]): On the one hand, ATIM can be used at home in any format (e.g., in a larger format) to plan the travel and to get familiar with the building, and on the other hand, on-site use with one's smartphone can be supported in a mobile way. In addition, gestures could be used to enable further interaction and learning of the map. In this paper, we first discuss user tasks of tactile indoor maps (TIM). We then present a proof-of-concept prototype that allows detailed information about a building to be obtained using audio and sonification while interacting with the TM with a digital pen. With our prototype, we demonstrate a process to automatically create ATIM based on OSM data and to use them together with a smartphone application. Furthermore, we got first feedback about the generated maps and the use of the app from one expert with blindness.

2 Interactive Tactile Maps

A number of approaches and prototypes enable interactive use of ATIM. Zeng et al. [11] provide a classification of approaches for interactive maps for the stationary and mobile use. In addition, Brock et al. [1] give an overview of interactive map projects of the last years. While the effectiveness of such systems combining tactile overlays with audio feedback has been numerously demonstrated (e.g. [2]), most existing solutions, as Brock et al. also noted [1], are not suitable for mobile use. Especially on site, however, it is usually of great importance for people with blindness to get information about the environment quickly, even if they already know the structure of the building. A common method is the use of touchscreens with a static tactile overlay (e.g. [2,7]). The overlayed tactile sheet thereby is often identified by QR-Codes. These methods not only provide a limited design space for interactions (primary double-tab gestures for detail-on-demand can be applied), but also pose the challenge of distinguishing between intended inputs and exploration of the tactile graphic (Midas touch problem). As a result, only a few touch gestures can usually be reliably recognized [7]. In addition, the format of the tactile map is limited to the extends of the device. The design of the maps have to be adapted to the size of specific devices which limits a flexible use of the maps. In addition, very few people with blindness use tablets when traveling to unfamiliar buildings [4].

Furthermore, most approaches focus on outdoor environments, where primarily streets and buildings were represented [1]. Indoor environments differ greatly from outdoor, representing complex structures, small and large rooms, details like doors and symbols as well as different levels of the building. The design of tactile materials have to be adapted for the purpose of the graphic, which is why specific research for ATIM is needed. In contrast, Engel et al. [3] compared two digital pens (TipToi and Neo Smartpen) to interact with audio-tactile charts. They argued that digital pens can be used with different formats, are suitable for the mobile use, low-cost, and enable different gestures, such as tap, double-tab, hold- and line-gesture. Audio feedback is given via a mobile phone so that users can interact with their familiar technology. Additionally, other modalities of the mobile phone (e.g. vibration, positioning) can also be used with the application. The authors evaluated the application of the technology with embossed prints; the suitability of swell paper has not yet been investigated. Furthermore, the design and automated creation of TIM for these technologies were not discussed yet.
In contrast, several approaches aim to develop an automation process for tactile maps (e.g. [5,9,10]). Štampach et al. [9] developed an automation tool to create tactile outdoor maps on the basis of ArcGIS. Furthermore, Tang et al. [10] developed a solution that is based on AutoCAD architecture floor plans to automate the creation of 3D-printed TIM for pre-journey tasks. Existing processes for map generation are often not accessible for people with blindness because they either require technological knowledge, use data sources that are not generally accessible (e.g. architectural building plans) or do not provide audio feedback. A comprehensive concept for the automatic creation of easy-to-use and especially mobile usable ATIM with the design of the same in mind, not exists yet.

3 Creating and Designing Audio-Tactile Indoor Maps

The design of tactile maps is related to the graphic type and as well to the purpose of use. The elements on the map relevant to users depend in particular on the intended use - i.e., what function the map is intended to perform. Therefore, we first identified specific tasks that users can perform with TIM.

1. **Getting an overview of the building:** Estimate the size, structure, shape and general parts of the building. For this task, at least main entrances of the building and walls are important. This knowledge is needed, for example, to decide which part of the map is relevant for further analysis, how building parts belong together, to recognize a known building, etc. This task is primarily performed in pre-journey planning phase.
2. **Checking the presence of certain targets/POIs in the building.:** For many users, it is particularly important in the pre-journey phase to know

whether a building has certain features (e.g., presence of an elevator, stairs, reception). Information about the accessibility of the building is particularly important for people with disabilities, e.g. to decide before the trip whether the building should be visited at all, or to recognize it on the basis of certain features. The structure and routing are less important for this purpose.
3. **Finding routes to known targets/POIs within the building**: In this scenario, the users know that a specific target is present in the building; first the target have to be found, and a route from current position to the target with the help of the map must be identified. Therefore, all names of targets and POIs on the map must be present. This task is more related to the mobile use of maps onsite in the building, but could also be part of the pre-journey planning phase.
4. **Finding routes to unknown/unspecific targets/POIs**: In contrast to the previously described task, multiple or no instances of an object may exist in the building in this scenario. An example is the search for a toilet in the building. This requires the user to find all available toilets on the map first and then decide which one is the nearest based on the map.

In the following, we will describe a basic prototype for ATIM by means of a digital pen that supports these tasks in an easy way and as well the automated creation of such.

3.1 Producing Audio-Tactile Indoor Maps with a Digital Pen

We decided to use digital pens to create audio-tactile maps because they are inexpensive, lightweight and easy-to-use as [3] pointed out. Like the authors suggested, we use the Neo Smartpen because this pen provides a SDK for the development of own applications for multiple operating systems, e.g. Android, IOS, Windows. Furthermore, the pen could be connected via Bluetooth with a smartphone to provide up-to-date information via audio. In addition, all functionalities and modalities of the smartphone can be used for interacting with the graphic (e.g. vibration, internet connecting, hardware power, audio output and input, positioning systems, etc.). This enables a wide range of applicable solutions for the development of applications for ATIM. For people with blindness in particular, it is further beneficial to be able to use their familiar devices for interaction.

Map Design. In order to represent an entire floor of a building for mobile purposes on an A4 sheet of paper, for example, the map elements must be generalized. For this purpose, we provide the outlines of the buildings as well as of rooms where the latter is thinner than the first. The main entry is represented with an arrow pointing to the entry. No symbols or Braille labels are shown on the map, as the required space is missing for most buildings. Only the title is shown in Braille above the map, but its content can also be accessed via audio. However, the location of POIs, such as stairs or elevators, is indicated by their outline. Accordingly, their meaning can only be determined with the help of the audio output. We also do not show doors in the walls of the rooms, for example, with a gap, because the length of the walls is often insufficient for this.

Combining Tactile Maps with Dot Pattern. For the realization of audio-tactile maps with the digital pen, tactile printouts are necessary on the one hand. In addition, the tactile printouts must be combined with the NCode-pattern, which is read by the pen using an infrared sensor to determine the position of the pen on the paper (see Fig. 1). The producer of the pen provides the NCode-pattern for different printing formats. The distinction between different sheets is encoded with NCode-pattern, so that the code can be assigned to a specific page. When printing, care must be taken to ensure that the NCode-pattern is printed on the sheet first, followed by the embossing or swelling. Otherwise, the dot pattern around the raised areas would not be printed correctly. We have tested this for swell paper and embossed graphics. The NCode-pattern should be printed in a resolution of at least 600 dpi. The NCode-pattern can simply be printed on the sheet, a calibration of the exact position is realized with the smartphone app using two calibration points. Afterward, in the case of embossed graphics, the sheet can be embossed with the map. When using swell paper, care must be taken to ensure that the NCode pattern does not swell, for example by adjusting the temperature of the fuser accordingly. In addition, when using a laser color printer, the black ink used to print the Ncode-pattern can be mixed from the color ink toner instead of using the black toner, since these areas do not swell. During our trials, we were able to combine both swell paper and embossed prints with the NCode-pattern in this way using common laser printers. We found that swell paper, due to its smooth surface, allows the pen to recognize the NCode-pattern less well than embossed printing. The pattern will also be destroyed faster. Using some sort of fixing spray might improve the recognition for both methods.

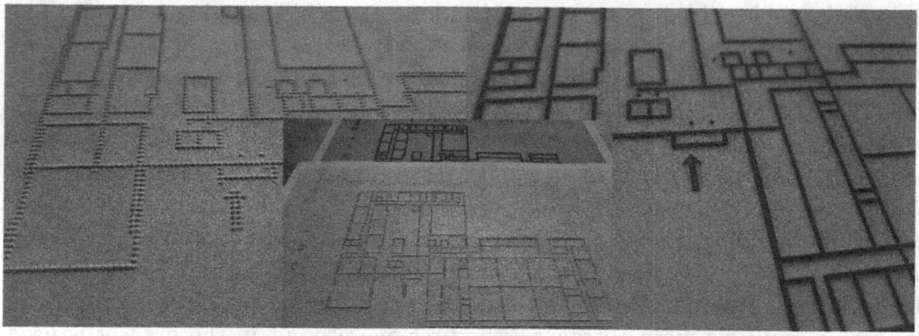

Fig. 1. Tactile indoor maps on embossed sheets (left) and swell paper (right) combined with NCode dot pattern.

Encoding of Information. Audio feedback in combination with tactile elements can be used to encode different types of information of the map: 1. Encode the same information related to tactile elements. 2. Encode additional information related to tactile elements. 3. Encode additional information not related to a tactile element. For example, the tactile graphic represents an elevator symbol while the audio feedback provides further information on the elevator. Our concept provides audio-feedback for all areas in the building where all three types of encoding will be supported.

Interaction Concept. Different gestures can be realized with the digital pen, such as single-tab, double-tab, line drawing or long-press. The interaction concept with the digital pen supports the information-seeking mantra [8], known from research in the field of data visualization. First, an overview is provided by the tactile outline of the building. The tactile representation supports the construction of a mental model of the general structure of the building. Zoom and filtering can't really be supported because the map is static. Instead, multiple modes are realized: The "Explore" mode provides details-on-demand via audio output. The "Search" mode allows the selection of a desired target in the building with the app. With the help of sonification, the user receives continuous audio feedback about the pen's current position in relation to the searched target. The pen is supposed to be moved over the map in order to get feedback about its position. The closer the pen is to the target, the higher becomes the frequency of the sound, comparable to a parking aid in a car. Details-on-demand are supported by the tab-gesture, which outputs the name or function of the selected element. Furthermore, the long-press-gesture provides details about the selected element, while the double-tab-gesture is used to provide specific accessibility features, such as speech output in elevators or Braille labels on stair handrails.

3.2 Prototype for Audio-Tactile Indoor Maps

We developed a basic prototype that enables the automated creation of rich, highly adaptable ATIM based on OSM indoor data (SIT tagging schema). The prototype consists of two applications (see Fig. 2): The first application, the "Tactile Renderer", is responsible for the generation of indoor maps which results in SVG-files that are optimized for the tactile print and include additional building semantics and characteristics (e.g. building layout, names, functions of rooms and POIs). The maps can be generated with a HTML-based user interface. The Tactile Renderer receives OSM data via the API. The data is filtered and outlines of the building, rooms and POIs are extracted and rendered with Python Geopandas. Next, the map is scaled to fit the selected format. Additionally, the building is rotated, so that it is aligned according to the main entrance. In the case of multiple main entrances, the first one present in the dataset is used as the starting point for the rotation. The orientation of the building is determined automatically based on its dimensions. The corresponding semantics of the building elements are added as attributes to the SVG-file. In addition, calibration points were added to the upper left and lower right corner of the sheet.

On the other hand, we developed a cross-platform mobile app "ATIM" that supports Android and IOS. The app can be connected with the digital pen via

Bluetooth and implements a parser for SVG-files that comes from the Tactile Renderer. For this, the SVG-files have to be added to the app manually. However, this step could also be automated by providing a shared folder for both or by using QR-codes as previous approaches demonstrated. After the desired map has been selected, a calibration step follows in which users are instructed to sequentially select two tactile calibration points in the top left and upper right corners of the sheet. After calibration, the map can be used to interact freely with the digital pen. The initial application further recognize the following gestures that were performed with the digital pen on the paper: Single-Tab, double-Tab, long-Tab and line drawing. Further gestures are possible (see [3]). Overall, we implemented the two modes for exploring building data described above (see Fig. 3). First, an exploration mode should support the user by getting detail-on-demand about specific building features by means of the tactile map (see Fig. 4). In this mode, the single-tab gesture is used to convey basic information about tactile elements, such as name or type of rooms. Double-tab is used to provide specific accessibility information of objects that were provided by OSM data, such as ramps, hazards, speech output in elevators. The long-press gesture provides additional detailed information, such as opening hours of the building, if available. These information were provided via audio-output and further can be read and repeated with the app. Gestures can also be used for other purposes. Here, we first focus on maps that avoid Braille labels and in that way represent the whole building on one A4 sheet. Moreover, it is also possible to produce maps in different formats and split it into multiple sheets.

The second mode is designed to support search tasks in buildings. First, the user can select a target from a list or search for a type of target (e.g. toilet) or a specific target in the building. In this way, users can determine whether the object they are looking for is located in the building. When the user now tabs

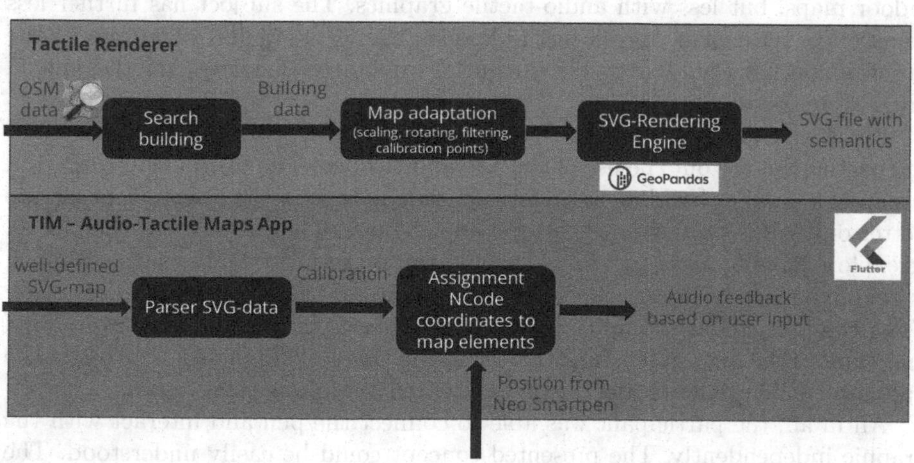

Fig. 2. Schematic representation of the two applications for automated creation and use of audio-tactile indoor maps.

the pen on the sheet, feedback is given by means of sonification, where beeps sound faster or slower depending on the distance of the pen from the searched target. When the target is reached, a continuous signal sounds. If several rooms match the search term (e.g. toilets), the search of all instances of the room is also possible with the sonification sound. The app further provides a real-time visual representation of the last selected position of the pen on the sheet (see Fig. 3). This enables the collaborative use of maps by people with and without sights and supports people with residual vision.

The described prototype demonstrates the implementation of an automated process to produce ATIM on swell paper and embossed ones. The use of the ATIM app is possible with any SVG-files as long as they are in the appropriate format. Beyond that, additional parser and building elements for reading SVG-files can also be implemented, allowing the flexible further development and use of the prototype. In a first step, we aim to evaluate the whole process and the usefulness of that technology for TIM. That is why, the prototype just provides basic functions that could be extended for further interaction concepts. However, the prototype is able to support users with important map tasks. Initially, a proof-of-concept-study with one experienced person with blindness was performed to get first feedback about the prototype.

3.3 Pilot Study

We evaluated the use of the smartphone app along with the exploration of tactile maps and the digital pen with an expert with blindness in a pilot study. In this study, we focus on the evaluation of an orientation map that represents a whole level of a building on one paper as described in Sect. 3.1. In addition, we first evaluated whether the map content can be understood by means of interaction. The participant has high experiences with tactile graphics and also with tactile indoor maps, but less with audio-tactile graphics. The subject has further less experiences with pens and is birth-blinded (age 30–40 years). The aim of the proof-of-concept study is to obtain initial qualitative feedback on the app in order to make adjustments.

First, we explained the whole concept, presented features of the app and let the participant try out the use of the app and the pen. The test person was given a map of a familiar building as an introduction in order to be able to concentrate better on the interaction with the app and the pen. The subject was then asked to explore an unfamiliar building. The recognition seems to be best when the pen is held in a steep position, which the participant got used to after short practice. Then the participant should connect the pen, select the desired map from a list and explore the map independently. Using the think-aloud method, errors in the app and challenges were identified. The search mode was then tested.

All in all, the participant was able to connect the pen and interact with the graphic independently. The presented concept could be easily understood. The participant noticed that the exploration mode and the search mode supports the understanding also for unknown buildings. In addition, accessibility weaknesses in the operation of the app were found, which can be easily eliminated. This results from the fact that the screenreader for Android and IOS works differently.

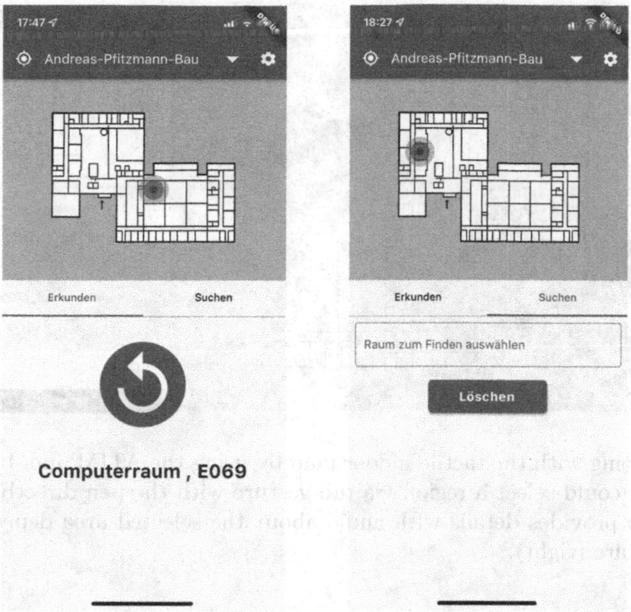

Fig. 3. Screenshot of the two modes provided by the ATIM app: Exploration mode to get detail-on-demand about selected elements (left). The search mode supports sonification to find map elements (right).

Therefore, the GUI should be optimized for both operating systems. Recognition of the NCode-pattern was not always reliable, so methods for fixing or better printing have to be examined in the future to improve recognition. In the user test, the recognition of the NCode-pattern with embossed maps was much better than on swell paper. Especially in very small rooms, the NCode-pattern could not always be reliably detected.

The participant proposed to use textures in rooms or floors to support better distinguishing between, them because the tactile map represents few orientation points. Moreover, the participant desired further input modalities, such as speech recognition, so that the interaction with the map would not be interrupted. The audio feedback, especially information about barriers and accessibility features, should also be adapted for output. While the current prototype was primarily designed to provide OSM data, future work should focus on a dictionary that provides a specific description of map elements based on the OSM data.

Since the time aspect is the most important aspect for the respondent on site in the building, the support by an assistant on site is preferred compared to the ATIM. In contrast, the participant would use the map for planning at home. Overall, practice is needed to use the pen and perform the gestures, especially if users have less experience with pens.

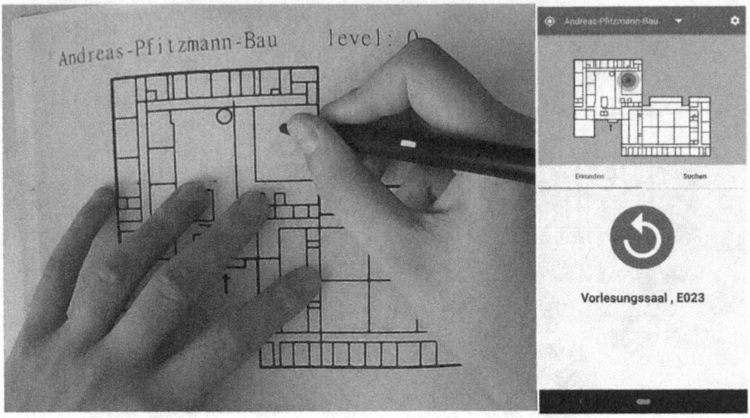

Fig. 4. Interacting with the tactile indoor map by using the ATIM app. In exploration mode, the user could select a region via tab-gesture with the pen directly on the map (left). The app provides details with audio about the selected area depending on the performed gesture (right).

4 Discussion and Outlook

In this paper, we first identified meaningful tasks that should be provided by indoor maps. We further demonstrated an automated generation process for highly adaptable ATIM that supports different user tasks of TIM. We showed on the basis of a first prototype that users with blindness could be able to interact with ATIM by means of a digital pen independently. The prototype allows the generation of easy-to-use ATIM that were generated on the basis of OSM data. It is limited by the data provided by OSM. The app can be flexibly extended to recognize other building elements and gestures.

For further developments, we would like to first improve the developed concept on the basis of the proof-of-concept study and then evaluate it with users with blindness for mobile and stationary use. A comparison of the effectiveness with pure tactile maps and identification of usable scenarios is necessary. Based on these findings, we will extend the interaction concept and investigate further the design of TIM for the use with a digital pen. The pen can be used beneficially especially for estimating distances on the map, which is often challenging.

The developed workflow forms the basis for the further development of automatically generated, low-cost, interactive audio-tactile indoor maps, which support people with blindness in orientating themselves in buildings. In the future, various extensions are feasible, such as the integration of further modalities.

Acknowledgment. The project is funded by the Federal Ministry of Labour and Social Affairs (BMAS) under the grant number 01KM151112. Many thanks to the participant of the study as well as to the students involved in the implementation of the Tactile Renderer as well as the ATIM mobile application.

References

1. Brock, A., Oriola, B., Truillet, P., Jouffrais, C., Picard, D.: Map design for visually impaired people: past, present, and future research. MEI-Médiation et information, pp. 117–129 (2013)
2. Brock, A.M., Truillet, P., Oriola, B., Picard, D., Jouffrais, C.: Interactivity improves usability of geographic maps for visually impaired people. Hum.-Comput. Interact. **30**(2), 156–194 (2015)
3. Engel, Christin, Konrad, Nadja, Weber, Gerhard: TouchPen: rich interaction technique for audio-tactile charts by means of digital pens. In: Miesenberger, Klaus, Manduchi, Roberto, Covarrubias Rodriguez, Mario, Peňáz, Petr (eds.) ICCHP 2020. LNCS, vol. 12376, pp. 446–455. Springer, Cham (2020). https://doi.org/10.1007/978-3-030-58796-3_52
4. Engel, C., Müller, K., Constantinescu, A., Loitsch, C., Petrausch, V., Weber, G., Stiefelhagen, R.: Travelling more independently: a requirements analysis for accessible journeys to unknown buildings for people with visual impairments. In: The 22nd International ACM SIGACCESS Conference on Computers and Accessibility. ASSETS 2020. Association for Computing Machinery, New York, NY, USA (2020). https://doi.org/10.1145/3373625.3417022
5. Hänßgen, D.: Haptosm-a system creating tactile maps for the blind and visually impaired. In: Proceedings of the Conference Universal Learning Design, pp. 49–56 (2014)
6. Lambert, L., Lederman, S.: An evaluation of the legibility and meaningfulness of potential map symbols. J. Vis. Impairment Blindness **83**(8), 397–403 (1989)
7. Melfi, G., Müller, K., Schwarz, T., Jaworek, G., Stiefelhagen, R.: Understanding what you feel: a mobile audio-tactile system for graphics used at schools with students with visual impairment. In: Proceedings of the 2020 CHI Conference on Human Factors in Computing Systems, pp. 1–12 (2020)
8. Shneiderman, B.: The eyes have it: a task by data type taxonomy for information visualizations. In: The Craft of Information Visualization, pp. 364–371. Elsevier (2003)
9. Štampach, R., Mulíčková, E.: Automated generation of tactile maps. J. Maps **12**(sup1), 532–540 (2016)
10. Tang, H., Tsering, N., Hu, F., Zhu, Z.: Automatic pre-journey indoor map generation using AutoCad floor plan. J. Tec. Pers. Disabil. **4**, 176–191 (2016)
11. Zeng, L., Weber, G.: Accessible maps for the visually impaired. In: CEUR Workshop Proceedings, vol. 792, pp. 61–71 (2011)

An Audio-Tactile System for Visually Impaired People to Explore Indoor Maps

Giuseppe Melfi(✉), Jean Baumgarten, Karin Müller, and Rainer Stiefelhagen

Karlsruhe Institute of Technology, Karlsruhe, Germany
{giuseppe.melfi,karin.e.mueller,rainer.stiefelhagen}@kit.edu
https://www.access.kit.edu

Abstract. Nowadays, a great amount of information is communicated in visual form. This excludes visually impaired people from easily accessing that information. A consequence is that they tend to limit their mobility due to lack of information. The goal of this work is to make indoor maps more accessible to help blind people preparing a trip to unknown buildings. In our approach, we further developed an interactive audio-tactile system to facilitate access to indoor maps. A study with blind participants showed that the prototype was well accepted and easy to use. The participants were able to achieve accurate mental models of the provided maps. A further comparison with sighted participants using visual maps showed no significant differences in the ability to describe the maps.

Keywords: Assistive technology · Audio-tactile graphics · Accessible indoor maps

1 Introduction

One of the major problems that blind people encounter concerns their mobility. While public transportation is getting more accessible, the destination might still be challenging to navigate without guidance. Before going to unknown buildings, it is important to familiarize yourself with the environment. This is especially true for people with blindness, as they can only perceive acoustically their immediate surroundings when entering a building. In large public buildings, information about the location of departments and offices is often provided by visual maps placed in the hall or in front of the building. These maps are intended for sighted visitors and not accessible to blind people. At this point, blind visitors would need help or preparation in advance to get knowledge about the layout of the building and where to find what they are looking for. When they lack the needed information, blind people often tend to limit their mobility and avoid areas they are unfamiliar with [1]. Tactile maps are one way to bridge the information gap for this target group. It has been shown that blind people are capable of building a mental map and orienting themselves like anyone else, if they have

K. Miesenberger et al. (Eds.): ICCHP-AAATE 2022, LNCS 13341, pp. 134–142, 2022.
https://doi.org/10.1007/978-3-031-08648-9_16

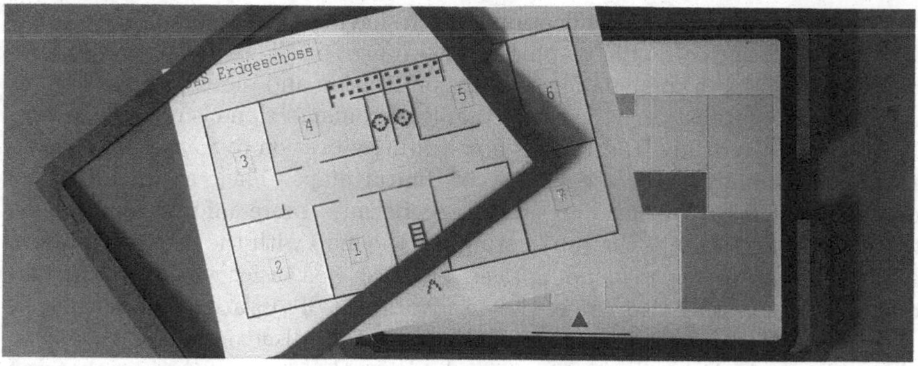

Fig. 1. The TPad system composed by an iPad Pro with the TPad app, a tactile indoor map and a frame to fix the map on the tablet.

the opportunity to get an accessible source of information and maps [2]. However, the information which can be included in a tactile map is very limited as tactile information, such as text in Braille or tactile symbols, need more space than text and symbols in visual maps. Therefore, systems that allow interaction with maps, e.g. by touch, are a good way to provide additional information.

In this work, we address the inaccessibility of indoor maps to blind people. To achieve this, new specific features have been added to the existing audio-tactile system TPad [6]. The system allows to put a tactile indoor map on an iPad Pro fixed by a frame and retrieves additional audio information about the map via touch to get a fast overview of the building. The system is shown in Fig. 1. Our new system provides auditory icons of the most important information and voice commands to enhance the interactivity of the system.

2 Related Work

A lot of research has already been conducted to provide accessible indoor maps to visually impaired people. Calle-Jimenez et al. [3] proposed a method to produce on-line SVG-based indoor maps that are designed to be explored by keyboard and screen readers. This approach has the disadvantage of not providing spatial information as the user loses the two-dimensional view of the map. The estimation of distances becomes difficult and even the relative positions of rooms can become challenging.

A more promising approach would be to use touch-sensitive devices coupled to audio feedback to provide spatial information. The GraViewer [4] used audio feedback to present floor plans on an iPad. The users can explore the plan with one finger and receive speech and audio feedback to navigate the map. This approach allows to explore a plan. However, the information about an indoor map must be reconstructed exclusively from many punctual audio feedback. This might not be enough for a good understanding of the explored material. Another study [9], also using image sonification, despite having good results, showed that participants preferred tactile graphics over sonification. This preference leads to the conclusion that a combination of both sonification and tactile graphics seems to be a good solution, since the use of tactile documents alone is not interactive.

A preliminary study [7] describes how adding vibration to complement audio feedback can improve the accessiblity of digital maps. Their approach allows zooming in a map, which is an advantage because more information can be stored. A disadvantage is that understanding the map with the help of vibration seems to be a relatively demanding task. The task was easier when the map was zoomed in, suggesting that one of the disadvantages of vibration feedback is the low resolution achieved with this technique. Another disadvantage is that most tablets do not include vibration motors, limiting the range of devices that can be used. In a similar manner, the GraVVITAS (Graphics Viewer using Vibration Interactive Touch and Speech) project [5] used a combination of audio and vibration feedback. Devices without vibration motors need to be used in combination with a haptic ring. The last two approaches share the disadvantage of not allowing two-hand exploration of the map, as the vibration can be felt by only one finger on the display.

The solution proposed in this paper addresses the issues discussed above and in particular meets the following requirements: two-hand exploration of the tactile map, a high resolution of the tactile component and an excellent degree of interactivity with the system.

3 Creating New Features for TPad

The first version of the TPad audio-tactile system was developed and tested specifically for the use with educational material [6]. In this section, we shortly describe the original TPad system. Then, we show how we improved the interaction methods by introducing the following new features to TPad: (i) two levels of information, and (ii) voice commands, i.e. map overview, unvisited elements, audio guided search. We also report on how we optimized the use of TPad by making it compatible with the VoiceOver screen reader.

Description of the Basic TPad System. TPad consists of a mobile application, installed on an iPad on which the digital document to be consulted is loaded. A frame allows to easily fix the tactile document on the tablet and thus can be explored with two hands like a normal tactile document. With a double-tap on a graphic element, it is possible to hear the text associated with that element, if the text is saved as description tag in the SVG input file.

Two Levels of Information. Each element present in the SVG file has two attributes: element title and description. The title was used to report to the user a short information about an element after a first double-tap, a second double-tap on the same element returns more detailed information contained in the description attribute.

Auditory Icons. In indoor maps, many elements are standard features such as stairs, restroom or entrance. We integrated the option to choose "Auditory icons" instead of natural language. Exploring the map with a single finger, when an interactive element is touched, an auditory icon will be automatically played. This allows the user to explore the map more quickly.

Voice Commands. To enhance the interactivity of the system, the following three features have been added which can be triggered via voice commands:

1) Map overview command. This command lists all interactive elements contained in a map. It allows the user to get an overview of the map by hearing a summary of all available elements they can interact with. The elements are grouped by type to reduce verbosity of the speech output.

2) Unvisited elements command. When exploring an interactive tactile map, it is possible that the users misses some information because they did not find some elements. The unvisited command returns a list of elements not yet explored. The app gives also a short description of the first three items of the list. At this point, the user can choose to be guided to one of these unvisited elements using the following search command.

3) Audio guided element search. At any time, the user can enter this mode using the voice command "*search*", for example "*search entrance*". In this mode, all interactive elements of the map are deactivated, except for the target one, to not disturb the search. By sliding a finger on the map first horizontally and then vertically (or vice versa), the user will receive two different sounds that will allow to locate the element on the map. The frequency of the sound changes depending on the distance from the target. Please note that this modality can be employed to signal temporary elements (e.g., construction work, temporary hazards) that do not have a tactile symbol and are only included in the updated digital version of a map.

Compatibility with VoiceOver. The current version of TPad was written in Swift using SwiftUI. One of the main benefits of this framework is the support for native accessibility features of the iPad. TPad is now compatible with VoiceOver and doesn't need an own accessibility feature. In this way, we avoid changing settings which is challenging for persons with visual impairment [8].

4 Indoor Map Interaction Using TPad

In this section, we describe in more detail how a user interacts with the system. We will assume the scenario in which a specific room is searched, as well as a way to reach it from the entrance. After loading the map and placing the corresponding tactile graphic on the device, a first possible interaction would be the "*map overview*" voice command. Then, using the "*audio guided element search*" feature, the main entrance to the building can be located quickly and with certainty. Now, the user begins to explore the tactile map by alternating between two-handed and single-finger exploration modalities. With the second modality, it is possible to distinguish the various interactive elements thanks to the auditory icons, and with a double tap more information will be read on demand. Once the user have located the room, the entrance, and the route from one to the other, they can choose to fully explore the map by invoking the command "*unvisited elements*" to get the list of the unexplored map elements.

5 User Study

To evaluate the described improvements on the TPad system, imaginary indoor maps from three buildings of increasing complexity were created. The complexity is defined by two parameters: the amount of rooms and the amount of symbols. The first map had 7 rooms and 4 tactile symbols, the second map 7 rooms and 9 symbols, and the third map 15 rooms and 13 symbols. The third map is shown in Fig. 2.

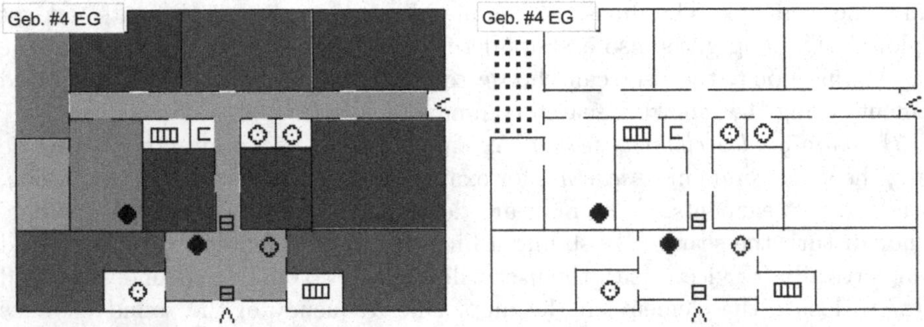

Fig. 2. The third indoor map used for the study. On the left the digital version of the map (SVG file). On the right the tactile version for the embosser. Circles with a dot represent restrooms, open triangles entrances, sequences of four rectangles stairs and of two rectangles steps, open squares elevators, empty circles receptions, filled circles POI.

5.1 Participants

Four blind people participated to the study. The age of the participants was in the range of 23–28 years old. All the participants were familiar with screen readers in general and with VoiceOver, the screen reader installed on the TPad system. One of them reported to use tactile materials weekly, two monthly and one even less. Only one participant reported to use tactile displays monthly, while the others reported to use them only seldom.

5.2 Method

Before starting with the tasks, participants were introduced to the system and its features. Using an indoor map of a simple building, participants familiarized with the system. When participants felt ready, they were asked to perform the same tasks for each of the three different indoor maps with increasing difficulty.

We provided the participants with a precise workflow to make sure that all available features were used.

Task 1. First they were asked to use the command "*map overview*" to get a summary of the map content, then they were free to explore the map using the audio-tactile system, without time limit.
Task 2. The participants were asked to describe the given map, while being allowed to continue using it. The time to provide the description was limited (60 s for the first map, 90 s for the second map, and 120 s for the third map). The audio of the descriptions has been recorded.
Task 3. The next step of the study was to ask the participants to search a given specific element in the map with the search command and describe the way out of the building from that point.
Task 4. For the first two maps, a search for a non-tactile elements was requested, to see if the implementation of the search was sufficient for non-tactile elements.

In the end, the participants were asked to use the command "*unvisited elements*", to note how many elements have not been explored. Before concluding the study, participants were asked to respond to evaluation questionnaires (SUS, NASA-TLX, features ranking, open questions).

6 Results

The descriptions of the three buildings provided by the participants (task 2) were transcribed and a score was calculated. Each map element contributed at most four points to the total score. One point was attributed for mentioning it and one for mentioning its correct location. Then, one point was given if the user recognized a particular shape of the room. The bottom left room in the building in Fig. 2 is an example: the room has a narrow entrance and gets bigger after that. The last point was attributed for mentioning additional information that is contained in the audio descriptions. If something is described wrongly a point is subtracted. This score is only intended to reflect the amount of correct information contained in the descriptions, and not weighted by its importance.

We also compared the maps' descriptions collected during the user study with the descriptions of the same buildings made by four sighted people. For that, we created visual maps with the same information. The comparison with the sighted participants' descriptions does not show significant differences in quality, as shown in Table 1. However, it must be mentioned that the blind participants were allowed to explore the maps as long as they wanted to compensate the lack of sight, as it is common in such studies or situations.

Table 1. Average score for the blind and sighted participants for each map.

Participants	Map 1	Map 2	Map 3
Blind	19.75	26	46
Sighted	19.25	28.75	47.5

The evaluation of the different tasks is very promising, as the descriptions given by the blind participants were of high quality and accuracy. Sometimes parts of the building were missing because the participants had forgotten them, but mostly this was due to the time pressure of the task and they were able to mention the missing elements afterwards. Also the description of the way out of the building after finding a specific location on the map (task 3) did not cause any difficulties. All participants were able to describe the correct way out. We report here one of the transcriptions relative to the third map (Fig. 2) starting from the restroom in the middle of the map: *"I walk out of the restroom to the top (of the map), then I can either (1) go left, very briefly along the corridor until it turns down, continue down the corridor, down the steps to the lobby, through there, down and to the entrance. The other option (2) is to walk from the restroom to the right along the corridor until I reach the side exit."*.

In a System Usability Scale, the system received a score of 83.75 (range 72.5–95). The results of NASA-TLX investigation, point out low values (lower than 10/20) for the sub-scales effort, frustration, mental, physical and temporal demand. For the self-estimated performance the average value was 16/20. Both the tools of investigation seem to indicate a usable system with an acceptable demanding load on the users.

The participants have been asked to rate the new features of the system in a scale from one (worst) to five (best). The average scores are reported in Table 2. Most of the features received a high ranking. Only the listing of all objects in the map seems not to be considered an interesting feature by the participants.

Table 2. Average rating the participants gave for the different features.

Feature	Rating
Search	4.75
Unknown	4.25
Auditory icons	4
Non tactile search	3.25
All objects	2.5

There is a limit on how much information should be placed on a map, otherwise some users may get lost in the complexity. However, the third indoor map, which was the most complex one, was considered as the upper limit of complexity by one user, one user was undecided, and the other two were confident that the system may be used with more complex buildings' maps. We observed that the system was quite well accepted by the participants of the study. They felt it was useful and some even enjoyed it. The main criticism to the system was about the lack of an alternative to the voice commands to interact with the new features of the system.

7 Conclusions and Future Work

We created an audio-tactile system that is intended to help visually impaired people in exploring indoor maps to prepare a visit to unknown buildings. A study was conducted testing the usability of the system and analyzing the quality of the participants' buildings descriptions. All blind participants were able to accurately describe most of the information contained in the maps, and the system performed well in terms of usability and workload. The descriptions were compared with a sample of descriptions from sighted users, and no obvious differences were found.

In future work, it would be interesting to investigate how participants manage to orient themselves in unfamiliar buildings after using the TPad to plan a visit. In addition, the possibility of splitting complex buildings into two maps could also be explored, as the participants' opinion differed on whether this would help or hinder the continuity of the map.

References

1. Brock, A., Jouffrais, C.: Interactive audio-tactile maps for visually impaired people. In: TACCESS, pp. 3–12 (2015)
2. Brock, A.M., Truillet, P., Oriola, B., Picard, D., Jouffrais, C.: Interactivity improves usability of geographic maps for visually impaired people. Human-Comput. Interact. **30**(2), 156–194 (2015)
3. Calle-Jimenez, T., Luján-Mora, S.: Accessible online indoor maps for blind and visually impaired users. In: ASSETS 2016, pp. 309–310 (2016)
4. Goncu, C., Madugalla, A., Marinai, S., Marriott, K.: Accessible on-line floor plans. In: WWW 2015, pp. 388–398 (2015)
5. Goncu, C., Marriott, K.: In: The 21st International ACM SIGACCESS Conference on Computers and Accessibility. New York, NY
6. Melfi, G., Müller, K., Schwarz, T., Jaworek, G., Stiefelhagen, R.: Understanding what you feel: a mobile audio-tactile system for graphics used at schools with students with visual impairment. In: CHI 2020, pp. 1–12 (2020)
7. Poppinga, B., Magnusson, C., Pielot, M., Rassmus-Gröhn, K.: Touchover map: audio-tactile exploration of interactive maps. In: MobileHCI 2011, pp. 545–550. ACM, New York, NY (2011)
8. Szpiro, S.F.A., Hashash, S., Zhao, Y., Azenkot, S.: How people with low vision access computing devices: understanding challenges and opportunities. In: ASSETS 2016, pp. 171–180. ACM, New York, NY (2016)

9. Wörtwein, T., Schauerte, B., Müller, K., Stiefelhagen, R.: Mobile interactive image sonification for the blind. In: Miesenberger, K., Bühler, C., Penaz, P. (eds.) ICCHP 2016. LNCS, vol. 9758, pp. 212–219. Springer, Cham (2016). https://doi.org/10.1007/978-3-319-41264-1_28

Supporting Independent Travelling for People with Visual Impairments in Buildings by Harmonizing Maps on Embossed Paper and Pin-Matrix Devices for Accessible Info-Points

Jan Schmalfuß-Schwarz(✉), Christin Engel, and Gerhard Weber

Fakultät Informatik, Technische Universität Dresden, Dresden, Germany
{jan.schmalfuss-schwarz,christin.engel,gerhard.weber}@tu-dresden.de

Abstract. Orientation in unknown buildings is a grand challenge for people with visual impairments in planned as well as in spontaneous scenarios. Therefore, it is necessary to develop solutions that support the whole travelling chain - on the one side the planning process for trips at home and on the other side the orientation process at a building. While different approaches exist for both contexts, in this paper we present a concept using two approaches together for planning and carrying out trips to unknown buildings. We focus on the one hand on tactile printed or embossed maps and on the other hand on digital tactile pin-matrix displays. The first type is suitable for pre-journey planning activities, while the second technology is designed for on-site use. Both approaches are able to provide spatial and configurational knowledge for the tactile sense. Based on this, we describe in this paper how both types could be harmonized to facilitate access to indoor maps in the given scenarios. We present prototypes for tactile indoor maps on embossed paper and demonstrate how a interaction on pin-matrix device can be designed and implemented to be used together and allow similar interaction with both.We propose providing dynamic maps as accessible info-points in buildings. Special focus is on the challenge of splitting tactile indoor maps into multiple views or sheets and how this can be achieved in a similar way with both methods.

Keywords: Accessibility · Visual impairments · Orientation · Indoor maps · Tactile maps · Swell paper · Embossed paper · Pin-matrix devices · Tactile user interfaces

1 Introduction

For people with visual impairments it is challenging to orientate themselves in unknown buildings. Independent travelling by people with visual impairments

J. Schmalfuß-Schwarz and C. Engel—Contributed equally to this research.

K. Miesenberger et al. (Eds.): ICCHP-AAATE 2022, LNCS 13341, pp. 143–152, 2022.
https://doi.org/10.1007/978-3-031-08648-9_17

therefore requires solutions for various scenarios, such as supporting the planning phase of a trip as well as spontaneous visits of unfamiliar buildings to address the complete itinerary from door to door [2]. Fröhlich et al. [3] describe the challenges that must be considered to address the various gaps in the development of accessible maps. When developing mobility-supporting applications for people with visual impairments the context of use and user needs have to be taken into account to realize meaningful support [2,10]. Several prior work pointed out the usefulness of tactile maps to support the orientation for people with visual impairments in unknown environments (e.g. [1,6,10]). Furthermore, Brock et al. [1] found that interactive map applications are more efficient than static applications [1]. However, many interactive solutions in this area are usually compromising, as they are largely based on static maps that have been augmented with another modality, in particular by using tablets (e.g. [1,7] or 3D-prints (e.g. [4]). In contrast, tactile pin-matrix displays are able to provide dynamic, highly-customizable tactile maps for people with visual impairments. While Zeng et al. [15] show the usefulness and the suitability for the mobile use of such devices for You-are-here maps of outdoor environments, orientation inside buildings is rarely addressed. An important advantage of this technology over static tactile overview maps is that changes can be realized quickly and thus the representation of up-to-date information is possible. In contrast, printed or embossed tactile maps can be used to get pre-familiar with unknown buildings and its structure. While tactile pin-matrix devices played a minor role for private use due to the high purchasing costs, their features make them especially suitable for use in buildings as interactive info-points. To address the complete trip - in particular planning a trip to an unknown building at home and orientate within the unknown building - we developed a concept that takes different approaches into account addressing indoor routes. We discuss three concepts for the tactile exploration process of buildings by supporting static and dynamic indoor maps. The first concept is based on printed or embossed tactile maps. The second one shows the adaption of tactile indoor maps for pin-matrix devices. The last one is an alternative approach for tactile pin-matrix displays, and serves in further research to compare the efficiency of the adapted approach. We also demonstrate our concept by means of a first prototype that represents dynamic tactile indoor maps and shows concepts how they can be implemented as accessible info-points in buildings.

2 State of the Art

Zeng and Weber introduced a classification of interactive map applications, where they identified the following five map types and discussed related advantages and disadvantages: *1. Printable Tactile Maps* [4], *2. Virtual Acoustic Maps* [13], *3. Virtual Tactile Maps*, *4. Augmented Paper-based Tactile Maps* [5,8,9] as well as *5. Braille Tactile Maps* [15]. In particular, both types *printable tactile maps* as analogue prints as well as embossed maps and *braille tactile maps*, such as the multitouch display Hyperflat[1] drive raised pins for tactile perception and are able to support audio output. While several approaches for *Augmented Paper-based Tactile Maps* enable interactivity and feedback via audio by using a tablet [14], braille tactile maps already offer an audio output or can be connected via Bluetooth to mobile devices to realize dynamic feedback and rich interaction. The latter requires the development of rich interaction concepts for dynamic, tactile devices to enable a fluid interaction with maps. In particular, concepts for changing the represented map and exploration of the same are needed.

Some approaches show how interaction with pin-matrix devices can be realized for mobile contexts as well. Zeng and Weber developed a location-aware prototype for mobile, interactive exploration of outdoor environments for people with visual impairments. Therefore, they explored tactile interaction techniques with maps, such panning and zooming to change the visible part of the map or different symbols to point out the user's orientation and to present buildings as well as audio output to inform about names of streets or bus stops. They describe that, "it is not suitable to replace the whole screen while panning" for the developed solution for outdoor environments, because "this might let users lose their previous focus and prevent them from maintaining their orientation" [15]. Furthermore, sixteen participants (eight legally blind people and eight blindfolded people) evaluate the system in a field study in two different real world scenarios which led to positive feedback. However, the authors pointed out the limited display space, which is challenging for large environments and the representation of symbols with pin-matrix displays [15]. While outdoor environments primarily focus on representing the structure of buildings and streets, non-visual orientation in indoor environments requires more structural details about the building [11]. A holistic interaction concept for dynamic tactile maps, especially for detailed indoor maps, is missing until now. In particular, it is unclear how indoor maps (including different floors and parts of the building) can be displayed with a pin-matrix device in such a way that the user is supported in understanding the entire building.

In order to represent the required information density on static tactile indoor maps, Trinh and Manduchi proposed a solution to provide static tactile indoor maps with multiple scales to explore unknown buildings before travelling as a special form of combined printable tactile maps.Therefore, the authors developed indoor maps with three scales of detail, representing the building structure, specific areas as well as the interior of rooms. The scales represent different levels of detail of information and support people with visual impairments during different phases of exploring a building [12]. This concept cannot be directly transferred to tactile pin-matrix devices, since less details can be tactilely displayed here due to the limited space and low resolution. An adaptation of the maps for these devices is therefore necessary, especially for connecting different views semantically with each other. While some approaches exist for static and dynamic building maps, the joint use of both media for planning and orientation

[1] Hyperflat device by the company Metec AG: https://metec-ag.de/produkte-graphik-display.php?p=hf (Last Access: 2022-02-04).

as well as the necessary design of the maps to be able to transfer seamless from one to the other medium has not been considered so far.

3 Concepts for Exploring Indoor Maps

One main challenge is the limited space of printable tactile maps and braille tactile maps, which restricts the represented amount of information (e.g. symbols, textures, rooms). To overcome this challenge, we propose different solutions for printable tactile maps and braille tactile maps to split the building into parts, while supporting the creation of a mental model of the building. Therefore, it is necessary to take the context of use as well as specific characteristics of printable tactile maps and braille tactile maps into account. For this, we compare both - approaches for the representation of indoor maps on pin-matrix devices as well as on multiple sheets (printable tactile maps). Since both methods can be used in an overall planning process - static maps for planning at home and use of info-points with a dynamic display in the building - special attention is given to how the user understand the concepts while using both techniques for planning trips to unfamiliar buildings for different purposes.

In the scenario addressed, it is assumed that people with visual impairments first prepare themselves at home for their journey to an unknown building with the help of static tactile maps. This allows to become familiar with the structure of the building, determine the location of desired destinations and form a mental model of the building. However, this map only includes the tactile building information. In order to provide the necessary symbols and labels, the map has been divided into several sheets. More detailed information is then only required in the building when people are on site. They can then interact with the dynamic pin-matrix device that is installed in the building. The display of the dynamic map should be designed in such a way that the users can recognize the map and have detailed information with audio output or look at the route through the building in more detail. Since the display is permanently installed in the building, the users also know the location of the map (you-are-here map). The dynamic display also requires a division of the entire map, which is harmonized with the static display.

3.1 Concept of Splitting for Printable Tactile Maps

Indoor maps are primarily large-scaled and represent doors, rooms, walls and specific characteristics of a building to provide features for orientation. For instance, Braille labels have a large size and cannot be scaled. For this reason, it is needed to split tactile maps of indoor environments into several pages to provide the required information. In addition, individual levels of complex buildings usually cannot be entirely represented on an A4 or A3 sheet, multiple sheets are often required to represent an entire building tactile. The number of sheets required per building depends on the selected scale and paper size. Here, the purpose of use must be taken into account. Smaller formats such as

A4 are more suitable for mobile use, while this also requires the representation of details. In each case, all parts of the map must have the same scale in order to be understandable.

The combination of the individual partial images to form an overall picture of the building, which is essential for independent navigation, therefore requires a high level of cognitive effort. To accomplish this successfully, concepts must be applied to convey how the parts of the map belong together. One advantage of using static tactile prints is that the sheets can be arranged together on a table to form an overall image. This should be supported by the design of the tactile maps.

In order to support the construction of a mental map of the entire building with partitioned tactile maps, it is at least necessary to identify the partial sheets correctly and to note this in the title, which will always be read first when exploring to identify the content of each sheet. The title should be placed at the top left. In our concept, we have therefore introduced a minimap representation, which allows to get an overall picture of the building as well as its structure and shape (see Fig. 1 right). The minimap is created for each floor and shows not only the building outline but also all the main entrances, as these are important for orientation. It is essential to make sure that the orientation of the minimap corresponds to those of the partial maps. The minimap also shows the distribution of the whole area over different partial maps. Fine dotted lines are separating the building parts from each other, and partial maps are identified by an ID serving as a reference in the title of each partial map. The minimap is especially helpful at the beginning of the exploration process to familiarize oneself with the partial maps provided and the structure of the building. After getting an overview, a detailed exploration of specific building features follows. For this, users have to explore the partial maps, find their configuration and are required to reference meaning of symbols, labels and textures within the legend. As a consequence, multiple focus switch between legend, minimap and partial maps are required which interrupts the exploration process and cause a high cognitive workload. To overcome this, we propose a concept to encode the configuration of the partial maps in a redundant way and make them available also directly on the parts of the map (see Fig. 1 left). Therefore, we provide indications at the border of each partial map, where the map continues at another page. Based on this information, the user can determine which partial map follows at which border of the current sheet, giving them a reference point during the exploration. To support the user in tracing lines across multiple sheets without losing orientation, even if rooms where splitted and represented on multiple sheets, indications on the edges of the sheet should be designed as a continuation of the lines so that they can be quickly recovered on the other sheet. Under this premise the sheets can be put together like a puzzle. In this way, redundant representations of rooms that were splitted at the edges of the sheet can be avoided. Furthermore, the whole exploration process, especially finding specific targets in the building, could be supported by adding page numbers to the legend, e.g. for the location of symbols. The usability of the maps can also be increased by taping the partial maps together or designing them as foldable maps.

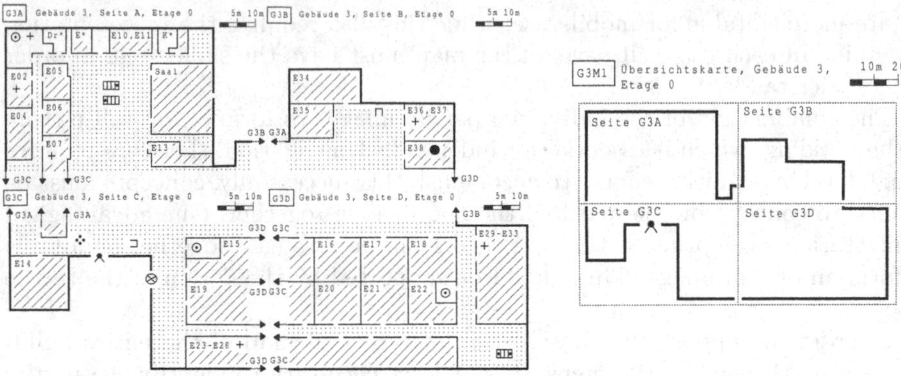

Fig. 1. Overview of the concept for splitting tactile static building maps into several pages. Left: Example with four partial maps which together represent one building level. Right: Minimap to provide an overview of the building and configuration of partial maps.

This concept for the design of multiple tactile indoor maps preserves the same scale to support the user in exploring complex buildings. Therefore, we support both - getting an overview of the building first, and then exploring details of specific areas while getting a mental model of the whole building. This layout technique could especially be used to get familiar with buildings in pre-planning phases. For orientation on-site in the building, exploring a couple of maps is not suitable.

3.2 Concepts of Exploring with Braille Tactile Maps

While the planning phase often provides enough time to explore details of the map, to learn the structure of the building and to determine available building features, other information are needed in the building. Here, the map is used to remember routes and structures or to get detailed information about specific objects in the building (detail-on-demand). This could be realized by providing permanently installed info-points with dynamic pin-matrix devices which can only show a few tactile details, but also support detail-on-demand through audio output. Moreover, they can be placed at various points in the building, where they show the current location as you-are-here maps. This would be possible with mobile usage of the devices with existing indoor localization methods (e.g. beacons), too. However, the private use of such devices is not yet common due to high prices.

Even with pin-matrix devices, it is necessary to split up maps of building and even floors because of the small display size. In contrast to printable tactile maps, users cannot combine different parts of the indoor map along the edges on braille tactile maps. For this reason, we propose a concept to switch between several parts of the map, where we focus on transferability of the designs, which is why we adapt the concept of splitting for printable tactile maps to reduce the cognitive workload and to simplify the usage of printable tactile maps at home and braille tactile maps on-site for people with visual impairments. Therefore, one solution is to use arrow keys to switch to the next part of the map - left, right, above or below the section currently displayed. The limitation that the user cannot puzzle the different parts together leads to the problem, that they have to reorient themselves in the new map part and to find the previous fingertip location along the swapping edge. That is, why we propose an overlapping layout for the different map parts (see Fig. 2a). Moreover, reorientation can be supported by representing the position of the last fingertip by flashing (periodically raising up and down pins on side of the new map) a tactile symbol like a circle. A second approach makes use of tactile guiding lines by raised pins which are shown between the swap of two map parts. In this case, the switch between map parts will be interrupted to navigate the user along a line to the previous position in the new area. After the connection point has been reached the updated indoor map view will be displayed.

In addition, we have implemented a first prototype that enables the splitting of indoor maps into parts on a tactile pin-matrix device. To execute this process, we use a mini computer as proxy server. It prepares the current view of the map and handles the user input of the tactile pin-matrix device. Therefore, we utilised an indoor data set from OpenStreetMap[2] of the TU Dresden (Dept. of Computer Science). The given indoor map data are published under open access. Moreover, in addition to the floor plan these OSM indoor maps contain accessibility information like the availability of speech output inside elevators.[3] Hence, the mini computer serves as instance between the tactile pin-matrix device and the data base used and pre-processes the georeferenced data for tactile presentation. Additionally, the current state of prototype allows users to switch between the different parts of the indoor map by panning and zooming the view (see Fig. 2b). SVG-files can be a second conceivable data base that contain semantics of the building. This architecture allows us to generate both - printed tactile maps and tactile maps on a pin matrix device - which are enriched with accessibility information by third-party. In that way we can harmonise the splitting process by given values and address changes in the accessibility of buildings over time.

Furthermore, the limited space of the display as well as the limitation of drawing symbols by the regular grid of the pins makes it imperative to use a second output modality. For this reason, we consider to connect the tactile pin-matrix display with a mobile phone by using Bluetooth to give an audio feedback to inform about map content. This enables the prospective opportunity, that for example user profiles can be transferred to the mobile phone to adapt the representation of the map as well as the incorporated information by the individual needs of different users without repeating setup processes.

Since several approaches are conceivable and Zeng and Weber discusses the problem of loosing the finger's reference point when updating the tactile display

[2] OpenStreetMap.org, https://www.openstreetmap.org, Access date: 31.03.2022.
[3] OpenLevelUp.net, https://openlevelup.net/#19/51.02546/13.72293, Access date: 31.03.2022.

completely, it is necessary to develop a second solution to compare the efficiency of the illustrated concept. Following these authors, a possible solution is a step-by-step panning, which is similar to the described exploration process for outdoor environments [15]. Therefore, we plan to implement a fixed sized window that can be moved step-by-step over a larger indoor map and is showing only a part of the map (see Figure 2c). In this scenario a user can focus his own position with one or both hands and scroll horizontally or vertically through the map by using arrow keys or speech input.

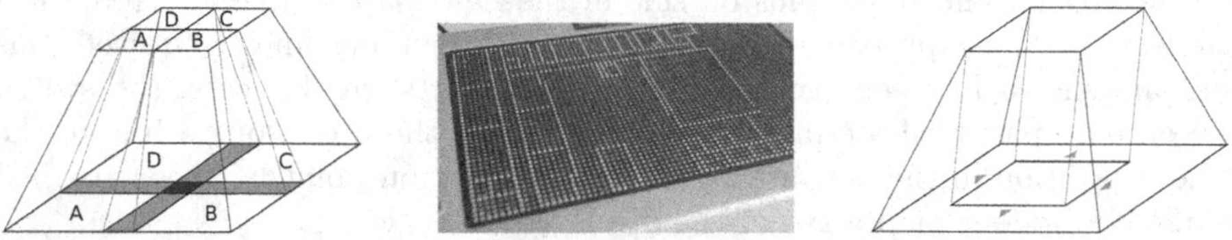

(a) Splitting scheme of a building in 4 parts for tactile pin displays, with overlapping parts

(b) Tactile pin displays with raised pins to draw a part of an indoor map of a building

(c) Window concept for tactile pin displays

Fig. 2. Different splitting schemas for braille tactile maps (a & c) and representation of a building part on a tactile pin display (b)

4 Conclusion and Future Work

A combination of printable and braille tactile maps for tactile exploration of indoor environments to support the planning and implementation phase overcomes the disadvantages of both technologies and thus supports people with visual impairments with independent orientation in buildings. Furthermore, since both approaches allow the representation of tactile indoor maps based on SVG files or indoor map data from OpenStreetMap, it is possible to harmonise them. This means, that the partitioning can be done in similar ways, so that they can be used together for trip planning and execution without a relearning process when switching between static and dynamic maps.

At the same time, it is necessary to consider the differences between the two kinds of map representations and to take them into account when implementing an overall system. For example, different approaches are required to combine a comprehensive map using partial maps split along the edges. In this context, printed tactile maps can be compared to an overall indoor map like a puzzle. In contrast, there is no possibility on pin-matrix devices to put the various map parts next to each other. Additionally, the output of extended information must also be differentiated, since displaying of complex tactile symbols on pin-matrix devices is severely limited.

Our concept is a first starting point for our research addressing accessible info-points in buildings and the simultaneous and fluid use of both. Accessible info-points enable access to building information for a wide range of users because it is directly available in the building. We will further develop a workflow that allows the generation of both - maps for embossers or swell paper and for the pin-matrix device based on the same data with harmonised design. Therefore, the usage of a mobile app to connect both can be beneficial. Moreover, a user centred design is essential to overcome gaps between the planning and implementation phase of travelling. For this reason, we want to evaluate our prototypes in real scenarios together with people with visual impairments and plan to use a pin-matrix device having a resolution of 10 dpi and a size of 76 to 48 pins.

Acknowledgement. This work was partially funded by the Federal Ministry of Labour and Social Affairs (BMAS) under the grant number 01KM151112.

References

1. Brock, A.M., Truillet, P., Oriola, B., Picard, D., Jouffrais, C.: Interactivity improves usability of geographic maps for visually impaired people. Human-Comput. Interaction **30**(2), 156–194 (2015)
2. Engel, C., Müller, K., Constantinescu, A., Loitsch, C., Petrausch, V., Weber, G., Stiefelhagen, R.: Travelling more independently: a requirements analysis for accessible journeys to unknown buildings for people with visual impairments. In: ASSETS 2020–22nd International ACM SIGACCESS Conference on Computers and Accessibility (2020). https://doi.org/10.1145/3373625.3417022
3. Froehlich, J.E., et al.: Grand challenges in accessible maps. Universal Interact. **26**(2), 78–81 (2019). https://doi.org/10.1145/3301657
4. Götzelmann, T., Eichler, L.: BlindWeb maps – an interactive web service for the selection and generation of personalized audio-tactile maps. In: Miesenberger, K., Bühler, C., Penaz, P. (eds.) ICCHP 2016. LNCS, vol. 9759, pp. 139–145. Springer, Cham (2016). https://doi.org/10.1007/978-3-319-41267-2_19
5. Ichikari, R., Yanagimachi, T., Kurata, T.: Augmented reality tactile map with hand gesture recognition. In: Miesenberger, K., Bühler, C., Penaz, P. (eds.) ICCHP 2016. LNCS, vol. 9759, pp. 123–130. Springer, Cham (2016). https://doi.org/10.1007/978-3-319-41267-2_17
6. Lambert, L., Lederman, S.: An evaluation of the legibility and meaningfulness of potential map symbols. J. Visual Impairment Blindness **83**(8), 397–403 (1989)
7. Melfi, G., Müller, K., Schwarz, T., Jaworek, G., Stiefelhagen, R.: Understanding what you feel: a mobile audio-tactile system for graphics used at schools with students with visual impairment. In: Proceedings of the 2020 CHI Conference on Human Factors in Computing Systems, pp. 1–12 (2020)
8. Papadopoulos, K., et al.: User requirements regarding information included in audio-tactile maps for individuals with blindness. In: Miesenberger, K., Bühler, C., Penaz, P. (eds.) ICCHP 2016. LNCS, vol. 9759, pp. 168–175. Springer, Cham (2016). https://doi.org/10.1007/978-3-319-41267-2_23
9. Poppinga, B., Magnusson, C., Pielot, M., Rassmus-Gröhn, K.: TouchOver map: Audio-tactile exploration of interactive maps. In: Mobile HCI 2011–13th International Conference on Human-Computer Interaction with Mobile Devices and Services, pp. 545–550 (2011). https://doi.org/10.1145/2037373.2037458
10. Rowell, J., Ungar, S.: Feeling our way: tactile map user requirements-a survey. In: International Cartographic Conference, La Coruna (2005)

11. Spindler, M., Weber, M., Prescher, D., Miao, M., Weber, Gerhard Ioannidis, G.: Translating floor plans into directions. In: International Conference on Computers for Handicapped Persons, pp. 59–66 (2012)
12. Trinh, V., Manduchi, R.: Feeling your way around: assessing the perceived utility of multi-scale indoor tactile maps. Conference on Human Factors in Computing Systems - Proceedings, pp. 1–8 (2020). https://doi.org/10.1145/3334480.3375200
13. Wörtwein, T., Schauerte, B., Müller, K., Stiefelhagen, R.: Mobile interactive image sonification for the blind. In: Miesenberger, K., Bühler, C., Penaz, P. (eds.) ICCHP 2016. LNCS, vol. 9758, pp. 212–219. Springer, Cham (2016). https://doi.org/10.1007/978-3-319-41264-1_28
14. Zeng, L., Weber, G.: Accessible maps for the visually impaired. CEUR Workshop Proceedings **792**, 61–71 (2011)
15. Zeng, L., Weber, G.: Exploration of location-aware you-are-here maps on a pin-matrix display. IEEE Trans. Hum.-Mach. Syst. **46**(1), 88–100 (2016). https://doi.org/10.1109/THMS.2015.2477999

The Accessible Tactile Indoor Maps (ATIM) Symbol Set: A Common Symbol Set for Different Printing Methods

Giuseppe Melfi(✉), Karin Müller, Gerhard Jaworek, and Rainer Stiefelhagen

Karlsruhe Institute of Technology, Karlsruhe, Germany
{giuseppe.melfi,karin.e.mueller,gerhard.jaworek,
rainer.stiefelhagen}@kit.edu
http://www.access.kit.edu

Abstract. In this paper, we describe a method on how to create a common tactile symbol set for printing methods which differ in resolution. We used a well-tested symbol set for swell paper as a basis and defined criteria on how to transfer the symbols to a different printing method. The method was developed in a user-centered design approach and assessed by a blind expert on tactile graphics resulting in the Accessible Tactile Indoor Maps (ATIM) symbol set. Moreover, we extracted the most important accessibility features for indoor environments and mapped them to distinct symbols. The presented method can also be useful for transfer to other printing techniques with a different resolution.

Keywords: Printing methods · Symbol set · Tactile maps

1 Introduction

Orientation in unknown environments is difficult for people with blindness. People with sight usually use visual maps to prepare a trip. However, this type of information is not accessible to blind people, who typically use a screen reader to read text information but these fail to interpret graphic information. As people with blindness use various combinations of their senses to obtain travel information such as tactile and audio information [7], graphical content needs to be described textually or transformed to a tactile graphic.

Tactile information can be retrieved from tactile graphics created by using different methods and materials. The most common method is the production of graphics with swell touch paper (aka microcapsule paper) [13]. This method uses a coated heat-sensitive special paper on which tactile information is printed in black ink using a copier or printer. Using a heating device, the areas of the paper printed in black expand and thus become tactile with the highest possible resolution. Other printing methods include using embossers, Braille printers that can print graphics, 3D printers or thermoform. Tactile graphics of the various printing methods differ primarily in their printing resolution and their degree of tactile impression.

K. Miesenberger et al. (Eds.): ICCHP-AAATE 2022, LNCS 13341, pp. 153–159, 2022.
https://doi.org/10.1007/978-3-031-08648-9_18

In our approach, we consider two different methods: Swell paper and embossed printing. We used well studied symbols on swell paper as a basis for developing the symbol set for our Accessible Tactile Indoor Maps (ATIM) symbol set. Moreover, we propose certain tactile symbols with a distinct meaning.

2 Related Work

Applications for people with disabilities for indoor environments are scarce because indoor maps usually do not include features about accessibility [6]. Especially for people with blindness, there is a lack of available tactile indoor maps [4]. Some approaches try to bridge this gap. For instance, [14] developed a map authoring tool for indoor environments to improve the availability of indoor maps.

Tactile maps contain point, line and area symbols. [13] showed that most people who create tactile maps use 10–15 distinct symbols per map where 3–4 were area and 3–4 line symbols. All others were point symbols. The discrimination of these point symbols is faster if they are build from simple geometry than more complex shapes such as polygons [10], and differs between the printing techniques (e.g. [9]). [5] analyzed the design of 58 indoor maps regarding the design of symbols, textures, lines, legend and Braille labels. They compared the common features and differences of the maps and found that some symbols such as stairs, elevators and exits share similar features. When analyzing this list, we found that many symbols are hardly not transferable to printing techniques with lower resolution.

The most similar to our approach are [3,12]. [3] compared symbols of three printing methods: 3D printing, swell paper and embossing on thicker paper. They used the same digital files derived from a 3D model for all three methods without any changes. The results show that symbols were best recognized for 3D printing, followed by swell paper and last by embossing. However, the disadvantage of their method is that they did not define criteria that exclude symbols that are not recognizable with lower resolution. It was to be expected that the symbols with the highest resolution will be best recognized [12] focused on area symbols and compared different production methods with diverse resolution.

3 Creation of a Tactile Symbol Set for Indoor Maps

The aim of our work was to create a full tactile symbol set that can be used for both printing tactile maps on swell paper as well as with an embosser with a lower resolution (20 DPI). We deployed a user-centered design process that selects and adapts an input symbol set for swell paper and returns a sub-set that can be recognized best despite the different printing techniques and resolutions. We applied our design process to the ATMAPS swell touch paper symbol set [1,11] and also compared them with sets mentioned in the literature [8,12]. (1) In a first step, we defined our criteria to select the symbols. (2) Then, we transferred the selected symbols to the second printing technique by adapting the shapes slightly. (3) In a third step, we tested the symbols that met these requirements with a blind expert on tactile graphics and improved the symbols exploiting expert knowledge about embossing.

3.1 Selection Criteria

The recognizability of graphical content in tactile graphics highly depend on the resolution of the printing technique. Curved or diagonal lines are stepped lines at low resolution. A symbol printed with a high resolution can be very recognizable, while at a low resolution it is no longer recognizable. Thus, we defined exclusion criteria to reduce the number of badly printable symbols with a lower resolution printing technique. As the selected symbol set should preserve recognizability in both printing techniques, the first criteria we have adopted was to chose symbols with a high ranking in the list of the best perceived symbols on swell paper [1,11]. Then, we avoided to choose symbols with complex shapes, too many details such as organic shapes with multiple unrelated elements, slanting lines and round curves and single dots, to avoid confusion with Braille. We also chose some symbols that can be rotated showing e.g. the direction of the door of an elevator or the main entrance[1].

3.2 Transfer to a Lower Resolution Printing Technique

At a resolution of 20 DPI, an A4 sheet consists of a 234×166 cells grid. Each cell is 1.27 mm and represents the smallest embossable element (a Braille dot - BD). The high-resolution symbols, created for swell paper, have been redrawn using the BD as dimension unit, e.g. a solid line can have a thickness of one BD (1.27 mm) or multiples.

To ensure the correct perception of a symbol, all its elements have to be separated by at least two BD (2.54 mm). For the point symbols, after having redrawn them applying the rules described above, we eliminated those with dimensions greater than 12 mm because they were too large to be perceived correctly with a fingertip.

3.3 Testing and Adaption of the Symbols

We used those tactile symbols for swell paper that are inline with the defined criteria and printed them with an embosser with 20 DPI. In a user-centered design process, the results were repeatedly improved and assessed by a blind expert for tactile graphics with experience in supporting people with blindness for over 20 years. The optimization of the symbols by excluding tactile noise in embossing were possible as we are aware of the special properties of the embosser. We extracted specific guidelines on how to place the symbols to avoid noise while embossing[2]. We tested for instance a full circle with the embosser resulting in pixelated edge. However, it still can be identified as a circle.

[1] Please note, that the [11] symbol set considers rotated symbols as different symbols.
[2] https://services.access.kit.edu/atim/.

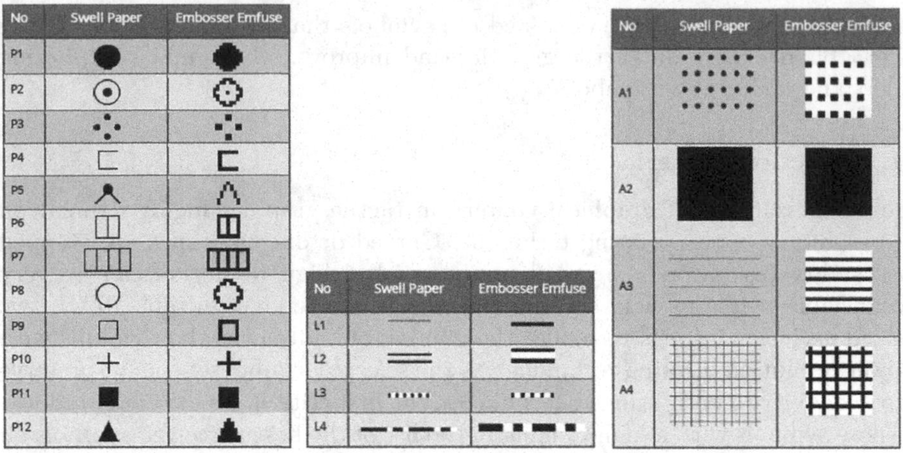

Fig. 1. The ATIM symbol set. Point symbols (left), line symbols (center), and area symbols (right) for swell paper and Emfuse embosser.

4 The ATIM Symbol Set

Each of the three panels in Fig. 1 show in three columns the id of the symbol, the symbol printed on swell paper and the symbol printed with an embosser. The best perceived and transferable point symbols P1-P12 from swell paper to a tactile embosser were P1 a filled circle, P2 a circle with a dot in the middle, P3 four dots forming a square standing on the corner, P4 a square with an open side, P5 two lines building a roof with a dot at the highest point, P6 two adjacent rectangles, P7 four adjacent rectangles, P8 an empty circle, P9 an empty square, P10 a cross, P11 a filled square, P12 a filled triangle. The four line symbols L1-L4 are L1 a solid line, L2 two solid parallel lines, L3 a dotted line and L4 a dash-dotted line. There are four area symbols A1-A4 where A1 is a uniformly dotted area, A2 a filled area, A3 an Area with parallel lines and A4 a checkered area.

4.1 Tactile Indoor Symbols with Distinct Semantics

The analysis of [5] showed that there is no consistent mapping between tactile symbols and their meaning. Thus, we created a subset of tactile symbols with distinct semantics with a group of experts on tactile graphics.

In a first step, we identified the most important features which should have a distinct meaning in order to understand an indoor map. We used the indoor environment features from ATMAPS [2] ordered by their significance. As they were very fine-grained, five accessibility experts categorized some of these features, e.g. revolving door was mapped to a door and a danger symbol. They also discussed about the tactile features which could express further information such as direction of the entrance to an elevator. The experts had experience with supporting students with visual impairments at least for over 5 up to 20 years. Four out of five were experts for creating tactile graphics.

Out of the 20 symbols, 11 features were mapped to an explicit symbol (see Table 1): services e.g. reception to P8, toilet to P2, entrance to P5, barrier/danger to P10, POI to P1, stairs to P7, elevator to P4, change of elevation (such as steps or ramps) to P6, outdoor e.g. balcony or terrace to A1, inaccessible areas to A2 and wall to L1. The first seven features were realized as point symbols (services, toilet, entrance, barrier, POI, stairs, elevator, change in elevation), two as area symbols (outdoor areas, inaccessible areas) and one as line symbol (wall).

Table 1. Mapping of features to tactile symbols

Feature	Symbol	Description
Services	P8	Circle
Toilet	P2	Circle with dot in the middle
Entrance	P5	Two lines building a roof with dot at highest point
Barrier/danger	P10	A cross
POI	P1	Filled circle
Stairs	P7	Four adjacent rectangles
Elevator	P4	Square with an open side
Change in elevation	P6 + P10	Two adjacent rectangles
Outdoor, e.g. balcony	A1	Uniformly dotted area
Inaccessible area	A2	Filled area
Wall	L1	Solid line

5 Recommendations to Use the Symbols

In order to prevent symbols from being embossed incorrectly, a number of steps must be followed. This will prevent "tactile noise" from forming around the symbols as shown in Fig. 2.

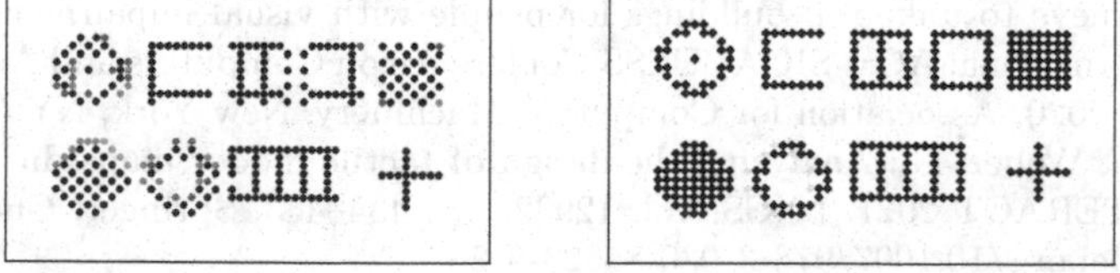

Fig. 2. Tactile preview of some symbols: on the right embossed correctly, on the left without using the recommended parameters

The symbols must not be scaled, the "chessboard pattern" feature[3] of the embosser must be disabled, the position of the symbols aligned with the grid described in Sect. 3.2. The point symbols can be rotated without losing quality by 90° and its multiples. This allows, for example, to make the opening of point P4 coincide with the elevator door it represents. Rotations of 45° should be limited as much as possible because they deteriorate the symbol, while still leaving it recognizable. Other angles of rotation should be avoided. To preserve the readability of the map, the same symbol should not be repeated several times in order to represent the real size of the element on the map. An exception is the symbol P6 (steps), which can be cloned and placed side by side several times to cover the entire front of the level change. Finally, the point P10 can be combined with other symbols to highlight a particular hazard associated with that element.

6 Conclusion

Using a user-centered approach, we were able to identify a set of criteria to transfer a well-tested symbol set for swell paper into a common tactile symbol set for printing methods with different resolutions. After extracting the most important accessibility features for indoor environments, they were mapped to distinct symbols of the Accessible Tactile Indoor Maps set. We believe that the presented method can also be useful for transfer to other printing techniques with a different resolution.

References

1. ATMAPS: Specification of symbols used on audio-tactile maps for individuals with blindness. testing results, March 2017. https://www.atmaps.eu/deliverables/ATMAPS-D_2_5-Testing_results_report.pdf
2. ATMAPS: Specification of symbols used on audio-tactile maps for individuals with blindness. user requirements specifications report, March 2017. https://www.atmaps.eu/deliverables/ATMAPS-D_2_1-User_requirements_and_specifications_report.pdf
3. Brittell, M.E., Lobben, A.K., Lawrence, M.M.: Usability evaluation of tactile map symbols across three production technologies. J. Vis. Impairment Blindness **112**(6), 745–758 (2018)
4. Engel, C., et al.: Travelling more independently: a requirements analysis for accessible journeys to unknown buildings for people with visual impairments. In: The 22nd International ACM SIGACCESS Conference on Computers and Accessibility. ASSETS 2020, Association for Computing Machinery, New York, NY (2020)
5. Engel, C., Weber, G.: Analyzing the design of tactile indoor maps. In: Ardito, C. (ed.) INTERACT 2021. LNCS, vol. 12932, pp. 434–443. Springer, Cham (2021). https://doi.org/10.1007/978-3-030-85623-6_26

[3] Some embossers have the ability to print surfaces by alternating tactile dots and spaces.

6. Froehlich, J.E., et al.: Grand challenges in accessible maps. Interactions **26**(2), 78–81 (2019)
7. Hersh, M.: Mental maps and the use of sensory information by blind and partially sighted people. ACM Trans. Access. Comput. **13**(2), 1-32 (2020)
8. Lobben, A., Lawrence, M.: The use of environmental features on tactile maps by navigators who are blind. Prof. Geogr. **64**(1), 95–108 (2012)
9. Martos, A., Kouroupetroglou, G., Argyropoulos, V., Papadopoulos, K.: Tactile identification of embossed lines and square areas in diverse dot heights by blind individuals. Univ. Access Inf. Soc. **20**(2), 333–342 (2020). https://doi.org/10.1007/s10209-020-00729-4
10. Ng, A., Chan, A.: Tactile symbol matching of different shape patterns: implications for shape coding of control devices. In: Proceedings of the International Multiconference of Engineers and Computer Scientists, vol. 2 (2014)
11. Papadopoulos, K., et al.: Specification of symbols used in audio-tactile maps for individuals with blindness. In: Miesenberger, K., Bühler, C., Penaz, P. (eds.) Computers Helping People with Special Needs, pp. 160–167. Springer International Publishing, Cham (2016)
12. Prescher, D., Bornschein, J., Weber, G.: Consistency of a tactile pattern set. ACM TACCESS **10**(2), 1–29 (2017)
13. Rowell, J., Ungar, S.: The world of touch: results of an international survey of tactile maps and symbols. Cartographic J. **40**(3), 259–263 (2003)
14. Trinh, V., Manduchi, R.: A multi-scale embossed map authoring tool for indoor environments. In: Miesenberger, K., Manduchi, R., Covarrubias Rodriguez, M., Peňáz, P. (eds.) Computers Helping People with Special Needs, pp. 459–466. Springer International Publishing, Cham (2020)

Indoor Navigation Assistance for Visually Impaired People via Dynamic SLAM and Panoptic Segmentation with an RGB-D Sensor

Wenyan Ou, Jiaming Zhang, Kunyu Peng, Kailun Yang(✉), Gerhard Jaworek, Karin Müller, and Rainer Stiefelhagen

Karlsruhe Institute of Technology, 76131 Karlsruhe, Germany
kailun.yang@kit.edu

Abstract. Exploring an unfamiliar indoor environment and avoiding obstacles is challenging for visually impaired people. Currently, several approaches achieve the avoidance of static obstacles based on the mapping of indoor scenes. To solve the issue of distinguishing dynamic obstacles, we propose an assistive system with an RGB-D sensor to detect dynamic information of a scene. Once the system captures an image, panoptic segmentation is performed to obtain the prior dynamic object information. With sparse feature points extracted from images and the depth information, poses of the user can be estimated. After the ego-motion estimation, the dynamic object can be identified and tracked. Then, poses and speed of tracked dynamic objects can be estimated, which are passed to the users through acoustic feedback.

Keywords: Navigation assistance · Dynamic SLAM · Panoptic segmentation · RGB-D sensor

1 Introduction

Human perception of the environment often takes an eye-based approach, which makes vision an indispensable part of daily life. People with visual impairments usually have very limited or no access to this channel. It is known that they mainly rely on information from other modalities to gain perception of the surroundings, the most important is hearing. Therefore, once the environment of visually impaired people is too noisy, their perception in environments with dynamic objects will be deviated, resulting in collisions with obstacles and even injuries, which greatly affects their daily life.

Besides, visually impaired people find it hard to maintain proper social distances from others during the Covid-19 pandemic [13]. Some assistance systems tackle this issue through Simultaneous Localization And Mapping (SLAM) and deep learning approaches [12,19], to provide accurate guidance to visually impaired people, but they are less effective in highly dynamic scenarios. To

K. Miesenberger et al. (Eds.): ICCHP-AAATE 2022, LNCS 13341, pp. 160–168, 2022.
https://doi.org/10.1007/978-3-031-08648-9_19

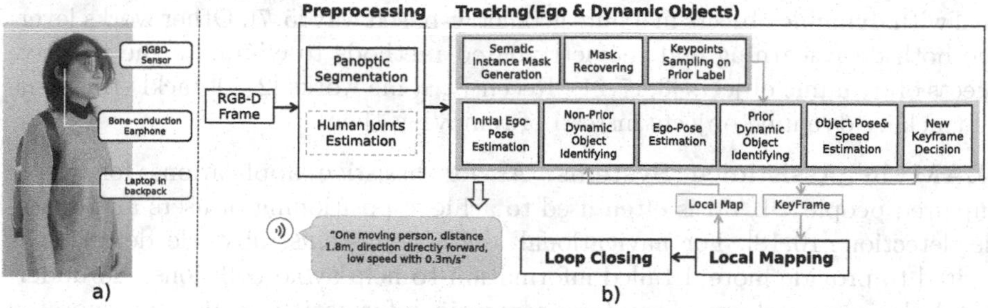

Fig. 1. (a) Our wearable devices designed for assisting people with visual impairments; (b) The proposed algorithm pipeline for navigation assistance.

address this problem, we propose a system to help people with visual impairments perceive dynamic objects in indoor environments and understand their motion.

Recently, research on SLAM has gradually shifted from traditional static environments to more diverse dynamic environments, which are closer to reality. According to the further processing of dynamic objects, current solutions can be divided into two categories. Some works directly discard the dynamic information as outliers [3,17]. Other works maintain them and jointly optimize the static map, pose of the camera, and dynamic objects in the scene [2,20].

In this work, we propose a novel indoor assistance system for visually impaired people while dealing with dynamic environments, of which the main structure is shown in Fig. 1. We develop a wearable assistance system based on an RGB-D sensor, which estimates the user's ego-pose, together with a static feature point map. The dynamic objects can be identified by the proposed system, and the average depth information to the user can be obtained. When the dynamic object belongs to a prior class, *e.g.*, *people*, it can also be tracked between frames. Moreover, the linear velocity of prior dynamic objects can be estimated and transmitted through the bone-conduction headphones located on our smart glasses system (see Fig. 1(a)) to the user.

In summary, our main contributions are: a wearable assistant system with an RGB-D sensor is proposed, and it can be used to achieve localization and mapping and help visually impaired people detect dynamic objects in indoor scenes and obtain corresponding motion cues.

2 Related Work

SLAM in a Dynamic Environment. In the past years, many visual SLAM systems were proposed and have a satisfactory performance, such as ORB-SLAM [14], DVO-SLAM [6], *etc.*. However, these visual SLAM systems are based on the assumption of a static- or a slightly dynamic environment. If there are highly dynamic objects in the environment - which is more closed to real-life scenarios - pose estimation and mapping may lead to poor results. Some approaches deal with dynamic objects in a pure geometry-based way [5,7]. Other works leverage both deep learning and geometry-based methods to eliminate the negative effects of dynamic objects [3,17,21]. Recently, some works [2,20] tackle this issue by tracking dynamic objects instead of removing them.

SLAM in Assistance Systems. As for assistive applications for visual impaired people, SLAM is often used to achieve positioning of users and obstacle detection [10,18]. For navigational assistive systems, obstacle detection is desired to provide more detailed information to help avoid collisions and understand the surroundings. Therefore, semantic information is also incorporated into a SLAM system to achieve semantic path- and destination finding [22]. Besides, a prior map with semantic information can be established by SLAM in advance for navigation systems in indoor environments [1,12] and can be later used for global path planning. Differing from these existing works, our work considers the localization and mapping in challenging dynamic environments and combines feature descriptors matching in ego-motion estimation and optical flow tracking in dynamic object motion estimation to guarantee valid tracking. Besides, our system can help seeing impaired people avoid collisions with diverse moving obstacles.

3 Method

Figure 1 (a) shows our assistant system consisting of a pair of smart glasses and a lightweight laptop. First, the surrounding environment of visual impaired people is captured by the aforementioned RGB-D sensor attached to the glasses in the wearable device. Then, panoptic segmentation of the RGB image is executed online on a laptop with a processor, and optionally human joint keypoint estimation will be performed. After the pre-processing step, the RGB-D image and the segmentation mask will be passed into the tracking module and further processed in the local mapping and loop closing modules. Focusing on the perspective of human-computer interaction, the information about the surroundings are delivered to the users, through the bone-conduction earphones on the glasses.

3.1 Preprocessing

PanopticFCN [11] is leveraged using the obtained RGB image as input. The output of panoptic segmentation consists of semantic- and instance-based masks, as visualized in Fig. 2(b). Since people tend to move dynamically in real-life indoor scenes, the annotation of *people* is set as prior dynamic. If a more accurate speed estimation of dynamic moving people is expected, the human joint keypoints' coordinates detected by OpenPose [4] can be generated as well. We select the joint keypoints on shoulder and middle hip, constraining the sampled points on the trunk body. So the points are more likely to be located on the slightly deformed parts of the body, enabling stable motion estimation.

3.2 Identifying Dynamic Objects

Dynamic objects that can be addressed by our system cover two categories, *i.e.*, prior dynamic objects like *people* or *pets*, and non-prior moving objects, *e.g.*, a carton passively moved by people as shown in Fig. 2(c). On the one hand, the non-prior dynamic object will be identified after the initial ego-pose estimation through the depth difference method, which is similar to [3]. The main difference between our approach and [3] is that the instance mask is directly leveraged to calculate the percentage of dynamic points in an object and identify if it is moving or not, rather than using region growing on depth images. On the other hand, 3D scene flow of sampled points on prior objects in consecutive frames is utilized to verify if a prior object is dynamic or not. When the magnitude of scene flow of a point is larger than a threshold, *i.e.*, 0.02 used in our work, the point will be regarded as dynamic. The object is regarded as a dynamic object if the percentage of dynamic points in the prior object is over a threshold (30%). Considering computational costs, only dynamic prior objects will be tracked and expected to be described with speed. The dynamic non-prior and static prior objects are feedback with the direction and averaged depth from the user.

Fig. 2. (a) RGB image; (b) Panoptic segmentation result; (c) Non-prior dynamic object; (d) Tracked points and the estimated speed of the prior dynamic person; (e) Top-view trajectory of the user and the moving person.

3.3 Ego-motion Estimation

We follow the same pipeline proposed by [14] to achieve ego-motion estimation. In our work, we add the step of "Non-Prior Dynamic Object Identifying" before tracking the local map. As for the mapping step, merely static points are considered as map points. Thanks to the excellent feature-based visual SLAM framework, we can estimate the ego-pose robustly and accurately, which is essential to the following dynamic object tracking.

3.4 Dynamic Objects Pose and Speed Estimation

We leverage a similar methodology as in [20] for the pose and speed estimation of the dynamic objects. Preparation procedure is firstly executed on the other thread while solving the ego-motion prediction. The potential dynamic objects with prior labels are numbered in the obtained panoptic segmentation mask respectively, while all the other pixels are annotated as 0. Then, the DIS optical flow [8] is used to find corresponding keypoints in the current frame. With this dense optical flow method, if a potential prior dynamic object appears in the mask of the last frame but fails to be segmented in the current frame, the object keypoints on the last frame can be tracked and recovered in the current frame. Those dynamic objects tracked by optical flow, as presented in Fig. 2(d), can be assigned unique track indices over time. To guarantee a sufficient tracking number of dynamic points, we sample every five points within an object mask. When the number of tracked points within a dynamic object decreases below the threshold, those sampled candidate points can be supplied.

After obtaining the ego-pose of current frame, the scene flow of points can be calculated. Therefore, the prior dynamic but actually remaining-static objects can be filtered according to the magnitude of scene flow. As for the initial pose estimation of dynamic objects, a better result with more inliers is selected from the EPnP method [9] or using the previous motion. Finally, further pose optimization and speed calculation as in [20] are used to obtain the final result.

4 Evaluation

We test our system on some sequences of public indoor TUM RGB-D dataset [16] and Bonn RGB-D dataset [15]. We select sequences with dynamic objects, including seated- and several walking people and *etc.*, to simulate real-life scenarios in the office or different rooms that are important for visually impaired people.

Quantitative Results of Pose Estimation. The experiments of evaluating the ego-motion are carried out. We choose RMSE of absolute trajectory- and relative pose error as error metrics, which indicates robustness of the system, as proposed by [16]. Table 1 presents the comparison between our system and the baseline framework ORB-SLAM2 [14] as well as the ORB-SLAM2 with prior semantic information. Our system shows better effectiveness in most cases, which verifies the superiority of our approach for highly dynamic indoor scenes. Since the dynamic objects in the sequences of TUM RGB-D dataset are mainly with the prior label 'people', so the difference between the latter two methods is small. For the slightly dynamic scenes like fr3/sitting rpy, ORB-SLAM2 has better performance, since it has more valid keypoints located on the people. However, the ATE of the latter two methods are relatively small. For the sequence crowed with three very fast moving and rotating people, the second method show a better result. But this method only maintains efficiency for sequences with prior dynamic objects. For the challenging sequences like moving nonobstructing box and moving obstructing box, our system shows a robust performance.

Table 1. Ego-motion comparison on the TUM and Bonn datasets. The top five sequences are from TUM, whereas the bottom six sequences are from Bonn. unit: ATE (m), RPE_t (m/frame), RPE_r (degree/frame). ORBv2: ORB-SLAM2 [14].

Sequences	ORBv2 (RGB-D)			ORBv2 with semantic			Our system		
	ATE	RPE_t	RPE_r	ATE	RPE_t	RPE_r	ATE	RPE_t	RPE_r
fr3/walking_static	0.271	0.026	0.515	**0.006**	0.006	0.174	**0.008**	0.006	0.175
fr3/walking_xyz	0.786	0.028	0.652	**0.016**	0.012	0.392	**0.015**	0.012	0.388
fr3/walking_halfsphere	0.481	0.024	0.603	**0.026**	0.015	0.434	**0.028**	0.013	0.417
fr3/walking_rpy	0.840	0.036	0.760	**0.036**	0.023	0.535	**0.033**	0.021	0.494
fr3/sitting_rpy	**0.019**	0.013	0.416	0.031	0.017	0.450	0.035	0.018	0.450
Crowd	1.179	0.132	3.191	**0.022**	0.014	0.654	0.035	0.014	0.634
moving_nonobstructing_box	0.383	0.023	0.931	0.084	0.028	0.986	**0.037**	0.023	0.735
moving_obstructing_box	0.471	0.022	1.139	0.342	0.017	1.082	**0.196**	0.045	1.616
person_tracking	0.632	0.030	1.581	**0.041**	0.021	1.513	**0.037**	0.021	1.507
person_tracking2	0.988	0.037	1.440	**0.048**	0.018	1.266	**0.042**	0.018	1.267
removing_nonobstructing_box	**0.019**	0.016	0.892	**0.015**	0.015	0.886	**0.016**	0.015	0.886

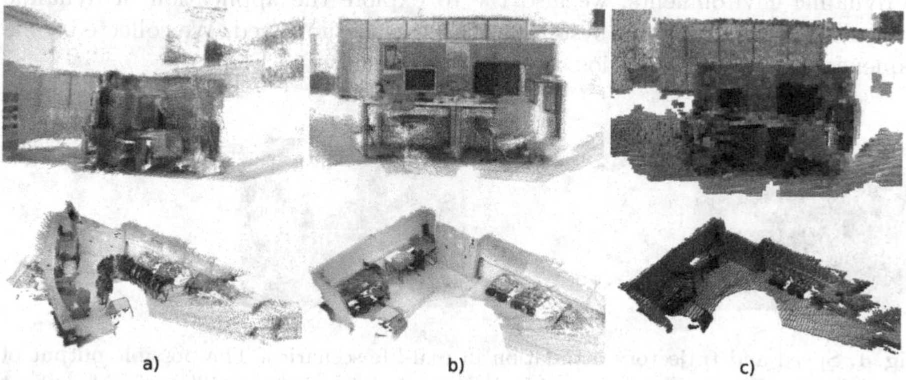

Fig. 3. Generated dense point map and octree map. (a) original dense point cloud map generated by ORB-SLAM2; (b) dense point cloud map generated by our system; (c) octree map based on our dense point cloud map, without filtering ground information.

Qualitative Results of Dynamic Object Estimation. Since the ground-truth information of the dynamic objects are not provided, a qualitative analysis of the estimation is presented in this section. We compute dynamic objects' speed as shown in Fig. 2(d). In the example scenario, the moving direction and speed of an on-coming or passing person are to be detected by the system and delivered to the user, so that they can react in time and avoid a collision.

To investigate the map built for further navigation tasks, we evaluate the mapping capacity of our system. Since the sparse point cloud map generated by ORB-SLAM2 can not be easily used in the practical application, we generate a dense point cloud map offline after obtaining the keyframe poses for the whole sequence. In Fig. 3, we have visualized the dense point cloud with or without the effect of dynamic objects. Moreover, we also generate octree maps based on the correct dense point cloud map, which are suitable for assistive functions. The overlapping prior dynamic objects (*person*) in the point cloud are removed and the valid map is generated. Here, one should note that during the whole sequence, the point cloud of the non-prior dynamic objects, such like the *chairs* in the left sequence, still remain two versions, *i.e.*, the position before it was moved by the person and the position when it became static again. Whether maintaining or deleting this kind of point cloud, a more complex strategy should be considered. For long-term SLAM systems, the map will be locally updated at a certain time.

Runtime Analysis. We test the average computational time of the system. The time excludes the part of panoptic segmentation and joint keypoints extraction, as this part totally depends on the GPU type and the selection of a certain neural network. And the time cost of our system is highly related to the number of tracked dynamic objects. For all the sequences, we achieve an average speed at 4–7 FPS on an i5-10210U CPU, which is reasonable for indoor navigation.

Real-life Scenarios. In addition to the function of localization and mapping in dynamic environments, we also try to explore the application of dynamic information in the assistive system for the visually impaired. We collected some sequences in real-life scenarios, two of them as shown in Fig. 4.

Fig. 4. Speed and trajectory estimation in real-life scenarios. The possible output of first scenario: One person on front side, low speed, 1.2 m distance; The possible output of second scenario: One person on right side, high speed, 1.6 m distance.

Our system can give several dynamic information of the prior dynamic object, including its number, average depth, position, pose, velocity, and possible moving direction. The depth value of a person can help the user maintain social distance in a public indoor environment like in a shopping mall. Moreover, when the moving object gets closer to the user and its speed is relatively fast, the reminder of potential risk can be passed to user. The object with high velocity is often dangerous for the visually impaired and this velocity information can enhance current obstacle avoidance modules that mainly use the depth information [12,19]. We also designed a questionnaire regarding the expected feedback form from our system. Through personal discussion and the results of the online questionnaire, the voice feedback of the system is preferred to be user-related and easily-understandable. The 'user-related' indicates that the moving object could affect the user's walking status in short time. For this case, the system should remind users of the potential risk with special signal tone.

5 Conclusion

In this work, an assistive system is developed to help people with visual impairments to understand dynamic changes in indoor scenes. The static keypoints obtained by sparse-feature visual SLAM are combined with dynamic keypoints, which are obtained by optical flow tracking. The former aims to estimate the ego-motion robustly and the latter supports the identifying and stable tracking of dynamic objects without additional object models. However, there are still some limitations of our system. Since the result of panoptic segmentation is hardly perfectly accurate, it leads to some errors when identifying the non-prior dynamic object. Additionally, the computational complexity of this system highly depends on the number of dynamic objects. Some methods of reducing the number of optimized parameters need to be integrated. For the future work, we intend to conduct user experience research, *i.e.*, invite visually impaired volunteers to use our devices and collect feedback, to further improve our system towards more holistic scene perception and reliable navigation assistance.

References

1. Bai, J., Liu, Z., Lin, Y., Li, Y., Lian, S., Liu, D.: Wearable travel aid for environment perception and navigation of visually impaired people. Electronics **8**(6), 697 (2019)
2. Bescós, B., Campos, C., Tardós, J.D., Neira, J.: DynaSLAM II: tightly-coupled multi-object tracking and SLAM. IEEE Robot. Autom. Lett. **6**(3), 5191–5198 (2021)
3. Bescós, B., Fácil, J.M., Civera, J., Neira, J.: DynaSLAM: tracking, mapping, and inpainting in dynamic scenes. IEEE Robot. Autom. Lett. **3**(4), 4076–4083 (2018)
4. Cao, Z., Hidalgo, G., Simon, T., Wei, S., Sheikh, Y.: OpenPose: realtime multi-person 2D pose estimation using part affinity fields. IEEE Trans. Pattern Anal. Mach. Intell. (2021)
5. Dai, W., Zhang, Y., Li, P., Fang, Z., Scherer, S.: RGB-D SLAM in dynamic environments using point correlations. IEEE Trans. Pattern Anal. Mach. Intell. **44**(1), 373–389 (2022)
6. Kerl, C., Sturm, J., Cremers, D.: Dense visual SLAM for RGB-D cameras. In: IROS, pp. 2100–2106 (2013)
7. Kim, D.H., Kim, J.H.: Effective background model-based RGB-D dense visual odometry in a dynamic environment. IEEE Trans. Robot. (2016)
8. Kroeger, T., Timofte, R., Dai, D., Van Gool, L.: Fast optical flow using dense inverse search. In: Leibe, B., Matas, J., Sebe, N., Welling, M. (eds.) ECCV 2016. LNCS, vol. 9908, pp. 471–488. Springer, Cham (2016). https://doi.org/10.1007/978-3-319-46493-0_29
9. Lepetit, V., Moreno-Noguer, F., Fua, P.: EPnP: an accurate O(n) solution to the PnP problem. Int. J. Comput. Vis. **81**(2), 155–166 (2009)
10. Li, B., et al.: Vision-based mobile indoor assistive navigation aid for blind people. IEEE Trans. Mob. Comput. **18**(3), 702–714 (2019)
11. Li, Y., et al.: Fully convolutional networks for panoptic segmentation. In: CVPR, pp. 214–223 (2021)

12. Liu, H., Liu, R., Yang, K., Zhang, J., Peng, K., Stiefelhagen, R.: HIDA: towards holistic indoor understanding for the visually impaired via semantic instance segmentation with a wearable solid-state LiDAR sensor. In: ICCVW, pp. 1780–1790 (2021)
13. Martinez, M., Yang, K., Constantinescu, A., Stiefelhagen, R.: Helping the blind to get through COVID-19: social distancing assistant using real-time semantic segmentation on RGB-D video. Sensors **20**(18), 5202 (2020)
14. Mur-Artal, R., Tardós, J.D.: ORB-SLAM2: An open-source SLAM system for monocular, stereo and RGB-D cameras. IEEE Trans. Robot. **33**(5), 1255–1262 (2017)
15. Palazzolo, E., Behley, J., Lottes, P., Giguère, P., Stachniss, C.: ReFusion: 3D reconstruction in dynamic environments for RGB-D cameras exploiting residuals. In: IROS, pp. 7855–7862 (2019)
16. Sturm, J., Engelhard, N., Endres, F., Burgard, W., Cremers, D.: A benchmark for the evaluation of RGB-D SLAM systems. In: IROS, pp. 573–580 (2012)
17. Yu, C., Liu, Z., Liu, X., Xie, F., Yang, Y., Wei, Q., Qiao, F.: DS-SLAM: a semantic visual SLAM towards dynamic environments. In: IROS, pp. 1168–1174 (2018)
18. Zhang, H., Ye, C.: An indoor wayfinding system based on geometric features aided graph SLAM for the visually impaired. IEEE Trans. Neural Syst. Rehabil. Eng. **29**(9), 1592–1604 (2017)
19. Zhang, J., Yang, K., Constantinescu, A., Peng, K., Müller, K., Stiefelhagen, R.: Trans4Trans: efficient transformer for transparent object segmentation to help visually impaired people navigate in the real world. In: ICCVW, pp. 1760–1770 (2021)
20. Zhang, J., Henein, M., Mahony, R.E., Ila, V.: VDO-SLAM: A visual dynamic object-aware SLAM system. arXiv preprint arXiv:2005.11052 (2020)
21. Zhang, T., Nakamura, Y.: PoseFusion: dense RGB-D SLAM in dynamic human environments. In: Xiao, J., Kröger, T., Khatib, O. (eds.) ISER 2018. SPAR, vol. 11, pp. 772–780. Springer, Cham (2020). https://doi.org/10.1007/978-3-030-33950-0_66
22. Zhuo, C., Liu, X., Kojima, M., Huang, Q., Arai, T.: A wearable navigation device for visually impaired people based on the real-time semantic visual SLAM system. Sensors **21**(4), 1536 (2021)

Accessible Adaptable Indoor Routing for People with Disabilities

Fabian Lüders, Julian Striegl(✉), Jan Schmalfuß-Schwarz, Claudia Loitsch, and Gerhard Weber

Fakultät Informatik, Technische Universität Dresden, Dresden, Germany
{julian.striegl,jan.schmalfuss-schwarz}@tu-dresden.de

Abstract. For people with disabilities, indoor routing approaches have to take the specific requirements of the target user group into account. Depending on the needs of the individual, certain objects and indoor features can present insurmountable barriers and hence, should be avoided when generating indoor routes. Research in the field of indoor routing for people with disabilities has been going on for several years, but most approaches focus on one specific disability and do not evaluate designed systems with the target user group. Therefore, we propose an accessible, adaptable indoor routing algorithm for people with disabilities. The designed system is evaluated in a user study with people with blindness and mobility impairments using a Wizard of Oz approach. Results indicate a good acceptance of the designed routing system.

Keywords: Indoor routing · Indoor navigation · Accessibility · Barriers · Openstreetmap · Visual impaired people · Mobility impaired people

1 Introduction

Mobility is one main aspect in our daily life and particularly involves way finding inside unknown as well as familiar buildings. For people with disabilities, mobility and most scenarios of traveling contain specific challenges. Requirements for mobility are highly heterogeneous, due to the diversity of people and contexts (e.g., previous experience, individual needs and complexity of buildings) [6]. In contrast, there are also specific requirements for adaptable routing solutions that apply to all potential users – independently of individual characteristics. Various studies have shown that humans mainly rely on uniquely identifiable landmarks in their environment in order to determine their current position [14,20]. Ross et al. [21] showed that referring to landmarks in navigation systems significantly increases the users' confidence and reduces the number of navigation errors made by them. The selection of these landmarks has to consider the individual sensory abilities, e.g., visually impaired people might need to rely on tactile or acoustic features rather than on visible ones. Ideally, an accessible route is characterized by containing no barriers that are insurmountable for the current navigation user at all. Schmalfuß-Schwarz et al. [22], however, showed that this optimization goal is

F. Lüders, J. Striegl and J. Schmalfuß-Schwarz—The authors contributed equally to this research.

K. Miesenberger et al. (Eds.): ICCHP-AAATE 2022, LNCS 13341, pp. 169–177, 2022.
https://doi.org/10.1007/978-3-031-08648-9_20

unreachable for many real-world applications. Therefore, they presented a classification scheme for barriers which distinguishes three types: insurmountable, individually insurmountable, and surmountable barriers. Consequently, an adaptable routing algorithm should completely avoid insurmountable barriers and reduce individually surmountable barriers in either their number or difficulty. To achieve this optimization goal, it is necessary to identify possible barriers for various user groups, categorize them, and represent them in map material or derived routing graphs. In addition, Froehlich et al. [8] describe the general importance of adaptable models of the real world, which are personalized to various users and address different needs, such as contents and details of provided information. Thus, adaption does not only mean to consider diverse types of barriers, but also to include a more comprehensive range of semantic data for ways and locations. This adaptable data can then be processed by route optimization algorithms.

Therefore, we propose a routing algorithm based on Points of Interest (POIs) and landmarks spanning a graph together with tag-annotated edges. These tags store semantic data representing accessibility features and other architectural characteristics. Each user can define sets of positive or negative tags, which are then used to compute an optimal way. The usage of landmarks particularly addresses one major difference of navigation in indoor environments compared to outdoor navigation: the difficulty of determining positions with high accuracy (as shown later). In this work, we especially focus on the specific requirements of two user groups: wheelchair users and blind people, in order to cover two major types of impairments – sensory and movement related impairments respectively. Nevertheless, the proposed algorithm is applicable for other user groups as well. Finally, we discuss a first user study to evaluate the calculated routes' adequacy and the algorithm's perceived usefulness.

2 State of the Art

Indoor navigation has been a focus of research for about four decades, yet numerous open challenges remain. One of the first prototypes, the *MOBIC* system (1996) provided a routing solution for visually impaired pedestrians [19]. Previous work also covered various sub-areas, such as building data acquisition and corresponding data structures, visualization and interaction techniques, and way finding strategies [3,27]. Nevertheless, there are still only few indoor navigation applications available, especially for people with special requirements [23,24]. Meanwhile, several studies have shown that these people demand to be supported more properly. Supporting their mobility in buildings could gain them more independence and is an important step towards increasing equality [6]. Indoor navigation has several differences comparing to outdoor routing solutions. There is, for instance, the need for using different positioning techniques, as satellite-based services (such as GPS) are mostly unavailable in buildings. These techniques, however, can generally be considered inaccurate in comparison to outdoor solutions [7,13]. This especially contradicts the fact that targets in indoor environments are located closer together. Thus, indoor navigation solutions require more sophisticated solutions for locating their users. While some precise indoor localization systems do exist – such as the multi-tier indoor navigation framework developed by Abu Doush et al. [1], utilizing a set of heterogeneous wireless localization techniques – those systems are only applicable in environments with a specialized infrastructure, and therefore not suitable for a widespread usage.

One main requirement for developing indoor routing solutions is the existence of appropriate map data. There are several data formats on the market which are capable of representing building structures, such as IndoorGML, CityGML, the Indoor Mapping Data Format (IMDF), Industry Foundation Classes (IFC), or the OpenStreetMap (OSM) data format [15,16]. While some of these formats represent geometrical structures of buildings, others can be used to describe a topological structure [2]. As routing algorithms depend on graph structures, the latter ones are more suitable in this case. Furthermore, it should be possible to store semantic data such as room types or accessibility features, which then can be used for adapting routes to personal needs. As Striegl et al. [23] showed, needed semantic data – especially on accessibility – is still lacking. Nevertheless, research on solutions to collect indoor accessibility information is ongoing. Projects such as *Wheelmap.org*[1], *AccessibleMaps*[2], and others [23] focus on the collection of accessibility information through semi-automatic indoor mapping techniques, image processing, deep learning, and crowd sourcing approaches. The collected data of those projects is partly available in the aforementioned data formats and can be used for an automated graph generation.

Finding optimized routes in graph structures is a well-known problem in computer science. Algorithms such as *Dijkstra's* or the one of *Bellman and Ford* solve this problem using cost annotations of edges in a routing graph [17]. However, classical algorithms only optimize routes regarding *one* criteria (path length, time to travel, minimum number of barriers etc.), which is insufficient for real-world problems such as the indoor navigation of people with special requirements [7,25]. An approach towards solving this challenge is the preprocessing of the routing graph, which generates single-value annotations out of multifactorial annotated graph edges. This preprocessing can be done in various ways, mainly depending on the type of data, which the routing graph is annotated with.

Völkel and Weber [25] proposed an approach to annotate routing graphs with vectors, modeling one attribute of the actual physical way the graph is representing with each of the vectors' entries. Such information could include the way length and expected traversal time, ground quality and slope, or usage frequency by other people [25]. The authors suggested a collaborative approach for data acquisition, which enables the users to rate path sections and environments. One slightly different approach for including accessibility information into routing graphs was presented by Dudas et al. [5] and includes the usage of an ontology. This ontology contains semantically structured concepts for expressing accessibility features of paths. Hashemi and Karimi [10] calculated an accessibility index based on the American Disability Act and applied it to the spatial model of buildings, thereby taking the accessibility of routes into account, when generating evacuation routes for people with disabilities. Unfortunately, while the needs of people with disabilities were taken into account in the system design, generated routes were not assessed by the target group. Park et al. [18] developed an IndoorGML extension for the indoor navigation of people with mobility impairments by assigning

[1] Wheelmap.org, https://wheelmap.org/, Access date: 22.03.2022.

[2] AccessibleMaps, https://www.accessiblemaps.de/, Access date: 22.03.2022.

accessibility thresholds to corridors, stairways, doorways, ramps, and elevators. They showed that routes for people with special mobility requirements can differ vastly from routes for people without mobility impairments. The usefulness of generated routes was not evaluated by people with disabilities. Weyrer et al. [26] developed a prototype of a door-to-door (indoor and outdoor) routing application for people with disabilities based on features extracted from the United Nations convention on the rights of persons with disabilities. The authors based their work on OSM data and illustrated two application scenarios: intermodal routing with transit transfers and the comparison of walk-only trips and intermodal routes. However, the system was not tested with people with disabilities. The concept of collaborative map annotation was also applied by Holone and Misund [11]. They use a coarse three-point scale (*good*, *uncomfortable*, *inaccessible*) by which the users can rate path sections. These ratings then are processed by a shortest path algorithm, which treats worse ratings as longer distances.

In summary, it can be said that there is ongoing research in the field of accessible indoor routing. Nevertheless, the design and evaluation of an adaptable routing algorithm considering the special characteristics of indoor-environments and specific accessibility features for people with disabilities still remains an open research question. This question therefore is addressed in the upcoming section.

3 Adaptable Indoor Routing for People with Disabilities

As a basis for the proposed algorithm, map data has to be transferred into an appropriate routing graph. This graph should then also be capable of holding semantic data, especially regarding accessibility features. Subsequently, the question is raised, which real-world elements should be represented by the graph's nodes or edges. Some existing indoor navigation solutions use a cell-based approach for this, where a node represents a certain area of a building, which in turn can be a room, floor, stair way etc. (cf. [16]). Other indoor way finding systems include technical features of positioning systems (e.g., Bluetooth beacons) in their routing graphs [4]. Outdoor navigation solutions i.a. use crucial points of streets, such as crossings, or start or end points. However, we decided to use a POI-based approach, in which every graph-node represents a special landmark inside the building (see Fig. 1). There are two main reasons for this decision:

- As indoor-positioning techniques in buildings are of poor accuracy (see above), navigation users can be supported to localize themselves by the system this way.
- Various studies have shown that referring to such landmarks increase the users' certainty during navigation (cf. [12,14,21]).

Two nodes of this graph are connected by an edge in case they are also directly accessible from each other in the real environment. The edges are then annotated with semantic data in the form of tag-sets, with each tag representing an accessibility feature of a path section. Those tags can be generic (e.g., 'accessible for wheelchair users'), but also more specialized, such as 'tactile paving' or 'elevator with speech output'.

The proposed algorithm is structured as follows:

1. *user input:* start and target nodes, positive and negative path tags (can be marked as 'optional' as well)

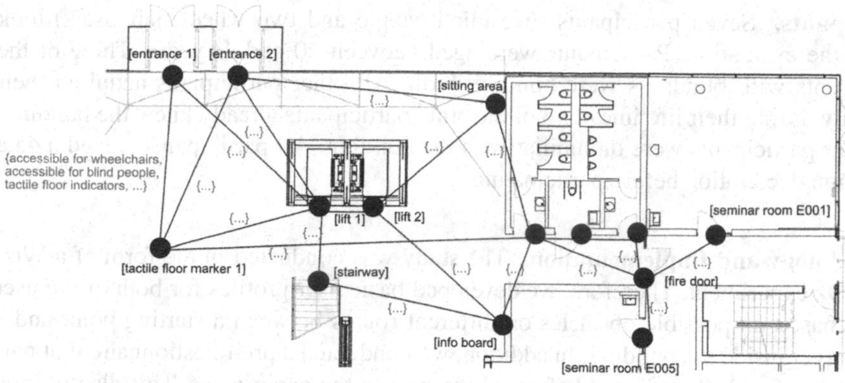

Fig. 1. Routing graph with uniquely identifiable landmarks as nodes. The edges are annotated with sets of semantic tags (some labels have been omitted for the sake of clarity).

2. *graph reduction:*
   (a) removal of all edges that do not hold all *positive* tags
   (b) removal of all edges with *negative* tags
3. *graph optimization:* starting from the path section's distance (given in meters), each *optional* positive/negative tag on an edge causes a decrease/increase of the section costs
4. *route finding:* a route finding algorithm determines a cost-minimizing route from start to target node, using the previously reduced and optimized graph structure
5. *generation of route description (optional):* extract user-relevant information from the calculated route (location names, accessibility information, expected barriers, etc.)

4 Evaluation Through a Pilot Study

We evaluated a preliminary prototype of the proposed routing algorithm within the target groups to validate its perceived usefulness and the quality of navigation information, which can be derived from the proposed data structure. Therefore, we chose a public building and generated indoor map data accordingly.

Location. As location for the pilot study the faculty of computer science at the TU Dresden was selected. The main reason for the selection was that there is already widely recorded open accessible indoor map data within *OpenStreetMap*[3]. Furthermore, various elements such as stairs already contain additional information regarding accessibility.[4] However, in order to implement the algorithm, the map data had to be expanded to include specific POIs for orientation.

[3] OpenStreetMap.org, https://www.openstreetmap.org, Access date: 31.03.2022.
[4] OpenLevelUp.net, https://openlevelup.net/#19/51.02546/13.72293, Access date: 31.03.2022.

Participants. Seven participants (five blind people and two wheelchair users) took part in the evaluation. Participants were aged between 20 and 44 years. Three of the participants with blindness were blind by birth. All other participants acquired their disability during their lifetime. Two of the blind participants already knew the building. All other participants were unfamiliar with the building. All participants signed a data protection declaration before participating.

Methodology and Implementation. The study was conducted in the form of a Wizard of Oz experiment. Therefore, we developed basic user profiles for both of the user groups based on possible obstacles on different routes between a starting point and a given target inside the building. In addition, we conducted a pre-questionnaire that participants were asked to fill out before taking part in the experiment. This also offered the opportunity to make certain adjustments to the profile. Participants with blindness had, for example, the possibility to choose if they prefer to use stairs or elevators or both equivalent. Based on the profile, an optimized route was computed for two scenarios with different start and end points. Therefore, we have implemented a server-client architecture so that we can push adapted user profiles with positive and negative terms (e.g. tactile paving) as well as a start and end point to the server, which computes the best route. Then, the algorithm is removing all edges, which contain negative terms, and is calculating the costs of all other edges based on the weight of their length, which will be manipulated by all terms that were marked as positive by the participants. Subsequently, a Dijkstra-Algorithm was used to compute the best route from the given start to the ending point. In both cases, participants were asked to follow the calculated route. Furthermore, to simulate a routing scenario, users were escorted by the facilitator, who read out pre-generated step-by-step instructions, which were compliant with the generated indoor route (see Table 1). Direct escort was necessary in order to be able to react to unforeseeable events in the real context, and thus not to endanger participants – especially subjects with blindness. After completing the experiment, a second questionnaire was used to get individual feedback about the computed route.

Results. All seven participants were able to reach given target locations using the read-out instructions. Both wheelchair users as well as three of the blind participants rated the given landmarks, and provided information, to be helpful for their indoor orientation. In contrast, the other two participants justified their poor rating with insufficient structural implementation of the building itself, such as missing Braille signs, difficult to find or unsatisfactory labeling with Braille, or unfavorable placed elevator buttons. For this reason, no direct conclusion can be derived from these statements on the quality of the algorithm. Moreover, two of the blind participants reported that they wish to select the mentioned POIs for orientation by themselves. Additionally, one blind participant suggested including further features as orientation points, for example the change of ground surface structure. Another request was that the distance between two landmarks should be given in meters in order to be able to estimate the distance. Finally, all participants could imagine using such a demonstrated system. However, there are still minor open points to be considered in a future design iteration.

Table 1. Examples of step-by-step instructions, which were read out to the participants

Instruction	Explanation
"You enter the building in a southerly direction through the main entrance."	Description of the current location (here main entrance)
"The stair has a handrail."	Additional accessibility information
"Go up the stairs by one floor to level 1."	Instructions for action and naming of the floor designation

Discussion. In order to improve the study's expressiveness, a more comprehensive follow-up study could be conducted, involving a larger and more diverse user group and a hands-on session with a further developed prototype. The system should therefore be deployed to an accessible mobile application featuring screen reader compatibility or the usage of voice user interfaces. Control groups may be acquired, helping to mitigate the impact of building features and individual sensory abilities on the user ratings. Similar to Giudice et al. [9], an experiment could be conducted with blind and sighted users out of which one group (including both blind and sighted subjects) is asked to use a real-time routing system, while the other group is not using such a system (serving as control).

5 Conclusion

In this paper, we presented an indoor routing algorithm that is capable of being adapted to the individual needs of users, in particular those with certain disabilities. One special aspect of indoor navigation in comparison to outdoor is the lack of accurate positioning techniques. We argued that users themselves can contribute to localization by referring to unique landmarks in their environment. An adaptable routing algorithm should take barriers and accessibility features into account. We therefore proposed a tag-annotated routing graph, which stores the necessary semantic data. The developed concept was evaluated in a first pilot study that indicated a good acceptance by participants.

Acknowledgement. This work was partially funded by the Federal Ministry of Labour and Social Affairs (BMAS) under the grant number 01KM151112.

References

1. Abu Doush, I., Alshatnawi, S., Al-Tamimi, A.K., Alhasan, B., Hamasha, S.: ISAB: integrated indoor navigation system for the blind. Interact. Comput. **29**(2), 181–202 (2016), ISSN 0953-5438
2. Afyouni, I., Ray, C., Christophe, C.: Spatial models for context-aware indoor navigation systems: a survey. J. Spatial Inf. Sci. **1**(4), 85–123 (2012)
3. Butz, A., Baus, J., Krüger, A., Lohse, M.: A hybrid indoor navigation system. In: Proceedings of the 6th International Conference on Intelligent User Interfaces, pp. 25–32, IUI 2001, Association for Computing Machinery (2001), ISBN 978-1-58113-325-7

4. Delnevo, G., Monti, L., Vignola, F., Salomoni, P., Mirri, S.: Almawhere: a prototype of accessible indoor wayfinding and navigation system. In: 2018 15th IEEE Annual Consumer Communications Networking Conference (CCNC), pp. 1–6 (2018)
5. Dudas, P.M., Ghafourian, M., Karimi, H.A.: ONALIN: ontology and algorithm for indoor routing. In: 2009 Tenth International Conference on Mobile Data Management: Systems, Services and Middleware, pp. 720–725 (2009), ISSN 2375–0324
6. Engel, C., et al.: Travelling more independently: a requirements analysis for accessible journeys to unknown buildings for people with visual impairments. In: The 22nd International ACM SIGACCESS Conference on Computers and Accessibility, pp. 1–11, ASSETS 2020, Association for Computing Machinery (2020), ISBN 978-1-4503-7103-2
7. Fallah, N., Apostolopoulos, I., Bekris, K., Folmer, E.: Indoor human navigation systems: a survey. Interact. Comput. **25**(1) (2013), ISSN 1873–7951
8. Froehlich, J.E., et al.: Grand challenges in accessible maps. Universal Interact. **26**(2), 78–81 (2019), ISSN 1072–5520
9. Giudice, N.A., Whalen, W.E., Riehle, T.H., Anderson, S.M., Doore, S.A.: Evaluation of an accessible, real-time, and infrastructure-free indoor navigation system by users who are blind in the mall of America. J. Vis. Visual Impairment Blindness **113**(2), 140–155 (2019)
10. Hashemi, M., Karimi, H.A.: Indoor spatial model and accessibility index for emergency evacuation of people with disabilities. J. Comput. Civil Eng. **30**(4), 04015056 (2016)
11. Holone, H., Misund, G.: People helping computers helping people: navigation for people with mobility problems by sharing accessibility annotations. In: Miesenberger, K., Klaus, J., Zagler, W., Karshmer, A. (eds.) ICCHP 2008. LNCS, vol. 5105, pp. 1093–1100. Springer, Heidelberg (2008). https://doi.org/10.1007/978-3-540-70540-6_164
12. Jeamwatthanachai, W., Wald, M., Wills, G.: Indoor navigation by blind people: behaviors and challenges in unfamiliar spaces and buildings. British J. Vis. Impairment **37**(2), 140–153 (2019)
13. Kunhoth, J., Karkar, A., Al-Maadeed, S., Al-Ali, A.: Indoor positioning and wayfinding systems: a survey. Human-centric Comput. Inf. Sci. **10**(1), 18 (2020), ISSN 2192–1962
14. May, A.J., Ross, T., Bayer, S.H., Tarkiainen, M.J.: Pedestrian navigation aids: information requirements and design implications. Pers. Ubiquitous Comput. **7**(6), 331–338 (2003), ISSN 1617–4909, 1617–4917
15. Mirvahabi, S.S., Abbaspour, R.A.: Automatic extraction of IndoorGML core model from OpenStreetMap. ISPRS - International Archives of the Photogrammetry, Remote Sensing and Spatial Information Sciences XL-1/W5, **40**, 459–462 (2015), ISSN 2194–9034
16. Open Geospatial Consortium: OGC® IndoorGML 1.1 (2020), https://docs.ogc.org/is/19-011r4/19-011r4.pdf. Accessed 1 Feb 2022
17. Ottmann, T., Widmayer, P.: Algorithmen und Datenstrukturen. Spektrum-Lehrbuch, Spektrum, Akad. Verl, 3, überarb. aufl edn. (1996), ISBN 978-3-8274-0110-6
18. Park, S., Yu, K., Kim, J.: Data model for IndoorGML extension to support indoor navigation of people with mobility disabilities. ISPRS Int. J. Geo-Inf. **9**(2), 66 (2020)
19. Petrie, H., Johnson, V., Strothotte, T., Raab, A., Fritz, S., Michel, R.: MoBIC: designing a travel aid for blind and elderly people. J. Navigation **49**(1), 45–52 (1996), ISSN 0373–4633, 1469–7785
20. Pielot, M., Boll, S.: "In Fifty Metres Turn Left": why turn-by-turn instructions fail pedestrians. In: Workshop at MobileHCI 2010, Tuesday, September 7, 2010, Lisbon, Portugal, pp. 26–28 (2010)
21. Ross, T., May, A., Thompson, S.: The use of landmarks in pedestrian navigation instructions and the effects of context. In: Brewster, S., Dunlop, M. (eds.) Mobile HCI 2004. LNCS, vol. 3160, pp. 300–304. Springer, Heidelberg (2004). https://doi.org/10.1007/978-3-540-28637-0_26

22. Schmalfuß-Schwarz, J., Loitsch, C., Weber, G.: Considering time-critical barriers in indoor routing for people with disabilities. In: Miesenberger, K., Manduchi, R., Covarrubias Rodriguez, M., Peňáz, P. (eds.) ICCHP 2020. LNCS, vol. 12377, pp. 315–322. Springer, Cham (2020). https://doi.org/10.1007/978-3-030-58805-2_37
23. Striegl, J., Lotisch, C., Schmalfuss-Schwarz, J., Weber, G.: Analysis of Indoor Maps accounting the needs of people with impairments. In: Miesenberger, K., Manduchi, R., Covarrubias Rodriguez, M., Peňáz, P. (eds.) ICCHP 2020. LNCS, vol. 12377, pp. 305–314. Springer, Cham (2020). https://doi.org/10.1007/978-3-030-58805-2_36
24. Swobodzinski, M., Raubal, M.: An indoor routing algorithm for the blind: development and comparison to a routing algorithm for the sighted. Int. J. Geographical Inf. Sci. **23**(10), 1315–1343 (2009), ISSN 1365–8816
25. Völkel, T., Weber, G.: RouteCheckr: personalized multicriteria routing for mobility impaired pedestrians. In: Proceedings of the 10th International ACM SIGACCESS Conference on Computers and Accessibility, pp. 185–192, Assets 2008, Association for Computing Machinery (2008), ISBN 978-1-59593-976-0
26. Weyrer, T.N., Hochmair, H.H., Paulus, G.: Intermodal door-to-door routing for people with physical impairments in a web-based, open-source platform. Transp. Res. Rec. **2469**(1), 108–119 (2014)
27. Zlatanova, S., Sithole, G., Nakagawa, M., Zhu, Q.: Problems in indoor mapping and modelling. ISPRS - International Archives of the Photogrammetry, Remote Sensing and Spatial Information Sciences XL-4/W4, 63–68 (2013), ISSN 2194–9034

Monocular Localization Using Invariant Image Feature Matching to Assist Navigation

Vikas Upadhyay(✉) and M. Balakrishnan

Indian Institute of Technology Delhi, New Delhi, India
vikas.upadhyay@cse.iitd.ac.in, mbala@iitd.ac.in

Abstract. Indoor positioning is critical for applications like navigation, tracking, monitoring, and accessibility. For the visually impaired this has a huge implication on independent mobility for accessing all types of services as well as social inclusion. The unavailability of indoor positioning solutions with adequate accuracy is a major constraint. The key reason for the lack of growth in indoor positioning systems is to do with the reliability of indoor positioning techniques and additional infrastructure costs along with maintenance overheads. We propose a novel single camera-based visual positioning solution for indoor spaces. Our method uses smart visual feature selection and matching in real-time using a monocular camera. We record and transform the video route information into spars and invariant point-based SURF features. To limit the real-time feature search and match data, the routes inside the buildings are broken into a connected graph. To find the position, confidence of a path increases if it founds a good feature match and decreases otherwise. Each query frame uses a K-nearest neighbor match with the existing databases to increase the confidence of matched path in subsequent frames. Results have shown a reliable positioning accuracy of ~ 2 meters in variable lighting conditions. We also investigated the error recovery of positioning systems where it easily re-positions the user within the neighboring edges. To promote crowdsourcing, proposed system can add more visual features to the database while performing the matching task.

Keywords: Visual positioning · Invariant feature · Localization

1 Introduction

Outdoor location-based services have shown significant growth over the past decade. Increasing reliability, as well as accuracy of global positioning system (GPS) have been a major driver in this success. However, GPS signals do not work inside a building, which leads to the need for alternate positioning technology for indoors. Indoor positioning is required for various applications including navigation, tracking, monitoring and accessibility. For people with visual impairment, localization, which is at the heart of indoor navigation techniques

K. Miesenberger et al. (Eds.): ICCHP-AAATE 2022, LNCS 13341, pp. 178–186, 2022.
https://doi.org/10.1007/978-3-031-08648-9_21

is essential for unassisted mobility in unfamiliar spaces including public buildings. The only option available to them today in a new surrounding is to use the walking canes for locating corridors and paths while constantly asking passerby for help with navigation. This clearly deprives them of their sense of independence as well as dignity. Researchers have presented various methods to support localization which can be broadly classified either as infrastructure-free or infrastructure dependent techniques [21]. Infrastructure-free techniques do not require additional investment in the existing infrastructure and it leverages the environment using various sensing mechanisms already available in the smartphone. WiFi-fingerprinting [15], visual light sensing [16], magnetic field sensing [14], dead-reckoning [25], visual positioning [17], LIDAR [6] are the popular infrastructure-free methods for indoor positioning. Most of these methods that have been presented in the literature have been tested in a controlled environments. On the other hand, infrastructure-dependent methods include deployment of additional sensors i.e. BLE [18] and UWB beacons [19], RFID, or visual tag [20] in the environment to support localization. A major challenge with sensor-based techniques is the poor reliability of wireless/radio frequency sensors in actual field. The performance of these sensors also depends significantly on the operating environment and heterogeneity among mobile devices. To support indoor navigation for people with visual impairment (PVIs), the existing methods for indoor positioning mostly rely on the use of well-placed BLE beacons inside a building [23]. However, limited positioning accuracy and additional infrastructure requirement are major barriers to scaling such techniques. So far none of the existing indoor positioning techniques have been proven at scale. On the other hand, infrastructure-free techniques have the potential to scale due to low implementation and maintenance costs.

Table 1. Problem summary: inputs, available tools and expected outputs

Input	Implemented algorithm	Expected outcome
Stream of images from pre-recorded paths	KNN matcher for a fast image to image matching	Match query image to a set point-feature data set.
A real-time query video	Lowe's ratio test	Finding the position of user
Feature Selection algorithm. We have used SURF	Other image matching confidence algorithms	Update position based on path confidence hypothesis

2 Related Work

Infrastructure free positioning techniques are emerging rapidly. Out of these, vision-based positioning has also gained attention for PVIs since it has potential for collision avoidance and it is also analogous to human localization [5]. Many of the vision-based techniques have been proposed that pack the SIFT features extracted from images into vectors of visual words [9] but constructing these visual words is complex and expensive [10]. Another method proposed is to use landmark feature-based indoor positioning [11] but the landmarks must be distinctive, repeatable and robust against noise. Other methods include topology-based approach [12] and stereo images [13]. Another approach uses convolution neural network (CNN)-based human detection using a camera to model the population density vs signal attenuation to improve positioning accuracy [24]. The accuracy of vision-based positioning techniques depends on camera resolution, lighting conditions, motion noise and unique point features for positioning. Despite the growing research in the field of visual positioning, very little is available in the open literature about real-life use cases and challenges faced by PVIs in using a such system. A brief summary of proposed solution is presented in the Table 1.

3 Creating Path Feature Graph Object

To achieve an image-based positioning inside a building, we need a visual feature graph of the building. In this proposed work, we first generate a SURF-based visual feature graph using pre-recorded video of possible routes inside a building. The confidence on how good two images are matching is a well-researched problem but empirically many indoor scenes resemble each other where basic image matching is not very effective. Hence we introduced a path-hypothesis based image matching algorithm that includes a temporal aspect to image matching. To find the position of the camera on a particular route, only distinct frames with unique features are required. We transform and store gray-scale images which are faster to operate and require less memory. For a particular path, pre-processing stage discards the frames having motion blur using the variance of the laplacian. This is because it is known that the more the variance of the laplacian, higher is the blurriness [3]. Pre-processing also ignores the frames having features less than a particular threshold. After removing frames with motion blur and lower invariant features, we perform a redundancy check for every frame using the SURF matcher and store distinct frames with time hypothesis for a particular path. This reduces the redundancy and features search domain. All the stored path data is annotated with a start node, end node and connecting edges over the given floor plan. This annotated path data is stored in a graph object. The information about the point feature descriptors serialized key points of the distinct frames of a path is stored in the same graph object. This graph object can be queried for matching a new series of incoming frames. For high-quality 720p edges videos for the ground floor (which contains 9 paths or 18 edges to and fro covering 110 m, as referred in the Fig. 1, left), graph object size was 20 MB including distinct images which can be reduced by storing point feature.

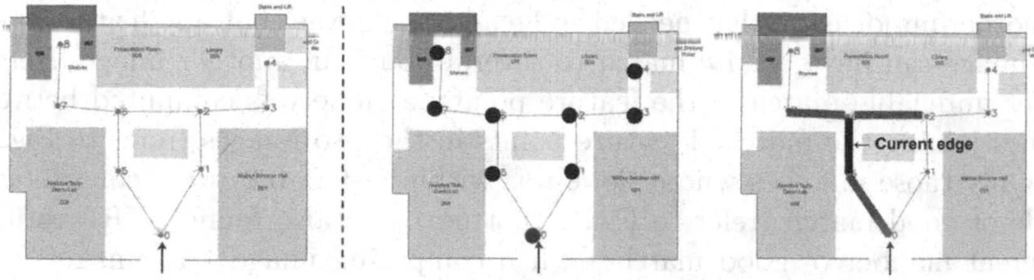

Fig. 1. Left: Generating route database; Right: Query domain for first edge indicated in black circle and after first stage indicated in black and blue line.

Image Based Localisation: In the initial approach, we had an array of edges that contained all possible edges with their confidence. To find the best match, a query frame gets en-queued on the possible edges with the highest confidence and moves to other edges only when the confidence of that edge decreases. Here, if a query frame keeps on getting a good match, edge confidence will keep increasing but keep decreasing in case of no matches. A real-time match was a problem in this approach because each possible edge had a different record for "i"(index of query video frames). In the case of distributed frames, getting continuous good matches was challenging. Thus it was required to use a slightly more brute force approach since image matching accuracy was more important than speed. To compute the similarity percentage match between two images, we tried SURF and SIFT with KNN as well as brute-force matcher and ORB with a brute-force matcher and used lowe's ratio test to filter the good matches [26]. We tried other approaches i.e. KAZE with cosine distance to filter good matches but the accuracy of the result was very poor. We also tried ASIFT matcher [1] which adjusts for relative orientation of two images and gives better matches [2] than SURF but at the same time very slow in processing speed that is not practically feasible. To process a 5 s video (at 2 FPS) on mobile device it took almost 60 s. Out of these, SURF with KNN matcher works best in accuracy and response time. There are certain practical problems while using SURF. If one of the images for matching is blurry or has fewer feature descriptors (i.e. a plain wall) as compared to the other, then the SURF returned a very large number of false matches. To overcome this limitation we have filtered blurred query images and dropped the images having feature descriptors less than a certain threshold.

Fig. 2. Top image: Point feature matches found using KNN + Lowe's test (shows more false match); Bottom image: Point feature matches found using KNN + Lowe's test + Slope greater than threshold removed (shows less false match)

Another major issue that needed to be addressed was that any feature point in an image can have a false match to several points in another image. Hence, to filter unreliable match of the feature points, a slope was computed between the lines joining the matched feature points in the two images (refer to Fig. 2, top). Only those matches whose slope was within (−0.2, 0.2) were considered a reliable or good match (refer to Fig. 2, bottom). We also found SURF returns a different number of good matches when comparing image 1 to image 2 and vice-versa. Hence, we compute a percent match using Eq. 1,

$$\%\,match = \frac{goodMatch(img1, img2) + goodMatch(img2, img1))}{(features(img1) + features(img2))}. \quad (1)$$

To prevent further matching of one feature to several, if ratio of two way good matches is outside (0.5, 2), select the features with least number to compute percent match using Eq. 2,

$$\%\,match = 2 \times \frac{min(goodMatch(img1, img2) + goodMatch(img2, img1))}{(features(img1) + features(img2)).} \quad (2)$$

Now for localization purposes, the smartphone camera is used to capture the video stream and is transferred to the host system at two frames per second in gray-scale. It is checked for motion blur using the variance of laplacian and its features are extracted using SURF. If found blurry, or its feature points are less than a certain threshold, then the frame is discarded and the next frame is picked up from the video stream. Proposed algorithm [22] uses best-found matches of the last five query frames to compute the position. If the fraction of matched features exceeds a certain value, a match is found. In the case of

Table 2. Path-hypothesis matching algorithm

Path confidence matching algorithm
Let query video frames F_1,F_2,..F_i ... as a sequence of incoming frames
For every path data-set i:
$Confidence = C_i$
Find first best match in i for F1,
let that be frame at t = k or If no match found, remove path as valid hypothesis
If : F_2 and frame $k + 1$ are also match (local maxima)
⇒ Increase confidence in path by factor f
Else if: F_2 and $k + 1$ are not a good match:
⇒ Decrease confidence by factor d and find the next best match for F_2 in i
Let that be $t = s$. Now, If confidence $< L\_bound$:
⇒Remove path as a valid hypothesis
If $highest\_confidence/Second\_highest\_confidence(for\ paths) > U\_Bound$:
⇒Select best path-hypothesis as path

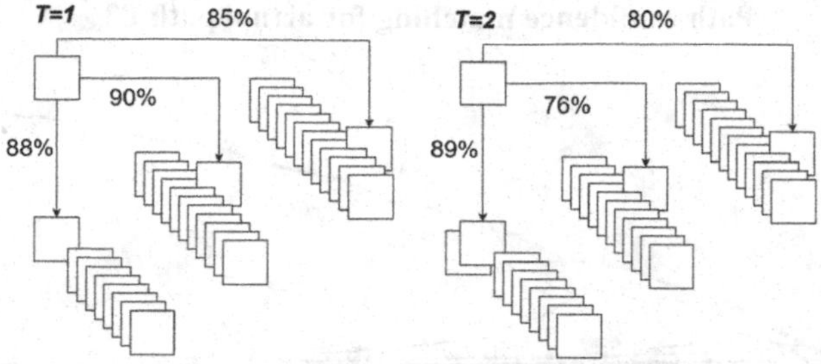

Fig. 3. A matching frames at t=1 and t=2 to path data-sets shows, central path loses matching hence getting down in confidence, while the other two are still a good match.

multiple matches, the highest fraction match is the best match. For finding the initial edge, the query frame is matched with the first frame of each edge, referred to as black dots in Fig. 1 (middle). Once the edge is found, the subsequent query frames are first compared with the features of the found edge (referred to as black edge in Fig. 1, right), and if no match is found the features of neighboring edges are compared (referred to as blue edge in Fig. 1, right). This can happen when the edge changes or the frame does not correspond to any frame in the database. To find the position in real-time, we increase the confidence of the path hypothesis having a higher matching threshold and decrease the confidence for other paths in time synchronization (refer to Fig. 3). At each query frame, the current location is calculated based on the mode of the best matches of the last 5 query frames. This ensures the accuracy of localisation in case of false matches, or if the camera is obstructed by random persons/objects for some time. The fraction of edge traversed can be calculated by dividing the time stamp of the best-matched frame (in the database) of the edge, by the timestamp of the last frame of the edge. For instance, if the frames in an edge are as given in the Table 3. Now, if the best matched frame number is 2, then the *fraction of edge traversed* $= 150/200 = 0.75$. This implies user's position is at $(3/4)^{th}$ of the edge. The information of the current edge and fraction traversed is used to display the current location of the user on the map. Path confidence matching result on ground truth path three for thirty frames at a rate of 2 frame/second as show in Fig. 4.

Table 3. Query and localisation

Frame number	0	1	2	3	4
Time stamp	0	55	150	172	200

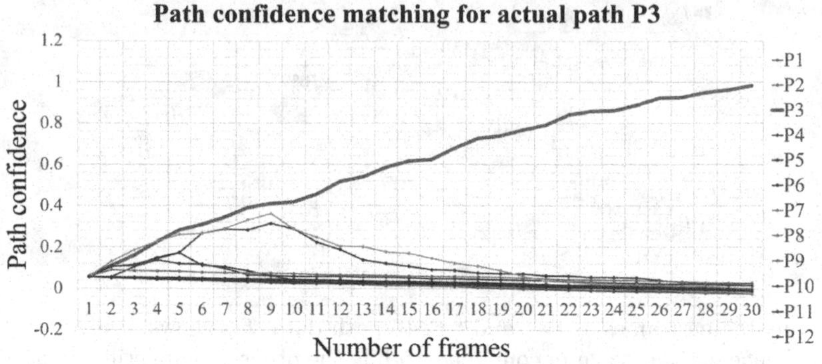

Fig. 4. Shows path confidence matching result for path three.

4 Current Limitations and Future Work

There are certain limitations to the existing method. (i) In the proposed method, the queried domain is limited. At each point, only the frames of current or adjoining edges can be queried due to its response time. If a large number of continuous frames do not get matched due to irregular frames in the query video, then the algorithm can catch up with the current location if the person is still on the last known edge or its adjoining edges. However, if a certain edge is missed completely because of no matches, then the algorithm fails because the person's current location will be out of the queried domain. (ii) The proposed point-feature matching is not very accurate. Though it yields good results, the representation on the map is only indicative of the best-matched frame in the current edge. Its accuracy depends on the best-found match among the frames of the edge, and the density of the database. (iii) Because image matching does not yield good results in varied lighting conditions, localization is reasonable only if the lighting conditions are somewhat similar to the lighting conditions used in creating the database. In spaces where sunlight plays an important role in lighting during the day, separate databases need to be created for a good match. (iv) Although SURF gives reasonable results, however feature detection was inconsistent in certain conditions. We tried using K means to club surf descriptors to generate a bag of words for images along every edge and train SVM [4]. We tested query images in the SVM where match results were accurate for paths with unique features but inaccurate along similar-looking paths. Crowded spaces and the walking speed of the camera were the other limitations that affect matching accuracy. Future improvements may include a pedometer and phone compass along with our algorithm to improve results. Placement of QR codes in strategic locations can further improve positioning accuracy. It may also be interesting to decode the available signages using OCR and integrate them into this methodology.

5 Conclusion

Real-time indoor positioning is a technically challenging problem. We presented a novel method to create a sparse and invariant feature set of possible routes inside a building using pre-recorded video of the routes. This video data can be crowd-sourced and fed to a feature extractor to generate these point features. Once we generate route features they are stored in a graph object and annotated over the floor plan. In the online route finding process, real-time frames are queried to match the point features to find the position. Our experimentation shows that multiple databases can be used to improve performance in variable lighting conditions. Our method has shown an ease of crowd sourcing because almost everyone is carrying a mobile with a camera. Along with modern object recognition capabilities, the proposed visual positioning can support various location-based services and improve indoor accessibility for PVIs.

Acknowledgements. This project was funded and supported by Assistech Lab, at IIT Delhi, India. We are thankful to student Subham, Vishal, and Sushant and other staff and researchers who contributed to this work.

References

1. Morel, J.-M., Yu, G.: ASIFT: a new framework for fully affine invariant image comparison. SIAM J. Imaging Sci. **2**(2), 438–469 (2009)
2. Huang, Y., et al.: Image-based localization for indoor environment using mobile phone. Int. Archives Photogrammetry, Remote Sens. Spatial Inf. Sci. **40**(4), 211 (2015)
3. Bansal, R., Raj, G., Choudhury, T.: Blur image detection using Laplacian operator and Open-CV. In: 2016 International Conference System Modeling & Advancement in Research Trends (SMART), IEEE (2016)
4. Kushalvyas.: Converting image to bag of words using KMeans on Surf Descriptors and training SVM to generate classes to group similar images. https://kushalvyas.github.io/BOV.html
5. Mautz, R.: Indoor positioning technologies (Doctoral dissertation, Habilitationsschrift ETH Zürich, 2012) (2012)
6. Li, K.H.: LiDAR-based Indoor Positioning System (2021)
7. Tardif, J.-P., Pavlidis, Y., Daniilidis, K.: Monocular visual odometry in urban environments using an omnidirectional camera. In: 2008 IEEE/RSJ International Conference on Intelligent Robots and Systems (2008)
8. Davison, A.J., et al.: MonoSLAM: real-time single camera SLAM. IEEE Trans. Pattern Anal. Mach. Intell. **29**(6), 1052–1067 (2007)
9. Sattler, T., Leibe, B., Kobbelt, L.: Fast image-based localization using direct 2D-to-3D matching. In: 2011 IEEE International Conference on Computer Vision (ICCV), pp. 667–674. IEEE (2011)
10. Li, Y., Snavely, N., Huttenlocher, D.P.: Location recognition using prioritized feature matching. In: Daniilidis, K., Maragos, P., Paragios, N. (eds.) ECCV 2010. LNCS, vol. 6312, pp. 791–804. Springer, Heidelberg (2010). https://doi.org/10.1007/978-3-642-15552-9_57

11. Sinha, D., Ahmed, M.T., Greenspan, M.: Image retrieval using landmark indexing for indoor navigation. In: 2014 Canadian Conference on Computer and Robot Vision (CRV), pp. 63–70 (2014)
12. Bay, H., Tuytelaars, T., Van Gool, L.: SURF: speeded up robust features. In: Leonardis, A., Bischof, H., Pinz, A. (eds.) ECCV 2006. LNCS, vol. 3951, pp. 404–417. Springer, Heidelberg (2006). https://doi.org/10.1007/11744023_32
13. Lategahn, H., Stiller, C.: Vision-only localization. IEEE Trans. Intell. Transp. Syst. **15**(3), 1246–1257 (2014)
14. Li, B., et al.: How feasible is the use of magnetic field alone for indoor positioning? In: International Conference on Indoor Positioning and Indoor Navigation (IPIN). IEEE (2012)
15. Husen, M.N., Sukhan, L.: Indoor human localization with orientation using WiFi fingerprinting. In: Proceedings of the 8th International Conference on Ubiquitous Information Management and Communication (2014)
16. Zhang, C., Zhang, X.: LiTell: robust indoor localization using unmodified light fixtures. In: Proceedings of the 22nd Annual International Conference on Mobile Computing and Networking (2016)
17. Deretey, E., et al.: Visual indoor positioning with a single camera using PnP. In: International Conference on Indoor Positioning and Indoor Navigation. IEEE (2015)
18. Jianyong, Z., et al.: RSSI based Bluetooth low energy indoor positioning. In: International Conference on Indoor Positioning and Indoor Navigation, IEEE (2014)
19. Molnár, M., Luspay, T.: Development of an UWB based indoor positioning system. In: 2020 28th Mediterranean Conference on Control and Automation. IEEE (2020)
20. Elgendy, M., Guzsvinecz, T., Sik-Lanyi, C.: Identification of markers in challenging conditions for people with visual impairment using convolutional neural network. Appl. Sci. **9**(23), 5110 (2019)
21. Lymberopoulos, D., Liu, J.: The microsoft indoor localization competition: experiences and lessons learned. IEEE Signal Process. Mag. **34**(5), 125–140 (2017)
22. Vikas Upadhyay, Assistech Lab, IIT Delhi, https://youtu.be/b8m0tymUQZc, Code Repo (2020). https://github.com/VikasAssistech/VisualPositioning
23. Upadhyay, V., Balakrishnan, M.: Accessibility of healthcare facility for persons with visual disability. In: 2021 IEEE International Conference on Pervasive Computing and Communications. IEEE (2021)
24. Jiao, J., et al.: A smartphone camera-based indoor positioning algorithm of crowded scenarios with the assistance of deep CNN. Sensors **17**(4), 704 (2017)
25. Kang, W., Han, Y.: SmartPDR: smartphone-based pedestrian dead reckoning for indoor localization. IEEE Sensors J. **15**(5), 2906–2916 (2014)
26. Bauer, J., Sünderhauf, N., Protzel, P.: Comparing several implementations of two recently published feature detectors. IFAC Proc. Vol. **40**(15), 143–148 (2007)

Can Route Previews Amplify Building Orientation for People with Visual Impairment?

Vikas Upadhyay[1(✉)], Tigmanshu Bhatnagar[2], Catherine Holloway[2], P.V.M. Rao[1], and M. Balakrishnan[1]

[1] Indian Institute of Technology Delhi, New Delhi, India
vikasjk@gmail.com

[2] University College London, London, UK

Abstract. Before visiting a new location, we often look at maps to build an a priori mental representation of the environment using landmarks and points of interest. No such options are easily available for persons with visual impairment (PVIs). As a result, PVIs are often dependent on others for assistance with any activities that require visiting unfamiliar spaces. This seriously constrains PVIs' social inclusion and ability and right to independently explore their environment. From our earlier studies with experienced PVIs, we explored existing way-finding strategies and the role of environmental cues in aiding orientation and mobility. Here, we build on these findings to propose a route preview assistance application for PVIs to improve building orientation by helping to create a mental representation of spaces they are planning to visit. We translated non-visual cues into potential landmarks and encoded them into a mapping tool - IncluMap. The mapped building data is used to generate an aural route preview. In the follow-up study with five PVI participants, we evaluated how route preview assistance can improve orientation and route knowledge. We show that even for longer routes (>50 m) with a relatively good number of cognitive landmarks (>5), participants were able to remember and build a mental map. We found cognitive landmarks were useful for PVIs to support re-localization and getting reassurance in complex indoor spaces. Based on these findings we believe that the proposed route preview assistance can be a useful tool to provide orientation and mobility training to PVIs.

Keywords: Accessibility · Route knowledge · Orientation · Cognitive maps

1 Introduction

Globally, there is more than 253 million population with visual impairment (PVIs). The rising adoption(approx. 60% population) of mobile technologies has aided in the independent outdoor navigation of PVI. Besides mainstream

K. Miesenberger et al. (Eds.): ICCHP-AAATE 2022, LNCS 13341, pp. 187–196, 2022.
https://doi.org/10.1007/978-3-031-08648-9_22

applications like Google Maps and Citymapper, mobile applications specifically for PVIs, such as Lazarillo, Blind Square, Soundscape [24], Nearby Explorer, Clue, have been developed to navigate outdoor and a few indoor spaces independently by following audio cues [26]. However, indoor navigation is not yet as advanced. A problem that exists within indoor spaces which we discovered in our earlier work, is the need for prior exploration of space ahead of visiting a new place to enable increased confidence in independent navigation [5]. Additionally, in low resource settings, building information changes frequently due to incremental design changes [5]. However, there is no suitable mechanism to create, update and deliver a new piece of building information digitally. Another key challenge is to locate the users inside a building to deliver the information in real-time. Smartphone GPS signals do not work either reliably or with the required accuracy inside a building to support localization. Thus, many other technologies for indoor localization like Bluetooth beacons, ultrasonic, RFID, and ultra-wideband(UWB) have emerged [21] over the years. Out of these, Bluetooth low-energy beacons are a popular choice for indoor localization. Even though it was originally designed for proximity detection, still its use is promising as it can achieve the required localization accuracy of 2 to 3 m. Indoor wayfinding and accessibility for PVIs require a range of localization accuracy (i.e. between 0.5 to 3 m) mainly defined by the task, nature of the route as well as the destination. Unfortunately, none of these techniques have been successful in creating and maintaining a uniform landscape for indoor localization coverage. As the indoor facilities and services are growing, the amount of information collected to support accessibility has also grown. The need for semantic information mapping, and accessible interfaces to communicate a priori journey plan has become even more apparent [2]. As current indoor navigation technologies have serious limitations, we need a solution that can reduce the need for additional infrastructure and help PVIs to access and plan their journey ahead. Our key contributions in this paper include *(i) Translation of real-world experience and practices followed by PVIs into accessible indoor maps. (ii) Automatic generation of route preview to improve orientation and route knowledge.* These two contributions can help transform the real-world information into a mental map for PVIs.

2 Related Work

The accessibility of the built environment has a significant impact on the independence and mobility of PVIs [6]. Most of the indoor spaces in low-resource countries are unstructured, where on-ground assistance - both human and technology, is constrained [7,8]. Over the past decade, pedestrian navigation and planning research has looked at the effect of different specifications for indoor landmarks (i.e. door, lift etc.) and associated data [11], the role of sequential mapping [12], localization [13], path planning [14], identification of decision points [15], strategic inclusion of signage [16], and modeling of indoor spaces [17]. Despite the growing need, there are very few recommendations that include real-world cues and experience supporting journey planning [18]. This real-world data is even more limited when referring to indoors, with only draft proposals [19]. In summary, the existing specifications [20] neither include comprehensive accessibility cues from the environment nor provide a mechanism to support journey planning for PVIs [18]. Some recent research has explored challenges for PVIs related to journey planning [9] including how people explore more open outside spaces [10]. Sato, Daisuke [1] presented NavCog3 - a specially designed app for PVIs which provides turn by turn instruction. Although, the amount of information provided in turn-by-turn instruction varies based on users' familiarity with the building. Joao Guerreiro, [3] presented a virtual-navigation app for PVIs to learn unfamiliar routes but does not evaluate what type of non-visual cues contribute to the mental map. Jaime, [22] presented an audio-based virtual environment for training and rehabilitation. Vishnu, [23] present NavStick, an audio navigation tool for virtual environments using a game controller. Globally there is no widely accepted solution exists for indoor journey planning for PVIs. The major reason for this is a highly customized approach that is being used for creating support for indoor wayfinding. None of the localization techniques have proven guaranteed accuracy and implemented successfully at scale. Another critical limitation is an overwhelming turn-by-turn instruction information causing a loss of user engagement in proposed solutions. The inclusion of building orientation and route preview is an additional challenge for these solutions. Based on these findings, the major research question we would like to answer is, *"if the cues from the environment can be provided in adequate detail and presented sequentially to the PVIs, can it be helpful in planning and accessing their journey independently"* [4].

3 Transferring Real-World into Cognitive Maps

Most of the indoor wayfinding research emphasises turn-by-turn navigation with a limited focus on improving building orientation and route knowledge for PVIs. This work is based on the outcome of a background study conducted with eight

Table 1. Cognitive attribute and associated environmental cues and landmarks

Cognitive attribute	Easy to remember non-visual cues and landmarks
Touch and Haptic	Door handles and opening, handrails, switches, and push buttons, fingerprint access, wall texture, etc.
Sound	Lift, escalators. humming sound of refrigerator, coffee maker, microwave, Water points, washroom, audio kiosk, printer
Smell	Coffee machine, canteen/cafeteria, etc.
Floor tactile	Change in floor levels, surfaces, ramps, stairs, floor-mat
Thermal and light	Change in lighting conditions or temperature
Protrusion	Window opening, surface obstacle of permanent nature

Information include physical and functional accessibility of cues and landmarks

experienced VI participants. The objective of the background study was to gain an insight into indoor accessibility challenges, behavior and practices followed by PVIs. Thematic summary of this study is presented in the Table 4 in Annexure-I. This includes themes related to building familiarity, orientation, cognitive landmarks, spatial characteristics, and route preview. Findings of environmental cues and landmarks based on the cognitive attribute (easy to correlate and remember) for PVIs are presented in the Table 1. PVIs learn these cues from the environment over a period of time. We translated these environmental cues into more clear and actionable information and encoded them into our custom map annotation tool named IncluMap[1]. Indoor maps generated using IncluMap incorporate landmarks and non-walking areas with their physical and functional properties. This map data is used to automatically compute route preview and is made available to PVIs in accessible text and audio. Users can also access and learn the information about services being offered on the map, operations and timings of various facilities at varying levels of detail based on their needs.

Table 2. Implementation details of orientation and route preview application.

Rectilinear path refinement over A*
P_s = **ShortestPath(S, D)** where S → Source and D → Destination Let $\{P_1, P_2, P_3, \ldots\}$ are the points belonging to shortest path P_{rl} = **ShortToRectilinear(P_s, d_t, θ_t)** Where $d_t \rightarrow$ distance threshold, $\theta_t \rightarrow$ angle threshold for all conjugate point (P_j, P_k) in path P_s find euclidean distance d_c and cosine angle θ_c between (P_j, P_k) if $d_c < d_t$ and $\theta_c < \theta_t \Rightarrow$ refined point $P_t = P_j$ + distance * sin(t) if $d_c < d_t$ and $\theta_c > \theta_t \Rightarrow$ refined point $P_t = P_j$ + distance * cos(t) Update $P_j \rightarrow P_t$ and $P_{rl} \rightarrow P_s$
Route preview P_k from refined path P_{rl}
P_k, generated using refined path P_{rl}, information priority I_p and users preferences U_k P_k = **CaptionRoute(P_{rl}, I_p, U_k)** where k is number of instructions in P_k P_k include Wayfinding, cognitive landmarks, and accessibility information
Application interfaces
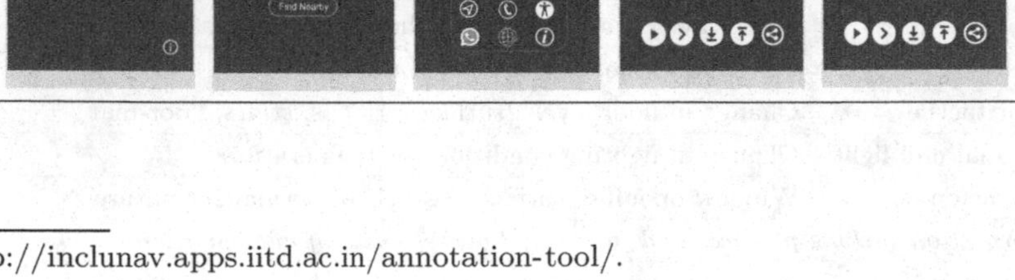

[1] http://inclunav.apps.iitd.ac.in/annotation-tool/.

Orientation and Route Preview Application. Annotated building data is used in an orientation and route preview application. Users can provide the source and destination information to extract and present an audio-based route preview. Over the application interface, users can orient themselves to a selected landmark virtually and explore the nearby points of interest in a particular direction using an electronic compass. The implementation details and application interfaces are presented in the Table 2.

4 Evaluation Study, Results and Discussion

Study Design: To understand the utility of orientation and route preview application, we conducted an evaluation study with five PVI participants. Prior consent was taken from all the participants to record the trials. This study was conducted in one of our campus buildings along with COVID precautions. In this study, we defined two goal-directed navigation routes with increasing complexity. (i) *Route one: Point A to point B, Length: 20 m, Total turns: 4, Landmarks: 3.* (ii) *Route two: Point A to Point B, Length: 60 m, Total turns: 6, Landmarks: 6* (ref. the figure in Table 3). Route-one preview is presented in the Table 3 which includes, positioning "P", orientation "O", navigational "N", Cognitive landmarks "CL", and accessibility information "A" (which includes obstacle, protrusion, micro-orientation, surface changes, service timings, contact, etc.). Audio-based route preview was provided to participants for both of the routes. Participants were asked to listen to the route preview a couple of times on both routes and perform the navigation task. During trials, we recorded route preview access frequency, travel time, and the route they followed was recorded. After the task completion, participants were interviewed about their experience and understanding of the mental map of the pilot routes.

Table 3. Shows pilot route and floor-plan on left and route one previews on right.

Route maps	Route preview
Route one Route two 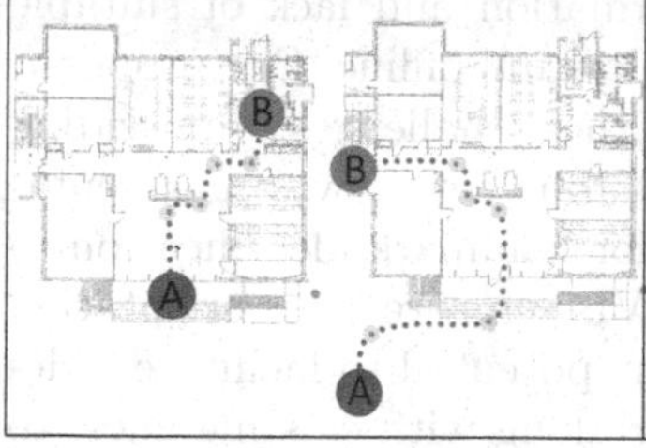	Push the glass door at front, (P, O, A, CL) Walk straight till glass wall, (N, CL) Assistech is on left, seminar room on right (O, L) Turn right, Walk a few steps and turn left (O, N) Walk straight till metal door, (O, N, CL) Turn right, walk a few steps, than turn left (L, O, N) You will pass by female washroom on right (O, N,CL) Destination water point is on right(O, P, CL) Drinking water is in right tap (A)

Results and Discussion: All the participants performed repeated navigation tasks three times over two given routes. For route one, the average number of times participants listened to route preview was 2.6, 2.4, and 1.4, with an average travel time of 80 s, 76 s, and 71 s over the 1st, 2nd, and 3rd attempts respectively. For route two, the average number of times they took route preview assistance was 4.2, 3.8, and 3.0 with an average travel time of 161 s, 154 s, and 142 s in 1st, 2nd, and 3rd attempts respectively. Detailed results and a summary of the evaluation study are presented in the Table 5 in Annexure-II. The follow-up interviews revealed participants were able to correlate the route preview with the actual environment and subsequent attempts reinforced the localization and their sense of confidence while minimizing the need for route preview. This was evident as participants listened to route preview after re-localization using cognitive landmarks. Another route preview design choice proposed by a participant was to include a subset of route previews for longer routes. Despite being a critical part of a journey requirement, route previews for indoor spaces have not been explored well. Our study has shown, even for complex routes, audio-based route preview at certain strategic locations can benefit PVIs. However, such audio, if generated, need local (regional) validation and a mechanism to adapt from one region to another. This is because the importance and familiarity of these landmarks can hugely differ from one region to another. The nature of smells in public places and the source of sounds are again very different in different countries/regions. The wider acceptability of way-finding solutions by the PVIs is challenging and it needs to be addressed holistically. It also includes outdoor-indoor-outdoor transitions along with the physical and functional accessibility of services provided there. There are no widely accepted standards to support indoor accessibility data, though some recent initiatives are emerging such as Wayfindr's open audio standard [25]. We believe, besides technical development, a more inclusive and comprehensive standard is required to govern indoor audio maps which can provide an orientation of complex indoor spaces to PVIs.

5 Conclusion

Indoor navigation researchers have contributed significantly to the literature over the past decade, however ground implementation has been limited. Reasons for this include unreliable indoor localization techniques, lack of standards, limited availability of indoor maps and accessibility information and lack of suitable interfaces to communicate them to PVIs - both online and offline. Our proposed advancement of IncluMap tries to overcome some of these challenges by providing a platform to annotate and automatically generate route previews and orientation information. We have presented an approach for landmark identification to represent the indoor environment that can help PVIs improve their orientation and route knowledge. These improvements have the potential to facilitate independent mobility of PVIs, using the route preview along with existing cues, to learn and build a mental representation before visiting unfamiliar spaces.

Acknowledgements. We are thankful to all the volunteers, staff members, and participants who actively contributed to the research, development and testing of tools used in this project. We also extend our gratitude to Assistech Lab, IIT Delhi, New Delhi, India for their logistic support.

Annexure - I: Background Study

Table 4. Thematic analysis of wayfinding experience and challenges.

(i) Building Familiarity: P2 mention, *We can have three categories, familiar buildings: visit two-three times or more in a month. Pseudo-familiar: visit once in two-three months. Unfamiliar building: visit once in six months or more.* Route preview and level of details in *turn-by-turn instructions can have Beginner, Knowledgeable and Expert mode*
(ii) Indoor Orientation and Cognitive Landmarks: P1 added, *The whole orientation depends on landmarks, We rely on tactile, sound, or smell because they are more reliable landmarks for orientation.* P4 mention, *To locate a room door, a foot mat outside it would help because I can guess where the door can be.* P2 added one interesting experience, *We also learn visual cues and refer this to sighted people if they ask.* P5 mention, *For indoors, sound landmarks are more often like an escalator, lift opening, the humming of a fan or if there is a water landmark that can be useful.* Orientation and route knowledge happen with the help of these landmarks after a while. Preview must include environmental cues and landmarks with sufficient details *Door: like a door must include, Opening type, material, timings, width, contact, etc.* with a choice of preference for PVIs
(iii) Spatial characteristics: *P8 mention, "in places where you can't trail a wall, tactile path, or a corridor, you quickly lose direction." P6 added, "airports have so much open space, there is no corridor anywhere and open space is always a challenge for me."* Tactile paths are useful in open spaces to get a direction but do not hint where it is leading. One can *break the open spaces using a floor-mat or tactile or digitally and create landmarks in it to support orientation*
(iv) Route Preview Assistance: P3 mentions *"route preview is very useful for small routes." Even for complex routes, it can be useful to orient and learn the routes in combination with real-time navigation.* P6 added, *"cognitive landmarks along a route are important for localization, orientation, referencing, reassurance and route knowledge."* P8 mentioned *"for longer routes, it mostly depends on the number of turns and whether landmarks are there in the route."* P2 added *"sometimes, I just want to know what is around me and what is in this direction, so I just want to explore the place."* Route preview can be very useful to explore new spaces virtually and especially when the timeline of the journey is critical

Annexure - II: Evaluation Study

Table 5. Evaluation study results and feedback from participants

	R1A1			**R1A2**			**R1A3**			**R2A1**			**R2A2**			**R2A3**		
PGA	T1	A1	C1	T2	A2	C2	T3	A3	C3	T1	A1	C1	T2	A2	C2	T3	A3	C3
P1M32	72	2	2	70	1	2	64	1	0	152	4	4	142	4	4	130	3	3
P2M44	88	3	3	82	3	3	77	2	0	170	5	5	164	5	5	152	4	3
P3F24	85	3	2	76	3	2	76	2	2	166	5	4	158	4	3	148	3	3
P4F21	70	2	2	68	2	2	62	1	1	160	3	3	162	3	3	150	2	2
P5M38	84	3	3	82	2	3	77	1	2	158	4	3	146	3	3	132	3	2
Avg.	**80**	**2.6**	2.4	**76**	**2.2**	2.4	**71**	**1.4**	1	**161**	**4.2**	3.8	**154**	**3.8**	3.6	**142**	**3**	2.6

Acronyms used, PGA: Participants, gender and age, T1: Task completion time(second) in first attempt, A1: Frequency of listening route-preview in first attempt, C: Frequency of listening route-preview at cues in first attempt, R1A1: Route one attempt one, etc.

Comments and Feedback from Evaluation Study

P1 mention, *I wish if I can listen to these overviews before visiting.* Some landmarks like glass doors and stairs were very helpful to localize and orient myself. P3 added, I found this preview interesting, I still remember route one which includes *a glass door, and wall than another metal door,* maybe after that, I need to listen to this route again. Another interesting input we got from P4, whenever I enter a corridor from an open space, ambient airflow gets changed. *This helps me to understand the pilot routes* where the initial part was open space then I moved to a corridor. Indoor spaces can be broken into their spatial characteristics. P2 added, *I would like to break the route-two preview into two sub-routes.* P1 was curious, *Can I explore my surrounding to my point of interest before listening to the route preview.* This will give me more freedom. P3 also mentioned *I would like to have more flexibility to explore my points of interest.* P5 mentioned *I feel we can replace turn by turn navigation with this.* I feel lost in following so many details in turn-by-turn navigation. I can listen to a route preview before visiting and then I can use the micro-routes for reassurance at some key locations

Other Inferences

People need an orientation before visiting while visiting they need sub-route audio maps and must include cognitive landmarks which are easy to identify in a building for PVIs. Complex routes can have a subset of mini routes. We found that on average, PVIs were able to remember 3 to 4 subsequent turns and 5 to 6 cognitive landmarks. It was clearly evident that cognitive route preview improves the route knowledge and reduces the requirement of reassurance almost at every turn to after 3 to 4 turns. There was a significant reduction in the frequency of listening to route previews in subsequent attempts. To get reassurance, most of the participants listened to a route preview whenever they do a self-localization or encounter a cognitive landmark

APIs and Demos

Annotation tool: http://inclunav.apps.iitd.ac.in/annotation-tool/

Manual: http://inclunav.apps.iitd.ac.in/annotation-tool/pdf-view

Preview application: https://inclunav.apps.iitd.ac.in/innav/

APIs: https://documenter.getpostman.com/view/2956893/TzJpiKeP

References

1. Sato, D., Oh, U., et al.: NavCog3 in the wild: Large-scale blind indoor navigation assistant with semantic features. ACM Trans. Accessible Comput. (TACCESS), **12**(3), 1–30 (2019)

2. Real, S., Araujo, A.: Navigation systems for the blind and visually impaired: past work, challenges, and open problems. Sensors **19**(15), 3404 (2019)
3. Guerreiro, J., Sato, D., et al.: Virtual navigation for blind people: transferring route knowledge to the real-World. Int. J. Human-Comput. Stud. **135**, 102369 (2020)
4. Devlin, A.S.: Wayfinding in healthcare facilities: contributions from environmental psychology. Behav. Sci. **4**(4), 423–436 (2014)
5. Upadhyay, V., Balakrishnan, M.: Accessibility of healthcare facility for persons with visual disability. In: 2021 IEEE International Conference on Pervasive Computing and Communications (2021)
6. Chanana, P.: Study of independent travel needs of persons with blindness and assistive technology solutions, IIT Delhi (2020)
7. Ahmed, N.: Wayfinding behavior in India. In: Abascal, J., Barbosa, S., Fetter, M., Gross, T., Palanque, P., Winckler, M. (eds.) INTERACT 2015. LNCS, vol. 9297, pp. 522–530. Springer, Cham (2015). https://doi.org/10.1007/978-3-319-22668-2_40
8. Upadhyay, V., Kumar, P.A., et al.: Retrofit framework for indoor mobility in unstructured spaces. Disability Design Innovation Workshop, CHI 2021
9. Abd Hamid, N.N., Edwards, A.D.: Facilitating route learning using interactive audio-tactile maps for blind and visually impaired people. In: CHI 2013 Extended Abstracts on Human Factors in Computing Systems (2013)
10. Bandukda, M., Holloway, C., Singh, A., Berthouze, N.: PLACES: a framework for supporting blind and partially, sighted people in outdoor leisure activities. In: The 22nd International ACM SIGACCESS Conference on Computers and Accessibility, pp. 1–13 (2020)
11. Pérez, J.E., Arrue, M., Kobayashi, M., Takagi, H., Asakawa, C.: Assessment of semantic taxonomies for blind indoor navigation based on a shopping center use case. In: Proceedings of the 14th International Web for All Conference, pp. 1–4 (2017)
12. Guerreiro, J., Ahmetovic, D., Kitani, K.M., Asakawa, C.: Virtual navigation for blind people: building sequential representations of the real-world. In: Proceedings of the 19th International ACM SIGACCESS Conference on Computers and Accessibility, pp. 280–289 (2017)
13. Ahmetovic, D., Murata, M., et al.: Achieving practical and accurate indoor navigation for people with visual impairments. In: Proceedings of the 14th International Web for All Conference, pp. 1–10 (2017)
14. Liu, L., Zlatanova, S.: A "door-to-door" path-finding approach for indoor navigation. In: Proceedings Gi4DM 2011: GeoInformation for Disaster Management, Antalya, Turkey, 3–8 May 2011 (2011)
15. Fallah, N., Apostolopoulos, I., Bekris, K., Folmer, E.: Indoor human navigation systems: a survey. Interact. Comput. **25**, 1 (2013)
16. Greenroyd, F.L., Hayward, R., Price, A., Demian, P., Sharma, S.: A tool for signage placement recommendation in hospitals based on wayfinding metrics. Indoor Built Environ. **27**(7), 925–937 (2018)
17. Worboys, M.: Modeling indoor space. In: Proceedings of the 3rd ACM SIGSPATIAL International Workshop on Indoor Spatial Awareness, pp. 1–6 (2011)
18. Giannoumis, G.A., Ferati, M., Pandya, U., Krivonos, D., Pey, T.: Usability of indoor network navigation solutions for persons with visual impairments. In: Langdon, P., Lazar, J., Heylighen, A., Dong, H. (eds.) CWUAAT 2018, pp. 135–145. Springer, Cham (2018). https://doi.org/10.1007/978-3-319-75028-6_12

19. Online. Draft Development Specification for Spatial Network Model for Pedestrians. https://www.mlit.go.jp/common/001177505.pdf, Director-General for Policy Planning, Ministry of Land, Infrastructure, Transport and Tourism
20. ITUTF Recommendation. ITU-Tf. 921. (2018)
21. Zafari, F., Gkelias, A., Leung, K.K.: A survey of indoor localization systems and technologies. IEEE Commun. Surv. Tutorials **21**(3), 2568–2599 (2019)
22. Sánchez, J., et al.: Navigation for the blind through audio-based virtual environments. In: CHI 2010 Extended Abstracts on Human Factors in Computing Systems, pp. 3409–3414 (2010)
23. Nair, V., Smith, B.A.: Toward self-directed navigation for people with visual impairments. In: Adjunct Publication of the 33rd Annual ACM Symposium on User Interface Software and Technology (2020)
24. Ross, A.S., et al.: Use cases and impact of audio-based virtual exploration. In: CHI 2019 Workshop on Hacking Blind Navigation (2019)
25. IABNNS, Recommendation, I. T. U. T. F. "ITU-Tf. 921."
26. Apps and Tech. For PVIs, 2021, https://www.noisyvision.org/2018/08/01/app-and-devices-for-blind-and-visually-impaired/. (Online)

Implementation and Innovation in the Area of Independent Mobility Through Digital Technologies

Implementation and Innovation in the Area of Independent Mobility Through Digital Technologies

Introduction to the Special Thematic Session

David Banes(✉)

David Banes Access and Inclusion Services, Trips Project, England, UK
david@davebanesaccess.org
http://www.trips-project.eu

Abstract. This STS explores contributions to the independent mobility of persons with disabilities. Mobility is often cited as a requirement of people with a disability seeking to increase opportunities for full access to education, employment and daily living. Recent innovations in assistive and accessible technologies suggest new ways in which navigation, orientation, and wayfinding can be accessible for people with a wide variety of needs, including those with cognitive, sensory, and physical impairments and the elderly.

The papers share insight and examples of the impact of emerging technologies, including location-based technologies, artificial intelligence, machine learning, and augmented mixed and virtual reality solutions. These offer opportunities for increasingly personalised, adaptive, and natural interfaces for access methods, including speech, audio, gestural and haptic approaches.

Such innovation is often based upon co-design requires appropriate service and training to be implemented across age, needs, and context. The STS discusses recent achievements in independent mobility through digital technologies, focusing on the technologies, forms of access, and associated services to support implementation, replication, and localisation.

Keywords: Disability · Accessibility · Assistive technology · Participatory · Co-design · Mobility · Transport · Travel · Independent living

1 Introduction

The guide to travel produced by the Australian government, Department of Infrastructure and Regional Development (2017) suggests that people with a disability are more likely to experience social and economic disadvantage because of more limited opportunities to earn income and the high cost (in proportion to their income) of their housing, travel, medical and other needs. In many cases, disability restricts people from driving a private vehicle, either through physical or cognitive ability or the lack of economic resources to own and operate a car. For many people, public transport's perceived or real inaccessibility leaves them reliant on family or friends or particular types of public transport

K. Miesenberger et al. (Eds.): ICCHP-AAATE 2022, LNCS 13341, pp. 199–206, 2022.
https://doi.org/10.1007/978-3-031-08648-9_23

such as the taxi system and the increasingly popular ride-share. This reliance on others to drive them where they want to go affects their ability to participate independently in many social, economic, or cultural aspects of the community.

Access to public transport opens up personal empowerment, social inclusion, and community participation opportunities. People can choose to travel to see friends and family and participate in social and cultural activities or other initiatives such as training or education. Accessible public transport allows individuals to travel based on their requirements (such as cost, time of day, the urgency of travel, length of the journey, interchanges, etc.) rather than relying on private transport options.

Public transport is cost-effective for individuals and the economy. Improving the accessibility of public transport can promote more efficient transport decisions by individuals and increase the customer base as more people can travel for work, business or study. This improves productivity and supports a stronger economy.

In the framework developed in the Australian model, the whole journey will include:

- Pre-journey planning: these are the decisions about using transportation based on available information.
- Journey start and end: these usually occur outside the transport system. For example, travelling from home to the stop, station, or terminal along a footpath, and then from the stop, station or terminal to the final destination.
- Transport stop/station: the dedicated or identified locations where transport services operate to and from.
- Transport service: the conveyance that enables the journey, the 'onboard experience', as well as the scheduling/routing of services
- Interchange: places where service or mode transfers take place.
- Return journey planning: reversing the journey for the return to origin or an onward journey to another place.
- Disruption to business-as-usual: this includes planned and unplanned disruption to transport services or along the journey start and end sections.
- Supporting infrastructure: this supports the journey and includes mid and end of trip infrastructures such as toilets, drinking fountains, wayfinding and seating

Throughout the STS, the researchers consider one or more stages of this journey and where emerging technologies describe impact and promote ease of access. The scope and scale of that research were significant, with a clear focus emerging on the design of vehicles themselves and the process of enhancing inclusion and a focus on some of the more intractable issues.

1.1 Co-design and Innovation in Mobility

Banes et al. (2022) describe how emerging technologies were introduced to panels in a series of co-design workshops held by the Trips Project. Each panel included people with a disability, transport operators and assistive technology specialists. Each prepared design concepts that outlined incremental or disruptive innovations to address one or more barriers identified during travel. The designs were prioritised according to feasibility and impact, and a priority list was prepared. The workshops identified innovations that could address one or more steps in planning and taking a journey. These divided into incremental innovations that seek to address specific travel barriers and disruptive innovations that often address the entire basis of travel and mobility.

In most cases, the most desired innovations were incremental, building upon current technologies on the market but applying them in new ways. These include accessible and inclusive travel planners. Many people with disabilities found that information about a journey was held in multiple locations. Since transport is a single process, there was a strong desire that planning technologies should reflect the need for a seamless process.

However, the workshops also invited participants to be creative and consider "big" ideas that would address many of the barriers they faced. In doing so, they identified the most critical emerging technologies, with the potential for impact upon travel and mobility in the short, medium and long term, as being

- Artificial Intelligence to analyse needs, anticipate problems and recommend solutions
- Internet of Things – communicating needs and requirements for travel to the vehicles
- Wearable technologies – reducing the need to address inaccessible sources of information and ticketing
- Robotics and Drones to create new forms of vehicles that utilise AI and the IoT for autonomous travel
- Natural interfaces simplify the interaction with infrastructure and systems

Many of the ideas developed were rooted in already available technologies or close to market release and hence had a good degree of feasibility. This raised further questions about the implementation and adoption of innovation within the sector.

1.2 Adoption of Innovation

Although it has been suggested that the most significant barrier to inclusion are attitudes and awareness (Siska 2019). With the growth of new technologies, we could include the need for imagination and creativity as a barrier to overcome. Banes et al. (2022) demonstrate how using a co-design methodology, workshop participants showed that ideas would flow in an open setting given time and space. By using well-formed tools to analyse ideas, priorities could be identified that could provide the basis of a business case for further investment to impact a diverse range of travellers.

König et al. (2022) undertook a further study into the impact of subjective technology adaptivity (STA) on the willingness of persons with disabilities to use emerging technologies. They confirmed that wearables, robots, augmented reality, and location-based alerts were the most preferred emerging technology systems. They note some variations depending on the type of disability observed in the degree of use intention. Some unexpected findings require further research, such as explaining the preference of visually impaired individuals for augmented reality.

In this study, age differences were observed only in relation to the intention to use wearables and location-based alerts and not for other technologies. Gender differences were minimal, with women showing a slightly higher preference for robots than men.

The disability often determines the level of intended use. For example, wearables demonstrated high use intention by persons with physical or multiple impairments but much lower for persons with hearing impairments.

It was shown that the resulting STA was comparable to the mean STA of the elderly in the study by Kamin and Lang (2013). However, the study suggested that people with disabilities assess the perceived adaptive utility of technologies more highly than the elderly. The paper shows that a disabled person's adaptivity to technology predicts the willingness to use assistive technologies. However, the relationship depends on the form of disability and the kind of technology.

These findings shed light on the role of perceived technology adaptivity in implementing and adopting future technologies. This may contribute to an improved understanding of the psychological mechanisms of using technology and may result in a new view on the widespread deficit model of disability (Dinishak 2016) and the rippled effects of the digital divide (Stendal 2012).

The results underline the importance of having a process for improving a person's adaptivity to technology. This might be formalised through education but may also depend upon the messaging of technology early adopters who may have a crucial role in influencing adoption rates.

1.3 Accessibility Standards and Legislation for Communicating Information

The willingness to adopt emerging technologies may be driven by clarity of message, impacting attitudes and awareness of benefits. Galinski (2022) explores the harmonisation of communication systems and platforms in implementing innovation through the lens of compatibility with accessibility standards and legislation. This challenge can cause dissatisfaction and leave the public transport user stranded and frustrated or completely discouraged. He notes that high-level recommendations for standardisation have identified a need to consider multilingualism, multimodality, and disabled persons' needs in all content development and management for over a decade. Alongside the content itself, this also necessitates consistency in both principles and methods to achieve more comprehensive content interoperability.

For many people with a disability, travel brings about anxiety. Irregular and unexpected situations in public transport require a timely connection to assistance directly or to interpreters to assist in communication. Standards-based technical interoperability of technologies with different information and content management systems can help address communication barriers. However, technical interoperability does not yet guarantee content interoperability. If the needs of persons with disabilities are included, he suggests that a new dimension is required, comprehensive content interoperability.

The methods, content providers, and tools to support such communication have implications beyond the domain of travel and mobility. The approaches generated could be used in other environments, such as smart cities, workplaces, and relevant language and communication services.

Increasing consistency of communication also should impact improved access to coherent information that is required to ease the burden of journey planning for many people with disabilities.

1.4 Routing and Journey Planning

To address this need, Darvishy, Hutter, and Mosimann (2022) investigate routing issues in relation to people with mobility impairments. They suggest an approach to personalised, accessible routing for people with mobility impairments and the information required to implement this, including curb cuts, inclination, path width, and additional barriers. In a case study for the city of Zurich, they analyse the availability of this information in OpenStreetMap (OSM) and investigate different approaches for collecting the missing accessibility data.

This accessibility data can implement routing apps for people with mobility impairments. Still, they also support city planners to consider future measures to improve urban accessibility. They suggest a methodology consisting of automated, semi-automated, crowd-based, and onsite data collection. Collecting and maintaining detailed and up-to-date accessibility information is time-consuming and costly. As a result, important accessibility data is generally missing from publicly available mapping databases such as OSM, which presents an obstacle to many people with disabilities who might wish to use such services. This paper envisions a routing algorithm that can incorporate the data and provide personalised, accessible paths from Point A to Point B, based on a user's specific mobility profile. A blended approach is suggested to collect this information, combining the exploitation of existing databases wherever possible with app-based crowdsourcing and manual data collection. Such integration and collection of data would lend themselves to using AI techniques to automate processes as much as possible.

1.5 The Final Leg of the Journey - Within Buildings

The end of a journey is not simply the arrival at a terminus or door to a building. Successful journies also often require entry to a location and navigation to a precise space. Constantinescu et al. (2022a) explore the experience and mitigations when travelling to unknown buildings and the benefits of accessibility features for indoor maps. They note that travelling independently in this context is difficult for people with disabilities due to a lack of information about the accessibility of indoor environments. They found that there are few freely available indoor maps of public buildings, as these are usually only at the disposal of the owners of the buildings. Only some information about buildings can be recorded in most open-source map projects. The authors collected accessibility features for buildings for people with different disabilities, sorted them, and aligned them with freely available features from OpenStreetMap and A11yJSON.

While some features can be already expressed in OSM, others need to be submitted to OSM or published as LinkedData. Their database represents a step toward standardising indoor accessibility features to help owners record the accessibility of their buildings more easily. Finally, end-users with disabilities will be able to make more informed decisions and travel to more accessible buildings.

Such data collection and curation are enhanced by acquiring surrounding visual information, as outlined for people with visual impairments by Iwamura et al. (2022). They note that recent advancements in recognition technology allow people with a visual impairment to obtain visual information from their surroundings using smartphone apps and assistive devices. However, taking a photo actively is not easy for people with visual impairment. To address this, they suggest an alternative approach of passive information acquisition (PIA). PIA has a tendency to transfer too much information to the user and they explore better ways for people with visual impairment to obtain only the information they want. The paper offers some useful insight into how to maximise the benefits of accessibility data collected to guide informed decision-making by persons with disabilities.

In a second paper, Constantinescu et al. (2022b) investigated some of these issues further by exploring textual descriptions of indoor spaces for people with little or no sight. They recognised that orientation in unknown environments is challenging for people with blindness. There is a lack of solutions for indoor environments. They propose a grammar for generating German textual descriptions of indoor environments for users with blindness. When visiting an unknown building, blind people usually travel with a sighted assistant or ask other people for the way. Engel et al. (2020) demonstrated that people with blindness would use textual descriptions of buildings if they were available to gain more independence. When travelling in an unknown building, information about the immediate surroundings, such as stairs, number of floors, or the location of doors, is particularly important, as it helps orient oneself.

This information needs to be provided, considering the user's location and orientation in a building. They created a description component for indoor environments by defining three grammar with different words order. The results suggest that a random order of words induces a higher cognitive load in a description. Users are especially frustrated by the inconsistency of the sentences.

Moreover, users repeatedly mentioned in their comments that they would like to be able to configure the textual descriptions. For instance, they wish to change the radius within which objects are conveyed or filter the objects depending on the situation. The different choices made by the participants, in terms of objects or how to convey the direction, also suggest that reconfigurability is paramount for a system designed for people with blindness.

1.6 Transference

A further issue that strongly influenced the adoption and successful implementation of emerging technologies and innovation related to the breadth and depth of the market. The economic and social case can be undermined if the innovation is believed to impact too small a sector of society. However, the paper by Boratyńska-Karpiej and Engel (2022) demonstrates that many of the barriers described by persons with disabilities are recognised by seniors aged over 65. In many cases, seniors opted not to use public transport in preference for being driven by family or by taxi. Many of the desired locations were equally shared. As suggested, seniors are willing to adopt new technology where the benefits are clear and obvious. Inclusive solutions for persons with a disability facilitated greater use by seniors, reducing carbon footprint and increasing footfall for public transport. As seniors were less like to travel at peak times driven by those journeying for employment and education, this might allow off-peak transport services to run more cost-effectively.

1.7 Summary

In conclusion, the papers within the STS recognise that a range of barriers can impact the ease of mobility for persons with disabilities. The research undertaken stresses the value that those with disabilities place upon both disruptive innovations that seek to provide new ways to travel and incremental innovation that addresses one or more specific challenges. Whilst much of the research described focuses on particular issues, they can be perceived as links in a mobility chain that, if implemented, will support further, more substantive innovation in the future.

References

Banes, D., Magni, R., Andrushevich, A., Hoogerwerf, E.J.: Emerging technologies and access to mobility through public transport: a review of potential impact upon people with a disability. In: Petz, A., Hoogerwerf, E.-J., Mavrou, K. (eds.) Assistive Technology, Accessibility and (e)Inclusion, ICCHP-AAATE 2022 Open Access Compendium, accepted for publication; online: https://www.icchp-aaate.org. Johannes Kepler University Linz, Austria (2022)

Department of Infrastructure and Regional Development: The Whole Journey: A Guide for Thinking beyond Compliance to Create Accessible Public Transport Journeys (2017)

Šiška, J., Beadle-Brown, J., Káňová, Š, Šumníková, P.: Social inclusion through community living: current situation, advances and gaps in policy, practice and research. Social Inclusion **6**(1), 94–109 (2018)

Miesenberger, K., Karshmer, A., Penaz, P., Zagler, W.: The impact of subjective technology adaptivity on the willingness of persons with disabilities to use emerging assistive technologies. In: Miesenberger, K., Kouroupetroglu, G., Mavrou, K., Manduchi, R., Covarrubias Rodriguez, M., Penaz, P. (eds.) Computers Helping People with Special Needs, LNCS. Springer, Cham (2022). https://doi.org/10.1007/978-3-642-31534-3

Kamin, S.T., Lang, F.R.: The subjective technology adaptivity inventory (STAI): a motivational measure of technology usage in old age. Gerontechnology **12**(1), 16–25 ((2013)

Dinishak, J. The deficit view and its critics. Disability Studies Quarterly **36**(4) (2016)

Galinski: H-H and H-M communication with and among disabled persons in public transport. In: Petz, A., Hoogerwerf, E.-J., Mavrou, K. (eds.) Assistive Technology, Accessibility and (e)Inclusion, ICCHP-AAATE 2022 Open Access Compendium, accepted for publication; online: https://www.icchp-aaate.org. Johannes Kepler University Linz, Austria (2022)

Darvishy, A., Hutter, H.P., Mosimann, R.: Towards personalised, accessible routing for people with mobility impairments. In: Miesenberger, K., Kouroupetroglu, G., Mavrou, K., Manduchi, R., Covarrubias Rodriguez, M., Penaz, P. (eds.) Computers Helping People with Special Needs, LNCS. Springer, Cham (2022). https://doi.org/10.1007/978-3-642-31534-3

Constantinescu, A., Muller, K., Loitsch, C., Zappe, S., Stiefelhagen, S.: Traveling to unknown buildings: accessibility features for indoor maps. In: Miesenberger, K., Kouroupetroglu, G., Mavrou, K., Manduchi, R., Covarrubias Rodriguez, M., Penaz, P. (eds.) Computers Helping People with Special Needs, LNCS. Springer, Cham (2022a). https://doi.org/10.1007/978-3-642-31534-3

Iwamura, M., Kawai, T., Takashima, T., Minatani, T., Kise, K. Acquiring surrounding visual information without taking photo actively for people with visual impairment, In: Miesenberger, K., Kouroupetroglu, G., Mavrou, K., Manduchi, R., Covarrubias Rodriguez, M., Penaz, P. (eds.) Computers Helping People with Special Needs, LNCS. Springer, Cham (2022). https://doi.org/10.1007/978-3-642-31534-3

Constantinescu, A., Neumann, E.M., Müller, K., Stiefelhagen, R.: Listening first: egocentric textual descriptions of indoor spaces for people with blindness. In: Miesenberger, K., Kouroupetroglu, G., Mavrou, K., Manduchi, R., Covarrubias Rodriguez, M., Penaz, P. (eds.) Computers Helping People with Special Needs, LNCS. Springer, Cham (2022b). https://doi.org/10.1007/978-3-642-31534-3

Engel, C., et al.: Travelling more independently: a requirements analysis for accessible journeys to unknown buildings for people with visual impairments. In: ASSETS '20. ACM, New York, NY, USA (2020)

Boratyńska-Karpiej, Engel: Transport for seniors - barriers and solutions on the example of Poland. In: Petz, A., Hoogerwerf, E.-J., Mavrou, K. (eds.) Assistive Technology, Accessibility and (e)Inclusion, ICCHP-AAATE 2022 Open Access Compendium, accepted for publication; online: https://www.icchp-aaate.org. Johannes Kepler University Linz, Austria (2022)

The Impact of Subjective Technology Adaptivity on the Willingness of Persons with Disabilities to Use Emerging Assistive Technologies: A European Perspective

Alexandra König[1(✉)], Laura Alčiauskaitė[2], and Tally Hatzakis[3]

[1] German Aerospace Center, Institute of Transportation Systems, Braunschweig, Germany
alexandra.koenig@dlr.de
[2] European Network on Independent Living, Brussels, Belgium
[3] Trilateral Research, Waterford, Ireland

Abstract. Emerging digital technologies like augmented reality (AR) hold promising prospects for people with disabilities. It remains, however, an open question how persons with disabilities respond to technological demands. The paper examines the potential impact of users' self-assessment of their own competence in using these technologies on users' responses by examining their *Subjective Technology Adaptivity* (STA) [1] and use intention to study the relationship between their self-assessed adaptivity and volitional technology use. To this end, data from 545 Europeans with different types of disabilities were collected based on an online survey. The research focused on six emerging assistive technologies related to mobility: accessible navigation systems, artificial intelligence alerts, wearables, robots, augmented reality and location-based alerts. The results show that the adaptivity to technology of people with disabilities predicts the use intention for emerging assistive technologies. There was, however, great variability depending on the type of disability. For example, a high STA of people with physical, visual, hearing or intellectual impairments predicted their willingness to use intention of AI-based alters but not for people with mental health issues or multiple impairments. Our findings shed new light on the role of perceived technology adaptivity of persons with disabilities for future technology use intention.

Keywords: Emerging technologies · Technology adaptivity · Disability research

1 Introduction

The emergence of new digital technologies is accompanied by a significant growth in the diversity and availability of assistive technologies. Advances in artificial intelligence, Big Data analytics for robotics or augmented reality offer promising perspectives for persons with disabilities in the next years [2–4]. However, we need to know more about the willingness of persons with disabilities to use emerging technologies and the determinants of their use intention. One approach to studying the determinants of technology

K. Miesenberger et al. (Eds.): ICCHP-AAATE 2022, LNCS 13341, pp. 207–214, 2022.
https://doi.org/10.1007/978-3-031-08648-9_24

use of persons with disabilities is the concept of digital capital [5], that is inspired by Bourdieu's (1997) notions of social and cultural capital [6] It can be described as a person's technological competencies and knowledge that enable her or him to use technology [7]. A related concept, that focusses on the individual's perception of its own abilities to deal with technologies, is the concept of Subjective Technology Adaptivity (STA), defined as "an individual's response to technological demands that are associated with improved competence, and with more frequent use of technology" [1, p. 16]. It was shown that the higher the score of the STA, the more interest in technological innovations and the more confidence while dealing with technology people exhibit [8]. It was shown that subjective technology adaptivity predicts technology use in higher age [1], but the concept has not been applied to the group of people with disabilities before. The paper aims to answer to the research question: Does adaptivity to technology predict the willingness of persons with disabilities to use emerging assistive technologies?

2 Methodology

2.1 Online Survey

To answer the research question, a survey study was conducted. The survey was conducted under the auspices of the European research project TRIPS (Transport Innovation for disabled People needs Satisfaction, https://trips-project.eu/). The survey focused on 13 future assistive technologies that were identified and reviewed within the TRIPS project [9]. For this paper, we report on six emerging technologies of wider appeal: accessible navigation systems, artificial intelligence (AI) alerts, wearables, robots, augmented reality (AR) and location-based alerts [10]. These technologies could potentially assist persons with various types of disabilities, as well as non-disabled users.

The survey items were based on preceding qualitative research that was conducted to identify barriers of current transport use for persons with disabilities [11]. Besides an English version, the questionnaire was translated into 14 languages (Bulgarian, Croatian, Dutch, French, German, Greek, Italian, Lithuanian, Polish, Portuguese, Romanian, Russian, Spanish and Swedish).

Use intention for the assistive technologies was measured using one single question (Would you use this system?) in a 5-point Likert scale with 1 = never, 2 = rarely, 3 = sometimes, 4 = frequently and 5 = always. Subjective technology adaptivity (STA) was measured using the Subjective Technology Adaptivity Inventory (STAI) [1]. STAI consists of 15 items regarding three dimensions: *Technology-related Goal-Engagement* (TGE), e.g., "I invest as much effort as I can until a device works as intended", *Perceived Adaptive Utility* (PAU), e.g., "Using modern technology helps me to master everyday life", *Perceived Safety of Technology* (PST), e.g., "I trust modern technology". Responses are given using a 5-point Likert scale (1 = strongly disagree, 5 = strongly agree) (Fig. 1).

The survey was conducted online via the project website, using the software SoSciSurvey. The survey was disseminated by TRIPS project partners and local disability user groups in seven EU cities and in European-wide NGOs working in the field of disability. More than 100 organizations had been contacted to disseminate the invitation to the survey via newsletter or social media. Data was collected from November 2020 until February 2021.

1. What do you think about the role of technology in your life?

Tick the option that represents your views best.

	strongly disagree	disagree	neutral	agree	strongly agree
Using modern technology helps me to make important decisions	○	○	○	○	○
Using modern technology helps me to master everyday life	○	○	○	○	○
Using modern technology supports my independence	○	○	○	○	○
Using modern technology helps me to be more efficient in my daily routines	○	○	○	○	○
I invest as much effort as I can until a device works as intended	○	○	○	○	○
I practice with a new device until I can use it as intended	○	○	○	○	○
I put in more effort when a new device is more difficult to use than expected	○	○	○	○	○

Fig. 1. Exemplary questions from the survey

2.2 Study Participants

Overall, 872 completed responses were submitted. After the exclusion of people from non-European countries and persons who do not identify themselves as having a disability, the final sample consisted of 545 participants from 21 European countries. The sample comprised 253 women (45.8%) and 284 men (51.4%, rest missing). While a large proportion of participants (87.7%) answered the survey themselves, 68 surveys (12.3%) were answered by another person on behalf of a disabled person. The average age of the sample was 46.4 years ($SD = 15.7$). Persons with physical impairments were by far the largest group of respondents regarding the type of disability (n = 297, 53.7%), followed by visual impairments (n = 85, 15.4%), multiple impairments (n = 85, 15.4%), hearing impairments (n = 45, 8.1%), intellectual disabilities (n = 17, 3.1%), mental health issues (n = 16, 2.9%) and others (n = 6, 1.1%). It should be noted that a person with multiple impairments was assigned once and not multiple times according to his or her various impairments. Most people did not specify their kind of physical impairment using the free text field, which results in a big and heterogeneous group of people with disabilities.

3 Results

3.1 Subjective Technology Adaptivity

According to Kamin & Lang (2013), the subjective technology adaptivity (STA) was calculated based on its components PAU, PST and TGE. Principal components analysis confirmed the three factors. The resulting STA was rather high with $M = 3.81$ ($SD = 0.72$). No significant differences in STA were identified between men ($M = 3.83$, $SD = 0.72$) and women ($M = 3.81$, $SD = 0.73$, ($t(535) = 0.26$, $p = .793$). Furthermore, no significant age effect was shown ($r < .01$, $p = .920$). However, the type of disability had an important effect on the STA ($F(5,539) = 3.648$, $p = .003$, $\eta p^2 = .033$). In detail, persons with visual impairments reported a significant higher STA ($M = 3.99$, $SD = 0.64$) than respondents with multiple impairments ($M = 3.61$, $SD = 0.81$, $p = .003$) (Fig. 2).

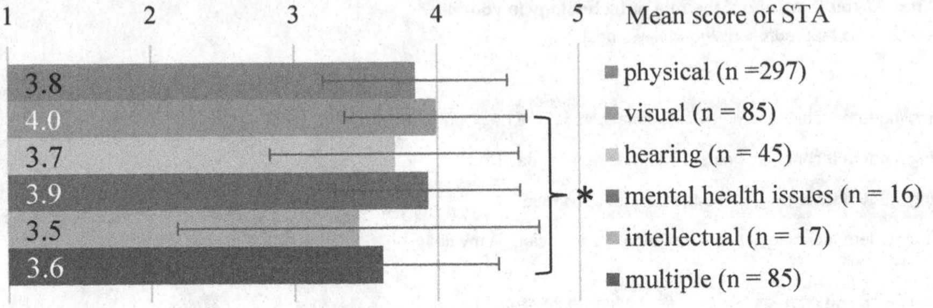

Fig. 2. Mean STA according to kind of disability. Significant differences are indicated by an asterisk ($p < .05$).

3.2 Use Intention for Emerging Technologies

Wearables, robots and location-based alerts were favored by the majority of respondents. A high use intention as stated by the selection of the option "frequently" or "always" was shown by 57.7% (n = 310) for wearables, 54% (n = 290) for robots, 47.1% (n = 253) for location-based alerts and 43,3% (n = 254) for augmented reality.

A descriptive analysis (Fig. 3) showed, that persons with multiple impairments showed a high use intention for all presented technologies, except accessible navigation systems that were deemed not applicable or unwilling to use them by 31.7% (n = 27). Persons with intellectual disabilities exhibited a high willingness to use to robots and a somewhat lower use intention to wearables and accessible navigation systems. Persons with mental health issues showed a similar high willingness to use for robots. Hearing-impaired individuals were particularly interested in artificial intelligence alerts and location-based alerts. Visually-impaired persons shared their high interest for artificial intelligence alerts and a furthermore showed a high willingness for accessible navigation systems and augmented reality. Persons with a physical impairment showed a high use intention for robots and wearables.

With regard to the relationship between the subjective technology adaptivity and the use intention for future assistive technologies, it was shown, that the correlation between the STA and the use intention was positive and significant for every assistive technology (Table 1). This implies that respondents who reported a higher subjective technology adaptivity are more willing to use the presented technologies in the future. A more detailed analysis regarding the effect disability on the relationship between STA and use intention based on linear regression showed, that the for physical impairments, the significant effect of STA on use intention remained appeared for all of the emerging mobility systems, but not for persons with mental health issues. As shown in Table 1, STA predicted the use intention for augmented reality for persons with physical ($r = .18, p = .001, f = .18$), visual ($r = .26, p = .015, f = .27$), and intellectual disabilities ($r = .48, p = .049, f = .55$), but not for the other groups. For respondents with multiple impairments, the significant relationship between STA and use intention was only shown for wearables ($r = .29$, $p = .007, f = .30$), and robots ($r = .22$, $p = .049, f = .23$). It should be emphasized, that the effect sizes of the relationship between the STA of persons with intellectual impairments and the use intention for AI-based alerts ($r = .55$,

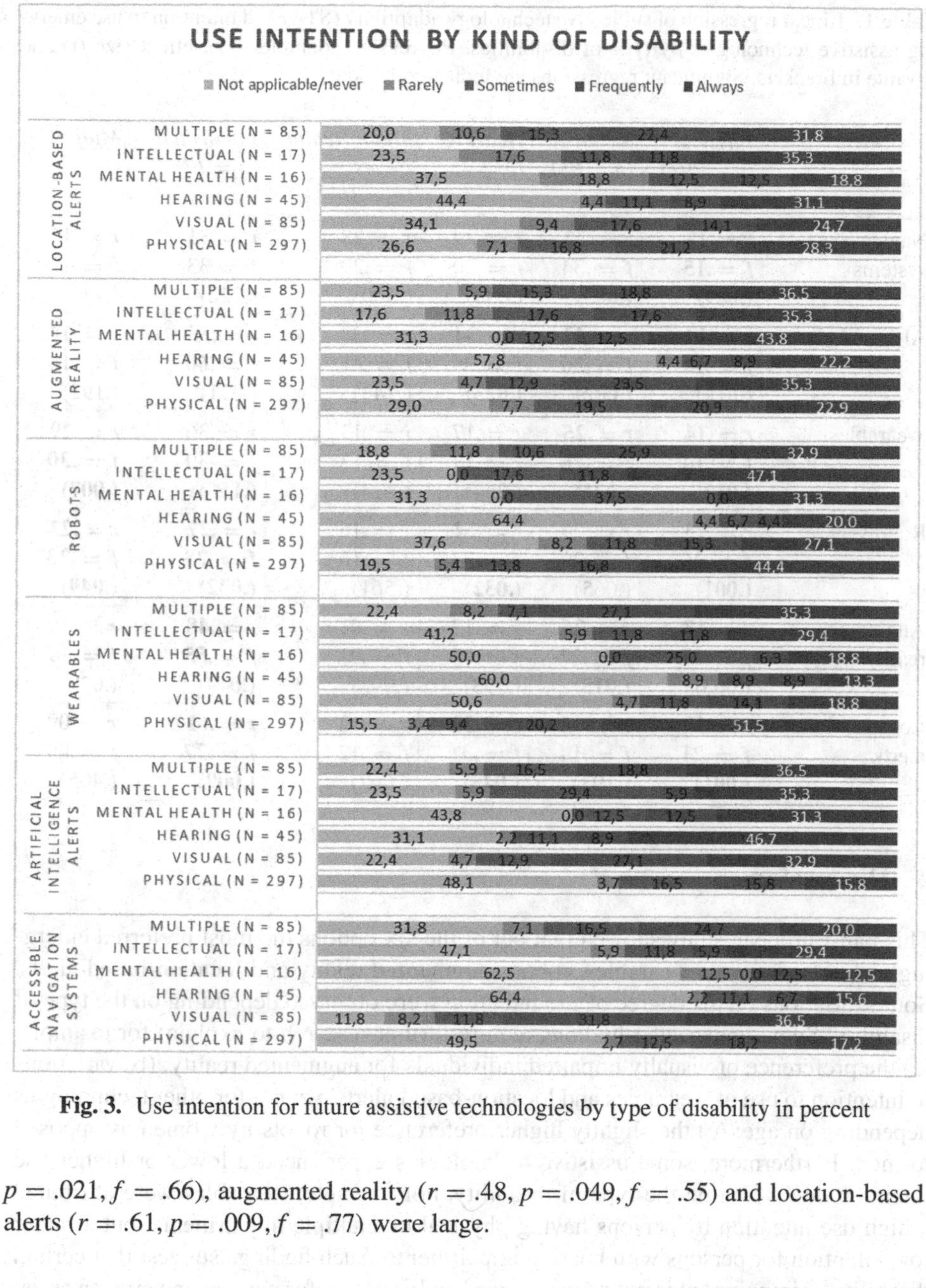

Fig. 3. Use intention for future assistive technologies by type of disability in percent

$p = .021, f = .66$), augmented reality ($r = .48, p = .049, f = .55$) and location-based alerts ($r = .61, p = .009, f = .77$) were large.

Table 1. Linear regression of subjective technology adaptivity (STA) and intention to use emerging assistive technologies by type of disabilities. Regression coefficient (r), effect size (f) and p-value in brackets. Significant regressions are indicated in bold.

	Physical (n = 297)	*Visual (n = 85)*	*Hearing (n = 45)*	*Ment. Health issues (n = 16)*	*Intellectual (n = 17)*	*Multiple (n = 85)*
Navigation systems	**r = .15 f = .15 (.009)**	**r = .32 f = .34 (.003)**	r = .29 f = .30 (.058)	r = .28 f = .29 (.300)	r = .31 f = .33 (.222)	r = .16 f = .16 (.141)
AI-based alerts	**r = .14 f = .14 (.019)**	**r = .34 f = .36 (.002)**	**r = .34 f = .36 (.023)**	r = .38 f = .41 (.143)	**r = .55 f = .66 (.021)**	r = .14 f = .14 (.192)
Wearables	**r = .14 f = .14 (.013)**	**r = .25 f = .26 (.021)**	r = .17 f = .17 (.254)	r = .13 f = .13 (.624)	r = .36 f = .39 (.155)	**r = .29 f = .30 (.007)**
Robots	**r = .25 f = .26 (.001)**	r = .20 f = .20 (.065)	**r = .32 f = .34 (.032)**	r = .16 f = .16 (.561)	**r = .27 f = .28 (.032)**	**r = .22 f = .23 (.049)**
Augmented reality	**r = .17 f = .17 (.003)**	**r = .26 f = .27 (.015)**	r = .13 f = .13 (.393)	r = .01 f = .01 (.998)	**r = .48 f = .55 (.049)**	r = .19 f = .19 (.078)
Location-based alerts	**r = .21 f = .21 (.001)**	r = .14 f = .14 (.193)	**r = .30 f = .31 (.043)**	r = .12 f = .12 (.667)	**r = .61 f = .77 (.009)**	r = .09 f = .09 (.405)

4 Discussion

This pan-European study showed that out of the six options the most preferred emerging technologies were wearables, robots, augmented reality and location-based alerts. Some variations on the degree of use intention were observed depending on the type of disability. Some unexpected findings require further research to explain; for example, (a) the preference of visually impaired individuals for augmented reality; (b) variations in intention to use of wearables and location-based alerts, yet not for other technologies depending on age; (c) the slightly higher preference for robots by women as opposed to men. Furthermore, some assistive technologies experienced a lower or higher use intention depending on the type of disability. For example, wearables were attributed a high use intention by persons having physical or multiple impairments, but a rather low intention for persons with hearing impairments. Such findings suggest that certain disability or impairment is not necessarily a key limitation for persons in using an assistive technology and perhaps other factors play an important role when it comes to use intention or alternative uses of such technologies are envisioned by users.

It was shown that the resulting STA was comparable to the mean STA of elderly in the study by [1]. However, the construct PAU showed a higher mean in this sample than in the group of elderly, indicating that persons with disabilities assess the perceived adaptive utility of technologies higher than elderly. However, comparable data of STA from a group of users who have no disability is still lacking.

With regard to the research question, it was shown that a disabled person's adaptivity to technology predicts the willingness to use emerging assistive technologies. However, the analyses indicate that the relationship depends on the type of disability and the kind of technology. Whereas STA was a significant predictor for the use intention of AI-based alters for people with physical, visual, hearing or intellectual impairments, it was not for people with mental health issues or multiple impairments. Interestingly, the effect sizes of the relationship between STA of people with intellectual impairments and the use intention for AI-based alerts, augmented reality and location-based alerts were high. It can be further concluded that the effect of subjective technology adaptivity on use intention for emerging mobility systems is not based on gender or age effects but more depending on the type of disability.

To conclude, our findings shed new light on the role of perceived technology adaptivity of persons with disability for future technology use intention. This may contribute to an improved understanding of psychological mechanisms of using technology and subsequently may result in a new view on the widespread deficit model of disability [12] and the rippled effects of the digital divide [13]. The results underline the importance of education for improving person's adaptivity to technology though equiping them with technological knowledge and improving their digital competences might help them to become more technical savvy and therefore, to be more open to new technology systems, which might help them to become more independent and overcome disability-related issues.

References

1. Kamin, S.T., Lang, F.R.: The subjective technology adaptivity inventory (STAI): A motivational measure of technology usage in old age. Gerontechnology **12**(1), 16–25 (2013)
2. Smith, P., Smith, L.: Artificial intelligence and disability: too much promise, yet too little substance? AI and Ethics **1**(1), 81–86 (2020). https://doi.org/10.1007/s43681-020-00004-5
3. Alshafeey, G.A., Lakulu, M.M., Chyad, M., Abdullah, A., Salem, G.: Augmented reality for the disabled: review articles. J. ICT Edu. **6**, 46–57 (2019)
4. Rashid, Z., Melià-Seguí, J., Pous, R., Peig, E.: Using augmented reality and internet of things to improve accessibility of people with motor disabilities in the context of smart cities. Futur. Gener. Comput. Syst. **76**, 248–261 (2016)
5. Selwyn, N.: Reconsidering political and popular understandings of the digital divide. New Media Soc. **6**(3), 341–362 (2004)
6. Bourdieu, P.: The forms of capital. In: Lauder, H., Brown, P., Stuart-Wells, A. (eds.) Education: Culture, Economy, Society. Halsey, pp. 46–58. Oxford University Press, Oxford (1997)
7. Seale, J.: When digital capital is not enough: reconsidering the digital lives of disabled university students. Learn. Media Technol. **38**(3), 256–269 (2013)
8. Kamin, S.T., Lang, F.R., Beyer, A.: Subjective technology adaptivity predicts technology use in old age. Gerontology **63**(4), 385–392 (2017)
9. Banes, D., et al.: D 3.4 report on assistive technologies trends impacts and related policies. Deliverable. https://trips-project.eu/wp-content/uploads/2020/10/TRIPS-D3.4-Report-on-Assistive-Technologies-Trends-Impacts-and-Related-Policies.pdf. Accessed 18 March 2022

10. Hatzakis, T.: D2.3 Quantitative survey report. Deliverable. https://trips-project.eu/wp-content/uploads/2021/04/D2.3-Quantitative-survey-report-1st-version-TRIPS.pdf. Accessed 18 March 2022
11. König, A., Seiler, A., Alčiauskaitė, L., Hatzakis, T.: A participatory qualitative analysis of barriers of public transport by persons with disabilities from seven European cities. J. Accessib. Design for All **11**(2), 295–321 (2021)
12. Dinishak, J.: The deficit view and its critics. Disab. Stud. Q. **36**(4), 5 (2016)
13. Stendal, K.: How do people with disability use and experience virtual worlds and ICT: a literature review. Virtu. Worlds Res. **5**(1), 1–12 (2012)

Towards Personalized Accessible Routing for People with Mobility Impairments

Alireza Darvishy(✉), Hans-Peter Hutter, and Roland Mosimann

Zurich University of Applied Sciences, 8400 Winterthur, Switzerland
{alireza.darvishy,hans-peter.hutter,roland.mosimann}@zhaw.ch

Abstract. This paper presents a vision for personalized accessible routing for people with mobility impairments and discusses which accessibility information is needed to realize this vision, such as curb cuts, inclination, path width, and additional information about various barriers. In a case study for the city of zurich, the paper first analyses how much of this accessibility information is available and in what quality in OpenStreetMap (OSM), and then investigates different approaches for collecting the missing accessibility data. This accessibility data can be used to implement novel routing apps for pedestrians with mobility impairments and can support city planners in considering future measures to improve urban accessibility. The main questions of this research are: What accessibility information is needed to allow for a personalized accessible routing? How can the missing accessibility data be collected efficiently? We suggest a methodology consisting of a combination of automated, semi-automated, crowd-based, and onsite data collection.

Keywords: Accessibility data · Accessible walking routes · People with mobility impairment · OpenStreetMap

1 Introduction

Mobility is an important aspect of a person's quality of life and independence. Many people, particularly people with disabilities and elderly persons, encounter everyday mobility barriers. For instance, a wheelchair user may not be able to take certain pedestrian routes due to a lack of curb cuts. A person using a walker may not be able to use a route that contains stairs, and an elderly person may have difficulties walking up sidewalks or roads that are too steep.

What's more, these barriers, combined with digital barriers, exclude many people from using mainstream mobility aids, like digital maps. Routing apps like Google Maps and services based on OpenStreetMap have embedded themselves into many people's daily lives, but none of these mainstream services reliably takes accessibility into account. As such, a route from A to B calculated by one of these apps may turn out to be completely inaccessible for a given user.

In 2006, the United Nations Convention on the Rights of Persons with Disabilities (CRPD) reaffirmed that all persons with disabilities must enjoy equal human rights and

K. Miesenberger et al. (Eds.): ICCHP-AAATE 2022, LNCS 13341, pp. 215–220, 2022.
https://doi.org/10.1007/978-3-031-08648-9_25

fundamental freedoms, including personal mobility [1]. This cannot be realized without equal access to digital maps and routing services.

We envision a mapping and routing service that automatically adapts to a user's accessibility needs. In order to offer such a service, two steps must be taken: First, it is necessary to collect key accessibility information, such as slope, sidewalk width, the presence of curb cuts, obstacles such as trees and poles, temporary barriers like construction sites, etc. The next step is to develop an algorithm that can use this information to calculate a personalized accessible route from point A to point B.

2 State of the Art in Accessible Routing

There are a number of research projects worldwide dealing with finding accessible walking routes. The University of Washington's Project Sidewalk, for example, invites people to virtually explore the Seattle region and validate accessibility features based on Google StreetView images [2]. The project website states that this data could be used to improve map routing accessibility. Another University of Washington group has developed AccessMap, a digital map which allows users to calculate routes from Point A to Point B in Seattle, taking into account slope and curb cuts [3]. The user can customize the settings by selecting maximum uphill and downhill slope, as well as indicating whether curb cuts are needed. Alternatively, the user can select one of the 3 preset profile types – wheelchair user, powered wheelchair user, or cane user – which have fixed slope and curb cut settings. A third such project is AccessPath, a project in the private sector which uses both manually collected and crowdsourced data to create accessible routing [4]. For this project, manual data is partially collected by a rolling device called PathMET, which aims to automatically measure features like sidewalk width and slope. At the current time of writing, this service still appears to be in development. To our knowledge, however, none of these mentioned projects provide their data publicly on open-source platforms such as OpenStreetMap or offer a routing that takes this information into account.

A potential open-source solution is offered by OpenRoutingService developed by HeiGIT, an online digital map which uses OpenStreetMap and other data sources to calculate routes from point A to point B, worldwide [5]. This service appears to allow users to enter accessibility criteria, such as maximum slope, maximum curb height and minimum sidewalk width. Unfortunately, for the vast majority of routes, no such data has actually been collected in the first place– as a result, the option to "customize" routing amounts to an illusion. Without alerting the user, the service actually ends up offering routes that do not fulfill the user's accessibility criteria, because it is missing the data to do so.

The most well-known open-source mapping project, OpenStreetMap [6], offers a public platform for collecting data, including accessibility information as well as various routing features. However, an investigation of the platform shows that there are very few accessibility-related data available on the platform. Furthermore, sidewalk information in OSM is often missing or only available as tags for road features, but no sidewalk measurements are available [7].

The well-known Google Maps offers a routing feature, but it only provides accessibility information in relation to public transportation for wheelchair users. For this, it uses publicly available accessibility information for certain bus, tram and train lines. Footpaths, however, are not guaranteed to be accessible.

Data within OSM is crowd-sourced. By nature, this data in more accurate and up to date in some regions than in others. In an ever-changing urban landscape, it is also never fully complete. For a reliable accessible footpath routing service, it is key to have up-to-date data such as slope and surface, and to make this data much more widely available.

3 Vision of Personalized Accessible Routing

Our vision for a personalized accessible routing is based on a user profile where the (dis-) abilities of the user can be specified, e.g. wheelchair width, maximum possible incline of a path, maximum step height, etc. With this information, the routing algorithm calculates the best route between two given points according to a specified criterion (e.g., distance or travel time). To that end, the routing algorithm needs detailed information about curb cuts, incline, step heights of stairs, surface characteristics, and path width, and other barriers. In order to streamline data collection and route calculations, only data will be gathered and considered that could actually present an accessibility issue, i.e. detailed path width data is not needed for every meter of sidewalk in the city – it only becomes relevant in spots where the path width is clearly below the recommended minimums.

For the outlined vision of a personalized accessible routing, certain OSM elements (described in Table 1) will require more information on specific features, e.g.:

- Height
- Curb-Style: Lowered/raised/flush/yes/no
- Presence/absence of ramps
- Ramp accessibility measurements (e.g. incline of the ramp)
- Presence of stairs/number of steps
- Individual step height
- How much space is left to pass a barrier: maxwidth:physical
- Minimum path width
- Maximum incline
- Surface type
- Smoothness

Table 1. OSM elements that need additional information for accessible routing

Element	Description
Curbs	Curbs appear along sidewalks. The routing must know whether a transition between sidewalk and street is blocked by a curb or is enabled by a curb cut. The most critical curbs are those at or near crossings
Steps	Steps occur along some pathways and are an obstacle for many pedestrians who rely on aids like wheelchairs or rollators. Some steps are accompanied by ramps that allows wheelchair users and others to pass. For the routing it is important to know where steps block a path and whether ramps are present
Barriers	Barriers can block the passing of vehicles or pedestrians. The routing must evaluate whether the user can pass the barrier, therefore only barriers that block the passage are considered relevant Includes: handrails, blocks, bump_gate, bus_trap, cattle_grid, cycle_barrier, debris, entrance, full-height_turnstile, gate, sliding_gate, hampshire_gate, horse_stile, kent_carriage_gap, kissing_gate, lift_gate, motorcycle_barrier, sally_port, spikes, stile, sump_buster, swing_gate, turnstile, wicket_gate, planter, yes, bollard, chain, jersey_barrier, tyres, curb, log, rope
Highway network	The highway network within OSM is broadly intended for all road users. The pedestrian network is a subset of this highway network. This selection of highways is taken from the OSM wiki about possible values on highways. The most critical information about highways that are useful to pedestrians are incline and the constitution of the surface Highway selection: - All highways with sidewalks on one or both sides - Residential Roads - Footways - Living streets - Service Roads - Pedestrian Zones - Tracks (Tracktype = g1) - Paths - Crossings - Elevators - Steps (separate)

4 Case Study Zurich

The case study of District 1 in Zurich seeks to better understand the efforts and methods needed to collect accessibility data for personalized routing. District 1 is the most heavily populated and frequented area of Zurich.

Status of Existing Accessibility Data in OSM

An analysis of the OSM data currently available for District 1 in the city of Zurich [7] reveals that the availability of accessibility data for the different OSM elements varies greatly, as it does in many other cities throughout Switzerland [8]. For instance, sidewalk surface type is recorded for 96% percent of the sidewalks, but sidewalk slope data is only available for 19% of segments. None of the "barrier"-type objects, such as gates and bollards, includes width information, i.e. the space left alongside, which would be needed to evaluate whether a given wheelchair can pass the barrier.

Data Collection Methodology

There are different possibilities for collecting the needed data. Some data will be derived from existing databases, e.g. incline information can be calculated from digital elevation models by swissALTI3D [9]. Other information, including step height or path width, can be measured remotely from detailed existing 3D street imagery [10].

The remaining missing information will be collected on-site via crowdsourcing through the following mobile apps:

- StreetComplete [11]: A mobile Android app used to complete selected tags on selected elements in OSM. Missing elements can be market with a note, that can be transformed into an element with a classical OSM editor like iD.
- AccessComplete [12]: A mobile app developed at ZHAW based on StreetComplete, with the addition that construction sites and other temporary barriers can be reported.

5 Conclusion

Collecting and maintaining detailed and up-to-date accessibility information is time-consuming and costly. As a result, important accessibility data is generally missing from publicly available mapping databases such as OSM, which presents an obstacle to many people with disabilities who might wish to use such services. This paper outlines the information needed to fill the gaps, and envisions a routing algorithm that can incorporate this data and provide personalized accessible paths from Point A to Point B, based on a user's specific mobility parameters. In order to collect this information as thoroughly and efficiently as possible, a blended approach is suggested, combining the exploitation of existing databases wherever possible with app-based crowdsourcing and manual data collection. Future works should additionally investigate the use of AI techniques to automate data collection as much as possible.

References

1. https://www.ohchr.org/en/hrbodies/crpd/pages/crpdindex.aspx
2. Saha, M., et al.: Project sidewalk: a web-based crowdsourcing tool for collecting sidewalk accessibility data at scale. In: CHI 2019: Proceedings of the 2019 CHI Conference on Human Factors in Computing Systems. Paper No.: 62, pp. 1–14, May 2019

3. Bolten, N., Caspi, A.: AccessMap website demonstration: individualized, accessible pedestrian trip planning at scale. In: The 21st International ACM SIGACCESS Conference on Computers and Accessibility (ASSETS 2019). Association for Computing Machinery, New York, NY, USA, pp. 676–678 (2019)
4. Sinagra, E.: Development of pathNav: A Pedestrian Navigation Tool that Utilizes Smart Data for Improved Accessibility and Walkability (No. Transit IDEA Project 87) (2019)
5. Open Route Service: https://openrouteservice.org/
6. Open Street Map: https://openstreetmap.org
7. Mobasheri, A.: OSM quality enrichment for wheelchair routing. PhD thesis. University of Heidelberg (2021)
8. Analysis of OSM data for accessible routing: https://colab.research.google.com/drive/1izbSSx4A12MFCOqxpPgRkivcBt4HuA6g
9. https://colab.research.google.com/drive/1STHM--XhrR7yaPm7OQFdLPCqBBRKsEJS?usp=sharing
10. SwissALTI3D Tool: https://www.swisstopo.admin.ch/en/geodata/height/alti3d.html
11. iNovitas Infra3D Service: https://www.inovitas.ch/en/products/overview
12. StreetComplete (open-source app): https://github.com/streetcomplete/StreetComplete
13. AccessComplete (open-source app): https://github.com/ZPAC-UZH/AccessComplete

Traveling to Unknown Buildings: Accessibility Features for Indoor Maps

Angela Constantinescu[1(✉)], Karin Müller[1(✉)], Claudia Loitsch[2], Sebastian Zappe[3], and Rainer Stiefelhagen[1]

[1] Karlsruhe Insitute of Technology, Karlsruhe, Germany
{angela.constantinescu,karin.e.mueller,rainer.stiefelhagen}@kit.edu
[2] Technische Universität Dresden, Dresden, Germany
claudia.loitsch@tu-dresden.de
[3] Sozialhelden e.V., Berlin, Germany
sebastian@sozialhelden.de

Abstract. Traveling independently to unknown buildings is difficult for people with disabilities, as there is a lack of information about accessibility of indoor environments. In particular, there are hardly any freely available indoor maps of public buildings. In this paper, we address the problem that there is no comprehensive list of information relevant to people with disabilities in indoor environments, which in turn can be used for indoor orientation and navigation systems.

We therefore collected in an extensive literature review around 820 indoor accessibility features relevant for people with disabilities. These were categorized and sorted in a database and mapped to OSM and A11yJSON. The database is publicly available and can serve as a basis for tag proposals to OSM, and as Linked Data (RDF).

Keywords: Accessibility · Indoor environments · Accessibility features

1 Introduction

Mobility is regarded as a core element of our society and is associated with freedom, particularly in the area of leisure [34]. But mobility is also taken for granted in the working environment: not everyone can travel to a meeting or conference at their will or even stay there overnight. People with disabilities, for instance, do not have the opportunity to freely choose their destinations, as many parts of the travel chain are not accessible [16,38]. One reason for this is that information about the buildings en route and at the destination is fragmentary.

Although there are many applications for outdoor environments, there is a great lack of knowledge about indoor accessibility [15]. Especially the knowledge about barriers and facilitators in a building is essential for orientation and navigation in indoor spaces. Data formats to describe physical accessibility exist, but a broadly used international standard is still lacking. Searching for this information requires a lot of time and is often not possible without help [15,33].

K. Miesenberger et al. (Eds.): ICCHP-AAATE 2022, LNCS 13341, pp. 221–228, 2022.
https://doi.org/10.1007/978-3-031-08648-9_26

However, a recent study showed that users with disabilities would like to navigate more independently [28] and would rather use technical applications while traveling [15].

Therefore, information about indoor environments in particular should be made available to people with disabilities to enable travel to unfamiliar buildings.

The general goal of this work is to improve orientation and mobility of people with different disabilities in buildings, by creating the prerequisites for accessibility information to be entered into indoor maps. Thus, we did an extensive literature review to collect accessibility criteria, features and hazards. Our main focus was on people with mobility and visual impairments. However, we gathered accessibility features for people with other disabilites as well if they were mentioned in our search results. We synchronized them in a database with features from Open Data approaches, namely OpenStreetMap (OSM) and A11yJSON, to reveal criteria that could not yet be mapped. The most important features will be proposed to OSM, and we will provide remaining ones as Linked Data.

2 Previous Work

In general, people with disabilities need information about a building and how to get to certain points inside it, in order to navigate well. However, to date there are only few indoor navigation applications [36], as: (1) localization in buildings is a problem, which is often solved by installing additional hardware such as beacons [23,29]; (2) there are hardly any indoor maps publicly available [40]; (3) indoor information relevant to people with disabilities can only be partially mapped so far, as many features have not been provided for.

A prerequisite for the development of indoor applications is that suitable information must be collected and defined [7]. This map-based information can be expressed by accessibility features of buildings. We define accessibility features in this context as anything that can either help or impede users with disability to orient themselves and navigate in indoor environments. For instance, [31] started to collect accessibility features such as hallways, stairways, doorways, ramps and elevators relevant for navigation of people with mobility impairments (MI) from various sources in IndoorGML, whereas [32] focused on people with visual impairments (VI).

With Semantic Web and Linked Open Data (LOD), the web has evolved from linked documents to a knowledge base where single data records are linkable as well [4], enabling queries on almost any kind of data, or to infer facts with technologies such as RDF, OWL or SPARQL. For the indoor domain, an ontology using LOD was developed by Simon-Nagy and Fleiner to support indoor navigation and to describe accessibility-relevant objects in buildings, in particular to describe width, height or quantity of objects [39]. Others investigated the adoption of ontologies for semantic routing requests [2,9], or specified an indoor navigation ontology to model movements of production assets [37]. While there are popular ontologies for discovering places of interest like the STI Accommodation Ontology [17,22] that has been integrated into the schema.org vocabulary, thus far, describing and connecting data about indoor environments with Semantic Web technologies (i.e. with LOD) has not been comprehensively addressed for the accessibility domain.

3 Literature Review on Accessibility Features

The main purpose of this literature review was to find accessibility features for indoor environments relevant to people with VI and MI. A first and quick review of literature beginning of 2020 yielded 15 studies containing indoor accessibility features [5,6,8,10,13,14,18,20,21,24,25,30,35,41,42]. Since we were not confident that we had found all relevant features, we searched various literature databases (Google Scholar, Science Direct, IEEExplore, SpringerLink, ACM DL) and Google Search to see whether a systematic literature review had already been performed. The keywords searched were: systematic, review, orientation, accessibility, indoor. Given that no relevant results were found, we concluded that such a systematic review most likely does not exist. We thus conducted a systematic literature review ourselves in April 2020.

Keyword Analysis. First, we performed a keyword analysis of already known, relevant literature. We searched five databases (ACM DL, SpringerLink, IEEExplore, ScienceDirect and Web of Science) and found 397 studies using the following final combination of keywords (see Table 1): *orientation AND ("visual impairment" OR "mobility impairment") AND indoor AND requirements AND unfamiliar AND map.*

Title and Abstract Analysis. In the next step, titles and abstracts of these studies were analyzed. Studies that obviously did not address orientation and/or mobility, navigation, or spatial awareness for people with VI and MI in indoor environments were discarded. Moreover, studies for which we could not get access to the full text were also excluded at this stage. Applying these criteria, 45 studies were found to be possibly relevant: 32 from ACM DL, 12 from SpringerLink and 1 from ScienceDirect.

Full Text Analysis. The full text of these 45 studies was analyzed according to the following inclusion/exclusion criteria:

Inclusion criteria: (1) Deals with VI or MI; AND (2) Mentions indoor features that affect orientation and/or mobility of one of the target groups.

Exclusion criteria: (1) Does not mention any accessibility features; (2) Duplicate; (3) A more relevant study by the same authors or project was already included.

Results of Literature Review. In the end, only 6 studies [3,11,12,36,43,44] contained accessibility features for people with VI or MI. Another 3 studies [26,27,32] were found in the references during the full text analysis, and 2 studies [1,19] were found during the systematic literature review, but with alternative searches, i.e. using different keywords. We also added the 15 sources found previously with the non-systematic search, giving a total of 26 studies. This final list contains both architectural standards and checklists [5,14,18], and research

Table 1. **(a)** Number of studies found in the five databases. **(b)** Number of relevant studies found for each target group in the three searches performed: simple, systematic and systematic review with alternative keywords. ALL: all disabilities; VI: visual impairment; MI: mobility impairment; *3 studies addressed both VI and MI, so they are counted twice in the total.

(a) Number of studies per database

Database	Number of studies
ACM DL	238
SpringerLink	128 (20 preview-only)
IEEExplore	0
ScienceDirect	31
Web of Science	0
	397 studies

(b) Number of studies per group

Search	ALL	VI	MI
Simple	4	5+3*	3+3*
Systematic	–	8	1
Systematic-alt.	–	2	–
Total	4	18*	7*

projects. When reviewing the latter, we considered end user involvement. The papers considered report comprehensive user studies with up to 53 [36], 95 [1] or even 120 endusers, namely people with disabilities [6].

Since some of the studies found addressed all disabilities (including e.g. hearing or cognitive impairments), without mentioning which features addressed which disability, we decided to create a single "complete" list for all disability types in order to keep track of all accessibility features.

4 Database of Accessibility Features for Maps

From our literature review described above, we obtained more than 820 indoor accessibility features and sub-features relevant for people with disabilities such as *door signs for next accessible entrance, automatic opening/closing mechanism of doors* or *car control buttons in Braille in elevators*. The complete list can be downloaded[1]. All features were translated to English, synonyms were merged, and finally categorized to the following nine categories: *way to building, general building information, building geometry, facility daily needs, general help for orientation, change of elevation, change in ground height, movables* and *security*. We found that other ways of categorization are difficult. For instance, a categorization in *dangerous* and *useful* is not possible in our case, because what is useful to a person in a wheelchair might be dangerous to a blind person. Besides, assessments such as *accessible, dangerous, useful* are very individual, even within the same user category.

Hierarchical Features. We noticed that some features were hierarchical (e.g. Stairs - handrail - location of handrail), others were categorized according to the particular interest of their authors, so we decided to create a hierarchical representation: category-feature-property. The categories emerged naturally after looking at the features. We took from all sources those categories that matched our data. After introducing all data, further levels in the hierarchy appeared: sub-properties and even sub-sub-properties.

[1] https://services.access.kit.edu/accessibility-features.

Structural Elements with Many Features. The building elements that have most features are *toilets* (97 features), *doorways* (90) and *rooms* (90), followed by *elevator* (64), *movables and furniture* (54), *signage* (53), *stairs* (45) and *floor/pathway* (40). Around 16% of the features describe dimensions such as height, width, length of paths, which are particularly relevant for people using wheelchairs, but also partly for people with blindness. Knowing the height of a doorbell or a towel dispenser in a restroom, for instance, makes it easier to find its exact location.

Difficult Features for Mapping. Besides the obvious architectural features such as dimensions and physical properties of building elements and movables, we also found some other interesting accessibility features, such as *audio* and *olfactory cues*, *quality of lighting* or *high contrast design*. Some of these features are difficult to map in solutions such as OSM, because they cannot be associated to a point or area in space, are ephemeral or cannot be measured. Especially the issue of measurement concerns several features. Other features such as *opening hours* could be mapped in the description of the building.

Analysis of OSM. Since we wanted to know which accessibility features can be mapped in OSM, we aligned the data to OSM features. Apart from dimensions, we found that another 16.3 % of the features can already be mapped in OSM. Some of them can be defined by using multiple OSM keys and tags. For instance, glass door can be described by *door=yes* and *material=glass*. Or, *maneuvering clearance in front of the ramp* can be expressed by *ramp=yes* and the space in front of the ramp by *width=x* and *length=y*. However, other tags need to be newly created, such as for reception or information desk, which are extremely important for people with VI for getting help on site. We are also currently building a user interface for our database to allow querying with query languages like SPARQL or Jekyll. As soon as it is available, we will publish it on our Website.

5 Discussion

In this section, we discuss limitations and describe lessons learned.

Bias towards Visual Impairment. Our study could be biased towards VI because of the original focus of our approach. Since it is possible that we have missed features, we encourage other experts to add to the list to help standardize accessibility features.

Language. Inconsistent domain vocabulary between the studies analyzed is an obstacle, as well as non-professional translations to English. Thus, concepts in our feature database might appear as duplicated synonyms.

Literature Reviews in Interdisciplinary Fields. Our systematic review yielded fewer results than expected, probably due to the unique search performed. We therefore recommend adapting keywords to each database and performing a complementary search in the best conference proceedings and journals in the different fields.

Mobility Impairment. We recommend not using "mobility impairment" for literature search, since it is often used in the context of VI instead of physical disability. We obtained better results when searching for "wheelchair", although not covering other mobility impairments.

Hierarchical Representation of Data. Our features include concepts that recur at different positions and levels in the table, with partially different subproperties. One example are signposts, which are scattered over 11 features. This shows that a hierarchical representation is not best suitable for our data. A better representation could be a flat or object-oriented one with "has" or "is" relationships, like in A11yJSON[2].

Profiles. Our categories can be used to filter profiles in future mobile applications for indoor orientation and navigation. Thus, they should not be excluded. A combination of a flat representation and category assignments could offer most advantages.

6 Conclusions and Future Work

In this work, we collected accessibility features for buildings for people with different disabilities, sorted them and aligned them with freely available features from OpenStreetMap and A11yJSON. While some of the features can be already expressed in OSM, others need to be submitted to OSM or published as LinkedData. Our database is a step forward towards the standardisation of indoor accessibility features, which will help owners to record the accessibility of their buildings more easily. Moreover, the features can serve as a basis for future mobility and orientation systems for people with disabilities. Finally, end users with disabilities will be able to make more informed decisions and travel to more accessible buildings.

Acknowledgements. We would like to thank Hanna Henke, Vanessa Petrausch and Gerhard Jaworek. The project is funded by the German Federal Ministry of Labour and Social Affairs (BMAS) under the grant number 01KM151112.

References

1. Alkhanifer, A., Ludi, S.: Towards a situation awareness design to improve visually impaired orientation in unfamiliar buildings: requirements elicitation study. In: Requirements Engineering Conference (RE) (2014)
2. Anagnostopoulos, C., et al.: OntoNav: a semantic indoor navigation system. In: SME 2005 (2005)
3. Banovic, N., et al.: Uncovering information needs for independent spatial learning for users who are visually impaired. In: ASSETS '13 (2013)
4. Bizer, C., et al.: Linked data: the story so far. In: Semantic Services, Interoperability and Web Applications: Emerging Concepts. IGI global (2011)

[2] https://a11yjson.org/ Retrieved on 23 June 2021.

5. Center, N.E.A.: ADA Checklist for Existing Facilities (2016)
6. Charitakis, K., Papadopoulos, K.: ATMAPS. User Requirements Specifications Report. In: Project ATMAPS: Specification of symbols used on audio-tactile maps for individuals with blindness (2017). https://www.atmaps.eu/deliverables/ATMAPS-D_2_1-User_requirements_and_specifications_report.pdf
7. Ding, C., et al.: A survey of open accessibility data. In: W4All, pp. 1–4 (2014)
8. Ding, D., et al.: Design considerations for a personalized wheelchair navigation system. In: EMBC '07 (2007)
9. Dudas, P.M., Ghafourian, M., Karimi, H.A.: ONALIN: ontology and algorithm for indoor routing. In: MDM 2009 (2009)
10. Dzafic, D., et al.: Towards an indoor traffic report-requirements for dynamic route planning for wheelchair users. In: IPIN 2012 (2012)
11. Fallah, N., et al.: The user as a sensor: navigating users with visual impairments in indoor spaces using tactile landmarks. In: CHI '12 (2012)
12. Goldschmidt, M.: Orientation and mobility training to people with visual impairments. In: Pissaloux, E., Velázquez, R. (eds.) Mobility of Visually Impaired People, pp. 237–261. Springer, Cham (2018). https://doi.org/10.1007/978-3-319-54446-5_8
13. Gomez, J., et al.: Navigating the workplace environment as a visually impaired person. In: UAHCI '16 (2016)
14. Grohmann, C., et al.: Kriterienkatalog zur Bewertung der baulichen Inklusion an Hochschulen. Sozial- und Gesundheitsbauten, Professur für Gebäudelehre und Entwerfen der Universität Dresden (2018)
15. Gupta, M., et al.: Towards more universal wayfinding technologies: navigation preferences across disabilities. In: CHI 2020 (2020)
16. Hara, K., et al.: The design of assistive location-based technologies for people with ambulatory disabilities: a formative study. In: CHI '16 (2016)
17. Hepp, M.: Accommodation ontology language reference. Technical report, Hepp Research GmbH, Innsbruck (2013)
18. Holfeld, M.: Barrierefreie Lebensräume: Bauen and Wohnen ohne Hindernisse. 2. überarbeitete Auflage. Beuth. DIN e.V. (2011)
19. Ivanov, R.: An approach for developing indoor navigation systems for visually impaired people using building information modeling. JAISE **9**(4), 449–467 (2017)
20. Jaunich, P.: m4guide-mobile multi-modal mobility guide AP 820. Auswertung der Befragung zur Ausgangssituation und den Anforderungen der Nutzer. BLIC (January 2014)
21. Jeamwatthanachai, W., et al.: Indoor navigation by blind people: behaviors and challenges in unfamiliar spaces and buildings. BJVI **5**, 140–153 (2019)
22. Kärle, E., Fensel, A., Toma, I., Fensel, D.: Why are there more hotels in Tyrol than in Austria? Analyzing schema.org usage in the hotel domain. In: Inversini, A., Schegg, R. (eds.) Information and Communication Technologies in Tourism 2016, pp. 99–112. Springer, Cham (2016). https://doi.org/10.1007/978-3-319-28231-2_8
23. Kim, J.E., Bessho, M., Kobayashi, S., Koshizuka, N., Sakamura, K.: Navigating visually impaired travelers in a large train station using smartphone and bluetooth low energy. In: SASC '16 (2016)
24. KIT and IOSB: Das System SmartCampus und das Projekt SmartCampus barrierefrei (2015). https://cm.tm.kit.edu/smartcampus.php. Accessed 18 June 2021
25. Mayordomo-Martínez, D., et al.: Sustainable accessibility: a mobile app for helping people with disabilities to search accessible shops. IJERPH **16**(4), 620 (2019)
26. McIntyre, L.: The way-finding journey within a large public building: a user centred study of the holistic way-finding experience across a range of visual ability. Ph.D. thesis, Univ. Dundee (2011)

27. Meyers, A.R., et al.: Barriers, facilitators, and access for wheelchair users: sbstantive and methodologic lessons from a pilot study of environmental effects. Soc. Sci. Med. **55**(8), 1435–1446 (2002)
28. Müller, K., Engel, C., Loitsch, C., Stiefelhagen, R., Weber, G.: Traveling more independently: a study on the diverse needs and challenges of people with visual or mobility impairments in unfamiliar indoor environments. ACM Trans. Access. Comput. **15**(2), 1–44 (2022). just accepted
29. Murata, M., Ahmetovic, D., Sato, D., Takagi, H., Kitani, K.M., Asakawa, C.: Smartphone-based indoor localization for blind navigation across building complexes. In: 2018 IEEE International Conference on Pervasive Computing and Communications (PerCom) (2018)
30. Park, J., et al.: Investigating the barriers in a typical journey by public transport users with disabilities. J. Transp. Health **10**, 361–368 (2018)
31. Park, S., Yu, K., Kim, J.: Data model for indoorgml extension to support indoor navigation of people with mobility disabilities. ISPRS Int. J. Geo-Inf. **9**(2) (2020)
32. Pérez, J.E., et al.: Assessment of semantic taxonomies for blind indoor navigation based on a shopping center use case. In: W4A 2017 (2017)
33. Quinones, P.A., Greene, T., Yang, R., Newman, M.: Supporting visually impaired navigation: a needs-finding study. In: CHI EA '11 (2011)
34. Sager, T.: Freedom as mobility: implications of the distinction between actual and potential travelling. Mobilities **1**(3), 465–488 (2006)
35. Saha, M., et al.: Closing the gap: designing for the last-few-meters wayfinding problem for people with visual impairments. In: ASSETS 2019 (2019)
36. Sato, D., et al.: NavCog3: an evaluation of a smartphone-based blind indoor navigation assistant with semantic features in a large-scale environment. In: ASSETS '17 (2017)
37. Scholz, J., Schabus, S.: An indoor navigation ontology for production assets in a production environment. In: Duckham, M., Pebesma, E., Stewart, K., Frank, A.U. (eds.) GIScience 2014. LNCS, vol. 8728, pp. 204–220. Springer, Cham (2014). https://doi.org/10.1007/978-3-319-11593-1_14
38. Shi, L., et al.: Understanding leisure travel motivations of travelers with acquired mobility impairments. Tour. Manag. **33**(1), 228–231 (2012)
39. Simon-Nagy, G., Fleiner, R.: Ontology extension for personalized accessible indoor navigation. In: Luca, D., Sirghi, L., Costin, C. (eds.) INTER-ACADEMIA 2017. AISC, vol. 660, pp. 281–288. Springer, Cham (2018). https://doi.org/10.1007/978-3-319-67459-9_35
40. Striegl, J., et al.: Analysis of indoor maps accounting the needs of people with impairments. In: ICCHP '20 (2020)
41. Thapar, N., et al.: A pilot study of functional access to public buildings and facilities for persons with impairments. Disabil. Rehabil. **26**, 280–289 (2004)
42. TUD: Ergebnis aus der Anforderungsanalyse AP2 (TUD): Konzeptionelles Datenmodell Version 4. Technical report, Projekt MOBILITY: Mobile zugängliche Lagepläne
43. Williams, M.A., et al.: Better supporting blind pedestrians and blind navigation technologies through accessible architecture. In: Designing Around People, pp. 237–246. Springer, Cham (2016). https://doi.org/10.1007/978-3-319-29498-8_25
44. Yang, R., et al.: Supporting spatial awareness and independent wayfinding for pedestrians with visual impairments. In: ASSETS 2011 (2011)

Acquiring Surrounding Visual Information Without Actively Taking Photos for People with Visual Impairment

Masakazu Iwamura[1(✉)], Takaaki Kawai[2], Keigo Takashima[2], Kazunori Minatani[3], and Koichi Kise[1]

[1] Graduate School of Informatics, Osaka Metropolitan University, Sakai, Japan
{masa.i,kise}@omu.ac.jp

[2] Graduate School of Engineering, Osaka Prefecture University, Sakai, Japan
sbb01097@st.osakafu-u.ac.jp

[3] The National Center for University Entrance Examinations, Tokyo, Japan
minatani@rd.dnc.ac.jp

Abstract. Recent advancements in recognition technology allow people with visual impairment to obtain visual information from their surroundings using smartphone apps and assistive devices. This paper points out a problem with this approach that has not attracted much attention. That is, the user is required to actively take a photo, which is not always easy for people with visual impairment. To address this problem, in contrast to the current standard approach, which we call active information acquisition, we propose passive information acquisition (PIA), which does not require the user to actively take a photo. However, PIA creates a new problem: the app tends to transfer too much information to the user. Therefore, this paper explores better ways for people with visual impairment toward obtaining only the desired visual information in PIA. Specifically, we experimented with nine people with visual impairment to evaluate seven information transmission methods, including information summarization and interactive communication methods.

Keywords: People with visual impairment · Object detection · Summarization · Information selection · Passive information acquisition

1 Introduction

Recognition technology has been employed to function as an eye for people with visual impairment in order to obtain visual information from their surroundings (e.g., [8,12–14]). It has been installed on smartphone apps (e.g., Seeing AI, Envision AI, and TapTapSee) and assistive devices (e.g., OrCam MyEye2 and Envision Glasses) as an indispensable tool. The tacit preconditions of using such apps and devices, however, require the user to actively take a photo using three steps:

K. Miesenberger et al. (Eds.): ICCHP-AAATE 2022, LNCS 13341, pp. 229–240, 2022.
https://doi.org/10.1007/978-3-031-08648-9_27

they must (1) notice a target object or textual information, (2) know its location, (3) take a picture by aiming their camera at that location. We call this standard framework *active information acquisition (AIA)*. A fundamental question that arises here is whether people with visual impairment can notice information around them and determine its location. Even if they succeed in determining the location, it is easy to predict that they will often face the difficulty of taking an appropriate picture for the recognition technology [4,7,9,11,16,19]. Thus, actively taking a photo is not always possible for people with visual impairment. However, this significant problem has not attracted much attention.

This paper focuses on the issue and introduces a new framework that enables the user to acquire the visual information from the user's surroundings without actively taking a photo. In contrast to the conventional AIA framework, we call the new framework *passive information acquisition (PIA)*. A possible method to actualize the PIA framework is to constantly photograph the user's surroundings and recognize all of them; constant recording by a camera (preferably, a wide field-of-view camera) can capture the user's surroundings to which the user is not easily able to pay attention. As a consequence, however, the user obtains a huge amount of surrounding visual information, which is substantially larger than the amount of those that can be processed by a conventional AIA framework. If such a large amount of information were constantly described, the user would be overwhelmed. Let us take the concrete example of object detection. Suppose that ten objects are detected every second through the constant recording and recognition; after one minute, 600 objects have been detected. This amount of information is too much to describe. However, it is likely that the same objects are detected multiple times. Therefore, if such duplication is suppressed by a summarization technique (say, *temporal summarization*), the amount of information conveyed to the user is greatly reduced. Even if the objects are not the same, some could be categorized into the same category, such as "drink bottles." In this case, instead of describing the name of each product, saying "drink bottles" would be more concise. We call this approach *semantic summarization*. These examples indicate that information summarization is crucial in the PIA framework. In this paper, we implemented the naive method (without using information summarization) and three information summarization methods, as shown in Fig. 1.

The discussion above opens the door to another problem that has been overlooked: when using the apps and devices, the user must keep listening to the voice verbally describing the recognition results, even though most of them are not meaningful to the user. Let us imagine that ten objects have been detected. Then, the user needs to evaluate the information about each of the ten objects one by one. In contrast to the behavior of sighted people, who can focus on the information of interest without evaluating everything in their sight, the current approach of the apps is far from efficient. A possible solution to this problem is to introduce *interactive communication*; the user requests information from the app, and then the app tells the requested information to the user. We use a question answering (QA) system to realize it. We prepared three interactive com-

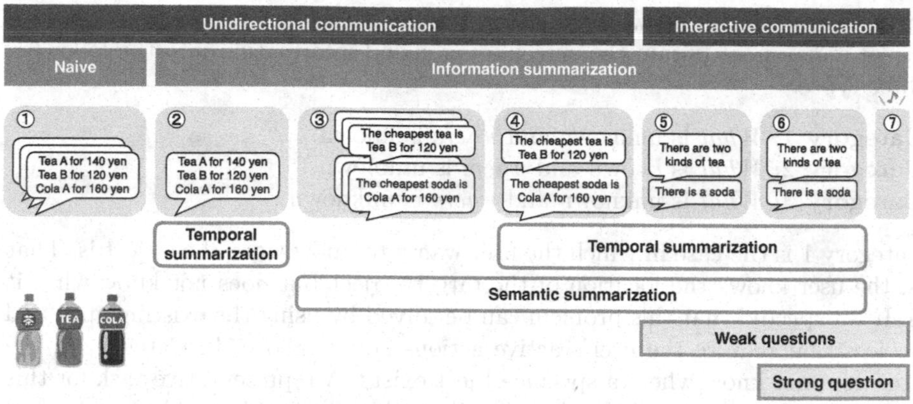

Fig. 1. Overview of the seven information transmission methods evaluated in the user study. Four unidirectional communication methods were designed to examine all four combinations of with/without temporal/semantic summarization. Three interactive communication methods are primarily compared with ④, which was the best among the four unidirectional communication methods in the subjective evaluation. In the figure, we present an example in which three drink bottles are recognized. Methods ① through ⑥ verbally describe the recognition results following the policy of each method. Method ⑦ does not verbally describe the recognition results. Instead, it just plays a ping sound to let the user know the system recognized something. If the user wants to know what it is, the user can ask the system. Otherwise, the user can ignore it. Methods ⑤, ⑥, and ⑦ accept weak questions. The weak questions do not directly ask which product is cheapest, but by combining the answers of the questions, the user can obtain the information about the cheapest product. Methods ⑥ and ⑦ also accept a strong question that directly asks which product is cheapest. Note that in the experiment, we used the names of actual products instead of abstract expressions such as "Tea A."

munication methods, as shown in Fig. 1. Note that we call the methods that do not use interactive communication, such as the four methods introduced above, *unidirectional communication* by contrast.

In this paper, as a test bed of the PIA framework, we implemented a voice guidance system using a wearable camera with a wide field-of-view lens. It is equipped with the functions of the seven information summarization and interactive communication methods. We experimentally evaluated the seven methods with nine people with visual impairment.

2 Related Work

We have introduced an idea related to the PIA framework [8]. In it, we consider two questions: "What is the object?" and "Where is the object?" The answers to the questions are limited to either *known* or *unknown*. For simplicity, let us denote "what the object is" by *what* and "where the object is" by *where*. Then, on the basis of their answers, we categorize the situations in which people with visual impairment obtain the surrounding visual information into the following three types.

Category 1: *What* is unknown and *where* is known.
Category 2: *What* is known and *where* is unknown.
Category 3: *What* is unknown and *where* is unknown.

Category 1 is the case in which the user wants to know what the object is. That is, the user knows the location of the target object but does not know what it is. It is expected that this problem can be solved by using the existing apps and devices that require the user's active actions stated above. In Category 2, the user does not know where a specific object exists. A representative task for this category is finding something. As a possible solution for this problem, a method that uses an omnidirectional camera has been considered [8]. In Category 3, the recognition target is unknown, so the user has no clues about its location. One example of this situation occurs when the user comes across unexpected information while walking around town. Among three categories, Category 1 corresponds to the AIA framework, and Categories 2 and 3 correspond to the PIA framework.

In the rest of this section, we survey existing approaches to summarize information obtained from recognition techniques.

Pseudo-visual Attention Approach: Sighted people instantly evaluate the importance of information coming in through their eyes. If the visual attention mechanism of sighted people could be reproduced on a computer, only the important information would be selected and summarized. Some visual attention mechanisms have been modeled [3,15,18].

Information Recommendation Approach: Information recommendation provides information derived from the user's preferences [5,17]. However, it requires a large amount of data to estimate the user's preferences.

Information Theory Approach: Bracha et al. [2] proposed an information theoretic approach, which is an unsupervised method to determine which label should be given priority in order to increase the amount of information.

QA Approach: In the QA approach, the user should be able to directly ask for any information needed. As related work, visual QA (also known as VQA) returns the correct answer when presented with an image and a question related to the image [1,6,10].

3 User Study

We asked nine people with visual impairment (six with complete blindness and three with low vision) to perform a pseudo-shopping task. The detailed profiles

Table 1. Participants' demographic information.

ID	Age	Sex	Visual impairment	Onset age
P1	36	F	Totally blind	15
P2	30	M	Totally blind	0
P3	27	F	Totally blind	3
P4	28	F	Light perception	0
P5	35	M	Low vision (left: light perception, right:0.01)	20
P6	31	F	Low vision (left: 0, right: 0.01)	18
P7	27	M	Totally blind	5
P8	47	M	Totally blind	20
P9	57	M	Low vision (left&right: 0.02, visual field: 10°)	42

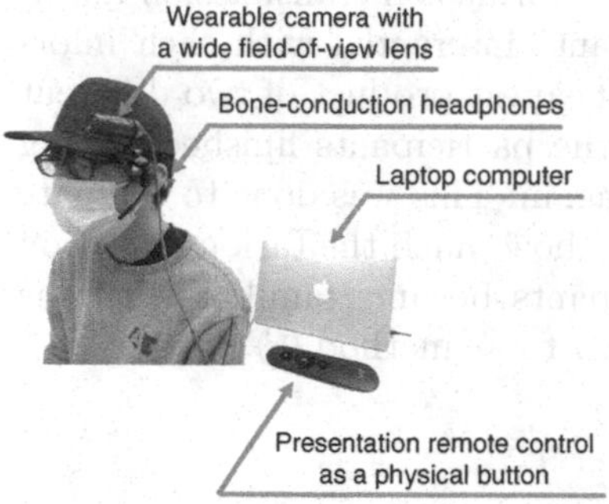

Fig. 2. Voice guidance system.

Fig. 3. Snapshot of the experiment.

of the participants are shown in Table 1. For quantitative evaluation, we asked them to perform the task of finding the cheapest product with the support of a voice guidance system, as shown in Fig. 2. The voice guidance system recognizes registered products every frame and basically reads aloud the names and prices of the recognized products. In the voice guidance system, we implemented seven information transmission methods that tell the user the recognition results differently, as shown in Fig. 1. Methods ⑤, ⑥, and ⑦ accept the following four weak questions: "What are the products that have been recognized?," "How much is (product name)?," "What are the categories that have been recognized?," and "What is the cheapest (category name)?" Methods ⑥ and ⑦ accept the following single strong question: "What is the cheapest product among all the recognized products?" The strong question is straightforward and easy to use for the user, but the system may not be ready to accept it; a strong question is specific and not frequently used in contrast to weak questions that are general and frequently used, which makes the cost and effort to prepare a strong question relatively high. Therefore, we also consider the case in which the user has to repeatedly ask weak questions until the desired information is obtained. This process places a relatively high cognitive load on the user.

A snapshot taken during the experiment is shown in Fig. 3. A participant wearing the voice guidance system sits on a chair in front of a table. A whiteboard is placed approximately 2 m away in front of the participant. An A0 paper on which 24 QR codes are printed is placed on the whiteboard. The QR codes are substitutes for products sold in a supermarket; when the voice guidance system recognizes a QR code, the system regards it as a registered product. We used QR codes to exclude as many effects caused by failure in recognition as possible. The voice guidance system runs on a laptop computer. Two experimenters, one of which appears on the left in the image, control the experiment. Although it is substantially different from shopping in actual daily life, we received feedback from some participants that the shopping in this experiment might be close to actual window shopping.

In the experiment, participants tested seven information transmission methods, referred to as methods ① to ⑦. Participants interacted with each information transmission method twice to buy the cheapest product of two different product types (i.e., a drink and snack). After the participants finished testing method ⑦, they were asked to test method ① again. This was done to evaluate the effect of the participants' familiarity; that is, how much the task completion time and the accuracy changed as the participants became familiar with the system. The second trial of method ① is referred to as method ①'.

3.1 Voice Guidance System

To evaluate information transmission methods, we implemented a voice guidance system using a wearable camera with a wide field-of-view lens, as shown in Fig. 2. This system was built using a combination of a wearable camera (Panasonic HX-A1H with a 150-degree field of view, 45 g), bone-conduction headphones (AfterShokz OPENCOMM, 23 g), and a presentation remote control (Logicool R500GR, 54 g) as a physical button. The wearable camera was connected by a cable to the laptop computer. The participant wore a cap, and the wearable camera was fixed with a mounting clip to the brim of the cap. The wearable camera reads the QR code that is associated with product information, and this information is described by voice through the bone-conduction headphones. Bone-conduction headphones were used for this experiment because it does not cover the ears and enables the participants to hear any instructions from the experimenters. When the participant felt uncomfortable or confused by listening to the large volume of product information, they could temporarily halt the verbal description at their own discretion using the physical button (presentation remote control). However, no participant used this function during the experiment. The verbal messages were spoken using Google Cloud Text-to-Speech. To recognize the QR codes, we used OpenCV and pyzbar, which are Python libraries.

Table 2. Subjective evaluation with a relative ranking. ">" indicates that the left is easier to use than the right, and "=" comparable. Hence, in general, the more to the left, the easier it is to use.

ID	Preference
P1	⑦ = ⑥ > ③ > ④ > ① > ② > ⑤
P2	⑦ = ⑥ > ⑤ > ④ > ③ > ② > ①
P3	⑦ > ⑥ > ④ > ⑤ > ③ > ② > ①
P4	⑦ > ⑥ > ⑤ = ④ > ③ > ② = ①
P5	⑦ > ⑥ > ⑤ > ④ > ② > ③ > ①
P6	⑦ = ⑥ > ⑤ > ③ > ④ > ② = ①
P7	⑦ = ⑥ > ⑤ > ③ > ④ = ② > ①
P8	⑦ > ⑥ > ⑤ > ④ > ③ > ② > ①
P9	⑦ > ⑥ > ④ > ③ > ① > ② > ⑤

3.2 Results and Discussion

The information transmission methods were subjectively and objectively evaluated.

Subjective Evaluation. Subjective evaluation of the information transmission methods was performed based on a relative ranking with comments. As mentioned above, seven information transmission methods were tested: methods ① to ⑦. After testing each method, an experimenter asked the participant about the relative rank of the method regarding ease of use and to comment on the method. Accumulating the relative ranks of the seven information transmission methods, we obtained the participants' preferences, as shown in Table 2.

Let us first focus on unidirectional communication methods (i.e., methods ① through ④). The table shows that almost all participants stated that methods ③ and ④ were easy to use. Both methods use semantic summarization, and therefore this proves the effectiveness of semantic summarization. In addition, comparing methods ① with ② and methods ③ with ④, methods ② and ④ were found to be preferred by most participants. Methods ② and ④ use temporal summarization, and therefore this proves the effectiveness of temporal summarization.

Next, we consider all methods. Comparing unidirectional communication methods and interactive communication methods, the table shows that interactive communication methods (i.e., methods ⑤ through ⑦) were preferred over unidirectional communication methods (i.e., methods ① through ④). All participants stated that method ⑦ was the best and method ⑥ was the second best, both of which allow the use of a strong question. By contrast, six participants ranked method ⑤ in third place, whereas three ranked lower (i.e., one ranked it in fourth place, and two ranked it last). This is because method ⑤ only allows

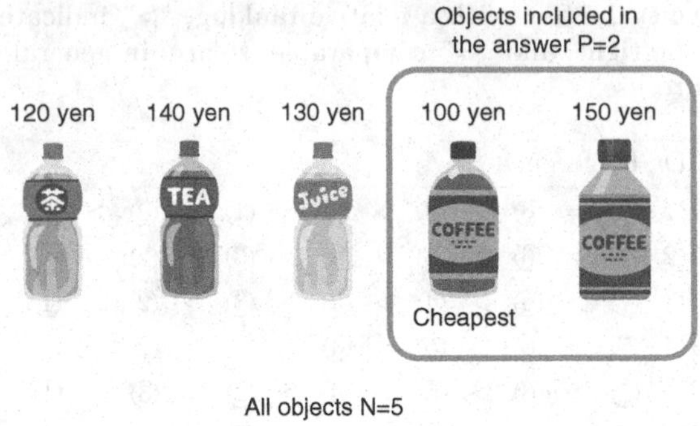

Fig. 4. Example calculation of the score defined by Eq. (1).

the use of weak questions. This implies that combining weak questions is not always comfortable for the users.

Objective Evaluation. The objective evaluation of the information transmission methods was performed based on the average time to complete the task and its accuracy, represented by a score.

The time to complete the task is defined as the time duration between the first recognition began on the voice guidance system and the participants raised their hand to state the name and price of the cheapest product. However, the experiment was terminated when the time exceeded 180 s, and the participants were requested to give their answer. The accuracy was measured by the score, which was defined in the range of 0% (the lowest) to 100% (the highest). Score Y is defined by

$$Y = \frac{1}{2}\frac{\log N - \log P}{\log N}X_{\text{name}} + \frac{1}{2}X_{\text{price}}, \tag{1}$$

where X_{name} and X_{price} respectively represent whether the answers for product name and price are correct; they are 1 if the answer is correct and 0 if it is incorrect. Furthermore, N is the number of all products and P is the number of the products not eliminated by the answers (see also Fig. 4), as described in detail below. The participants often described the product ambiguously, for instance, "It was a tea-type drink for 120 yen." This ambiguity had two causes: 1) the existence of long or similar product names; and 2) the participants tended to forget the product names when they focused on the prices. Thus, judging an answer as correct or incorrect hinders the meaningful evaluation of the accuracy. Therefore, we take into account the intermediate states in the manner of information theory. For example, as shown in Fig. 4, we consider the case in which the participant answered, "Some coffee is the cheapest for 100 yen." In this case, from the answer, we can reduce the candidate products from all $N = 5$ objects to $P = 2$ objects, and the cheapest product is included in the candidate products. Thus, $X_{\text{name}} = 1$. In addition, the participant's answer for the cheapest

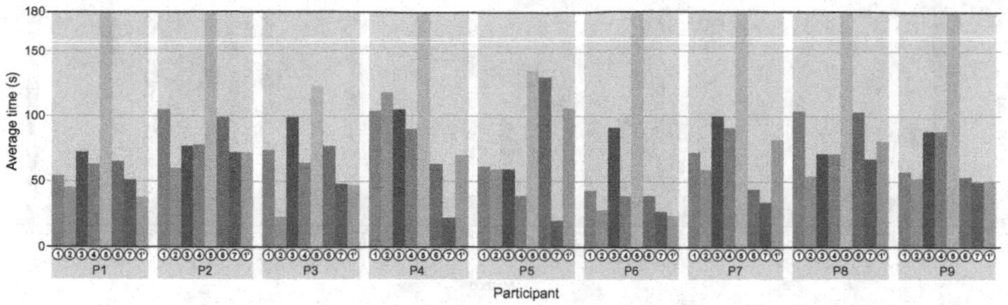

Fig. 5. Average time to complete the task for each participant.

price is correct, thus $X_{\text{price}} = 1$. Following the idea of information theory, the answer reduced the ambiguity of $N = 5$ products to the ambiguity of $P = 2$ products. Therefore, the information provided by the answer is $\log N - \log P$. To normalize this score so that it ranges between 0 and 1, we divide it by its maximum value, $\log N$, to obtain the first term of (Eq. 1). As a consequence, the score is $Y = 0.78$ in this case.

Regarding the average time to complete the task, we found that it depends more on the participants than the information transmission methods. Therefore, we visualized the average time to complete the task for each participant in Fig. 5. Focusing on unidirectional communication methods, Participants P1, P5, P6, and P9, whose vision became impaired to its current level relatively recently, required around 60 s to complete the task, which was less than the times of the other five participants. Focusing on interactive communication methods, all participants except for P3 and P5 spent 180 s for method ⑤. When using that method, to obtain the cheapest product, the participant repeatedly needs to combine two questions: "What are the categories that have been recognized?" and "What is the cheapest (category name)?" This process places a relatively high cognitive load on the user because the user needs to remember the category list as well as the name and price of the cheapest product thus far. By contrast, methods ⑥ and ⑦, which allow the use of a strong question, required much less time. Owing to the existence of the strong question, the participants could easily identify the cheapest product using the strong question. This implies the power of interactive communication methods. Comparing methods ① and ①' (the second trial of method ①), all participants except for P5 and P7 reduced the time in the latter trial. On average, it was reduced by 13%. This indicates that the participants quickly became used to the experiments. However, even taking this effect into account, the consideration mentioned above is not affected. We predicted that the participant with congenital blindness might be more tolerant to verbal information acquisition, but we did not confirm such a correlation. We received feedback that participant P6, who had low vision, had seen the product used in the experiment before, so that it was much easier to imagine the product and obtain the information.

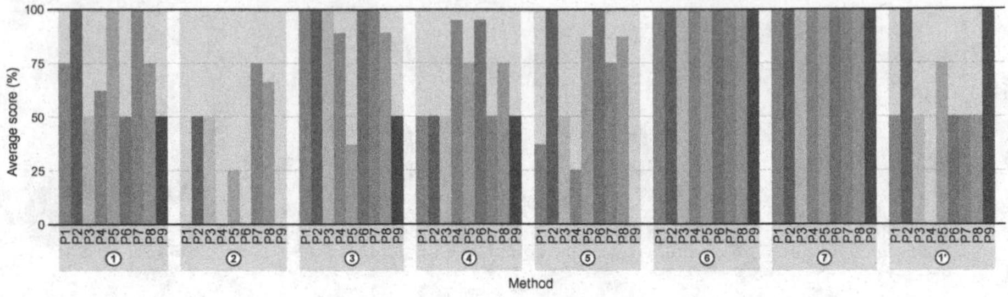

Fig. 6. Average score for each information transmission method.

Figure 6 visualizes the average score for each information transmission method. Let us focus on unidirectional communication methods first. We obtained different results depending whether temporal summarization was used. The scores of methods ② and ④, which use temporal summarization and a verbal description only once were low, whereas those of methods ① and ③, which do not use temporal summarization and verbally describe the results repeatedly were high. It is believed that this score difference is explained by the fact that the participants were not allowed to reconfirm the product name when they failed to catch it or forgot it. A notable result was obtained for method ②, for which the scores of four participants were 0. This seems to be a typical disadvantage of temporal summarization. Next, let us focus on interactive communication methods. Methods ⑥ and ⑦, which allow the use of a strong question, achieved 100% for all participants. This implies the ease of use of the strong question. In contrast, the scores of method ⑤, which allow the use of only weak questions, were worse than those of methods ⑥ and ⑦. A significant difference in the scores depending on participants arose because of the termination of the experiment at the upper time limit; when the time exceeded 180 s, participants were requested to give an answer even if they had no idea which answer was correct.

4 Conclusions

With regard to using smartphone apps and assistive devices supporting people with visual impairment to obtain visual information from the surroundings, this paper pointed out two problems that have not attracted much attention. The first problem is that the user is required to actively take a picture as an implicit precondition. However, this is not always possible for people with visual impairment. Therefore, we proposed a new framework called *passive information acquisition (PIA)* that is independent of the active actions performed by the users. The proposed PIA framework can be actualized by constantly recording the user's surroundings and recognizing all the images. A downside of this framework is that it can obtain a huge amount of surrounding visual information, which may overwhelm the user. Thus, information summarization is crucial. Another problem is that the user must constantly listen to the voice describing aloud the recognition results when using assistive apps and devices. Compared with sighted people, who can focus on the information of interest without evaluating everything in their sight, people with visual impairment must use methods that are far less efficient. A possible solution to this problem is to introduce *interactive communication* using a question answering (QA) system, where the user requests information from the recognition system, and then the recognition system tells the requested information to the user.

We conducted an experiment with nine people with visual impairment and asked them to perform a pseudo-shopping scenario. In the experiment, we examined four unidirectional communication methods that were designed to examine all four combinations of with/without temporal/semantic summarization. These methods were subjectively evaluated with relative rankings and objectively evaluated based on the task completion time and accuracy. As a result, the method with both temporal and semantic summarization was the best in the subjective evaluation. Although this method was not the best in the objective evaluation, the effectiveness of temporal summarization was confirmed.

We also examined three interactive communication methods. Comparing the interactive communication methods with the unidirectional communication methods, we found that the methods that allow a strong question to be used were the best in the subjective evaluation. These methods were also the best with respect to accuracy in the objective evaluation. However, the method that allows only weak questions was not always better than the best unidirectional communication method both in the subjective and objective evaluations.

Acknowledgments. This work was supported by JSPS Kakenhi Grant Number 20H04212.

References

1. Antol, S., et al.: VQA: visual question answering. In: Proceedings of the IEEE International Conference on Computer Vision, pp. 2425–2433 (2015)
2. Bracha, L., Chechik, G.: Informative object annotations: tell me something i don't know. In: Proceedings of the IEEE/CVF Conference on Computer Vision and Pattern Recognition (CVPR) (2019)
3. Broadbent, D.E.: Perception and Communication. Elsevier, Amsterdam (2013)
4. Chiu, T.Y., Zhao, Y., Gurari, D.: Assessing image quality issues for real-world problems. In: Proceedings of the IEEE/CVF Conference on Computer Vision and Pattern Recognition (CVPR), pp. 3643–3653 (2020). https://doi.org/10.1109/CVPR42600.2020.00370
5. Davidson, J., et al.: The youtube video recommendation system. In: Proceedings of the Fourth ACM Conference on Recommender Systems, pp. 293–296 (2010). https://doi.org/10.1145/1864708.1864770
6. Gurari, D., et al.: VizWiz grand challenge: answering visual questions from blind people. In: Proceedings of the IEEE Conference on Computer Vision and Pattern Recognition (CVPR) (2018)

7. Iwamura, M., Hirabayashi, N., Cheng, Z., Minatani, K., Kise, K.: VisPhoto: photography for people with visual impairment as post-production of omni-directional camera image. In: Extended Abstracts of the 2020 CHI Conference on Human Factors in Computing Systems, pp. 1–9 (2020). https://doi.org/10.1145/3334480.3382983
8. Iwamura, M., Inoue, Y., Minatani, K., Kise, K.: Suitable camera and rotation navigation for people with visual impairment on looking for something using object detection technique. In: Proceedings of the 17th International Conference on Computers Helping People with Special Needs (ICCHP 2020) (2020). https://doi.org/10.1007/978-3-030-58796-3_57
9. Jayant, C., Ji, H., White, S., Bigham, J.P.: Supporting blind photography. In: Proceedings of the 13th International ACM SIGACCESS Conference on Computers and Accessibility, pp. 203–210 (2011). https://doi.org/10.1145/2049536.2049573
10. Jiang, H., Misra, I., Rohrbach, M., Learned-Miller, E., Chen, X.: In defense of grid features for visual question answering. In: Proceedings of the CVPR (2020)
11. Kacorri, H., Kitani, K.M., Bigham, J.P., Asakawa, C.: People with visual impairment training personal object recognizers: feasibility and challenges. In: Proceedings of the CHI Conference on Human Factors in Computing Systems. ACM Press (2017). https://doi.org/10.1145/3025453.3025899
12. Kayukawa, S., et al.: BBeep: a sonic collision avoidance system for blind travellers and nearby pedestrians. In: Proceedings of the 2019 CHI Conference on Human Factors in Computing Systems, pp. 1–12 (2019). https://doi.org/10.1145/3290605.3300282
13. Kayukawa, S., Ishihara, T., Takagi, H., Morishima, S., Asakawa, C.: BlindPilot: a robotic local navigation system that leads blind people to a landmark object. In: Extended Abstracts of the 2020 CHI Conference on Human Factors in Computing Systems, pp. 1–9 (2020). https://doi.org/10.1145/3334480.3382925
14. Kayukawa, S., Takagi, H., Guerreiro, J.A., Morishima, S., Asakawa, C.: Smartphone-based assistance for blind people to stand in lines. In: Proceedings of the CHI Extended Abstracts, pp. 1–8 (2020). https://doi.org/10.1145/3334480.3382954
15. Lavie, N., Tsal, Y.: Perceptual load as a major determinant of the locus of selection in visual attention. Percept. Psychophys. **56**(2), 183–197 (1994)
16. Lee, K., Hong, J., Pimento, S., Jarjue, E., Kacorri, H.: Revisiting blind photography in the context of teachable object recognizers. In: Proceedings of the 21st International ACM SIGACCESS Conference on Computers and Accessibility, pp. 83–95 (2019). https://doi.org/10.1145/3308561.3353799
17. Thorat, P.B., Goudar, R., Barve, S.: Survey on collaborative filtering, content-based filtering and hybrid recommendation system. Int. J. Comput. Appl. **110**(4), 31–36 (2015)
18. Treisman, A.M.: Contextual cues in selective listening. Q. J. Exp. Psychol. **12**(4), 242–248 (1960)
19. Vázquez, M., Steinfeld, A.: Helping visually impaired users properly aim a camera. In: Proceedings of the 14th International ACM SIGACCESS Conference on Computers and Accessibility, pp. 95–102 (2012). https://doi.org/10.1145/2384916.2384934

Listening First: Egocentric Textual Descriptions of Indoor Spaces for People with Blindness

Angela Constantinescu(✉), Eva-Maria Neumann, Karin Müller(✉), Gerhard Jaworek, and Rainer Stiefelhagen(✉)

Karlsruhe Institute of Technology, Karlsruhe, Germany
{angela.constantinescu,karin.e.mueller,gerhard.jaworek, rainer.stiefelhagen}@kit.edu
http://www.access.kit.edu

Abstract. Orientation in unknown environments is challenging for people with. Especially in indoor environments, there are very few systems that support navigation but almost none for orientation. Thus, we propose a grammar for generating German textual descriptions of indoor environments for users with blindness. We utilize an egocentric approach taking into account the user's location and orientation in the building. To investigate what word order is preferred, we compare descriptions generated by three different grammars. We also examine what strategies people with blindness pursue to orient themselves in buildings. We test our concept in an online user study with people with blindness. Our study shows that egocentric information should be brief, always following the same structure and allow for customization.

Keywords: Textual descriptions · Indoor maps · Blindness

1 Introduction

Traveling independently in indoor environments is an unsolved problem for people with blindness. When visiting an unknown building, blind people usually travel with a sighted assistant or ask other people for the way. Engel *et al* [10] showed that people with blindness would use textual descriptions of buildings if they were available, in order to gain more independence. When travelling in an unknown building, information about the immediate surroundings, such as stairs, number of floors or the location of doors, tactile labels are particularly important, as it helps orient oneself [2]. This information needs to be provided from an egocentric point of view taking into account the user's location and orientation in a building. The research questions we are investigating are: (1) *How should indoor environments be described from an egocentric perspective to a blind person in German?* and (2) *Is there an effect of using different word*

A. Constantinescu, E.-M. Neumann—Equal contribution.

K. Miesenberger et al. (Eds.): ICCHP-AAATE 2022, LNCS 13341, pp. 241–249, 2022.
https://doi.org/10.1007/978-3-031-08648-9_28

orders in egocentric descriptions? Since blind people mainly use their hearing in order to navigate safely, any speech output interface must be designed very carefully and should meet the needs of the user group as (i) the output must not overload the users, or put their safety at risk; (ii) blind users need other information than sighted people to orient themselves in unknown environments. Thus, a balance between too much and not enough information must be found, taking into account the users' own preferences and capabilities. *The users should be informed in the right amount at the right timing about the surrounding environment during navigation. To be effective, the navigation solution is advised to focus on conveying specific environmental information* [1,7].

In this work, we create different grammars for automatically generating egocentric descriptions of indoor maps in German from OpenStreetMap[1] to help blind users orient themselves in unknown buildings. By creating the grammar in a user-centered way, we make sure that it fulfills the strict requirements of the users. Our study shows that information about the direct indoor environment should be brief, always following the same structure and allow for customization.

2 Related Work

Navigation systems have been in the focus of research for over 30 years now. There are several surveys that give a good overview, from various points of view. In 2020 alone, there were several journal articles that reviewed navigation solutions for people with visual impairments either indoors [6,13,15], or both indoors and outdoors [7]. However, the interface is hardly ever considered. In [11], a grammar for *turn-by-turn instructions* is created in a user centered approach by analyzing route descriptions made by blind people. Objects on the route are mentioned, but the focus is on navigation, rather than a description of the immediate environment. Another approach [1] specifies a grammar for turn-by-turn navigation instructions, but for *outdoors*. In [8], textual descriptions of floor plans are automatically generated, in an allocentric approach. This means, that the entire plan is described independently of the user perspective. While such descriptions are useful for *planning* a trip to an unfamiliar building, they are not useful for on-site orientation, where egocentric information is needed as described in our approach. A very similar approach had been previously tried by [12]. The approach that comes closest to specifying a grammar for egocentric textual descriptions of indoor spaces is the one by Yang *et al* [16]. Their Talking Points 3 system reads aloud a list of points of interest (POIs) around the user. Their system can be used both indoors and outdoors. Although they do not formally specify a grammar, they describe many of its components. Some details, however, remain unspecified. Our work complements their efforts and tries to close this gap. We include newer findings with respect to parts of the grammar and answer open questions in a user-centered way. We focus on a solution tailored to the German language.

[1] OpenStreetMap. https://www.openstreetmap.org, Retrieved February 01, 2022.

To our knowledge, until now there is no approach that analyses the output of current systems for egocentric descriptions and tests different versions of a generation component based on a grammar.

3 Design of an Egocentric Description Component

In this section, we describe how we designed the grammar for egocentric descriptions of an area within a building. We first analyze previous literature and then design three grammar versions to learn how the descriptions should be created.

3.1 Analysis of Literature and Existing Solutions

We performed an analysis of previous literature, including one online user study and a focus group previously carried out within our project. Additionally, we studied the output of three existing apps for indoor navigation and orientation: Blindsquare[2], BFW Smartinfo[3], RightHear[4]. Table 1 shows the results of our analysis regarding the amount of information, word order, output of distance and direction.

Table 1. Overview of some of the rules for textual descriptions found in literature and existing Apps or prototypes.

Textual description rule	Reference
Object then Direction	Blindsquare
Direction then Object	[16]
Distance then Direction	[1], Blindsquare,
Direction then Distance	[1,4,11], RightHear
Object should contain details	[9]
Distance in fixed unit (*e.g* meter, feet)	[11,16], Blindsquare, BFW SmartInfo
Distance in steps	[11,14]
Direction as clock	[5,14], Blindsquare, BFW Smartinfo
Direction as degrees	[5], Blindsquare
Direction as left/right	[5,12], Blindsquare, BFW Smartinfo
Direction as cardinal points	[3], Blindsquare

2 Blindsquare. https://www.blindsquare.com/, Retrieved 3 February 2022.
3 BFW Smartinfo. http://smartinfo.bfw-wuerzburg.de/, Retrieved 3 February 2022.
4 RightHear. https://www.right-hear.com/, Retrieved 3 February 2022.

3.2 Specification of the Grammar

German word order is quite flexible and in certain contexts, words in phrases can appear at various positions. Thus, we created three grammar versions for the generation of the descriptions: (1) object followed by direction and distance (ObDirDis), (2) object followed by distance then direction (ObDisDir), (3) random word and sentence order (Random) as a baseline. The word order of the third grammar changes randomly for each sentence and reflects an arbitrary order, as it could be given by people. Table 2 shows the rules of the three different grammars, expressed as regular expressions. The descriptions are as short as possible to reduce the cognitive load.

Table 2. Main parts of the three grammars with different word order expressed as regular expressions: (1) Object Direction Distance (ObDirDis), (2) Object Distance Direction (ObDisDir) and (3) arbitrary word order (Random)

Grammar ObDirDis:	([Details]* Object [Details]* Direction Distance)^n
Grammar ObDisDir:	([Details]* Object [Details]* Distance Direction)^n
Grammar Random:	Permutations of Object (incl details), Direction and Distance

Objects can contain details such as *name*, *number*, *ladies'* or *men* in case of restrooms. For example, in *German: Treppen TR06 zu Stockwerken 0–3*; *English: staircase TR06 to floors 0–3*, the object *staircase* has both a name, *TR06*, and additional information about where it leads to, *0–3*.

Table 3 displays a condensed egocentric description of a floor generated by the three grammars. In column 1, the object is followed by direction and distance. The sentences are listed according to the position of the respective object, clockwise, starting with 10 o'clock (front left). Column 2 is the same except that Distance and Direction are permuted. The third grammar uses random word order for each sentence, and random sentence order.

Table 3. Example of a partial description of one of the buildings generated by two grammar versions: Object-Direction-Distance (ObDirDis), and random word order (Random) in German (G) and its translation in English (E). The Object-Distance-Direction grammar is not described as the output is identical to the first grammar except with the permutation of direction and distance.

Grammar 1: Object-Direction-Distance	Grammar 3: Random Word Order
G: Raum 109 auf 11 Uhr in 11 Metern.	G: Raum 109 auf 11 Uhr in 11 Metern.
E: Room 109 at 11 o'clock in 11 meters.	**E: Room 109 at 11 o'clock** in 11 meters.
G: Damentoilette auf 1 Uhr in 15 Metern.	G: Auf 1 Uhr Damentoilette in 15 Metern.
E: Ladies' restroom at 1 o'clock in 15 meters.	**E: At 1 o'clock, ladies restroom** in 15 meters.
G: Gang F02 auf 2 Uhr in 18 Metern.	G: In 18 Metern auf 2 Uhr Gang F02.
E: Corridor F02 at 2 o'clock in 18 meters.	**E:** In 18 meters **at 2 o'clock corridor F02.**
G: Haupteingang auf 6 Uhr in 1 Metern.	G: Haupteingang in 1 Metern auf 6 Uhr.
E: Main entrance at 6 o'clock in 1 meter.	**E: E: Main entrance** in 1 meter **at 6 o'clock.**

4 User Study

We evaluated our approach in an online study consisting of the following three parts: (1) demographic questions, (2) orientation strategies in buildings and users' preferences, as well as (3) the evaluation of three different generation components (grammars) for egocentric descriptions. The study was planned in a user-centered way with the involvement of three accessibility experts, one of whom with blindness. The implementation of the study was done in the SoSciSurvey platform running on university servers. We evaluate the effectiveness of egocentric descriptions in terms of the mental map they induce, and efficiency in terms of the users' cognitive load.

Thus, our study hypotheses are: (1) **Hypothesis 1:** Egocentric descriptions are effective in building a mental map of an indoor environment. (2) **Hypothesis 2:** There is a difference in efficiency - cognitive load - between egocentric descriptions with random word order, as usually provided by natural persons (as one of the most popular strategies used by blind people when walking in unknown buildings is asking other people for the way), and a predefined egocentric description generated by a structured grammar.

Participants. The study was sent per email to people with visual impairments who agreed to be contacted by ACCESS@KIT. Nine people with blindness answered the questions of the first two parts of the study. Six out of nine completed the full questionnaire. The ages of all nine ranged between 18 and 67 years; five of them were male and four female; six were blind from birth.

Orientation Strategies and Users' Preferences. In the second part, we asked about the participants' travel practices, if they want to travel more often alone, their use of digital navigation aids and their orientation strategies inside of buildings. Moreover, we asked about their preferences on how directions should be expressed in buildings, which information should be announced and in what radius.

Evaluation of the Generation Components for Egocentric Descriptions. In the third part, the three grammars detailed in Sect. 3.2 are used to generate German egocentric descriptions of three different buildings. The order of the grammars, as well as the combination grammar and building, were randomized. After each grammar the participants were asked several questions. The aim was to learn if a certain structure i.e. word order has an influence on the cognitive load of a user. Moreover, we investigated whether the grammars help to get an idea of where objects are located and if they build a mental map. Finally, we wanted to clarify user preferences regarding some grammar components.

5 Results

In this section, we report on the results of the orientation strategies, the participants' preferences on how direction should be announced, the radius and number of described objects. We also describe the results of the mental map task, the cognitive load, and refer to useful user comments.

Orientation Strategies in Indoor Environments. Independence from other people is an important aspect for people with blindness. Most of the participants would like to visit buildings on their own. Hearing and using natural guidance systems is an important way to gather information about the surroundings. However, if there are no people or too many people in a building, this source of information is gone which points at the importance of descriptions.

User Preferences to Direction, Radius and Objects. For conveying the direction, six participants prefer the clock system, while three the left/right directions. According to P1, *"directions like right or back left are easier in theory, but you also have fewer subdivisions."* No user has chosen degrees or cardinal points. Seven participants answered the question about the radius within which to convey objects. The answers were very diverse: two prefer 5 m, two others 2–20 m, one 5–20 m, one 20–30 m, one said "variable" and one wanted to have all prominent objects *in the room*, irrespective of the distance; alternatively, when looking for an object, either 3 m, or 5 m for larger lobbys. When asked what objects should be included in the descriptions, all participants selected *room*, *stairs* and *entrance* - see Table 4. Each one selected between 8 and 15 objects out of 17, with an average of 11.7.

Table 4. Number of participants who selected the given objects

Auswahl	Room	Stairs	Entrance	Toilets	Door	Corridor	Eating place	Open area	Info point	Shopping	Steps	Emergency exit	Tactile paving	Elevator	Ramp	Accessible toilets
Anzahl	9	9	9	8	8	7	7	7	7	6	6	6	5	5	3	2

Mental Map. In order to assess the mental maps that the users formed of the building parts described, the users were asked to describe their mental map or, in other words, their perception of the described environment. We analyzed the written descriptions by assigning 1 point for each correctly named object, 3 points for a correct object-direction combination, and –1 points for a false object. The grammar version Object-Direction-Distance obtained 137 points from all six participants, while the other two versions, Object-Distance-Direction and Random obtained each 132 points, namely on average 74.2% of the maximum possible score. On average, each participant named 25.6 objects from 30 in total. Moreover, relations between objects were built ("the entrance is right across [the toilets]") and details, which were not included in the descriptions, were being deduced: "I am standing in a long hallway", "semi-circular foyer". Thus, we

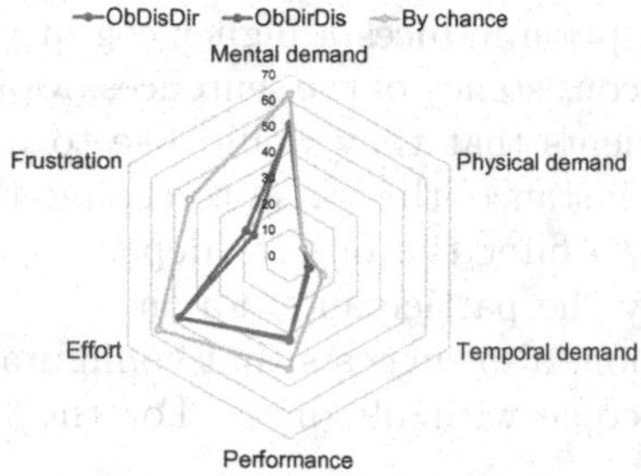

Fig. 1. Results of Raw NASA-TLX of the three grammars with different word order: (1) object, direction, distance (ObDirDis) (2) object, distance and direction (ObDisDir), (3) arbitrary word order (Random). Please note that the scale for performance is counter-intuitive, a higher score being worse.

conclude that the users could build a mental map with the egocentric descriptions provided, and thus Hypothesis 1 is accepted.

Cognitive Load with Raw NASA-TLX. We administered the raw NASA-TLX to assess the cognitive load of the users with respect to the three grammars. The results show that using an arbitrary word order resulted in an increased cognitive load as displayed in Fig. 1. The users felt particularly frustrated when no fixed word order was used. Mental demand, performance and effort are also slightly higher for the random sentences. The other two grammar versions have almost identical scores. We thus conclude that Hypothesis 2 is accepted. Additionally, since the cognitive load for the two fixed grammars was low, we state that fixed descriptions are efficient and do not overload the user.

User Comments. Participant P4 described their own orientation strategy in a building: "*I orient myself by listening, to people you hear and what they do such as opening doors, talking on the phone, using elevators or stairs, so to all sounds that say something about the room conditions. Also, whether the room is large or small. After that, I orient myself to walls and the doors.*" The same participant, P4, mentioned some requirements for descriptions made by people in buildings, which also suit generated textual descriptions: "*They have to be structured and accurate and reflect the information I need.*"

Another participant, P5, suggests one additional function of the system: *I can imagine a system that only mentions the objects clockwise and I can then go to the desired object and get more information there, such as how many meters or is there a wall between them.*

6 Conclusion

We created an egocentric description component for indoor environments by defining three grammars with different words order. We evaluated our concept in an online study with blind participants. The results suggest that a random order of words in a description induces a higher cognitive load. Users are especially frustrated by the inconsistency of the sentences. Moreover, users repeatedly mentioned in their comments that they would like to be able to configure the textual descriptions. For instance, they wish to change the radius within which objects are conveyed or to filter the objects depending on the situation. The different choices made by the participants, for instance in terms of objects or how to convey the direction, also suggests that configurability is paramount for a system designed for people with blindness. For the future, a test in a real environment is planned.

Acknowledgements. This work was funded by the German Federal Ministry of Labour and Social Affairs (BMAS) under the grant number 01KM151112.

References

1. Constantinescu, A., Petrausch, V., Müller, K., Stiefelhagen, R.: Towards a standardized grammar for navigation systems for persons with visual impairments. In: ASSETS 2019, pp. 539–541. ACM, New York, NY, USA (2019)
2. Engel, C., et al.: Travelling more independently: a requirements analysis for accessible journeys to unknown buildings for people with visual impairments. In: ASSETS 2020, pp. 1–11. ACM, New York, NY, USA (2020)
3. Goyal, S., Bhavsar, S., Patel, S., Chattopadhyay, C., Bhatnagar, G.: SUGAMAN: describing floor plans for visually impaired by annotation learning and proximity-based grammar. IET Image Process. **13**(13), 2623–2635 (2019)
4. Jain, D.: Path-guided indoor navigation for the visually impaired using minimal building retrofitting. In: ASSETS 2014, pp. 225–232. ACM, New York, NY, USA (2014)
5. Kamikubo, R., Kato, N., Higuchi, K., Yonetani, R., Sato, Y.: Support strategies for remote guides in assisting people with visual impairments for effective indoor navigation. In: CHI 2020, pp. 1–12. ACM, New York, NY, USA (2020)
6. Kandalan, R.N., Namuduri, K.: Techniques for constructing indoor navigation systems for the visually impaired: a review. IEEE Trans. Hum.-Mach. Syst. **50**(18) (2020)
7. Kuriakose, B., Shrestha, R., Sandnes, F.E.: Tools and technologies for blind and visually impaired navigation support: a review. IETE Tech. Rev. **39**(1), 1–16 (2020)
8. Madugalla, A., Marriott, K., Marinai, S., Capobianco, S., Goncu, C.: Creating accessible online floor plans for visually impaired readers. TACCESS **13**(4), 1–37 (2020)
9. May, K.R., Tomlinson, B.J., Ma, X., Roberts, P., Walker, B.N.: Spotlights and soundscapes: on the design of mixed reality auditory environments for persons with visual impairment. ACM Trans. Access. Comput. **13**(2), 1–47 (2020)
10. Müller, K., Engel, C., Loitsch, C., Stiefelhagen, R., Weber, G.: Traveling more independently: a study on the diverse needs and challenges of people with visual or mobility impairments in unfamiliar indoor environments. ACM Trans. Access. Comput. **15**(2), 1–44 (2022). just accepted
11. Nicolau, H., Jorge, J., Guerreiro, T.: Blobby: how to guide a blind person. In: CHI EA 2009, pp. 3601–3606. ACM, New York, NY, USA (2009)

12. Paladugu, D.A., Maguluri, H.B., Tian, Q., Li, B.: Automated description generation for indoor floor maps. In: ASSETS 2012, pp. 211–212. ACM, New York, NY, USA (2012)
13. Plikynas, D., Zvironas, A., Budrionis, A., Gudauskis, M.: Indoor navigation systems for visually impaired persons: mapping the features of existing technologies to user needs. Sensors **20**(3) (2020)
14. Sato, D., et al.: Navcog3 in the wild: large-scale blind indoor navigation assistant with semantic features. TACCESS **12**(3), 1–30 (2019)
15. Simões, W.C.S.S., Machado, G.S., Sales, A.M.A., De Lucena, M.M., Jazdi, N., De Lucena, V.F.: A review of technologies and techniques for indoor navigation systems for the visually impaired. Sensors **20**(14) (2020)
16. Yang, R., et al.: Supporting spatial awareness and independent wayfinding for pedestrians with visual impairments. In: ASSETS 2011, pp. 27–34. ACM, New York, NY, USA (2011)

Haptic and Digital Access to Art and Artefacts

Non-visual Access to an Interactive 3D Map

James M. Coughlan[1(✉)], Brandon Biggs[1,2], and Huiying Shen[1]

[1] The Smith-Kettlewell Eye Research Institute, San Francisco, CA, USA
{Coughlan,brandon.biggs,hshen}@ski.org

[2] Georgia Institute of Technology, Atlanta, GA, USA

Abstract. Maps are indispensable for helping people learn about unfamiliar environments and plan trips. While tactile (2D) and 3D maps offer non-visual map access to people who are blind or visually impaired (BVI), this access is greatly enhanced by adding interactivity to the maps: when the user points at a feature of interest on the map, the name and other information about the feature is read aloud in audio. We explore how the use of an interactive 3D map of a playground, containing over seventy play structures and other features, affects spatial learning and cognition. Specifically, we perform experiments in which four blind participants answer questions about the map to evaluate their grasp of three types of spatial knowledge: landmark, route and survey. The results of these experiments demonstrate that participants are able to acquire this knowledge, most of which would be inaccessible without the interactivity of the map.

Keywords: Assistive devices · Accessibility · Augmented reality · Audio labeling · Visual impairment · Blindness · Low vision

1 State of the Art and Related Technology

Tactile (2D) and 3D maps offer non-visual map access to blind or visually impaired (BVI) people, filling an important gap left by available navigation tools. GPS-enabled smartphone apps like Google Maps offer fully accessible turn-by-turn directions, but they don't convey the spatial layout of the environment to users who can't see the mobile device screen, which has been shown to hinder navigational understanding [1]. Other GPS-enabled apps such as BlindSquare[1] and Microsoft SoundScape[2] give real-time information about the user's surroundings but don't replace the information contained in a map – which can be explored freely offline, in a comfortable setting (such as one's home or office), and without having to be physically present in the region represented by the map. Similarly, while verbal descriptions of routes can be read aloud using a screen reader, they don't convey spatial layout information except in very simple cases.

An alternative approach to providing non-visual map access is the vibro-audio map (VAM) [2], which displays geographic information on a tablet device by issuing vibrations and sounds when the user's finger contacts a geographic feature such as a path or

[1] https://www.blindsquare.com/about/.

[2] https://www.microsoft.com/en-us/research/product/soundscape/.

K. Miesenberger et al. (Eds.): ICCHP-AAATE 2022, LNCS 13341, pp. 253–260, 2022.
https://doi.org/10.1007/978-3-031-08648-9_29

junction on the tablet screen. Digital auditory maps [3], which allow a user to explore a map on a computer (e.g., moving around the map by pressing the left, right, up and down arrow keys) and hear a combination of speech and sounds to indicate geographic information, are another promising approach to accessing maps non-visually. However, both of these approaches have the disadvantage that the user is unable to feel the map with their hands and explore the shapes of objects and routes on the map tactilely, which is what BVI users desire in an ideal map [4].

Raised-line tactile maps (such as the commercially available and customizable TMAP [5]) offer direct access to the spatial information encoded in a map, but important semantic information such as the names of streets and buildings is typically represented using braille. Space limitations usually necessitate the use of braille abbreviations coupled with an extensive key; users often have difficulty interpreting these abbreviations, which force them to alternate between the map itself and the key, thereby disrupting the process of exploring the map. 3D tactile maps are an alternative that facilitate easier learning of the environment represented by the map [6], but placing braille on 3D maps is time-consuming and expensive. Moreover, braille is inaccessible to the large majority of people with visual impairments who don't read it[3].

An effective way to circumvent the limitations of braille labels is to substitute them with audio labels, i.e., by making the map interactive, which may be accomplished in several ways. For instance, tactile maps may be overlaid on a touch-sensitive tablet (e.g., Touch Graphics T3[4]). Alternatively, special 3D models can be built with touch-sensing capabilities (such as those made by Touch Graphics), but these require a significant amount of custom hardware. By contrast, computer vision may be used to add audio labels to virtually any tactile or 3D map [7, 8], with the benefit that an existing map can be used with little or no modifications to the map itself.

While studies such as [9] have explored the benefits of adding interactivity to tactile maps, little or no work has been done to our knowledge focusing on the impact of adding interactivity to 3D maps. Our study focuses on a 3D map of a playground, using audio labels provided by the CamIO system for audio labeling [8], extending the co-design in [4] and the work performed in [10]. This map was originally a cardboard prototype that allowed BVI participants to give feedback on what else they wanted in a 3D model. They requested more information around pathways, and details on the small walls that were located around the playground. An early version of CamIO was also used in this version to digitally label objects. The new version of the model (based on the 3D-printed prototype shown in Fig. 1) includes all the requested tactile features, and a significantly improved CamIO.

We explore the use of an interactive 3D map, in which pointing a handheld stylus at a location on the map triggers the announcement of a specific audio label about that location (for instance, pointing at a small rocking horse structure triggers the announcement "rocking horse"). The map is a 1/100 scale 3D-printed nylon model of an actual playground, and the interactive system contains over seventy audio labeled features, including playground structures and features such as paths. We conducted a pilot experiment with one blind participant to assess the functionality of the system and the design

[3] https://nfb.org/images/nfb/documents/pdf/braille_literacy_report_web.pdf.

[4] https://www.touchgraphics.com/education/t3.

of the formal experiment, and made improvements based on this pilot experiment to both the functionality and the experimental design. Formal experiments were then conducted with four additional blind participants, who were tasked with answering questions about the 3D map, demonstrating their grasp of three types of spatial knowledge: landmark, route and survey.

2 Overview of Interactive 3D Map System

This section summarizes the functioning of the interactive 3D map system. Specifics about the user studies are presented in subsequent sections.

Fig. 1. 3D playground map shown with stylus held by user to point at a feature on the map.

Our study is based on a 3D-printed map (see Fig. 1) representing an actual playground in Palo Alto, California. The map measures roughly 59 cm × 76 cm horizontally, with the highest point about 14 cm. It is a 1/100 scale model of the playground containing over seventy features, such as “disk swings”, “climbing loops”, “playhouse”, “Ava’s bridge” and “climbing giraffe”. The 3D map was designed so that the shapes of the features are as familiar as possible and could either be recognized by touch, or are intuitive enough to be easily remembered once they are introduced.

To make the 3D map interactive, we used the CamIO system [8] to create audio labels for the features on the map. Using this approach, an iPhone is mounted rigidly above the 3D map so that the iPhone camera views it in its entirety. Computer vision algorithms run on the iPhone to analyze the scene, specifically determining where the tip of a handheld stylus (Fig. 1) lies in relation to the 3D map. Whenever the stylus tip touches a feature of interest (referred to as a “hotspot” in [8]), the corresponding audio label is read aloud using text-to-speech.

Next we describe the stylus in more detail. The stylus is made of a foam cube 3 in. wide, covered with barcode marker patterns printed on paper, and attached to a stick for the user to hold. Computer vision algorithms estimate the *pose* (3D translation and 3D rotation) of the stylus and of the 3D map (which is also framed with printed barcode marker patterns for this purpose) in each camera frame, allowing the system to track the 3D location of the stylus tip relative to the map. The stylus was designed with barcode marker patterns large enough to be clearly resolved by the camera, but small enough to be mounted on a pointing stick that is easily grasped. (We are currently experimenting with a more durable and compact 3D-printed stylus with a 2-in.-wide cube on top.)

Since the actual playground is organized into seven zones, which are groupings of related playground structures (such as the "Tot Zone" and "Swinging and Swaying Zone"), we created special audio labels for these zones. The audio label for each zone is triggered whenever the stylus tip falls inside a volume of space roughly 12–20 cm above the structures contained in the zone.

3 Pilot Experiment

Before embarking on formal experiments with BVI participants, we conducted a pilot experiment with one BVI participant (female, age 29, blind with very limited form perception) to determine how well the 3D interactive map works and to assess if any changes should be made to the system or our prototype experimental design.

3.1 Procedure

At the beginning of the pilot experiment, we briefly described the overall layout of the map and explained how to use the stylus to trigger the audio labels. Next we asked the participant to spend 5 min familiarizing herself with the map, and then asked her to perform three groups of tasks to assess three specific types of knowledge that can be obtained from maps [9, 11]: (a) *landmark knowledge*, which is the awareness of specific locations in an environment; (b) *route knowledge*, which is knowledge about how to traverse one or more specific routes; and (c) *survey knowledge*, which is knowledge of how landmarks and routes relate to one another spatially. We note that survey knowledge is useful for creating robust mental maps of the environment, which facilitate independent navigation of the environment [9]. Spatial knowledge was assessed in multiple trials asking the participant to locate specific locations on the map, trace walking routes from one location to another, and specify cardinal directions (north/south/east/west) from one location to another.

Here we describe the spatial knowledge questions in detail. The landmark knowledge tasks asked the participant to find all seven zones, and each task required them to identify two structures in each zone by name (except for one specific zone that contained few structures). For each route task, the participant was given a starting feature and destination feature, and was told to find each feature and to trace the shortest walking path from the start to destination using their finger or the stylus (without walking over walls or through structures or other barriers). Finally, each survey task specified a starting feature and destination feature, and the participant was asked to find these features and then to indicate the direction (as the crow flies, i.e., along a straight path irrespective of barriers such as walls) that the destination was located in relative to the start. The starting and destination features were chosen so that the directions connecting them were always aligned to the four cardinal directions defined by the rectangular map; the participant was allowed to specify the direction by saying "north", "south", "east" or "west" or else "12 o'clock", "3 o'clock", "6 o'clock" or "9 o'clock".

Next the participant completed an SUS questionnaire [12] (with its language adapted to BVI participants [9]). Finally, the experimenter conducted a semi-structured interview in which the participant was asked what works well/needs improvement/works poorly in the system, how they use the stylus, how much information the shapes on the 3D map provide by themselves (without the audio labels) and how they might want descriptive information about each object on the map presented.

3.2 Results

The participant was indeed capable of finding some map features – and of reasoning about them spatially when the features were correctly located. However, in this pilot study the experimenter gave hints to her because it was very difficult for her to find many features (especially given that there are over seventy of them on the map and the system offered no way of guiding her to each feature). Indeed, the SUS score was 60, which indicates that the system was only partially usable. In the semi-structured interview, the participant reported that the overall concept of the interactive 3D map was sound, and that the features were well labeled, but that it was easy to get lost in the map, and noted confusion relating to certain features (such as slides) being present in multiple zones. She noted that she tended to alternate between exploring with both hands (without holding the stylus), and then picking up the stylus to obtain information about a specific structure. In addition, she suggested that detailed descriptions of a structure could be triggered by having the stylus tip dwell on the structure after the name was announced.

To address the challenge of having to search among over seventy structures, in the formal experiments we modified the zone announcements to include not only the zone names but also a listing of important features in each zone. We noticed that the zone announcements were not always triggered reliably, so we improved the CamIO software in such a way that not only increased how reliably zone announcements were triggered but also decreased the incidence of announcements being halted prematurely (due to noise in the estimation of the stylus tip location). Based on the performance of the participant in the pilot experiment, we set time-out periods for each task in the formal experiments (described in the next section).

Finally, the SUS was omitted in the formal experiments due to the difficulty of evaluating only the interactivity of the system (as opposed to factors beyond our control such as the design of the actual playground itself), and also to save time.

4 Formal Experiments

After the pilot experiment, we conducted formal experiments to confirm the usability of the improved interactive map system and to assess how using the system affects spatial learning and cognition.

4.1 Procedure

The formal experiments were conducted with four additional BVI participants ranging in age from 31–75 years old (2 male, 2 female, all blind: three with no form perception and one with some form perception in one eye). These experiments were similar to the pilot experiment, except that the audio labeling of zones was improved (as described in the previous section) and no hints were given to the participant during the formal trials. In the brief training phase of the experiment, we explained to the participants that the zone announcements functioned as directory listings, and could be used to locate specific structures more efficiently than exhaustively searching the entire map. We set the following time-out periods for the formal tasks: 2 min for each landmark task, 3 min for each landmark/route task and 3 min for each landmark/survey task.

4.2 Results

The results of the formal trials demonstrate that participants were able to acquire spatial knowledge (which would likely be inaccessible without the audio labels due to the absence of braille on the 3D map) *without hints* from the experimenter. (We speculate that this success was partly due to the listing of important zone features in the zone announcements, which enabled participants to search for features more efficiently than exhaustively searching the entire map.) Specifically, out of 23 total questions about spatial knowledge for each participant, the numbers of correct responses for the four participants were 22, 19, 14 and 21; we note that nearly all incorrect responses occurred when trials timed out (i.e., when the participant was unable to find a given feature in the allowed time).

We analyzed one component of this spatial knowledge statistically, the cardinal direction estimates, which relate specifically to survey knowledge. These estimates were reported in all trials that didn't time out, and they were *correct every time they were reported*. For each participant, the resulting 100% correct cardinal direction estimate rate is well above the chance success rate of 25% (implied by four possible cardinal directions). This is confirmed by a two-tailed binomial test [13] (with null hypothesis probabilities of 25% for correct estimates and 75% for incorrect estimates) for each participant, with all p-values equaling 2.5×10^{-4} or lower, ruling out the null hypothesis that the cardinal directions were estimated by chance.

In the semi-structured interviews, participants expressed positive feedback about the overall approach of the interactive 3D map, including the usefulness of the zone announcements, and noted that many of the structures had shapes that made them recognizable, or at least easy to remember once learned. Three participants said they alternated between exploring by hand without the stylus and using the stylus to get information about a structure of interest, while another said he preferred to hold the stylus while exploring with both hands. They described some issues that need improvement, including the difficulty fitting the stylus tip in some crowded locations of the map; important items (such as the drinking fountain) that have audio labels but are difficult to find since they are not listed in any zone announcement; audio label announcements that sometimes stutter or halt prematurely; how the large cube on top of the stylus sometimes makes it difficult to hold the stylus; and the need for explicit guidance to specific destinations.

When asked for an appropriate way to trigger the announcement of detailed information about a feature, some suggested having the stylus tip dwell at a feature, while others suggested a stylus double-tap gesture.

5 Conclusions and Future Work

We have described experiments with BVI participants using an interactive 3D map that is a scale model of an actual playground. These experiments not only confirm the usability of the interactive map but also demonstrate the ability of the participants to non-visually learn spatial information represented by the map, assessed in terms of landmark, route and survey knowledge. The approach highlights the advantages of creating interactivity with computer vision, which allows audio labels to be created for an existing 3D model without having to modify the model physically (aside from attaching barcode markers to the corners of the model). We note that the audio labels can include as much information as desired, and they are fully accessible even to BVI people who don't read braille.

Future work will include exploring the implementation of hand/finger tracking algorithms to eliminate the need for a stylus; offering audio labels in multiple languages; experimenting with an interface accessible to deaf-blind users; and providing audio instructions to guide the user to a desired destination on the map (perhaps using an approach similar to [14]). A bronze version of the interactive map is planned for permanent installation (including a stylus and rigidly mounted iOS device) at the actual playground. After the map installation is complete, we will perform user experiments to assess the impact that the interactive 3D map has on physical navigation of the playground.

Acknowledgments. The authors gratefully acknowledge support from NIH grant 5R01EY025332 and NIDILRR grant 90RE5024–01-00. We would like to thank the Magical Bridge Foundation for funding the development of the 3D-printed map.

References

1. Giudice, N.A.: Navigating without vision: Principles of blind spatial cognition. Edward Elgar Publishing, In Handbook of Behavioral and Cognitive Geography (2018)
2. Giudice, N.A., Guenther, B.A., Jensen, N.A., Haase, K.N.: Cognitive mapping without vision: comparing wayfinding performance after learning from digital touchscreen-based multimodal maps vs. embossed tactile overlays. Front. Hum. Neurosci. **14**, 87 (2020). https://doi.org/10.3389/fnhum.2020.00087
3. Biggs, B., Coughlan, J.M., Coppin, P.: Design and evaluation of an audio game-inspired auditory map interface. In: 25th International Conference on Auditory Display (ICAD 2019). Northumbria University, Newcastle-upon-Tyne, UK (June 2019)
4. Biggs, B.: Designing accessible nonvisual maps. OCAD University (2019) Retrieved from http://openresearch.ocadu.ca/id/eprint/2606
5. Biggs, B., Pitcher-Cooper, C., Coughlan, J.M.: Getting in touch with tactile map automated production: evaluating impact and areas for improvement. J. Technol. Persons with Disabilities **10** (2022)

6. Holloway, L., Marriott, K., Butler, M.: Accessible maps for the blind: comparing 3D printed models with tactile graphics. In: Proceedings of the 2018 CHI conference on human factors in computing systems, pp. 1–13 (April 2018)
7. Shi, L., McLachlan, R., Zhao, Y., Azenkot, S.: Magic touch: interacting with 3D printed graphics. In: Proceedings of the 18th International ACM SIGACCESS Conference on Computers and Accessibility, pp. 329–330 (Oct 2016)
8. Coughlan, J.M., Shen, H., Biggs, B.: Towards accessible audio labeling of 3D objects. J. Technol. Persons with Disabilities **8** (2020)
9. Brock, A.M., Truillet, P., Oriola, B., Picard, D., Jouffrais, C.: Interactivity improves usability of geographic maps for visually impaired people. Human-Computer Interact **30**(2), 156–194 (2015)
10. Biggs, B., Coughlan, J.M., Coppin, P.: Design and evaluation of an interactive 3D map. Rehabilit. Eng. Assistive Technol. Soc. North America (2021)
11. Siegel, A.W., White, S.H.: The development of spatial representations of large-scale environments. Adv. Child Dev. Behav. **10**, 9–55 (1975)
12. Brooke, J.: SUS: a retrospective. J. Usability Stud. **8**(2), 29–40 (2013)
13. Howell, D.C.: Statistical methods for psychology. Cengage Learning (2012)
14. Coughlan, J.M., Biggs, B., Rivière, M.-A., Shen, H.: An audio-based 3D spatial guidance AR system for blind users. In: 17th International Conference on Computers Helping People with Special Needs (ICCHP '20) (Sept 2020)

Development of Tabletop Models of Internal Organs for Anatomy Learning of the Visually Impaired

Moeka Shinoda[1], Akihiro Koike[1], Sayaka Teraguchi[2], and Yoshinori Teshima[3](✉)

[1] Master's Program in Innovative Mechanical and Electronic Engineering, Chiba Institute of Technology, 2-17-1 Tsudanuma, Narashino 275-0016, Chiba, Japan
18a2059qw@s.chibakoudai.jp

[2] Hiroshima Central Special Support School, 2-1-4 Hesakasenzoku, Higashiku, Hiroshima 732-0009, Hiroshima, Japan
s-teraguchik977277@hiroshima-c.ed.jp

[3] Department of Innovative Mechanical and Electronic Engineering, Chiba Institute of Technology, 2-17-1 Tsudanuma, Narashino 275-0016, Chiba, Japan
yoshinori.teshima@it-chiba.ac.jp

Abstract. In this study, we developed two types of tabletop models of internal organs as tactile teaching materials that can be used by the visually impaired when learning anatomy. The first one is a model in which parts of the internal organs that do not have connectional relationships are placed in a concave area of a pedestal. The second one is a model in which parts of the internal organs have a connectional relationship. Parts of the organs were connected using connecting pins, holes, and rubber tubes. A connected respiratory system, a connected digestive system, and a connected urinary system are also placed in the concave areas of the pedestal. Evaluation experiments conducted on the two types of tactile teaching materials revealed that the second model is a better teaching material in terms of placement stability and an understanding of the connectional relationship of internal organs.

1 Introduction

For the visually impaired to properly understand different shapes, an appropriate three-dimensional model applied as a tactile teaching material is required. For example, a service allowing the creation and use of tactile maps has been offered to the visually impaired and their caregivers [1–3]. Moreover, studies have been conducted on the use of 3D printers to help the visually impaired [4–6].

To date, many 3D teaching materials have been developed for the visually impaired [7], including models of mathematical curved surfaces [8], enlarged models of plankton skeletons [9], heart models [10], and tactile globes [11]. Thus, various targets have been developed for this purpose.

In the physical therapy department of a school for the blind, students with visual impairments aiming to become licensed masseurs, or acupuncture or moxibustion therapists, learn anatomy to understand the structure and function of the human body. However, commercially available organ models, which are almost at the real scale, are unsuitable for beginners learning anatomy. The authors developed prototypes of enlarged skull

K. Miesenberger et al. (Eds.): ICCHP-AAATE 2022, LNCS 13341, pp. 261–269, 2022.
https://doi.org/10.1007/978-3-031-08648-9_30

model, myofibril model, stretch reflex model, hepatic lobule model, crystalline lens model, ear model, and cardiac valve membrane models. The developed prototypes were utilized by visually impaired students at Hiroshima Central Special Support School.

In this paper, we report the development of a tabletop model of internal organs that enables visually impaired students to learn the position and shape of internal organs by touch, as well as the results of an evaluation experiment conducted on the models.

2 Method

In the development of a tabletop internal-organ model, it is important to make the model of an appropriate size and adequately simplify the shapes of the organs. In terms of size, commercially available organ models are almost at the actual scale and are thus too large to be provided to each student. The model was therefore reduced to a size that could be used on a desk. Commercially available models have complicated shapes that reflect those of the actual organs and, when downscaled, provide too much information for beginners. They should therefore be appropriately simplified. The degree of such simplification was not determined automatically, but was chosen through interactions between model developers and teachers in the educational field.

Through this development process, two tabletop internal-organ models (Models A and B) were developed in this study. Model A consists of 12 organs (i.e., lungs, trachea, heart, esophagus, stomach, spleen, liver, duodenum, pancreas, small intestine, large intestine, and kidneys). These organs have no connectional relationships and are simply placed in the concave portions of the pedestal. Figures 1(a) and 1(b) show photographs of the pedestal and placed organ parts of Model A. Model B consists of 13 organs (i.e., lungs, trachea, heart, esophagus, stomach, spleen, liver, duodenum, pancreas, small intestine, large intestine, kidneys, ureter, and bladder), which were placed in several connected forms in the concave portions of the pedestal. Figures 1(c) and 1(d) show photographs of the pedestal and placed organ parts of Model B. The details of the model development are as follows (note, however, that we mainly describe Model B owing to space limitations).

2.1 Model Development Policy

The authors improved the initial model based on feedback from the visually impaired who tried out the initial model, and the shape of each organ was modified using 3D CAD (Autodesk Fusion 360). Model B was designed such that the organ parts could be connected to each other with pins or rubber tubes to help understand the connectional relationships among the organs.

2.2 Model Creation Using Additive Manufacturing

To create the models, 3D printers (Microboard Technology, Afinia H800+, and Afinia H +1) were used. Model A was made of a PLA filament, and Model B was made of an ABS filament. Because the connecting pins of Model B were fine and easily damaged, their strength was retained by increasing the modeling density. After modeling all organ parts, both Models A and B were placed on the pedestals to check for any problems, such as interference between organs, and then adjusted overall.

The organ models of Model B are shown in Figs. 2, 3, 4, 5 and 6 and Fig. 7. Parts of the respiratory (trachea and two lungs) and circulatory (heart and spleen) systems are colored red, parts of the digestive system (esophagus, stomach, liver, duodenum, pancreas, small intestine, and large intestine) are colored yellow, and parts of the urinary system (kidneys, ureter, and bladder) are colored blue. Figure 7 show the connectional relationships for each organ system. Coloring the organ parts is helpful for both partially and fully sighted individuals in distinguishing the different organ systems and understanding each system as a unit.

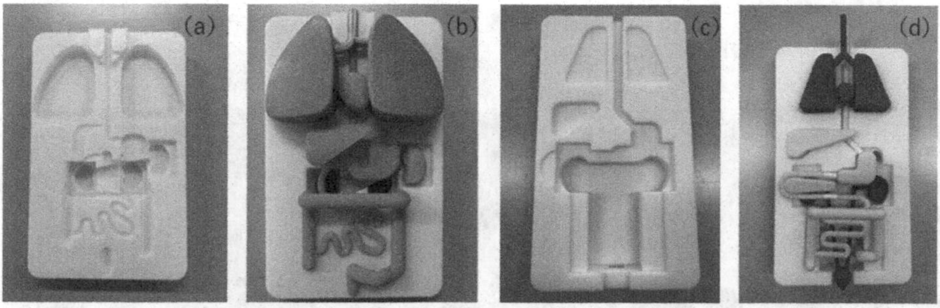

Fig. 1. (a) A pedestal of Model-A. The models of the internal organs are not placed in the pedestal. The size of the pedestal is 190 mm (length) × 120 mm (width) × 25 mm (height). (b) A pedestal of Model-A and all parts placed inside. (c) A pedestal of Model-B. The models of the internal organs are not placed in the pedestal. The size of the pedestal is 210 mm (length) × 120 mm (width) × 28 mm (height). (d) A pedestal of Model-B and all parts placed inside.

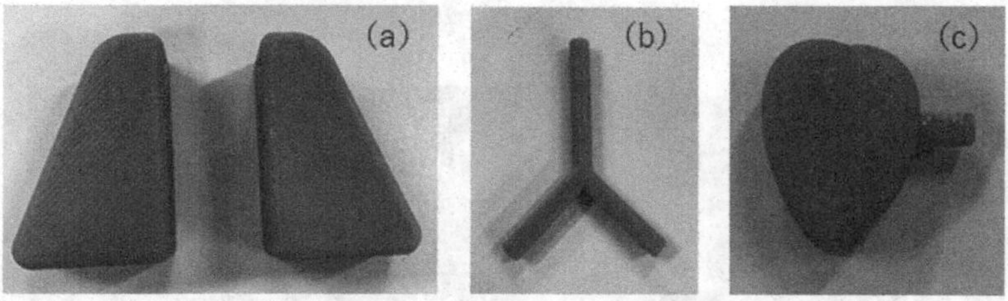

Fig. 2. (a) Two lungs (model): The right lung has a hole on the inner surface for connecting to the trachea. The left lung has two holes on the inner surface, one of which connects to the trachea and the other connects to the heart. (b) Trachea (model): The two prisms below the bifurcation are connected into the holes on the sides of both lungs. (c) Heart (model): A fixing pin for insertion into the left lung protrudes toward the right.

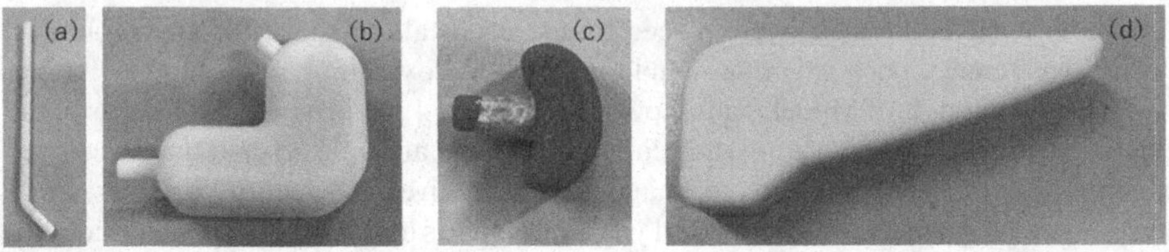

Fig. 3. (a) Esophagus (model): A rubber tube is installed at the bottom end to connect the entrance pin of the stomach. (b) Stomach (model): An entrance pin (upper) connects to the esophagus and an exit pin (lower) connects to the duodenum. (c) Spleen (model): A fixing pin for insertion into the stomach protrudes toward the left. (d) Liver (model): The left lobe (right side of the figure) is thin. The right lobe is thick and fits into the concave portion of the pedestal.

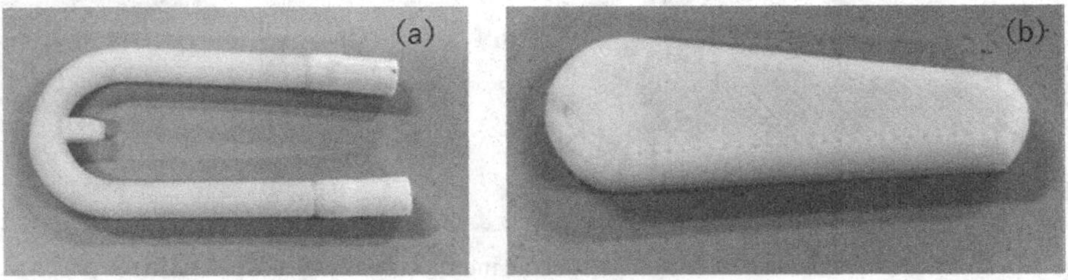

Fig. 4. (a) Duodenum (model): The rubber tube at the upper right end connects to the exit pin of the stomach, and the rubber tube at the lower right end connects to the entrance pin of the small intestine. There is a fixing pin inside the curve to insert into a hole of the pancreas. (b) Pancreas (model): There is a hole on the left side to insert a fixing pin of the duodenum.

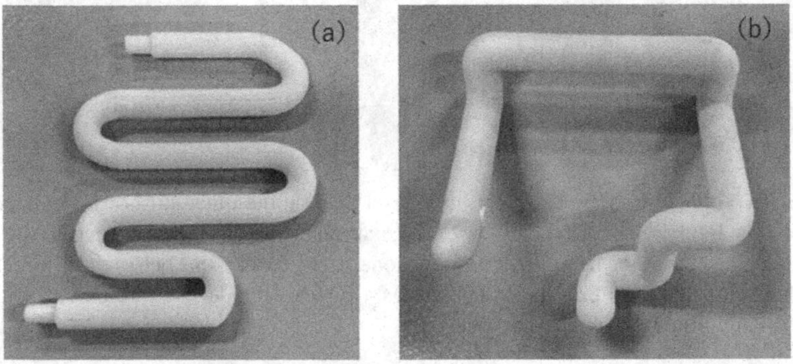

Fig. 5. (a) Small intestine (model): An entrance pin (upper end) connects to the duodenum and an exit pin (lower end) connects to the large intestine. (b). Large intestine (model): A hole for connecting an exit pin of the small intestine is installed in front of the left side (rubber tube embedded).

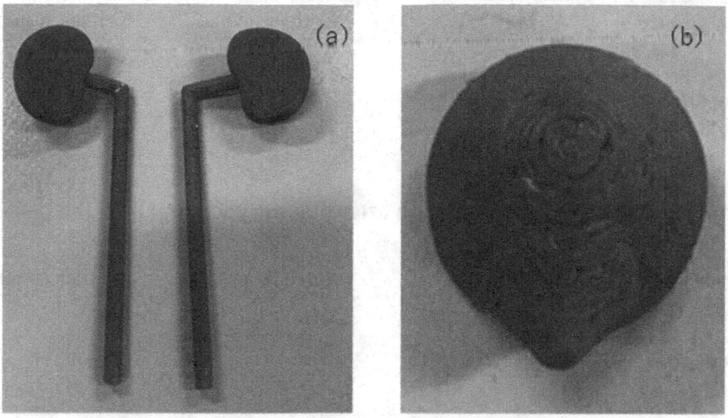

Fig. 6. (a) Kidney and ureter (model): The model of the kidney and ureter is pre-combined. (b) Bladder (model): There are two holes on the upper side of the bladder model for connecting the two ureters. The narrowed part on the lower side represents the urine outlet. (Color figure online)

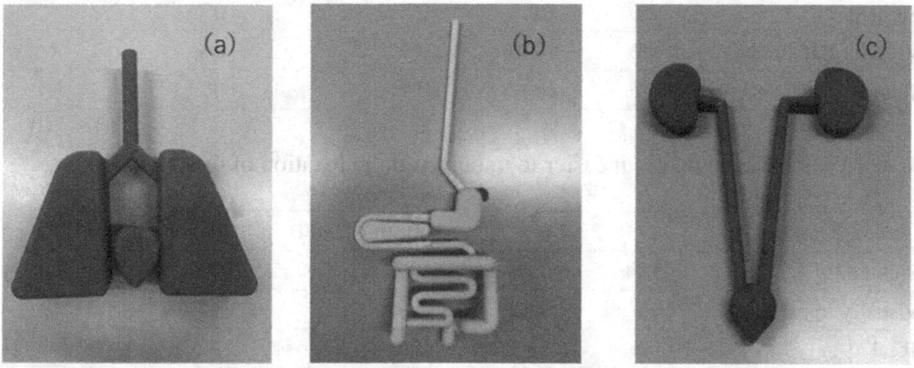

Fig. 7. (a) A unit in which the respiratory system and the heart are fixed. (b) A unit in which the digestive system and the spleen are fixed. (c) A unit of the urinary system. (Color figure online)

3 Evaluation Experiments

An evaluation was conducted on 12 subjects using Models A and B developed in this study. Six sighted adults wearing eye masks participated in the evaluation. The tester described the models and asked the subjects questions. It took approximately 75 min per subject to describe and conduct a listening-based investigation of the models. A similar survey was also conducted with six visually impaired people who were blind or amblyopic. In the survey of the visually impaired, the questionees read the description about the two anatomy models before the survey and touched the models for a few minutes just before the survey. The tester only asked questions in the survey, and each survey lasted 10–30 min. The results when comparing Models A and B are presented below.

Q1 Which model has a stable connection between organs?

Choices/Questionee	A	B	Both A and B	Neither A nor B
Sighted	0%	66%	34%	0%
Visually impaired	0%	100%	0%	0%
Total	0%	83%	17%	0%

Q2 Which model has a stable position after placing each organ on the pedestal?

Choices/Questionee	A	B	Both A and B	Neither A nor B
Sighted	34%	66%	0%	0%
Visually impaired	0%	100%	0%	0%
Total	17%	83%	0%	0%

Q3 Which model makes it easier to understand the connection of the organs?

Choices/Questionee	A	B	Both A and B	Neither A nor B
Sighted	0%	100%	0%	0%
Visually impaired	0%	100%	0%	0%
Total	0%	100%	0%	0%

Q4 Which model makes it easier to understand the location of the organs?

Choices/Questionee	A	B	Both A and B	Neither A nor B
Sighted	34%	66%	0%	0%
Visually impaired	0%	83%	0%	17%
Total	17%	74.5%	0%	8.5%

Q5 Which model is more suitable for self-operation?

Choices/Questionee	A	B	Both A and B	Neither A nor B
Sighted	33%	17%	33%	17%
Visually impaired	0%	83%	0%	17%
Total	16.5%	50%	16.5%	17%

Several observations were made during the evaluation experiment. For Model A, there were two subjects who could not accurately distinguish between the top and bottom of the heart. The kidneys and spleen were difficult to distinguish because their shapes and sizes were similar. The small intestine, pancreas, stomach, and spleen were also difficult to locate because there was no gap between them and the concave area of the pedestal. After placing the liver and large intestine in the concave area of the pedestal, the subjects frequently shifted them from the correct position. For Model B, the connections were mostly successful. However, for the connection between the small and large intestines, the interference between them hindered the connection task. When the end of the ureter was connected to the hole in the bladder, the connection was unstable because the current holes in the bladder were shallow. Because the large intestine and ureter switch positions dorsabdominally, it is necessary to temporarily lift the bladder and place the anus on the dorsal side when placing the large intestine and anus in the pedestal. Only half of the subjects conducted this task independently.

4 Discussion

From the results of Q1 and Q2, Model B was found to be superior to Model A in terms of the stability of the connection and arrangement of each organ part. We considered that connecting multiple organs into a unit would result in the stability of the arrangement. As a natural result, all subjects chose Model B for Q3 because the organ parts of Model A were not connected to each other; that is, they were independent, whereas the organ parts of Model B were able to connect with each other with rubber tubes or pins. For Q4, most subjects chose Model B. The organ parts were connected to each other before being placed on the pedestal in Model B, and thus it was considered that the connectional relationship between the organs could be more clearly imagined by the subjects. According to Q5, 67% of the subjects responded that Model A could be used without assistance, whereas 33% of the subjects answered that Model B could be used without assistance. The percentage of respondents who preferred Model A was the highest in Q5. This might be because most of the subjects were unable to connect the small intestine and the large intestine by themselves for Model B.

In a future study, modification of the shapes of the small intestine and large intestine can solve this problem and eliminate the interference of the parts during the connection task. Based on indications from the teachers of a school for the blind, we plan to make further improvements to Model B. In particular, the following three aspects will be applied: First, we will modify the shapes of the small and large intestines and improve the connectional holes of the bladder. In addition, we will place the duodenum and pancreas deeper than the current positions such that the duodenum will contact the right kidney and the pancreas will contact the left kidney. As a result, the stomach will be located in the correct position, that is, the front of the pancreas. Third, we will assign different colors to the heart and respiratory system. In Model B, both the circulatory system (the heart and spleen) and the respiratory system (the lungs and trachea) are colored in red. In a future study, we plan to change the color of the respiratory system from red to green, incorporating the opinions of the subjects.

5 Conclusion

In this study, we developed two types of models with the aim of providing tabletop models of internal organs that can be used by visually impaired students when learning anatomy. One is a model in which the parts of the internal organs do not have connectional relationships, and the other is a model in which the parts of the internal organs have such relationships. Evaluation experiments conducted on the two types of tactile teaching materials clarified that the model with a connectional relationship was a better teaching material in terms of placement stability and understanding the connectional relationship of the internal organs.

Acknowledgments. YT would like to thank Dr. Hisao Honda for his helpful comments on improving the tactile model. This study was partially supported by a Grant-in-Aid for Scientific Research (A) (18200049) and Research (C) (20K04226) from the Japan Society for the Promotion of Science (JSPS). We would like to thank Editage (www.editage.com) for the English language editing.

References

1. Minatani, K., et al.: Tactile map automated creation system to enhance the mobility of blind persons - its design concept and evaluation through experiment. ICCHP 2010, LNCS, vol. 6180, pp. 534–540. Springer, Heidelberg (2010)
2. Watanabe, T., Yamaguchi, T., Koda, S., Minatani, K.: Tactile Map Automated Creation System Using OpenStreetMap. In: Miesenberger, K., Fels, D., Archambault, D., Peňáz, P., Zagler, W. (eds.) ICCHP 2014. LNCS, vol. 8548, pp. 42–49. Springer, Cham (2014). https://doi.org/10.1007/978-3-319-08599-9_7
3. Watanabe, T., Yamaguchi, T.: Six-and-a-half-year practice of tactile map creation service. Stud Health Technol Inform. **242**, 687–694 (2017)
4. Minatani, K.: An Analysis and Proposal of 3D Printing Applications for the Visually Impaired. Stud Health Technol Inform. **242**, 918–921 (2017)
5. Minatani, K.: A Proposed Method for Producing Embossed Dots Graphics with a 3D Printer. In: Miesenberger, K., Kouroupetroglou, G. (eds.) ICCHP 2018. LNCS, vol. 10897, pp. 143–148. Springer, Cham (2018). https://doi.org/10.1007/978-3-319-94274-2_20
6. Minatani, K.: Examining visually impaired people's embossed dots graphics with a 3D printer: physical measurements and tactile observation assessments. AHFE 2018, AISC, vol. 794, pp. 960–969. Springer, Cham (2018)
7. Teshima, Y.: Three-dimensional tactile models for blind people and recognition of 3D objects by touch. ICCHP 2010, LNCS, vol. 6180, pp. 513–514. Springer, Heidelberg (2010)
8. Teshima, Y., et al.: Models of Mathematically Defined Curved Surfaces for Tactile Learning. In: Miesenberger, K., Klaus, J., Zagler, W., Karshmer, A. (eds.) ICCHP 2010. LNCS, vol. 6180, pp. 515–522. Springer, Heidelberg (2010). https://doi.org/10.1007/978-3-642-14100-3_77
9. Teshima, et al.: Enlarged skelton models of plankton for tactile teaching. ICCHP 2010, LNCS, vol. 6180, pp. 523–526. Springer, Heidelberg (2010)
10. Yamazawa, K., et al.: Three-Dimensional Model Fabricated by Layered Manufacturing for Visually Handicapped Persons to Trace Heart Shape. In: Miesenberger, K., Karshmer, A., Penaz, P., Zagler, W. (eds.) ICCHP 2012. LNCS, vol. 7383, pp. 505–508. Springer, Heidelberg (2012). https://doi.org/10.1007/978-3-642-31534-3_74
11. Teshima, Y., et al.: Development of Tactile Globe by Additive Manufacturing. In: Miesenberger, K., Manduchi, R., Covarrubias Rodriguez, M., Peňáz, P. (eds.) ICCHP 2020. LNCS, vol. 12376, pp. 419–426. Springer, Cham (2020). https://doi.org/10.1007/978-3-030-58796-3_49

Semi-automatic Contour "Gist" Creation for Museum Painting Tactile Exploration

Son Duy Dao(✉), Ngoc-Tan Truong, Edwige Pissaloux, Katerine Romeo, and Lilia Djoussouf

LITIS, University of Rouen Normandy, Rouen, France
{son-duy.dao,edwige.pissaloux}@univ-rouen.fr

Abstract. Contour "gist" creation (i.e., creating a simplified contour which represents an object) is always required in helping Visually Impaired People (VIP) to do an effective tactile exploration on painting images in a museum. However, this process is very labor intensive, and the existing contour/edge detection algorithms in the literature are not capable of creating the contour "gist" models automatically. In this paper, a method for semi-automatic contour "gist" creation for museum painting tactile exploration is proposed. It uses 2 databases (original image database and contour "gist" model database), an object detection algorithm (deep learning), and object-contour "gist" model matching algorithm. The output of this method would be transferred to Force-Feedback Tablet (F2T) (an original tactile device) to allow the VIP to explore the museum paintings more effectively.

Keywords: Contour gist creation · Force-feedback tablet · Tactile exploration · Visually impaired people

1 Introduction

The World Health Organization (WHO) [1] estimated that there are about 2.2 billion people with vision impairment and blindness (Visually Impaired People or VIP) in the world. The vision impairment and blindness severely impact the life quality of many people, and contribute to walking difficulty and social isolation. For example, several societal activities such as a visit of museums and artworks perception are almost inaccessible for the VIP. Moreover, museum access for the VIP audiences is generally designed exclusively for them by sighted curators and specialist access providers. This 'top-down' provision not only excludes the VIP visitors from shared (inclusive) museum experiences with their sighted peers, it also means they have little or no choice about when, how and to what they are granted access. Furthermore, in the limited instances where accessible provision is provided for the VIP audiences, it is almost always low-tech and restricted to a tiny fraction of the institution's holdings.

Paintings are important parts of any museum. Currently, audio descriptions and 3D models for tactile exploration are the most common solutions which allow the VIP to access to the museum paintings. However, these solutions have several drawbacks such as the sequential and passive audio descriptions which are not adapted to different visitors,

K. Miesenberger et al. (Eds.): ICCHP-AAATE 2022, LNCS 13341, pp. 270–277, 2022.
https://doi.org/10.1007/978-3-031-08648-9_31

expensive 3D models with too many details for tactile exploration. Therefore, simplified and selective representations of the museum paintings for active tactile exploration are required. The classical automatic methods fail to provide such simplified and selective representations [2]. That is why the "gist" concept is used here as the "essential meaning" may be lost.

"Gist" is a global first impression of an image [3]. The "gist" representation of an image is a representation in which only a few important objects and/or information are considered. The "gist" representation can be seen as a global and rough "map" of an image. In this paper, contour "gist" model is defined as a simplified contour which represents an object. An example of the contour "gist" model is shown in Fig. 1, in which the left image (a) is a scene of the Bayeux Tapestry, XI century (France); while the right image (b) represents its contour "gist" model [4].

Fig. 1. An example of contour "gist" model [4]

There have been a significant number of contour/edge detection algorithms in the literature. In a research of Yang *et al.* [5], a convolutional encoder–decoder framework to extract image contours supported by a generative adversarial network to improve the contour quality was developed. In a research of Al-Bande *et al.* [6], an object localization technique with deep learning was proposed to improve fetal head contour detection. Zhang, Lin, and Li [7] developed a biologically-inspired model applying binocular disparity and receptive field dynamics for contour detection. A robust contour detection operator with combined push-pull inhibition and surround suppression was proposed by Melotti *et al.* [8]. Nevertheless, applying the existing automatic contour/edge detection algorithms to create the contour "gist" representation of an image as shown in Fig. 1 is still very challenging. To overcome this challenge, this paper proposes a semi-automatic contour "gist" creation for museum painting tactile exploration. Section 2 identifies the challenges that the existing approaches in the literature are facing. Section 3 presents the proposed method for the semi-automatic contour "gist" creation. Finally some conclusions and the future works are given in Sect. 4.

2 Current Challenges

Although, a significant number of automatic contour/edge detection algorithms exist in the literature, they fail to create the contour "gist" model of a museum image as shown in Fig. 1. Currently, we are facing 3 challenges as follows:

+ The objects in the image in the museum are usually very unique (e.g., very old boats, very old animals, very old church, very old people, very old building, etc.). Therefore, the specific data-base is required in order to recognize such objects.
+ The existing contour/edge detection algorithms in the literature are not capable of removing some internal contour/edge (a typical result shown in Fig. 2, for example). As results, more powerful methods, which can eliminate useless edges, for the complex object recognitions are necessary.
+ Currently, an algorithm for automatic contour "gist" creation does not exist in the literature.

To overcome above limitations, an innovative approach for semi-automatic contour "gist" creation for museum painting tactile exploration will be presented in the next Section.

Fig. 2. A typical result from an automatic contour/edge detection algorithm [9]

3 Proposed Approach for Semi-automatic Contour "Gist" Creation

The proposed approach for semi-automatic contour "gist" creation for museum painting tactile exploration is shown in Fig. 3. As can be seen from Fig. 3, there are two databases, namely original image database and contour "gist" model database. In addition, there is an object detection algorithm which must be trained in the image database. Furthermore, an object-contour "gist" model matching algorithm is used to decide the correct contour "gist" model(s) to be displayed on the computer. Once the whole processing performed, the computer will send the gist to Force-Feedback Tablet (F2T) for the manual exploration via F2T joystick as shown in Fig. 4. It should be noted that in this approach, contour "gist" model database must be manually prepared in advance. To the best authors' knowledge, no existing contour/edge algorithms in the literature can do it automatically – because the contour "gist" for the VIP tactile exploration must be very simple and very easy to understand. Sometimes, we have to move and/or separate the objects a little bit to make the contour "gist" understandable by the VIP. For example, if we do not separate the bird from the man as shown in Fig. 3, it would be very hard to the VIP to image and understand the contour.

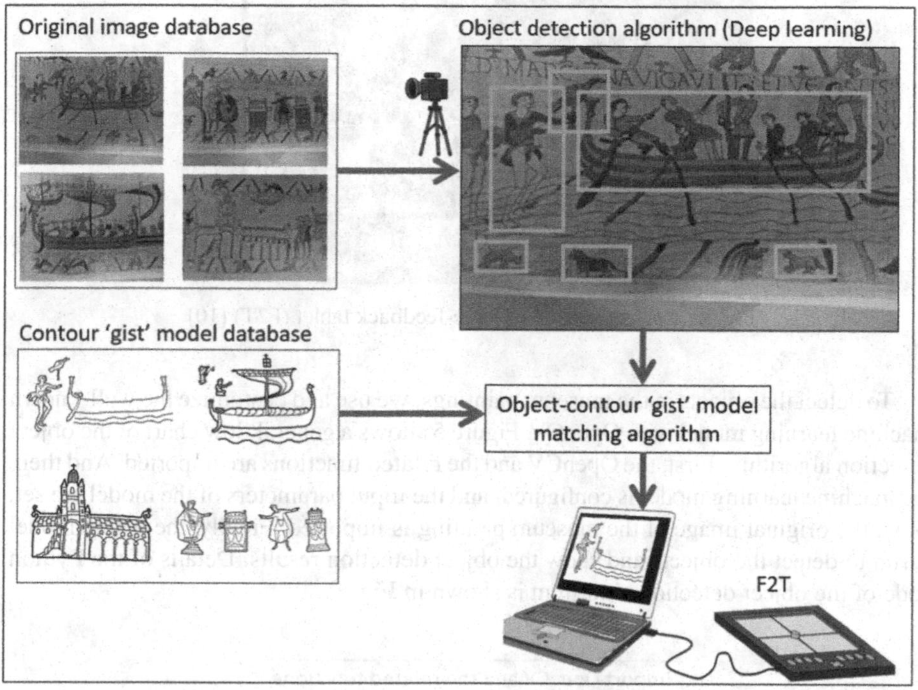

Fig. 3. Proposed approach for semi-automatic contour "gist" creation

F2T is a new haptic device, based on force-feedback principle, used to help the VIP to access and interact with 2D data. Figure 4 shows the current version of our F2T prototype. Each F2T has a flat thumbstick mounted on a 2D actuated support, enabling force feedback effects on the user's finger. More specifically, the flat thumbstick measures the user's intended movements independently from mobile support's actual movements, enabling highly interactive effects, static and dynamic effects, or guidances. For example, when a VIP touches the thumbstick of the F2T, he/she can follow the contour(s) being displayed in the connected computer as illustrated in Fig. 3, i.e., doing the tactile exploration. With the combination of the tactile exploration using F2T and audio description, the VIP can enjoy the paintings in the museum better. As a result, museum visiting experience of the VIP would be significantly enhanced. For more details about the working principle and technical aspects of the F2T, it is advised to refer to [10].

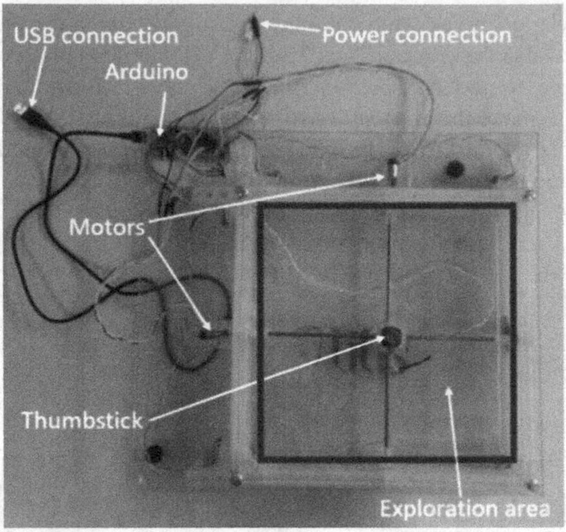

Fig. 4. Current version of force-feedback tablet (F2T) [10]

To detect the objects in the museum paintings, we use and customize the well-known machine learning model with OpenCV. Figure 5 shows a general flow chart of the object detection algorithm. First, the OpenCV and the related functions are imported. And then, the machine learning model is configured, and the input parameters of the model are set. Next, the original image of the museum painting is imported. Finally, the whole model is run to detect the objects and show the object detection results. Details of the Python code of the object detection algorithm is shown in Fig. 6.

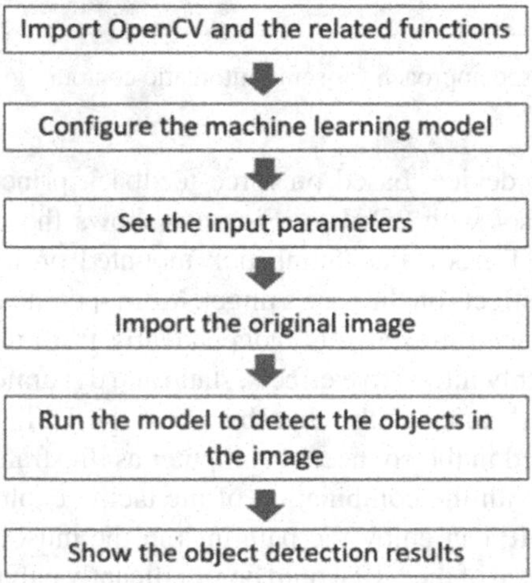

Fig. 5. Flow chart of the object detection algorithm

```
import cv2
import matplotlib.pyplot as plt
config_file = 'ssd_mobilenet_v3_large_coco_2020_01_14.pbtxt'
frozen_model = 'frozen_inference_graph.pb'

model =cv2.dnn_DetectionModel(frozen_model,config_file)
classLabels = []
file_name = 'Labels.txt'
with open (file_name, 'rt') as fpt:
    classLabels = fpt.read().rstrip('\n').split('\n')

model.setInputSize(110,110)
model.setInputScale(1/127.5)
model.setInputMean((127.5,127.5,127.5))
model.setInputSwapRB(True)

img = cv2.imread('p26.png')
plt.imshow(cv2.cvtColor(img,cv2.COLOR_BGR2RGB))
ClassIndex, confidece, bbox = model.detect(img,confThreshold=0.22)
font_scale = 2
font = cv2.FONT_HERSHEY_PLAIN
for ClassInd, conf, boxes in zip(ClassIndex.flatten(),confidece.flatten(),bbox):
    cv2.rectangle(img,boxes,(0,0,255), 2)
    cv2.putText(img,classLabels[ClassInd-1],(boxes[0]+10,boxes[1]+40),font, fontScale=font_scale,color=(0,0,255), thickness=3)
    print(classLabels[ClassInd-1])

plt.imshow(cv2.cvtColor(img,cv2.COLOR_BGR2RGB))
```

Fig. 6. Python code of the object detection algorithm using OpenCV library [11]

Some test results of the object detection algorithm are shown in Fig. 7. As it can be seen from Fig. 7 that the algorithm can detect the boat and some people, but it is still not perfect because some other people and a small boat are still missing. That is why we are working on the algorithm training and customization on the dataset from museum paintings to make it more effective. As mentioned before, the objects in the museum paintings are usually very unique (very old boats, animals, people, etc.). Therefore, the specific dataset is required in order to recognize such objects.

File Edit View Insert Cell Kernel Widgets Help Fiable | Python 3 (ipykernel)

▶ Exécuter ■ C ⏩ Code

```
    cv2.putText(img,classLabels[ClassInd-1],(boxes[0]+10,boxes[1]+40),font, fontScale=font_scale,color=(0,0,255), thickness=3)
    print(classLabels[ClassInd-1])

plt.imshow(cv2.cvtColor(img,cv2.COLOR_BGR2RGB))
```

```
Objects detected are:
person
person
person
person
boat
person
Out[62]: <matplotlib.image.AxesImage at 0x17799afed00>
```

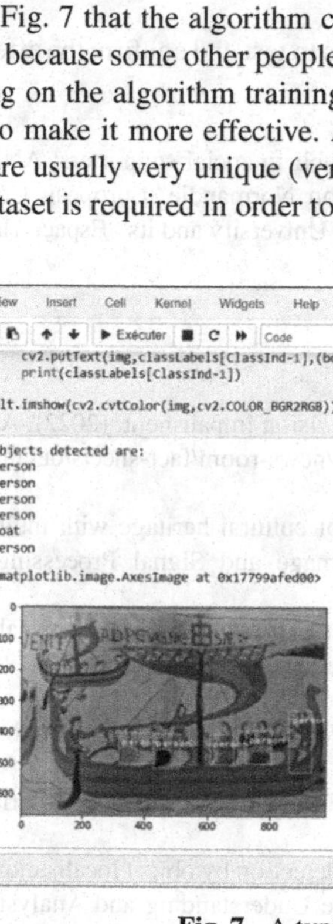


```
Entrée [ ]:
```

Fig. 7. A typical object detection result

It is noted that this is on-going research project, and it has not been fully complete yet. Although, we have made some progress on F2T prototype as shown in Fig. 4, the object detection algorithm using OpenCV as shown in Figs. 5 and 6, and some experiment results as shown in Fig. 7, the final version of the object detection algorithm as well as the object-contour "gist" model matching algorithm have not been finalized yet. In this paper, we would like to raise a hard and interesting problem related to tactile exploration for the VIP and propose an idea for a possible solution. Shortly, we will setup the experiments to test and to confirm the effectiveness of the proposed approach. We admit this limitation and mention it as our future work in Sect. 4.

4 Conclusions and Future Works

In this paper, a new method for semi-automatic contour "gist" creation for museum painting tactile exploration was proposed. The proposed method has two databases (namely original image database and contour "gist" model database), one camera, one object detection algorithm (deep learning), one object-contour "gist" model matching algorithm, and one Force-Feedback Table (F2T). The proposed approach can allow the Visually Impaired People (VIP) to do an effective tactile exploration on painting images in a museum.

In our future work, we will setup the experiments to test and confirm the effectiveness of the proposed approach.

Acknowledgement. The authors would like to thank their financial supporters: ANR (Agence Nationale de Recherche), Normandy University, Région Normandie, European Commission, CNRS and MEAE (France Embassy in London), Rouen University and its "Espace Handicap".

References

1. World Health Organization (WHO): Blindness and vision impairment. (2022). Accessed on 31 Jan 2022; Available from: https://www.who.int/news-room/fact-sheets/detail/blindness-and-visual-impairment
2. Souradi, A., et al.: Towards the tactile discovery of cultural heritage with multi-approach segmentation. In: International Conference on Image and Signal Processing. Springer International Publishing (2020)
3. Groen, I.I.A., et al.: From image statistics to scene gist: evoked neural activity reveals transition from low-level natural image structure to scene category. J. Neurosci. **33**(48), 18814–18824 (2013)
4. La Tapisserie de Bayeux. (2022). Accessed on 05 Feb 02 022. Available from: https://www.bayeuxmuseum.com/la-tapisserie-de-bayeux/
5. Yang, H., et al.: ContourGAN: image contour detection with generative adversarial network. Knowl.-Based Syst. **164**, 21–28 (2019)
6. Al-Bander, B., et al.: Improving fetal head contour detection by object localisation with deep learning. In: Annual Conference on Medical Image Understanding and Analysis. Springer International Publishing (2020)
7. Zhang, Q., Lin, C., Li, F.: Application of binocular disparity and receptive field dynamics: a biologically-inspired model for contour detection. Pattern Recogn. **110**, 107657 (2021)

8. Melotti, D., et al.: A robust contour detection operator with combined push-pull inhibition and surround suppression. Inf. Sci. **524**, 229–240 (2020)
9. Roussel, L.: Contribution to assisting the (re-)presentation of works of art to the visually impaired Master's thesis. Université de Rouen Normandie, Litis (2021)
10. Gay, S.L., et al.: F2T: a novel force-feedback haptic architecture delivering 2D data to visually impaired people. IEEE Access **9**, 94901–94911 (2021)
11. OpenCV: TensorFlow Object Detection API (2022). Accessed on 29 Feb 2022. Available from: https://github.com/opencv/opencv/wiki/TensorFlow-Object-Detection-API

Inclusive Multimodal Discovery of Cultural Heritage: Listen and Touch

Katerine Romeo[1](✉), Hannah Thompson[2], and Marion Chottin[3]

[1] LITIS, University of Rouen Normandy, Rouen, France
katerine.romeo@univ-rouen.fr
[2] Royal Holloway University of London, London, United Kingdom
[3] IHRIM, CNRS-ENS Lyon, Lyon, France

Abstract. Museums around the world present their collections mainly to visual perception without the possibility of hearing or touching paintings, sculptures and artworks (Size, fragility). It has now become a priority to promote inclusive approaches to issues related to accessibility. Audio and tactile perceptions are often complementary. The figurative elements of the paintings are difficult to describe with words but can be presented tactilely. Other elements cannot be perceived via touch, for example colors, light, some links between elements; but these elements and the feelings they arouse can be evoked via audio-description. We present our tests of objective and sensorial audio description. Then we propose tactile exploration with the use of Force Feedback Tablet (F2T) to discover the general shape of some elements in a painting and complete the perception with an inclusive audio-description.

Keywords: Multimodal perception · Inclusiveness · Accessibility · Audio-description · Force-feedback

1 Introduction

Today, around the world, some museums offer mediation devices for visually impaired people (VIP). The majority of these devices consist of guided tours by lecturers trained, more or less well, in "visual impairment" [1]. During these visits, a speaker describes some paintings, and sometimes also provides relief drawings to touch, made from these works, or some of the objects or materials that are on the canvas, or even three-dimensional transpositions (such as the multisensory case of the *Petit Palais* (Paris, France) which contains the 3D transposition of "The Sweeper" by Pieter Janssens Elinga). Rarely, some works are accompanied in situ by their tactile reproductions [2]. Finally, several museums have recently made available audio guides that are supposed to be accessible to blind and visually impaired people, which differ from traditional audio guides by the fact that they add a description of the work to the commentary [3].

K. Miesenberger et al. (Eds.): ICCHP-AAATE 2022, LNCS 13341, pp. 278–285, 2022.
https://doi.org/10.1007/978-3-031-08648-9_32

The insufficiency of these devices can be analyzed according to 6 points:

1) The principle of guided tours, organized on a very occasional basis, often on weekdays when blind and visually impaired people work, does not guarantee equal access [4] which is a right according to the "disability" law in France.
2) The quality of the descriptions depends on the skills of the speakers, whose "visual disability" training, which is not compulsory, has generally not been carried out, or not properly [5].
3) These descriptions are always intertwined with historical and contextual elements, which deprives the VIP of access to the purely sensorial / imaginative / aesthetic / subjective experience of the artwork.
4) Tactile models, are both expensive and voluminous, and are considered to be too few to justify a trip to the museums that offer them [5].
5) In rare cases where tactile transpositions (e.g. the tactile artworks of the Musée du quai Branly (Paris, France)) are offered to visitors, several people cannot explore the same artwork at the same time, contrary to what happens with the sense of sight, which brings a sharing of experience [6].
6) Most of these devices generate frustration because they aim above all at the identification of pictorial elements and the transmission of the historical and artistic context of the work, and not at arousing an aesthetic experience [5].

We propose in this article, to combine listening and touch for a multisensory perception that increases the impact and memorability of the work. To effectively bring together these two modes of transmission, we present in this article the use of figurative and non-figurative elements (Sect. 2) with the multisensory approach. The inclusive descriptive audio approach is explained in Sect. 3, and the tactile approach with force feedback and finger guidance is introduced in Sect. 4, followed by the Conclusion and Perspectives.

2 Multisensory Approach

The figurative elements of the paintings are difficult to describe with words, but can be presented tactilely. Nonfigurative elements could not be perceived via touch, for example colors, light, some links between elements; but these elements and the feelings they arouse can be evoked via audio-description.

No description will evoke in the mind a representation perfectly similar to the original work – and this is for at least two reasons:

1) the nature of language, whose words can only be general, where the sensations are always particular (we can distinguish indefinitely by words the different forms of mouth, which we will not be able to reproduce the absolutely singular one of the beloved woman – cf. the story told by Diderot in Encyclopedia [7].
2) the nature of the imagination, the limits of which Descartes already pointed out:

"If I want to think of a chiliagon, although I understand that it is a figure consisting of a thousand sides just as well as I understand the triangle to be a three-sided figure, I do not in the same way imagine the thousand sides or see them as if they were present before me" [8].

If it is possible for us to mentally represent simple figures, our imagination quickly reaches its limits for complex figures. In short, a description of figures and their arrangement on the canvas will never arouse in the mind what their tracing arouses on sensitivity – hence the importance of tactile transposition.

Conversely, touch alone is not enough:

1) It is rare that touch alone can identify on its own what is being felt.
2) Some elements could not be perceived via touch, for example colors, light, some links between elements and facial expressions;

If tactile transpositions allow an understanding of the overall composition of the painting, its lines of force, and the painted shapes, they obviously fail to transmit what Aristotle called "the sensorial proper to the sight", namely the colors, and all that is correlated to them: the light, the gaze of the characters, the shadows that give its perspective to a painting, etc.

These elements and the feelings they arouse can be evoked via audio-description.

It is therefore necessary to articulate listening and touch: articulation of a global tactile presentation and an audio description that completes it at level 1) of the general framework of the work or scene; 2) the meaning of what one touches; 3) particular elements that were removed during tactile transposition; 4) visual elements (colors, light, etc.); 5) historical knowledge.

3 Inclusive Descriptive Audio Approach

In 2018, the TETMOST consortium organized a series of workshops, during which descriptions of paintings were co-written with blind, partially blind and sighted people. These descriptions were intended to provoke an aesthetic experience through listening.

After being read and amended by the specialist of Aboriginal painting Philippe Peltier, a sample of these descriptions was listened to by 27 persons with various visual capacities: 11 people who are early blind, 8 people who are late blind, 5 visually impaired persons and 3 blindfolded persons. Each of them listened to two audio descriptions of the same painting, one of the following: "The Dream of the Snake" by "W. Tjapaltjarri or "Ord River, Bow River, Denham River," by R. Thomas. The first description was "objective", describing the elements very briefly with some essential details. The second description of the same painting was "sensorial" with more picturesque details and feelings felts in view of this painting.

It has been found that colors and other visual elements can be by means of language 1) imagined by the visually impaired people who have already seen and have preserved visual memories; 2) felt in their own way by early blind people who have never seen: colors are associated with feelings, abstract ideas, tactile experiences, etc.

And thus, we can say descriptions of visual elements produce a true aesthetic experience. Alison Eardley shows that audio descriptions arouse in sighted people also truly aesthetic experiences [9]. Audio descriptions of visual elements bring an inclusive approach and take in consideration the expectations of everyone.

On the emotion aroused by the audio description, Table 1. gives the answers for the question "Listening to this audio description, have you lived an experience, an aesthetic pleasure?" Sometimes people have not had any aesthetic experience, sometimes they have had one after listening to both types of audio description.

Table 1 gives all the diversity of preference of people with or without visual impairment between objective and sensorial audio descriptions (AD). It can be observed that sensorial audio descriptions were preferred by a majority.

The majority of visually impaired and blind participants preferred sensorial audio descriptions. Late blind people who saw the colors chose 75% of sensorial audio descriptions compared to 25% of objective audio descriptions, which is the same percentage for the sighted blindfolded participants; while the early blind participants were divided in their choice (45% chose the objective audio description, 55% the one that was sensorial). We can observe that a painting can elicit an aesthetic experience even in people who have never seen.

Table 1. Answers to the question: "Listening to this audio description, have you lived an experience, an aesthetic pleasure?". N.B. Sometimes people have not had any aesthetic experience, sometimes they have had one after listening to both types of audio description.

Preference	Dream of the snake		River Ord, river Bow, river Denham	
	"objective" AD	"sensorial" AD	"objective" AD	"sensorial" AD
Early Blind Persons: 11	2	4	3	2
Late Blind Persons: 7	1	1	1	5
Visually impaired Persons: 6		2		2
Sighted blinded Persons: 4		2	1	1

4 Tactile Approach

The first advantage of touch, is to make the pictorial forms feel as they are on the painting and not in an approximate way as an audio description presents.

The tactile aspect of an artwork may bring also the motion sensitivity of touch: feeling the undulation of a wave, the movement of a walking horse, etc. But as it was said earlier in Sect. 2, some tactile elements miss information like color or context. And we need simplified shapes for easy transcription of artworks to tactile perception [10]. Segmentation of various elements in the painting could be done semi-automatically under the direction of museum curators.

For a multisensory approach we propose a Force-feedback tablet, F2T [11] which can react to the user's movements and apply a force against or in-line with the movement of the user's finger according to the characteristic properties of the element on the painting (Fig. 1).

To complement the audio description, F2T can:

1) Give a first impression (gist). The user can explore freely the entire space of the painting image on the tablet which is a square of $25cm^2$. Some areas could be defined as walls or boundaries of the explored shape [12].
2) Guide the finger in the exploration. Simple geometric shapes are easy to recognize, but when the exploration becomes more complex, the guidance mode can shorten the exploration time.
3) Offer interactivity. Finger exploration can be accompanied by short audio descriptions of the elements touched virtually through the thumbstick.
4) Create edges and reliefs. The boundaries or profile of the explored element can't be crossed with the finger for a better understanding of the outline or with a relief that can be crossed with a tactile illusion of slope.
5) Create flow or rail effects. These effects are useful for keeping the finger in a predetermined path on the picture of the painting. Force feedback gives the feeling of resistance when the finger moves away from the path and a feeling of acceleration when the finger is on the path.
6) Create attractor. The finger is attracted to a particular element of the artwork.
7) Create textures. Texture effects are produced with force feedback by creating a feeling of resistance (solid friction, liquid friction) [13].

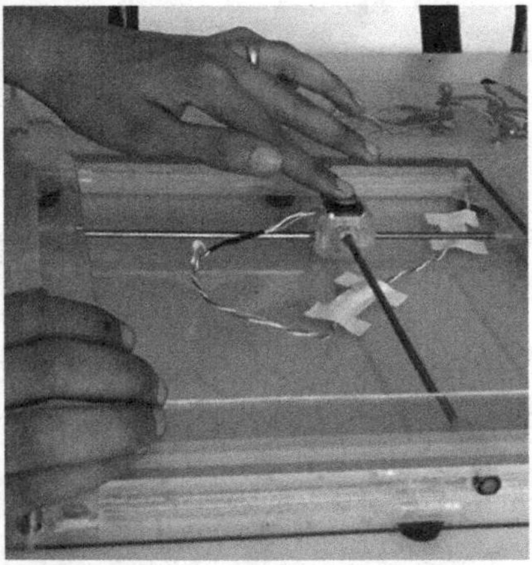

Fig. 1. F2T, force feedback tablet used by a blindfolded participant during a test. The thumbstick guides the finger around the shape of an element of a picture.

These movements associated with the audio description provide an original emergence of perceptions (gist), and stimulate imagination. People with visual disabilities and sighted blindfolded people who participated in our tests faithfully described the figures discovered with the finger guided by the thumbstick [13]. Participants expressed satisfaction at having freely explored the surface of the F2T tablet in addition to being guided [12] even if it takes longer.

To illustrate the articulation of listening and touch, two examples of tactile paths are given in Figs. 2A and 3A, for the audio description of these elements in the painting "The dream of the snake". The path is represented with a green line, it can start if the user wishes to be guided during the audio description and can be repeated if necessary.

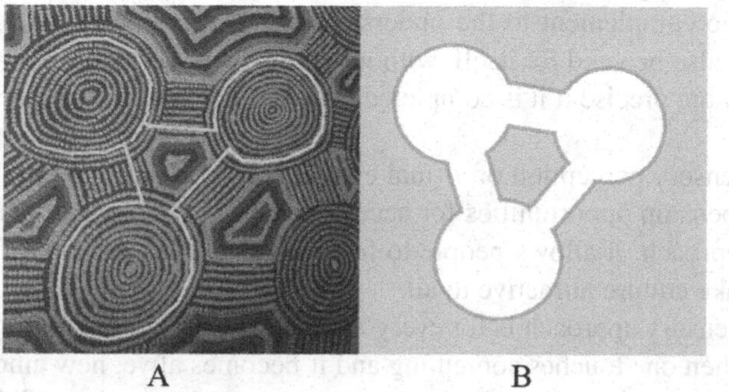

Fig. 2. Tactile path in the painting "The dream of the snake". The guided path helps the VIP to explore quickly the outline of some elements as shown in the left image. The same path can be explored freely following the white area in the image on the right.

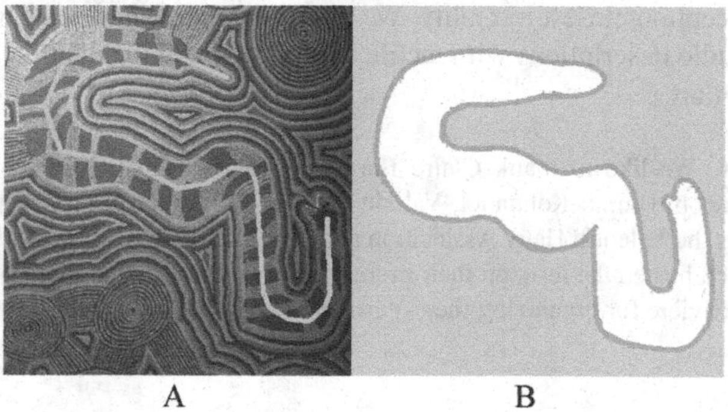

Fig. 3. On the left image, a tactile guided path of the shape of the snake gives the curves as it is painted. The outline of the image on the right can be explored freely moving the thumbstick in the white area.

If the user wishes to explore freely and at his own pace the different elements of the painting after listening to the audio description, it is possible to take an element and explore it to understand its shape. The tactile images are generated by the contours of the elements, the concentric circles connected with lines (Fig. 2B) and the shape of the snake (Fig. 3B). The outline of the elements can be followed with the finger inside the green colored space that can't be crossed. The user's finger is brought to the white surface as at the start of the tactile path. In these examples, the contour exploration was chosen from the inside so that the user virtually "touches" the element. It is possible to reverse as in the case of exploration of a human profile where one can "touch" the outline of the nose, etc.

5 Conclusion

In this article, we present a new approach to articulating inclusive audio description and virtual tactile exploration of artworks. We confirm that the audio description is an indispensable complement to the understanding of the artwork with touch. Audio description can also be valid for itself, without vision, without touch. But the perception of the work is more precise if it is completed by a tactile representation according to the user's choice.

The multisensory perception of virtual elements can be practiced in the museum or at home and opens up opportunities for access to culture for prevented audiences. It is an inclusive approach, it allows people to feel new emotions in front of a work of art and aims to make culture attractive to all.

This multisensory approach is for everyone, not just visually impaired persons, so it is inclusive. When one touches something and it becomes alive, new emotions emerge, these are expressed as words and allow exchanges on the content of the painting or artwork.

Our research continues on the paintings of the Museum of Quai Branly, the Bayeux Tapestry and the hangings of the Apocalypse at the Château of Angers. Each work of art has its specificities and the methods of audio and tactile description must be adapted to create the perception closest to reality. We plan to organize new tests to improve the articulation of audio descriptions with tactile exploration and to adapt them to different types of works of art.

Acknowledgment. We like to thank Claire Bartoli, Patrick Crespel, Nadine Dutier, Claude Gilbert, Maryse Jacob, Hamid Kohandel, Valérie Pasquet for organization and participation to the tests, as well as the Valentin Haüy Assiciation and the Federation of Blind and Amblyopes of France (FAF) which hosted the tests on their premises. We thank Edwige Pissaloux, Simon Gay and Marc-Aurèle Rivière for organizing the experiments with F2T.

References

1. Reichhart, F., Lomo, A.: L'offre culturelle française à l'épreuve de la cécité : étude de cas de l'accessibilité au musée. Canadian Journal of Disability Studies **8**(6) (Dec 2019)
2. Mariage, A.: Les médiations tactiles: elargir l'accès aux collections muséales pour le public handicapé visuel. Mémoire M2, Ecole du Louvre, Paris (June 2020)
3. Chauvey, V.: Texts in museums for non-sighted visitors: how to approach content and format choices?, La letter de l'OCIM, Musées, Patrimoine et Culture scientifiques et techniques **132**, 40–47 (Nov-Dec 2010) https://doi.org/10.4000/ocim.391
4. Thompson, H.: Recent Work in Critical Disability Studies. Edinburgh University Press, Paragraph **41**(2), 233–244 (2018)

5. Dhrif, R.: L'Accès aux Musées chez les Déficients Visuels: Entre Variété de l'Offre et Complexité des Besoins, Mémoire M2. Université Paris 13 (2018)
6. Romeo, K., Chottin, M., Ancet, P., Pissaloux, E.: Access to artworks and its mediation by and for visually impaired person. Int. Conf. Comp. Help. People, pp. 233–236. ICCHP (2018)
7. Diderot, D.: ENCYCLOPEDIE, In: Diderot, D., D'Alembert, J. (eds.) Encyclopédie ou Dictionnaire raisonné des sciences, des arts et des métiers, vol. 5, p. 639b (1755)
8. Descartes, R.: Méditations métaphysiques [1641]. In: Cottingham, J., Stoothoff, R., Murdoch, D. (eds.) The Philosophical Writings of Descartes, translated, vol. 2, p. 50. Cambridge University Press
9. Hutchinson, R., Eardley, A.F.: Inclusive museum audio guides: 'guided looking' through audio description enhances memorability of artworks for sighted audiences. Museum Management and Curatorship (2021). https://doi.org/10.1080/09647775.2021.1891563
10. Romeo, K., Chottin, M., Ancet, P., Lecomte, C., Pissaloux, E.: Simplification of painting images for tactile perception by visually impaired persons. In: Int. Conf. Computers Helping People, pp. 251-257. ICCHP (2018)
11. Gay, S., Rivière, M.-A., Pissaloux, E.: Towards haptic surface devices with force feedback for visually impaired people. In: Int. Conf. Comp. Helping People, pp. 259–266. ICCHP (2018)
12. Romeo, K., Gay, S., Rivière, M.-A., Pissaloux, E.: Exploring maps with touch: an inclusive haptic device, In: Petz, A., Miesenberger, K., (eds.) Future Perspectives of AT, eAccessibility and eInclusion, pp. 93–98. ICCHP Open Access Compendium (2020)
13. Gay, S.L., Pissaloux, E., Romeo, K., Truong, N.-T.: F2T: a novel force-feedback haptic architecture delivering 2D data to visually impaired people. IEEE Access **9**, 94901–94911 (2021). https://doi.org/10.1109/ACCESS.2021.3091441

Accessibility of Co-located Meetings

Accessibility of Co-Located Meetings

Introduction to the Special Thematic Session

Andreas Kunz[1(✉)], Reinhard Koutny[2], and Klaus Miesenberger[2]

[1] Innovation Center Virtual Reality, ETH Zurich, Zurich, Switzerland
kunz@iwf.mavt.ethz.ch

[2] Institut Integriert Studieren, Johannes Kepler University, Linz, Austria
{Reinhard.Koutny,Klaus.Miesenberger}@jku.at

https://www.icvr.ethz.ch,
https://www.jku.at/institut-integriert-studieren/

Abstract. Non-verbal communication is an important carrier of information. Even though the spoken word can be heard by blind and visually impaired persons, up to 60% of the overall information still remains inaccessibly to them due to its visual character [11]. However, there is a wide spectrum of non-verbal communication elements, and not all of them are of the same importance. In particular for group meetings, facial expressions and pointing gestures are relevant, which need to be captured, interpreted and output to the blind and visually impaired person.

This session first gives a systematic approach to gather the accessibility requirements for blind and visually impaired persons, from which two typical requirements are selected and discussed in more detail. Here, solutions for capturing and interpreting are provided, and finally the session introduces a concept for accessible user interfaces.

Keywords: Emotion recognition · Pointing gesture detection · Non-verbal communication

1 Introduction

Team meetings do not employ the spoken word only, but also heavily rely on visual information that is spatially distributed in a room, and to which sighted persons refer to by gesturing. Moreover, body language plays an important role for information exchange, but also for unconsciously managing a conversation. In particular, body language often refers to spatially distributed information such as different whiteboards or screens, but also to locations of other users (see Fig. 1). Thus, blind and visually impaired persons face two problems at the same time: (i) they lack important information for social communication, and (ii) they have to localize information that is spatially distributed.

A promising approach to overcome these issues could be a completely virtual meeting in a virtual environment, in which all participant are represented as avatars. Such a virtual meeting room would keep the spacial information distribution as this is helpful to the sighted users, but it also allows a blind and

K. Miesenberger et al. (Eds.): ICCHP-AAATE 2022, LNCS 13341, pp. 289–294, 2022.
https://doi.org/10.1007/978-3-031-08648-9_33

Fig. 1. Typical meeting room with multiple interaction spaces.

visually impaired person to retrieve information in the appropriate way e.g., by localisation movements using his or her smartphone, which would not be possible in a collocated meeting within a physical space.

However, such a virtual meeting room can only be as good as sensors allow capturing sighted persons' behavior such as facial expressions or referring gestures. Also, the further post-processing of the acquired data is important to avoid an overflow of information for the blind and visually impaired person on the one hand, but also to guarantee that no important information gets lost or modified on the other hand.

This special thematic session thus introduces a first overall approach if a digital accessible meeting room.

2 Accessibility Needs to Non-verbal Communication [15]

Enforced by the pandemics, many team meetings were held virtually, either through videoconferencing systems, or completely in a virtual environment such as the Metaverse using avatars [14]. It is most likely that such an IT-based communication will not disappear in the post-pandemic era. The supporting IT experienced a significant technological boost and is now able to support multi-user collaboration over the network in high quality. However, non-verbal communication and spatial information that is inherent to such team meetings might still be difficult to access by blind and visually impaired persons due to several reasons, e.g., low bandwidth that reduces audio fidelity, or too complex technical capabilities to capture and interpret non-verbal communication elements from the sighted persons. Consequently, a social interaction between sighted and visually impaired persons is hardly possible [5].

For such a social interaction - regardless whether it would be in a videoconferencing system or in a virtual environment - additional non-verbal cues such as facial expressions or pointing gestures need to captured, interpreted and displayed to the blind and visually impaired person [12,13].

To support the most important non-verbal communication elements for social interaction in the future, the needs were acquired in a semi-structured interview with blind and visually impaired persons. Here, the most important elements were stated to be: (i) gaze and gaze direction, (ii) facial expressions, (iii) gestures, (iv) audio, and (v) touch. These communication channels - if not directly accessible - need to be captured, interpreted and displayed to the blind and visually impaired persons.

3 Facial Expressions and Emotion Recognition [9]

Facial expressions together with verbal intonation help to better understand a reaction or attention of a user in a meeting. They are thus important for a social interaction [2]. Regardless whether a team meeting is done through a videoconferencing system or in a virtual environment, facial expressions have to be recognized, categorized, and then displayed to the blind and visually impaired person. While emotions could also be detected from the voice pitch, i.e., from a frequency shift of the upper formant frequencies [16], this might not be possible because of a low bandwidth that does not allow transferring high frequencies, or simply because a user is doing facial expressions without speaking. Instead, a video signal from a user's webcam is taken and fed into a neural network such as a convolutional neural network [10]. Such networks are then trained with publicly available datasets such as AFEW[1] and deliver seven possible classes of facial expressions. However, these emotion classes are much too detailed for a team meeting and would overwhelm a blind and visually impaired person with information. In order to reduce the amount of emotion information, the seven different classes are clustered into the three categories "positive", "neutral", and "negative". After training the network with these new classes, facial expression taken with a regular webcam could be analyzed, and then the emotions were recognized with 97% (positive), 99% (neutral), and 64% (negative). The results could then either be displayed directly to the blind and visually impaired person, or they could be used to animate the facial expressions of an avatar in a virtual environment (see Sect. 2). To further reduce the information flow to the blind and visually impaired person, the "neutral" state could be neglected, since it doesn't give any further information to the spoken word.

4 Gesture Detection [3]

Within a conversation, sighted persons frequently use gestures to refer to objects in the nearby environment. Since these gestures cannot be accessed by blind and visually impaired persons, there is a need for detection and interpretation [4]. While also for gesture detection and interpretation deep learning approaches

[1] https://cs.anu.edu.au/few/AFEW.html.

exist, they are not applicable to referring gestures, e.g., on artifacts on a whiteboard, since here also the environment has to be taken into account. In particular for pointing gestures on a whiteboard's content, a high accuracy in detecting them is required to precisely display the corresponding artifact's content to the blind and visually impaired person [1,8]. However, the precision relies on various factors such as pointing accuracy, tracking accuracy, amount and position of artifacts on the whiteboard, etc. When referring to whiteboard content, mainly the three gestures "pointing", "pairing", and "grouping" are used. Mapping these gestures as trajectory on the whiteboard, the gestures mainly differ in their radii, in the angle between two succeeding tangents, and in the fact whether they enclose an artifact or not. Now, the user will interact for example in a virtual environment (see Sect. 2) on a virtual whiteboard (see Fig. 2).

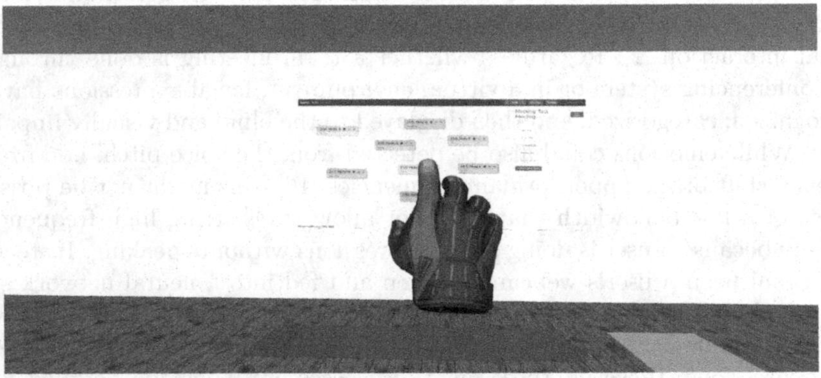

Fig. 2. User performing a pointing gesture in a virtual environment.

Within the virtual environment shown in Fig. 2, in total 1350 different actions were performed, from which 44% were recognized correctly. The main reason for not detecting more gestures correctly is in the fact that users typically did not perform pointing gestures very accurately. However, even false recognition (26%) does not necessarily mean that it completely irritates the blind and visually impaired person, but it might just be a misinterpretation of a grouping by a pairing gesture or vice-versa, which still preserves the overall context. During the measurements, it never happened that the recognized gestures refer to a completely different region of the whiteboard.

5 User Interface Concept [6]

So far, the achieved information can be made accessible using standard interfaces such as a Braille display. However, in a group conversation there are also a lot of referring gestures to general spatial information in the nearby environment, which have to be made accessible to the blind and visually impaired persons. In some previous approaches, this spatial information was mapped on the audio channel, which was then overloaded very quickly [7]. Thus, new approaches are proposed that offer a sufficiently high spatial resolution in order to localize objects in the near environment.

A first approach is to map the virtual meeting room on a web interface, on which blind and visually impaired persons could access important information by simply using a screen reader. In the web interface, e.g., the content of a digital whiteboard could be represented, as well as other users, their emotions and where they are pointing at.

A second approach employs a smartphone which translates the distance to an object, e.g., an artifact on a whiteboard, to vibration bursts with increasing repetition frequency the closer the smartphone comes to an artifact on the virtual whiteboard in front of the blind and visually impaired user. When selecting an artifact such as a card, the smartphone can be used to read out the content of this note, but also to manipulate the note e.g., by moving it to a different position on the virtual whiteboard.

A third approach also uses a vibration feedback to locate objects in the environment, but now the user wears a smartwatch as an output device.

The three proposed hardware settings are currently undergoing user studies for optimizing the overall system and to include feedback from blind and visually impaired users.

6 Summary

This special thematic session addresses a virtual collaboration environment that captures sighted users' facial expression as an indicator of their emotional state, and their pointing gestures. After an interpretation of the acquired measurements, the information is displayed on novel interface concepts to the blind and visually impaired person.

References

1. Dhingra, N., Valli, E., Kunz, A.: Recognition and localisation of pointing gestures using a RGB-D camera. In: Stephanidis, C., Antona, M. (eds.) HCII 2020. CCIS, vol. 1224, pp. 205–212. Springer, Cham (2020). https://doi.org/10.1007/978-3-030-50726-8_27
2. El-Gayyar, M., ElYamany, H.F., Gaber, T., Hassanien, A.E.: Social network framework for deaf and blind people based on cloud computing. In: 2013 Federated Conference on Computer Science and Information Systems, pp. 1313–1319. IEEE (2013)
3. Gorobets, V., Merkle, C., Kunz, A.: Pointing, pairing and grouping gesture recognition in virtual reality. In: Computers Helping People with Special Needs, 18th International Conference; Joint Conference ICCHP-AAATE, Lecco, Italy, Proceedings. Springer (2022)
4. Kane, S.K., Wobbrock, J.O., Ladner, R.E.: Usable gestures for blind people: understanding preference and performance. In: Proceedings of the SIGCHI Conference on Human Factors in Computing Systems, pp. 413–422 (2011)

5. Kim, J.: VIVR: presence of immersive interaction for visual impairment virtual reality. IEEE Access **8**, 196151–196159 (2020)
6. Koutny, R., Miesenberger, K.: Accessible user interface concept for business meeting tool support including spatial and non-verbal information for blind and visually impaired people. In: Computers Helping People with Special Needs, 18th International Conference; Joint Conference ICCHP-AAATE, Lecco, Italy, Proceedings. Springer (2022)
7. Kunz, A., et al.: Accessibility of brainstorming sessions for blind people. In: Miesenberger, K., Fels, D., Archambault, D., Peňáz, P., Zagler, W. (eds.) ICCHP 2014. LNCS, vol. 8547, pp. 237–244. Springer, Cham (2014). https://doi.org/10.1007/978-3-319-08596-8_38
8. Liechti, S., Dhingra, N., Kunz, A.: Detection and localisation of pointing, pairing and grouping gestures for brainstorming meeting applications. In: Stephanidis, C., Antona, M., Ntoa, S. (eds.) HCII 2021. CCIS, vol. 1420, pp. 22–29. Springer, Cham (2021). https://doi.org/10.1007/978-3-030-78642-7_4
9. Lutfallah, M., Käch, B., Hirt, C., Kunz, A.: Emotion recognition - a tool to improve meeting experience for visually impaired. In: Computers Helping People with Special Needs, 18th International Conference; Joint Conference ICCHP-AAATE, Lecco, Italy, Proceedings. Springer (2022)
10. Marinoiu, E., Zanfir, M., Olaru, V., Sminchisescu, C.: 3D human sensing, action and emotion recognition in robot assisted therapy of children with autism. In: Proceedings of the IEEE Conference on Computer Vision and Pattern Recognition, pp. 2158–2167 (2018)
11. Mehrabian, A., Ferris, S.: Inference of attitudes from nonverbal communication in two channels. J. Consult. Clin. Psychol. **3**, 248–252 (1967)
12. Oh Kruzic, C., Kruzic, D., Herrera, F., Bailenson, J.: Facial expressions contribute more than body movements to conversational outcomes in avatar-mediated virtual environments. Sci. Rep. **10**(1), 1–23 (2020)
13. Roth, D., Klelnbeck, C., Feigl, T., Mutschler, C., Latoschik, M.E.: Beyond replication: augmenting social behaviors in multi-user virtual realities. In: 2018 IEEE Conference on Virtual Reality and 3D User Interfaces (VR), pp. 215–222. IEEE (2018)
14. Tu, J.: Meetings in the Metaverse: Exploring Online Meeting Spaces through Meaningful Interactions in Gather. Town. Master's thesis, University of Waterloo (2022)
15. Wieland, M., Thevin, L., Machulla, T.: Non-verbal communication and joint attention between people with and without visual impairments. guidelines for inclusive conversations in virtual realities. In: Computers Helping People with Special Needs, 18th International Conference; Joint Conference ICCHP-AAATE, Lecco, Italy, Proceedings. Springer (2022)
16. Yildirim, S., et al.: An acoustic study of emotions expressed in speech. In: Proceedings of the Eighth International Conference on Spoken Language Processing (2004)

Non-verbal Communication and Joint Attention Between People with and Without Visual Impairments: Deriving Guidelines for Inclusive Conversations in Virtual Realities

Markus Wieland[1(✉)], Lauren Thevin[2], Albrecht Schmidt[1], and Tonja Machulla[1,3]

[1] LMU Munich, 80337 Munich, Germany
{markus.wieland,albrecht.schmidt}@ifi.lmu.de
[2] Université Catholique de l'Ouest, Angers, France
lthevin@uco.fr
[3] TU Dortmund University, 44227 Dortmund, Germany
tonja.machulla@tu-dortmund.de

Abstract. With the emergence of mainstream virtual reality (VR) platforms for social interactions, non-verbal communicative cues are increasingly being transmitted into the virtual environment. Since VR is primarily a visual medium, accessible VR solutions are required for people with visual impairments (PVI). However, existing propositions do not take into account social interactions, and therefore PVI are excluded from this type of experience. To address this issue, we conducted semi-structured interviews with eleven participants, seven of whom were PVI and four of whom were partners or close friends without visual impairments, to explore how non-verbal cues and joint attention are used and perceived in everyday social situations and conversations. Our goal was to provide guidelines for inclusive conversations in virtual environments for PVI. Our findings suggest that gaze, head direction, head movements, and facial expressions are important for both groups in conversations but often difficult to identify visually for PVI. From our findings, we provide concrete suggestions for the design of social VR spaces, inclusive to PVI.

1 Introduction

Social interactions are an emergent topic in virtual reality (VR). In 3D virtual spaces like Altspace VR, Rec Room and Horizon Worlds, people can interact with each other and also play games together. For realistic social interactions in VR the design of embodied virtual avatars is increasingly important [3]. This also includes non-verbal communication such as gaze, facial expressions, gestures, haptics, body posture, distance, and general noises. Today's technology makes it possible to integrate such non-verbal cues into 3D virtual spaces for better social interaction [2]. However, current VR applications have a strong focus

K. Miesenberger et al. (Eds.): ICCHP-AAATE 2022, LNCS 13341, pp. 295–304, 2022.
https://doi.org/10.1007/978-3-031-08648-9_34

on increasing the visual fidelity of such cues. As a result, people with visual impairments (PVI) profit only to a limited extent from these advances.

Various adaptations and tools have been proposed to increase the accessibility of VR for PVI. However, they focus on facilitating navigation through VR environments and the interaction with inanimate elements of the virtual scene but not on social interactions [4,8,15,17,18]. To successfully initiate social VR experiences, the user needs to be able to detect the presence of others and identify them if already acquainted. In real life situations, PVI employ a broad range of multisensory cues to achieve this task, some of which could already be integrated into present VR applications (for guidelines for inclusive avatars see [13]). Additionally, non-verbal communication cues, including those that facilitate joint attention, are an integral part of social interactions. Joint attention refers to the notion of drawing another person's attention to an object or situation. In persons without visual impairment, this is mostly achieved through gaze [9]. The communication through gaze has an evolutionary origin and initiating actions on the basis of others' gaze directions is more pronounced in humans than in other primates [5,14]. In real-world interactions, non-verbal communication and joint attention are likely to be used between persons with and without visual impairment. This should be reflected in virtual social experiences.

In the present work, we focus on non-verbal communication between PVI and others and how attention is jointly directed to objects or situations in real-world settings. A total of eleven people were interviewed in a semi-structured interview. Seven of them were PVI and four were their partners or friends who did not have a visual impairment. From the results, we propose guidelines for the design of representations of non-verbal communication and interaction cues inclusive to persons with and without visual impairment.

2 Related Work

Self-presentation is an important factor for social interactions in VR. Personalized avatars as well as realistic photogrammetry 3D scans are perceived as more human-like compared to an abstract avatar, resulting in a higher virtual body ownership [7,16]. Further, non-verbal cues in VR contribute to more engaging social interactions. Seeing facial expressions and bodily gestures of an avatar in VR lead to a more positive interaction experience [10]. Augmenting eye contact, joint attention, and grouping in social interactions in VR increased the perception of social presence [12]. In sum, combining realistic avatars with non-verbal communication signals can enhance the experience of an social interactions in VR. However, PVI do not profit from these types of non-verbal cues because they are designed specifically for visual perception. So far, attempts to increase VR accessibility for PVI focus on improving the interaction with the physical VR environment. To aid navigation, a cane was developed that provides a physical resistance when touching objects in VR, gives tactile and auditory feedback resembling real world sounds of the cane [17]. In another VR application for PVI the environment is generated entirely through sounds and PVI can walk through and perceive the environment [15]. SeeingVR provides tools such as a magnification lens, edge enhancement or text to speech that PVI can apply in VR [18]. PVI with macular degeneration can use a tool that increases the color and brightness in their central vision in VR [8]. The proposed studies help PVI navigate and explore virtual environments, but do not assist them in social interactions in VR.

3 Methods and Participants

We studied how social cues are used by PVI and partners without visual impairments in real-world scenarios, with the goal to propose implementations in VR. The study was conducted as a semi-structured interview, consisting of 22 questions for the PVI and 14 questions for their partners and friends. The questions were divided into the following six categories: gaze and head direction, facial expressions, gestures, sense of hearing, sense of touch, and joint attention. The respective categories asked whether this type of communication channel is used and how it is perceived. Seven PVI (four female, three male; average age of 56 years with a standard deviation of 23 years) and four sighted persons (one female, three male; average age 60 years with a standard deviation of 24 years) participated in the interview. The detailed overview about the PVI can be seen in Table 1. Note that except for P7, all participants are "blind" according to WHO classification [1]. Interviews were conducted online via Zoom in German and recorded with permission for further analysis. The interviews with the partners were conducted separately. All participants were financially compensated for their participation.

Table 1. Vision conditions of the seven PVI

ID	Sex	Age	Diagnosis	Residual Vision
P1	w	67	Inherited retinal degeneration	5%
P2	w	84	Age-related macular degeneration	5%
P3	m	48	Retinal detachment since birth	2%
P4	m	69	Myopia	2%
P5	w	29	Nystagmus since birth	3–5%
P6	m	69	Albinismus since birth	5%
P7	w	24	Stargardt	15%

4 Results

We grouped our results into six categories of non-verbal communication: gaze and head direction, facial expressions, gestures, sense of hearing, sense of touch, and joint attention. In each subsection, we first summarize the statements of the seven PVI, followed by supplementary statements of the four partners, and subsequently the guidelines for inclusive conversations for PVI in VR. Numerals in brackets indicate the number of participants who mentioned a specific theme.

4.1 Using and Perceiving Gaze and Head Direction

Participants with VI: Gaze, head direction, and head gestures are communicative cues that are difficult to perceive. The direction of the head is more perceptible than the gaze (5) than vice versa (1) and language is used to orient oneself in a conversation (1). Participants report that they consider gaze to be important (5) (P1, "It is theoretically important for me, but only very limited perceivable") and that they try to look their conversational partner in the eye (7). For example, P4 said "I do this for the reason that I signal readiness to receive". This is in spite of the fact that most cannot perceive their counterpart's eyes or gaze direction (6). All report to be familiar with situations where persons communicate through gaze alone but that they would typically use other cues such as giggling or the sound of clearing one's throat (4), movements (1) or another uncommon reaction (1) of their partner. One person stated not using alternative ways of communication. With regard to head direction, few persons are able to make use of this cue directly (2) and some are able to infer it from changes in the acoustics in their partner's speech, i.e., sound direction (4). Head gestures, such as nodding and shaking for negation, are perceivable by one person; all others reported that it depends on distance, context, and light conditions. It helped if these gestures were done more consciously and conspicuously than usual and accompanied verbally. One PVI also said that their close friends do not use head gestures during conversation, illustrating an adaptation of the social environment. All persons reported that the perception of gaze and head direction is influenced by light conditions (7) in a conversation. Lighting is in general problematic because too much light such as daylight or candles can be blinding (P6, "When there is a candle on the table, it blinds me.") and too little light worsens perception and the interlocutor has to talk more (5). Further, perception is poor when the interlocutor sits with their back to the window (2).

Sighted Partners: Partners stated that both parties always tried to look at each other during a conversation (4) and eye contact is important for them (3). One person said "I miss that, of course [eye contact with the partner]. When my partner is sitting across from me at the table, my partner doesn't see if I'm making faces if I'm laughing, angry, or crying anyway. My partner really does not see such things.", which shows the feeling of missing eye contact with the partner. One sighted partner said eye contact was important, while the PVI responded by not knowing for sure because it was not perceivable. Several sighted partners do not know whether the partner relies more on sight or on the head direction (3) whereas one sighted responded with head direction. In the perception of gaze and head direction under different lighting conditions, there are no differences in the PVI perceived by the sighted partners (4).

Guidelines for Inclusive Conversations: Eye contact is important for both groups in a conversation. Therefore, conversations in VR should provide multisensory cues based on gaze, head direction, and head movement. For example, when another person approaches a PVI for a conversation, an auditory cue could help the PVI to know that a person wants to talk to them and is trying to make eye contact. During a conversation, movements such as a head nodding could be represented with significantly larger animations and accompanied acoustically. Further, the virtual environment could offer adjustable light settings for single elements to adapt contrasts.

4.2 Using and Perceiving Facial Expressions

Participants with VI: PVI use facial expressions in standard ways and without conscious intention (7). In others, facial expressions are not perceivable in conversations (4) unless there is good lighting (1), the interlocutor is close (1) (P5, "When my partner does something funny with his face, he comes right in front of my face"), or well known (1). Emotions that are typically conveyed by the face are directly inquired for (4) or perceived through other cues such as voice, breathing, sighing, and posture (3) (P5, "For example, if someone becomes very emotional, the person speaks more slowly or pauses more when speaking, I notice that. This means that the person may not be doing so well at the moment.").

Sighted Partners: The use of facial expressions during a conversation is confirmed by the sighted partners (4). They themselves use their facial expressions in conversation with their partner as with all other conversational partners (2), to a lesser degree (1), or not at all (1).

Guidelines for Inclusive Conversations: Facial expressions are mostly not perceivable to PVI, so they use other cues. Thus, the information should be communicated with multisensory cues. For example, the facial expression of the conversation partner could be recognized and then played back with audio cues or joyful facial expressions are accompanied by soft background music. Further, an automatic magnifier could be integrated that enlarges the face of the conversation partner and displays it in good lighting conditions.

4.3 Using and Perceiving Gestures

Participants with VI: The use of gestures (6) can be divided into semaphoric, deictic, and gesticulation gestures. Some PVI use various forms of gestures and therefore multiple mentioning was possible. Semaphoric gestures are hand gestures that stand for specific meanings. They are occasionally used, such as in the form of thumbs up (2) and semaphoric emoticons on a smartphone (1) (P3, "Some gestures I can imagine a certain way based on this description [screen reader] alone."). Deictic gestures, i.e., pointing, are only used when the location is well known (2) (P5, "[...] if it is a place I know well, then I point to it. But I think I say that in the context that, it is on the cabinet."). Further, gesticulations are used to express themselves in a conversation (2) and one of the PVI learned the concept of gesticulation from an early teacher. One PVI does not use gestures at all. Several factors have an influence on the perception of gestures and multiple mentioning was possible: the bigger, expressive, and flailing the gesture, the better it can be perceived (4) (P1, "The bigger they are [gestures], the better I can perceive them."), light conditions and the change of colors through the light during a gesture (2), distance (2), air flow (2), context (1), and moving fabric of clothes (1). The recognition of two different gestures in one movement (e.g., semaphoric and then deictic) depends on distance, light condition and whether the attention is focused on the interlocutor (5), if the object for a deictic gesture is known in advance (1), would be ignored unless the interlocutor expresses it verbally (1).

Sighted Partners: The use of gestures in conversation with the partner is divided into normal use (2), less use (1) and no use at all (1). Gesture recognition for the PVI partner is only possible under the following conditions: when the partner is nearby (2), when something is pointed at and accompanied verbally at the same time (1). One sighted person mentioned that the partner is not able to recognize gestures.

Guidelines for Inclusive Conversations: Recognizing gestures for PVI is possible under certain conditions. In order to aid PVI to recognize gestures, the virtual environment should enhance semaphoric or deictic gestures with a larger representation of the gestures and with accompanying sounds. The connection between a deictic gesture to an object could be indicated with a high-contrast ray and announced verbally. Enhanced gesticulation could be used to personalize the avatars of social partners for easier identification.

4.4 Using Sense of Hearing

Participants with VI: Hearing is used for different tasks in a conversation: recognize behavior (4), recognize mood (1) (P5, "It is also important how the voice changes. For example, I can hear how someone smiles, so I know how the voice changes if I know the person."), to draw conclusions about the interlocutor (1), and to infer the posture of the interlocutor, since people speak differently in different postures, and then in turn infer behavior (1). Non-communicative sounds of the interlocutor in a conversation are perceived as distracting and disturbing (3), or as interesting, because conclusions about the interlocutor can be drawn from it (1). However, general noises are not paid attention to (2) and it also depends on the context of the conversation (1).

Sighted Partners: The participants reported that they do not use consciously sounds in a conversation with their partners (4) and they do not consciously change their voice to add more emotion to what they say (3), except for one participant.

Guidelines for Inclusive Conversations: Since the voice in a conversation can provide important information about the behavior of the interlocutor, it should be possible to eliminate disturbing noises or background sounds. However, for people who consciously use sounds of the conversation partner to find out about behavior, sounds such as footsteps or a nervous shaking should be integrated or presented as a multisensory cue.

4.5 Using Sense of Touch

Participants with VI: The sense of touch is used in conversations only with friends (3) and when socially appropriate (1), to find out how serious the communication is meant through hugs and handshakes (1) (P4, "what I just always want to know is how serious it is meant, and that is also important for further communication"), or to attract attention in a conversation (1). One person state not to use the sense of touch in social interactions. When participants were asked if they were touched in a conversation and how they felt about it, they reported that it only occurs with friends (3), and it is fine as a sign of attention (1). Whereas it is sometimes annoying when people approach the PVI and ask if help is needed (1) (P6, "I sometimes have problems keeping people off my back. They think I have bad eyesight, and then they always come close to me.") and it also occurs that no touch at all takes place during a conversation (2).

Sighted Partners: The sense of touch is used according to general social norms (2) or to a lesser degree (2) in conversation with the partner.

Guidelines for Inclusive Conversations: The sense of touch is used socially appropriately and is also expected from the interlocutor. In a virtual environment, functions can be used that allow touch only after the person being touched has given permission or the function could be activated for friends so that they can touch each other or approach each other closely.

4.6 Joint Attention

Participants with VI: When participants are handed an object, it is recognized verbally (3) and by the movement of the body or arm (3) (P1, "I would perceive it visually. I think the person can only give it to me if the person sits close enough to me.") or by placing the object directly in the hand (1), but it is also difficult to recognize without verbal cues (1). The situation in which the participants are made aware of objects or situations in their environment usually happens with verbal cues (3), but this does not occur often because they know where everything is located in their environment (2) (P5, "In my apartment, I just know where everything is.") and objects are often placed directly in front of them (1). In public, the participants are verbally made aware of objects or situations (7), and further they indicated that they are additionally made aware by touch (2). If participants wanted to draw the attention of others to an object or situation in their environment, it happens verbally (4), with gestures because the partner no longer hears well (1), with deictic gestures but only if the location of the object is known (1) and getting closer to the object (1) (P7, "I do not really point at objects that you can hold in your hand. Instead, I usually get very close to the object I want to show or draw attention to.").

Sighted Partners: The partner's attention to an object or situation is drawn via verbal cues (3) and this does not occur often in the home environment because the partner knows where the objects are located (1). In addition, it was mentioned that the partner's attention is unintentionally drawn to something by making noises (1) ("When I drink in the kitchen, my partner hears that too and asks for a glass of water or something."). The sighted partner are made aware of objects or situations by their partners through verbal cues (2) and if the partner knows where the object is with a deictic gesture, otherwise verbally (1). However, it was also reported that one's attention is not drawn to an object or situation by one's partner because sighted people can see everything (1) ("My partner cannot direct my attention to any objects. It only works the other way around."). In terms of a difference in non-verbal cues when talking to their PVI partner or a sighted person, it was mentioned that less gestures are used (2) ("I use fewer gestures because I know they are ineffective with my partner."), no eye contact although it is important for them as a couple (1) and communication is generally more verbal, but this is usually done unconsciously (1) ("Communication shifts to the verbal level, but this happens rather unconsciously. You just adapt and somehow it becomes automatic without thinking about it.").

Guidelines for Inclusive Conversations: Verbal cues to objects or situations are necessary for joint interactions. To focus joint attention on an object or situation, short automatic verbal cues could be given. In addition, a high-contrast visual and auditory signal related to the PVI head direction and the sighted interlocutor's gaze could signal that both are attending to the same object in a collaborative interaction to establish joint attention. Further, verbal cues to an object or situation could automatically lead to a deictic gesture of the PVI's avatar toward the object or situation.

5 Discussion

Here, we presented the results of an interview with eleven participants regarding non-verbal communication and joint attention. The findings are used to propose guidelines for inclusive conversations in virtual environments for PVI. Our recommendations and examples include translating behaviors, verbalizations, and appearances into different formats. VR offers the opportunity to make various visual cues perceivable to PVI in a conversation. For example, by integrating facial expressions[1] into social VR environments, they can be made perceivable

[1] www.vive.com/us/accessory/facial-tracker/.

through other sensory cues, establishing bidirectional communication. However, the wide range of possibilities offered by VR also raises privacy issues. Both interlocutors need to know that their behavior, verbalizations, and appearances translate into different formats and commit to these inclusive conversations. Future work should address how to make VR accessible to PVI by also transferring existing real-world aids, such as eye-gaze glasses that provide tactile feedback when viewing at a PVI, to VR [11] or augmenting facial expressions [6]. In addition, a set of tools could be provided for inclusive conversations in VR that can be automatically integrated into an existing VR application similar to the approach of the toolbox SeeingVR [18]. Our future research will address the development and evaluation of different supporting methods for non-verbal signals for PVI in VR.

Acknowledgments. Research was supported by the BMBF (project HIVE: grant no. 16SV8183). We would also like to thank the reviewers and ACs for their work and valuable feedback.

References

1. Blindness and vision impairment: World Health Organization (2021). https://www.who.int/news-room/fact-sheets/detail/blindness-and-visual-impairment
2. Cha, H.S., Choi, S.J., Im, C.H.: Real-time recognition of facial expressions using facial electromyograms recorded around the eyes for social virtual reality applications. IEEE Access **8**, 62065–62075 (2020)
3. Freeman, G., Maloney, D.: Body, avatar, and me: the presentation and perception of self in social virtual reality. Proc. ACM Hum.-Comput. Interact. **4**(CSCW3), 1–27 (2021)
4. Kim, J.: VIVR: presence of immersive interaction for visual impairment virtual reality. IEEE Access **8**, 196151–196159 (2020)
5. Kobayashi, H., Kohshima, S.: Unique morphology of the human eye and its adaptive meaning: comparative studies on external morphology of the primate eye. J. Hum. Evol. **40**(5), 419–435 (2001)
6. Lang, F., Schmidt, A., Machulla, T.: Augmented reality for people with low vision: symbolic and alphanumeric representation of information. In: Miesenberger, K., Manduchi, R., Covarrubias Rodriguez, M., Peňáz, P. (eds.) ICCHP 2020. LNCS, vol. 12376, pp. 146–156. Springer, Cham (2020). https://doi.org/10.1007/978-3-030-58796-3_19
7. Latoschik, M.E., Roth, D., Gall, D., Achenbach, J., Waltemate, T., Botsch, M.: The effect of avatar realism in immersive social virtual realities. In: Proceedings of the 23rd ACM Symposium on Virtual Reality Software and Technology, pp. 1–10. ACM, Gothenburg Sweden (2017)
8. Masnadi, S., Williamson, B., Gonzalez, A.N.V., LaViola, J.J.: VRiAssist: an eye-tracked virtual reality low vision assistance tool. In: 2020 IEEE Conference on Virtual Reality and 3D User Interfaces Abstracts and Workshops (VRW), pp. 808–809. IEEE, Atlanta, GA, USA (2020)
9. Mundy, P., Newell, L.: Attention, joint attention, and social cognition. Curr. Dir. Psychol. Sci. **16**(5), 269–274 (2007)

10. Oh Kruzic, C., Kruzic, D., Herrera, F., Bailenson, J.: Facial expressions contribute more than body movements to conversational outcomes in avatar-mediated virtual environments. Sci. Rep. **10**(1), 20626 (2020)
11. Qiu, S., Hu, J., Han, T., Osawa, H., Rauterberg, M.: An evaluation of a wearable assistive device for augmenting social interactions. IEEE Access **8**, 164661–164677 (2020)
12. Roth, D., Klelnbeck, C., Feigl, T., Mutschler, C., Latoschik, M.E.: Beyond replication: augmenting social behaviors in multi-user virtual realities. In: 2018 IEEE Conference on Virtual Reality and 3D User Interfaces (VR), pp. 215–222. IEEE, Tuebingen/Reutlingen, Germany (2018)
13. Thevin, L., Machulla, T.: Guidelines for inclusive avatars and agents: how persons with visual impairments detect and recognize others and their activities. In: Miesenberger, K., Manduchi, R., Covarrubias Rodriguez, M., Peňáz, P. (eds.) ICCHP 2020. LNCS, vol. 12376, pp. 164–175. Springer, Cham (2020). https://doi.org/10.1007/978-3-030-58796-3_21
14. Tomasello, M., Hare, B., Lehmann, H., Call, J.: Reliance on head versus eyes in the gaze following of great apes and human infants: the cooperative eye hypothesis. J. Hum. Evol. **52**(3), 314–320 (2007)
15. Torres-Gil, M.A., Casanova-Gonzalez, O., Gonzalez-Mora, J.L.: Applications of virtual reality for visually impaired people. WSEAS Trans. Comput. **9**(2), 184–193 (2010)
16. Waltemate, T., Gall, D., Roth, D., Botsch, M., Latoschik, M.E.: The impact of avatar personalization and immersion on virtual body ownership, presence, and emotional response. IEEE Trans. Vis. Comput. Graph. **24**(4), 1643–1652 (2018)
17. Zhao, Y., et al.: Enabling people with visual impairments to navigate virtual reality with a haptic and auditory cane simulation. In: Proceedings of the 2018 CHI Conference on Human Factors in Computing Systems, pp. 1–14. ACM, Montreal, QC, Canada (2018)
18. Zhao, Y., Cutrell, E., Holz, C., Morris, M.R., Ofek, E., Wilson, A.D.: SeeingVR: a set of tools to make virtual reality more accessible to people with low vision. In: Proceedings of the 2019 CHI Conference on Human Factors in Computing Systems, pp. 1–14. ACM, Glasgow, Scotland, UK (2019)

Emotion Recognition - A Tool to Improve Meeting Experience for Visually Impaired

Mathieu Lutfallah(✉), Benno Käch, Christian Hirt, and Andreas Kunz

Swiss Federal Institute of Technology, Zurich, Switzerland
{lutfallah,kaech,hirtc,kunz}@iwf.mavt.ethz.ch
https://www.icvr.ethz.ch/index_EN

Abstract. Facial expressions play an important role in human communication since they enrich spoken information and help convey additional sentiments e.g. mood. Among others, they non-verbally express a partner's agreement or disagreement to spoken information. Further, together with the audio signal, humans can even detect nuances of changes in a person's mood. However, facial expressions remain inaccessible to the blind and visually impaired, and also the voice signal alone might not carry enough mood information.

Emotion recognition research mainly focused on detecting one of seven emotion classes. Such emotions are too detailed, and having an overall impression of primary emotional states such as positive, negative, or neutral is more beneficial for the visually impaired person in a lively discussion within a team. Thus, this paper introduces an emotion recognition system that allows a real-time detection of the emotions "agree", "neutral", and "disagree", which are seen as the most important ones during a lively discussion. The proposed system relies on a combination of neural networks that allow extracting emotional states while leveraging the temporal information from videos.

Keywords: Emotion recognition · Neural networks · Non-verbal communication

1 Introduction

Emotion Recognition (ER) is a significant component of non-verbal communication. It allows perceiving another person's reactions, intentions, honest opinion, and mood. Humans recognize emotions by relying on facial expression, voice intonation, and spoken words among other tools. However, blind and visually impaired people cannot perceive the non-verbal cues i.e. the facial expressions [9]. This means that ER's advantages, e.g. to better interpret the reaction and intention of a person they are interacting with [5], are inaccessible for visually impaired people. The following work proposes a solution to this problem focused on in-person and mixed team meetings.

This work was commonly funded by DFG, FWF, and SNF under No. 211500647.

K. Miesenberger et al. (Eds.): ICCHP-AAATE 2022, LNCS 13341, pp. 305–312, 2022.
https://doi.org/10.1007/978-3-031-08648-9_35

Integration of visually impaired people can be improved using Artificial Intelligence (AI) performing ER, which is then conveyed to them. However, ER using AI is challenging. Despite the universality of facial expressions indicating the seven basic human emotions, facial emotional expressions might differ due to the variation in emotional expressivity across cultures and facial features and appearance across ethnicities. In addition, humans are capable of a certain degree to control their facial emotion expression. Previous research mainly focused on ER using video clips taken from movies such as the Acted Facial Expressions In The Wild (AFEW) dataset[1]. This dataset presents clips with distinctively different illuminations and background conditions. The clips are labeled with seven emotions i.e. happy, sad, surprise, angry, fear, neutral, and disgust. However, such emotions are too detailed, and having an impression of primary emotional states such as positive, negative, or neutral is more beneficial for the visually impaired persons in a lively discussion within a team.

In this paper, we focus on video-based facial emotion detection due to two main reasons. First, online meetings could lead to bad audio due to compression or bad microphone, which in turn reduces the visually impaired person's ability to recognize the emotion of the speaker because of missing the upper formant frequencies [17]. Second, it is interesting to detect the emotion of participants who are not speaking and convey that information to the blind and visually impaired participants.

This paper introduces a tool that allows social interaction to be enhanced by making facial expressions accessible to visually impaired people, which is important for communicating sympathy and understanding. After summarizing related work in this field, we will explain our approach in more detail. The remainder of the paper then gives a summary and an outlook on future work.

2 Related Work

To encourage research in ER through AI technology, various groups have created datasets that comprise images, videos, and dialogues with corresponding labels of emotions. In the case of discrete labels, various emotion schemes have been proposed. For example, Ekman [4] defines six universal emotions that are anger, disgust, fear, happiness, sadness, and surprise. However, some datasets such as the EMOTIC [13] dataset, include up to 26 emotion categories.

The EmotiW [2] competition uses the AFEW dataset. The task in this competition is to assign one of seven emotion labels e.g. anger, disgust, fear, happiness, neutrality, sadness, and surprise to each short video clip in the dataset. Unlike other facial expression datasets, the subjects cover a wide age range i.e. 1–70 years, which makes it generic in terms of age. In this competition, state-of-the-art methods were presented for ER and compared based on the test accuracy. The overall accuracy is computed by averaging the accuracy of correct predictions across all classes. Before the rise of the popularity of deep neural networks, frame-level handcraft features were wildly utilized for ER in images.

[1] https://cs.anu.edu.au/few/AFEW.html.

One method proposed to extract a new feature descriptor is called Histogram of Oriented Gradients from Three Orthogonal Planes [1]. They achieved a test accuracy of 45.21% while working with the seven emotion classes. Currently, the neural network based approach generates state-of-the-art performance in all categories of ER from videos to audio and dialogues. The winning method [8] of EmotiW 2017 achieved a 60.03% accuracy. The method consisted of evaluating four networks to extract features from images and a classifier based on audio.

Another dataset is CK+ [11] which consists of the facial expressions of 210 adults, which were recorded using two synchronized Panasonic AG-7500 cameras. The individuals were asked to express a specific emotion which was then labeled regarding the expressed emotion. The clips consist of a couple of frames that start from a neutral facial expression and peak in the frame of the expressed emotion. Samples of this dataset are shown in Fig. 1. These images are close to what can be expected in a meeting since they show a regular background with good lighting conditions.

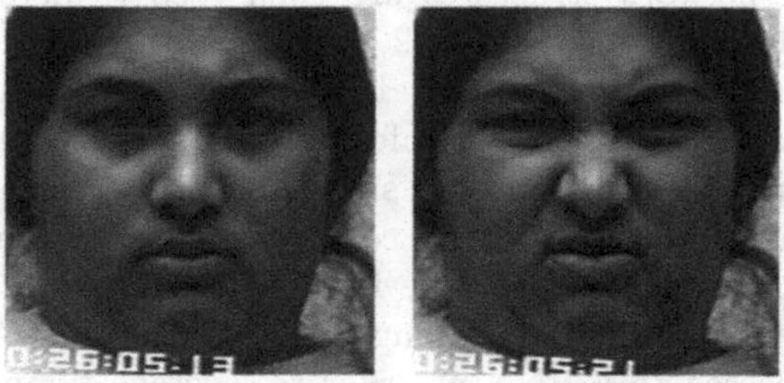

Fig. 1. Example frames of the CK+ dataset at the start of a video and at the end [11].

State-of-the-art methods have been developed for ER, however what is still missing is applications for ER. In one experiment by Marinoiu et al. [12], researchers explore how convolutional neural networks (CNN) can detect the action performed by an autistic child as well as the emotion they are expressing. This would help to design robots that are perceptive to emotion and capable of interacting with autistic children, providing them with a better social experience and helping them to improve. Another application of ER is to help IOT systems interact with users [3]. Moreover, researchers [7] have found that using ER can help in learning environments to maintain student interest.

3 Contribution

To help visually impaired people accessing facial expressions in a net-based meeting, a tool was developed that allows detecting facial expressions, deriving emotional states from them, and delivering the results to the participants. For this, we leveraged state of the art neural networks and public datasets and tailored them for our use case. These datasets contain general emotion categories such as the ones mentioned before.

The pipeline of the tool is to record frames from the facial expression of each participant and then feed those frames into the neural network composed of a CNN, a recurrent neural network (RNN) and a multi-layered perceptron (MLP). Before that, the network required training using the public datasets. To utilize these datasets, we need to cluster the categories of videos they present. The individual steps are explained more in detail in the next sections.

3.1 Network Structure

A video stream of the participant in the meeting is fed to the tool. The first step is to sample the video into frames followed by cropping the images around the face of the participant. The dlib library[2] was used to detect the faces. The images are then cropped and sized to 224×224 px. Three frames were fed to the network per clip.

State-of-the-art network structures are then used to detect the emotions. The neural network used, shown in Fig. 2, consists of three parts: feature extractor, fusion, and classifier. The *feature extractor* reduces the dimensionality of the image thus taking out redundant information and keeping only useful one. Resnet-18 [6] was used for this purpose since it gave the best results compared to the VGG [15] network. The output consists of three feature vectors corresponding to the three images that were fed into the network. The *fusion* part combines the features from the three images. The feature vectors extracted from these images are passed to a RNN in order to leverage temporal information. In this work, the gated recurrent network (GRU) is used to combine the information. The three feature vectors are fed sequentially to the GRU allowing to merge information across time. As an output, we get three new feature vectors which are averaged. The *classifier* predicts the probability of the sample belonging to each category of emotions. This is done by taking the averaged feature vector and assigning three scalar values for each emotion class. An MLP with three layers is used to determine these numbers, which are then passed to a soft-max function for normalization. The normalized values are interpreted as the probability of the sample being part of the corresponding class.

3.2 Clustering of Classes

During net-based meetings, only few classes of emotions are expected. Participants in a meeting are mainly neutral except for a few frames where another emotion is shown. Thus, a more general classification of participants' facial expressions is required. The classification includes three classes of emotions i.e. neutral, positive and negative. The public datasets with seven categories need to be adapted to these classes to remove the need to create a new dataset. This

[2] http://dlib.net/.

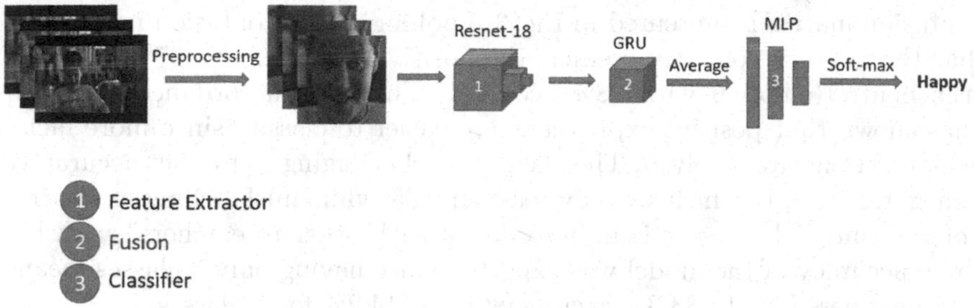

Fig. 2. Pipeline of the tool showing the different types of neural networks used.

can be done by summarizing these categories to have a more general interpretation. As mentioned in Sect. 2, AFEW and CK+ provide samples that are labeled based on seven categories. Thus, we have to group those categories into the three classes we want. The positive group will consist of the happy, surprise categories while the negative one will be formed of the sadness, anger, disgust, and fear categories. The neutral class is already found in the AFEW dataset but that is not the case in CK+ since its replaced by the contempt class. However, as mentioned in Sect. 2, the first frames of the clips are used as neutral frames.

3.3 Network Training

We used the AFEW dataset as pre-training data despite that movie clips present social conditions different to the context of meetings. Pre-training allows having better initial weights for the model thus allowing a better generalization of the model [14]. After pre-training the network using this aforementioned dataset, the network weights were fine-tuned on the CK+ dataset since it shows images of people clearly expressing emotions. Furthermore, these clips were made in more similar environment conditions to our net-based meetings.

One issue we faced is that the network is trained on an imbalanced dataset since the neutral class has much less samples than the negative class as the negative cluster comprises four types of videos which represent sadness, anger, disgust, and fear. Having an unbalanced dataset causes the network to learn only a few of the classes and never predict those with a small number of training samples. To overcome this, we used a weighted loss function, which weights a misclassification on a minority class more strongly than on a majority class. This means that the loss is increased if a neutral sample is misclassified, while the loss is decreased if the negative sample is misclassified.

4 Evaluation and Discussion

The accuracy is computed by feeding clips of videos which were not used for training from the CK+ into the network and then counting the number of correct predictions. The network gave us an 88.8% accuracy on the CK+ dataset and the confusion matrix is presented in Fig. 3. Looking at the confusion matrix, we see that the network correctly predicts the positive emotion with 97% accuracy and the neutral emotion with 98% accuracy. This is in accordance with [10] who has shown that positive expressions are easier to classify since more facial expression actions are involved. The class most challenging to predict accurately is the negative one, in which we only reached 64% while mislabelling as neutral 30% of the time. This result is in accordance with other researchers' work [8]. The high accuracy of the model was expected since having only 3 classes means the random guess lead to 33.3% accuracy versus 14.2% for 7 classes.

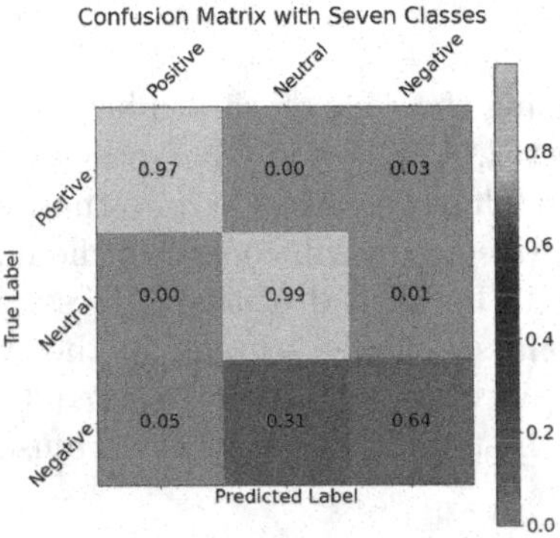

Fig. 3. Confusion matrix for tertiary classification.

The current tool allows displaying the results on a graphic interface as shown in Fig. 4. The scores are shown in terms of a histogram and a smiley face which indicates the emotion. This latter information can later be conveyed to the visually impaired person as a three-stage signal using a Braille display.

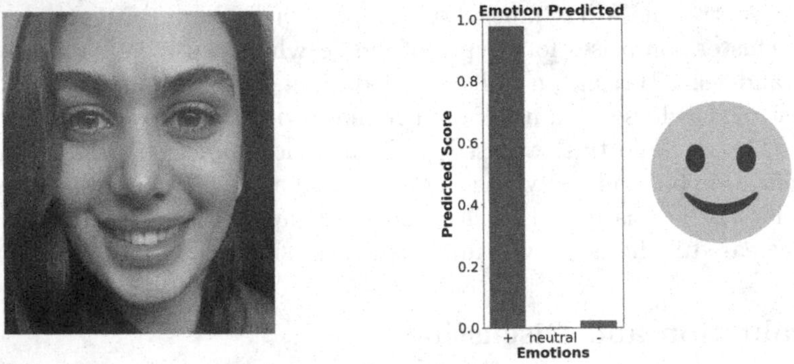

Fig. 4. Happy output of the real-time application.

Interestingly, the network mainly relies on relating specific facial actions to emotions. The network mimic the human ER system, e.g., if teeth are shown or the mouth is shaped in an upward arc, it directly relates to the emotion of happiness. Conversely, the upper part of the face is used to detect sadness since furrowing the eyebrows is usually representative of a negative expression. The absence of any of these two previous features indicate a neutral emotion.

5 Conclusion and Future Work

We introduce a tool that is able to recognize emotional states in a net-based team meeting and by this to enhance visually impaired person's experience in a conversation. This work proves the possibility of using publicly available datasets used for ER to develop such a tool for visually impaired people by clustering the emotion categories to more generic ones. This improvement allows saving time and avoiding the need to develop specific datasets for our use case.

Further investigation can be done on novel network structures and fusion schemes. Resnext [16] is a variation of Resnet that surpasses the latter structure and shows promising results for various tasks. In addition, 3D convolutional networks would be a good extension for our test case since we have data evolving over time. However, these networks still require a lot of memory and large datasets to be functional.

Moreover, a reliable method to output the emotional states to the visually impaired person needs to be investigated. Since the output of recognized emotional states is reduced to a three-stage signal, only two stages need to be output (positive and negative), while the neutral state corresponds to "no output". For this approach, a user study is needed to evaluate the efficiency of the tool in terms of improving the visually impaired people experience. However, due to the pandemic situation this was left as future work.

References

1. Chen, J., Chen, Z., Chi, Z., Fu, H.: Emotion recognition in the wild with feature fusion and multiple kernel learning. In: Proceedings of the 16th International Conference on Multimodal Interaction, pp. 508–513. ICMI 2014, Association for Computing Machinery, New York, NY, USA (2014). https://doi.org/10.1145/2663204.2666277
2. Dhall, A., Goecke, R., Joshi, J., Wagner, M., Gedeon, T.: Emotion recognition in the wild challenge (EmotiW) challenge and workshop summary. In: Proceedings of the 15th ACM on International conference on multimodal interaction, pp. 371–372. ICMI 2013, Association for Computing Machinery, New York, NY, USA (2013). https://doi.org/10.1145/2522848.2531749
3. Dzedzickis, A., Kaklauskas, A., Bucinskas, V.: Human emotion recognition: review of sensors and methods. Sensors **20**(3) (2020). https://doi.org/10.3390/s20030592
4. Ekman, P.: An argument for basic emotions. Cogn. Emot. **6**(3–4), 169–200 (1992)

5. El-Gayyar, M., ElYamany, H.F., Gaber, T., Hassanien, A.E.: Social network framework for deaf and blind people based on cloud computing. In: 2013 Federated Conference on Computer Science and Information Systems, pp. 1313–1319. IEEE (2013)
6. He, K., Zhang, X., Ren, S., Sun, J.: Deep residual learning for image recognition. CoRR abs/1512.03385 (2015). http://arxiv.org/abs/1512.03385
7. Kaklauskas, A., et al.: Affective tutoring system for built environment management. Comput. Educ. **82**, 202–216 (2015). https://doi.org/10.1016/j.compedu.2014.11.016, https://www.sciencedirect.com/science/article/pii/S0360131514002693
8. Knyazev, B., Shvetsov, R., Efremova, N., Kuharenko, A.: Convolutional neural networks pretrained on large face recognition datasets for emotion classification from video. CoRR abs/1711.04598 (2017). http://arxiv.org/abs/1711.04598
9. Kunz, A., et al.: Accessibility of brainstorming sessions for blind people. In: Miesenberger, K., Fels, D., Archambault, D., Peňáz, P., Zagler, W. (eds.) ICCHP 2014. LNCS, vol. 8547, pp. 237–244. Springer, Cham (2014). https://doi.org/10.1007/978-3-319-08596-8_38
10. Li, S., et al.: Bi-modality fusion for emotion recognition in the wild. In: 2019 International Conference on Multimodal Interaction, pp. 589–594. ICMI 2019, Association for Computing Machinery, New York, NY, USA (2019). https://doi.org/10.1145/3340555.3355719
11. Lucey, P., Cohn, J.F., Kanade, T., Saragih, J., Ambadar, Z., Matthews, I.: The extended Cohn-Kanade dataset (CK+): a complete dataset for action unit and emotion-specified expression. In: 2010 IEEE Computer Society Conference on Computer Vision and Pattern Recognition-Workshops, pp. 94–101 (2010). https://doi.org/10.1109/CVPRW.2010.5543262
12. Marinoiu, E., Zanfir, M., Olaru, V., Sminchisescu, C.: 3D human sensing, action and emotion recognition in robot assisted therapy of children with autism. In: Proceedings of the IEEE Conference on Computer Vision and Pattern Recognition, pp. 2158–2167 (2018)
13. Mittal, T., Guhan, P., Bhattacharya, U., Chandra, R., Bera, A., Manocha, D.: Emoticon: context-aware multimodal emotion recognition using frege's principle. CoRR abs/2003.06692 (2020). https://arxiv.org/abs/2003.06692
14. Peng, A.Y., Koh, Y.S., Riddle, P.J., Pfahringer, B.: Using supervised pretraining to improve generalization of neural networks on binary classification problems. In: ECML/PKDD (2018)
15. Simonyan, K., Zisserman, A.: Very deep convolutional networks for large-scale image recognition. In: Bengio, Y., LeCun, Y. (eds.) 3rd International Conference on Learning Representations, ICLR 2015, San Diego, CA, USA, 7–9 May 2015, Conference Track Proceedings (2015). http://arxiv.org/abs/1409.1556
16. Xie, S., Girshick, R., Dollar, P., Tu, Z., He, K.: Aggregated residual transformations for deep neural networks. In: Proceedings of the IEEE Conference on Computer Vision and Pattern Recognition (CVPR), July 2017
17. Yildirim, S., et al.: An acoustic study of emotions expressed in speech. In: Eighth International Conference on Spoken Language Processing (2004)

Pointing, Pairing and Grouping Gesture Recognition in Virtual Reality

Valentina Gorobets(✉), Cecily Merkle, and Andreas Kunz

Swiss Federal Institute of Technology, Zurich, Switzerland
{gorobets,kunz}@iwf.mavt.ethz.ch
https://www.icvr.ethz.ch/index_EN

Abstract. During a team discussion, participants frequently perform pointing, pairing, or grouping gestures on artifacts on a whiteboard. While the content of the whiteboard is accessible to the blind and visually impaired people, the referring deictic gestures are not. This paper thus introduces an improved algorithm to detect such gestures and to classify them. Since deictic gestures such as pointing, pairing and grouping are performed by sighted users only, we used a VR environment for the development of the gesture recognition algorithm and for the subsequent user studies.

Keywords: Virtual reality · Gesture recognition · Non-verbal communication · Deictic gestures · Integration

1 Introduction

Lively discussions among people heavily rely on non-verbal communication, such as deictic gestures, facial expressions, body poses etc. Following Mehrabian and Ferris [11], such non-verbal communication could make up to 55% of the overall information exchange. Among these non-verbal communication elements, deictic gestures become particularly important when referring to common artifacts in a team meeting such as a whiteboard. Deictic gestures are used to support information exchange and are intuitively performed and understood by sighted people. However, blind and visually impaired people (BVIP) can not access these deictic gestures, and thus there is a need for detection and interpretation as stated by Kane et al. [7]. While detecting and interpreting gestures in an easy task for human being, machines need sophisticated algorithms to reliably detect gestures and to avoid erroneous output to the BVIP.

This paper thus introduces an improved algorithm for gesture detection. For this, the paper is structured as follows: Sect. 2 introduced previous work in this field, followed by Sect. 3, in which our algorithm is explained more in detail, together with the technical setup and a description of our user study. The remainder of the paper gives a statistical evaluation in Sect. 4, before we discuss the results in Sect. 5. Finally, we conclude our paper with a summary and an outlook on future work in Sect. 6.

This work was commonly funded by DFG, FWF, and SNF under No. 211500647.

K. Miesenberger et al. (Eds.): ICCHP-AAATE 2022, LNCS 13341, pp. 313–320, 2022.
https://doi.org/10.1007/978-3-031-08648-9_36

2 Related Work

Tracking and interpreting deictic gestures has been researched since many years. Research on gestures can be basically divided into 2D and 3D gestures with regard to the interaction space. A comprehensive overview on gestures is given by van den Hoven and and Mazalek [6]. Gesture detection is researched in various application fields. Hofemann et al. [5] for instance use pointing gestures to instruct a robot which part to pick from a table, while pointing gestures were studied in a student-tutor relationship by Sathayanarayana et al. [14]. Besides possible applications of detecting pointing gestures, the pointing accuracy was also intensively studied, e.g., in [1,4].

For detecting hand gestures and interpreting them, recent research employs deep learning algorithms that can detect from incoming video streams. However, training such deep learning networks requires a large data set of annotated gestures, which is a time consuming procedure [13]. Such deep learning networks were again applied to human-robot interaction [12], but also to meeting environments [3] or classroom settings [10,15].

However, there is only little work related to gestures in team meetings, and how to analyze different kinds of gestures to be output to BVIP. A first approach was introduced by Kunz et al. [8] who detected pointing gestures on artifacts on a horizontal workspace. Later, pointing gestures on artifacts on a vertical screen were detected using an Microsoft Kinect depth cam [2], and recently an HTC Vive tracking system was used to track hand gestures and to distinguish them into pointing, pairing, and grouping as the most relevant ones for referring to objects (cards) on a whiteboard [9].

3 Methodology

Our work builds upon the work from Liechti et al. [9] who detected and distinguished three different gestures on a whiteboard: pointing, pairing, and grouping. While this work proved that a distinction of deictic gestures based on tracking signals is in general possible, the accuracy was rather low. This was due to wrongly detected artifacts by the algorithm, position dependency of the pointing person with regard to the whiteboard, and a virtual pointing ray defined by the user's forearm.

Although the envisioned application of our algorithm is to detect deictic gestures by sighted persons in a team meeting together with visually impaired people, we completed the optimization of the algorithm in a Virtual Environment (VE). A VE allows for more replicable conditions in the user study (see also Sect. 3.3).

3.1 Technical Setup

Our technical setup consists of the HTC Vive Pro head-mounted display (HMD) and two HTC Vive trackers. The HMD is used for displaying the VE only, while its tracking capabilities were not used. Instead, a tracker was attached to the user's head, while the other was attached to the user's wrist. Unlike in [9], the virtual pointing ray is thus calculated from the user's eye position (the top of the head minus an offset) and the user's hand, which eventually is the more precise approach.

3.2 Detection Algorithms

The performed gestures by the user will generate a virtual pointing ray that invisibly intersects with the virtual whiteboard. Thus an invisible trajectory is drawn on the whiteboard. The trajectory consists of points that are generated with a certain spawn rate while pointing, and then interconnected with straight lines. This trajectory will be evaluated by our algorithm and then categorized as "pairing" (indicate a connection between two cards), "grouping" (indicating a cluster of multiple cards), or "pointing" (indicating a single card) (see also Fig. 1).

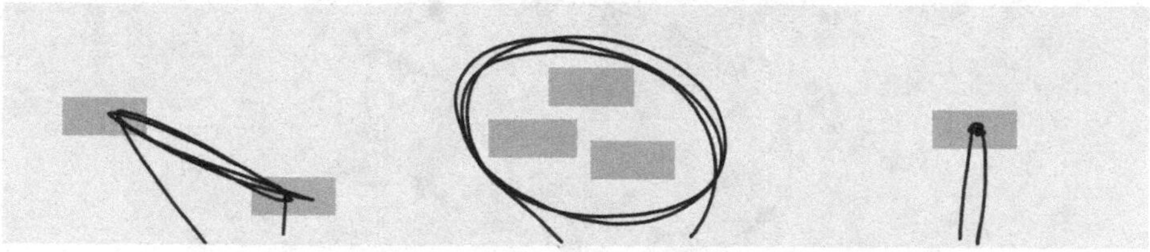

Fig. 1. Pairing, grouping and pointing gestures gestures to be detected.

Detection of Pairing Gesture. A pairing gesture is assumed to have an elliptic-shaped trajectory as shown in Fig. 1 (left) and that the regions close to the elliptic focal points determine the two cards to be paired (see Fig. 2a (left)). In order to determine these regions of the ellipse, the curvature used. The ellipse is discretized by the so-called "recognition spheres", that are generated by a given spawn rate while the user is gesturing (see Fig. 2a (right)). Subsequent spheres are interconnected by straight lines, and the angle between two subsequent lines is determined. The two lines that include the maximum angle are defined by in total three points, from which they one in common. This point is the "corner sphere" and supposed to be on a card. The radius of this sphere is then virtually increased to cope with imprecise pointing of the user. Thus, the detection of pairing gestures can be tuned by two parameters: the threshold for the angular change, and the radius of the corner sphere. The values were empirically determined in a separate pilot study to be $\alpha = 100°$ and $r = 0.3$ m.

Detection of Grouping Gestures. In case α is always below the set threshold, then a grouping gesture is assumed. For the grouping gesture detection, all sphere positions are recorded, and the extreme values of the x- and y-coordinates define four coordinates of a boundary box, in which the grouped notes re-assumed (see Fig. 2b).

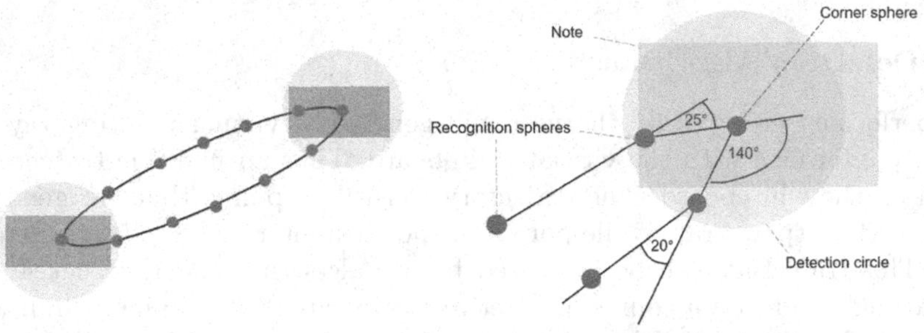

(a) Pairing gesture to be detected.

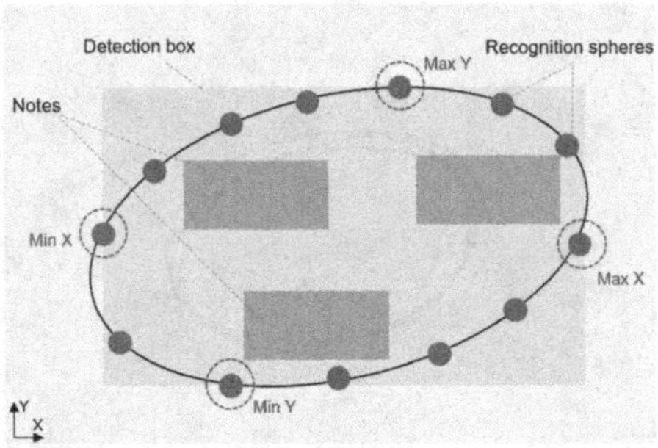

(b) Grouping gesture to be detected.

Fig. 2. Detection of pairing and grouping gestures.

Detection of Pointing Gestures. The pointing gesture on a note is simply detected in a temporal manner. If a note is hit by subsequent detection spheres for more than 2 s, it will be detected as pointing.

3.3 Virtual Environment (VE) Design

For creating the VE and interactions within it, we used Unity game engine. Three different zones (see Fig. 3) represent three distance classes in relation to the whiteboard. We wanted to investigate if the distance or the position of the user affects the recognition algorithm and if it does, then in which manner. The top-down view of the VE illustrates the distances from the center of the whiteboard to the center of each zone: the center of the cyan zone is located 2.5 m from the whiteboard, the center of the yellow zone is 1 m away, the center of the magenta zone is 3.3 m. The yellow zone is used to perform gestures next to the whiteboard, the cyan zone represents further distance, and the magenta zone was used to test gestures that are performed from the side. The virtual whiteboard is represented by the user interface proposed by [8] in our VE.

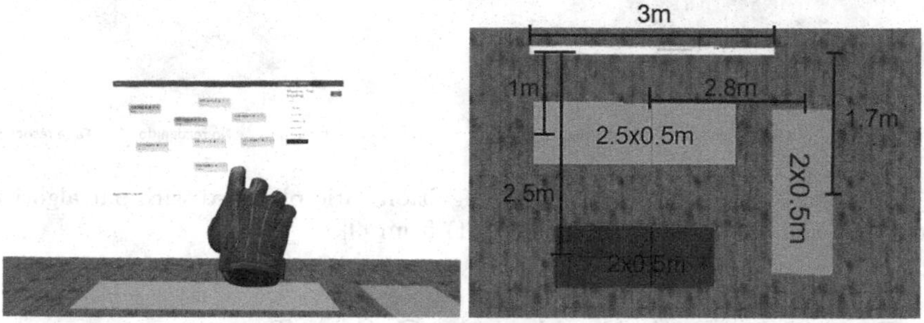

Fig. 3. User's perspective in the HMD and top-down view on the distance zones. (Color figure online)

3.4 Experiment Design

To test and compare the improvements of our algorithm compared to [9], we designed our experiment in the following manner. First, we gave a short introduction to the participants and collected the data obtained from the initial questionnaires. Second, they were asked to perform a particular gesture, following the oral instructions given by the experimenter. Therefore, we consider those instructions as the ground truth for the recognition algorithm.

Participants. We conducted the user study with 30 right-handed participants from 19 to 31 years old. There were 4 females and 26 males with normal or corrected-to-normal vision. We didn't include blind and visually people because the intention of this user study is to test the recognition algorithm we proposed, which can be done with the sighted people only.

4 Results

There are three possible outcomes: the algorithm recognized the gesture correctly, incorrectly or it didn't recognize anything while the gesture was performed.

4.1 Overall Recognition Ratio

Each participant performs 45 gestures during the experiment: 15 pointing, 15 pairing, and 15 grouping gestures. This gives a total number of 450 gestures of each type. Therefore, the total number of the performed gestures among all 30 participants is 1350. Our algorithm correctly recognized 44% of all gestures, 30% of the gestures were not recognized, and 26% were recognized wrongly. The results were then compared to the ones from [9] (see Fig. 4).

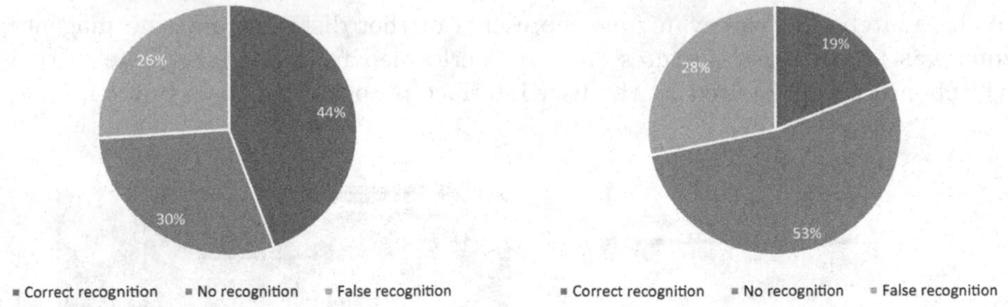

Fig. 4. Side by side comparison of the recognition ratio obtained with our algorithm (on the left) and the algorithm (on the right) from [9].

4.2 Recognition Ratio Based on the Gesture Type

As some of the gestures are easier to recognize than others, we decided to investigate how the recognition ratio depends on the gesture type. We assumed that the pointing gesture will have the highest ratio as it is performed with only one note. Figure 5a gives an overview of the recognition ratio for pointing, pairing and grouping gestures.

4.3 Recognition Ratio Based on the Distance Zones

As it was discussed in Sect. 3.3, we tested our algorithm in three different zones to study if the user position affects the recognition algorithm. The results are presented on Fig. 5b. As it can be observed from Fig. 5b, gesturing from the side has the lowest recognition rate of 37% among all three zones. Zones in which participants stand in front of the whiteboard show better recognition results: 45% when the gestures are performed from a longer distance and 51% when participants stand right next to the whiteboard.

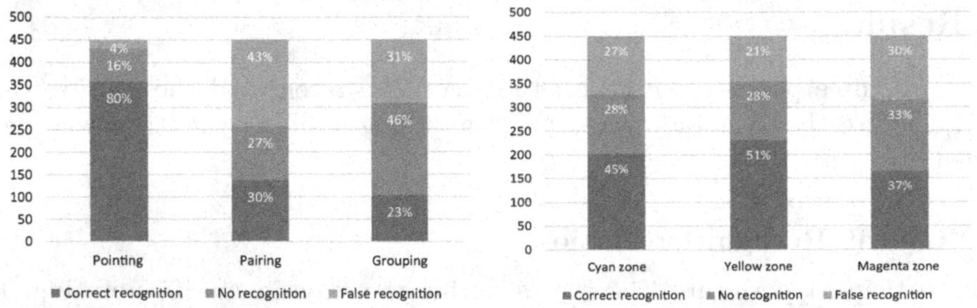

(a) Recognition ratio based on the gesture type.

(b) Recognition ratio based on the distance zones.

Fig. 5. Recognition ratio for various study conditions.

5 Discussion

False recognition for pairing and grouping gestures (see Fig. 5a) was usually caused by the inclusion of additional notes that were close to the notes involved in the performed gesture. Another reason for the low recognition rate for the pairing gesture is caused by the user behavior. We assumed that during pairing two notes participants will do it repeatedly. However, during the experiment we observed that some participants were pairing two notes by pointing at them successively. In this case, pairing gesture was either not recognized, or recognized false. Pointing was also not recognized if pointing gestures were performed very fast, since the time threshold for the start of the pointing gesture recognition was not reached.

Our algorithm performs worse for the gesturing from the side. However, it could also be caused by the inaccurate gesturing of the participants. Due to their position, it is more difficult to "aim" and perform an accurate gesture when they face the whiteboard from the side.

6 Summary and Outlook

In this paper, we described an approach for the pointing, pairing and grouping gestures recognition. We investigated the overall recognition ratio for all performed gestures, and how it changes depending on the gesture type and the position to the whiteboard.

For future work, we will decouple the results of the recognition algorithm from the performance of human gesturing. Such decoupling will allow us to test the initial accuracy of the algorithm without considering differences caused by different gesturing behavior. The next steps will also include transferring this algorithm to the real life scenario by creating a virtual twin of the real setup and using only two trackers without the HMD to recognise the performed gestures. Next, an interface to communicate gesturing information to blind and visually impaired people will be implemented.

References

1. Akkil, D., Isokoski, P.: Accuracy of interpreting pointing gestures in egocentric view. In: Proceedings of the 2016 ACM International Joint Conference on Pervasive and Ubiquitous Computing. ACM, September 2016. https://doi.org/10.1145/2971648.2971687
2. Dhingra, N., Valli, E., Kunz, A.: Recognition and localisation of pointing gestures using a RGB-D camera. In: Stephanidis, C., Antona, M. (eds.) HCII 2020. CCIS, vol. 1224, pp. 205–212. Springer, Cham (2020). https://doi.org/10.1007/978-3-030-50726-8_27
3. Hassink, N., Schopman, M.: Gesture recognition in a meeting environment. Master's thesis, University of Twente (2006)

4. Herbort, O., Krause, L.-M., Kunde, W.: Perspective determines the production and interpretation of pointing gestures. Psychon. Bull. Rev. **28**(2), 641–648 (2020). https://doi.org/10.3758/s13423-020-01823-7
5. Hofemann, N., Fritsch, J., Sagerer, G.: Recognition of deictic gestures with context. In: Rasmussen, C.E., Bülthoff, H.H., Schölkopf, B., Giese, M.A. (eds.) DAGM 2004. LNCS, vol. 3175, pp. 334–341. Springer, Heidelberg (2004). https://doi.org/10.1007/978-3-540-28649-3_41
6. van den Hoven, E., Mazalek, A.: Grasping gestures: gesturing with physical artifacts. AI EDAM **25**(3), 255–271 (2011)
7. Kane, S.K., Wobbrock, J.O., Ladner, R.E.: Usable gestures for blind people: understanding preference and performance. In: Proceedings of the SIGCHI Conference on Human Factors in Computing Systems, pp. 413–422. ACM, New York (2011). https://doi.org/10.1145/1978942.1979001
8. Kunz, A., Alavi, A., Sinn, P.: Integrating pointing gesture detection for enhancing brainstorming meetings using Kinect and pixelsense. Procedia CIRP **25**, 205–212 (2014)
9. Liechti, S., Dhingra, N., Kunz, A.: Detection and localisation of pointing, pairing and grouping gestures for brainstorming meeting applications. In: Stephanidis, C., Antona, M., Ntoa, S. (eds.) HCII 2021. CCIS, vol. 1420, pp. 22–29. Springer, Cham (2021). https://doi.org/10.1007/978-3-030-78642-7_4
10. Liu, T., Chen, Z., Wang, X.: Automatic instructional pointing gesture recognition by machine learning in the intelligent learning environment. In: Proceedings of the 2019 4th International Conference on Distance Education and Learning, pp. 153–157 (2019)
11. Mehrabian, A., Ferris, S.R.: Inference of attitudes from nonverbal communication in two channels. J. Consult. Psychol. **31**(3), 248–252 (1967). https://doi.org/10.1037/h0024648
12. Pizzuto, G., Cangelosi, A.: Exploring deep models for comprehension of deictic gesture-word combinations in cognitive robotics. In: 2019 International Joint Conference on Neural Networks (IJCNN), pp. 1–7. IEEE (2019)
13. Ripperda, J., Drijvers, L., Holler, J.: Speeding up the detection of non-iconic and iconic gestures (SPUDNIG): a toolkit for the automatic detection of hand movements and gestures in video data. Behav. Res. Methods **52**(4), 1783–1794 (2020). https://doi.org/10.3758/s13428-020-01350-2
14. Sathayanarayana, S., et al.: Towards automated understanding of student-tutor interactions using visual deictic gestures. In: Proceedings of the IEEE Conference on Computer Vision and Pattern Recognition Workshops, pp. 474–481 (2014)
15. Wang, J., Liu, T., Wang, X.: Human hand gesture recognition with convolutional neural networks for k-12 double-teachers instruction mode classroom. Infrared Phys. Technol. **111**, 103464 (2020)

Accessible User Interface Concept for Business Meeting Tool Support Including Spatial and Non-verbal Information for Blind and Visually Impaired People

Reinhard Koutny(✉) and Klaus Miesenberger

Institut Integriert Studieren, Johannes Kepler University Linz, Altenbergerstraße 69, 4040 Linz, Austria
{reinhard.koutny,klaus.miesenberger}@jku.at

Abstract. Business meetings play an essential role in many people's work life. Although, business meetings have changed over time, especially tools, which are used to support the process, slowly moving from traditional means like flipcharts to more modern, digital alternatives, some aspects stayed the same: Visual information is used to gather thoughts, support arguments and lead the discussion. These kinds of information used to be completely inaccessible to blind and visually impaired people (BVIP) and still are, for the most part. Even though, the movement towards digitalization facilitates accessibility, no fully accessible tool support for business meetings is available. Additionally, non-verbal communication and spatial information is heavily used as well. People use mimic and gestures, and they refer to objects or other people by pointing at them. BVIP miss out on this type of information as well. Ultimately, BVIP have a significant disadvantage during business meetings and very often during their entire professional life. Research efforts have tried to mitigate single aspects of this situation, but no comprehensive user interface approach has be developed. This paper presents a user interface approach, as part of the MAPVI project [1], that allows BVIP access visual, non-verbal and spatial information of business meetings in a user-friendly manner, using only off-the-shelf hardware. Additionally, it presents results of user tests of this novel user interface.

Keywords: Business meetings · Brainstorming meetings · Blind and visually impaired people · User interface design

1 Introduction

Communication between multiple humans talking to each other in person does not only consist of the spoken language and the auditory channel to convey information. It includes multiple channels. The most obvious one is the visual sense, which provides additional information on multiple levels, often referred to as a key part of "non-verbal communication". People constantly refer to the real world, which is often done by gestures, by referring to its visual appearance or location in space or a combination of

K. Miesenberger et al. (Eds.): ICCHP-AAATE 2022, LNCS 13341, pp. 321–328, 2022.
https://doi.org/10.1007/978-3-031-08648-9_37

both commonly called deictic gestures. Common artifacts being descripted or referred to during conversations are objects, persons, location, or processes/actions.

In addition, non-verbal communication plays a crucial role in face-to-face conversations as well. In particular, facial expressions, postures, gestures and body language in general convey manifold complementary information, describing the underlying meaning of the spoken words, the feelings and emotions of the speaker, and other people that are part of a group conversation and often put statements into perspective, sometimes even negate the actual meaning of them (e.g. the concept of sarcasm).

However, not every persons has the same capabilities and might be restricted in to which degree they can use their senses for communication. For instance BVIP cannot use or are limited in using their visual sense and are therefore at risk to miss important information. In particular, group conversations are a major problem. Conversations only involving two persons, one of them is blind and the other one is sighted, the sighted person will most likely adapt to the situation and try avoiding gestures, which require the visual sense, or rather additionally describe important information, e.g. gestures, verbally.

Group conversations, on the other hand, where most of the participants are sighted, tend to be much more challenging in terms of equal access. Frequently, sighted people will fall back to behavioral patterns to make heavy use of gestures and body language to convey information when they specifically talk to a sighted person in a group, while the blind person is still passively participating listening and missing out on a decisive junk of information.

In particular, group conversations at business meetings with all of their visual artifacts and references to the real world introduce a vast multi-dimensional information space, which is impossible to adequately explore for blind persons by traditional methods only using their acoustic sense due to the enormous complexity of this kind of information.

2 Related Work

A broad variety of tools to support business meetings is available. They help to record discussions, structure thoughts and support presenters with their arguments. Traditionally, analog whiteboards, sketching tables or flipcharts were used, while in recent years a slow change towards digital means has taken place. Modern meeting rooms are equipped as a minimum standard with digital projectors to show PowerPoint presentation to other participants, but wall-mounted touchscreens are commonly used as well. While the shift to digital tools theoretically provides accessibility for BVIP to some extent, the reality looks much different. Most tools, file formats and documents do not consider this target group adequately, which leads to a situation were sometimes solely textual information, and if provided alt-texts, can be read, but the spatial arrangement of items on a slide or whiteboard is inaccessible. However, this information is crucial to understand the context of the textual information, which is then confusing at best and straight inaccessible most of the time.

For decades, researchers have developed approaches to solve or at least mitigate these issues. Earlier approaches used mice and keyboards, some even optically tracked pens [2] and PDAs [3] to feed information to the system and share it on an electronic whiteboard. More recently, researchers have developed an approach facilitating a back-projected interactive table and interactive vertical screens. An overview, which goes into more detail can be found here [3, 4].

Still, visual aids of business meetings are only one source of information. Spatial aspects of the meeting and the venue, including the position of physical objects and other participants offer a much greater challenge to understandably present but give important context to conversation as well. Research efforts have been concerned with world exploration techniques for BVIP [5–9]. One issue that has been repeatedly identified, also in previous projects [10], is that the auditory channel of a BVIP can be overloaded quickly. This channel is used more intensely in general, in comparison to a sighted person. Therefore, it is of utmost importance for a user interface to limit the amount of information transmitted via this channel. Otherwise, the user ends up choose to either operating the user interface or listening to the conversation. In business meetings, this is barely an option. Consequentially, other approaches were explored. One direction is the adaption of regular Braille displays, which usually display one-dimensional text in a haptic manner. Hyperbraille was facilitated in this context [11] and offers in contrast a two-dimensional array of braille elements, which allows to display 2D content, and was even extended with audio notifications by adopting tangible interaction concepts [10]. This device, however, comes with some drawbacks - most notably the relatively low resolution, the size and weight, and the high price.

Therefore, the goal of this work is to provide a user interface concept to access business meeting information including spatial and non-verbal aspects. The tracking, especially of non-verbal information, is part of the MAPVI project, but is out of scope of this paper. Functional prototypes co-developed and tested by community of BVIP only using off-the-shelf hardware help to determine the benefit of this approach.

3 The Scenario

Business meetings can look different, depending on the context, the company and the profession. Acknowledging this fact, the MAPVI project has defined a scenario as an example business meeting, which is considered to offer a broad variety of types of information; namely a brainstorming meeting. In this scenario, multiple persons are gathered in the meeting room, and multiple persons are participating remotely. One or more of these participants can be BVIPs. The meeting room is equipped with multiple screens holding information. In particular, these screens contain notes arranged on 2D planes. The position of these notes holds a certain meaning and these notes can also be grouped and linked to each other. In the meeting room, participants are primarily gathered around a table, but they can also walk up to screens and point at them to emphasize on an argument or to moderate the discussion.

Looking at this scenario, two different 2D information spaces can be identified:

One information space is the meeting room itself, where participants have certain positions, perform gestures and reference at objects in the same room by pointing at them.

The second information space are the white boards: notes are arranged with the arrangement holding a certain meaning, depending on the context.

4 User Interface Concept

While parts of this information can be described textually and therefore presented to BVIP in an accessible way, usually with the help of screenreaders in combination with text-to-speech output or braille diplays, the implicit information deriving from the arrangements of entities in the two 2D information spaces cannot be conveyed in an understandable manner. Therefore, the user interface concept adds user interfaces to deal with this issue.

In particular, three user interfaces have been created to let participants of meetings, including blind and visually impaired ones, not only gain access to all information of such meetings, but also allow equally contribute to the conversation.

4.1 Web Interface

The first user interface is the web interface, which displays a visual whiteboard to sighted people, but also allows blind people to gain access to all textual information of the whiteboard, the notes. Besides that, it allows, especially blind people to retrieve information about real-world aspects of the meeting, including the participants, their names and what kind of gestures they are currently performing. This web interface is fully accessible, for BVIP using screenreaders, as well as sighted keyboard users. Furthermore, it is responsive which means that users can operate it on tablets, smartphones or on regular screens with high zoom levels to mitigate weak eyesight.

4.2 Smartphone

While the web interface grants access to a broad variety of information and is fully accessible, some types of information, in particular spatial information, simply cannot be convey in an understandable manner to BVIP. As there are two different 2D information spaces, two separate user interfaces were created to make both of them accessible. The first user interface uses off-the-shelf smartphones using Google AR-Core [12] to create a haptic VR representation of the whiteboard in front of the user. This representation can be described as a virtual wall erected in front of the user, with objects on it. These objects correspond in position to notes on the whiteboard of the web interface. The user can explore the same whiteboard with the smartphone in hand be simple moving the hand. If the hand approaches a note, the phone starts vibrating in short bursts, getting stronger the closer it gets. If the phone virtually touches a note, the device continuously vibrates. Additionally, the phone announces via text to speech the name of the note. In addition to the exploration of the whiteboard, the user can perform several actions on a virtual note using the hardware volume buttons on the phone with short and long presses. One action is to retrieve addition information, like the body text of the note. Another action is moving and rotation the note be pressing and holding a button and moving the phone. This way, blind and visually impaired users can intuitively manipulate the position and orientation of notes, which would not be possible otherwise. Finally yet importantly, users can highlight either single notes by the press of a button, or show a visually cursor for sighted people to highlight whole regions. This is helpful and necessary to not only limit BVIP to the role of retrieve information and participating in meetings, but also moderating the meeting and creating their own information and manipulating existing one.

4.3 Smartwatch

Since the smartphone UI approach only covers the information space of whiteboards, a third UI has been developed facilitating off-the-shelf smartwatches. It allows blind and visually impaired participants to explore the physical meeting room. The user has the smartwatch strapped to his or her hand and receives information of persons or objects he or she is pointing at. By swiping the hand across the room, the user can explore the whole room. The smartwatch starts to vibrate if a person or object is in pointing direction. It is also possible to search for specific persons or objects. This can be triggered in the web interface. After this the smartwatch switches to a specific mode and the vibration gets stronger, the closer the direction is to the actual direction of the object or person.

5 Methodology

User tests are undertaken in three stages:

5.1 Stage 1

In collaboration with two peer researchers, the first prototypes of these three user interfaces were tested, examined and improved.

5.2 Stage 2

The user interfaces described above will be tested in a next step by a small group (about 5 persons) of other blind users. The goal is to further improve the usability and accessibility and to avoid an "over-optimization" for only a few users (the peer researchers). Two of these user studies are considered useful for each of the three user interfaces (in total six user studies). Peer researchers are being involved and support the user studies. Between the individual user studies, the user interfaces will be further improved based on the findings of the previous user study. A single iteration of a user study consists of five parts:

- Training: The project is explained to the participants of the user studies and a short introduction to the concept of operation of the user interface is given.
- Evaluation: Participants are given tasks to perform. Recordings are made with their consent (video, time, error rate…).
- Feedback: Participants fill out a questionnaire. Here they can state what they liked, what they didn't like and what and how they would improve parts of the user interface in their opinion.

- Analysis: The feedback as well as the recordings are analyzed and aggregated. Suggestions for improvement are created and weighted based on this.
- UI improvement: The improvement suggestions will be implemented for the next iteration of the user studies depending on impact, effort and other criteria.

5.3 Stage 3

Finally, a large user study will be conducted (possibly divided into several sessions, depending on the current Corona regulations). The goal is to have the user interfaces tested by a group of users that is as large as possible (about 10 people) in order to obtain quantitatively meaningful insights into the added value of these user interfaces. Peer researchers are involved and support the user studies.

Current Status of User Tests and Preliminary Results

User studies are being held and are about to enter stage 2. The first stage showed promising results for the overall user interface concept as well as for the three different user interfaces themselves. The web interface, while being still a novelty as fully accessibly whiteboard and meeting support tool, is the user interface, which is the most traditional one in terms of concept of operations. Therefore, it is considered by both peer researchers to be on a very high level of accessibility and usability with only minor suggestions for improvement e.g. regarding the naming of menu element. These suggestions are being implemented with the next iteration of the prototype.

The feedback regarding the smartphone user interface, which allows to haptically explore whiteboards, has been positive as well. Both peer researchers see great potential in the user interface concept to explore 2D spatial information in general and have suggested to adapt this concept to other contexts as well, for example education. However, due to the nature of this user interface, there is the larger space for improvement and multiple suggestions were mentioned, which will be implemented after prioritization. One suggestion was that the range of motion should be configurable by the user. This means the user should be able to define how large the area in front of him or her is, that is used to represent the whiteboard. A smaller area has the benefit, that less space around the user is required to explore the whole whiteboard, but it also means that notes are closer to each other, which seems to increase the error rate, especially with more notes on the whiteboard. Another request was that it would be beneficially for a user if there was the option to do a guided walkthrough through all of the notes.

Regarding the smartwatch user interface, which allows to explore the actual meeting room, the feedback was again quite positive and was found to be rather intuitive. However, one suggestion was, to add, in addition to vibrations, also acoustic feedback if an object or person is directly in pointing direction.

Currently, stage one of the user test has ended and stage two is about to start. Due to COVID- related issue stages two and three were postponed, with stage two starting in mid of April.

6 Conclusion

In the extended abstract of this paper, we presented a complete user interface concept for accessible business meetings with blind and visually impaired people as equal collaborators. This concept does not treat blind and visually impaired participants as someone who can only receive information others created, but it allows them to understand spatial information, create and manipulate it. In addition to the concept, we presented functional prototypes for each user interface and preliminary tests of the ongoing user tests. We expect the full results of the user tests including stage two and three to be available in summer.

Acknowledgements. This project (MAPVI) including this publication was funded by the Austrian Science Fund (FWF): I 3741-N31.

References

1. Gunther, S., et al.: MAPVI. In: Makedon. F. (ed.) Proceedings of the PETRA'19, 12th ACM International Conference on Pervasive Technologies related to Assistive Environments, Rhodes, Greece June 05–07, pp. 343–352. ACM = Association for Computing Machinery, New York (2019). https://doi.org/10.1145/3316782.3322747
2. Elrod, S., et al.: Liveboard. In: Bauersfeld, P., Bennett, J., Lynch, G. (eds.) Proceedings of the SIGCHI conference on Human factors in computing systems - CHI '92, pp. 599–607. ACM Press, New York, New York, USA (1992). https://doi.org/10.1145/142750.143052
3. Magerkurth, C., Prante, T.: „Metaplan" für die westentasche: mobile computerunterstützung für kreativitätssitzungen. In: Oberquelle, H., Oppermann, R., Krause, J. (eds.) Mensch & Computer 2001: 1. Fachübergreifende Konferenz, pp. 163–171. Vieweg+Teubner Verlag, Wiesbaden (2001). https://doi.org/10.1007/978-3-322-80108-1_18
4. Lahlou, S. (ed.): Designing user friendly augmented work environments. From meeting rooms to digital collaborative spaces. Computer supported cooperative work. Springer, London, New York (2009)
5. Bolt, R.A.: Put-that-there. In: Thomas, J.J., Ellis, R.A., Kriloff, H.Z. (eds.) Proceedings of the 7th annual conference on Computer graphics and interactive techniques - SIGGRAPH '80, pp. 262–270. ACM Press, New York, New York, USA (1980). https://doi.org/10.1145/800250.807503
6. Brock, M., Kristensson, P.O.: Supporting blind navigation using depth sensing and sonification. In: Mattern, F., Santini, S., Canny, J.F., Langheinrich, M., Rekimoto, J. (eds.) Proceedings of the 2013 ACM conference on Pervasive and ubiquitous computing adjunct publication, pp. 255–258. ACM, New York, NY, USA (08 Sept 2013). https://doi.org/10.1145/2494091.2494173
7. Geronazzo, M., Bedin, A., Brayda, L., Campus, C., Avanzini, F.: Interactive spatial sonification for non-visual exploration of virtual maps. Int. J. Hum Comput Stud. **85**, 4–15 (2016). https://doi.org/10.1016/j.ijhcs.2015.08.004
8. Guo, A., et al.: VizLens. In: Rekimoto, J., Igarashi, T., Wobbrock, J.O., Avrahami, D. (eds.) Proceedings of the 29th Annual Symposium on User Interface Software and Technology, pp. 651–664. ACM, New York, NY, USA (16 Oct 2016). https://doi.org/10.1145/2984511.2984518

9. Willis, S., Helal, S.: RFID Information grid for blind navigation and wayfinding. In: Ninth IEEE International Symposium on Wearable Computers (ISWC'05), pp. 34–37. IEEE (2005). https://doi.org/10.1109/ISWC.2005.46
10. Kunz, A., et al.: Accessibility of Brainstorming Sessions for Blind People. In: Miesenberger, K., Fels, D., Archambault, D., Peňáz, P., Zagler, W. (eds.) ICCHP 2014. LNCS, vol. 8547, pp. 237–244. Springer, Cham (2014). https://doi.org/10.1007/978-3-319-08596-8_38
11. Pölzer, S., Miesenberger, K.: A Tactile Presentation Method of Mind Maps in Co-located Meetings. undefined, vol. (2014)
12. Google Developers: Build new augmented reality experiences that seamlessly blend the digital and physical worlds (2020). https://developers.google.com/ar

Interactions for Text Input and Alternative Pointing

Study of User Behavior When Using a List of Predicted Words

Mathieu Raynal[1(✉)] and Georges Badr[2]

[1] ELIPSE Team, IRIT Lab, University of Toulouse, Toulouse, France
mathieu.raynal@irit.fr
[2] TICKET LAB, Antonine University, Baabda, Lebanon
georges.badr@ua.edu.lb

Abstract. In this article, we present a study on the user's gaze tracking during a text input task on a soft keyboard associated with a word prediction list. The purpose of this study is to investigate user strategies for using the prediction list. When does he watch it? How frequently? Does he look at the whole list? our first results shows that the user only looks at the top of the list. Therefore, it does not use the prediction list optimally and enters more characters on the soft keyboard. Moreover, typing on the soft keyboard is also penalized by the presence of the list next to the keyboard because the user looks at it without necessarily using it. This sub-optimal use of the list coupled with slower input on the soft keyboard therefore results in a slower average input speed on the soft keyboard associated with a list.

Keywords: Words list · Soft keyboard · Text entry · Gaze tracking

1 Introduction

With the increasing use of digital devices (desktops, laptops, smartphones, tablets, etc.), text input or data entry has become a major task in our daily lives, whether for work (writing documents) or to communicate (emails, social networks, etc.). For these typing tasks, we usually use a physical keyboard. When the device we use does not have a physical keyboard, it is generally replaced by a so-called soft keyboard (or virtual keyboard): a software keyboard is an on-screen keyboard with which the user can interact either through a touch screen or by using a pointing device. For people with motor impairment of the upper limbs, the only way to type on a computer is the soft keyboard. They can manipulate it with a pointing device adapted to their motor abilities (joystick, eye and/or head tracking system [4,6,10], etc.).

In these situations, typing on a soft keyboard is much slower than it can be on a physical keyboard. However, to increase typing speed, soft keyboards are often coupled with word prediction systems to improve text input speed. Soft keyboards coupled with a word prediction list are the best known and most widespread systems [7,8]. These suggest the most likely words for a given prefix.

K. Miesenberger et al. (Eds.): ICCHP-AAATE 2022, LNCS 13341, pp. 331–337, 2022.
https://doi.org/10.1007/978-3-031-08648-9_38

The results suggested by these systems are then offered in the form of a list near the soft keyboard. The advantage of using this type of system is to minimize the number of actions to be carried out: rather than entering all the characters of the word, the user can select the word as soon as it appears in the list. The faster the word appears in the list, the fewer actions the user will have to perform to enter a word.

However, these word lists can be counterproductive if the word does not appear in the list or if it appears late. Indeed, the user must regularly look at the list to see if the word he wishes to enter is in the list. Several works have been carried out on lists to study the importance of characteristics such as the position of the list on the screen, the items size or the number of items in the list [3,5,11]. However, these works do not explain why the use of the list remains detrimental for the user as soon as he has a high typing speed on the software keyboard.

2 Method

2.1 Participants

We recruited 8 participants. Six were male, two were female. Ages ranged from 21 to 43 years.

2.2 Apparatus

The experiment required the use of two desktop computers. The first is used to run the experiment. The experiment tasks were presented using the E-Assiste platform [9]. All the software tools used (presentation banner, keyboard, prediction list) are implemented in Java. The second computer is used to drive the gaze tracking system and save the data from this tracking system. The gaze tracking system used is EyeLink2.

2.3 Procedure

Our study consisted of entering 40 words that we had chosen according to the number of characters to be entered before they appeared in the list and their position in the list when they appeared. We have therefore chosen words that appear after 2, 4, 6 and 8 characters typed and in the first, third, fifth and seventh positions in the list. We have chosen 2 words for each of the "number of characters"/"position" pairs. In addition to these 32 words, we have chosen eight words that do not appear in the list. Finally, we chose to compare the use of the same soft keyboard with or without the word list.

Participants were instructed to enter the words as quickly as possible. The word to copy was presented on a line, and the text input by the participant appeared on the line below (see Fig. 1). Text entry errors were not displayed on the screen. Instead, there was visual and auditory feedback signaling the error.

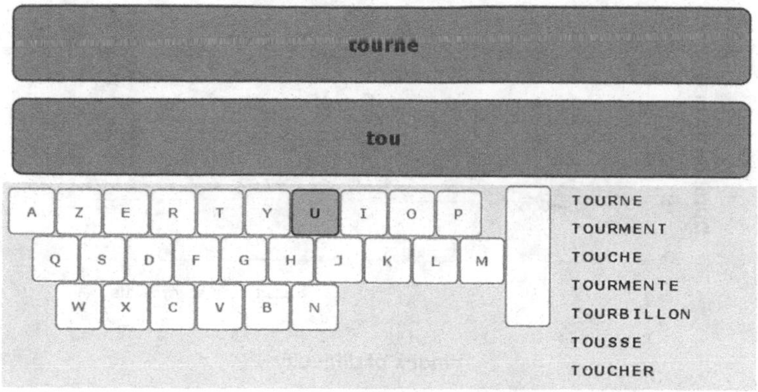

Fig. 1. Experiment tasks presented on the E-Assiste platform

The cursor did not move until the participant entered the correct character. At the end of each word, participants hit the Space bar. Our prediction list is a vertical list of seven items where the words are ranked according to their frequency of appearance (not in alphabetical order). Only words of more than 6 characters are displayed there.

2.4 Design

The eight participants had two exercises to perform. Each exercise corresponded to a copy task of 40 words. One exercise was performed with the AZERTY soft keyboard alone and the other exercise was performed with the same keyboard coupled to the prediction list. The participants were divided into two groups of four. One group started with the keyboard alone and then performed the exercise with the list, while the other group performed the exercises in reverse order.

3 Results and Discussion

3.1 Text Entry Speed

On average, participants were faster with the keyboard alone than with the keyboard coupled with the list. Indeed, they entered on average a character every 815 ms against 911 ms to enter a character with the list. This difference between the two devices is statistically significant ($F_{1,6} = 21.987$ with $p < 0.005$).

The Fig. 2 shows that regardless of the index of difficulty of the pointing task, the user took an average of 100 ms longer to type the desired character. The red and blue lines represent the time required to enter a character, depending on the difficulty of reaching it, respectively with the keyboard alone and with the same keyboard coupled to a words list. The index of difficulty depends on the distance to be traveled to reach the key and the key size.

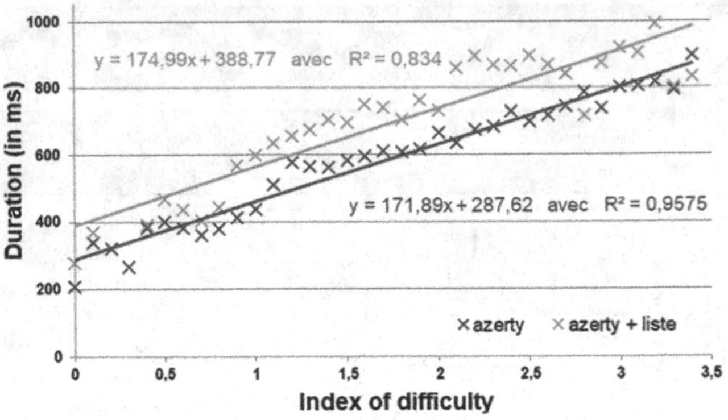

Fig. 2. Time to enter a character depending on the difficulty of reaching the corresponding key (Color figure online)

3.2 Gaze Fixations on the Words List

On the soft keyboard with the prediction list, we can also see that the average time to type a character increases proportionally to the number of characters typed on the keyboard (cf. Fig. 3a). This observation can be explained by the analysis of gaze tracking. Indeed, we can see that the more characters the user enters on the keyboard, the more the number of gaze fixations on the words list increases (see Fig. 3b).

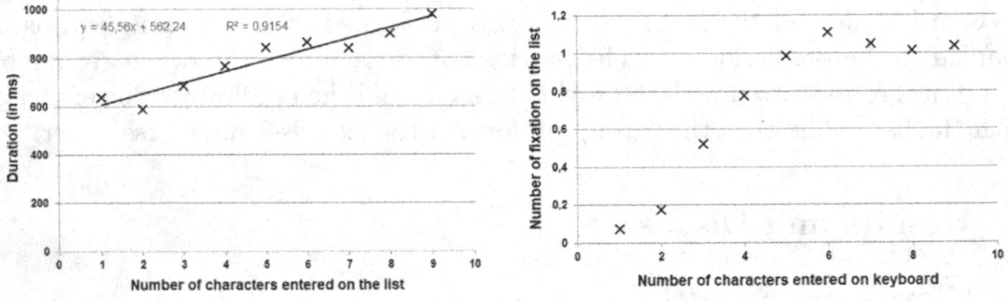

(a) Fixation time depending on the progress in the word

(b) Average number of fixations depending on the number of characters entered

Fig. 3. Main results on gaze fixations on the word list

We can also notice that the user does not use the words in the list on average one time out of 3 (left bar in the Fig. 4), and even if the word appears quickly in the word list, the user selects few words in the list before having entered at least 4 characters on the keyboard. The word list is mainly used between the 4th and 6th character entered (cf. Fig. 4).

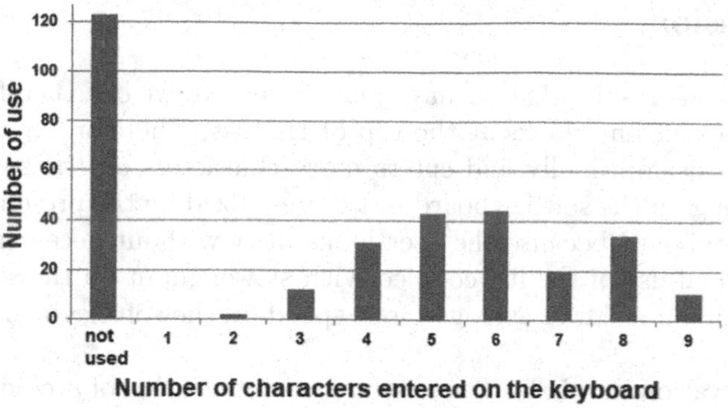

Fig. 4. Selection from the list according to the number of characters already entered

Finally, it also appears that the user tends to be concerned only with the top part of the list. The Fig. 5a presents the fixation rate on the top part of the list, i.e. the first 3 items (blue bar in the Fig. 5a) and the fixation rate on the lower part of the list, i.e. the last 4 items (red bars in the Fig. 5a). We can notice that the majority of fixations performed on the list are located on the first elements of the list, especially when the user only fixes the list once or twice (approximately 90%) when typing the word.

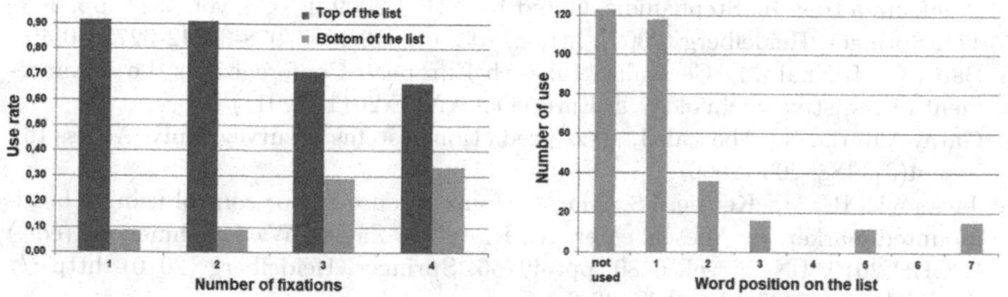

(a) Gaze position in the list

(b) Use of the list according to the position of the word

Fig. 5. Main results of user behavior during an input task (Color figure online)

This also results when selecting the words from the list. Users mainly select the word in the list when it is in the first position in the list (see Fig. 5).

4 Conclusion

To summarize the results that we have just presented, we can therefore say that in general the user only looks at the top of the list. Therefore, it does not use the prediction list optimally and enters more characters on the soft keyboard. However, typing on the soft keyboard is also penalized by the presence of the list next to the keyboard because the user looks at it without necessarily using it. This sub-optimal use of the list coupled with slower input on the soft keyboard therefore results in a slower average input speed on the soft keyboard associated with a list.

This observation should lead us to study the integration of prediction systems into text input systems. Proposing the words is not enough because the user cannot use them every time he looks at the list. One solution is therefore to facilitate the use of the results of the prediction. WordTree [1] and Centralist [2] are an example of a solution allowing to select only a part of the proposed words.

Acknowledgments. This work is partially funded by the AAC4All project (ANR grant: ANR-21-CE19-0051).

References

1. Badr, G., Raynal, M.: WordTree: results of a word prediction system presented thanks to a tree. In: Stephanidis, C. (ed.) UAHCI 2009. LNCS, vol. 5616, pp. 463–471. Springer, Heidelberg (2009). https://doi.org/10.1007/978-3-642-02713-0_49
2. Badr, G., Raynal, M.: Centralist. In: 11th European Conference for the Advancement of Assistive Technology in Europe (AAATE 2011) (2011)
3. Garay-Vitoria, N., Abascal, J.: Text prediction systems: a survey. Univ. Access Inf. Soc. **4**(3), 188–203 (2006)
4. Javanovic, R., MacKenzie, I.S.: MarkerMouse: mouse cursor control using a head-mounted marker. In: Miesenberger, K., Klaus, J., Zagler, W., Karshmer, A. (eds.) ICCHP 2010. LNCS, vol. 6180, pp. 49–56. Springer, Heidelberg (2010). https://doi.org/10.1007/978-3-642-14100-3_9
5. Koester, H.H., Levine, S.: Model simulations of user performance with word prediction. Augmentative Altern. Commun. **14**(1), 25–36 (1998)
6. Majaranta, P., MacKenzie, I.S., Aula, A., Räiha, K.J.: Auditory and visual feedback during eye typing. In: Extended Abstracts of the ACM Conference on Human Factors in Computing Systems - CHI 2003, pp. 766–767. ACM, New York (2003)
7. Masui, T.: POBox: an efficient text input method for handheld and ubiquitous computers. In: Gellersen, H.-W. (ed.) HUC 1999. LNCS, vol. 1707, pp. 289–300. Springer, Heidelberg (1999). https://doi.org/10.1007/3-540-48157-5_27
8. Maurel, D., Le Pévédic, B.: The syntactic prediction with token automata: application to handias system. Theoret. Comput. Sci. **267**(1–2), 121–129 (2001)
9. Raynal, M., Maubert, S., Vigouroux, N., Vella, F., Magnien, L.: E-Assiste: a platform allowing evaluation of text input systems. In: 3rd International Conference on Universal Access in Human-Computer Interaction (UAHCI 2005). Las Vegas (2005)

10. Rodrigues, A.S., da Costa, V.K., Cardoso, R.C., Machado, M.B., Machado, M.B., Tavares, T.A.: Evaluation of a head-tracking pointing device for users with motor disabilities. In: Proceedings of the 10th International Conference on Pervasive Technologies Related to Assistive Environments, pp. 156–162 (2017)
11. Sad, H.H., Poirier, F.: Modeling word selection in predictive text entry. In: Jacko, J.A. (ed.) HCI 2009. LNCS, vol. 5611, pp. 725–734. Springer, Heidelberg (2009). https://doi.org/10.1007/978-3-642-02577-8_80

TBS³: Two-Bar Single-Switch Scanning for Target Selection

Mathieu Raynal[1(✉)] and I. Scott MacKenzie[2]

[1] ELIPSE Team, IRIT Lab, University of Toulouse, Toulouse, France
mathieu.raynal@irit.fr
[2] Electrical Engineering and Computer Science, York University, Toronto, Canada
mack@yorku.ca

Abstract. We present a two-dimensional (2D) pointing technique for motor-impaired users who generally use single-input switch. The technique, called TBS³ for "two-bar single-switch scanning", uses two bars and proceeds in two steps: moving a vertical bar then moving a horizontal bar. The user starts and stops each bar by activating the single input switch. Selection is made at the intersection of the two bars when the horizontal bar is stopped by the user. We present two variations of the technique. In the first ("one-way"), the bars move only in one direction, and return to their origin after each selection. In the second ("button"), the user controls the direction by a selecting an on-screen soft button before bar movements starts. The techniques were evaluated in a experiment with twelve participants using the 2D target-selection task described in ISO 9241-411. Due to the two-stage pointing process, the task was inherently slow with a mean movement time of 8.4 s per trial. The mean error rate was just under 10% with the one-way method (8.0%) more accurate than the button method (11.1%). Throughput was 0.31 bps overall with values of 0.26 bps for the one-way method and 0.36 bps for the button method.

Keywords: Motor disability · Pointing technique · Single-switch scanning · Assistive technologies

1 Introduction

Since the 1980s and the emergence of the Apple Macintosh, graphical user interface have become the standard interface on traditional computers. These interfaces use a pointing device to interact in applications, to point and select elements to access different functionalities. The mouse and the trackpad are the main pointing devices for desktop and laptop computers, respectively. However, users with severe motor impairments cannot operate these devices.

In this paper, we propose a pointing technique using single-switch input and inspired by an interaction technique used on virtual keyboards. Indeed, to enter text, motor-impaired users often use a soft keyboard combined with single-switch

K. Miesenberger et al. (Eds.): ICCHP-AAATE 2022, LNCS 13341, pp. 338–346, 2022.
https://doi.org/10.1007/978-3-031-08648-9_39

scanning – a so-called "scanning soft keyboard". The cursor moves automatically from zone and when the cursor is on the right zone, the user validates it through an input action.

We propose a new pointing technique based on the automatic scanning of two bars (one horizontal and one vertical) controlled by a single input switch. We describe the principle of our interaction technique, and the different possibilities of interaction afforded. To validate this technique, we performed an evaluation with pointing tasks following recommendations for the evaluation of pointing devices [3,9]. We describe the methodology of our evaluation followed by analyses of the results and suggestions for further improvements and research.

2 Related Work

Alternative pointing devices have been proposed to provide access for motor-impaired users. The most common are those using eye-tracking [10] or head-tracking techniques [8]. However, these devices have drawbacks: eye-tracking systems require the user to fixate on the element they want to select. Other techniques based on EEG signals [6] or contraction signals of voluntary muscles using EMG [5] have also been studied to bring WIMP interaction to the most severely disabled people. Alternatives using face tracking [4] or a keypad [1] have also been proposed.

3 TBS^3: Two-Bar Single-Switch Scanning

3.1 Principle

Our implementation for single-switch scanning works with a vertical bar and a horizontal bar (see figures below). The bars move automatically over the width of the screen for the vertical bar and the height for the horizontal bar. The pointer is at the intersection of the two bars.

Pointing is done in two main steps: first, moving the vertical bar, then moving the horizontal bar. The user presses a single input switch to start the automatic movement of the vertical bar. Then, the user presses the same input switch again to stop the first bar. Stopping the vertical bar automatically starts the movement of the horizontal bar. Finally, the user stops this bar when desired by pressing the single input switch again. Stopping the second bar then generates a click at the coordinates of the intersection of the two bars. Along with this simple description of two-bar single-switch scanning, there are additional possibilities to enhance interaction.

3.2 "One-Way" Version

We implemented a first version called "one-way" where the vertical bar starts from the left of the screen and moves from left to right. The horizontal bar starts at the top of the screen and moves down.

Two options were considered for the start of a new pointing task. The first is to start the bars from the position of the last pointing, while the second option is to restart the bars from the origin.

When a bar reaches the end of the screen, we offer two modes: "go/return" mode wherein the bar continues in the opposite direction and "circular" mode wherein the bar starts again from the origin of the screen.

3.3 "Button" Version

In the "one-way" version, the user cannot choose the direction of bar movement. If the selected element is close to the bars but in the opposite direction to movement, the user must wait until the bar travels across the entire screen before returning to the element. Similarly, if the element is in the second part of the screen, the bars must travel a long distance before arriving at the element.

To overcome these problems, before the start of each scan, we implemented a "button" version which offers two soft buttons displayed in the center of the bar to allow the user to choose the movement direction (see Fig. 1). Button focus automatically alternates between the two buttons until the user makes a selection to set the direction of movement. This done by pressing the single input switch when the desired direction button is highlighted. The bars start from the center of the screen. Thus, the user can choose the direction of movement of the bars. Although an extra scanning step is required, this makes it possible to divide-by-two the distance required to reach the desired element.

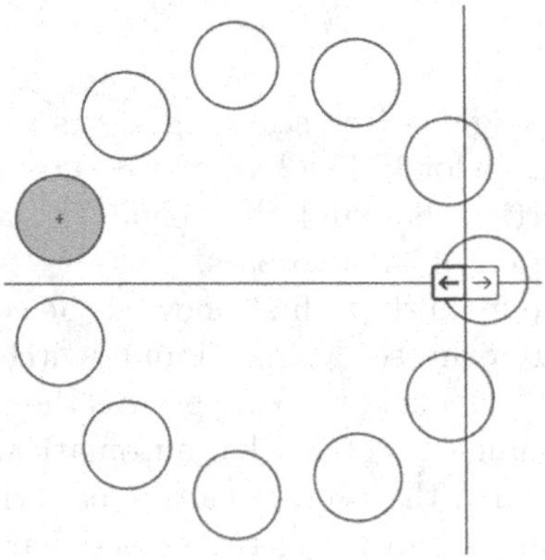

Fig. 1. "Button" version

4 Method

The goal of our user study was to empirically evaluate TBS^3, our two-bar single-switch scanning technique, and compare the two implementation methods described above ("one-way", "button"). The "one-way" method was combined with "origin" starting mode and the "button" method was combined with the "last pointing" starting mode. A 2D Fitts' law task conforming to ISO 9241-411 was used with three movement amplitudes combined with three target widths. Our hypothesis is that, even if the "button" version requires one more input actions, moving the bars in both directions will yield better results.

4.1 Participants

We recruited 12 participants from the first author's university campus. Nine were male, three were female. Ages ranged from 18 to 43 yrs.

4.2 Apparatus

The experiment was conducted on a Dell Latitude 5490 laptop with a resolution of 1024 × 768 pixels. The experiment tasks were presented using a modified version of GoFitts[1], a Java application implementing the 2D Fitts' law task (see Fig. 2). GoFitts includes additional utilities such as FittsTrace which plots the cursor trace data captured during trials.

The 2D task presented 11 targets per sequence, combining three movement amplitudes (100, 200, 400 pixels) with three target widths (20, 40, 80 pixels). Amplitude and width were included to ensure the conditions covered a range of task difficulties. The result is nine sequences for each test condition with IDs ranging from $\log_2(\frac{100}{80}+1) = 1.17$ bits to $\log_2(\frac{400}{20}+1) = 4.39$ bits.

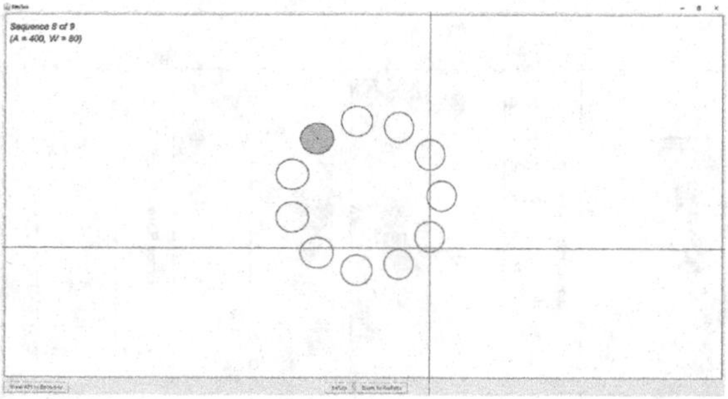

Fig. 2. 2D Fitts' law task in the modified GoFitts application with an amplitude of 400 pixels and a target width of 80 pixels

4.3 Procedure

The software and experiment were explained and demonstrated, following which testing began. Testing took a little under one hour per participant. Before each method, participants could test the method as much as they wanted (they generally performed 2 or 3 target selections).

[1] https://www.yorku.ca/mack/FittsLawSoftware/.

4.4 Design

The experiment was a 2×3×3 within-subjects design. The independent variables and levels were Pointing Method ("one way", "button"), Amplitude (100, 200, 400 pixels), and Width (20, 40, 80 pixels).

For each sequence, 11 targets appeared. The dependent variables were throughput (bps), movement time (ms), error rate (%). There were two groups for counterbalancing, one starting with the "one way" and the other starting with "button". The total number of trials was 2376 ($= 2 \times 3 \times 3 \times 11 \times 12$).

5 Results and Discussion

5.1 Throughput

The main performance measure in ISO 9241-411 is throughput (TP) [3,9], measured in bits/second (bps). TP is calculated over a sequence of trials as the ID-MT ratio: $TP = ID_e/MT$. The standard specifies calculating throughput using the effective index of difficulty (ID_e). The calculation includes an adjustment for accuracy to reflect the spatial variability in responses: $ID_e = \log_2(A_e/W_e + 1)$ with $W_e = 4.133 \times SD_x$.

Selecting with TBS[3] had a mean throughput of 0.306 bps. By pointing method, the means were 0.256 bps and 0.356 bps for one-way and button, respectively. This represents a 39% performance advantage for button. The effect of selection method on throughput was statistically significant ($F_{1,10} = 19.89, p = .0012$).

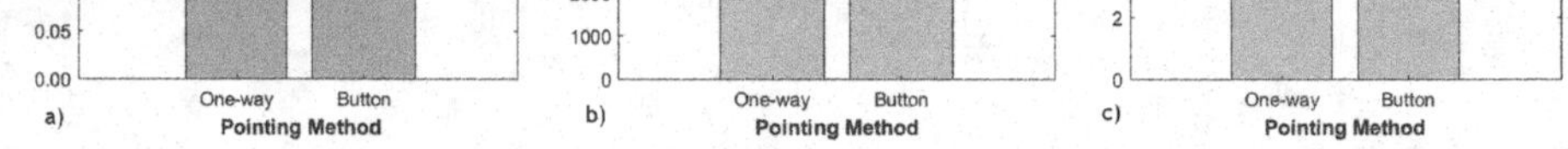

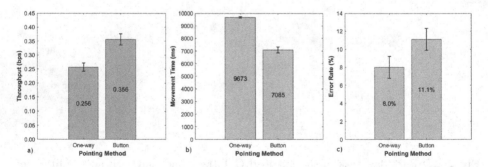

Fig. 3. a) Throughput (bps) by pointing method; b) Movement time by pointing method; c) Error rate by pointing method. Error bars show ±1 SE

The throughput values are low compared to a mouse [9]. But, we are here in the context of motor impairment, and these values are comparable with those reported in similar work [1,2]. On the other hand, the participants did not control the speed of movement of the two bars. The speed of the bars had been empirically fixed at 3 pixels per 20 ms. This movement speed could be adjusted to each user according to their abilities – a topic for future study.

5.2 Movement Time and Error Rate

The speed and accuracy of the techniques are combined in the throughput calculation, but it is interesting to examine both separately. Indeed, we can see in Fig. 3b that the speed is dependent on the technique in the same way as the throughput: the participants were faster with the button version than with the one way version (7085 ms and 9673 ms, respectively for a reduction of 27%), and this in a significant way ($F_{1,10} = 36.50, p = .0001$).

On the other hand, the error rate shows an opposite trend: Participants were more precise with the one-way method than with button method (8% and 11.1%, respectively), but this difference was not statistically significant. Several errors were observed with the button version when a bar was positioned correctly after the previous click. Indeed, the bars remain in the same position (whereas they are positioned at the origin with one-way) and users are forced to choose a direction of movement. If the bar was already well placed, it was necessary to click twice very quickly (or to let the bar go back and forth). Several participants made mistakes when trying to do two clicks very fast. Possible solutions include adding a third button to allow the user not to move the bar, or using a lower velocity for the initial movement of the bar.

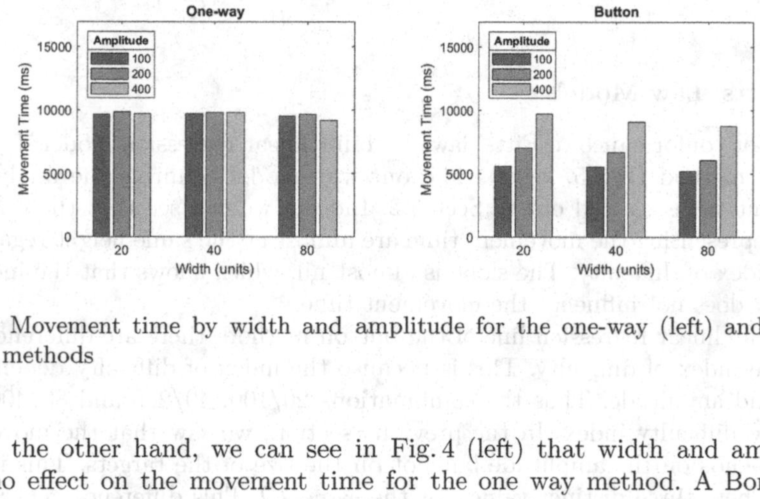

Fig. 4. Movement time by width and amplitude for the one-way (left) and button (right) methods

On the other hand, we can see in Fig. 4 (left) that width and amplitude have no effect on the movement time for the one way method. A Bonferroni multiple-comparisons test confirmed that none of the pairwise differences were statistically significant ($p > .05$). This is because the bars are always positioned at the origin after each click. Therefore, the distance actually traveled is always that between the upper left corner of the screen and the target. This effect is not found with the button version: The bars remain at the position of the last click; so, the distance between the targets influences the movement time to reach the target.

5.3 Cursor Trace Examples

Figure 5 (left) shows an example of pointer traces for the button method. The traces are straight horizontal or vertical lines, which reveal the functioning of the pointing method where the movements of the pointer are guided by successive rectilinear movements of the vertical then horizontal bar.

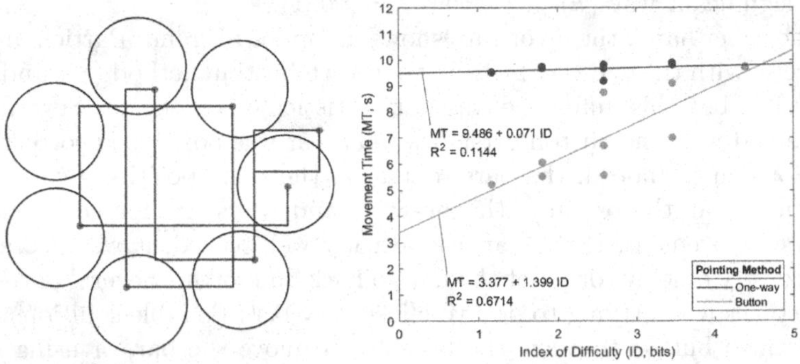

Fig. 5. At left, example pointer trace for button version; at right, Fitts' law models for one-way (blue line) and button (red line) methods (Color figure online)

5.4 Fitts' Law Models

To test for conformance to Fitts' law, we built linear regression models for each pointing method (Fig. 5, right). The one-way model confirms the analysis of movement times carried out in Sect. 5.2. Indeed, we can see that the different points representing the movement time are almost at the same height regardless of the index of difficulty. The slope is almost nil, which shows that the index of difficulty does not influence the movement time.

For the linear regression line of the button method, there are differences for the same index of difficulty. This is because the index of difficulty depends on width and amplitude. Thus the combinations 20/100, 40/200 and 80/400 give the same difficulty index. In the previous section, we saw that the movement time depends on the amplitude but not on the size of the targets. This is why we have here three distinct values for the same *ID*. This difference generates a lower value of the correlation coefficient.

6 Conclusion and Future Work

Single-switch scanning is designed to make pointing easier for users who have limited motor skills and cannot easily use pointing devices that require continuous movement. We propose in this article two methods. The first (one-way) always moves the bars in the same direction. With each click, the bars start again from the origin. This version is slower, but users make fewer errors. The second (button) allows users to choose the direction of movement. Thus the bars are not repositioned after each click. This allows users to go faster from target to target.

Currently, the user can only perform one type of event when stopping the horizontal bar: a single click. In a future version, we will allow the user to choose the event to perform: "do nothing", "click", "double click", "press", "release", "right click". As for the direction buttons, options will be presented in a pie menu and will be accessible via scanning. Finally, another area of improvement will be the displacement of the pointer. Rather than having two bars, we will present a "software joystick", as described by Raynal et al. [7], where the user selects the direction after an automatic rotation of the "stick" around the axis. This will move the pointer directly in one direction, not necessarily horizontal or vertical.

References

1. Felzer, T., MacKenzie, I.S., Magee, J.: Comparison of two methods to control the mouse using a keypad. In: Miesenberger, K., Bühler, C., Penaz, P. (eds.) ICCHP 2016. LNCS, vol. 9759, pp. 511–518. Springer, Cham (2016). https://doi.org/10.1007/978-3-319-41267-2_72
2. Hassan, M., Magee, J., MacKenzie, I.S.: A Fitts' law evaluation of hands-free and hands-on input on a laptop computer. In: Antona, M., Stephanidis, C. (eds.) HCII 2019. LNCS, vol. 11573, pp. 234–249. Springer, Cham (2019). https://doi.org/10.1007/978-3-030-23563-5_20
3. ISO: Evaluation methods for the design of physical input devices - ISO/TC 9241–411: 2012(E). Report Report Number ISO/TS 9241–411:2102(E), International Organisation for Standardisation (2012)
4. Magee, J., Felzer, T., MacKenzie, I.S.: Camera Mouse + ClickerAID: dwell vs. single-muscle click actuation in mouse-replacement interfaces. In: Antona, M., Stephanidis, C. (eds.) UAHCI 2015. LNCS, vol. 9175, pp. 74–84. Springer, Cham (2015). https://doi.org/10.1007/978-3-319-20678-3_8
5. Perez-Maldonado, C., Wexler, A.S., Joshi, S.S.: Two-dimensional cursor-to-target control from single muscle site sEMG signals. IEEE Trans. Neural Syst. Rehabil. Eng. **18**(2), 203–209 (2010)
6. Pinheiro, C.G., Naves, E.L., Pino, P., Losson, E., Andrade, A.O., Bourhis, G.: Alternative communication systems for people with severe motor disabilities: a survey. Biomed. Eng. Online **10**(1), 1–28 (2011)
7. Raynal, M., Gauffre, G., Bach, C., Schmitt, B., Dubois, E.: Tactile camera vs. tangible camera: taking advantage of small physical artefacts to navigate into large data collection. In: Proceedings of NordiCHI 2010, pp. 373–382. ACM, New York (2010)
8. Rodrigues, A.S., da Costa, V.K., Cardoso, R.C., Machado, M.B., Machado, M.B., Tavares, T.A.: Evaluation of a head-tracking pointing device for users with motor disabilities. In: Proceedings of PETRA 2017, pp. 156–162. ACM, New York (2017)

9. Soukoreff, R.W., MacKenzie, I.S.: Towards a standard for pointing device evaluation, perspectives on 27 years of Fitts' law research in HCI. Int. J. Hum. Comput. Stud. **61**(6), 751–789 (2004)
10. Zhang, X., MacKenzie, I.S.: Evaluating eye tracking with ISO 9241 - Part 9. In: Jacko, J.A. (ed.) HCI 2007. LNCS, vol. 4552, pp. 779–788. Springer, Heidelberg (2007). https://doi.org/10.1007/978-3-540-73110-8_85

Impact of Using an Eye-Gaze Technology by a Young Adult with Severe Cerebral Palsy Without Speech

Yu-Hsin Hsieh[1(✉)], Mats Granlund[2], Ai-Wen Hwang[3], and Helena Hemmingsson[1]

[1] Department of Special Education, Stockholm University, Stockholm, Sweden
yu-hsin.hsieh@specped.su.se

[2] CHILD, School of Health and Welfare, Jönköping University, Jönköping, Sweden

[3] Graduate Institute of Early Intervention, College of Medicine, Chang-Gung University, Tao-Yuan City, Taiwan

Abstract. This case study explores an eye-gaze technology intervention for a young adult with severe physical and speech difficulties and visual impairments. Data were collected over a six-month intervention period encompassing measures on pupil's occupational performance of computer activities and psychosocial impact, and interviews with the user, the parents, and the teacher on the technology acceptability. The results showed that the six-month intervention enhanced the pupil's performance in three computer activities and led to a positive psychosocial impact. The parent and teacher described the intervention as appropriate to increase the pupil's self-expression and interaction with others, and there was no adverse event during the study period. The pupil demonstrated motivation to use the eye-gaze technology after the intervention continuously. In conclusion, this study shows that a young adult with severe motor impairments and visual problems can benefit from using eye-gaze technology to increase participation in leisure activities, communication, and social interactions.

Keywords: Communication · Computer activity · Gaze-controlled computer · Participation · Severe motor · Speech impairment

1 Introduction

Individuals with severe motor and speech impairments experience participation restrictions in communication, interpersonal interactions, education, and recreation [1]. They were reported to engage in fewer activities and tend to have a lower diversity of activities in community participation than same-age peers [2, 3]. Computer assistive technology provides access for individuals with severe disabilities to participate in communication and learning, which is emphasized as a fundamental right by the Convention on the Rights of Persons with Disabilities [4]. Eye-gaze technology is a feasible method to access a computer via eye movements, applying an infrared camera to calculate the direction of eye gaze, which enables individuals to perform computer activities in play, communication, or learning [5, 6]. Compared to other access methods such as a switch, eye-gaze

K. Miesenberger et al. (Eds.): ICCHP-AAATE 2022, LNCS 13341, pp. 347–354, 2022.
https://doi.org/10.1007/978-3-031-08648-9_40

technology could be less demanding and a reliable method concerning the restricted abilities of persons with severe motor impairments to control a computer through hands, head, or other body parts [5]. Studies have demonstrated the effectiveness of applying eye-gaze technology for adults with amyotrophic lateral sclerosis [6]. A few longitudinal studies in children and youths showed increased participation in computer activities and communicative interactions [7, 8]. However, there was insufficient research on whether the eye-gaze technology could benefit young adults with severe motor and speech difficulties and visual impairments and to what extent the individual can use the technology and perform activities in everyday situations.

This article reports on a case study with a young adult with severe cerebral palsy and visual and cognitive impairments who was a novel user of eye-gaze technology that started to learn for six months. This study referred to the International Classification of Functioning, Disability and Health (ICF) [9], focusing on the enablement of participation and the environmental factor, applying eye-gaze technology and services to support an individual's functioning and participation in leisure, communication, and interactions. The aim was to explore the impacts of a six-month intervention for this non-verbal young adult with severe disabilities on the performance of computer activities, psychosocial impacts, and the acceptability of using the technology in everyday contexts.

2 Methods

This case study is part of an eye-gaze technology intervention research in Taiwan. It involves a young adult with severe cerebral palsy who was followed with repeated outcome measurements before, during, and after a six-month intervention. Ethical approval was obtained for the study (201812EM004, Dnr 2019-04902).

2.1 Participant Profile

The young adult, 22 years old, male, has a diagnosis of spastic cerebral palsy with severe gross motor, fine motor, and communication function restrictions based on the Gross Motor Function Classification System [10], the Manual Ability Classification System [11], and the Communication Function Classification System [12]. He has visual impairment of strabismus, nystagmus, and myopia and unspecified cognitive impairments according to medical records. He had low-eye control skills gazing for target selection on a screen (accuracy $<10\%$) based on Compass Aim Test [13] initially. He showed understanding of simple instructions in a routine conversation and mostly used nonverbal communication through vocalization, facial expressions, or looking to express his needs or interact with familiar people. He had tried other computer interfaces (such as a switch) but showed limited functional use. An occupational therapist evaluated him as a candidate for and in need of eye-gaze technology. He attended an adult day center during weekdays, which provides daily life skills training, leisure activity, and community participation program.

2.2 Eye-Gaze Technology Intervention

The six-month eye-gaze technology intervention was introduced in the center, including eye-gaze devices and services. After three months, his parents were motivated to use it at home as well.

The participant was provided with an add-on eye-gaze device, Tobii PCEye Mini (Tobii Dynavox Ltd.), for a laptop computer. The software included play/leisure program and individualized content with dynamic pages in communication, learning, and leisure activities (e.g., music, photos) tailored to the participant's interests and needs. In total, there were about 125 symbols/pictures in the application. High contrast colors, specific arrangements of cell display, and a shorter time for gaze activation were applied regarding the visual problems.

Service delivery used a collaborative approach, involving the special educator in the center, his parents, one occupational therapist, and the researcher. There was one planning meeting for joint goal setting and planning intervention and one follow-up meeting to review progress and modify strategies. Twelve times individual support to the teacher and parents were provided by the therapist and the researcher jointly to promote the technology uptake in everyday contexts.

2.3 Procedure and Measurements

Data were collected at baseline (26 days, using the computer as usual), at the three-month intervention (T2), and after the six-month intervention (T3).

The performance in computer activities was assessed by the Canadian Occupational Performance Measure (COPM) [14] using a proxy report. The parent and teacher were interviewed to rate the level of the participant's performance and their satisfaction with his performance for each activity using the performance and satisfaction scales, from 1 (low) to 10 (high). The functional independence was measured by the Chinese version of the Psychosocial Impact of Assistive Devices Scale (PIADS) [15] on the impact of eye-gaze technology versus low-tech devices from the perspective of the teacher, with a rating scale from -3 (maximum negative impact) to $+3$ (maximum positive impact). It includes three subscales, competency, adaptability, and self-esteem. After the intervention, the parent and teacher received interviews on their perceived acceptability of supporting the participant's use of eye-gaze technology. The young adult was interviewed on his favorite activities when using the technology.

2.4 Data Analysis

Descriptive analysis reported the changes in the average score on the two scales of COPM at T2 and T3 from baseline and each subscale score of PIADS at baseline and T3. Clinically important differences of the COPM were defined as a score change of two points or more [14]. The minimal clinically important difference of each subscale of PIADS was defined as 0.50 score change [16]. Interview data were transcribed and analyzed using content analysis [17].

3 Results

3.1 Improved Performance in Computer Activities

Three activities were determined at the beginning of the intervention, including (1) engaging in computer game activities for at least 10–15 min each time, (2) commenting on activity through communication pages in group sessions, and (3) choosing pop music to interact with classmates/teachers during leisure time. The teacher's and the parent's ratings on the pupil's performance showed clinical significance for two activities at T2 (score change = 3–4) and all activities at T3 (score change = 6–7). After the six-month intervention for all activities, their satisfaction ratings with the pupil's performance reached clinical significance (score change on the satisfaction scale = 4–5).

3.2 Improved Psychosocial Impact

As displayed in Fig. 1, the results showed that the participant increased in functional independence after introducing the eye-gaze technology. The score changes in the three subscales (Competence, Adaptability, and Self-esteem) were 1.25 to 1.67. The findings indicated an overall positive psychosocial impact of eye-gaze technology and achieved a minimal clinically important difference in the three domains.

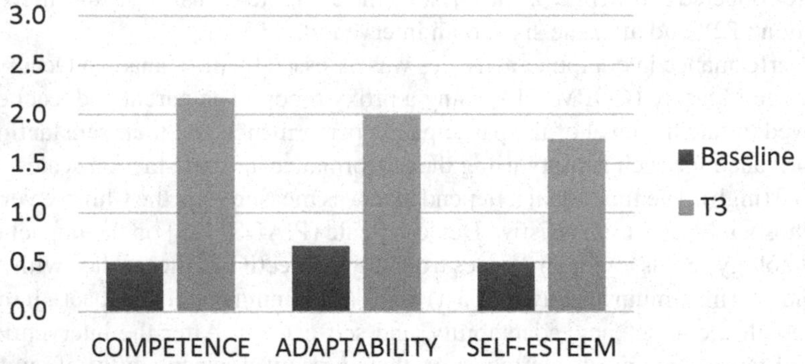

Fig. 1. Subscale scores of PIADS at baseline (using low-tech pictures) and T3 (eye-gaze technology).

3.3 User and His Teacher's and Parents' Acceptability

The participant used eye-gaze technology to respond that he felt interested in using the technology to perform computer activities. His favorite activities were choosing music to share with peers and painting. He also expressed that he wanted to continue to learn eye-gaze technology.

The parents and teacher described that eye-gaze technology is appropriate for increasing young adults' participation and control in computer activities. It offers opportunities to communicate what he wants and self-determination, unlike in the past, showing passive and waiting for the caregivers' total assistance. His teacher and parents described that using the technology enhances others to understand his thoughts as the communication pages on a screen and voice out functions of the software enhanced the clarity of his communication messages, reducing the time for guessing. The stakeholders reported no adverse events during the intervention phase, although the pupil appeared tiresome easily at the beginning of the intervention. His eye stamina developed from practicing gaze control on computer games. He expanded the visual search field on a screen, from focusing only on the lower part of the screen to searching the whole area. Both the parents and teacher observed his faster speed and longer gaze time when selecting an object on a screen. The teacher mentioned that he enjoyed using EGAT to interact with peers and got a sense of accomplishment from mutual interactions. The teacher reported that the pupil showed more confidence and engagement from relying on others to be "translators" to demonstrating his agency during group activities. Overall, the teachers and parents reported the eye-gaze device as sensitive to detecting the user's eyes, and the activity content meets the pupil's needs and preferences.

4 Discussion

This study shows positive findings that a young adult with severe and multiple disabilities and visual impairments learned to use eye-gaze technology to conduct meaningful activities in everyday circumstances. He showed improved performance in playing games, making comments, and utilizing the technology in interactions with peers. The effects were also found in the changes of the three psychosocial domains, indicating eye-gaze technology helps the pupil develop functional independence and self-confidence. The findings were supported by the parents' and teacher's descriptive comments. They perceived a positive influence on the pupil's self-expression, agency, and social interactions with others. Notably, the pupil expressed motivation to use eye-gaze technology continuously. The findings combining quantitative and qualitative outcomes support the usability of eye-gaze technology for the young adult to increase participation in leisure, communication, and interactions, and the key stakeholders showed satisfaction with the pupil's changes in performance.

This study entails that providing eye-gaze technology as environmental alternations could partially compensate for severe motor impairments and facilitate participating in everyday activities through a computer for pupils with severe motor and speech difficulties [9]. For clinical implications, it is essential to provide opportunities to trial eye-gaze technology for pupils with severe motor and speech impairments with limited functional use of other aided methods for communication. Novice users with visual problems might easily demonstrate tiredness at the initial learning stage; hence, offering short breaks with use, appropriate head positioning, and motivating activities with careful display arrangement would be crucial to ease the demand for eye control. It is important to bear in mind that pupils require time and practice to develop gaze control skills and communication competencies and also rely on the opportunities the key stakeholders provided to use the technology for varied communication purposes and to discover potential activities they could perform and benefit from [5, 18]. Therefore, continuous team support to parents and teachers is essential in adapting strategies and content to fit the pupil's skill development and varied needs across time [7].

This study as a case report has limitations for generalizability, and the results need to be interpreted with caution. Concerning the heterogeneity in this small group, future studies could apply a single-case research design [19] to provide more robust evidence and consider including objective measures for participation in computer activities such as the measurement of computer engagement on specific activities at baseline, during, and after the intervention. This study involved the key stakeholders in the application of eye-gaze technology and incorporated the user's interests into the design of activities; however, the user did not participate in the development of the intervention. Future research is worth considering different methods to collect credible views of pupils [20] to enhance a user-centered approach. Eye-gaze technology has the potential to be a practical method to gather the user's perspectives on the intervention process, given that the user could access a computer to express their thoughts with context-fitting content. A longitudinal follow-up study is also critical to evaluate the long-term effects of using eye-gaze technology across situations.

In conclusion, the results indicate that eye-gaze technology can be introduced to young adults with severe disabilities and visual impairments to enhance self-expression and social interactions.

Acknowledgements. The authors would like to thank the participant and his parents, teachers and therapist for participating in this study. We thank Tobii and Boyang Medical Technology for supporting the eye-gaze device and software during the study period. We are grateful for the grant support by the Stiftelsen Clas Groschinskys Minnesfond, Stiftelsen Kempe-Carlgrenska Fonden, Folke Bernadotte Stiftelsen, and Helge Ax:son Johnsons Stiftelse. The funders had no role in the study process or writing of the article.

References

1. Mei, C., et al.: Activities and participation of children with cerebral palsy: parent perspectives. Disabil. Rehabil. **37**(23), 2164–2173 (2015). https://doi.org/10.3109/09638288.2014.999164
2. Hwang, A.W., et al.: Participation of children with disabilities in Taiwan: the gap between independence and frequency. PLoS ONE **10**(5), e0126693 (2015). https://doi.org/10.1371/journal.pone.0126693
3. van Campen, C., Iedema, J.: Are persons with physical disabilities who participate in society healthier and happier? Structural equation modelling of objective participation and subjective well-being. Qual. Life Res. **16**(4), 635–645 (2007). https://doi.org/10.1007/s11136-006-9147-3
4. The United Nations: Convention on the Rights of Persons with Disabilities. https://www.un.org/development/desa/disabilities/convention-on-the-rights-of-persons-with-disabilities.html. Accessed 21 Mar 2022
5. Hemmingsson, H., Borgestig, M.: Usability of eye-gaze controlled computers in Sweden: a total population survey. Int. J. Environ. Res. Public Health **17**(5), 1639 (2020). https://doi.org/10.3390/ijerph17051639

6. Majaranta, P., Donegan, M.: Introduction to gaze interaction. In: Majaranta, P., et al. (eds.) Gaze Interaction and Applications of Eye Tracking: Advances in Assistive Technologies, pp. 1–9. IGI Global, Hershey (2012)
7. Borgestig, M., Sandqvist, J., Ahlsten, G., Falkmer, T., Hemmingsson, H.: Gaze-based assistive technology in daily activities in children with severe physical impairments-an intervention study. Dev. Neurorehabil. **20**(3), 129–141 (2017). https://doi.org/10.3109/17518423.2015.1132281
8. Hsieh, Y.-H., et al.: Communicative interaction with and without eye-gaze technology between children and youths with complex needs and their communication partners. Int. J. Environ. Res. Public Health **18**(10), 5134 (2021). https://doi.org/10.3390/ijerph18105134
9. World Health Organization: International Classification of Functioning, Disability and Health (ICF). WHO, Geneva (2001)
10. Palisano, R.J., Rosenbaum, P., Bartlett, D., Livingston, M.H.: Content validity of the expanded and revised Gross Motor Function Classification System. Dev. Med. Child Neurol. **50**, 744–750 (2008). https://doi.org/10.1111/j.1469-8749.2008.03089.x
11. Eliasson, A.-C., et al.: The Manual Ability Classification System (MACS) for children with cerebral palsy: scale development and evidence of validity and reliability. Dev. Med. Child Neurol. **48**, 549–554 (2006). https://doi.org/10.1017/S0012162206001162
12. Hidecker, M.J., et al.: Developing and validating the Communication Function Classification System for individuals with cerebral palsy. Dev. Med. Child Neurol. **53**(8), 704–710 (2011). https://doi.org/10.1111/j.1469-8749.2011.03996.x
13. Koester, H.H., Simpson, R.C., Spaeth, D., LoPresti, E.: Reliability and validity of Compass software for access assessment. In: Proceedings of RESNA 2007 Annual Conference. RESNA Press, Arlington (2007)
14. Law, M., Baptiste, S., Carswell, A., McColl, M.A., Polatajko, H., Pollock, N.: Canadian Occupational Performance Measure, 4th edn. CAOT Publications ACE, Ottowa (2005)
15. Hsieh, Y.J., Lenker, J.A.: The Psychosocial Impact of Assistive Devices Scale (PIADS): translation and psychometric evaluation of a Chinese (Taiwanese) version. Disabil. Rehabil. Assist. Technol. **1**(1–2), 49–57 (2006). https://doi.org/10.1080/09638280500167217
16. Vessoyan, K., Steckle, G., Easton, B., Nichols, M., Mok Siu, V., McDougall, J.: Using eye-tracking technology for communication in Rett syndrome: perceptions of impact. Augment. Altern. Commun. **34**(3), 230–241 (2018). https://doi.org/10.1080/07434618.2018.1462848
17. Kyngäs, H., Mikkonen, K., Kääriäinen, M. (eds.): The Application of Content Analysis in Nursing Science Research. Springer, Cham (2020). https://doi.org/10.1007/978-3-030-30199-6
18. Light, J., et al.: Challenges and opportunities in augmentative and alternative communication: research and technology development to enhance communication and participation for individuals with complex communication needs. Augment. Altern. Commun. **35**(1), 1–12 (2019). https://doi.org/10.1080/07434618.2018.1556732
19. Kazdin, A.E.: Single-Case Research Designs: Methods for Clinical and Applied Settings. Oxford University Press, New York (2021)
20. Wang, R.H., et al.: The time is now: a FASTER approach to generate research evidence for technology-based interventions in the field of disability and rehabilitation. Arch. Phys. Med. Rehabil. **102**(9), 1848–1859 (2021). https://doi.org/10.1016/j.apmr.2021.04.009

Proposal of "micro:bit PC" Powered by Numeric Key Programming for both Visually Impaired and Sighted Elementary School Students

Yoshihiko Kimuro(✉), Taishi Takiuchi, Ken'ichi Furusato, and Takafumi Ienaga

Fukuoka Institute of Technology, 3-30-1, Wajiro-Higashi, Higashi-ku, Fukuoka-shi, Fukuoka-ken 811-0295, Japan
kimuro@fit.ac.jp

Abstract. In the informational society, elementary school students are expected to learn programming. The BBC micro:bit, which has many sensors, is employed as one of the programming materials. However, MakeCode, which is a block programming editor of the micro:bit, is not accessible for visually impaired yet. Regarding this problem, we have proposed a new and easy programming environment for a mobile robot kit involving the micro:bit. The environment does not require any PC or tablet so visually impaired students can use it. Therefore, visually impaired students were able to obtain the programming skill within 15 min at maximum from their first touch of the robot. In this paper, we explain on the details of the command set of our robot and how to use the sensors of the micro:bit with our programming environment for the robot kit.

Keywords: micro:bit · Visually impaired · Programming · Robot kit · Elementary school

1 Introduction

In the informational society, we citizens are required to learn programming because we should come to know what we can do with a computer and what we cannot. This applies to even an elementary school student who is visually impaired or not. It is thought that the BBC micro:bit microprocessor board is used as one of the good educational materials for learning programming. However, almost all programming tools for beginners employ graphical user interface [1], so visually impaired students cannot use such programming tools easily. This is also applied to Microsoft MakeCode for the micro:bit. In fact, the micro:bit organization says on their web site the MakeCode is not accessible for visually impaired yet.

In order to resolve this problem, many researchers have studied on programming languages, programming environments and programming materials for the

K. Miesenberger et al. (Eds.): ICCHP-AAATE 2022, LNCS 13341, pp. 355–362, 2022.
https://doi.org/10.1007/978-3-031-08648-9_41

visually impaired [2]. Concerning the micro:bit, A. Hadwen-Bennett has proposed a programming method for the micro:bit, which uses a screen reader and Python language [3]. However, it seems that Python language is difficult for elementally school students and non-native learners of English. On the other hand, some researchers have tried to improve the block programming environment. In such environments, block programming elements are represented as physical blocks with RFID tags or QR code tag attached. The constitution of blocks with tags is translated into a corresponding programming code, and then the translated code is executed on the computer. However, these methods require more complex skills to use the tag readers and translation software. This is just a new barrier. From the perspective of physical programming, J. D. Oliveria et al. focused on using robots in programming education and surveyed relating many papers [4]. As the result of the survey, they pointed out the effectiveness of robots and some recommendations on robot programming for the visually impaired. Unfortunately, it was more difficult to use the robot such as “LEGO” for the visually impaired than the sighted. Therefore, the accessibility of a robot for visually impaired should be as simple as for sighted

2 Our Idea

To resolve the above problems, we have proposed the numeric key programming [5]. The most unique characteristic of our programming environment is that only twelve keys are required like phone buttons or numeric key pads. Ten numeric keys, which are from 0 to 9, are for making codes, and remaining two keys are for input “RUN” and “Reset” commands. Using this characteristic, a mobile robot can be programmed by Text-Based Language (TBL). In our previous study, we designed this programming environment for Arduino. In this study, we have designed the almost same one for the BBC micro:bit.

The BBC micro:bit is a pocket-sized codable computer with some built-in sensors and BLE wireless communication. Moreover, there are two buttons for an input device, and a 5×5 LED array for output. Furthermore, in many cases of the micro:bit kits, a buzzer is added to the micro:bit in order to beep or play musical scale. Accordingly, these characteristics will be expected to arouse visually impaired learners’ interest.

The BBC micro:bit device can be plugged into a PC using a USB cable and programmed using some different programming environments, i.e. a block editor (MakeCode, Scratch), Python and JavaScript(Fig. 1a). In our idea, these programming environments are replaced with the numeric key programming (Fig. 1b).

Figure 2 shows the overview of our mobile robot, which has the micro:bit microprocessor board and a small keypad. In the following sections, we will explain on the detail of command sets of our programmable robot and how to use sensors of the micro:bit.

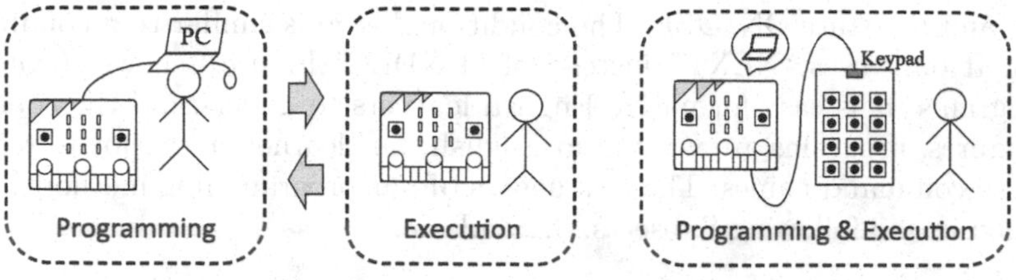

(a) Conventional method (b) Proposed method

Fig. 1. The micro:bit programming style

Fig. 2. Programmable robot involving the micro:bit "TAMIYA crawler type robot"

3 Specification of Our Programmable Robot

3.1 Command Set

A command set of our robot has five basic commands, which are motion- and sound-related, and three flow control commands, which are "For," "If" and "While" statements (Table 1).

The basic commands consist of "opcode" and "operand," that is a two-word command. Using a one digit number, namely from "0" to "9," working time of transition and rotation of the robot can be programmed. In the sound command, a number means a musical scale. Moreover, if "0" is set at a certain basic command as an operand, the command works as not stop-command but random motion.

As flow control commands of our mobile robot, there are three statements, i.e., loop (For), conditional branch (If), and conditional loop (While). The loop procedure executes sequential statements sandwiched with "FOR n" and "NEXT" by n times. In the case of "FOR 0," this FOR block behaves as an infinite loop. The conditional branch is described by a block structure with "IF condition" and "ENDIF." A conditional expression consists of identifier of sensors and the state ON/OFF. The conditional loop is similar to a conditional branch. It only uses "NEXT" instead of "ENDIF." Figure 3 shows some sample programs. It is easy for native English learners to understand the codes. In these figures, programs are written in English, but learners need not to remember these command names. The uniqueness of our programming method will be explained in the following Subsects. 3.2 and 3.3.

Table 1. Robot programming commands

Category	Command	Parameter	Description
Basic	FW	d	Move Forward (0:random)
	BK	d	Move Backward (0:random)
	LR	d	CCW rotation (0:random)
	RR	d	CW rotation (0:random)
	BEEP	d	Musical scale (0:random)
Control	FOR	d	Loop block (d:times, 0:inf)
	NEXT	-	End of Loop or While block
	IF	Sensor ID & State	Conditional branch block
	ELSE	-	Else clause
	ENDIF	-	End of IF block
Operation	RUN/STOP	-	Execution/Temporal stop
	RESET	-	Clear program memory

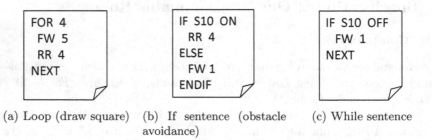

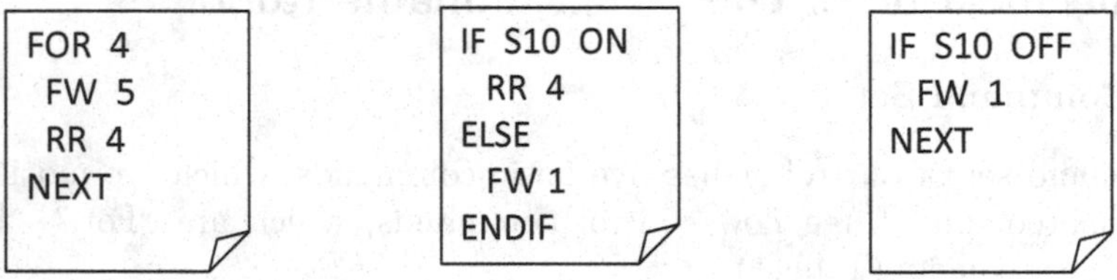

(a) Loop (draw square) (b) If sentence (obstacle avoidance) (c) While sentence

Fig. 3. Sample programs (Note: S10 means the sonar detected some objects within 10 cm.)

3.2 Programming Method

The numeric keypad we employed is just similar to a button layout of the telephone, which is common in the world, so visually impaired students can understand it easily too. For accessibility of the keypad for the visually impaired, only a convex part on the "5" key is prepared.

The robot commands "forward," "backward," "turn left," and "turn right" are located at in front, in back, at left and at right of a center key "5" respectively (Fig. 4). Namely, key layout directly means motion commands. The key "5" is used for the sound command in our system.

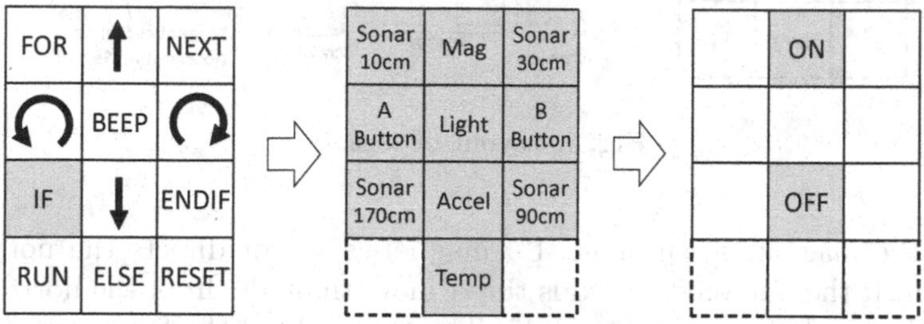

Fig. 4. Commands layout and its state transition

The flow control commands are located at the rest of the above keys. For example, "FOR" and "NEXT" are set at "1" and "3" keys respectively. "IF" and "ENDIF" are set at "7" and "9" respectively. "ELSE" is assigned at "0" remained last. The position of keys for choosing sensors is shown in the 3rd figure from the left on Fig. 4. We can use two buttons and 5 sensors. We will explain about these sensors in Subsect. 3.3. "RUN/STOP" button and "Reset" button are set at the right and left of "0."

3.3 Sensors of the micro:bit

Sensors of the robot and the micro:bit are assigned as follows (Fig. 5). A sonar sensor is used for detecting the range from the front of the robot to surrounding obstacles so that Sonar is set at "1" and "3" respectively. This layout using "1" and "3" is used for touch sensor in other mobile robots. "7" and "9" key is used for Ir sensor using line trace in our previous mobile robot system, so also sonar at set at these keys.

The A and B buttons, which are located at the left and right of the micro:bit board, are set at "4" and "6" respectively. Light sensor of the micro:bit uses LED array locating at the center of the micro:bit board. So, Light sensor is set at "5" key. Magnetics sensor is set at "2" at the above of "5" key. This is because the north is on top. Acceleration sensor of the micro:bit is set at "8." It is analogy of gravity causing dropping. A remaining temperature sensor is set at "0. "

In our programmable robot system, all sensors are used as binarized sensors. This means that sensor's value is 0 or 1. So, to use various sensors, we have to decide an adequate threshold level in each sensor. Table 2 shows a ON condition of each sensor. A and B button are able to have two states, "Pressed (1)" or "No Pressed (0)." States of Light sensor are "Bright (1)" and "Dark (0)." Its threshold value is set automatically during the execution of the program. When

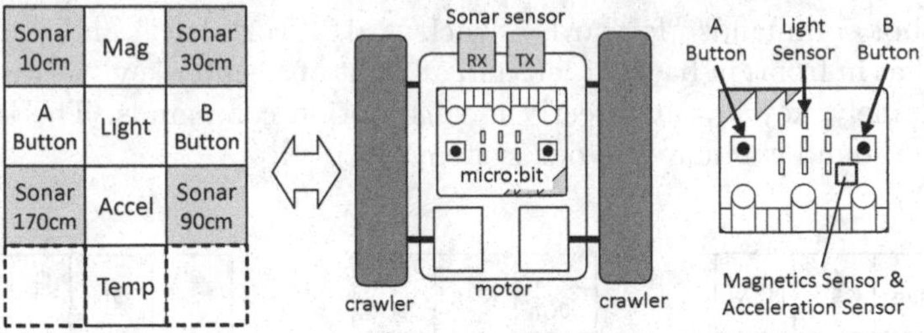

Fig. 5. Layout of sensors

state of the magnetics sensor is "1", magnetics sensor directs the north with 30° width. If the micro:bit board is tilted more than 45° from the horizontal or shaken, the accelerometer state is "1". The threshold of the temperature sensor is set at ±5° from 25°.

Table 2. Sensors and conditions

Sensor	ON condition
Sonar	Fixed detecting range
A, B button	Pressed
Light	Brightness
Magnetic sensor	±15[deg] from the north
Accelerometer	Tilted at 45[deg] or shaken
Temperature	±5 over from 25 °C

3.4 Implementation

The base of our mobile robot (Fig. 2) is a toy robot (ITEM 7021) released by TAMIYA Co. This robot kit has the micro:bit (v1.5). two DC motors, a sonar sensor, and a buzzer. We added the numeric keypad (I2C 4 × 4 keypad I-LOGIC) to the base robot kit.

A firmware for a command interpreter explained at the Sect. 3.1 and 3.2 is installed on the micro:bit board. The program codes input from the keypad are automatically stored in the flash memory of nRF51822 chip on the micro:bit board (v1.5) (Fig. 6). Therefore, the learner does not have to remember the SAVE command. Now, our firmware can store 256 program steps at maximum. The depth of nesting of each FOR, IF, WHILE is 10.

4 Evaluation

We evaluated our robot system from the following two viewpoints. One is whether or not visually impaired students are able to understand the usage

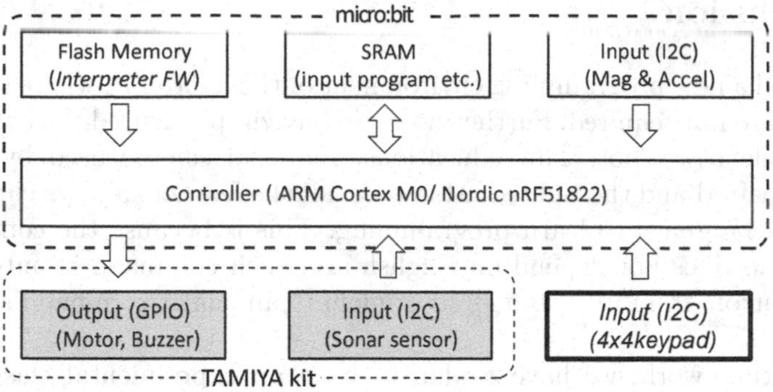

Fig. 6. Block diagram

of this system, including the key layout that corresponds to the sensors. The other is whether they use the sensors after understanding the characteristics of the sensor.

Our past research already confirmed a part of the former question. All six students, who have total blindness or low vision and were over 6 years old, were able to make sequential codes and executed them on the robots within 15 min at maximum from their first touch of the robots [5].

In the experimental class, we also confirmed that visually impaired junior high school students can create flow control programs. However, we have not verified anything about the sensors of the micro:bit (Table 2) yet.

Therefore, in order to verify the above two questions, we rented our robots to Fukuoka Blind Elementary School. The students use them as they want, and the supporter, who is a teacher of Fukuoka Blind Elementary School, teaches students various robot programs using sensors. Up to now, we have received reports from the supporter, and based on those reports, we have made the following considerations.

- The students could easily use the buttons and light sensor. It seems that the students were able to recognize the corresponding key position on the keypad because they could recognize it by touching the sensors.
- For students, their understanding of the magnetic and acceleration sensor seemed to depend on the science curriculum in the elementary grades.
- Visually impaired learners were familiar with the sonar sensor, because they knew the electronic white cane.

As a next step, we plan to have an experimental class to obtain a deeper understanding of the relationship between the learner's understandings of the sensors and the key layouts corresponding to the sensors.

5 Conclusion

We proposed a new programming environment of the micro:bit, where any PCs or tablet PCs are not required. Furthermore, we have implemented the environment into a mobile toy robot. This educational material can be used by both the visually impaired and the sighted. Moreover, all the learners always can use their own mother language to learn programming. This is because the command set of the system does not depend on English and each command is only assigned into one button from "0" to "9" so students can make command's name by themselves.

As a future work, we have a plan to have an experimental class at blind elementally schools to verify the validity of the sensor layout of our micro:bit programming system. In addition to this, we will design a stand-alone micro:bit PC programming environment in order to use the edge connector of the micro:bit as I/O ports.

References

1. Bau, D., Gray, J., Kelleher, C., Sheldon, J., Turbak, F.: Learnable programming: blocks and beyond. Commun. ACM **60**(6), 72–80 (2017)
2. Hadwen-Bennett, A., Sentance, S., Morrison, C.: Making programming accessible learners with visual impairments: a literature review. Int. J. Comput. Sci. Educ. Sch. **2**(2), 3–13 (2018)
3. Hadwen-Bennett, A.: BBC micro:bit for Visually Impaired Learners, 31 January 2022. http://physicalcomputing.co.uk/2018/01/03/bbc-microbit-for-visually-impaired-learners/
4. Damasio Oliveira, J., de Borba Campos, M., de Morais Amory, A., Manssour, I.H.: Teaching robot programming activities for visually impaired students: a systematic review. In: Antona, M., Stephanidis, C. (eds.) UAHCI 2017. LNCS, vol. 10279, pp. 155–167. Springer, Cham (2017). https://doi.org/10.1007/978-3-319-58700-4_14
5. Kimuro, Y., Ienaga, T.: Numeric Key Programming: Programmable Robot Kit for both Visually Impaired and Sighted Elementary School Students, ICCHP2020 (2020)

Extended Mouth/Tongue Gesture Recognition Module for People with Severe Motor Dysfunction

Ikushi Yoda[1(✉)], Kazuyuki Itoh[2(✉)], and Tsuyoshi Nakayama[2(✉)]

[1] Advanced Industrial Science and Technology (AIST), Tsukuba 305-8560, Japan
i-yoda@aist.go.jp

[2] Research Institute, National Rehabilitation Center for Persons with Disabilities, Tokorozawa 359-8555, Japan

Abstract. We researched gesture interfaces for people with motor dysfunction who cannot use normal interface switches. For this purpose, we have developed nine gesture recognition modules. One of them is the tongue recognition module that detects whether the tongue is in or out for the switch interface. In the process of collecting data on various types of mouth and tongue gestures and user's demands, we discovered three useful types of mouth-related gestures: mouth open/close, tongue in/out, and movement around the lips. These gestures are also useful when performed simultaneously. We conducted several experiments using data of people with motor dysfunction and inspected the conditions for real use. Furthermore, we conducted a basic experiment with healthy people to recognize three gestures simultaneously.

Keywords: Gesture interface · Gesture recognition · Mouth interface · Assistive technology

1 Introduction

People with severe motor dysfunction cannot use existing computer interfaces due to spasticity, involuntary movements, etc. We developed a gesture-based switch interface [1–5] that utilizes a commercially available RGB-D camera. The system's software recognizes gestures from 2D and 3D images, enabling the system to be customized for each user more easily than hardware-based systems.

We used a RGB-D camera to collect data on the types of gestures that severely quadriplegic people want to use in an interface. The data included both moving RGB images and depth (range) images. A total of 1663 gestures were collected from 78 individuals with motor dysfunction, and voluntary movements were classified on the basis of body part. We developed seven recognition modules dependent on body part (Head, Wink, Tongue, Shoulder, Finger, Knee, and Foot) and two site independent ones (Front object and Slight movement). Table 1 shows all gesture recognition modules. Users select a few suitable modules, and the system learns the user's gesture to enable them to use their own gesture as a switch interface. We describe the extended mouth/tongue gesture module in this paper.

K. Miesenberger et al. (Eds.): ICCHP-AAATE 2022, LNCS 13341, pp. 363–370, 2022.
https://doi.org/10.1007/978-3-031-08648-9_42

Table 1. Recognition modules.

Recognition module	Gesture	Body part
Head	Head left/right, up/down	Head
Wink	Big wink	Eye
Tongue	*Tongue in/out*	*Tongue*
Shoulder	Shoulder up/down, forward/back	Shoulder
Finger	Bending fingers	Finger
Knee	Open and close legs	Knee
Foot	Foot step	Foot
Front object	Movement of the closest part of the camera	Site independence e.g., tips of a foot, hand, and upper arm
Slight movement	Slight movement of specified area	Site independence e.g., fingers and hands

2 Tongue Gesture Recognition Module

For tongue gesture recognition, we simply determine whether a user is sticking out their tongue deliberately or not; the switch is turned on when the tongue remains out within a certain area.

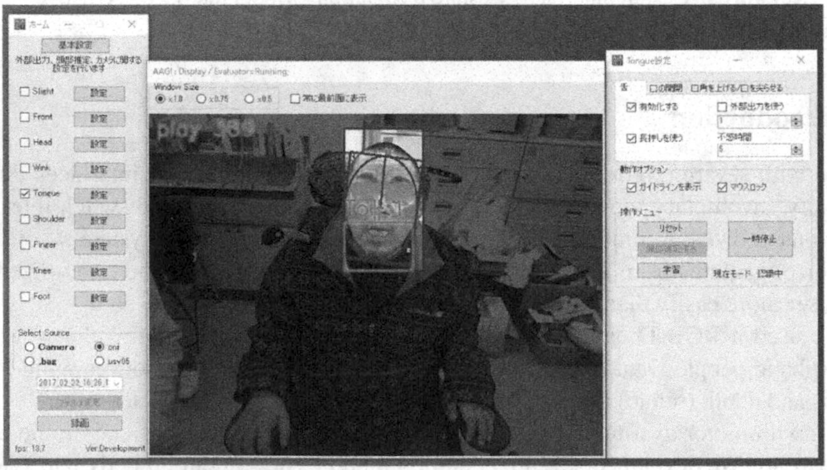

Fig. 1. Application windows (tongue switch on). (Color figure online)

We describe the algorithm of the tongue gesture recognition module as follows. The system first detects the head position by utilizing 3D information. Then, the mouth position is continuously detected and tracked from the head position, color, and movement.

If the tongue sticks out over a certain area, the switch turns on. Figure 1 shows all applications windows for the system. The blue ellipse represents the head position, and the red rectangle represents the mouth position. The system continuously monitors the tongue's in/out position in this rectangle. As each user's gestures are clearly different, the system requires 10 gestures to be learned. The example shown in Fig. 1 shows that the tongue switch is on. A user can specify to which control to assign the tongue switch, for example a key press or mouth control button. Furthermore, he/she can specify whether the key or button is "pushed" or "pushed and held."

3 Extension of Mouth/Tongue Gesture Module

When first collecting data, we assumed that recognizing whether a user's tongues is in or out was considered to be the most stable, and subsequently developed the tongue gesture recognition module. However, after continued data collection, various issues were determined. In particular, a number of people cannot stick out or retract their tongue and only open and close their mouth. A few people said that they were ashamed of opening their mouth or sticking their tongue out in public. After considering all data and opinions, we developed three recognition methods: mouth open/close, sticking out/retracting tongue, and movement around lips. For all three methods, the system first estimates the head position and then the mouth position.

3.1 Mouth Open/Close

This method was developed for users who cannot move their tongue, but can open and close their mouth. The system always monitors the line between the upper and lower lips and the hole of the mouth in 3D. As each person's gestures are different, the systems requires 10 gestures to be learned using depth and color images. This method is useful when a key or button needs to be held.

3.2 Sticking Out/Retracting Tongue

This method was developed for users who cannot open and close their mouth smoothly or do not want to stick out their tongue. The system learns movements such as raising the corners of the mouth or moving the area around the lips. As such movements are momentary, this method cannot be applied to holding a key or button. The system also requires 10 gestures to be learned.

3.3 Movement Around Lips

This method was developed for users who cannot open and close their mouth smoothly or do not want to stick out their tongue. The system learns movements such as raising the corners of the mouth or moving the area around the lips. As such movements are momentary, this method cannot be applied to holding a key or button. The system also requires 10 gestures to be learned.

3.4 Simultaneous Use of Three Gestures

Although we assumed that users would use only one method at a time, we confirmed experimentally that using three methods simultaneously is useful. This means the system can distinguish three kinds of gestures. Although the healthy people can use three methods simultaneously, we cannot estimate if it would be possible for people with severe motor dysfunction to do the same. In the future, we plan to perform data collection from people with motor dysfunction assuming such simultaneous use. We evaluated the potential recognition of the switches from the data we currently collected. Furthermore, we conducted a basic experiment with three healthy people to recognize three gestures simultaneously.

4 Evaluation Experiment

4.1 Experiment with Collected Data from Motor Dysfunction People

We recorded a total of 184 videos consisting of 43 people. The mean shooting time per shot was one minute, and an average of nine gesture occurrences were included in one shooting. In the initial stage of this study, the setting method of the camera itself was a problem, and the viewing position and angle of a person varied. Therefore, we evaluated the data from 34 shots based on the size and angle of the target area in the videos. Table 2 shows the total recognition results and Fig. 2 shows recognition examples.

For the mouth open/close gesture, because the movement requires the whole chin to move down, the final success rate is 7/13. The recognition is depended on the depth information. Therefore, if the mouth position estimation fails, gesture recognition tends to become more difficult.

For the sticking out/retracting tongue gesture, if the head position is successfully estimated, the mouth position estimation can be completely successful. However, the final success rate is less than 50%. This is mainly due to tongue colour and size. We believe that increasing the image resolution and improving the lighting conditions can resolve this issue.

For the movement around lips gesture, the success rate of the mouth position estimation is less than 50%. However, the system recognized a wider area around the lips, so the recognition was successful.

If the head and mouth positions are estimated correctly, the recognition rates in the three methods would be accurate. The causes for failure in the head position estimation are due to small head sizes and bad viewing angles. We confirmed that the three methods are effective if the image resolution is over a certain size and the viewing angle to the head is correct.

We considered the conditions of objects and their size in images through all results carefully. For high accurate recognition, the medium close-up shot (bust shot) and the front view without rotation are needed in VGA size image basically.

Table 2. Total result to recognition.

Gesture	Number of estimations	Success of head position estimation	Success of mouth position estimation	Number of final successes
Mouth open/close	13	12	6	7
Sticking out/retracting tongue	13	7	7	3
Movement around lips	8	8	3	8
Total	34	27	16	18

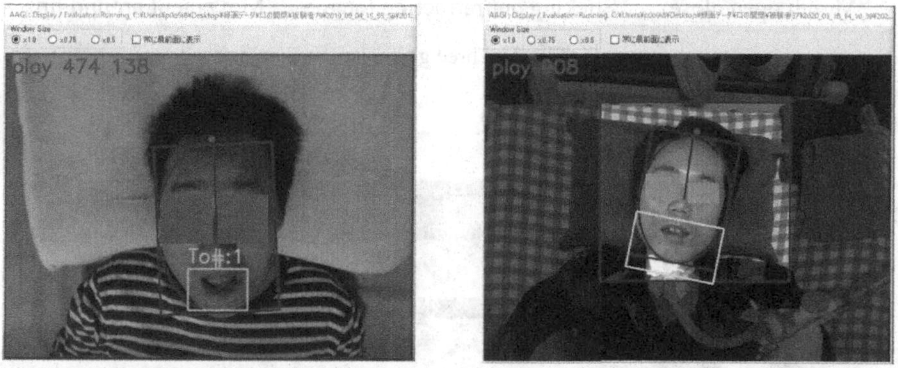

Fig. 2. Recognition examples (left: recognition of mouth opening, right: failure in the exact mouth position estimation within the yellow rectangle). (Color figure online)

4.2 Experiment with the Healthy People for Recognizing Three Gestures Simultaneously

To consider the possibility of recognizing three simultaneous gestures, we conducted a simple experiment for simultaneous learning and recognition with three healthy people as participants. For the learning, the system used the Gesture Music application we developed to learn each gesture individually. Figure 3 shows the three gestures and Fig. 4 shows a screenshot of Gesture Music. The gestures shown in Fig. 3 represent mouth open/close, sticking out/retracting tongue, and movement around lips. The rectangles in each image represent three estimated areas.

During the learning by Gesture Music, the participants performed a gesture when a circle reached the line of the left-hand side. The participants performed each gesture 10 times. After the learning, the participants played Gesture Music using the three gestures, and we evaluated the recognition results through visual observation. Figure 5 shows the recognition result. In the figure, the five bars for each gesture represent the total number of gestures, the number of correct results, the number of lacking extractions, the number of missed recognitions, and the number of overextractions from the left-hand side.

The recognition result of the sticking out/retracting tongue gesture is 100% and the number of overextractions is 6. In addition, the simple recognition rate of the movement around lips gesture is 61% and the number of overextractions is 20. Because the system must recognize three gestures simultaneously, the recognition result is insufficient. However, if the system only must recognize one gesture, the total recognition result is over 90% for three gestures.

Mouth open/close Sticking out/retracting tongue Movement around lips

Fig. 3. Three gestures.

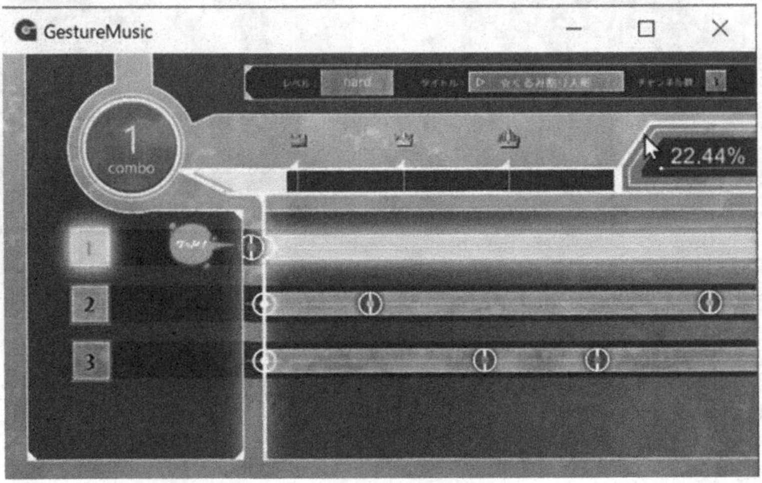

Fig. 4. Gesture Music for learning and evaluation.

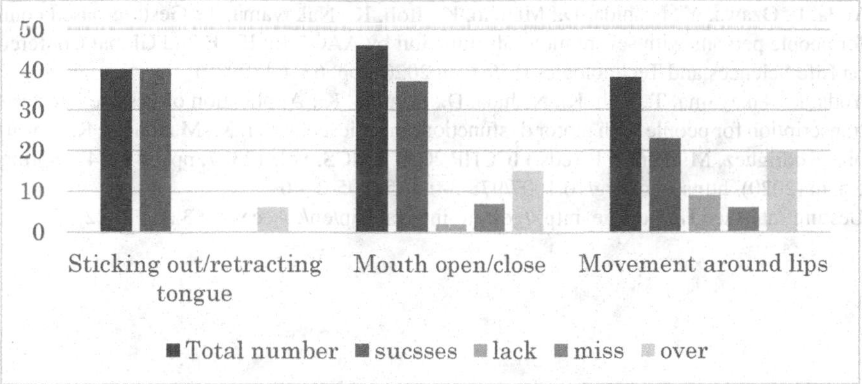

Fig. 5. Result of simultaneously recognizing three gestures.

5 Conclusion and Future Works

We have extended our tongue gesture recognition module that was developed for only sticking out/retracting a user's tongue. We have developed three methods: mouth open/close, sticking out/retracting tongue, and movement around lips. If a healthy participant uses the recognition module, they can use the three methods only using mouth and tongue movements simultaneously.

We conducted an evaluation experiment utilizing collected data. If the head and mouth positions are estimated correctly, the recognition rates in the three methods would be accurate. This means that if the image resolution and viewing angle of the head is good, this method could be useful for real users. We plan to conduct an evaluation experiment on suitable settings and improve the recognition module in the future.

The simultaneous recognition of three gestures needs to be improved. The main problems are a lack of accuracy for mouse position estimation, the similarity of the mouse motions of the three gestures, and so on. However, we believe the position estimation accuracy can be improved. Furthermore, missed recognitions can be reduced if the recognition time can be extended by a few frames.

We hope to promote the use of this software to real users around the world [6].

References

1. Yoda, I., Itoh, K., Nakayama, T.: Collection and classification of gestures from people with severe motor dysfunction for developing modular gesture interface. In: Antona, M., Stephanidis, C. (eds.) UAHCI 2015. LNCS, vol. 9176, pp. 58–68. Springer, Cham (2015). https://doi.org/10.1007/978-3-319-20681-3_6
2. Yoda, I., Ito, K., Nakayama, T.: Long-term evaluation of a modular gesture interface at home for persons with severe motor dysfunction. In: Antona, M., Stephanidis, C. (eds.) UAHCI 2016. LNCS, vol. 9738, pp. 102–114. Springer, Cham (2016). https://doi.org/10.1007/978-3-319-40244-4_11
3. Yoda, I., Itoh, K., Nakayama, T.: Modular gesture interface for people with severe motor dysfunction: foot recognition. In: Proceedings of AAATE 2017, (Harnessing the Power of Technology to Improve Lives), pp. 725–732. IOS Press (2017)

4. Yoda, I., Ozawa, Y., Nishida, D., Mizuno, K., Itoh, K., Nakayama, T.: Gesture-based control for people persons with severe motor dysfunction by AAGI. In: IEEE 2nd Global Conference on Life Sciences and Technologies (LifeTech 2020), pp. 63–64 (2020)
5. Yoda, I., Nakayama, T., Itoh, K., Nishida, D., Mizuno, K.: Application of gesture interface to transcription for people with motor dysfunction. In: Miesenberger, K., Manduchi, R., Covarrubias Rodriguez, M., Peňáz, P. (eds.) ICCHP 2020. LNCS, vol. 12377, pp. 343–347. Springer, Cham (2020). https://doi.org/10.1007/978-3-030-58805-2_40
6. Gesture Interface Homepage. http://gesture-interface.jp/en/. Accessed 3 Apr 2022

Accessible Hands-Free Input Methods for VR Games

Fiona Heilemann(✉), Gottfried Zimmermann, and Patrick Münster

Responsive Media Experience Research Group, Stuttgart Media Univertity, Stuttgart, Germany
fiona.heilemann@web.de
https://www.hdm-stuttgart.de/remex

Abstract. New ways to interact with VR environments come with both opportunities and challenges for accessibility. In this work, we summarize different possible hands-free input methods to play a VR game and investigate their applicability. Using a serious game as a Proof of Concept we implemented five focus methods (head-tracking, scanning, head-movement, eye-tracking and voice control) and three activation methods (button, dwelling and blink) exemplary using the Oculus Go standalone VR headset and the Unity game engine. We analyzed the suitability of these methods in a pre-study that excluded head movements for controlling the game based on user feedback. The remaining input methods were evaluated in an explorative user study in terms of operability and ease of use.

Keywords: Virtual reality · Game accessibility · Hands-free · Head-tracking · Scanning · Eye-tracking · Voice control

1 Hands-Free Input Methods in VR

Making games accessible is a more complex task than the accessibility of software or web applications. Even more work has to be put into making accessible games in Virtual Reality. VR applications are mainly realized through a Head-Mounted Display (HMD) which uses head-tracking and special controllers for manipulation and navigation. However, the sensors in HMDs also allow the implementation of non-standard forms of input and output that are not possible with standard devices and offer new possibilities for people with motor impairment. In previous studies, hands-free interaction proved a good alternative and desirable by users [17]. A hands-free game, as we present in this work, can prevent or reduce several of the barriers listed by Ian Hamilton [4]. Because no controller has to be held, the range, strength or presence of the hands, fingers and arms is not a prerequisite. Some input methods like eye-tracking or voice control do not require the head to move. Offering scanning can eliminate the need for accuracy or precise movements.

K. Miesenberger et al. (Eds.): ICCHP-AAATE 2022, LNCS 13341, pp. 371–379, 2022.
https://doi.org/10.1007/978-3-031-08648-9_43

1.1 Head-Tracking

The use of a VR-headsets gyroscope allows tracking exactly how the user moves their head. The data is used to show a so-called reticle (crosshair) in the direction of view. This way, head-tracking gives an analog input with a continuous movement similar to a mouse controlled by how the user moves their head around. This method is not to be confused with eye-tracking, even if it is sometimes called "gaze". For implementing this method, we use the Oculus Integration package [9]. In combination with head-tracking, so-called "dwelling" is often used. It means an element that was focused with the reticle is activated after a certain amount of time. The user has to dwell on the element to select it. What visualizations are suitable to show the passing of time for dwelling in VR was evaluated by Kim et al. [8]. They conclude that a circular slider (ring) is the preferred method which we also use. Head-tracking is, besides speech, one of the already widely used and wanted input methods in VR applications [8]. Holderied [7] compared such head-tracking with two controller-based input methods and found that it was rated the best by users and was also the fastest. Kim et al. [8] cite multiple sources showing a gaze-based interface is a "core element" in interacting with VR.

1.2 Scanning

To control a game with a single or two inputs only we use scanning. Each interactable element is focused one after another and the user can select the right one. We try out two different versions in which the transition between elements can be done. One is button-based, which means the user actively triggers the transition from one element to the next by pressing a hardware button. Pressing a controller's hardware button can be superseded with different special devices and also does not necessarily have to be a physical button but could be any kind of voluntary input. To make the feeling of using the game hands-free easy and authentic we use a page turner pedal as a trigger to be stepped on with the foot. The other method is a time-based approach, where the transition between elements is made automatically after a customizable amount of time. However, not every application can be used by simply alternating elements. Some require a more precise method. In the game we used for this study it is not feasible to iterate over all possible elements that can be selected. Therefore a new method had to be found. For this, Apple introduced what they call point scanning [1]. The screen is scanned by two lines or divided into a row-column grid. We use a similar approach in this work, where the user places a horizontal and a vertical line and the element where they cross is selected. Two studies that use scanning are Sarker et al. [11] and H. Singh and J. Singh [13]. They use a combination of scanning and blinks as an alternative input on a desktop PC.

1.3 Head-Movement

We use head gestures for scanning with discrete input. By moving the head in four directions (up, down, left, right), the user can mark the desired element.

The difference to regular scanning is that the head's movement allows for more dimensionality. Instead of only selecting the next element in a row of elements, the user can go backward or up and down. Different head gestures can be recognized by HMDs reading the rotation from the gyroscope. Head-movements have been explored as an input method for non-VR applications by different sources collected by Yan et al. [18]. Vogl et al. [17] note that head gestures might get uncomfortable for complex interactions.

1.4 Eye-Tracking

Because the user already wears a HMD, including an eye-tracking device is simple for VR. With the help of cameras that track the movement of the eyes, it is possible to know where the user is looking and to select items in a program. The cameras can also detect when a user is blinking, which is an alternative way of voluntary input for activating things. The components to use eye-tracking and recognize blinks in Unity are provided by the Pupil Labs Unity package [10]. Tobii [16] provides a collection of games that can be played in combination with eye-tracking. However, most of them only use eye-tracking as a supplementary input method e.g. aiming or adapting the view.

1.5 Voice Control

For implementing a voice control system no special hardware is needed as most HMDs already offer voice control or have a built-in microphone. Speech recognition is one of the more frequently offered input methods for games. However, the rate of misunderstood words is often high and gets worse in noisy environments [18]. To enable the control via voice commands, we used the GameVoiceControl Plugin available in the Unity Asset Store [15]. It allows for simple voice recognition without needing an internet connection. In a comparison of interactions with HMDs Vogl et al. [17] concluded that speech is the most desired interaction technique. In most games, voice commands are only used to enhance input.

1.6 Other Input Methods

In addition to the methods we present in this work, various other hands-free methods are conceivable. One tracking method that has not been explored much as an input method for better accessibility is face tracking. The tracking of the face in VR bears a challenge when wearing a bulky HMD. Therefore, some studies only recognize the lower half of the face [19]. Another innovative example of a possible new input method is using different kinds of breath to activate special attacks in a game introduced by Sra, Xu, and Maes [14]. Physiological signals used as input that were already tested are the heart rate, muscle movements and brainwaves. A Brain-Computer-Interface (BCI) allows getting information directly from the brain through measuring brain activity and muscle movement with electrodes on the scalp. This can be used as input for physical objects (like robotic arms) but also computer games. There are various methods to measure brain signals, the most popular being Electroencephalogram (EEG) [2]. Among others, Coogan and He [3] successfully controlled a VR environment in Unity with a combination of BCI signals and physical input.

2 Implementation and Validation

Not all input methods that are hands-free are suitable for controlling a VR game. The studies of Kim et al. [8] and Vogl et al. [17] indicate that the most frequently used hands-free input methods for games are head-tracking (gaze) and voice control. However, no study is currently known to us comparing multiple hands-free input combinations as it is done here. To test the introduced input methods, we developed a simple demo application (Fig. 1a) and changed an existing game (Fig. 1b). We distinguish between focus and activation methods to cross-test various method combinations. A focus method specifies how a user puts an element into focus, thus selecting or highlighting it. The activation method is the user's interaction to trigger the action of the focused object or button. The tested focus methods were: head-tracking, button-based scanning, time-based scanning, head-movement, eye-tracking and voice control. As activation methods, we chose dwelling, a button press on the foot pedal and blinking. The goal of the two studies was not to find the best method, but to show which aspects need to be considered when using hands-free input methods to play a VR game.

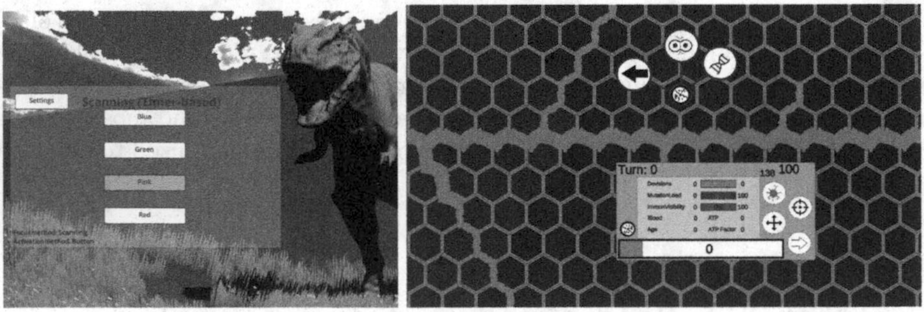

(a) Demo application (b) Main application: BioVR

Fig. 1. Screenshots of the two programs used for the studies

2.1 Demo Application and Pre-study

The demo program is a simple VR application that was used for a pre-study, testing if and how the methods can be implemented and used in a small context. The demo program consists of a menu with four buttons and a view for different settings. When pressed, the buttons activate a simple action by changing the color of a GameObject. The settings-view allows the user to choose method combinations. Depending on the input method, different versions and values can be chosen to customize the method.

In an explorative within-group pre-study with five participants, we evaluated the input methods' suitability for this minimal VR application. For this study it is assumed that typical user characteristics like gender, age, profession, or income do not influence the outcome. All participants had used a VR headset before the test. Because of the small scope of this study a selection of convenience was used to recruit the five participants. Therefore, the user group consisted of acquaintances of the authors with no disabilities. This was accepted because the goal of the study was to help identify which methods and method-combinations are suitable for the later game BioVR and to find the basic quantitative limits for the various input methods. The methods were tested if they can be adequately used by the user and how they are perceived. Data was collected via think-aloud and by asking the participants how comfortable a method is and how efficient they feel using it. Quantitative data was collected in the form of the settings values.

This study showed that it is possible to realize all introduced input methods with Unity for the Oculus Go and that users are able to control a simple menu with them in a VR environment. The result of the asked questions and think-aloud allow the following conclusions to be drawn: The two scanning methods, eye-tracking and voice control had mediocre or no valuable results. Head-tracking had exceptional good comments and ratings in both categories whereas head-movements were rated very poorly and perceived as uncomfortable. From this, we concluded that the head-movement method is not suitable for a complex and lengthy game, which is why this method was excluded from further research. Additionally, the settings values chosen by the participants were used to determine the default values the settings should have in the subsequent study.

2.2 Main Application and Main-Study

Our overall goal of the main program and study was to show how different hands-free input methods can be implemented and used inside an already existing game in VR. BioVR is a serious game developed in cooperation with the Institute of Pharmacy and Molecular Biotechnology at Heidelberg University [5]. The game's topic is the functioning, structure and life cycle of cancer cells. It is a strategic game that is played in turns. To demonstrate how the introduced hands-free input methods can be implemented and used in a real VR game we changed the game to be playable with the introduced methods. In summary, there was no or little change needed for the head-tracking and eye-tracking, while the scanning and voice control had to be extended with point scanning. A setup scene is shown on start-up before the actual game. The user can customize the game by choosing a method combination and different settings.

Based on this game we constructed a user study. The study used a mixture of a within-group and between-group test design. As in the pre-study all participants were recruited from private acquaintances of the authors and employees of Stuttgart Media University. In total, 12 participants were recruited for this study: eight men and four women in the age range from 22 to 53 (average age: 36). Demographic data that might influence the study, meaning gender, age and experience with VR, was collected. The evaluation of the demographic data showed that both gender and age had no influence on how users experienced the tested methods. Any unfairness in experience was avoided by giving each participant an explanation about the headset and time to get used to it. Again, the participants had no disability. However, they were not given a controller and were not allowed to use their hands in any form to simulate the use case of people with motor impairment of the hands or arms. Therefore, the results are valid as a Proof of Concept and can and should be used as a basis for further studies including the target group of people with disabilities. Each participant played the game three times with a consistent focus method but alternating activation methods. As the study was designed as an explorative test, it did not measure quantitative data. Data was collected through a questionnaire including the short version of the User Experience Questionnaire (UEQ) [12]. It contained questions about the usability of the input methods and direct ratings and comparisons. Comments during the tests were also taken into account.

In conclusion, all input methods were generally usable and people were able to execute all possible features of the game without major issues within the scope of our study. For the focus methods, the results confirmed the ones from the pre-study. The head-tracking was rated exceptionally good and very few mistakes were made by users. The eye-tracking was rated similarly good. The other methods were rated mediocre which can be due to the point-scanning that led to more mistakes. The UEQ rated the quality of the activation methods by pragmatic and hedonic quality. For both categories the overall rating of all three activation methods (dwelling, button and blink) was predominantly good or mediocre. While the button method had very high ratings in pragmatic quality and came in last at the hedonic rating, the opposite was true for the blink method. This shows that pressing a simple button might be the most practical, but people are very used to it and more enthusiastic about non-standard methods. Outside the UEQ the majority of the participants preferred the activation by button. The blink method was the least liked but with only a slight difference to dwelling.

3 Conclusion

In this work, we use the new input possibilities VR offers to eliminate game barriers. This is demonstrated by making a game playable hands-free with different input methods. From the implementation, we can conclude that all introduced methods except head-movements can be implemented and used for a VR game. It was possible to adapt the game BioVR to be completely played with the introduced methods. Depending on the method, different amounts of effort and additional features were necessary for the existing game. Based on the users' combined feedback, we summarize the results for each tested input method in

Table 1. Summarized conclusion of the evaluation of all input methods. The rating scale refers to the methods in relation to one another.

Method	Rating	Note
Head-tracking	Very good	Best rated focus method, very comfortable and efficient, also easy to use. If the game and head-mobility allows it, this should be the preferred alternative method to offer in VR games
Head-movement	Very bad	Very uncomfortable for the head/neck. Not suitable to control a VR game and should be used with caution
Scanning	Mediocre	Can be used to interact with a game. If possible a button-based approach is preferable. The suitability depends on whether point scanning is necessary. More suitable for simple applications
Eye-tracking	Good	Positive overall ratings and comments; recognition is good. Can be exhausting for the eyes in the long run. Good alternative for head-tracking if the head's mobility is limited. The only method that needs special hardware, a cable, wifi-connection and calibration
Voice control	Mediocre	Recognition takes too long and high error rate in this study. Good method otherwise. Very dependent on personal preferences. Most promising for future improvement
Dwelling	Mediocre	Mixed ratings, good alternative if a button press is not possible. The dwelling time has to be customizable in any case
Button	Very good	Best activation method overall, excellent ratings. Compared to the other methods it lacks in hedonic quality. If used, alternative hardware devices need to be supported
Blink	Bad	Most interesting activation method. Hard to use and prone to errors which leads to bad pragmatic rating and annoyance or exhaustion. Usage is only suitable as an alternative if necessary

Table 1. It takes into account all results from the pre-study and the main-study as well as results from questionnaires and the think-aloud. The results have to be looked at with caution, as the testing number was smaller than optimal because of the COVID-19 pandemic restrictions. Nevertheless, they give insight into the suitability of the different methods and there are many starting points for follow-up studies. In any case, when making games more accessible, we should not commit to a single input method and people with disabilities should be able to choose which method they want to use [6].

References

1. Apple Support: Use Switch Control to navigate your iPhone, iPad, or iPod touch (2019). https://support.apple.com/en-us/HT201370
2. Cattan, G., Mendoza, C., Andreev, A., Congedo, M.: Recommendations for integrating a P300-based brain computer interface in virtual reality environments for gaming **7**(2), 34 (2018). https://doi.org/10.3390/computers7020034
3. Coogan, C.G., He, B.: Brain-computer interface control in a virtual reality environment and applications for the Internet of Things **6**, 10840–10849 (2018). https://doi.org/10.1109/ACCESS.2018.2809453
4. Hamilton, I.: A practitioner reflection on accessibility in virtual reality environments. Comput. Games J. **7**(2), 63–74 (2018). https://doi.org/10.1007/s40869-018-0061-z
5. Heidelberg University: Institute of Pharmacy and Molecular Biotechnology (2021). https://www.ipmb.uni-heidelberg.de/index_en.html
6. Heilemann, F.: Accessible hands-free input methods for a serious VR game: Development and evaluation (2021). https://hdms.bsz-bw.de/frontdoor/index/index/start/0/rows/10/sortfield/score/sortorder/desc/searchtype/simple/query/heilemann/docId/6641
7. Holderied, H.: Evaluation of Interaction Concepts in Virtual Reality Applications (2017). https://doi.org/10.18420/IN2017_254
8. Kim, M., Lee, J., Jeon, C., Kim, J.: A study on interaction of gaze pointer-based user interface in mobile virtual reality environment **9**(9), 189 (2017). https://doi.org/10.3390/sym9090189
9. Oculus: Oculus Integration (2017). https://assetstore.unity.com/packages/tools/integration/oculus-integration-82022
10. Pupil Labs GmbH: GitHub — Release HMD-Eyes v1.3 pupil-labs/hmd-eyes (2020). https://github.com/pupil-labs/hmd-eyes/releases
11. Sarker, S., Mazumder, M., Rahman, S., Rabbi, M.A.: An assistive HCI system based on block scanning objects using eye blinks (2019)
12. Schrepp, M., Hindersks, A., Thomaschewaki, J.: User Experience Questionnaire (UEQ) (2018). https://www.ueq-online.org/
13. Singh, H., Singh, J.: Object acquisition and selection using automatic scanning and eye blinks in an HCI system. J. Multimodal User Interfaces **13**(4), 405–417 (2019). https://doi.org/10.1007/s12193-019-00303-0
14. Sra, M., Xu, X., Maes, P.: BreathVR: leveraging breathing as a directly controlled interface for virtual reality games. In: Mandryk, R., Hancock, M., Perry, M., Cox, A. (eds.) Proceedings of the 2018 CHI Conference on Human Factors in Computing Systems - CHI 2018. pp. 1–12. ACM Press (2018). https://doi.org/10.1145/3173574.3173914
15. Stendal Syndrome Studio: Game Voice Control [Offline speech recognition] (2020). https://assetstore.unity.com/packages/tools/audio/game-voice-control-offline-speech-recognition-178047
16. Tobii Gaming: PC Games with Eye Tracking gameplay (2021). https://gaming.tobii.com/games/
17. Vogl, A., Louveton, N., McCall, R., Billinghurst, M., Haller, M.: Understanding the everyday use of head-worn computers. In: 2015 8th International Conference on Human System Interaction (HSI), pp. 213–219. IEEE (2015). https://doi.org/10.1109/HSI.2015.7170668

18. Yan, Y., Yu, C., Yi, X., Shi, Y.: HeadGesture **2**(4), 1–23 (2018). https://doi.org/10.1145/3287076
19. Yu, J., Park, J.: Real-time facial tracking in virtual reality. In: Liu, E., de Joya, J.M. (eds.) SIGGRAPH ASIA 2016 VR Showcase. p. 1. Association for Computing Machinery-Digital Library and ACM Special Interest Group on Computer Graphics and Interactive Techniques. ACM (2016). https://doi.org/10.1145/2996376.2996390

Gaze-Contingent Screen Magnification Control: A Preliminary Study

Roberto Manduchi[1(✉)] and Susana Chung[2]

[1] University of California, Santa Cruz, USA
manduchi@ucsc.edu
[2] University of California, Berkeley, USA

Abstract. People with low vision often use screen magnification software. Screen magnification requires continuous control of the onscreen content by moving the focus of magnification with the mouse or the trackpad. In this contribution, we explore the possibility of controlling the focus of magnification by means of the user's own eye gaze, which is measured by a commercial gaze tracker. We conducted two small experimental studies with individuals with impaired central vision, who used two screen magnification modalities to read two different types of documents. In the first study, mouse tracks and gaze point tracks were collected during manual control for later analysis. In the second study, the center of magnification was controlled by the user's own gaze, using two different control mechanisms. This preliminary study highlights the potentials and shortcomings of gaze-contingent screen magnification control for easier access of onscreen content with low vision.

Keywords: Screen magnification · Eye gaze tracking · Gaze-contingent display

1 Introduction

Many people living with low vision use screen magnifiers to read documents and web pages on a computer. As more and more textual content is consumed online rather than in printed form, screen magnifiers are taking on the role of more traditional desktop video magnifiers (sometime called CCTV magnifiers), which have been used for decades to access printed text In many ways, a screen magnifier functions like a magnifying glass – while being purely software-based. It is the tool of choice for those individuals with some functional vision who do not need to (or choose not to) resort to screen readers. Multiple types of screen magnification are available on the market, either integrated in operating systems (Windows or MacOS), or in the form of specialized software such as ZoomText or MAGic.

Screen magnification is a powerful access technology, but it is not without its shortcomings. The common crux of screen magnification is that it requires continuous manual scrolling (using the mouse or trackpad) in order to move the focus of magnification (located at the mouse cursor), which determines the portion of the document to be magnified. Continuous scrolling of magnified content may represent a burden for the viewer

K. Miesenberger et al. (Eds.): ICCHP-AAATE 2022, LNCS 13341, pp. 380–387, 2022.
https://doi.org/10.1007/978-3-031-08648-9_44

(*page navigation problem* [4]). Manual scrolling often results in slow reading [8] and can be challenging for those who don't have full motor control of their hands.

The need for continuous manual scrolling of the magnified content could be mitigated by technology designed to assist the user in moving the focus of magnification. In this contribution, we propose a new system of gaze-based magnification control. The proposed system enables scrolling control by means of the viewer's own gaze, which is computed by an eye gaze tracker. This hands-free modality has the potential to afford a more natural experience when reading onscreen content than standard approaches that require use of mouse or trackpad.

This contribution describes two studies, comprising an initial data collection experiment, followed by a preliminary test of simple gaze-contingent magnification control algorithms. In Study 1, six participants with low vision operated two types of customized screen magnification software to read text from two onscreen documents. The application recorded the mouse tracks as well as the gaze point tracks, which were measured by an IR gaze tracking device. This study was meant to inform the design of a mechanism that uses gaze data to control the location of the focus of magnification. In Study 2, three simple mechanisms of gaze-contingent magnification control were tested by three participants with low vision. The goal of this preliminary study was to evaluate the feasibility of gaze-based magnification control, and to provide indications for future research in this direction.

2 Related Work

Prior research (e.g., [7, 8]) studied the performance of onscreen reading for people with low vision (sequential reading as well as non-sequential skipping or skimming modalities [5]) using different types of magnification mechanisms, with outcomes expressed in terms of reading speed or error rates.

Gaze-contingent mechanisms for image enhancement/magnification are designed to process images at the location of the gaze point, or possibly at the preferred retinal locus of individuals with central field loss. Various image processing functions have been considered in the literature, including: "bubble" (or "fisheye" [3]) filters, which shift the image area hidden by a scotoma to a nearby peripheral area [1]; band-limited contrast enhancement [13]; adjustment of letter spacing to minimize "crowding" in peripheral areas [1]; and Region of Augmented Vision selection and magnification [2]. For the systems cited above to work, a high-precision gaze tracker (with resolution as high as 0.1°) is generally needed [14]. This normally requires head stabilization (e.g., by means of a chin rest) to ensure precise gaze tracking, or implementation in a head-mounted display. The need for head stabilization or head-mounted display greatly reduces the practical appeal of such devices. In contrast, we aim to build a system that is easy to use in a natural viewing setting, and that could benefit a variety of users with low vision, rather than only those with central field loss. By employing a relatively large screen lens or full screen magnification, rather than a highly localized "bubble", we afford the use of low-accuracy gaze trackers that do not require expensive hardware, and allow for some amount of head motion during reading. Experiments pairing a gaze tracker with magnification software were presented in [10–12]. These systems are similar to the Screen Lens–Integrative (SL–I) modality discussed in Sect. 4.1.

3 Study 1: Data Acquisition

3.1 Method

Participants. We recruited six participants with low vision for this study from the optometry clinic in our university. The participants had varying prior experience with screen magnification. P1, P4 and P6 were accustomed to magnifying the content of a Word document by "zooming" on the trackpad. P2 regularly used the AI Squared ZoomText Reader software (P4 also used this software on occasion). P3 mentioned that she normally increased the font size of a document (Ctrl + on Mac) for better reading. P5, who rarely used a computer, never used screen magnification before. Two participants (P1 and P2) used eyeglasses during the experiment.

Apparatus. We created a screen magnification software application for Windows 10, using the Magnification API and the Tobii EyeX Engine. The application ran on a Dell Latitude 3470 laptop computer, with screen size of 31 $\times$ 17.5 cm, and resolution of 1366 $\times$ 768 pixels. The computer was connected to a Tobii X2-30 eye tracker, attached to the lower edge of the screen. The X2-30 tracker captures data at 30 Hz and has nominal accuracy of 0.4° in ideal situations. It does not require head stabilization, which makes it suitable for "real world" applications. For the eye tracker to function correctly, a per-user prior calibration phase is necessary. This operation, which may take a few minutes, requires the user to follow with their gaze a dot moving on the screen, until prompted by the system that calibration has been completed.

Our application allows one to select between full screen (FS) and screen lens (SL) (sometimes called picture-in-picture) magnification. Full screen magnification expands the content of the whole screen around the focus of magnification (FoM), which coincides with the location of the mouse cursor. This results in only a portion of the onscreen content being visible within the screen viewport. Screen lens magnification uses the paradigm of a magnifying glass to only enlarge a rectangular portion of the screen (note that also in this case, the FoM coincides with the location of the cursor as controlled by the mouse). In both modalities, participants were able to select the desired magnification factor (over a logarithmic scale) using the keyboard. For the screen lens modality, participants were able to vary the width and the height of the rectangular "lens", still using the keyboard. The application captured all mouse movements as well as all measured gaze points (i.e., the points on the screen where gaze was directed, as estimated by the gaze tracker).

Experiments. Each participant underwent a sequence of four trials. In each trial, participants were asked to read two paragraphs each from two Word documents using a specific screen magnification modality. Two types of documents were considered: a 1-column document, and a 3-column document. Text was displayed with a 9-point Helvetica font, with single line spacing and a whole blank line between paragraphs. The single-column document had 0.5″ left and right margins. The three-column document had columns with width of 1.67″ and spacing of 0.5″ between columns. In the first two trials, participants accessed the single-column document, first with full screen magnification (first two paragraphs) then with screen lens magnification (next two paragraphs). They repeated the same sequence in the last two trials, this time on the three-column document.

3.2 Results

General Observations. All participants (except for the one who was excluded from the experiment, as mentioned earlier) were able to successfully complete all trials. The magnification factor α chosen by the participants ranged from 2.25 (P1) to 11.4 (P2, P3, P4) trials. The chosen lens size varied from 455 × 192 pixels (P1) to 1366 × 308 pixels (P3). The aspect ratio (width/height) of the lens varied from 1.2 (P2) to 4.4 (P3).

Reading Speed. When computing reading speeds, we considered the total number of standard-length words in the paragraphs being read, where the number of standard-length words in a paragraph is defined to be the total number of characters (including spaces and punctuation) divided by 6 [Carver 1990]. We observed a large variation in reading speed, from 14 words per minute (P5, screen lens, 1 column) to 208 words per minute (P6, full screen, 3 columns). Analysis of the data using paired t-test shows that the average reading speed for the 3-column document using screen lens was faster than for the 1-column document using full screen magnification ($p = 0.03$) or screen lens ($p = 0.04$). In addition, the average reading speed for the 3-column document using full screen magnification was found to be significantly larger than for the 1-column document using the screen lens modality. The mean reading speeds measured over all trials for these 5 participants was 42.3 words/minute, which is consistent with what found in [8] (mouse mode, low vision subjects, 44 words/minute).

Gaze Tracking Quality. Even though all participants successfully completed the calibration phase, analysis of the data collected shows that gaze tracking was successful (as defined by an effective reading rate of 20 Hz or more on average) only for four of the six participants: P1, P2 (except for the first trial,) P4, and P6. No useful gaze data could be obtained for P3 and for P5 (except for one trial, wherein the reading rate for P5 reached 5 readings per second.)

Mouse Motion/Eye Gaze Tracks. Figure 1 (left column) shows the recorded mouse (FoM) tracks and gaze tracks, superimposed on the un-magnified screen, for a set of representative trials. The figure also shows the plots of the X- and Y-coordinate of the gaze point samples as a function of time, as well as of the location of the element looked at in the un-magnified screen. Not surprisingly, gaze points are located close to the FoM in the case of screen lens (SL) magnification. This is clearly seen in the plots, and confirmed by the moderate ($\rho \geq 0.4$) to strong ($\rho \geq 0.6$) correlation coefficients measured between gaze point and FoM, with the notable exception of P6 for the 3-column document. P6 chose to use a wide window with a relatively low magnification (2.59), such that the window contained the whole width of the magnified column, requiring almost no horizontal motion of the window during reading. For what concerns correlation under full screen (FS) magnification, results varied from moderate correlation in the 1-column case for P1 and P6, to very weak correlation ($|\rho|<0.2$) in the other cases.

4 Study 2: Gaze-Based Control

4.1 Method

Participants. This study included two participants from Study 1 (P2, P6) and a new participant (P7), who was not part of Study 1 (see Fig. 1). Of note, P2 underwent the Study 2 experiment one year after the Study 1 experiment, while P6 did both experiments in the same day.

Apparatus. We developed two simple systems for gaze-based control of full screen magnification, and one system for screen lens control, as described below.

Full Screen–Dead Zone (FS–DZ). With this control modality, the onscreen content is scrolled only when the user's gaze point is outside of a central rectangular region (*dead*

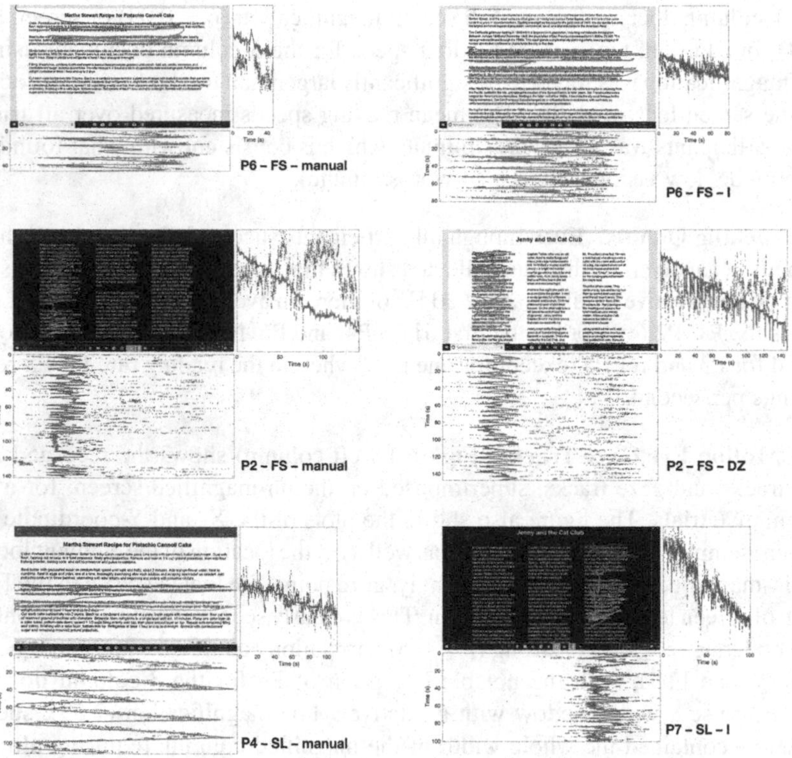

Fig. 1. Sample data from our trials from different participants. The colored line on the (unmagnified) screenshots represents the track of the FoM (with color changing from purple to yellow as a function of time). The X- and Y-coordinate of the recorded gaze points are shown as blue dots at the bottom and to the right, respectively, of the screenshots. The same plots show the coordinates of $p(t)$, the location on the un-magnified screen of the element been looked at. Left column: manual control with full screen (FS) or screen lens (LS) magnification. Right column: gaze-contingent control using the FS-DZ, FS-I, or SL-I algorithms. (Color figure online)

zone). Eight *scroll zones* are defined bordering the dead zone (the scroll zones are invisible to the user). When gaze fixates on a scroll zone, the onscreen content is scrolled with constant velocity towards the opposite size of the screen. For example, if one is reading a line of magnified text, and reaches the rightmost scroll zone, the FoM is moved to the right (note that the screen content appears to move in the opposite direction of the FoM). The onscreen text thus moves to the left, making more magnified content available within the viewport for reading. In order to move to the beginning of the next line, one needs to look intently at the left edge of the screen, causing the FoM to move to the left and the magnified content to the right. In the implementation used for our tests, the dead zone was set to be small, with horizontal and vertical sizes equal to 1/10 of the corresponding screen size. In practice, this meant that the screen content was scrolled most of the time. The horizontal and/or vertical component of the FoM velocity (when gaze was in a scroll zone) was set equal to $600/\alpha$ pixels per second (where α is the magnification factor). The only exception was when gaze falls on the leftmost scroll zone, in which case the (horizontal) velocity was doubled. This was done to facilitate moving to the beginning of the new line, which requires full scroll of the screen content to the right.

Full Screen–Integrative (FS–I). Inspired by classic control theory, this mechanism implements an integrative controller. The general idea is to move the FoM such that the user, while reading text, is led to "naturally" gaze at a fixed location, that is chosen to be the center of the screen. If $g(t)$ is the location of the gaze point at time t, and $m(t)$ is the location of the FoM, the algorithm moves the FoM with velocity $v_m(t)$ defined by: $e(t) = g(t) - s$; $v_m(t) = \gamma e(t)$ where s is the location of the center of the screen, and γ is a positive coefficient set to $0.1/\alpha$. If gaze remains fixed at the center of the screen, the FoM also remains static. As soon as one moves their gaze to the right (e.g., while reading a line of text), the FoM also moves right, effectively scrolling the screen content to the left, with a speed that depends on the distance of the gaze point to the center of the screen. In order to reduce the risk of continuous motion due to small saccades (which could lead to motion sickness [9]), the error term is checked against a threshold (i.e., the X- or Y- component of $e(t)$ is set to 0 if its magnitude is smaller than a positive constant ϵ_X or ϵ_Y). In our experiments, we set ϵ_X and ϵ_Y equal to 1/20 of the width and height of the screen, respectively. This effectively creates a dead zone identical to that of the FS-DZ algorithm. The main difference between the two is that, while the velocity in a scroll zone is constant for FS-DZ, it can be controlled in FS-I by moving one's gaze closer or farther away from the screen center.

Screen Lens–Integrative (SL–I). For the case of screen lens magnification, we implemented an algorithm identical to FS–I, with the critical difference that the FoM $m(t)$ is made to smoothly move towards the current gaze point $g(t)$, rather than towards the center of the screen. This is obtained by simply replacing $e(t)$ as defined above with $g(t) - m(t)$. For this case, the extent of the dead zone is set to a much smaller value.

Experiment. The experiment was conducted in a very similar way to Study 1. The same computer and gaze tracker were used, with the difference that a mouse was not made available, as the participants were tasked with reading magnified text only using gaze-based control. Participants attempted to read two paragraphs from the 1-column document using FS-DZ, then the next two paragraph using FS-I, and the final two paragraph using SL-I. The process was then repeated for the 3-column document.

4.2 Results

All three participants were able to use both systems for gaze-based full screen magnification control (FS–DZ and FS–I) without any particular difficulty (although P2 struggled while reading the 3-column document under FS-I). However, gaze-based control for the screen lens modality (SL–I) was found to be very challenging. Only P6 was able to complete the trials on both documents, while P7 was only successful in the 3-column document. P2 was not able to complete either trial with SL-I. The reading speed was within the range of those recorded for mouse-based control, except for P6 using SL-I, in which case the reading speed was substantially lower than for the equivalent trials with mouse control. Failure to use SL-I appeared to be caused by over-compensation when the lens was not centered where desired, which often resulted in loss of control.

All three participants complained of some fatigue and of a somewhat "unnatural" reading experience while using gaze-based control. No participant felt motion sickness. Sample mouse and gaze tracks are shown in Fig. 1 (right column).

5 Conclusions

We presented a preliminary study on the feasibility of a system that relies on the user's gaze direction to control the focus of magnification of a screen magnifier. This analysis may inform the future design of a gaze-contingent magnification control.

While our Study 2 showed that gaze-contingent magnification control is feasible (at least in the full screen modality), more research is needed on the design of effortless, ergonomic, and natural gaze-based control mechanisms. Based on our experience with this system, we believe that gaze-based magnification control should be built around two critical components: (1) a predictor of the element p in the un-magnified screen the user is interested in looking at; and (2) a mechanism to decide the location $\hat{p}$ where to map this element after magnification. From these two values, an appropriate location m for the FoM can be derived. For what concerns the second component (finding an appropriate location $\hat{p}$ for the magnified element), different strategies are available. For example, one may choose to maintain an almost stable gaze location, while moving the FoM $m(t)$ such that the desired text position $p(t)$ at all times falls, after magnification, on the same or similar screen location $\hat{p}$: $m(t) = (\alpha p(t) - \hat{p})/(\alpha - 1)$, where α is the magnification factor. In this case, one may expect little correlation between gaze point and FoM. At the other end of the spectrum, one may control the FoM such that one's gaze is led to follow the text line exactly as it would without magnification, i.e. $g(t) = p(t)$. This can be obtained by ensuring that the FoM always falls on the location in the un-magnified screen of the text element currently being gazed at ($m(t) = p(t) = g(t)$). From our analysis of the gaze tracks vis-à-vis the mouse tracks from our Study 1, no patterns emerged supporting either mechanism, suggesting that our participants chose control strategies that are in the middle ground between these two extremes. Ultimately, any control mechanism needs to be validated by proper user studies, which should include qualitative subjective measures besides standard quantitative metrics such as reading speed.

Acknowledgment. Research reported in this publication was supported by the National Eye Institute of the National Institutes of Health under award number R01EY030952-01A1. The content is solely the responsibility of the authors and does not necessarily represent the official views of the National Institutes of Health.

References

1. Aguilar, C., Castet, E.: Use of a gaze-contingent augmented-vision aid to improve reading with central field loss. Invest. Ophthalmol. Vis. Sci. **53**(14), 4390 (2012)
2. Aguilar, C., Castet, E.: Evaluation of a gaze-controlled vision enhancement system for reading in visually impaired people. PLoS ONE **12**(4), e0174910 (2017)
3. Ashmore, M., Duchowski, A., Shoemaker, G.: Efficient eye pointing with a fisheye lens. In: Proceedings of Graphics Interface 2005 (2005)
4. Beckmann, P., Legge, G.: Psychophysics of reading – XIV. The page navigation problem in using magnifiers. Vis. Res. **36**(22), 3723–3733 (1996)
5. Bruggeman, H., Legge, G.: Psychophysics of reading-XIX. Hypertext search and retrieval with low vision. Proc. IEEE **90**(1), 94–103 (2002)
6. Carver, R.P.: Reading Rate: A Review of Research and Theory. Academic Press, San Diego (1990)
7. Hallett, E.C., Dick, W., Jewett, T., Vu, K.-P.: How screen magnification with and without word-wrapping affects the user experience of adults with low vision. In: Ahram, T., Falcão, C. (eds.) AHFE 2017. AISC, vol. 607, pp. 665–674. Springer, Cham (2018). https://doi.org/10.1007/978-3-319-60492-3_63
8. Harland, S., Legge, G., Luebker, A.: Psycophysics of reading: XVII. Low-vision performances with four types of electronically magnified text. Optom. Vis. Sci. **75**(3), 183–190 (1998)
9. Hoeft, R., Buff, W., Cook, E., Stanney, K., Wilson, S.: Improving assistive technologies for the visually impaired: minimizing the side effects of magnification products. In: Proceedings of the Human Factors and Ergonomics Society Annual Meeting (2002)
10. Maus, N., Rutledge, D., Al-Khazraji, S., Bailey, R., Ovesdotter Alm, C., Shinohara, K.: Gaze-guided Magnification for Individuals with Vision Impairments. In: Extended Abstracts of the 2020 CHI Conference on Human Factors in Computing Systems (2020)
11. Pölzer, S., Gander, E., Miesenberger, K.: Gaze based magnification to assist visually impaired persons. In: Miesenberger, K., Kouroupetroglou, G. (eds.) ICCHP 2018. LNCS, vol. 10897, pp. 333–337. Springer, Cham (2018). https://doi.org/10.1007/978-3-319-94274-2_46
12. Schwarz, T., Akbarioroumieh, A., Melfi, G., Stiefelhagen, R.: Developing a magnification prototype based on head and eye-tracking for persons with low vision. In: Miesenberger, K., Manduchi, R., Covarrubias Rodriguez, M., Peňáz, P. (eds.) ICCHP 2020. LNCS, vol. 12376, pp. 354–363. Springer, Cham (2020). https://doi.org/10.1007/978-3-030-58796-3_42
13. Wallis, T., Dorr, M., Bex, P.: Sensitivity to gaze-contingent contrast increments in naturalistic movies: an exploratory report and model comparison. J. Vis. **15**(8), 3 (2015)
14. Werblin, F., et al.: Gaze-directed magnification: developing a head-mounted, wide field, immersive electronic low vision aid. In: ARVO Annual Meeting Abstract (2015)

Pardon? An Overview of the Current State and Requirements of Voice User Interfaces for Blind and Visually Impaired Users

Christina Oumard, Julian Kreimeier, and Timo Götzelmann(✉)

Nuremberg Institute of Technology, Nuremberg, Germany
{oumardch67627,julian.kreimeier,timo.goetzelmann}@th-nuernberg.de

Abstract. People with special needs like blind and visually impaired (BVI) people can particularly benefit from using voice assistants providing spoken information input and output in everyday life. However, it is crucial to understand their needs and include them in developing accessible and useful assistance systems. By conducting an online survey with 146 BVI people, this paper revealed that common voice assistants like *Apple's Siri* or *Amazon's Alexa* are used by a majority of BVI people and are also considered helpful. In particular, features in audio entertainment, internet access, and everyday life practical things like weather queries, time-related information (e.g., setting an alarm clock), checking calendar entries, and taking notes are particularly often used and appreciated. The participants also indicated that the integration of smart home devices, the optimization of existing functionalities, and voice input are important. Still, also potentially negative aspects such as data privacy and data security are relevant. Therefore, it seems particularly interesting to implement offline data processing as far as possible. Our results contribute to this development by providing an overview of empirically collected requirements for functions and implementation-related aspects.

Keywords: Voice assistant · Blind and visually impaired people · Requirements

Voice assistants can be a valuable tool for blind and visually impaired (BVI) people to output and input spoken information. Such information can be everyday issues, such as checking the weather at a certain place, the current time, and what appointments are coming up. But, it is also important to be able to create appointments and reminders, for example. Voice assistants (also known as a voice user interfaces) are widespread and available in the non-accessibility-focused consumer market, e.g., on the move in the form of *Apple's Siri* or at home with *Amazon's Alexa*. However, mostly consumer devices are designed for sighted users and do not address accessibility aspects. To this end, the correct speech recognition is crucial, and the technical infrastructure required for

K. Miesenberger et al. (Eds.): ICCHP-AAATE 2022, LNCS 13341, pp. 388–398, 2022.
https://doi.org/10.1007/978-3-031-08648-9_45

this is usually implemented via an online connection to corresponding servers with powerful computing capabilities [13,31]. Conventional assistants such as *Amazon Alexa*, only work with an online connection because of the online computed speech recognition. However, this implementation involves considerable data security and privacy issues, see, for example, the definitions of Phelps et al. [22]). There are different approaches to ensure data privacy and security in the most efficient way [26,32], frameworks to test them [8,14] or general investigations regarding privacy norms [17]. Worldwide smart speaker sales increased from 4.6 million units in the fourth quarter of 2016 to 58.2 million in the fourth quarter of 2021 [1]. This trend was also predicted to a lesser extent by Statista in 2016. The increase was predicted from 390 million users of digital assistants in 2015, and 504 million in 2016 to 1831 million people in 2021 [25].

In this context, the question arises whether, how, and why such assistance systems are also suitable for BVI persons and what has to be done for an even better acceptance and benefit in everyday life. Towards answering this question, our contribution gives an overview of the current state of the use of voice assistants for BVI users and the requirements for functionalities. After discussing related work under technical and requirements analysis aspects, the content, implementation, and results of our online survey with BVI participants are presented. Finally, the paper's main findings are summarized, and recommendations for future work are derived.

1 Related Work

1.1 Voice Assistants

To the authors' best knowledge, three proof of concepts of offline speech interfaces [18,20,21] and eight related assistants already developed for people who are visually impaired are known, presented in detail in the following.

The system *Sarah* [18] and Petraitytes' voice assistant [21] describe designs of voice user interfaces and have not implemented any voice assistant features yet. While *Sarah* can run with offline modules (e.g., *PocketSphinx*, *MaryTTS*, *spaCy*) as well as with online modules (e.g., *wit.ai*, *Ivona*, *Mycroft*), it also allows text as an input and is not limited to speech input. *PIPPA* only works with the offline engines *DeepSpeech* for speech recognition, *RASA* dialog management and *Mozilla* TTS. The system is limited to the uncustomized vocabulary and also needs a spellchecker to compensate for minor errors in the speech-to-text (STT) model. The offline smart speaker *Pippa* [20] also uses *Mozillas' DeepSpeech* for speech recognition and has already some assistive features like controlling the lights.

Felix et al. [9], Chen et al. [7] and Kulhalli et al. [13] introduce *Android* application, that provide features like image and currency recognition [9], outdoor navigation with falling detection, information service for weather, news, date, calculator, playing music [7], and controlling commands for the smartphone [13]. While the voice assistants of Felix et al. and Chen et al. [7,9] only work with an internet connection, the personal assistant from Kulhalli et al. [13]

can recognize the user speech input offline, but only processes given commands like "open application" or "send text SMS to respective person" which must be known to the user.

Weeratunga et al. [31] and Bose et al. [4] developed systems that provide online speech recognition by the *Google* API and the offline module *pyttsx* for text to speech. Nethra [31] also provides an alternative offline speech recognition with a limited vocabulary. These assistants allow the user to interact with computers and internet-based services [31] and to send and receive mails, get the daily news, weather forecast, and manage reminders, alarms, and notes [4].

The only entirely offline working systems are the *Android* application intelligent eye [3] (providing light and color detection and object and banknote recognition) and the intelligent home automation for physically challenged people [11,23,29] (offering features like Wikipedia, news, weather, movies, a module that responses definitions of requested words, find my phone module, and a joke module), and the smart assistant of Tahoun et al. [30] (including an object, color and text recognition and distance algorithm calculating the distance to an object using an ultrasonic sensor). The intelligent eye and the smart assistant do not have a voice input module and can only be operated via buttons. In terms of design, the intelligent home automation comes closest to our approach but only possesses a query processor and no dialog management. In addition, it is generally designed for physically challenged people and therefore not focused on especially blind and visually impaired users.

When developing assistive devices, it is crucial to consider the users' requirements and the technical implementation details. The following section presents existing reviews, questionnaires, and their main findings.

1.2 Surveys on Voice Assistants

There are several survey and review papers, e.g., on how fundamental metaphors and guidelines for designing voice assistants might empower and constrain visually impaired users [5], on the risk and potential of voice assistants [12], and concerns from the users' perspective [6].

Voice assistants have a high potential to support blind users, but entail usability and accessibility issues by complex commands, receiving appropriate non-visual feedback, and correcting errors during interaction [2]. However, "blind screen reader users are the "power users" of voice interfaces, and centering them in the design process can generate better tools for a variety of users." To this end, Branham et al. [5] performed a qualitative review of known voice-activated personal assistants' design guidelines by *Amazon*, *Google*, *Microsoft*, *Apple*, and *Alibaba* and how fundamental metaphors and guidelines for designing voice assistants might empower and constrain visually impaired users. The length and complexity suggested in the guidelines do not adequately describe the cognitive abilities of blind users since many blind people are superior to sighted in serial memory tasks and are better at remembering longer sequences of words. Thus, blind users may be able to correctly interpret and retrieve longer and more complex speech responses. In an interview by Abdolrahmani et al. in

2018, 14 adult blind participants that were experienced with voice-activated virtual assistants appreciated these systems on the one hand due to a reduction of needed time with spoken input compared to a touch screen or keyboard. On the other hand, mobile voice assistants were said to tend to misinterpret the user's command, especially in noisy public environments. Other problems are the non-availability of refining the recognition of special names and the limited time for spoken input. The assistant's spoken feedback can often be too detailed, unnecessary, irrelevant, or, conversely, did not provide sufficient information to answer the question. Ideally, such aspects should be adjustable by each user individually. Moreover, no reaction after the wake-word or unrequested activation can be obstructive, especially if the visual feedback (e.g., *Amazon Echo's* light ring cannot be seen. However, data privacy and security issues are considered acceptable for the functionality offered.

Apart from accessibility and enginerring issues, an market research survey in 2019 revealed that from 1021 (sighted) participants between 18 and 69 years, 62% have already used a virtual assistant, of which 52% are satisfied with the functions. The most often used skills are requesting information from, for example, *Google*, playing music, getting weather reports and reminders of dates [24]. With consumer devices, another survey from 2021 identified *Amazon Echo* as most *Alexa* disseminated (78 %), followed by *Apple HomePod* (*Siri*) and *Google Home* (*Google Assistant*) with 12 % each [27].

Klein et al. [12] presented 2020 a questionnaire with 115 (sighted) participants, of which 87,8% have access to at least one voice assistant, and 51.5% use one device. *Google Assistant* is most frequently used, followed by *Amazon's Alexa* and *Apple's Siri* and 30,61% use a voice assistant several times a day or week, and 19,38% have a weekly or monthly usage times. But apart from gaining more popularity and momentum, concerns about smart speakers and intelligent voice assistants remain. However, interestingly, such privacy aspects are less pronounced among cell phone users than in the domestic smart home context [16].

A 2018 study identified several reasons impeding the use of voice assistants: Security concerns, gathering a lot of data, autonomy and transparency when accessing information [28], where data privacy [6] and possible data misuse and monitoring [12] is not only most important, but also well-founded [14,15]. With offline data processing as far as possible, such problems can be systemically avoided.

2 Online Survey

2.1 Method

To identify requirements for an offline voice user interface with offline speech processing, the following overall research questions were presented to blind and visually impaired (BVI) participants in an accessible online survey.

- How many BVI people use voice assistants?

- Which systems and features do BVI people use, and which ones are most helpful?
- What are positive and negative experiences with voice assistants?
- What features are missing?

The URL to the electronic, qualitative, and partially standardized questionnaire was sent via Email to BVI people organizations within Germany and contacted already known BVI participants from previous experiments.

In detail, the survey consists of seven pages and fourteen questions (see Fig. 1) and is organized on the individual pages as follows:

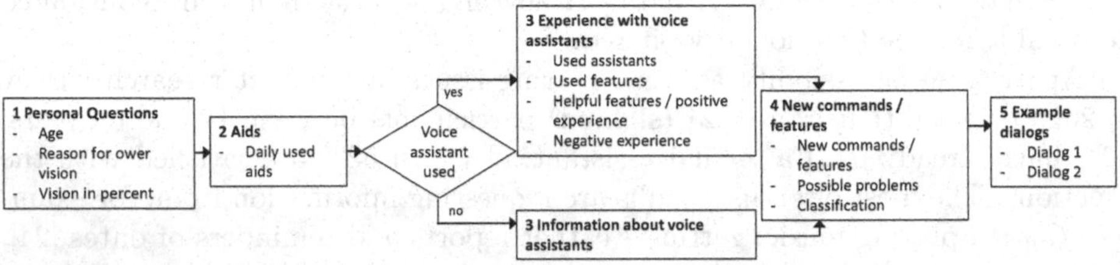

Fig. 1. Flowchart of the questionnaire procedure.

(1) Demographics data (age, reason and data for vision impairment)
(2) Assistive devices (daily used aids and used voice assistants)
(3) Voice assistant experience (used systems and features, if applicable)
(4) Voice assistant data (new commands and features, possible problems, classification)
(5) Two self considered example dialogs (understanding user expressions)

SoSci Survey was used as the survey platform. To ensure accessibility, a telephone number was provided by which the survey could also be conducted on the phone.

2.2 Participants

The survey was conducted with $n = 146$ participants between 18 and 82 years with a mean age of 52 ± 14 years. 61% of the participants are blind, and 93% have a maximum vision of 5%.

2.3 Results and Discussion

As a first step, invalid data (e.g., an incomplete questionnaires set or facetious answers) was deleted, and non-consistent data (e.g., the year of birth or age, or remaining vision and synonymous reasons) was manually converted to the same format, it necessary. The given answers were clustered into often used, helpful, and new features to identify characteristics on features.

Categories that were mentioned more than four times were added to the list of features to be implemented (see Fig. 2 step 2). When determining how often particular features were mentioned, it was ensured that a category was only counted once per person, even if they named several items from this group. For example, if a person said he or she uses the music and radio skill, the corresponding category auditory entertainment was only calculated once. Afterward, features were again omitted that can be replaced by frequently used tools and therefore do not necessarily create added value (e.g., sending an SMS message or using the telephone, step 3). This resulted in the final selection of features to be implemented (step 4).

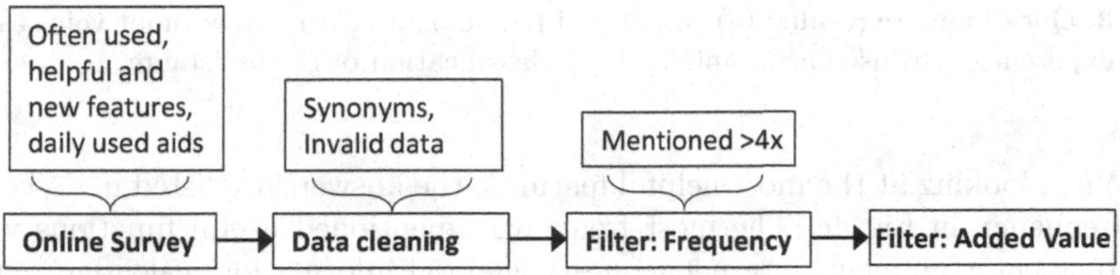

Fig. 2. Procedure for the evaluation of the questionnaire on the use and experience of voice assistants.

Experiences with Voice Assistants. The majority (88%) of participants have already used a voice assistant, and 86% consider such systems as helpful, while some participants consider them as not useful (3%), a toy (9%), or don't know (2%). Figure 3 shows that most of them used *Siri*, *Amazon's Alexa* or the *Google* system. Some participants named screen readers (e.g., *JAWS*) when asked for voice assistant experience, which is, per definition, not a voice assistant because they are rather used to solve predefined tasks with commands instead of operating a dialog system.

When looking at the most used features, the answers are listed in descending frequency in Fig. 4a. Auditory entertainment, Internet requests and gathering information, asking for weather forecast, setting an alarm clock, managing the calendar, setting a timer, using telephony, dictation function, asking for the current time, receiving the news, playing games, controlling the smartphone, using smart home features and identifying locations and opening times were stated. The group auditory entertainment includes answers like music, audio film, audiobook, TV media, and podcasts. In addition, several Internet search engines like *Google* and *Wikipedia* and general questions were grouped into the category of internet requests. Only information asked again via specific pages, such as a train timetable or news, was left as a single category. The category of home automation includes controlling the blinds, lights, heating, sockets, air conditioning, or a robot vacuum cleaner.

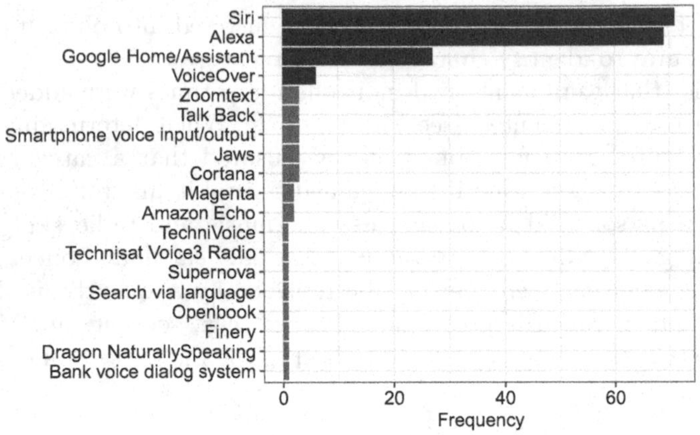

Fig. 3. Questionnaire results: (a) Number of participants with and without voice assistant experience, (b) used assistants and (c) classification of the assistants

When looking at the most helpful features, the answers are listed in descending frequency in Fig. 4c. The most frequently mentioned useful functions were auditory entertainment, internet requests, general information, calendar, alarm clock, weather, timer, time, telephony, TV, sending messages, dictation function, news, home automation, calculator, and pedestrian navigation with time and distance information. In addition to the actual functions, many also stated that they particularly appreciate the operation speed and independence through Voice Assistance. They also sometimes need fewer devices or do not have to search for them.

When it comes to new features with an added value for daily living, most participants mentioned features within home automation, i.e., controlling other devices like light, television, shutter, and kitchen appliances. Also, a better and louder public transport timetable, another navigation method through the systems menu, and more specific internet requests were stated. It was also submitted to provide better indoor and outdoor navigation with voice commands, object recognition, and pedestrian routes. Some named the ability to read documents, displays, and packaging aloud, managing notes and shopping lists, address book, and phone numbers. It was also mentioned that the listing of locations such as restaurants, delivery services, or stores could be changed/improved by providing specified filters and changing the order of the presented sequence. Some also mentioned that they would like to order from supermarkets, get information about desired food, translate a given sentence or word, or even use the assistant with other languages. At least some suggest providing a description of named environments and objects.

Besides positive experiences, used features, and new ideas, negative criticism of voice assistants were wrong text detection, issues during a poor internet connection, and wrong interpretation of the detected input. Some participants also complained that the assistant sometimes does not react or has concerns about data protection and security and continuous listening of third parties. Furthermore, linguistic problems such as similar English and German words, technical words, proper names, or accents were mentioned.

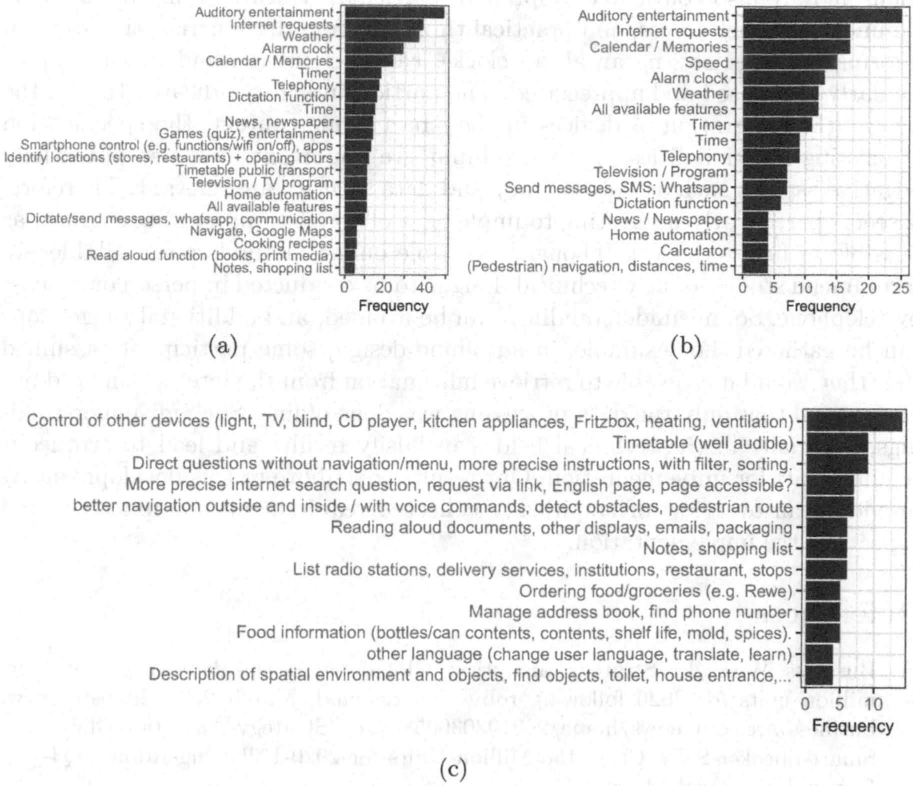

Fig. 4. Questionnaire results: Histogram to (a) often used, (b) helpful features and (c) proposals

The results are broadly consistent with those of previous surveys, such as the affinity or subjective suitability of *Apple* devices in the area of accessibility [10,19]. The users wished for factual questions, directions/location of a place, speech-to-text conversion, and setting a timer [16]. The *Statista* survey on the used functions of virtual assistants in 2019 shows similar skills in a similar order. Blind and visually impaired people also frequently use the assistant to set an alarm clock or timer and ask for the time.

3 Conclusion and Future Work

Especially for marginalized groups like blind and visually impaired (BVI) people, voice assistants can be a helpful tool to facilitate their everyday life through spoken input and output of information. However, it is important to understand their needs and include them in developing accessible and useful assistance systems. In this paper, a survey with 146 BVI persons revealed that common voice assistants like *Apple's Siri* or *Amazon's Alexa* are also used by a majority of them and are also considered helpful. In particular, features from audio entertainment, internet access, and practical things like weather queries, time-related information (e.g., setting an alarm clock), calendar entries, and notes are particularly often used and appreciated. The participants also indicated that in the future, the integration of devices in the smart home context, the specification of existing functionalities, and voice input are important, but also potentially negative aspects such as data privacy and data security are relevant. Therefore, it seems particularly interesting to implement offline data processing as much as possible in future devices. Though accessible online methods are available, we recommend studies of new technical designs to be conducted in person or at least by telephone. So, misunderstandings can be avoided, and additional suggestions can be gathered. For example, in an offline design, some participants assumed that they would not be able to retrieve information from the internet and did not understand that only the data processing was done offline. Such misunderstandings, especially in the technical field, can falsify results and lead to erroneous requirements for implementation. Our results contribute to this development by providing an overview of empirically collected requirements for functions and aspects of the implementation.

References

1. Business Wire, I.: Strategy analytics: Global smart speaker sales cross 150 million units for 2020 following robust q4 demand, March 2021. https://www.businesswire.com/news/home/20210303005852/en/Strategy-Analytics-Global-Smart-Speaker-Sales-Cross-150-Million-Units-for-2020-Following-Robust-Q4-Demand. Accessed 14 Sep 2021
2. Abdolrahmani, A., Mukkath, R., Kuber, R., Branham, S.M.: Blind people are power users: An argument for centering blind users in design of voice interfaces. UMBC Student Collection (2020)
3. Awad, M., El Haddad, J., Khneisser, E., Mahmoud, T., Yaacoub, E., Malli, M.: Intelligent eye: a mobile application for assisting blind people. In: 2018 IEEE Middle East and North Africa Communications Conference (MENACOMM), pp. 1–6. IEEE (2018)
4. Bose, P., Malpthak, A., Bansal, U., Harsola, A.: Digital assistant for the blind. In: 2017 2nd International Conference for Convergence in Technology (I2CT), pp. 1250–1253. IEEE (2017)
5. Branham, S.M., Mukkath Roy, A.R.: Reading between the guidelines: how commercial voice assistant guidelines hinder accessibility for blind users. In: The 21st International ACM SIGACCESS Conference on Computers and Accessibility, pp. 446–458 (2019)
6. Burbach, L., Halbach, P., Plettenberg, N., Nakayama, J., Ziefle, M., Valdez, A.C.: "Hey, siri", "ok, google", "alexa". Acceptance-relevant factors of virtual voice-assistants. In: 2019 IEEE International Professional Communication Conference (ProComm), pp. 101–111. IEEE (2019)

7. Chen, R., Tian, Z., Liu, H., Zhao, F., Zhang, S., Liu, H.: Construction of a voice driven life assistant system for visually impaired people. In: 2018 International Conference on Artificial Intelligence and Big Data (ICAIBD), pp. 87–92. IEEE (2018)
8. Chung, H., Park, J., Lee, S.: Digital forensic approaches for Amazon Alexa ecosystem. Digit. Investig. **22**, S15–S25 (2017)
9. Felix, S.M., Kumar, S., Veeramuthu, A.: A smart personal AI assistant for visually impaired people. In: 2018 2nd International Conference on Trends in Electronics and Informatics (ICOEI), pp. 1245–1250. IEEE (2018)
10. Griffin-Shirley, N., et al.: A survey on the use of mobile applications for people who are visually impaired. J. Vis. Impair. Blind. **111**(4), 307–323 (2017)
11. Kamala, M., Bhanusree, G., Dullapally, M., Thakkar, P., Patel, R.: Offline voice recognition with low cost implementation based intelligent home automation system. J. Eng. Sci. (JES) **11**(11), 133–136 (2020)
12. Klein, A.M., Hinderks, A., Rauschenberger, M., Thomaschewski, J.: Exploring voice assistant risks and potential with technology-based users. In: WEBIST, pp. 147–154 (2020)
13. Kulhalli, K.V., Sirbi, K., Patankar, M.A.J.: Personal assistant with voice recognition intelligence. Int. J. Eng. Res. Technol. (IJERT) **10**(1), 416–419 (2017)
14. Liao, S., Wilson, C., Cheng, L., Hu, H., Deng, H.: Measuring the effectiveness of privacy policies for voice assistant applications. In: Annual Computer Security Applications Conference, pp. 856–869 (2020)
15. Liao, S., Wilson, C., Cheng, L., Hu, H., Deng, H.: Problematic privacy policies of voice assistant applications. IEEE Secur. Privacy **19**, 66–73 (2021)
16. Liao, Y., Vitak, J., Kumar, P., Zimmer, M., Kritikos, K.: Understanding the role of privacy and trust in intelligent personal assistant adoption. In: Taylor, N.G., Christian-Lamb, C., Martin, M.H., Nardi, B. (eds.) iConference 2019. LNCS, vol. 11420, pp. 102–113. Springer, Cham (2019). https://doi.org/10.1007/978-3-030-15742-5_9
17. Martin, K.: Understanding privacy online: development of a social contract approach to privacy. J. Bus. Ethics **137**(3), 551–569 (2016)
18. Micha: Diy Sprachsteuerung (fast) komplett offline, February 2017. https://duke.de/2017/02/diy-sprachsteuerung-fast-komplett-offline/. Accessed 13 May 2021
19. Morris, J., Mueller, J.: Blind and deaf consumer preferences for Android and iOS Smartphones. In: Langdon, P.M., Lazar, J., Heylighen, A., Dong, H. (eds.) Inclusive Designing, pp. 69–79. Springer, Cham (2014). https://doi.org/10.1007/978-3-319-05095-9_7
20. Peinl, R.: Smart speaker ohne cloud, January 2019. https://smarthome-franken.org/wp-content/uploads/2019/02/Peinl-2019-Forschungspaper_Smart-Speaker.pdf. Accessed 13 May 2021
21. Petraityte, J.: How to build a voice assistant with open source rasa and Mozilla tools, August 2019. https://blog.rasa.com/how-to-build-a-voice-assistant-with-open-source-rasa-and-mozilla-tools/. Accessed 13 May 2021
22. Phelps, J., Nowak, G., Ferrell, E.: Privacy concerns and consumer willingness to provide personal information. J. Public Policy Market. **19**(1), 27–41 (2000)
23. Prasanna, G., Ramadass, N.: Low cost home automation using offline speech recognition. Int. J. Signal Process. Syst. **2**(2), 96–101 (2014)
24. Regenthal, J.: Statista survey: Smart speakers and virtual assistants 2019, March 2021. https://de.statista.com/statistik/studie/id/61562/dokument/smart-speaker-und-virtuelle-assistenten/. accessed 14 Sep 2021

25. Richter, F.: Forecast for the use of virtual digital assistants worldwide by 2021, August 2016. https://de.statista.com/infografik/5627/nutzung-von-digitalen-virtuellen-assistenten/. Accessed 14 Sep 2021
26. Singh, A.K., Gupta, I.: Online information leaker identification scheme for secure data sharing. Multimedia Tools Appl. **79**(41), 31165–31182 (2020)
27. Statista Global Consumer Survery: Germany: Most popular smart speaker brands in 2021, August 2021. https://de.statista.com/prognosen/999790/deutschland-beliebteste-smart-speaker-marken. Accessed 14 Sep 2021
28. Statista Research Department: Survey on reasons for not using voice assistants in Germany 2018, February 2021. https://de.statista.com/statistik/daten/studie/872316/umfrage/gruende-fuer-die-nichtnutzung-von-sprachassistenten-in-deutschland/. Accessed 14 Sep 2021
29. Suresh, S., Rao, Y.S.: Modelling of secured voice recognition based automatic control system. Int. J. Emerg. Technol. Comput. Sci. Electron. (IJETCSE) **13**(2), 140–144 (2015)
30. Tahoun, N., Awad, A., Bonny, T.: Smart assistant for blind and visually impaired people. In: Proceedings of the 2019 3rd International Conference on Advances in Artificial Intelligence, pp. 227–231 (2019)
31. Weeratunga, A., Jayawardana, S., Hasindu, P., Prashan, W., Thelijjagoda, S.: Project Nethra-an intelligent assistant for the visually disabled to interact with internet services. In: 2015 IEEE 10th International Conference on Industrial and Information Systems (ICIIS), pp. 55–59. IEEE (2015)
32. Yang, C.N., Lai, J.B.: Protecting data privacy and security for cloud computing based on secret sharing. In: 2013 International Symposium on Biometrics and Security Technologies, pp. 259–266. IEEE (2013)

Learning a Head-Tracking Pointing Interface

Muratcan Cicek and Roberto Manduchi(✉)

University of California, Santa Cruz, USA
mcicek@ucsc.edu, manduchi@soe.ucsc.edu

Abstract. For people with poor upper limb mobility or control, interaction with a computer may be facilitated by adaptive and alternative interfaces. Visual head tracking has proven to be a viable pointing interface, which can be used when use of the mouse or trackpad is challenging. We are interested in new mechanisms to map the user's head motion to a pointer location on the screen. Towards this goal, we collected a data set of videos of participants as they were moving their head while following the motion of a marker on the screen. This data set could be used to training a machine learning system for pointing interface. We believe that by learning on real examples, this system may provide a more natural and satisfactory interface than current systems based on pre-defined algorithms.

1 Introduction

Interacting with a computer via traditional interface mechanisms requires good upper limb and hand control. For people with motor impairment, tasks such as typing and pointing (moving the pointer with the mouse or a trackpad) may become difficult or impossible [24]. Assistive technology solutions for computer interaction are designed to receive user input in alternative ways, or through entirely different channels such as sound or vision. For example, dictation systems can be used in lieu of typing, but only if the user has understandable speech (e.g., they may be useless for someone with dysarthria). As for pointing, computer vision-based head tracking has gained popularity in recent years, with several applications using this technology already available [2,6,15,17,18]. These systems use a camera (e.g., embedded in a computer screen) to track the user's head motion using computer vision algorithms. Typically, measurements are taken in terms of a "face box" or of a specific facial figure (e.g. the nose tip [4]). These measurements are then mapped to the pointer location in the screen using a pre-defined algorithm.

A main drawback of this approach is that the mapping from head motion to pointer location is not necessarily representative of the user's intent. For example, moving one's head to the right may lead to a rightwards motion of the pointer that is faster than what the user intended. This may result in an overshoot, which then needs to be corrected by a leftward head motion. In practice, the

K. Miesenberger et al. (Eds.): ICCHP-AAATE 2022, LNCS 13341, pp. 399–406, 2022.
https://doi.org/10.1007/978-3-031-08648-9_46

user needs to learn to use the system with head patterns that may not feel "natural". While these algorithms typically afford some parameter tuning, the general mapping mechanism remains unchanged.

We propose a user-centric approach to designing a pointing algorithm based on head tracking. Rather than imposing a pre-defined algorithm mapping head position to pointer position, we would like to learn a flexible mechanism that adapts to the user's intent. As a first step towards this goal, we created a data set where the measured data (head position from video frames) is associated with the desired location of the pointer. To build such a data set, we resorted to the following strategy. We showed a well-visible marker (a white disk) moving on the screen in specific patterns. While watching the marker moving, participants were asked to move their head "as if" they were controlling the marker themselves. Images were collected by a screen-embedded camera, and time-registered with the location of the marker on the screen at each time. We believe that the videos thus recorded are representative examples of the way participants would move their head if asked to move the cursor to replicate the same trajectories traversed by the pattern they saw moving on the screen.

This paper describe our data collection strategy, which was accomplished remotely due to COVID-19 social distancing constraints. We also present examples of the dynamic of a specific facial feature (the nose tip) while participants were following different trajectories of the pattern in the screen, and provide a simple analysis of the variance of the location measured for this feature across participants.

2 Related Work

There are various head-based pointing methods developed by the researchers including physical head-mounted styluses like Finger-nose [21] for touchscreens, and new sophisticated products like Quha Zono [20] and Glassouse [10]. In addition physical styluses, there are also software-based solutions [3,6,15,17,18] thanks to the front cameras and the advancements in Computer Vision. Vision-based head-based pointing shares the same fundamental with the gaze-based mechanisms [12,16,19] but instead it tracks the movement of the head rather than eye balls. Comparisons between head-based and gaze-based interactions [1,13] suggest that head-based techniques are more voluntary, stable and have greater accuracy while gaze-based techniques may be faster for some specific tasks like typing [9].

Most of the visual-based head-based pointing solutions rely on off-the-shelf face tracking algorithms to capture user feedback (i.e. head movement) and convert this input into pointing coordinates on the screen. We know that Enable Viacam [17] benefits from the Haar Cascade algorithm [25] for face detection by evaluating its source code. Camera Mouse [3] also allows users to choose the input mechanism for pointing. Besides face tracking, it also includes point tracking based on simple optical flow calculation. In this setting, users can determine a small patch on their face and the software tries to keep track of this patch on the following frames. On the other hand, HeadGazeLib [5] utilizes the depth sensors of the device the locate user face with respect to the camera. While other methods [4,15] use advanced deep learning algorithms to detect and track the facial features from RGB images, their conversion functions are again tailored by the developers and involve no machine learning. To the best of our knowledge, there is no visual-based head-based pointing solution that aims to learn pointing from user's appearance directly.

3 Data Collection

We recruited 8 participants (3 female) from our university. One participant has a motor impairment due to cerebral palsy, and is a regular user of head-based pointing technology. Although this is a relatively small sample size, it is adequate for a proof-of-concept. We will consider a larger set of participants (including more participants with motor impairment) in future work. The goal of this study was to collect videos of the participants as they moved their head, following the path of a small white disk shown on their computer screen. The participants were instructed to pretend that they were controlling the white disk with their head motion. They were asked to not just follow the disk with their eye gaze, but by moving their head. No other instructions (e.g., how much to move their head, whether to rotate it vs. move it, etc.) were given. Hence, we can assume that the head motion of each participant was as "natural" and spontaneous as it could be.

We first generated a number of "trajectory videos" with a small white disk moving along a predetermined trajectory against a black background. Some of these trajectories were repeated at a slower velocity. Some trajectories included "pause" points, where the disk would stop for one second. Participants were able to see the future path of the disk (shown with dimmed brightness), so that they would know in advance where the disk would move next. Examples of disk trajectories are shown in Fig. 1. Note that in all trajectories, the disk started and ended at the center of the screen. We uploaded these trajectory videos (17 in total) on YouTube and created separate playlists for each participant, with the order of the video randomly permuted for each playlist.

The study was conducted remotely due to the social distancing requirements imposed by the COVID-19 pandemic. We utilized the Zoom platform to run the data collection sessions, including recording the participants' visual input during the pointing tasks. For each participant, we scheduled a one-hour online meeting via Zoom. We collected information about the computer they would use for the test, whether they would use the embedded camera in the screen or an external camera, the screen size and resolution. In the teleconference, we explained to each participant how the test would be conducted, then asked them to go to the YouTube site at the playlist assigned to them, and to expand the browser window to fulls screen. In this way, participants would only interact with the moving disk in the trajectory videos, while images of their head were taken by the camera and recorded in the cloud via Zoom.

Consecutive trajectory videos within the playlist were separated by 10 s intervals. Participants could use these intervals of time to briefly rest, and they were also allowed to pause the playlist in between trajectory videos. An acoustic signal was played at the beginning and at the end of each trajectory video in the playlist. This was used to synchronize the video displayed to the user, with the video of the user recorded via Zoom ("user video"). These user videos were recorded at a resolution of 1280 × 720 pixels and at a rate of 25 frames per second. The whole session for each participant as recorded by Zoom was exported as a single video for simplicity. We then cropped individual user videos, using as reference the acoustic signal recorded at the beginning and at the end of each trajectory video. In this way, we obtained pairs of synchronized trajectory-user videos, to be used for our analysis. 17 such video pairs were recorded for each user. We had to discard only 2 such video pairs, one due to noticeable latency caused by Zoom, and one because the video was mistakenly interrupted by the experimenter. In total, we obtained 136 synchronized video pairs from 8 separate participants, with the length of the user videos varying between 536 and 2267 frames.

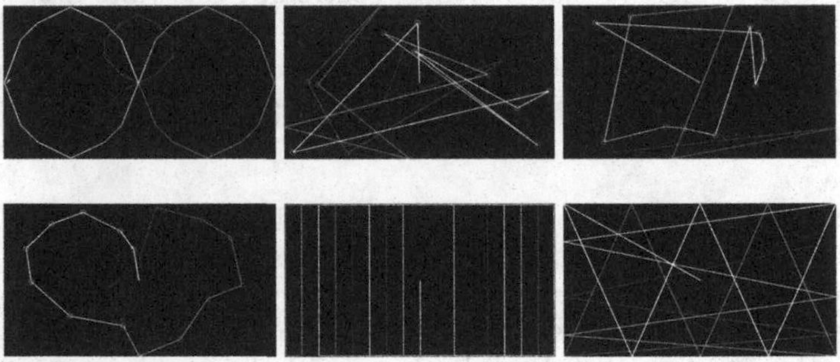

Fig. 1. Samples of trajectory videos. The whole trajectory of the white disk is visible, with lighter color indicating earlier locations in the trajectory. Small circles correspond to location where the white disk stopped for one second.

4 Head Motion Computation

One of the goals of this study is to explore whether the motion of the white disk on the screen could be predicted from the user video. For this purpose, we first extracted a number of visual "features", that can be used to describe the user head's motion. These features can then be mapped, using suitable machine learning mechanisms, to the position of the disk on the screen.

A very simple, though perhaps not very informative, feature is the location of the "face box", defined as a rectangle encompassing the whole face image [7,14,23]. A richer description can be obtained by identifying specific facial landmarks. We experimented with three state-of-the-art facial landmark detection models [11,26,27]. For example, Fig. 2 shows the location of the facial

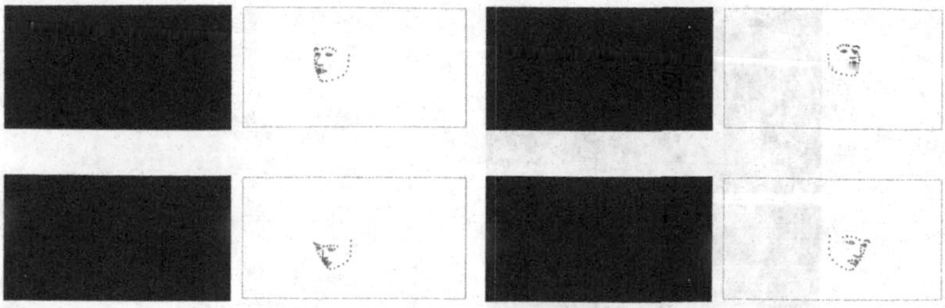

Fig. 2. Facial landmarks produced by the PFLD algorithm [11] for one of the participants, taken at the time the white disk appeared in the location shown in the left half of the figure.

landmarks produced by the PFLD algorithm [11] for one of the participants, at the times when the white disk being followed was situated in vicinity of the four corners of the screen.

A higher-level feature that we will consider in future work is the pose (3-D location + orientation) of the user's head, which can be computed using 3-D deformable models (e.g., [8,22,28]).

5 Trajectories Analysis

It is instructive to compare the trajectory of the visual features being tracked, against that of the white disk on the screen. This can provide some intuition about how a user would move their head in relation to the desired pointer location. In Fig. 3, we show the trajectory of a specific facial feature, the user's nose tip, for two participants (P2 and P6), viz-a-viz the trajectory of the white disk. Note that the nose tip location has been used successfully for head-based pointing control in prior work [4]. While the trajectories of the nose tips may vaguely resemble the trajectory of the white disk on the screen, it is clear that a precise one-to-one positional mapping would be hard if not impossible.

The trajectories of the nose tip feature shown in Fig. 3 are clearly different across the two considered participants. This is to be expected, since the dynamic of head motion associated with tracking the white disk on the screen is completely subjective (remember that participants were not given instructions about how to move their head). In some cases (see e.g. the last case of Fig. 3), a positional bias is visible (possibly because the users positioned themselves at different locations in front of the camera). In these cases, the bias could be easily recovered and compensated for.

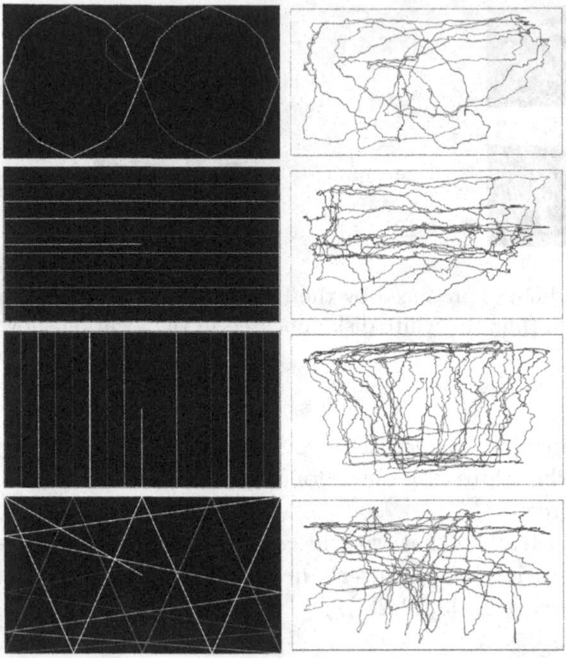

Fig. 3. Trajectories of the nose tip features for two different participants (P2 and P6) associated with the white disk trajectories shown in the left half of each row.

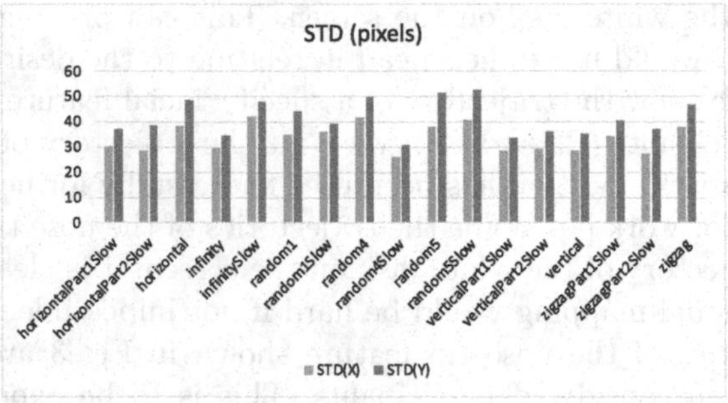

Fig. 4. Average standard deviation of the X and Y coordinate of the nose tip across participants for each trajectory video.

In order to quantify the difference between trajectories across participants, we computed a measure of variance as follows. For each trajectory video, we measured, at each time, the variance in the X and Y coordinate of the nose tip location across all participants. (We excluded P5 in this analysis, as facial feature detection was unreliable for this participant.) Then, we computed the average of these variances over the whole trajectory. The squared root of the average variance (i.e., the standard deviation) for the X and Y coordinates of the nose tip are plotted for each trajectory video in Fig. 4. These values vary between 28 and 42 pixel for X, and between 31 and 53 pixels for Y (remember that the recorded images have resolution of 1280×720 pixels.)

6 Conclusions

This paper presents a unique data set collected for the purpose of understanding the different head motion dynamics adopted by different participants while imagining to control a moving disk on a screen. We are currently using this data set to train a machine learning system that can predict the desired location of the cursor based on the user's head motion. Our hope is that, by learning from videos collected in response to a stimulus on the screen, this system can do a better job of mapping image feature to cursor locations than current, hand-tailored algorithms.

Our initial analysis of the collected data shows that there is a fairly large variance of the location of facial features (e.g., the nose tip) across participants while following the same disk trajectory. This suggests that a certain degree of personalization may be necessary, in order to adjust the algorithm to the specific head dynamics of each user.

References

1. Bates, R., Istance, H.O.: Why are eye mice unpopular? A detailed comparison of head and eye controlled assistive technology pointing devices. Univers. Access Inf. Soc. **2**(3), 280–290 (2003)
2. Betke, M., Gips, J., Fleming, P.: The camera mouse: visual tracking of body features to provide computer access for people with severe disabilities. IEEE Trans. Neural Syst. Rehabil. Eng. **10**(1), 1–10 (2002)
3. of Boston College, T.: Cameramouse (2018). http://www.cameramouse.org/. Accessed 31 Jan 2022
4. Cicek, M., Dave, A., Feng, W., Huang, M.X., Haines, J.K., Nichols, J.: Designing and evaluating head-based pointing on smartphones for people with motor impairments. In: The 22nd International ACM SIGACCESS Conference on Computers and Accessibility, ASSETS 2020 (2020)
5. Cicek, M., Xie, J., Wang, Q., Piramuthu, R.: Mobile head tracking for ecommerce and beyond. Electron. Imaging **2020**(3), 303–1 (2020)
6. Corporation, O.I.: Headmouse nano (2017). http://www.orin.com/access/headmouse/. Accessed 31 Jan 2022
7. Deng, J., Guo, J., Zhou, Y., Yu, J., Kotsia, I., Zafeiriou, S.: Retinaface: single-stage dense face localisation in the wild. CoRR (2019). http://arxiv.org/abs/1905.00641
8. Fanelli, G., Gall, J., Van Gool, L.: Real time head pose estimation with random regression forests. In: CVPR 2011, pp. 617–624. IEEE (2011)
9. Gizatdinova, Y., Špakov, O., Surakka, V.: Comparison of video-based pointing and selection techniques for hands-free text entry. In: Proceedings of the ACM International Working Conference on Advanced Visual Interfaces, pp. 132–139 (2012)
10. Glassouse: Glassouse assistive device (2018). http://glassouse.com/. Accessed 17 July 2018

11. Guo, X., et al.: PFLD: a practical facial landmark detector. CoRR (2019). http://arxiv.org/abs/1902.10859
12. Inc., A.: Use switch control to navigate your iphone, ipad, or ipod touch (2018). https://support.apple.com/en-us/ht201370. Accessed 15 July 2018
13. Kytö, M., Ens, B., Piumsomboon, T., Lee, G.A., Billinghurst, M.: Pinpointing: precise head-and eye-based target selection for augmented reality. In: Proceedings of the 2018 ACM CHI Conference on Human Factors in Computing Systems, p. 81 (2018)
14. Li, J., et al.: DSFD: dual shot face detector. CoRR (2018). http://arxiv.org/abs/1810.10220
15. LLC, P.D.: Smylemouse (2016). https://smylemouse.com/. Accessed 31 Jan 2022
16. Majaranta, P.: Gaze Interaction and Applications of Eye Tracking: Advances in Assistive Technologies: Advances in Assistive Technologies. IGI Global (2011). https://doi.org/10.4018/978-1-61350-098-9
17. Mauri, C.: Enable viacam (2017). http://eviacam.crea-si.com/index.php. Accessed 31 Jan 2022
18. Mauri, C.: Eva facial mouse (2018). https://github.com/cmauri/eva_facial_mouse. Accessed 31 Jan 2022
19. MyGaze: Mygaze assistive (2018). http://www.mygaze.com/products/mygaze-assistive/. Accessed 16 July 2018
20. Oy, Q.: Quha zono (2018). http://www.quha.com/products-2/zono/. Accessed 15 July 2018
21. Polacek, O., Grill, T., Tscheligi, M.: Nosetapping: what else can you do with your nose? In: Proceedings of the 12th ACM International Conference on Mobile and Ubiquitous Multimedia (2013)
22. Ruiz, N., Chong, E., Rehg, J.M.: Fine-grained head pose estimation without key-points. In: Proceedings of the IEEE Conference on Computer Vision and Pattern Recognition Workshops, pp. 2074–2083 (2018)
23. Tang, X., Du, D.K., He, Z., Liu, J.: Pyramidbox: a context-assisted single shot face detector. CoRR (2018). http://arxiv.org/abs/1803.07737
24. Turturici, M., Fanucci, L.: Inertial human interface device for smartphone and tablet dedicated to people with motor disability. In: Volume 33: Assistive Technology: From Research to Practice. Assistive Technology Research Series (2013). https://doi.org/10.3233/978-1-61499-304-9-494
25. Viola, P., Jones, M.: Rapid object detection using a boosted cascade of simple features. In: Proceedings of the 2001 IEEE Computer Society Conference on Computer Vision and Pattern Recognition, CVPR 2001, vol. 1, pp. I-I. IEEE (2001)
26. Wang, X., Bo, L., Li, F.: Adaptive wing loss for robust face alignment via heatmap regression. CoRR (2019). http://arxiv.org/abs/1904.07399
27. Wu, W., Qian, C., Yang, S., Wang, Q., Cai, Y., Zhou, Q.: Look at boundary: a boundary-aware face alignment algorithm. CoRR (2018). http://arxiv.org/abs/1805.10483
28. Yang, T.Y., Chen, Y.T., Lin, Y.Y., Chuang, Y.Y.: Fsa-net: learning fine-grained structure aggregation for head pose estimation from a single image. In: Proceedings of the IEEE/CVF Conference on Computer Vision and Pattern Recognition, pp. 1087–1096 (2019)

Cognitive Disabilities and Accessibility

Cognitive Disabilities and Accessibility

Introduction to the Special Thematic Session

Klaus Miesenberger[1](✉), Susanne Dirks[2], Christian Bühler[2], and Peter Heumader[1]

[1] Institute Integriert Studieren, Johannes Kepler University, Altenbergerstraße 69, Linz, Austria
{klaus.miesenberger,peter.heumader}@jku.at
[2] TU Dortmund University, 44227 Dortmund, Germany
{susanne.dirks,christian.buehler}@tu-dortmund.de

Abstract. This STS, following a series of STSs and sessions on Cognitive Disabilities and Accessibility in ICCHP over more than two decades, documents the development on how the neurodivergent people and their support/care sector develops in defining and addressing needs towards R&D for both Accessibility and Assistive Technologies (AT). It reports on progress in guidelines, standards, methods, techniques, and tools for addressing Accessibility. And it gives a comprehensive overview to new and innovative AT solutions and service provision models for better participation, including studies and reflection on efficiency, effectiveness and impact on social inclusion and quality of life. This is accompanied by reflections on socio-economic, business and policy/political developments.

Keywords: Cognitive disabilities · Cognitive Accessibility · Assistive technology · Digital inclusion

1 Introduction and Context

Since its start in the late 1980ies ICCHP has been giving a particular focus to Cognitive Accessibility [e.g. 1, 2] and for 8 years now it promotes a Special Thematic Session on the topic [3–5]. The series of STSs provides a comprehensive overview to the developments, highlights, and hot topics in Cognitive Accessibility and ATs. The session for this edition called for ideas, research, development, project, practice, and evaluation related to

- Digital technologies (software, apps, ATs) for people with cognitive impairments
- Cognitive Accessibility of everyday technologies and eLearning environments
- eLearning environments for learners with learning difficulties (accessible MOOCs, LMS, VLEs)
- Participatory software development
- Digital support systems for people with dementia
- Use of Augmented Reality, Virtual Reality or Gaming elements in digital technologies for people with learning disabilities

K. Miesenberger et al. (Eds.): ICCHP-AAATE 2022, LNCS 13341, pp. 409–416, 2022.
https://doi.org/10.1007/978-3-031-08648-9_47

The potential of digital technology, the HCI, the Internet and the upcoming technical developments framing the digital society [6] for people with disabilities has been recognized at political and following this at legal level [e.g., 7–9]. We see a considerable advance in the public awareness for AT and Accessibility at all levels. A large number of countries have ratified the UN Convention on the Rights of Persons with Disabilities (UNCRPD) [7], and WCAG 2.1 [10] has become the world standard for creating accessible digital content, entering as a reference in legislation. The United Nations 2030 Agenda for Sustainable Development has called on all member states to take action to end poverty and disadvantage. Of the 17 defined goals, goal 10 ('Reduce inequality within and among countries') focuses directly on improving social, economic, and political inclusion of people with disabilities [11].

The potential is taken up for personal quality of life and participation in all domains by people with disabilities and their sector. More and more the Accessibility requirements addressed at mainstream developers and designers are accepted as a business opportunity both in terms of reaching out to all potential clients and also to include diversity into the workforce. This makes the progress in Accessibility and AT remarkable. We see mainstream ICT taking up Accessibility, supported by a growing number of consulting and expert companies and organizations. We see more and better assistive functionalities integrated in mainstream products and more and better specialized ATs for addressing specific and personal requirements of users, as documented also in these proceedings [12].

Basically, this situation also holds true for Cognitive Accessibility and AT for supporting cognitive access. But still we can identify a gap between general Accessibility and AT developments as outlined above and the lagging behind Cognitive Accessibility. This target group, or better to say, the broad group of users with neurodivergent challenges, has been underrepresented in the Accessibility and AT field, what is seen in the only recent catching up in the standardization efforts of Accessibility [e.g., 14]. Core reasons are on the on hand that people with cognitive disabilities lack in power of representing themselves and expressing their needs and on the other hand the complexity of parametrizing the diversity of requirements, defining according guidelines and standards and allowing efficient and large-scale implementation of Accessibility. Allowing and supporting personalization of content (responsibility of designers, developers, and content authors) and making the actual implementation of Accessibility part of the service delivery process have been outlined as the key factors for progress.

This STS supports taking up these challenges, documents and discusses domains as layout adaption, tools supporting the production and integration of Plain and Easy Language, symbol, picture, videos or other dynamic content as e.g., 3D. At a more basic level, a better and more efficient integration of methods and tools known from other groups of people with disabilities as e.g., speech output, screen/layout adaption and other tools supporting reading, writing, calculating, planning, memorizing and other cognitive tasks is still to be researched [e.g., 12, 13]. We explore new ideas of using upcoming technologies as Artificial Intelligence for user tracking and profiling to better adapt content and interaction for understandability, Smart Environments for integrating cognitive support features in everyday life (e.g., education, work, travel, leisure, culture, religion, politics, administration) or new Assistive Technologies (AT) for overcoming functional limitations.

2 Addressing the Broad Aspects of Cognitive Accessibility: Neurodiversity

With this, the STS contributes to structuring the broad diversity of issues outlined over the years, which can be summarized and categorized today following the W3C/WAI working group on Cognitive Accessibility [14] and recently published in a Pilot Study on Inclusive Web-Accessibility for Persons with Cognitive Disabilities by Funka for the European Commission [15]:

- Reading
- Writing
- Understanding
- Calculation
- Focusing on a task or information, keeping the focus
- Managing tasks
- Memory
- Managing time (planning, allocating, and controlling)
- Managing choices (evaluating options, deciding)

These efforts in structuring more granular functional challenges and support needs, which are considerably divers in and cross user groups, define a good orientation what Accessibility and ATs have to address to better adapt to personal requirements.

3 Contribution to Cognitive Disabilities and Accessibility

This year the session includes publications accepted for the Open Access Compendium of ICCHP, publishing scientific papers which are not so much on engineering and technology but more service, care, policy, and practice. Together the contributions complement and prolongate the series of STSs making it a unique collection and resource. The following provides a cross-publication discussion of contributions to the STS.

3.1 User Requirements, Profiling and Personalization

Research in Cognitive Accessibility and AT is still very much focused on user requirements, as also the number of papers submitted underlines. This is in line with the ongoing discussions on guidelines and standardization where the identified gap of including the requirements of users from the neurodivergent spectrum is addressed [e.g., 14].

The user study "Living at home with dementia: a multi-stakeholder perspective on challenges during the night" [16] provides new insights and evidence on the challenges of the growing group of people living with dementia. The study identifies core domains to be addressed with Accessibility and AT for end users and the caring environment. A focus is to be given on good structuring day and night activities for relaxation and sleep quality. The results underline once more the need of a person-centered approach respecting the environmental, personal, and mental factors including habits and behaviors. Collecting and documenting them in time for later sharing and use by all stakeholders is to be addressed in ICT, AT, and Accessibility.

In a similar domain the CAREPATH project (see paper in this chapter) includes a user centered study on designing tools for person-centered health care, addressed at people with Mild Cognitive Impairment (MCI). This includes monitoring, data collecting and self-caring features. The results of interviews with patients and informal caregivers underline the broad diversity of requirements and the need of personalization.

Otto (see paper in this chapter) discusses data-driven user profiling and personalization in an application called Tiimo. It presents a study on 50 participants to characterize time management behavior of the broad group of neurodivergent users for scheduling applications. The results allow improving time management tools and defining next steps towards more granular management of tasks and subtasks.

Hauser [17] presents a study on user requirements forming the starting point for an e-counselling and e-learning app for parents with children having Attention Deficit Hyperactivity Disorder (ADHD). The focus in on the needs of care givers, parents and therapists identifying what support is needed to successful deal with the situation. Motivation for self-care and organization (e.g., diet, contacts to organizations and experts, peer-groups) and information on ADHD and methods, tools and techniques for awareness and understanding are identified as key domains. Better understanding ADHD through the use of new media (e.g., videos) is to be addressed. Low-level access to information is proven as a key requirement to improve the situation by using the available state of the art and allowing and educated selection from what is available.

3.2 Language Use and Language Technology

An important set of methods, techniques, tools, and services for Cognitive Accessibility and ATs is related to translation of content into Easy to Read or Plain Language and annotating content with symbols, pictures, videos and/or other dynamic content supporting access. In terms of tools, an initial focus on automation (e.g., translation, annotation) with AI based tools is to be accompanied with approaches integrating technology into service provision infrastructures.

Suárez-Figueroa (see paper in this chapter) presents an approach of using easy to read for adapting captions. Many user groups of captions are challenged due to the complexity of the content in captions and easy to read might be an approach to make captions better usable and accessible. A user study identified handling repetitions as a key domain which will allow better copying with the amount of information. This led to a new method for handling repetitions for better comprehension of captions.

In her second contribution, Suárez-Figueroa [18] addresses the issue of understanding content when reading by developing a novel approach for auto-adapting micro poems. A comparative study showed that subjects responded with different questions to the adapted poems due to differing affects as emotions, memories, or judgements. The study concludes with an outline of the effects of adaptation on emotions what invites to consider the approach for other content domains.

Striegl (see paper in this chapter) focusses on the usability of voice assistant-based CBT (Computer Based Training) for Age-related Depression. Testing with 14 users voice assistants for CBT showed the potential for reducing depression and the importance of respecting preferences (e.g., voice assistance over chat pots), in particular for older users. Empathy is identified as a core issue in design and use of ATs.

In a closely related study, Gotthardt (see paper in this chapter) provides evidence on the usefulness of voice-based CBT for students and the effect of empathy-driven dialog management on treating depression.

Abend [19] discusses the use and uptake of services in easy to read and also sign language in the German speaking area based. The study includes examples of web content made available at web pages of the federal administration. This allows analyzing the effect of linguistic patterns of Web language and rules for easy to read on behavior of users and defining further research demands and approaches.

3.3 ATs, Applications and Service Provision Support for People with Cognitive Disabilities

Since years the need for R&D for better and more effective tools both for users and the caring environment is underlined in the STS. Manifold approaches discuss new ideas and concepts of tools addressing the needs of both target groups in service provision.

Bosse [20] outlines the potential and viability of using Virtual Reality (VR) as a method and tool for cognitive ATs, Cognitive Accessibility and service provision. The study analyses the grade of immersion and the level of action in VR. The study with 20 end users is based on adaption of VR use cases, training, and empowerment of users. The result demands for accessible design thinking and transferability to other domains.

ACCESS+ is a museum application for people with Cognitive Disabilities, also including Augmenting and Alternative Communication (AAC) features. Soares Guedes (see paper in this chapter) describes and discusses a user centered approach from ideation to testing and redesign and respecting recommendations from experts.

3.4 Cognitive Accessibility and AT for Autism

Autism is gaining more attention in Accessibility and AT since several years, also seen in the series of this STS. This underlines the potential of accessible ICT and AT for this user group. It outlines the viability and usefulness of existing Cognitive Accessibility and AT approaches for this user group facilitating new and innovative solutions.

Early identification of cognitive challenges of children, which might be related to autism, is of key importance for successful interventions and therefore for successful application of Accessibility measures and AT. Cesario [21] addresses this need by a tool for supporting pre-school teachers in identifying early signs of autism spectrum disorder. A mobile application (NEMO) helping in observing and analyzing is presented. A user centered approach, taken the broad state of the art into account, has been taken in a cyclic development approach.

Sik Lanyi [22] presents "InfoBase", a user-friendly online database to support people with autism for the Hungarian National Autistic Association (HNAA). The paper discusses the diverse media, organizations and services included and the design process again allowing to learn and transfer results to other R&D approaches. A good overview and easy access to AT and features supporting cognitive access is needed.

Covarubias (see paper in this chapter) discusses examples of Augmented Reality games for children with autism spectrum disorders. By researching and taking up the potential of XR/VR/AR approaches to support attention and memorizing are explored. Psycho-cognitive aspects of symbolic and semantic storage are considered which can be better addressed in 3D environments.

Sacchi [23] presents a review on AT available and in use for workers with autism. He underlines the availability of many tools which are to be considered and identifies issues and domains to close the gap in comparison to the actual level of use.

4 Discussion

Once more a very positive trend towards more interest and effort in taking up the challenges of Cognitive Accessibility, ATs and more efficient and professional digitally supported service provision is identified. The sector is on its way to catch up with the identified gap and lag in Accessibility and AT. Progress is seen in providing a user-focused, data driven and usable base for better guidelines, standards and targeted policies as well as administrative measures. It is in particular important to highlight, that R&D becomes better able to address the diversity of needs in the neurodivergent spectrum by supporting personalization and selection of functionalities. But there is still evidence for the need of measures to make the information society more accessible also for these groups through enhanced Accessibility, ATs and service provision.

The flexibility and adaptability of systems based on user requirements studies, predefining possibilities for tracking and AI for better understanding and managing the needs, allows addressing complex context of these target groups including users, their care and support environment and the intended inclusive settings in everyday life. The focus on service provision and reflecting on the wholistic situation underlines the better and more comprehensive understanding of Cognitive Accessibility in its technical, social, psych-cognitive but also organizational dimensions. This let us expect targeted future R&D and upcoming solutions in the near future.

Cognitive Accessibility is on its way to play its role at equal level in the Accessibility and AT movement.

Acknowledgement. This session and this introduction have been facilitated in the frame of the Easy Reading project, which received funding from the European Union's Horizon 2020 research and innovation program under grant agreement No. 780529.

References

1. Chapter/Session: Easy to web between science of education, information design and (speech) technology. In: Miesenberger, K., Karshmer, A., Penaz, P., Zagler, W. (eds.) ICCHP 2012,

Part II. LNCS, vol 7383, p. 361ff, Springer, Heidelberg. https://doi.org/10.1007/978-3-642-31534-3
2. Chapters/Sessions: Towards e-inclusion for people with intellectual disabilities, People with cognitive disabilities: AT, ICT & AAC. In: Miesenberger, K., Fels, D., Archambault, D., Penaz, P., Zagler, W. (eds.) ICCHP 2014, Part I. LNCS, vol 8547, pp.157ff, 448ff. Springer, Heidelberg. https://doi.org/10.1007/978-3-319-08596-8
3. Edler, C.: Towards e-Inclusion for people with intellectual disabilities: introduction to the special thematic session. In: Miesenberger, K., Bühler, C., Penaz, P. (eds.) ICCHP 2016. LNCS, vol 9759, p. 285ff. Springer, Heidelberg. https://doi.org/10.1007/978-3-319-41267-2
4. Dirks, S., Bühler, C., Edler, C.: Digital inclusion through accessible technologies - introduction to the special thematic session. In: Miesenberger, K., Kouroupetroglou, G. (eds.) ICCHP 2018, Part I. LNCS, vol. 10896, p. 404ff. Springer, Cham (2018). https://doi.org/10.1007/978-3-319-94277-3_67
5. Dirks, S., Bühler, C., Edler, C., Miesenberger, K., Heumader, P.: Cognitive disabilities and accessibility - pushing the boundaries of inclusion using digital technologies and accessible eLearning environments. In: Miesenberger, K., Manduchi, R., Covarrubias Rodriguez, M., Peňáz, P. (eds.) ICCHP 2020, Part II. LNCS, vol. 12377, p. 42ff. Springer, Cham (2020). https://doi.org/10.1007/978-3-030-58805-2_6
6. Miesenberger, K.: Best practice in design for all. In: Stephanidis, C. (ed.) The Universal Access Handbook. CRC Press, Boca Raton (2009)
7. United Nations: Convention on the Rights of People with Disabilities 2006, April 2022. https://www.un.org/development/desa/disabilities/convention-on-the-rights-of-persons-with-disabilities.html
8. ETSI/European Commission: Accessibility requirements for ICT products and services, April 2022. https://www.etsi.org/deliver/etsi_en/301500_301599/301549/03.02.01_60/en_301549v030201p.pdf
9. European Commission: European Accessibility Act (EAA), April 2022. https://ec.europa.eu/social/main.jsp?catId=1202
10. W3C/WAI/ISO: Web Content Accessibility Guidelines (WCAG) 2.1, ISO/IEC 40500:2012 Web Content Accessibility Guidelines 2.0, April 2022. https://www.w3.org/TR/WCAG21/
11. United Nations Sustainable Development Goals, Goal 10 – Reduce inequality within and among countries, June 2020. https://sustainabledevelopment.un.org/sdg10
12. Miesenberger, K., Edler, C., Heumader, P., Petz, A.: Tools and applications for cognitive accessibility. In: Yesilada, Y., Harper, S. (eds.) Web Accessibility: A Foundation for Research. HIS, pp. 523–546. Springer, London (2019). https://doi.org/10.1007/978-1-4471-7440-0_28
13. Dirks, S., Bühler, C.: Participation and autonomy for users with ABI through easy social media access. In: Cudd, P., de Witte, L.P. (eds.) Harnessing the Power of Technology to Improve Lives. Proceedings of the 14th European Conference on the Advancements of Assistive Technology. Studies in Health Technology and Informatics, vol. 242. IOS Press (2017)
14. W3C/WAI: Cognitive and Learning Disabilities Accessibility Task Force (Coga TF) of the AG WG and APA WG, April 2022. https://www.w3.org/WAI/GL/task-forces/coga
15. Kjellstrand, S., Laurin, S., Mohamed, S., Chowdhury, N.: Pilot Project Study: Inclusive Web-Accessibility for Persons with Cognitive Disabilities. European Commission, Directorate-General for Communications Networks, Content and Technology, Luxembourg (2020)
16. Sponselee, A.: Living at home with dementia: a multi-stakeholder perspective on challenges during the night. In: Petz, A., Hoogerwerf, E.-J., Mavrou, K. (eds.) Assistive Technology, Accessibility and (e)Inclusion, ICCHP-AAATE 2022 Open Access Compendium (accepted for publication). https://www.icchp-aaate.org. Johannes Kepler University Linz, Austria

17. Hauser, C.: User requirements for an e-Counselling and e-Learning app for parents with children with attention deficit hyperactivity disorder. In: Petz, A., Hoogerwerf, E.-J., Mavrou, K. (eds.) Assistive Technology, Accessibility and (e)Inclusion, ICCHP-AATE 2022 Open Access Compendium (accepted for publication). https://www.icchp-aaate.org. Johannes Kepler University Linz, Austria
18. Suárez-Figueroa, M.C.: Shall the easy-to-read adaptation of micropoems affect emotions? In: Petz, A., Hoogerwerf, E.-J., Mavrou, K. (eds.) Assistive Technology, Accessibility and (e)Inclusion, ICCHP-AATE 2022 Open Access Compendium (accepted for publication). https://www.icchp-aaate.org. Johannes Kepler University Linz, Austria
19. Abend, S.: Who uses online services in easy-to-read language and German sign language and how? In: Petz, A., Hoogerwerf, E.-J., Mavrou, K. (eds.) Assistive Technology, Accessibility and (e)Inclusion, ICCHP-AATE 2022 Open Access Compendium (accepted for publication). https://www.icchp-aaate.org. Johannes Kepler University Linz, Austria
20. Bosse, I.: Virtual reality for children with special needs. In: Petz, A., Hoogerwerf, E.-J., Mavrou, K. (eds.) Assistive Technology, Accessibility and (e)Inclusion, ICCHP-AATE 2022 Open Access Compendium (accepted for publication). https://www.icchp-aaate.org. Johannes Kepler University Linz, Austria
21. Cesario, L.: Towards a mobile application to support pre-school teachers observing early signs of autism spectrum disorder. In: Petz, A., Hoogerwerf, E.-J., Mavrou, K. (eds.) Assistive Technology, Accessibility and (e)Inclusion, ICCHP-AATE 2022 Open Access Compendium (accepted for publication). https://www.icchp-aaate.org. Johannes Kepler University Linz, Austria
22. Sik Lanyi, C.: "InfoBase" - design a user-friendly online database to support people with autism. In: Petz, A., Hoogerwerf, E.-J., Mavrou, K. (eds.) Assistive Technology, Accessibility and (e)Inclusion, ICCHP-AATE 2022 Open Access Compendium (accepted for publication). https://www.icchp-aaate.org. Johannes Kepler University Linz, Austria
23. Sacchi, F.: Promoting labour market inclusion: a review of assistive technologies for workers with autism spectrum disorder. In: Petz, A., Hoogerwerf, E.-J., Mavrou, K. (eds.) Assistive Technology, Accessibility and (e)Inclusion, ICCHP-AATE 2022 Open Access Compendium (accepted for publication). https://www.icchp-aaate.org. Johannes Kepler University Linz, Austria

First Attempt to an Easy-to-Read Adaptation of Repetitions in Captions

Mari Carmen Suárez-Figueroa[1(✉)], Isam Diab[1], Álvaro González[1], and Jesica Rivero-Espinosa[2]

[1] Ontology Engineering Group (OEG), Universidad Politécnica de Madrid (UPM), Madrid, Spain
mcsuarez@fi.upm.es, isam.diab@upm.es, a.gsanz@alumnos.upm.es
[2] Inserta Innovación, Madrid, Spain
jrivero@fundaciononce.es

Abstract. Subtitles of audiovisual content produced in the same language as the oral discourse are called captions. Such type of subtitles is crucial to ensure that audiovisual resources have inclusive and equal access for people with functional diversity. When talking about people with reading comprehension difficulties, captions must be written in easy reading. During the subtitling process, it is important to bear in mind that the oral mode includes some unique characteristics such as the use of punctual reiterations or redundancies. However, excessive repetition in the written mode slows down reading and makes it difficult to understand. Currently, repetition is not considered as a problematic aspect in the Easy-to-Read (E2R) Methodology, since this linguistic resource is not frequent in the written mode. Despite this, we believe that some features of the oral mode, such as repetitions, should be considered within the captioning process. Hence, our current research is focused on discovering whether captions with repetitions, coming from the oral mode, can be a problem for people with cognitive disabilities. To achieve such a goal, we performed a user study whose main goal is to find out whether people with reading comprehension difficulties prefer audiovisual captions with or without repetitions. Initial findings indicate that captions without repetitions are the most preferred ones. For this reason, we have also created a method for automatically adapting repetitions in captions following an E2R approach.

Keywords: Easy-to-Read methodology · Lexical repetitions · Captions

1 Introduction

One way of achieving accessibility in audiovisual resources, such as video content, live streams or video conferencing, is to provide captions or intralinguistic subtitles. According to the W3C Web Accessibility Initiative, captions are a text

K. Miesenberger et al. (Eds.): ICCHP-AAATE 2022, LNCS 13341, pp. 417–424, 2022.
https://doi.org/10.1007/978-3-031-08648-9_48

version of the speech and non-speech audio information needed to understand the content[1], mainly by people who are deaf and hard-of-hearing.

During the subtitling process a balance between text cohesion and text length is needed. There are two main strategies to accomplish such a balance [12]: (a) the reduction of linguistic redundancy to a minimum and (b) the omission of certain elements which are not essential for understanding the message. Both strategies refer to the so-called "intrasemiotic redundancy" [11], and are related to spoken language features, such as repetitions and false starts. According to [1], any changes performed during the subtitling process must ensure the coherence and final understanding of the subtitling.

As already mentioned, captions and, thus, the intralingual subtitling process are mainly focused on helping people with hearing difficulties. In order to provide inclusive and equal access to audiovisual resources to people with cognitive disabilities or reading comprehension difficulties, it is also crucial to guarantee cognitive accessibility. There are two main approaches to accomplish such an accessibility: (a) applying text simplification and (b) applying the Easy-to-Read (E2R) Methodology. On the one hand, text simplification [3] has as goal to make text easier to read without significantly impacting the content; on the other hand, the main goal of the E2R Methodology [2] is to present clear and easily understood documents for people with cognitive or intellectual disabilities, among others.

Regarding the adaptation of captions following the E2R Methodology, the so-called E2R captions, it is worth mentioning (a) a study for the identification of cues and types of information to create subtitles for people with intellectual disabilities [16]; (b) a study for determining which type of subtitles (subtitles for the deaf and hard-of-hearing or E2R captions) is preferred by elderly people [14]; and (c) a study to identify the potential benefits of adopting E2R subtitles for immersive media [6].

However, to the best of our knowledge, there is no specific research on how typical features of oral discourse, such as repetitions, are treated in E2R captions. Repetitions in the oral mode are used with a clear emphatic intent; however, repetitions in the written mode could slow down reading and make it difficult to understand. Currently, repetitions are not considered as a problem in the E2R Methodology, since this linguistic element is not frequent in written texts.

To cover the identified gap, we pose the following research question: "What are the reading preferences of people with reading comprehension difficulties or with cognitive impairments regarding subtitles in E2R? Do they prefer reading subtitles with repetitions or reading subtitles without repetitions?". Given that our main goal is to discover whether repetitions affect the understanding of the message, we focus on the so-called lexical repetitions[2], since such repetitions are used to put emphasis on the meaning [8]. For answering our research question, we conducted a user study grounded on the belief that treating repetitions in E2R captions will be beneficial in order to have more cognitive accessible captions.

[1] https://www.w3.org/WAI/media/av/captions/.

[2] We do not consider phonological or morphological ones.

After the analysis of our study, findings indicate that study participants consider captions without repetitions as the easiest and the most preferred reading option. Based on these results, we decided (a) to create a method for adapting lexical repetitions in captions written in Spanish with an E2R approach and (b) to implement a proof of concept based on such a method.

The rest of the paper is organized as follows: Sect. 2 is devoted to the state of the art on explaining the repetition as a linguistic phenomenon and presenting automatic approaches for its identification. In Sect. 3 we describe the user study performed; while Sect. 4 presents our contributions for automatically adapting lexical repetitions in captions written in Spanish with an E2R approach. Finally, we show some conclusions and future work.

2 State of the Art

Since we developed a method to automatically detect repetition occurrences in subtitles and adapt them into E2R versions, as mentioned in Sect. 1, this section is devoted to (a) describing the repetition as a linguistic phenomenon (definition, functions and typology), and (b) summarizing the automatic approaches carried out regarding the identification of repetitions.

In broad terms, repetition is a linguistic phenomenon which consists of reiterating in its formal aspect a part or the totality of the elements of a previous segment or utterance, with possible modifications (e.g. of intonation or deictic units) and with variations in the semantic and pragmatic meaning of the new segment with respect to the previous one [9]. In addition, lexical reiteration is a constant in natural languages [8], i.e. it is not specific to a particular language typology, but presents a universal nature in human language.

The repeated use of words, or word pattern (rhyme, alliteration, anaphora, parallelism, etc.), is a powerful rhetorical instrument for producing emphasis, intensity, clarity, or exaggeration. Indeed, as numerous researchers agree [17], speakers reiterate a word or phrase to gain time (stalling), link the content of an utterance to preceding utterances (cohesion), ensure the sense of the content (coherence), indicate that they are simply listening, show understanding or surprise (connection), express agreement or disagreement (affiliation), clarify a previous statement (interaction), self-correct or correct their interlocutor or imitate her/him (parody), hold or yield a turn, or for other purposes.

Besides these rhetorical and pragmatic functions of the repetition, it has also been analysed its syntactic formalisation, i.e. which linguistic elements constitute the repetition and how they are combined. Since our study addresses repetition occurrences in Spanish, we have considered some syntax aspects in that language. In this sense, authors [8,10] identified three main types of syntactic structures in Spanish. Firstly, (1) juxtaposition, where the lexical repetition occurs immediately adjacent to the emphasised word class. The predominant combinations are verb + verb (e.g. ***Corriendo corriendo*** *llegarás más lejos*[3]) and adjective +

[3] Literal Translation: *Running running you will get further.*; Translation Sense: *You will get further by running hard.*

adjective (e.g. *Me encantan los claveles* ***rojos rojos***[4]). In the second structure, (2) coordination, the lexical repetition occurs through the interposition of a linking element. Such a link could be of three types: a conjunction (e.g. *No paró de* ***comer y comer***[5]), a relative -pronoun or adverb- (e.g. *Pondremos arroz para comer* ***venga quien venga***[6]), or a preposition (e.g. *No me quejaré,* ***a pesar de los pesares***[7]). Finally, (3) anteposition is the third scheme proposed. Such a structure achieves the focalisation of the highlighted element, i.e. a kind of semantic underlining (e.g. *¡Hombre!* ***Comer come***, *pero muy poco*[8]).

To the best of our knowledge, attempts on identifying repetition occurrences in an automatic way are scarce. One of those research works [4] proposed an automatic detection system of self-repetitions in a human-machine dialogue. In this line, the study by [5], following the same procedure, presented a method for the automatic detection and characterization of the so-called other-repetitions, particularly in the context of spontaneous French dialogues. Both research works [4,5] based their methods on a two-stages process. Firstly, a set of candidates are proposed by using a pattern matching search. The second step filters those candidates to accept or reject them by (a) using information from syntax, semantic and acoustic levels [4], or (b) establishing a set of rules [5].

In addition to those, several neural network-based approaches for repetition detection have been reported during the last years. On the one hand, repetitions have been detected in disordered speech: (a) in [15] the automatic detection of syllable repetition is one of the important parameters in assessing the stuttered speech objectively; and (b) in [7] automatic detection of repetitions serves as a preprocessing step in the method proposed to improve dysarthric speech to text alignment. And, on the other hand, in [13] repetitions are detected in Spoken Dialogue Systems (SDS). This work assumes that repetitions can be a symptom of problematic communication in SDS, and thus, a sign of problematic turns. The approach combines the alignment score obtained using phonetic distances with dialogue-related features to improve repetition detection.

Nevertheless, according to our latest knowledge, there are not existing approaches handling the automatic transformation of lexical repetitions into simpler structures in order to facilitate the reading comprehension process.

3 User Study

This user study intended to answer the research question presented in Sect. 1. Thus, the goal of such a study was two-fold: on one hand, it sought to find out whether people with reading comprehension problems or with cognitive

[4] Lit. Transl.: *I love red red carnations.*; Transl. Sense: *I do love red carnations.*
[5] Lit. Transl.: *He did not stop eating and eating.*; Transl. Sense: *He ate too much.*
[6] Lit. Transl. and Transl. Sense: *We will cook rice whoever comes.*
[7] Lit. Transl. and Transl. Sense: *I will not complain despite the odds.*
[8] Lit. Transl.: **Sure! Eat, she does eat, but not much.*; Transl. Sense: *Sure! She does eat, but not much.* (Henceforth, the asterisk symbol (*) will be used to indicate ungrammatical structures).

impairments prefer audiovisual captions with or without repetitions; and, on the other hand, the study aimed at identifying the most prefer captions from a set of captions with and without repetitions[9]. For this purpose, we developed a questionnaire written in Spanish and implemented as a Google Form[10]. Such a questionnaire was launched in January 2022 through mailing lists of autonomic federations and associations of people with cognitive impairments in Spain.

The questionnaire is divided into two main parts: (1) a section that includes questions for capturing data about which captions are easier or better understood; and (2) a final part with questions related to the participants' demographics, knowledge, background, and experience. In the first part of the questionnaire, participants were asked about their preferences with respect to the simplicity of groups of short sentences written in Spanish coming from oral conversations that could be captions in audiovisual resources. Each group includes an original sentence with lexical repetitions (e.g. *Tuvo* ***bastante bastante*** *suerte en el examen*[11]) and one or more sentences that are the result of adapting lexical repetitions in the original sentence with an E2R approach in mind (e.g. *Tuvo una suerte en el examen notable*, *Tuvo una suerte notable en el examen*, and *Tuvo mucha suerte en el examen*). This part of the questionnaire is composed of 16 questions of which 12 include sentences with juxtaposition repetitions and four include sentences with coordination repetitions. We put our efforts of these types of repetitions because the other type (anteposition) has a less redundancy character, since the repetition is not literal (e.g. ***Entender, entiendo***, *pero no hablo*[12]). The collection of sentences used in the questionnaire was built using two oral corpus: COSER[13] and C-Or-DiAL[14].

The 86 participants (47 female, 37 male, and 2 participants who preferred not to provide gender information) included representatives from 4 different autonomous communities in Spain: Andalucía (39.5%), Comunidad Valenciana (37.2%), Madrid (22.1%), and one participant from Galicia. Most of the participants (41.9%) had a medium level of reading comprehension, whereas 38.4% had a high level and 11.6% a low level[15]. Regarding the age range, half of the participants ranged from 31 to 45 years old, 29.1% from 18 to 30, 16.3% were from 46 to 60, and one participant was over 60 years old. With respect to their impairments, most of the participants (73.8%) have an intellectual disability, followed by those (7.1%) with an intellectual disability and a mental disease, and those (7.1%) who have intellectual and physical disabilities.

Findings indicate that, overall, participants prefer reading captions without lexical repetitions. The most preferred caption in the 16 questions was always one

[9] To measure the level of participants' comprehension is out of the scope of this paper.
[10] https://forms.gle/9R8ET2NDszcGf5eL8.
[11] Lit. Transl.: *She had quite a lot of luck in the test.*; Transl. Sense: *She was quite lucky in the test.*
[12] Lit. Transl.: **Understand, I do understand, but I do not speak [this language]*.; Transl. Sense: *I do understand it, but I do not speak [this language].*
[13] http://www.corpusrural.es/index.php.
[14] http://lablita.it/app/cordial/corpus.php.
[15] Some participants declined to supply their level, while others did not know about it.

of the adapted sentences. It is also worth noting that the highest percentage for the selection of a caption with lexical repetitions was 10.5% (only 9 participants out of 86). These data reply our research question presented in Sect. 1 and reveals that participants' preferences can be classified into the following scenarios: **Scenario A.** Captions that are adapted by removing repetitions. In this case, we can distinguish between (a) a total removal, which means that all the repeated elements are deleted (e.g. original caption: *Tengo* ***muy muy*** *pocas ganas de ver a Jose*, adapted caption: *Tengo Ø pocas ganas de ver a Jose*); and (b) a partial removal, which stands for deleting a specific number of repeated elements so the result is a caption with just one element (e.g. original caption: *Encantada de conocerte, Ana, ¿eres de un pueblo o de* ***Madrid Madrid****?*, adapted caption: *Encantada de conocerte, Ana, ¿eres de un pueblo o de Madrid?*); and **Scenario B.** Captions that are adapted by replacing repetitions with other synonym linguistic structures (e.g. original caption: *Luis tuvo* ***bastante bastante*** *suerte en el examen*, adapted caption: *Luis tuvo mucha suerte en el examen*). It is worth mentioning that the first scenario was significantly more selected (62.5%) than the second one (37.5%) when we analyzed the whole questionnaire.

In more specific detail, this first approximation suggests that these two scenarios are related to the semantic intensity of the reiterated elements. That is, lexical repetitions can express two types of intensification: quantitative or qualitative. The former is achieved by means of semantically gradable words; the latter, on the other hand, occurs when the repeated element does not accept any sort of gradation. In this sense, we observe that the replacement of the repetition structure presented in Scenario B occurs with gradable elements (evoking quantitative intensification), such as, for instance, quantifying adverbs or qualifying adjectives. In this case, participants' preference tends to either (a) replace the reiterated item with another one semantically higher on the graded scale (e.g. *bastante bastante* > *mucha*), or (b) rephrase the structure by adding an element expressing intensity (e.g. *bonita, bonita, especialmente bonita* > *muy bonita*).

On the other hand, the removal (both total and partial) of the repetition raised in Scenario A occurs with (1) high-intensity gradable elements, since it is not necessary to increase their semantic feature [+intensity] by a lexical reiteration (e.g. *muchas muchas* > *muchas*); with (2) non-gradable elements (evoking qualitative intensification), such as proper nouns (e.g. *de Madrid Madrid* > *de Madrid*). Note that in this example Scenario A cannot arise due to the non-semantic gradation of the elements (e.g. **de muy Madrid*). And, finally, with (3) the so-called false starts in the form of discourse markers (e.g. *sí, sí, claro, claro* > *Ø*), whose function is purely conversational and whose meaning is subtle.

4 Proposal for E2R Adaptations of Lexical Repetitions

Our method for adapting lexical repetitions with an E2R approach is composed of the following activities: (1) Natural Language Processing (NLP), which includes tokenization and part of speech tagging of the original sentence (the one including repetitions), (2) repetition identification, and (3) repetition substitution. In more detail, the repetition identification activity relies on a pattern recognition task and on a repetition verification task. On the one hand, the pattern recognition task is focused on the following patterns: (a) A A (e.g. *La casa está* ***vieja vieja***[16]) y (b) A, A, (y) A (e.g. *Antonio está enfadado porque siempre cena* ***verduras, verduras, y nada más que verduras***[17]). On the other hand, the repetition verification tasks calculates the semantic distance to verify the situation. The activity of substituting repetitions can imply two different types of substitutions: (a) simple substitution, which refers to the elimination of the repeated linguistic structure (this case corresponds to Scenario A) and (b) complex substitution, which involves a replacement of the repeated linguistic structure and a subsequent rephrasing (this case corresponds to Scenario B).

We have developed a web service for adapting repetitions to E2R, based on the aforementioned method. Such a service requires as input a sentence written in Spanish and provides as output an easier version of the original sentence in which repetitions have been adapted with an E2R approach in mind. The service has been implemented in Python and is using spaCy[18] for the NLP tasks.

5 Conclusions and Future Work

In this work, we investigated whether people with reading comprehension difficulties prefer reading subtitles with repetitions or reading subtitles without repetitions. From a general perspective, the user study we carried out suggests that participants consider captions without repetitions as the easiest and the most preferred reading option. Additionally, the data gathered have contributed to identifying the better way to adapt captions with repetitions following an E2R approach. In this sense, it seems that an E2R-based strategy for adapting captions with repetitions should include a decision between removing repetitions and replacing repetitions with other synonym linguistic structures. According with these insights we created a method for adapting lexical repetitions in captions written in Spanish with an E2R approach, that has been implemented as a proof of concept. Our future work includes (a) an analysis of survey data to identify whether demographic aspects have any influence on responses, (b) a deep analysis of the two scenarios to obtain more knowledge about their linguistic features, and (c) the extension of our method with the further outcomes.

Acknowledgements. This research has been financed by Asociación Inserta Innovación (part of Grupo Social Once) through Prosvasi Ciencia y Tecnología Para La Inclusión, A.I.E., within the project ACCESSJOBS. We would like to thank Plena Inclusión España for its help in organizing the study with users, as well as the Federations of Organizations of people with intellectual or developmental disabilities in Madrid, Comunidad Valenciana y Andalucía for their participation in the study.

---

[16] Lit. Transl.: *The house is old old.*; Transl. Sense: *The house is very old.*

[17] Lit. Transl.: *Antonio is angry because he always eats vegetables, vegetables and nothing but vegetables for dinner.*; Transl. Sense: *Antonio is angry because he always eats vegetables for dinner.*

[18] https://spacy.io/.

References

1. AENOR: Subtitulado para personas sordas y personas con discapacidad auditiva (UNE 153010:2012) (2012)
2. AENOR: Lectura fácil. pautas y recomendaciones para la elaboración de documentos (UNE 153101:2018 EX) (2018)
3. Alva-Manchego, F., Scarton, C., Specia, L.: Data-driven sentence simplification: survey and benchmark. Comput. Linguist. **46**(1), 135–187 (2020). https://doi.org/10.1162/coli_a_00370
4. Bear, J., Dowding, J., Shriberg, E.: Integrating multiple knowledge sources for detection and correction of repairs in human-computer dialog. In: 30th Annual Meeting of the Association for Computational Linguistics, pp. 56–63 (1992)
5. Bigi, B., Bertrand, R., Guardiola, M.: Automatic detection of other-repetition occurrences: application to French conversational Speech. In: The 9th edition of the Language Resources and Evaluation Conference, Reykjavik, Iceland, pp. 836–842 (2014)
6. Climent, M.M., Soler-Vilageliu, O., Vila, I.F., Langa, S.F.: Vr360 subtitling: requirements, technology and user experience. IEEE Access **9**, 2819–2838 (2021)
7. Diwakar, G., Karjigi, V.: Improving speech to text alignment based on repetition detection for dysarthric speech. Circuits Syst. Signal Process. **39**(11), 5543–5567 (2020). https://doi.org/10.1007/s00034-020-01419-5
8. Escandell-Vidal, V.: Sobre las reduplicaciones léxicas. Lingüística Española Actual **13**, 71–86 (1991)
9. Garcés Gómez, P.: La repetición: formas y funciones en el discurso oral. Archivo de filología aragonesa **59–60**, 437–456 (2004)
10. García-Page Sánchez, M.: Formas de superlación en español, la repetición. Anuario Galego de Filoloxía **24**, 133–157 (1997)
11. Gottlieb, H.: Subtitles, translation & idioms. Ph.D. thesis, University of Copenhagen (1997). OCLC: 872545808
12. Howard, L.J.: Film subtitling: a challenge for the translator. In: V Encuentros complutenses en torno a la traducción: del 22 al 26 de febrero de 1994. pp. 581–588. Editorial Complutense (1995)
13. Lopes, J., et al.: Detecting repetitions in spoken dialogue systems using phonetic distances. In: Interspeech 2015, pp. 1805–1809. ISCA (2015). https://doi.org/10.21437/Interspeech.2015-60
14. Oncins, E., Bernabé, R., Montagud, M., Uzquiza, V.A.: Accessible scenic arts and virtual reality: a pilot study with aged people about user preferences when reading subtitles in immersive environments. MonTI. Monografías de Traducción e Interpretación **12**, 214–241 (2020). https://doi.org/10.6035/MonTI.2020.12.07
15. Ravikumar, K.M., Reddy, B., Rajagopal, R., Nagaraj, H.C.: Automatic detection of syllable repetition in read speech for objective assessment of stuttered disfluencies. Int. J. Electr. Comput. Eng. **36**, 270–273 (2008)
16. Rodríguez, T.A.: Traducción audiovisual accesible a personas con discapacidad intelectual mediante el uso de subtítulos adaptados. Estudios de Traducción **4**, 199–209 (2014). https://doi.org/10.5209/rev_ESTR.2014.v4.45376
17. Sergio, F.S.: Repetition in dialogue interpreting. In: Kellet, C.J. (ed.) Interpreting Across Genres: Multiple Research Perspectives (2012)

ACCESS+: Designing a Museum Application for People with Intellectual Disabilities

Leandro Soares Guedes[1(✉)], Valentina Ferrari[1], Marilina Mastrogiuseppe[2], Stefania Span[3], and Monica Landoni[1]

[1] Università della Svizzera italiana (USI), Lugano, Switzerland
{leandro.soares.guedes,valentina.ferrari,monica.landoni}@usi.ch
[2] University of Trieste, Trieste, Italy
[3] Cooperativa Sociale Trieste Integrazione a m. Anffas Onlus, Trieste, Italy
https://www.luxia.inf.usi.ch/

Abstract. Inclusive solutions are essential to improve the user experience and overall accessibility. They contribute to the independence and participation of people with disabilities and can be designed for a wide variety of contexts. In this paper, we describe a design cycle from ideation to testing and redesign of ACCESS+, an accessible application to navigate through museum content focusing on people with Intellectual Disabilities (ID). We have focused on personalized and inclusive features so that users could tailor to their needs and preferences icons and font sizes, labels, and backgrounds. Also, users could make sense of the text by looking at symbols via Augmentative and Alternative Communication (AAC), and by listening to text-to-speech of full text with highlight, tone, and pitch configuration. Finally, users could provide different forms of feedback: ratings and comments. We conducted heuristic evaluations with an educator and a psychologist, both specialists in inclusive education, redesigning the interface and moving from a system to a user-friendly terminology. We also followed the specialists' suggestions and made the icons and text of the UI more accessible.

Keywords: Design · Accessibility · Application · Museum · Intellectual Disabilities

1 Introduction

Communication is an essential aspect of our daily lives. The majority of people rely on oral communication, although we also have nonverbal, visual, and written forms.

Technology plays an important role in daily communication by helping people express themselves, learn and access information. When designing and developing technology, accessible solutions contribute to the independence and empowerment of people with intellectual disabilities. Further, they improve the user

K. Miesenberger et al. (Eds.): ICCHP-AAATE 2022, LNCS 13341, pp. 425–431, 2022.
https://doi.org/10.1007/978-3-031-08648-9_49

experience and access to information about cultural heritage sites, like museums and exhibitions.

The museums are crucial for in-person cultural acquisition and learning, but are their digital versions accessible for people with intellectual disabilities? In this work, we designed an accessible application called ACCESS+ as a means to find an answer to this question. We focus on people with intellectual disabilities and the features that could help them interact with technology.

2 Related works

Accessible design can help everyone, not just those with a disability [5]. Nevertheless, existing technical solutions only partially cover the needs of users with Intellectual Disabilities (ID) [3].

Cultural heritage sites are adopting strategies to improve accessibility and participation for all. Involving people with ID in this process contributes to investigating their perceptions and obstacles to accessing knowledge.

The readability and comprehensibility of textual resources are important aspects. Mastrogiuseppe et al. [7] designed and ran a questionnaire using the easy-to-read criteria and assessed perception and physical interaction, language and symbols, content comprehension, and engagement.

Users with different reading abilities can take advantage of the museum content using multisensory experiences [9] and assistive technologies. Examples include instructive applications, tangible objects, augmented reality, and Alternative and Augmentative Communication (AAC).

In the ID community, some people take advantage of an AAC system. Sutherland et al. [11] applied a survey in New Zealand to understand the importance and need for AAC among adults with ID. The study concluded that they have a substantial need for AAC systems.

The design, development, and evaluation are not straightforward activities, and we can take advantage of a multidisciplinary framework [6]. When possible, co-design [8] activities help devise applications to support people with intellectual disabilities (ID). Also, we can benefit from improvisation [10] to deal with challenging and unpredictable situations.

3 Designing an Accessible Museum Application

The ACCESS+ application seeks to enhance access to the museum content with an accessible solution designed with people with intellectual disabilities in mind.

We had several meetings with experts and participants to define the application requirements. The participants belong to a special school in Trieste - Italy, where the age range is from 17 years old. We conducted online meetings and in-person research visits in the previous year to acquire empirical knowledge and develop closer contact with the participants. This long-lasting experience made us realize that several user interface elements are not intuitive for people with ID.

In partnership with the Natural History Museum of Trieste, also located in Italy, we designed ACCESS+. We developed the current content of the application in two different languages (English and Italian). However, we present only the English version here to keep it consistent with the paper language. For research purposes, the application content was limited to the topics the participants were learning and could further appreciate in guided visits. The application in its first version includes already several features that could help people with ID during their interactions.

When designing the ACCESS+, we aimed for a simple, consistent, and customizable design [3,5]. We used conventional mobile application designs (e.g., top bar, burger menu icon, left side menu list) to structure the content. We wanted the application to be similar and consistent to what the users might have already seen/used or may see/use in the future. Regarding fonts, spacing, colors, and dimensions, we referenced the WCAG 2.1 and other W3C/WAI guidelines [1].

We developed ACCESS+ using an open-source UI software development kit called Flutter [4]. This choice allowed us to develop a cross-platform application, in particular, we wanted to be able to deploy for Android, iOS, and the web. Moreover, the application design is responsive so that we can easily use it on mobile, tablet, and desktops. All those technical decisions have been made in order to have a coherent design among different platforms and screen sizes.

We implemented a variety of customizations to allow participants to adapt the interface to their needs (Figures 1a, 1b, 1c).

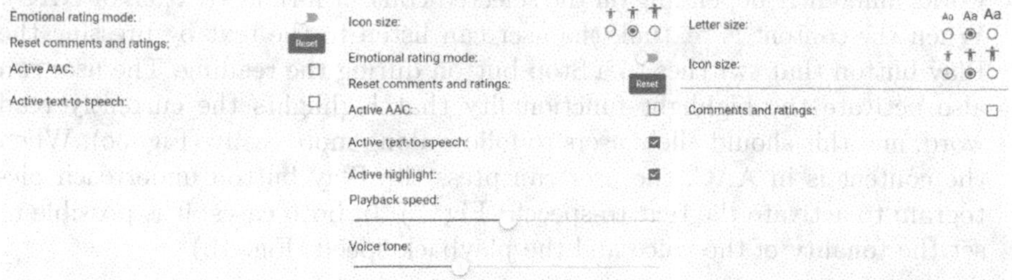

(a) First prototype (b) Full menu (1a) (c) Redesigned page

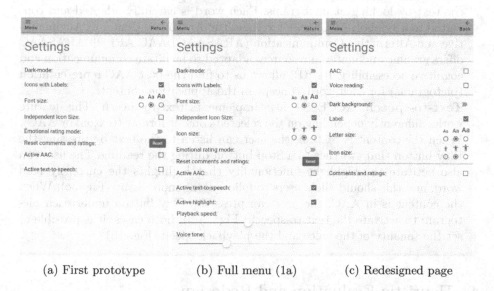

Fig. 1. ACCESS+ Settings page before and after Redesign.

- **Light and Dark modes**. Both modalities have a high contrast between background and text and background and accent color. We limited the range of colors to three (background, text, and accent) for simplicity matters. Except for the emotional rating icons coloring (we will explain the reason below).
- **Three size options**. It is possible to enlarge or reduce the size of the text and icons (together or independently) according to the user's needs. However, we predefined the dimensions to avoid the content overflowing and becoming confusing to the user.
- **Icons labelling**. To support the understanding of standard icons (e.g., arrows, menu button, play button, etc.), we decided to add a textual label so that, even if the users do not recognize the icons, they have a textual alternative to understanding them. Nonetheless, the setting is optional so that users that can not read or find the addition of labels more confusing than helpful can hide the labels.
- **Different feedback options**. The user can give feedback by written comment, rating, or both.
- **Different rating scales**. The user can set the preferred rate scale. Either the Likert-scale Star Assessment (Fig. 3b) or the Emotional Assessment (Fig. 3a). We decided to emphasize negative, neutral, and positive emotions by coloring the icons red, yellow, and green since the differences between the three icons might not be recognisable by some users.
- **Textual content and AAC**. The application allows users to access content in textual form or its AAC representation (Fig. 2). AAC (mainly used by non-hearing and non-speaking users) allows people with ID to make sense of the text by looking at pictograms. Each word is carefully adapted and converted to a symbol. ACCESS+ leverages the Aragonese Center of Augmentative and Alternative Communication (ARASAAC) AAC API [2]. ARASAAC offers graphic and material resources adapted to facilitate communication and cognitive accessibility. Its API allows us to find the best AAC representation (pictograms) for each word/concept in the application content.
- **Text-to-speech**. ACCESS+ also implements text-to-speech. This feature works differently depending on the selected content format (textual or AAC). When the content is textual, the user can listen to the text by pressing the Play button that switches to a Stop button during the reading. The user can also activate the highlight functionality that highlights the currently read word, and this should allow users to follow along more easily (Fig. 3c). When the content is in AAC, the user can press the Play button under each pictogram to activate the text-to-speech (Fig. 2). In both cases, it is possible to set the tonality of the voice and the playback speed (Fig. 1b).

4 Heuristic Evaluation and Redesign

We asked two special education experts to analyze the first prototype and give feedback about possible improvements. One of them is an educator, and the other

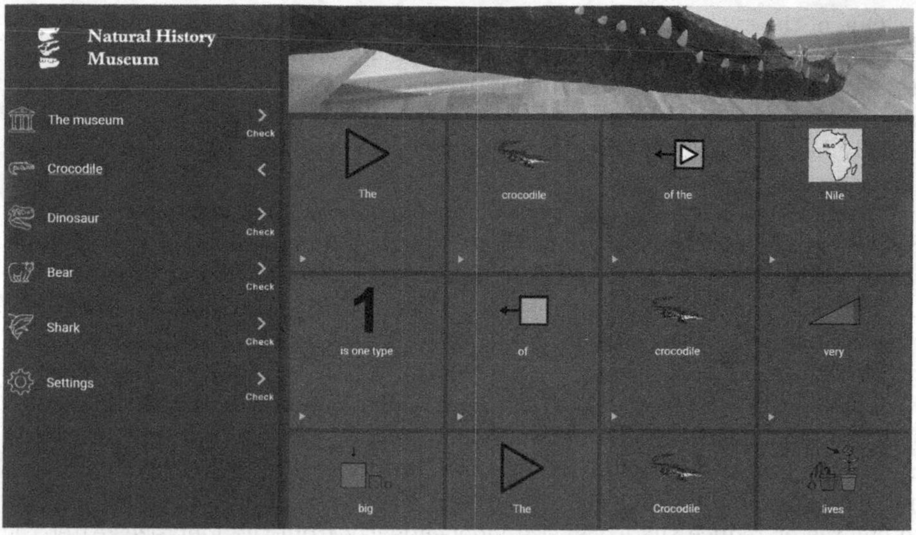

Fig. 2. AAC feature with Dark Mode and Landscape tablet orientation.

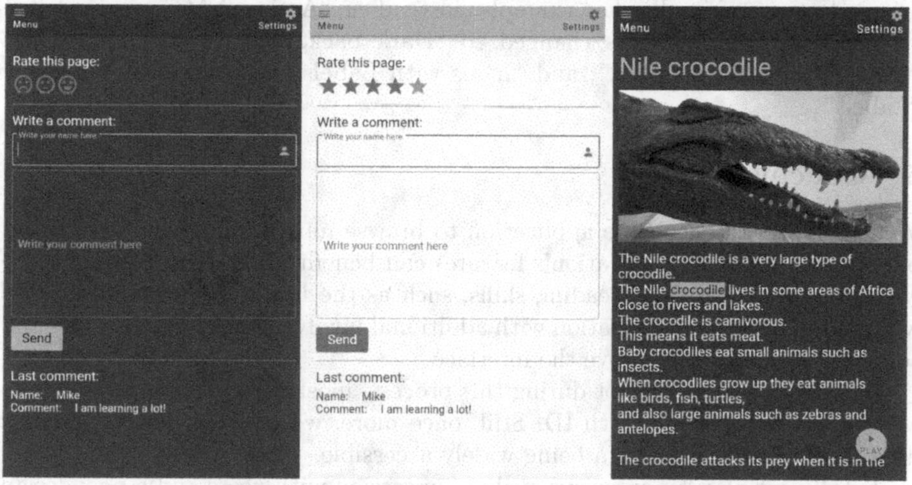

(a) Emotional Assessment (b) Likert-scale Assessment (c) Text-to-speech feature

Fig. 3. ACCESS+ rating modes, comment section and text-to-speech feature highlighting text. (Color figure online)

is a psychologist with long-term experience working with people with intellectual disabilities. Unfortunately, due to the COVID-19 pandemic, we could not proceed to an in-person co-design session and evaluation while designing and developing this app.

One of the experts noticed that the text in easy-to-read language had incorrect line wraps. The line's wraps play an essential role in pacing text and making it easy to understand. Regrettably, viewing on a small device such as a smartphone makes it difficult to structure the sentences precisely, and the experts have already had this problem on other occasions. We made some improvements on this aspect.

Another feedback was related to the evaluation and comment elements. Experts mentioned that it would be interesting to understand if the different rating formats and comment sections will be intuitive to grasp or disruptive.

The next consideration was relative to how intuitive the icons could be. The start and stop AAC icons seem intuitive from the experts' perspective, but it requires future investigation.

The experts described the settings page layout as problematic. We redesigned the page organization to be more straightforward. For example, the setting to change the icon size was hidden in the first prototype (Fig. 1a). This information not readily available would have forced users to take an extra step to be able to enlarge or reduce the icons' size independently from the font size. After the redesign, the setting is immediately available (Fig. 1c).

We redesigned and changed the terms used in the interface from being system-oriented to user-friendly. For example: instead of "Active AAC" we used just "AAC"; "Dark-mode" was changed to "Dark background"; we changed the "Return" button to "Back"; and "Icons with Labels" was modified to simply "Labels".

5 Conclusions

We developed an accessible application to browse museum content focusing on people with ID. The application's features can benefit all users, including those with limited or emerging reading skills, such as the illiterate and children. We will require further investigation with additional involvement of participants and co-design sessions to improve the interface.

Further, we learned a lot during this process, mostly about how to fruitfully collaborate with people with ID. Still, once more, we realized how technology used in museums is far from being widely accessible.

Finally, we plan an extensive evaluation session with users and a new design cycle as future works. Some suggestions for extra features include: providing additional descriptions of items on display; implementing the possibility for visitors to record themself expressing their opinion on the visit; integrating an augmented reality functionality; adding a button to change the orientation of the screen; providing a setting to hide the side menu to increase focus on main content; making sure all buttons have labels and are intuitive to select; and enabling visitors to make drawings inspired by the exhibition, in a sort of atelier modality.

Acknowledgements. We would like to thank SNSF, USI and its UROP Internship program for funding this research.

References

1. Mobile Accessibility: How wcag 2.0 and other w3c/wai guidelines apply to mobile (2015). https://www.w3.org/TR/mobile-accessibility-mapping/#other-w3c-wai-guidelines-related-to-mobile
2. ARASAAC: Aragonese center of augmentative and alternative communication. https://arasaac.org/
3. Dekelver, J., Kultsova, M., Shabalina, O., Borblik, J., Pidoprigora, A., Romanenko, R.: Design of mobile applications for people with intellectual disabilities. Creat. Intell. Technol. Data Sci. **535**, 823–836 (2015)
4. Google: Flutter - build apps for any screen. https://flutter.dev/
5. Mariger, H.: Cognitive disabilities and the web: where accessibility and usability meet. National Center on Disability and Access to Education (NCDAE) Resources (2006)
6. Mastrogiuseppe, M., Soares Guedes, L., Span, S., Clementi, P., Landoni, M.: Reconceptualizing inclusion in museum spaces: a multidisciplinary framework. In: ICERI2021 Proceedings, 14th annual International Conference of Education, Research and Innovation, IATED, pp. 7225–7233 (November 2021). https://doi.org/10.21125/iceri.2021.1620
7. Mastrogiuseppe, M., Span, S., Bortolotti, E.: Improving accessibility to cultural heritage for people with intellectual disabilities: a tool for observing the obstacles and facilitators for the access to knowledge. Alter **15**(2), 113–123 (2021). https://doi.org/10.1016/j.alter.2020.06.016, https://www.sciencedirect.com/science/article/pii/S1875067220300651
8. Sitbon, L., Farhin, S.: Co-designing interactive applications with adults with intellectual disability: a case study. In: Proceedings of the 29th Australian Conference on Computer-Human Interaction, OZCHI 2017, pp. 487–491. Association for Computing Machinery, New York (2017). https://doi.org/10.1145/3152771.3156163
9. Soares Guedes, L.: Designing multisensory experiences for users with different reading abilities visiting a museum. SIGACCESS Access. Comput. (129) (2021). https://doi.org/10.1145/3458055.3458058
10. Soares Guedes, L., Landoni, M.: Meeting participants with intellectual disabilities during covid-19 pandemic: challenges and improvisation. In: The 23rd International ACM SIGACCESS Conference on Computers and Accessibility, ASSETS 2021. Association for Computing Machinery, New York (2021). https://doi.org/10.1145/3441852.3476566
11. Sutherland, D., et al.: Survey of AAC needs for adults with intellectual disability in New Zealand. J. Dev. Phys. Disabil. **26**(1), 115–122 (2014)

Investigating the Usability of Voice Assistant-Based CBT for Age-Related Depression

Julian Striegl(✉), Marie Gotthardt, Claudia Loitsch, and Gerhard Weber

Chair of Human-Computer Interaction, TU Dresden,
Nöthnitzer Straße 46, 01187 Dresden, Germany
{julian.striegl,marie.gotthardt1,claudia.loitsch,
gerhard.weber}@tu-dresden.de

Abstract. To combat the global shortage of mental health services, new solutions - such as computerized therapy options - have to be found. While research in this field has been ongoing for several decades and approaches such as chatbot-based cognitive behavioral therapy (CBT) have already shown to be effective in reducing symptoms of depression for younger adults, voice assistant-based (VA-based) approaches have thus far not been investigated deeply. However, especially for elderly people with depression VA-based systems could yield benefits - such as the avoidance of physical accessibility issues. Therefore, we propose the design of a VA-based system capable of delivering selected methods from CBT to elderly users with depression in order to investigate its usability. To assess the usability of the conceptualized system in comparison to a chatbot-based approach we conducted a randomized controlled A/B testing experiment with 14 participants. Results indicate a good usability and acceptance of the designed system and a preference for the delivery of CBT-methods via voice assistant rather than via chatbot, especially among elderly participants.

Keywords: Human-computer interaction · Speech · Voice interaction · Voice assistants · Conversational agents · Cognitive behavioral therapy · Affective disorders · Depression · Usability

1 Introduction

The prevalence of mental health problems has been increasing in the past decades worldwide [10]. Over their lifespan, 29% of the global population is affected by some form of mental disorder [36], with affective disorders, such as depression and anxiety disorders, being the most common forms [29]. As Denecke et al. [12] emphasized, we further have a global shortage of professionals delivering mental health services. As a result, affected individuals often face long waiting periods before they can receive adequate treatment [9] and less than half receive proper treatment at all [17]. This can be especially harmful for people with age-related depression, as there is presumably a high rate of under-reporting due to the high stigmatization of the illness in elderly people and as the risk for suicide rises strongly in relation to age [15]. Therefore, new

K. Miesenberger et al. (Eds.): ICCHP-AAATE 2022, LNCS 13341, pp. 432–441, 2022.
https://doi.org/10.1007/978-3-031-08648-9_50

solutions have to be found to provide low threshold, scalable forms of mental health support. Those solutions should be applicable to different forms of mental health problems and should be accessible and usable by a broad and diverse user base.

To cope with the shortage of face-to-face therapy options and the rising prevalence of mental disorders, research on internet-based therapy approaches has been going on for several decades. Approaches exist in the form of online psychotherapy, email-based, app-based, or chat-based therapy solutions. While some solutions provide automated therapeutic methods for self-guided interventions, others function as a communication medium between therapist and patient and are intended to be used adjunct to therapy [7,26]. As they are easy to access and discrete in usage, those solutions provide one possible strategy to encounter the issue of increasing mental health problems [3]. As a next step, CA-based therapy has become one focus of research in this area. The primary type of psychotherapy implemented digitally is CBT [6]. In recent years several internet-based CBT solutions have been shown to be effective in improving depressive symptoms and life satisfaction [2,25,28,39]. CBT is based on the assumption that cognitive distortions contribute to the development and maintenance of mental illnesses [5,14]. Therefore, the central goal of CBT is to identify the patient's problematic patterns in cognition and behavior to modify those through cognitive reconstruction and behavior changes. As a trans-diagnostic intervention, CBT can be successfully applied to many psychiatric conditions, as its underlying principals apply to anxiety disorders, depression, eating disorders and paranoid delusions [38]. Nevertheless, from its beginnings CBT was created with a focus on depressive disorders [41]. In mental health, conversational agents (CAs) such as chatbots (CBs) and voice assistants (VAs) can be a more interactive way to inform patients on CBT techniques and provide information on mental well being [10]. Furthermore, CAs can help to reduce cost, improve efficiency and reduce time spent assessing the well being of patients [22]. Moreover, CAs can be used as a more user friendly way of screening for mental health issues in comparison to diagnostic scales [10]. While existing CA-based solutions showed promising results, the usability of VA-based CBT with a standalone voice user interface (VUI) has not yet been analyzed - especially not with elderly users. This is, however, crucial, as a good usability leads to better acceptance and therapy adherence [32]. Therefore, we propose a novel concept for VA-based CBT for elderly people with an onset depressive disorder and investigate the perceived usability with the target group. Specifically, we want to investigate how the usability of a VA-based system for CBT delivery compares to the usability of CB-based CBT delivery.

In Sect. 2 the current state of research of CA-based CBT will be laid out. Subsequently, Sect. 3 introduces the conceptualization and interaction design of a CA capable of delivering selected CBT methods. Section 4 describes a conducted study, followed by a thorough discussion of results, implications and shortcomings. Section 5 completes the paper through a concise conclusion and an indication of future work.

2 State of the Art

CBs for mental health counseling have already been proposed and first studies have shown promising results regarding acceptance and efficacy [10,12,18]. However, CB-based solutions can have disadvantages for people with visual or other impairments and accessibility guidelines for CBs have yet to be established [35]. Furthermore, certain user groups might prefer speech as an interaction modality. Concerning the elderly, for example, studies indicate that VUIs are favored over conventional user interfaces due to the simplicity of speech interaction and the avoidance of physical accessibility issues [30,42]. Additionally, this user group often lacks media competence and therefore the usage of graphical user interfaces in the context of therapy can be challenging due to missing skills necessary for interacting with computerized therapy systems [24].

Wysa is a CB developed by Becky et al. [23]. The system's goal is to increase mental resilience through text-based conversations. In 2017 a study was conducted to investigate the efficacy of the CB in mediating CBT techniques to increase the mental well being of users. Participants that used the app in between measurements of their mental state had a significant improvement in depressive symptoms in comparison to control.

Fitzpatrick et al. [18] designed and implemented a CB called *Woebot* intended for daily usage. Each interaction with Woebot consists of a short inquiry about the user's current activity and mood followed by a short CBT-based learning session. The efficacy of the application for treatment of depression and anxiety was shown in a randomized controlled trial.

An application designed to support mental health through VA technology was proposed by Bhat et al. [8]. The plant-shaped device combined with an Alexa VA called *PlantBot* was specifically designed for young adults receiving behavioral activation therapy for depression to remind them of their therapeutic tasks at home. On PlantBot, a LED-panel indicates what the user has to do - e.g. start a conversation with Alexa - and provides feedback to the user in combination with a suitable sound. Through the VA, the user receives instructions for tasks to be performed. The usability of PlantBot was evaluated in two studies revealing that the proposed approach showed a good acceptance and usability by participants with depressive symptoms. However, to what extent these results are transferable to elderly users is still unclear.

To summarize, existing approaches indicate a good acceptance and efficacy of CA-based CBT for depression treatment, but standalone VA-based systems for CBT have not yet been proposed and their usability in comparison to CB-based solutions is still unknown. The upcoming Section will hence describe the concept and prototype of a VA-based system in order to investigate the perceived usability in comparison to a CB-based CBT approach.

3 Design and Prototype of a VA for CBT Delivery

A thorough analysis of related research (cf. Sect. 2) and of the context of use resulted in several insights. First, most computerized CBT systems follow the structure of a classical face-to-face therapy session to convey their content. Moreover, several of the before mentioned solutions had a mental health assessment of users in order to hinder suicidal people from using the system and rather connect them to a suicide prevention hotline. This is crucial to ensure the safety of users, as suicide risk increases 30-fold for people with depression compared to the general population [20] and the suicide risk for elderly people is particularly high [15]. Additionally, the system should clearly indicate that the usage of a CA-based system for CBT is not intended as a replacement for face-to-face therapy with mental health specialists [18]. Furthermore, as the system is intended for elderly users, guidelines for the design of VUIs for elderly people have to be taken into account [19,37]. Based on related research, three CBT tools were identified as suitable for a VA-based CBT session: A mood journal [11], a radio play with multiple choice questions as a psycho educational component [27,40], and a short meditation practice to end the session [21,31].

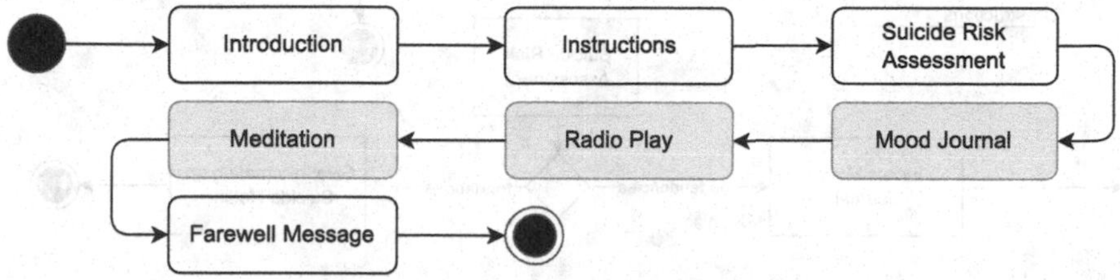

Fig. 1. Conceptualized structure of a VA-based CBT session.

The system introduces itself at the beginning of each session. As a female voice and a personalized name seem to be favorable for the acceptance of VA systems by elderly users [33,42], we chose a female persona for the VA. Upon introduction, the system stresses that it is not intended as a therapy replacement and is not a real human, but an automated CA. Subsequently, on first usage an introduction is given to the user (see Fig. 1), explaining possible interactions with the system and the structure of the following session to ensure self-descriptiveness, expectation conformity and user learnability (as suggested by Ferland et al. [16]). Afterwards, users are asked if suicidal thoughts occurred recently. If so, users are urged to call the suicide prevention hotline, the telephone number to said service is given and the session is terminated. Otherwise, the system leads the user through the before mentioned CBT tools. An excerpt of the designed dialog management can be seen in Fig. 2. The session is finalized through a farewell message and the user is asked to set a date and reminder for the next planned session.

4 Evaluation: Comparing the Usability of CB-Based Versus VA-Based CBT

In order to assess the usability (cf. ISO 9241-11 [13]) of the developed system we conducted a randomized controlled A/B testing experiment, mainly focusing on two central research questions: **1.** How does the usability of a VA-based CBT system compare to a CB-based CBT system? **2.** Are there differences in perceived usability between older and younger users? Requirements of elderly participants were taken into account in the design of the conducted user study, following guidelines for user testing with elderly subjects [34]. Senior participants were recruited by contacting nursing facilities and through social media. Additionally, younger participants were recruited through social media. All participants had to sign a privacy policy and consent form to comply with data protection provisions.

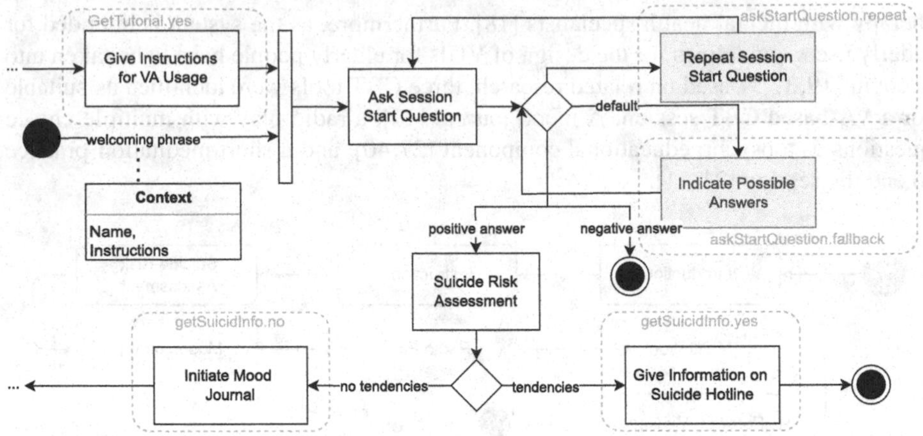

Fig. 2. Activity diagram showing an excerpt of the implemented dialog management strategy, including the therapy session start and suicide assessment components. Intents are indicated through dotted boxes.

4.1 Participants

Overall, 14 participants took part in the study (8 females and 6 males). The average age of participants was 57.57 years (ranging from 26 to 83), with 9 participants being over the age of 60. 57% of participants had either been depressive and in therapy in the past or had close relatives with depression. However, none of the participants were diagnosed with depression during the study period in order to comply with ethical concerns. The implications of this predicament will be discussed later. 50% of participants had no prior experience with CAs.

4.2 Methodology and Material

Participants were pseudorandomly assigned to either the CB group or the VA group, to keep the age distribution in both groups approximately equal. Thereby, the interaction modality (CB or VA) and age were independent variables, with questionnaire results (system usability scale result) being the dependent variable. After an introduction to the concept (see Fig. 1), participants had to fill out 5-point Likert scale questionnaires (ranging from 1 := completely disagree, to 5 := completely agree) on demographic information, technological affinity and on their opinion of the presented concept. Afterwards, participants had an independent hands-on session with the prototype in absence of the facilitator (to factor out social desirability effects). Both testing groups were provided with the same CA and content, differentiating only in the interaction modality (VA in group A and CB in group B). The user test was followed by a questionnaire on the usability - using the system usability scale (SUS) - and by a semi structured interview as a formative evaluation (e.g. to gather suggestions for additional functionalities). Due to the global COVID-19 pandemic, rigorous hygiene precautions had to be taken into account. Therefore, the questionnaire and conducted semi-structured interview were carried out online, the VA was provided through a telephone gateway and the CB version as a web application to enable test subjects to participate in the study remotely.

4.3 Results

Concept Evaluation: Overall, the concept of a CA-based system for CBT was well received by participants. Participants indicated that they were interested in talking to the system (median (ME): 4, mode (MO): 5) and that they would appreciate it, if a VA was able to support them during depressive episodes (ME: 4, MO:4). The relative majority of participants assessed the system to be capable of reducing the supply bottleneck of psychological care (43%).

Table 1. Mean SUS scores in VA and CB group for participants in different age groups

VA Group			CB Group		
Age ≥ 60	Age < 60	Mean	Age ≥ 60	Age < 60	Mean
75	75	75	51	71	61

Comparison Between Group A and B: The SUS is a widely used standardized questionnaire for assessing perceived usability through a scale from 0 to 100 (with ≥60 indicating a usability above average and ≥70 indicating a good usability) [4]. SUS measurements showed differences between VA and CB group, especially in relation to age (see Table 1). In the VA group the usability was rated as good (SUS: 75) and in the CB group as mediocre (SUS: 51) by participants over the age of 60. Additionally, over all age groups the VA condition had a SUS score of 75 and the CB condition had a score of 61. Furthermore, participants had to answer a questionnaire specific to the therapeutic context. While participants of the VA group could imagine using the system in case of a depressive episode (median: 4, mode: 4), the opinion with the CB-based prototype, especially among seniors, was scattered (median: 2.5, mode: [1,2,3,5]) and overall in the CB group the opinion was rather neutral (median: 3.5, mode: 5). Additionally, the progress subjects achieved with the prototype during the CA-based therapy session was tracked. In the VA group subjects over the age of 60 finished on average 90% of the therapy session. While seniors in the CB group finished only 58%. For younger participants (age <60) the difference between groups was smaller (92% for VA condition, 72% for CB condition).

4.4 Discussion

The concept and developed prototype were positively received by the majority of test subjects. 10 out of 14 participants found the system useful and assessed the system to be able to support people with depression. Direct comparison of age groups revealed that younger people rated the concept and prototype slightly better than seniors. It was also found that the evaluation of the prototype was dependent on the evaluation of the concept. Subjects who found the overall concept of VA-based CBT unsuitable or did not support the idea of computer-based therapy generally, also rated the usability of the prototype lower than those who rated the concept positively. In particular, subjects who suffered from depression themselves or had close acquaintances or family members with depression showed high interest in the concept and prototype. The fact that the evaluation of the concept affected the evaluation of usability should be viewed critically. Subjects who themselves or their relatives are affected by the therapy supply bottleneck may have rated the usability better and thus falsify the result. Conversely, people who rated usability negatively because of the concept could falsify the result in the opposite direction. A larger sample size could reduce such potential biases in a followup study. Overall, the usability of the VA-based prototype (SUS: 75), was rated better than the usability of the CB prototype (SUS: 61). For the group of elderly participants, scores were even further apart (75 for VA group and 51 for CB group). In both variants most of the test persons reached the end of the therapy session. This is a good indicator that the prototype was intuitive for the target group and that errors could be avoided or corrected through the implemented dialog management. The majority of subjects also indicated in the semi-structured interview that they preferred or would have preferred to talk to the system rather than write with the system. In addition, two seniors in the CB group dropped out of the therapy session after only a few minutes, stating that they were frustrated by the time needed for typing.

It is important to point out that the user study was conducted with only 14 participants. While 57% of participants had either been depressive in the past or had close relatives with depression, non of them were diagnosed with depression at the time of study. A followup study should therefore be conducted with people diagnosed with depression and with a higher number of participants in both groups. While results were highly promising, the focus of this study was to investigate the usability of VA-based CBT delivery in comparison to CB-based CBT systems. Similar to related CA-based therapy approaches [1], the effect of this novel form of CBT delivery on psychological well being should be further investigated, as the so far existing evidence is not sufficient enough to show clinical importance.

5 Conclusion

This study investigated a novel approach for VA-based CBT delivery for elderly people with depression. Therefore, a first concept of a VA-based CBT session was designed, implemented and used to conduct a randomized controlled A/B testing experiment. The concept was well received by the majority of participants and results indicate a good usability of the designed system. In particular, results indicate a preference for the delivery of CBT-methods via VA rather than CB, especially among elderly participants. Future studies should investigate the usability and acceptance of VA-based CBT delivery over a longer time period. Moreover, the efficacy of the system on the reduction of depressive symptoms in the target group should be examined. For this purpose the system should be extended by further CBT-based courses and exercises in order to provide subsequent CBT sessions via VA.

Acknowledgement. Preliminary work for the presented study has been done by Dennis Körte.

References

1. Abd-Alrazaq, A.A., Rababeh, A., Alajlani, M., Bewick, B.M., Househ, M.: Effectiveness and safety of using chatbots to improve mental health: systematic review and meta-analysis. J. Med. Internet Res. **22**(7), e16021 (2020)
2. Andersson, G.: Randomised controlled non-inferiority trial with 3-year follow-up of internet-delivered versus face-to-face group cognitive behavioural therapy for depression. J. Affect. Disord. **151**(3), 986–994 (2013)
3. Auerbach, R.P., et al.: WHO world mental health surveys international college student project: prevalence and distribution of mental disorders. J. Abnormal Psychol. **127**(7), 623–638 (2018)
4. Bangor, A., Kortum, P., Miller, J.: Determining what individual SUS scores mean: adding an adjective rating scale. J. Usabil. Stud. **4**(3), 114–123 (2009)
5. Beck, A.T.: Cognitive therapy: nature and relation to behavior therapy - republished article. Behav. Therapy **47**(6), 776–784 (1970)
6. Becker, T.D., Torous, J.B.: Recent developments in digital mental health interventions for college and university students. Curr. Treat. Opt. Psychiat. **6**(3), 210–220 (2019). https://doi.org/10.1007/s40501-019-00178-8
7. Berger, T.: Internetbasierte Interventionen bei psychischen Störungen. Hogrefe Verlag, Fortschritte der Psychotherapie (2015)
8. Bhat, A.S., Boersma, C., Meijer, M.J., Dokter, M., Bohlmeijer, E., Li, J.: Plant robot for at-home behavioral activation therapy reminders to young adults with depression. ACM Trans. Human-Robot Interact. **10**(3), 1–21 (2021)
9. Bower, P., Gilbody, S.: Stepped care in psychological therapies: access, effectiveness and efficiency: narrative literature review. Brit. J. Psychiat. **186**(1), 11–17 (2005)
10. Cameron, G., et al.: Towards a chatbot for digital counselling. In: HCI 2017: Digital Make Believe - Proceedings of the 31st International BCS Human Computer Interaction Conference, HCI 2017, July 2017 (2017)
11. Clabby, J.F.: Helping depressed adolescents: a menu of cognitive-behavioral procedures for primary care. Primary Care Comp. J. Clin. Psychiat. **8**(3), 131 (2006)
12. Denecke, K., Vaaheesan, S., Arulnathan, A.: A mental health chatbot for regulating emotions (sermo) - concept and usability test. IEEE Trans. Emerg. Topics Comput. **9**(3), 1170–1182 (2021)
13. DIN, E.: 9241–11: Ergonomische anforderungen für bürotätigkeiten mit bildschirmgeräten. teil 11: Anforderungen an die gebrauchstauglichkeit; leitsätze. Berlin: Beuth (1999)
14. Ellis, A.: Reason and Emotion in Psychotherapy. L. Stuart (1962)
15. Fellgiebel, A., Hautzinger, M.: Altersdepression. Springer, Heidelberg (2017). https://doi.org/10.1007/978-3-662-53697-1
16. Ferland, L., Huffstutler, T., Rice, J., Zheng, J., Ni, S., Gini, M.: Evaluating older users' experiences with commercial dialogue systems: implications for future design and development. arXiv preprint arXiv:1902.04393 (2019)
17. Ferrari, A.J., et al.: Burden of depressive disorders by country, sex, age, and year: findings from the global burden of disease study 2010. PLoS Med. **10**(11), e1001547 (2013)
18. Fitzpatrick, K.K., Darcy, A., Vierhile, M.: Delivering cognitive behavior therapy to young adults with symptoms of depression and anxiety using a fully automated conversational agent (woebot): a randomized controlled trial. JMIR Mental Health **4**(2), e19 (2017)

19. Gollasch, D., Weber, G.: Age-related differences in preferences for using voice assistants. In: Mensch Und Computer 2021, MuC 2021, pp. 156–167. Association for Computing Machinery, New York (2021)
20. Harris, E.C., Barraclough, B.: Suicide as an outcome for mental disorders: a meta-analysis. Brit. J. Psychiat. **170**(A meta–MAR.), 205–228 (1997)
21. Hofmann, S.G., Sawyer, A.T., Fang, A.: The empirical status of the "new wave" of cognitive behavioral therapy. Psychiat. Clinics **33**(3), 701–710 (2010)
22. ILIĆ, D., MARKOVIĆ, B.: Possibilities, limitations and economic aspects of artificial intelligence applications in healtcare. Ecoforum J. **5**(1) (2016)
23. Inkster, B., Sarda, S., Subramanian, V.: An empathy-driven, conversational artificial intelligence agent (WYSA) for digital mental well-being: real-world data evaluation mixed-methods study. JMIR Mhealth Uhealth **6**(11), e12106 (2018)
24. Knowles, S.E., Lovell, K., Bower, P., Gilbody, S., Littlewood, E., Lester, H.: Patient experience of computerised therapy for depression in primary care. BMJ Open **5**(11), e008581 (2015)
25. Krämer, R., Köhler, S.: Evaluation of the online-based self-help programme "Selfapy" in patients with unipolar depression: study protocol for a randomized, blinded parallel group dismantling study. Trials **22**(1), 1–10 (2021)
26. Lattie, E.G., Adkins, E.C., Winquist, N., Stiles-Shields, C., Wafford, Q.E., Graham, A.K.: Digital mental health interventions for depression, anxiety, and enhancement of psychological well-being among college students: Systematic review. J. Med. Internet Res. **21**(7), e12869 (2019)
27. Margraf, J., Schneider, S.: Lehrbuch der Verhaltenstherapie, Band 1. Springer, Heidelberg (2018)
28. Martinengo, L., et al.: Self-guided cognitive behavioral therapy apps for depression: Systematic assessment of features, functionality, and congruence with evidence. J. Med. Internet Res. **23**(7), e27619 (2021)
29. Organization, W.H.: Depression and other common mental disorders: global health estimates. World Health Organization, Technical documents (2017)
30. Pradhan, A., Mehta, K., Findlater, L.: "Accessibility came by accident": use of voice-controlled intelligent personal assistants by people with disabilities. Special Care Dentist **27**(4), 154–157 (2007)
31. Ramel, W., Goldin, P.R., Carmona, P.E., McQuaid, J.R.: The effects of mindfulness meditation on cognitive processes and affect in patients with past depression. Cogn. Therapy Res. **28**(4), 433–455 (2004)
32. Rismawan, W., Marchira, C.R., Rahmat, I.: Usability, acceptability, and adherence rates of mobile application interventions for prevention or treatment of depression: a systematic review. J. Psychosoc. Nurs. Mental Health Serv. **59**(2), 41–47 (2021)
33. Schlögl, S., Chollet, G., Garschall, M., Tscheligi, M., Legouverneur, G.: Exploring voice user interfaces for seniors. In: Proceedings of the 6th International Conference on PErvasive Technologies Related to Assistive Environments, PETRA 2013. Association for Computing Machinery, New York (2013)
34. Silva, P.A., Nunes, F.: 3 × 7 usability testing guidelines for older adults. In: Proceedings of the 3rd Mexican Workshop on Human Computer Interaction (MexIHC 2010), pp. 1–8 (2010)
35. Stanley, J., Brink, R., Valiton, A., Bostic, T., Scollan, B.: Chatbot accessibility guidance: a review and way forward. In: Yang, X.-S., Sherratt, S., Dey, N., Joshi, A. (eds.) Proceedings of Sixth International Congress on Information and Communication Technology. LNNS, vol. 216, pp. 919–942. Springer, Singapore (2022). https://doi.org/10.1007/978-981-16-1781-2_80

36. Steel, Z., Marnane, C., Iranpour, C., Chey, T., Jackson, J.W., Patel, V., Silove, D.: The global prevalence of common mental disorders: a systematic review and meta-analysis 1980–2013. Int. J. Epidemiol. **43**(2), 476–493 (2014)
37. Striegl, J., Gollasch, D., Loitsch, C., Weber, G.: Designing vuis for social assistance robots for people with dementia. In: Schneegass, S., Pfleging, B., Kern, D. (eds.) Mensch und Computer 2021 - Tagungsband, pp. 155–165. ACM, New York (2021)
38. Van Der Gaag, M.: The efficacy of CBT for severe mental illness and the challenge of dissemination in routine care (2014)
39. Voderholzer, U., Beintner, I., Backes, B., Esguerra, E., Hessler-Kaufmann, J.B.: Implementing videoconference CBT for depression in routine outpatient care: outcome, working alliance, and influence of patients' technology commitment. Verhaltenstherapie **31**(3), 238–247 (2021)
40. Wagner, R.F.: Rollenspiel und rollentausch in der kognitiven verhaltenstherapie. Zeitschrift für Psychodrama und Soziometrie **2**(1), 69–77 (2003)
41. Wills, F., Plata, G.: Kognitive Therapie nach Aaron T. Beck: Therapeutische Skills kompakt. Junfermann Verlag (2014)
42. Wulf, L., Garschall, M., Himmelsbach, J., Tscheligi, M.: Hands free - care free. In: Proceedings of the NordiCHI 2014: The 8th Nordic Conference on Human-Computer Interaction: Fun, Fast, Foundational, pp. 203–206 (2014)

Data-Driven User Profiling and Personalization in Tiimo: Towards Characterizing Time Management Behaviors of Neurodivergent Users of a Scheduling Application

Sofie Otto[1(✉)], Brian Bemman[1], Lykke Brogaard Bertel[1], Hendrik Knoche[1], and Helene Lassen Nørlem[2]

[1] Aalborg University, Aalborg, Denmark
{sio,lykke}@plan.aau.dk, {bb,hk}@create.aau.dk
[2] Tiimo, Copenhagen, Denmark
hln@tiimo.dk

Abstract. Deficits with time management and other cognitive functions can stem from multiple causes and be found across different diagnostic conditions. At the same time, cognitive function can differ within diagnostic classes, which calls for adaptable and personalized assistance. A great deal of literature on cognitive assistive technology (CAT) focus on diagnostic populations rather than cognitive impairments across different conditions. This study reports the initial steps towards a data-driven approach to map out the characteristics and behavior of users of a time management app, Tiimo, originally targeting children with ADHD. Based on results from a questionnaire and analysis of user activity data, findings indicate a tendency of attracting a more heterogeneous user population compared to the originally intended target group, thus supporting the need for a more complex and data-driven 'design for all' approach to CAT rather than delimitations based on diagnostic groups. Preliminary findings from the analysis of activity data across user groups and diagnoses show that users generally schedule fewer than five daily activities and most often in the morning, suggesting a potential emphasis on support particularly during morning routines. However, the analysis also highlights the need for more data points to enable assessment of progress, motivation, and effectiveness of the technology. Next steps include a more detailed analysis of user activity that takes different types of behavior and other relevant factors into account by applying NLP to further develop data-driven approaches to user profiling and personalization in time management apps for neurodivergent users.

Keywords: Cognitive assistive technology · Time management · Task completion · Design for all · Data-driven user profiling and personalization

K. Miesenberger et al. (Eds.): ICCHP-AAATE 2022, LNCS 13341, pp. 442–450, 2022.
https://doi.org/10.1007/978-3-031-08648-9_51

1 Introduction

Time management is a higher-level cognitive function that involves the ordering of events in a chronological sequence and the allocation of time to events and activities [1], which is an essential function for perceived control of time, job satisfaction, and health [2]. The International Classification of Functioning, Disability and Health (ICF) defines higher-level cognitive functions as mental functions especially dependent on the frontal lobes of the brain, which include a broad range of goal-directed behaviors such as time management as well as organization and planning functions [1]. Impairment in higher-level cognitive functions is often seen in people with cognitive disabilities, and the functional capabilities and consequences of impairment can differ substantially within and across different diagnostic populations. Applications of assistive technology for cognition (ATC) or cognitive assistive technology (CAT) can help compensate for cognitive impairments and alleviate barriers to daily life participation. However, ATC/CAT are often conceptualized in accordance with diagnostic classes (e.g., dementia), which can be problematic because similar cognitive deficits can be found across different clinical populations [3]. O'Neill and Gillespie [3] propose an alternative framework based on the specific cognitive functions being assisted, e.g., higher-level cognitive functions, thus encouraging a shift towards 'design for all', which constitutes the underlying conceptualization of this paper.

1.1 Time Management and the Tiimo App

Applications supporting time management include prompting systems informing the user that an action should be taken through visual, verbal, or auditory cues, and time management technologies aiding the planning, prioritizing, and execution of daily and time-dependent tasks [4]. Tiimo is a research-based combined task management and prompting system designed in close collaboration with families and experts as a tool to support children with attention deficit hyperactivity disorder (ADHD) navigate daily challenges through structure and predictability [5]. The smartwatch application utilizes a visual timeline, persuasive visual reminders, checklists, and icons among other behavioral design elements to support executive function and motivate the user to build and stick to daily routines. Since its launch in 2018, the application has gained a large userbase representing 65 different countries. Apart from a need for support in managing time, little is known about the users, as the system does not automatically collect personal information regarding age, health, or potential diagnosis. However, raw data on activities, checklists and routines, their time slots as well as the users' progress is stored – an extensive data collection constituting a potentially valuable source of insight into the behaviors of neurodivergent users with time management support needs.

This paper reports the preliminary findings from a two-step approach to map out the characteristics and behavior of users of an assistive technology originally targeting children with ADHD and their families. The initial data collection is based on an online questionnaire and user activity data from the app. The two-step approach intends to generate insights into 1) who the users are and motivating factors to start using the technology, and 2) what characterizes their actual behavior when interacting with the app, for the purpose of investigating if and how these insights might potentially contribute to improvements and accommodation of their needs.

2 Related Work

In recent years, ATC/CAT have been developed and investigated as compensation for difficulties related to higher-level cognitive functions with the aim of helping different target groups cope with daily life demands. Since the point of departure in the current research is focused on mobile high-tech intervention, the following section will present related work centered around mobile technologies supporting relevant higher-level cognitive functions.

Time management functions have previously been supported through different mobile technologies, including an iPod Touch personal digital assistant (PDA) targeting adults with ASD in a work context [6], a smartphone application supporting children with attention deficit disorder (ADD) in both private and school context' [7], and location-specific tangible objects connected to a web-based interface supporting children with ADHD during morning routines [8, 9]. Assistive features included to-do lists, video-based task-sequencing prompts [6], real-time monitoring and progress tracking [7-9], and task reminders [6, 7]. The support of task management though PDAs have been investigated for adults with acquired brain injury (ABI) in a cognitive rehabilitation setting [10], high school students with autism spectrum disorder (ASD) in everyday life tasks [11], and middle school students with ASD in the completion of novel tasks and transition within and between tasks [12]. PDA features included reminder, to-do-list, address book and predefined scripts [10, 11], and combined auditory and visual prompt levels [12].

Aside from time and task management, other functions have been of focus in the described studies, e.g., organization and planning functions supported by to-do-lists and automatic planning features and memory functions supported by PDA reminders [6, 8–10]. Research approaches and methods included a delayed randomized control trial [6], system design and pilot testing [7], initial stages of a user-centered design process [8] and evaluation [9], randomized parallel-group study [10], quasi-experimental study [11], and multiple probe experimental design [12].

2.1 Data-driven User Profiling Across Diagnoses

As it appears from the research above, mobile ACT/CAT are often developed and investigated as aids for specific diagnostic populations and supporting different cognitive functions, either separately or combined with others. However, the needs and characteristics of people within specific diagnostic groups can differ substantially, while specific cognitive impairments can be found across a variety of diagnoses, and correspondingly, interventions and research targeting a single diagnostic group may be beneficial to another [3]. A systematic review of ICT-based assistive technology for impaired cognition found that mobile prompting systems can improve task execution for different diagnostic groups with shared activity limitations [13], while another systematic review of cognitive function and ATC found that reminder and micro-prompting systems are effective in supporting organization and planning functions for most clinical populations targeted [14]. Thus, similar outcomes are often detected across diagnostic classes, which underlines the importance of addressing neurodivergence according to the type of impairment or need rather than a specific diagnosis alone. The current study will contribute with an examination of an implemented ATC/CAT developed for a specific target group (children with ADHD) but addressing general difficulties with time management, and a data-driven approach to analyzing the extensive collection of user activity data across cognitive conditions or diagnoses. By mapping out user characteristics and behaviors, the aim is to generate insights into the potential of data-driven user profiling and personalization to further inform and improve the Tiimo app specifically, as well as mobile ATC/CAT in general.

3 Data Collection and Methodology

The initial data collection is based on a two-step approach to map out general user characteristics and behavior using a self-completion questionnaire and user activity data. The questionnaire was administered to newly registered users of Tiimo in welcoming emails from October 2021 to January 2022 via Google Forms. The purpose of the questionnaire was to generate insights into the characteristics and motivation of newly registered users through a three-part structure. The first part focused on the motivation, onboarding experience and general usage of the app through close-ended questions, while the second part collected information regarding the users' cognitive and health-related condition. The third part collected personal information through close-ended questions related to age, gender, occupation, and country of residence, as well as open-ended questions welcoming general feedback based on their initial experiences from using the application.

Subsequently, activity data from a subset of Tiimo users from approximately the same time period as the questionnaire was analyzed to characterize user behavior based on their actual interaction with the technology. This is accomplished by looking at basic descriptive statistics concerning users along various dimensions regarding, for example, how frequently they schedule activities, what activities they find important to schedule, or what time of the day these activities occur. The analysis is based on fully anonymized data collected from 70,018 current Tiimo user profiles during the period from 2021-01-01 to 2021-11-30. Table 1 shows an anonymized sample of data and relevant headings for a typical Tiimo user profile.

Table 1. Anonymized sample of activity data and relevant headings for a typical user profile.

ProfileId	Title	Starttime	Endtime	Created
anonymizedUserProfileID	Eat dinner	2021-10-02 19:00:00	2021-10-02 20:00:00	2021-09-21 08:42:17

The 'ProfileId' field in Table 1 indicates the unique user ID provided by Tiimo for each of their users' profiles. The 'Title' field indicates the shortened description of the scheduled activity that may be created by the user or Tiimo while the 'StartTime' and 'EndTime' fields indicate the starting and ending time of that scheduled activity, respectively.

4 Preliminary Findings and Discussion

4.1 User Characteristics

A total of 50 respondents completed the survey between October 2021 and January 2022. The results show a high dispersion in age, ranging from 16 to 71 (median = 33), geographical setting, and occupation type. The vast majority (n = 48) reported themselves as the primary user of Tiimo, while one reported their partner/spouse, and one reported their child(ren). Furthermore, the respondents were asked if the primary user of Tiimo was either diagnosed or self-diagnosed with any cognitive disabilities. The majority (n = 33) identified with ADHD, out of which nearly half reported comorbid disorders such as dyslexia, generalized anxiety, and intellectual disability. A large portion identified with ASD (n = 20), out of which only four reported no comorbid disorders. Furthermore, several respondents reported the primary user as neurotypical (n = 6) or "not sure" (n = 7). These findings indicate a great diversity and interest from a heterogeneous group of users compared to Tiimo's original target group. This emphasizes the problem of delimiting ATC/CAT according to a single diagnostic and age specific group, as the technology appears to attract other groups of neurodivergent users, including self-diagnosed groups and neurotypical users. A common goal for the respondents was to create structure throughout the day (n = 48) as well as to build and stick to routines (n = 43).

From the open-ended questions inviting general feedback, several respondents expressed an overall preliminary satisfaction with the technology, while others emphasized barriers in meeting their needs, such as an insufficient amount of initial training and confusion in differentiating between activities and routines. Some respondents also emphasized the potential of built-in suggestions for how to e.g., break down the day and come up with activities and routines, since, as one respondent noted "I often find it easier when solutions to problems are presented in this way, as I can struggle to think of them myself". However, developing suggestions that meet the needs of a diverse group of neurodivergent users is a difficult task, as there is no 'one-size-fits-all' solution. Thus, future potential may include efforts to tailor suggestions based on the users' needs, preferences, and past behavior.

While findings from this initial questionnaire reflect only local patterns of user characteristics based on a small sample of novice users and thus do not provide conclusions on usage and the actual effectiveness of the technology, initial steps towards realizing this potential are taken by creating an overview of user characteristics and behavior. The next steps towards a more comprehensive mapping of user characteristics include a follow-up questionnaire that inquire into the following usage and experience of the same users, as they have moved from novice to more experienced users.

4.2 Descriptive Statistics of Activity Data

In our preliminary analysis of activity data, basic descriptive statistics will be applied in the analysis of 'typical' Tiimo user profiles, e.g., in terms of what and how many activities they schedule each day and where in the day these activities occur. Figure 1 shows the frequency of Tiimo user profiles' median number of daily (repeated or not) scheduled activities and the relative frequency of all such daily activities (morning, afternoon, and evening).

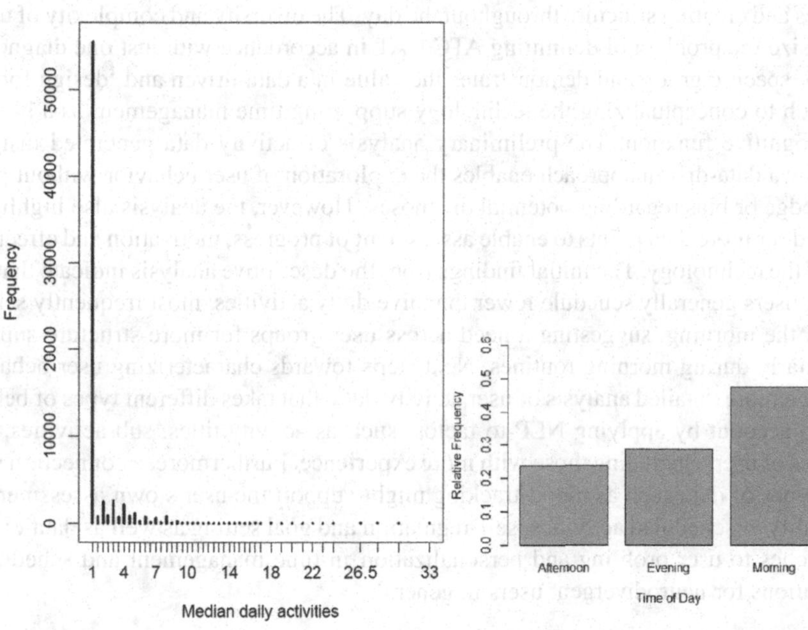

Fig. 1. Frequency of user profiles' median number of daily scheduled activities (left) and the relative frequency of all daily activities according to the time of day (right).

One will note that the vast majority of Tiimo user profiles have scheduled fewer than 5 median daily activities while in the graph shown at right, nearly 50 percent of all daily scheduled activities occur in the morning. The next steps towards characterizing user behavior include a more detailed analysis that explores the potential of clustering activities, e.g., by applying NLP to analyze factors such as titles and whether the activities are divided into sub activities, as well as when the activities are created and the actual progress of completing activities. Finally, it will be relevant to investigate whether the users are motivated to continue using the technology and the potential usefulness in enabling users to self-monitor, self-regulate and set goals based on their own activity data.

5 Conclusion and Future Work

This paper presented preliminary findings from of a two-step data-driven approach to identifying characteristics and behaviors of users of the Tiimo time management and prompting system. Although the technology was originally developed to support children with ADHD, findings from the questionnaire indicate that the app attracts a more heterogeneous population of mostly neurodivergent users, who share a goal of building routines and creating structure throughout the day. The diversity and complexity of users emphasize the problem of delimiting ATC/CAT in accordance with just one diagnostic and age specific group and demonstrates the value in a data-driven and 'design for all' approach to conceptualizing the technology supporting time management as a higher-level cognitive function. The preliminary analysis of activity data generated insights into how a data-driven approach enables the exploration of user behavior without prior knowledge or bias regarding potential diagnoses. However, the analysis also highlights the need for more data points to enable assessment of progress, motivation and effectiveness of the technology. The initial findings from the descriptive analysis indicate that the current users generally schedule fewer than five daily activities, most frequently scheduled in the morning, suggesting a need across user groups for more structure-support particularly during morning routines. Next steps towards characterizing user behavior include a more detailed analysis of user activity data, that takes different types of behavior into account by applying NLP to factors such as activity titles, sub activities, and progress of users, including those with more experience. Furthermore, a connection with other types of data such as mood-tracking might support the user's own assessment of the quality of scheduled activities, self-regulation and goal setting as well as data-driven approaches to user profiling and personalization in time management and scheduling applications for neurodivergent users in general.

References

1. World Health Organization: International Classification of Functioning, Disability and Health (ICF), Geneva (2001)
2. Claessens, B.J.C., van Eerde, W., Rutte, C.G., Roe, R.A.: A review of the time management literature. Pers. Rev. **36**(2), 255–276 (2007). https://doi.org/10.1108/00483480710726136
3. O'Neill, B., Gillespie, A.: Assistive Technology for Cognition: A Handbook for Clinicians and Developers, 1 edn. Psychology Press, Taylor & Francis Group, London, New York (2015)
4. Cook, A.M., Polgar, J.M.: Assistive Technologies- E-Book: Principles and Practice. Elsevier Health Sciences (2014)
5. Tiimo: Research and strategies. https://www.tiimoapp.com/research/. Accessed 06 Feb 2022
6. Gentry, T., Kriner, R., Sima, A., McDonough, J., Wehman, P.: Reducing the need for personal supports among workers with autism using an ipod touch as an assistive technology: delayed randomized control trial. J. Autism Dev. Disord. **45**(3), 669–684 (2014). https://doi.org/10.1007/s10803-014-2221-8
7. Alonso Molinero, A., Jorge Hernández, F., Méndez Zorrilla, A., García Zapirain, B.: Technological solution for improving time management skills using an android application for children with ADD. In: Bravo, J., Hervás, R., Rodríguez, M. (eds.) IWAAL 2012. LNCS, vol. 7657, pp. 431–434. Springer, Heidelberg (2012). https://doi.org/10.1007/978-3-642-35395-6_58
8. Weisberg, O., et al.: TangiPlan: designing an assistive technology to enhance executive functioning among children with ADHD: In: Proceedings of the 2014 Conference on Interaction Design and Children, Aarhus, Denmark, pp. 293–296 (2014). https://doi.org/10.1145/2593968.2610475
9. Zuckerman, O., Gal-Oz, A., Tamir, N., Kopelman-Rubin, D.: Initial validation of an assistive technology to enhance executive functioning among children with ADHD: In: Proceedings of the 14th International Conference on Interaction Design and Children, Boston Massachusetts, pp. 299–302 (2015). https://doi.org/10.1145/2771839.2771901
10. De Joode, E.A., Van Heugten, C.M., Verhey, F.R.J., Van Boxtel, M.P.J.: Effectiveness of an electronic cognitive aid in patients with acquired brain injury: a multicentre randomised parallel-group study. Neuropsychol. Rehabil. **23**(1), 133–156 (2013). https://doi.org/10.1080/09602011.2012.726632
11. Gentry, T., Wallace, J., Kvarfordt, C., Lynch, K.B.: Personal digital assistants as cognitive aids for high school students with autism: results of a community-based trial. J. Vocat. Rehabil. **32**(2), 101–107 (2010). https://doi.org/10.3233/JVR-2010-0499
12. Mechling, L.C., Savidge, E.J.: Using a personal digital assistant to increase completion of novel tasks and independent transitioning by students with autism spectrum disorder. J. Autism Dev. Disord. **41**(6), 687–704 (2011). https://doi.org/10.1007/s10803-010-1088-6
13. Brandt, Å., Jensen, M.P., Søberg, M.S., Andersen, S.D., Sund, T.: Information and communication technology-based assistive technology to compensate for impaired cognition in everyday life: a systematic review: disabil. Rehabil. Assist. Technol. **15**(7), 810–824 (2020). https://doi.org/10.1080/17483107.2020.1765032

14. Gillespie, A., Best, C., O'Neill, B.: Cognitive function and assistive technology for cognition: a systematic review. J. Int. Neuropsychol. Soc. **18**(1), 1–19 (2012). https://doi.org/10.1017/S1355617711001548

Voice Assistant-Based CBT for Depression in Students: Effects of Empathy-Driven Dialog Management

Marie Gotthardt(✉), Julian Striegl, Claudia Loitsch, and Gerhard Weber

Chair of Human-Computer Interaction, TU Dresden,
Nöthnitzer Straße 46, 01187 Dresden, Germany
{marie.gotthardt1,julian.striegl,claudia.loitsch,
gerhard.weber}@tu-dresden.de

Abstract. With a rising number of students with depression, new low-threshold solutions have to be found to strengthen the resilience against and help those affected by mental disorders. One approach lies in the usage of chatbots (CBs) to provide tools based in cognitive behavioral therapy (CBT) that can be used independently in order to reduce symptoms of depression. To ensure the adherence to such systems, a good usability and acceptance is important. Conversational agents (CAs) that provide CBT-based content should further be sensitive to the users emotional state, as empathy is one central aspect of therapy. While promising research has been going on in the field of CB-based empathy-driven CBT, voice assistant-based (VA-based) solutions have thus far not been investigated deeply. Therefore, we propose a VA-based, empathy-driven system, capable of delivering selected methods from CBT to students with depression.

To assess the effects of empathy-driven dialog management on perceived usability and acceptance, we conducted a single blind randomized controlled A/B testing experiment with 10 participants. While the application of empathetical dialog management shows no benefits to the usability and acceptance, results overall indicate a good usability and acceptance of the system in the target group.

Keywords: Human-computer interaction · Speech · Voice interaction · Voice assistants · Conversational agents · Cognitive behavioral therapy · Affective disorders · Depression · Usability

1 Introduction

Connected to the rising prevalence of mental health problems, there is an increasing gap between the demand for mental health care and the resources of health services [7]. As patients are subject to substantial delays when waiting for therapy [7,9] new ways of combating this global shortage of mental health services have to be found. One possible solution lies in the usage of conversational agents (CAs). CAs can be used to overcome

M. Gotthardt and J. Striegl—The authors contributed equally to this research.

K. Miesenberger et al. (Eds.): ICCHP-AAATE 2022, LNCS 13341, pp. 451–461, 2022.
https://doi.org/10.1007/978-3-031-08648-9_52

certain barriers, such as long waiting lists and geographical problems that prohibit the attendance of face-to-face counseling [7]. Additionally, CAs offer unique benefits to mental health, such as being continuously available, responding to context of both the user and the user's language, the capacity to give responses based on clinically relevant mental health theories and the avoidance of stigmatization of affected individuals [23]. However, thus far CAs are not deployed widely and research to assess the potential impact of this type of assistive technology in mental health is still in its early stages [23]. For young adults, the lack of professional support services poses a major problem since precisely the age group between 17 and 25 visits health care professionals particularly rarely [15]. Hence, low-threshold services are needed that reach those affected in an early stage of mental health problems, such as depression [15]. In Germany, every sixth student is affected by mental health problems [15] and the prevalence of depressive disorders is especially high in adolescents and people in their 20s in comparison to other age groups [19]. Most students are at this critical age. In addition to the general consequences which depression may cause, students might face further challenges in the academic context. Deroma et al. [10] revealed that depressive symptoms in students are associated with lower academic performance. Hunt el al. [17] found a connection between depression and higher drop-out rates. The psychological strain on students further worsened through the COVID-19 pandemic due to the lack of social contacts [1].

Empathy-driven chatbots (CBs) using methods based in cognitive behavioral therapy (CBT) for mental health counseling have already been proposed and first studies have shown the efficacy in treating symptoms of depression [7,9,13,18]. The central goal of CBT is to identify the patient's problematic patterns in cognition and behavior in order to modify those through cognitive reconstruction and behavior changes [3,12]. While it can be applied to many psychiatric conditions, from its beginnings CBT was created with a focus on depressive disorders [34]. However, so far there is no research on how empathy-driven dialogues affect the usability and acceptance of voice assistant (VA) based CBT. Therefore, we address this gap by proposing the concept for an empathy-driven VA-based CBT system for the mental support of students with depression. The usability and acceptance of the concept is evaluated through a user study with the target group based on a developed prototype. Specifically, the effects of emotion sensitivity on usability and acceptance are investigated through a single blind randomized controlled A/B testing experiment.

In Sect. 2 the fundamentals of emotion sensitive CA-based CBT will be laid out, while incorporating the current state of research. Subsequently, Sect. 3 will introduce the concept and prototype of an empathy-driven VA capable of delivering CBT-related psycho-education to students. Section 4 will describe the methodology, execution and results of a conducted study to investigate the effects of sentiment recognition and empathy-driven dialog management on the acceptance and usability of the created system. Consequently, implications and shortcomings will be discussed. Section 5 will complete the paper through a concise conclusion and an indication of future work.

2 State of the Art: Empathy-Driven CA-Based CBT

Norcross et al. [33] demonstrated, that regardless of the type of psychotherapy chosen for treatment, the therapeutic relationship plays a crucial role in therapy outcome. Among others, empathy has been identified as an effective element of the therapeutic relationship [11]. Hence, there has been ongoing research with empathy-driven CBs and Embodied Conversational Agents (ECAs) delivering chosen methods based in CBT.

Wysa is an empathy-driven CA that aims to increase mental resilience and uses sentiment recognition and dialog adaptation in text-based conversations[1]. In 2017 a study was conducted by Becky et al. [18] to investigate the efficacy of the CA in mediating techniques based in positive psychology and CBT in order to increase the mental well being of users. Participants that used the app in between measurements of their mental state had a significant improvement in depressive symptoms in comparison to control.

Fitzpatrick et al. [13] designed and implemented a CA called *Woebot* as a CB application intended for daily usage. The therapeutic approach of the application consists of psycho-educational content oriented toward self-help for CBT and therapeutic process-oriented features. These include, among others, empathetic responses, meaning that Woebot adapts its responses to the user's mood, and tailoring, meaning that the content provided to the user is also adapted to their mood. The conversational style is based on both the dynamics of social interactions and clinical decision making. Fitzpatrick et al. evaluated the feasibility, acceptability and preliminary efficacy of Woebot on a sample of college students with symptoms of anxiety and depression. The results indicated that Woebot could be a suitable option of CBT delivery.

Miranda et al. [22] developed a mobile-based ECA for detecting and preventing suicidal behavior called *HelPath*. Users can make inputs only through predefined interaction options with the GUI. Each interaction is organized as a short therapy session, starting with a query of the user's current mood. The subsequent procedure of therapy sessions may vary depending on two factors. Firstly, the user is able to decide, which kind of activity they want to do. Secondly, the application is designed to respond empathetically in order to increase the success of the therapeutic interventions. One of the strategies for generating empathetic reactions includes explaining and suggesting suitable CBT activities based on the user's emotional state. This empathetic strategy also contributes to the variability of therapy sessions. Another empathy-driven strategy implemented in HelPath is the generation of emotional feedback to the user's utterances. To identify the user's emotional state from their utterances, the cognitive appraisal theory of emotions [28] is used. Usability, adherence and acceptability of HelPath was evaluated in a study with individuals affected by suicidal thoughts [22]. The results indicated, that HelPath is perceived as emotionally competent and participants evaluated its level of adherence as positive [22].

Ring et al. [25] proposed an ECA that communicates CBT principles verbally and non-verbally to users with the goal of recreating face-to-face conversations. The system's interface allows speech input as well as input via touch screen. However, user input is constrained to pre-formulated answers that can be chosen. Two sub-systems are used for speech recognition and to detect affect from user input. The basic building

[1] Wysa Ltd., https://www.wysa.io/, Access date: 04.02.2022.

block of the affect detection system consists of a classifier which assigns the user's utterance to one of three valence categories (happy, neutral and sad). In addition, the user's facial expression is used for affect detection. The generation of empathetic responses to negative affect relies on Russell's circumplex model of emotion [27]. For empathetic responses, suitable items are picked from a hand-created list of responses. The feasibility and acceptance of the counseling system was evaluated in a pilot study on young individuals aged 18 to 28, who had symptoms of depression [25]. The study showed that the system is capable of evoking and responding to the affective state of users in real time and that the users felt understood by the agent [25].

In summary, while there has been promising research in the field of empathy-driven CB-based and ECA-based therapy approaches, research on the effects of empathy-driven dialogues in VA-based systems for CBT on usability and acceptance is still lacking.

3 Design and Prototype of an Empathy-Driven VA for CBT Delivery

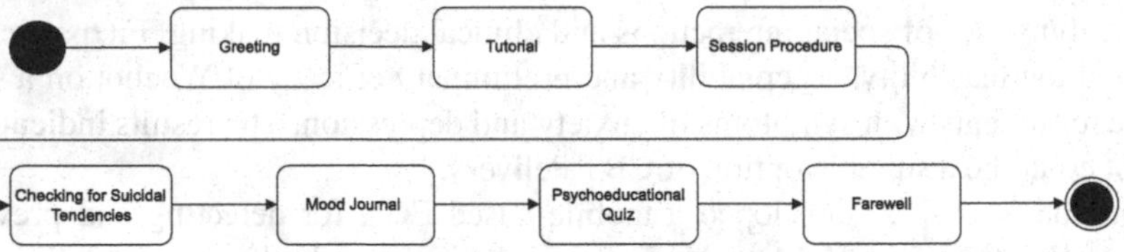

Fig. 1. Procedure of initial therapy session

We designed an empathy-driven VA capable of delivering psycho educational content as one selected method from CBT to students in a human centered design approach, based on a thorough analysis of related work and of the context of use. The interactions with the VA are designed as short therapy sessions. In order to track the course of depressive symptoms of users, they are asked to evaluate the severity of their symptoms before the actual therapy session starts. If the user's scores indicate that they suffer from severe depression, they are encouraged to seek professional psychological help and the session terminates. Afterwards, the user is asked about their current emotional state. Following the concept of Ghandehrioun et al. [14], the user's utterances are classified into an extended version of Russell's circumplex model [27] to identify the user's emotional state. The extension of the circumplex model includes the addition of a neutral category to the four quadrants and the inclusion of more mood-describing words to make the model more precise. The system adapts its response accordingly to the identified emotional category. Therefore, different empathetic techniques are used i.e. mirroring, empathetic listening, cheering up or calming [30]. As a sentiment recognition strategy a rule-based approach is used. Hence, keywords describing the user's mood are looked up in lexical resources and matched to emotions. Subsequently, therapeutic content is delivered in a quiz format, containing content regarding depression and CBT, to support long-term retention of information as shown by Roediger and Butler [26]. During the quiz, the user is given statements about depression, psychotherapy and psychological treatment possibilities and has to decide, if those statements are true or false. Afterwards, the user is given immediate feedback on the correctness of their answer through empathetic responses - as those have been shown to be important for the therapeutic relationship [11,21] as well as for the interaction with CAs in general [8]. Hence, feedback is adapted depending on the correctness of the user's answer and detailed information on the respective CBT-related topic is given. To ensure controllability and customizability as important interaction design principles [29], the user is able to chose a quiz on a specific CBT-based topic during the course of the interaction with the system. The procedure of the VA-based therapy session can be seen in Fig. 1.

4 Evaluation of Acceptance and Usability

To assess the usability and acceptance (cf. ISO 9241-11 [31]) of the developed system we conducted a single blind randomized controlled A/B testing experiment. Specifically, we wanted to investigate, how empathy-driven dialog management affects usability and acceptance of the system in students. Participants were recruited using social media. All participants had to sign a privacy policy and consent form in order to comply with data protection provisions.

4.1 Participants

To be eligible to participate in the study, subjects had to be a current or recent student and be able to speak German fluently (as system's utterances were in German). While symptoms of depression were measured during testing using the Patient Health Questionnaire (PHQ9) [20], none of the participants were diagnosed with a current depressive episode before taking part in the study in order to comply with ethical concerns. The implications of this predicament will be discussed later. Although, 16 participants took part in the study, 6 participants had to be excluded due to incomplete data provision. Overall, 10 subjects completed the survey and testing (5 females and 5 males). The average age of participants was 25,6 (ranging from 21 to 30).

4.2 Methodology and Material

Subjects were randomly assigned to test either an empathy-driven VA delivering psycho-educational content (as described in Sect. 3) in group A or to a VA without empathetic dialog management, delivering the same psycho-educational content, in group B. The existence of different experimental groups was not disclosed to participants. To measure differences in usability, the System Usability Scale (SUS) [2] was used. Consumer satisfaction and acceptance in the context of digital mental health interventions was assessed using the adapted Client Satisfaction Questionnaire for internet-based interventions (CSQ-I) [6]. The Net Promoter Score (NPS) [16] was applied as an additional indication of the perceived usability and acceptance. As subjects' technology commitment might effect their assessment of acceptance and usability of the proposed system, it was measured using the subscales *technology acceptance* and *technology competence belief* of a questionnaire for measuring technology commitment (TB) [24]. Participants first had to answer questionnaires regarding demographic information, experience with depression and psychotherapy, the PHQ9, the subscales of the TB, and experience with VAs. Afterwards, participants tested the VA-based system (provided with either the empathetic or the non-empathetic version). Finally, participants had to fill out the SUS, CSQ-I, items included as a manipulation check and the NPS. Furthermore, they were given the opportunity to provide additional feedback.

4.3 Results

PHQ9 scores ranged from 1 to 16, whereby scores ranged from 2 to 7 in the experimental group and from 1 to 16 in the control group. Referring to Kroenke et al. [20], these scores indicate that all subjects in the experimental group showed none or mild depressive symptoms while in the control group, one subject showed moderate depressive symptoms and one even showed moderately severe symptoms . However, differences between groups in depressive symptoms were not significant ($M_{exp} = 4.0$, $SD_{exp} = 1.9$; $M_{contr} = 8.0$, $SD_{contr} = 5.02$, $p = .17$).

Regarding the technology commitment, no significant differences could be found between groups either, neither in the subscale *technology acceptance* ($M_{exp} = 12.6$, $SD_{exp} = 3.93$; $M_{contr} = 15.6$, $SD_{contr} = 3.26$, $p = .27$) nor in the subscale *technology competence beliefs* ($M_{exp} = 17.4$, $SD_{exp} = 2.65$; $M_{contr} = 18.2$, $SD_{contr} = 3.12$, $p = .71$), although the control group showed slightly higher values in both subscales.

The second part of the survey contained the SUS, the CSQ-I, items for manipulation check and the NPS. Overall, the mean SUS score was 79.25 ($SD_{overall} = 10.67$), indicating a usability above average[2]. While no significant differences were found regarding SUS scores between groups ($p = .95$), the control group rated the usability slightly higher than the experimental group ($M_{exp} = 79.0$, $SD_{exp} = 9.82$; $M_{contr} = 79.5$, $SD_{contr} = 11.45$).

Similar results were found regarding the CSQ-I. The mean CSQ-I score over all subjects was 23.7 ($SD_{overall} = 4.86$) and while no significant differences were found between groups ($p = .13$), the control group assessed the application slightly higher than the experimental group ($M_{experimental} = 21.2$, $SD_{exp} = 4.58$; $M_{contr} = 26.2$, $SD_{contr} = 3.71$). Regarding the items used for manipulation check, significant differences occurred only for the item asking how well subjects felt understood by the respective VA (item *Comprehension Skills*), whereby the comprehension skills of the neutrally acting VA were rated higher than those of the emapthetically acting one ($M_{exp} = 2.6$, $SD_{exp} = 0.49$; $M_{contr} = 4.0$, $SD_{contr} = 0.89$, $p = .025$). When asked for rating the appropriateness of the VA's answers, the assessments in both groups were exactly the same ($M_{exp} = 4.2$, $SD_{exp} = 0.4$; $M_{contr} = 4.2$, $SD_{contr} = 0.4$). For the assessment of perceived aloofness, no significant differences between groups could be found either ($p = 0.76$) although participants of the experimental group gave slightly smaller ratings ($M_{exp} = 2.2$, $SD_{exp} = 1.17$; $M_{contr} = 2.4$, $SD_{contr} = 0.49$). The overall NPS was -10. When considering

[2] Usability.gov,https://www.usability.gov/how-to-and-tools/methods/system-usability-scale.html, Access date: 26.03.2022.

both groups separately, the NPS was higher in the control group ($\text{NPS}_{contr} = 20$) than in the experimental group ($\text{NPS}_{exp} = -40$).

4.4 Discussion

On sample level, a SUS score above average and a CSQ-I score above mean were obtained, indicating a high usability and acceptance of the proposed application. Those results support other research indicating that VA technology seems suitable for delivering psychotherapy digitally [4,32]. Nevertheless, here presented application differs from those proposed within other studies. In contrast to a VA-based application supporting young adults receiving behavioral activation therapy for depression treatment in doing their therapeutic homework, here proposed application does not require users to already receive therapy [4]. Thereby, it addresses the problem of insufficient treatment options and provides more versatile possibilities of use.

Striegl et al. (2022) [32] also proposed a VA-based application which does not require users to receive therapy as a preliminary for its use. However, this application was intended to be used by elderly individuals suffering from depression whereas the application proposed here is intended to be used by students. Furthermore, as Striegl et al. (2022) [32] did not investigate the influence of empathetic DM on users' usability ratings, they only equipped their VA with rudimentary empathetic capabilities.

Although SUS scores and CSQ-I scores were high, the overall NPS score was -10 indicating that subjects would rather not recommend the proposed application. Furthermore, no significant differences in SUS scores and CSQ-I scores could be found between groups meaning that the implementation of empathetic DM did not have effects on subjects' usability and acceptance ratings. However, among manipulation check items, significant differences were found in the item *Comprehension Skills*, whereby control group ratings were higher than those in the experimental group.

Several implications could be derived from the obtained results. First, within this study, empathetic DM might have not influenced subjects' usability and acceptance assessment. However, the strategies chosen for equipping the proposed application with empathetic abilities might have not been sufficient, as the neutrally acting prototype was perceived as being better in understanding subjects than the empathetically acting prototype. The other manipulation check results - which indicate that the empathetically acting prototype was not perceived as less aloof and its reactions were not assessed as more appropriate - further support this hypothesis. Additionally, mixed findings exist in this area of research in general. Ghandeharioun et al. (2019) [14] also used a control group design evaluating an empathetically responding and a neutrally responding mental health application and could not find any significant differences between groups. However, instead of using questionnaires requiring subjective evaluations, they used behavioral data as indicators for group differences. Bickmore et al. (2005) [5], on the other hand, found beneficial effects of the implementation of relational strategies such as empathy on working alliance and the desire to keep working with their proposed application continuously. However, this study is only partly comparable as it investigated a computer agent supporting users in changing automated health behavior, whereas the here presented study focused on a VA-based application delivering CBT.

Overall, it is difficult to compare the here presented results to those of other studies in the field of empathetic conversational agents, as most other research relies on different implementation and/or assessment methods. Therefore, further research is needed in this area.

A major limitation concerning the evaluation procedure and the obtained results of this study lies in the occurrence of several technical problems. Those problems negatively affected the evaluation in different ways. First, technical problems lead to the exclusion of participants resulting in a final sample size of only 10 subjects (5 in each group). A further consequence was that several testings had to be accompanied by the facilitator, which might have led to social desirability biases. Additionally, some participants could not interact with the VA properly which might have influenced their perception of the VA negatively. As those problems did not occur equally distributed over groups, they potentially influenced the evaluation systematically and thereby negatively influenced the internal validity of this study. Furthermore, they might have contributed to higher SUS, CSQ-I and NPS scores in the control group. Additionally, as stated before, while several of the participants showed singes of mild to in one case even moderately severe symptoms of depression, none of the test subjects were diagnosed with depression before taking part in the study. A followup study should therefore be carried out with students with diagnosed depression and with an improved prototypical system.

5 Conclusion

Within this study, no significant effects could be found between a group testing an empathetically acting VA and a group testing a neutrally acting VA delivering chosen CBT-based methods to students with depression. This could indicate that the implementation of empathetic DM does not influence the usability and acceptance of VA-based CBT delivery. With reference to the manipulation check results, another explanation might be that the selected strategies to implement empathetic behavior were not sufficient. Nevertheless, definite conclusions cannot be drawn as several technical problems - resulting in a small sample size and a potential systematic bias - impaired the evaluation. Therefore, a follow-up study with a larger sample size should investigate whether the proposed strategies are suitable to implement empathetic behavior in VAs and whether empathetic DM influences the usability and acceptance of VA-based CBT delivery.

Despite those problems, the obtained results on sample level are highly promising regarding the suitability of VA-based CBT delivery to students with depression. Additionally to high usability and acceptance ratings, qualitative feedback was very encouraging and emphasized the importance of research in the area of digital solutions for students with depression.

References

1. Adam-Gutsch, D., Paschel, F., Ophardt, D., Huck, J.: Studieren im corona-online-semester: Bericht zur befragung der lehramtsstudierenden der technischen universität berlin im sommersemester 2020. Tech. rep., Technische Universität Berlin (2021), http://dx.doi.org/10.14279/depositonce-11343
2. Bangor, A., Kortum, P.T., Miller, J.T.: An empirical evaluation of the system usability scale. Intl. Journal of Human-Computer Interaction **24**(6), 574–594 (2008)
3. Beck, A.T.: Cognitive Therapy: Nature and Relation to Behavior Therapy - Republished Article. Behavior Therapy **47**(6), 776–784 (1970)
4. Bhat, A.S., Boersma, C., Meijer, M.J., Dokter, M., Bohlmeijer, E., Li, J.: Plant Robot for At-Home Behavioral Activation Therapy Reminders to Young Adults with Depression. ACM Transactions on Human-Robot Interaction 10(3) (2021)
5. Bickmore, T., Gruber, A., Picard, R.: Establishing the computer–patient working alliance in automated health behavior change interventions. Patient Education and Counseling **59**(1), 21–30 (2005). https://doi.org/10.1016/j.pec.2004.09.008, https://www.sciencedirect.com/science/article/pii/S0738399104003076
6. Boß, L., Lehr, D., Reis, D., Vis, C., Riper, H., Berking, M., Ebert, D.D., et al.: Reliability and validity of assessing user satisfaction with web-based health interventions. Journal of medical Internet research **18**(8), e5952 (2016)
7. Cameron, G., Cameron, D.M., Megaw, G., Bond, R.B., Mulvenna, M., O'Neill, S.B., Armour, C., McTear, M.: Towards a chatbot for digital counselling. HCI 2017: Digital Make Believe - Proceedings of the 31st International BCS Human Computer Interaction Conference, HCI 2017 2017-July (2017), https://www.scienceopen.com/hosted-document?doi=10.14236/ewic/HCI2017.24
8. Casas, J., Spring, T., Daher, K., Mugellini, E., Khaled, O.A., Cudré-Mauroux, P.: Enhancing conversational agents with empathic abilities. In: Proceedings of the 21st ACM International Conference on Intelligent Virtual Agents. pp. 41–47 (2021)
9. Denecke, K., Vaaheesan, S., Arulnathan, A.: A Mental Health Chatbot for Regulating Emotions (SERMO) - Concept and Usability Test. IEEE Transactions on Emerging Topics in Computing **9**(3), 1170–1182 (2021)
10. Deroma, V.M., Leach, J.B., Leverett, J.P.: The Relationship Between Depression and College Academic Performance. College Student Journal 43(2), 325–334 (2009), publisher: Project Innovation Inc
11. Elliott, R., Bohart, A.C., Watson, J.C., Murphy, D.: Therapist Empathy and Client Outcome: An Updated Meta-Analysis. Psychotherapy **55**(4), 399–410 (2018)
12. Ellis, Ellis, A.: Reason and Emotion in Psychotherapy. L. Stuart (1962)
13. Fitzpatrick, K.K., Darcy, A., Vierhile, M.: Delivering Cognitive Behavior Therapy to Young Adults With Symptoms of Depression and Anxiety Using a Fully Automated Conversational Agent (Woebot): A Randomized Controlled Trial. JMIR Mental Health 4(2) (2017)
14. Ghandeharioun, A., McDuff, D., Czerwinski, M., Rowan, K.: Emma: An emotion-aware wellbeing chatbot. In: 2019 8th International Conference on Affective Computing and Intelligent Interaction (ACII). pp. 1–7. IEEE (2019)
15. Grobe, T. G., Steinmann, S., Szecsenyi, J.: Arztreport 2018 — BARMER. Schriftenreihe zur Gesundheitsanalyse (2018)
16. Hamilton, D., Lane, J.V., Gaston, P., Patton, J., Macdonald, D., Simpson, A., Howie, C.: Assessing treatment outcomes using a single question: the net promoter score. The bone & joint journal **96**(5), 622–628 (2014)
17. Hunt, J., Eisenberg, D., Kilbourne, A.M.: Consequences of receipt of a psychiatric diagnosis for completion of college. Psychiatric Services 61(4), 399–404 (2010), https://pubmed.ncbi.nlm.nih.gov/20360280/

18. Inkster, B., Sarda, S., Subramanian, V.: An empathy-driven, conversational artificial intelligence agent (wysa) for digital mental well-being: Real-world data evaluation mixed-methods study. JMIR Mhealth Uhealth 6(11), e12106 (Nov 2018), https://doi.org/10.2196/12106
19. Kessler, R.C., Berglund, P., Demler, O., Jin, R., Merikangas, K.R., Walters, E.E.: Lifetime prevalence and age-of-onset distributions of DSM-IV disorders in the National Comorbidity Survey Replication. Archives of General Psychiatry **62**(6), 593–602 (2005)
20. Kroenke, K., Spitzer, R.L., Williams, J.B.: The phq-9: validity of a brief depression severity measure. Journal of general internal medicine **16**(9), 606–613 (2001)
21. Leahy, R.L.: The therapeutic relationship in cognitive-behavioral therapy. Behavioural and Cognitive Psychotherapy **36**(6), 769–777 (2008)
22. Martínez-Miranda, J., Martínez, A., Ramos, R., Aguilar, H., Jiménez, L., Arias, H., Rosales, G., Valencia, E.: Assessment of users' acceptability of a mobile-based embodied conversational agent for the prevention and detection of suicidal behaviour. Journal of Medical Systems **43**(8), 1–18 (2019)
23. Miner, A., Chow, A., Adler, S., Zaitsev, I., Tero, P., Darcy, A., Paepcke, A.: Conversational agents and mental health: Theory-informed assessment of language and affect. HAI 2016 - Proceedings of the 4th International Conference on Human Agent Interaction pp. 123–130 (2016)
24. Neyer, F.J., Felber, J., Gebhardt, C.: Entwicklung und validierung einer kurzskala zur erfassung von technikbereitschaft. Diagnostica (2012)
25. Ring, L., Bickmore, T., Pedrelli, P.: An affectively aware virtual therapist for depression counseling. In: ACM SIGCHI Conference on Human Factors in Computing Systems (CHI) workshop on Computing and Mental Health. pp. 01951–12 (2016)
26. Roediger, H.L., III., Butler, A.C.: The critical role of retrieval practice in long-term retention. Trends in cognitive sciences **15**(1), 20–27 (2011)
27. Russell, J.A.: A circumplex model of affect. Journal of Personality and Social Psychology **39**(6), 1161–1178 (1980)
28. Scherer, K., Schorr, A., Johnstone, T.: Appraisal Processes in Emotion: Theory, Methods. Research, Oup Usa (2001)
29. Schneider, W.: Ergonomische Gestaltung von Benutzungsschnittstellen: Kommentar zur Grundsatznorm DIN EN ISO 9241–110. Beuth Verlag (2008)
30. Spring, T., Casas, J., Daher, K., Mugellini, E., Abou Khaled, O.: Empathic response generation in chatbots. In: SwissText (2019)
31. Standardization, I.O.F.: Ergonomische anforderungen für bürotätigkeiten mit bildschirmgeräten teil 11: Anforderungen an die gebrauchstauglichkeit (1999)
32. Striegl, J., Gotthardt, M., Loitsch, C.: Investigating the Usability of Voice Assistant-based CBT for Age-related Depression. In: Computers Helping People with Special Needs. pp. 1–8. Springer International Publishing (2022)
33. Wampold, B., Norcross, J., Lambert, M.: Psychotherapy Relationships That Work. Oxford University Press, Oxford, United Kingdom (2019)
34. Wills, F., Plata, G.: Kognitive Therapie nach Aaron T. Therapeutische Skills kompakt. Junfermann Verlag, Beck (2014)

Augmented Reality Game for Children with Autism Spectrum Disorder

Mario Covarrubias Rodriguez[3(✉)], Shefali Mehta[2], and Milton Carlos Elias-Espinosa[1]

[1] Tecnológico de Monterrey, Escuela de Ingeniería y Ciencias, Mexico City, Mexico
[2] School of Design, Politecnico di Milano, 20156 Milan, Italy
[3] Virtual Prototyping and Augmented Reality Lab, Department of Mechanical Engineering, Lecco Campus, Politecnico di Milano, Milan, Italy
mario.covarrubias@polimi.it

Abstract. Games play an important role in the development of children. Especially when it comes to children with special needs like autism, it is important to have a different approach when it comes to learning. Shapes and colours are the most important fundamental skills that help in the recognition of objects around and help with letters and words. Balloon Pop is an application that is designed keeping in mind the requirements of children diagnosed with autism. The paper gives an idea of the user's needs and requirements and shows how the project solves the problem with augmented reality game design. The goal of the project is to design a game for autistic children that will help them learn the abstract concept of shapes and colours. The Digital game-based learning methodology (DGBL) is used in developing the game. The paper consists of the design rules that have been followed in designing for better interaction along with hardware and software architecture describing the flow of the project. Also, at last, the test and evaluation and 8 users have been done by using the System Usability Scale (SUS) tool. The application has been proven to be helpful for children along with parents/therapists to achieve the goal to make children interact and communicate freely, increase focus, and learn the abstract concepts of shapes and colour easily.

Keywords: Autism · Augmented reality · Game · Children · Balloon pop

1 Introduction

Autistic Spectrum Disorder (ASD) is a neuro developmental condition characterized [1] by persistent difficulties in communication and social interaction along with a restriction in interests and the presence of repetitive behaviours [2]. It is characterized by repetitive behaviours, lack of focus, and difficulties in social interaction [3]. Specifically, in this area, AR has shown some advantages with respect to more traditional interventions, as it allows individuals with ASD to

K. Miesenberger et al. (Eds.): ICCHP-AAATE 2022, LNCS 13341, pp. 462–467, 2022.
https://doi.org/10.1007/978-3-031-08648-9_53

be treated in more ecological and realistic environments that may be manipulated and adapted to the specific and heterogeneous characteristics that children and adolescents with ASD exhibit [4]. Nowadays, children are more exposed to technology than in the past. They interact with devices on an everyday basis and affinity toward the use of technology by children is quite noticeable [5]. In recent days, Augmented Reality has been a boost in the competitive digital market. The mobile gaming industry has evolved drastically over time, and children amidst the new generation find them-self more and more engaged and comfortable with this technology since it provides a virtual learning experience [6]. Balloon Pop is an Augmented reality-based game that is designed keeping in mind the needs of children with Autism Spectrum. The idea is to create an augmented reality-based game to teach kids the skills they need to feel calmer and more interactive, at the same time learning skills through a fun gaming activity. The project concentrates on building an AR application that kids could love. Such an application needs to be effective and tap into the kids' fascination and interest in technology, allowing for self-paced learning and individualized feedback. Another benefit of the application would be its scalability.

2 Objective

Balloon Pop is an application that is designed keeping in mind the needs of children diagnosed with autism. The goal of the project is to design a game for autistic children that will help them learn the abstract concept of shapes and colors. AR application game help kids interact by virtually experiencing and making the learning process more fun and engaging. The idea is to create a fun interactive AR game that can be easily used at homes by children, at schools by teachers, and by therapists. The project aims at:

- Visual learning: Gaining curiosity in the children to reason out the things they see and also helping them learn in an interactive way.
- Providing safe space: As children with autism don't easily feel secure in a changing environment, providing them with their own safe space is important.
- Keep up attention through gamification: Motivating the child to learn more by the process of gamification, different levels, and scoreboard. This also makes the overall process fun and engaging for the child.
- Repetitive process: Children with autism have a habit of repeating things, be it any task or routine. They feel comfortable in repetitive activity as they get more and more familiar with the process which in turn makes them learn faster.
- Improving communication skills: Children with ASD have difficulty communicating with others. They may not understand hand signals, or make eye contact, and have trouble reading facial expressions and understanding gestures. So in this case the aim is to make them slowly comfortable enough to communicate freely with other people around, by letting them feel comfortable.

- Sensory processing: It is a method used to perceive and respond to daily sensory stimuli. With the help of AR, creating an interactive application where the child interacts with the real world which makes it easier to generalize real-life situations through digital content.
- Problem-solving skills: By creating different levels of difficulty in the game application that helps the child learn problem-solving. By creating an environment to interact with the child at the same time to solve a given problem.

3 Method

The Digital game-based learning methodology (DGBL) is used in developing the game. The design rules have been followed in designing for better interaction along with hardware and software architecture describing the flow of the project. The game is designed using an easy interface for the user to understand it without difficulty as can be seen from Fig. 1.

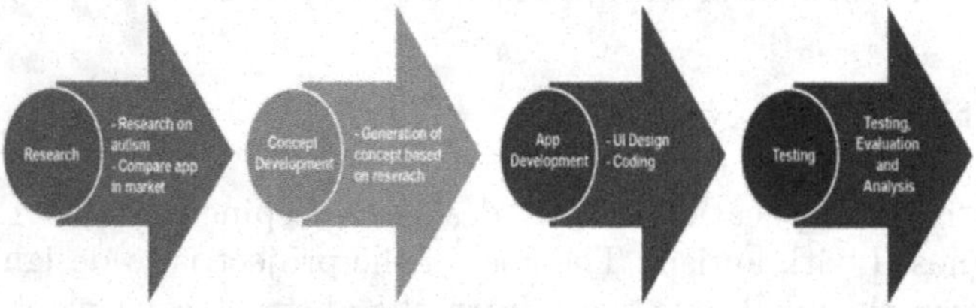

Fig. 1. First prototype of the mechanical arm.

4 Data Collection Process and Quality Assessment

The personal interview was conducted for a deeper understanding of the user's needs, and key points were taken into consideration while designing the application. The conversation was carried out with the parent of the child to understand the perspective for better analysing the challenges faced by them in everyday life. Following is an abstract of one of these conversations: ***"Stefano is a mild autistic child studying in primary school. He is currently doing a special day class which is a special education classroom with a teacher and therapist who have a smaller setting for children. Four times a week he goes there to learn, socialize and have interactive sessions. Stefano struggled to focus on a task for a long time. He gets bored very quickly. But he is good with repetitive things as it helps in building confidence in him. He doesn't really like human touch a lot and feels scared when hugged or touched. He is very sensitive to loud music, doesn't like others touching his toys. He likes to play Legos, and since the pandemic, he likes to play games on mobile as his therapy session was online. Playing with balloons and bubbles distract his mind and make him calmer and hence more interactive."***

Following are the questions asked through Google survey:

1. At what age the child was diagnosed with autism?
2. Does s/he interact with you?
3. Does s/he come up to you spontaneously for a chat?
4. Does s/he notice unusual details that others miss?
5. Does s/he like to do things over and over again, in the same way, all the time?
6. Can s/he keep a 2-way conversation going?
7. Can s/he read appropriately for his/her age?
8. What makes him/her calm down?
9. What kind of game helps him/her learn more effectively?
10. Is it hard for him/her to focus?
11. Does s/he have difficulty understanding rules?
12. Does s/he have strength in noticing patterns/shapes?

After the research was conducted the key finding that came out was that the children with autism have difficulty in interacting with others and they hardly initiate conversation. Many children showed difficulty in understanding complex rules, and some have good observation to notice unusual details. Many children find it hard to focus and concentrate when they play with objects that are familiar to them since they feel safe. Objects like balloons, bubbles are children favorite and even therapist uses them for their sessions to help them calm down.

5 Results

The Balloon Pop application was tested and has been validated by using the System Usability Scale (SUS). The parents/teachers assisting the 10 children with autism were asked to score the following set of questions from SUS that range from strongly agrees to strongly disagree. This group of children have started a focus learning program at Politecnico di Milano, Lecco Campus. Every Wednesday from 14.00 to 16.00 each child whit his/her assistant professor comes to the Virtual Prototyping and Augmented Reality Lab to perform different activities in order to increase the cognitive and motor capabilities. From the use of collaborative robots, Virtual and Augmented Reality applications like the Balloon Pop one.

All the children were different when it came to the severity of the autism spectrum. Every child reacted in a non-identical way to the game. The learning curve was different for every child. Some children were very quiet and liked to be in their own space as can be seen from Fig. 2.

Most importantly it helped them to have a bond to communicate better, at the same time having their own safe place with technology. Some children were very vocal and got distracted very easily. What seemed to be common among them was the interest in technology and predilection for visual objects around them. The game can be easily installed on all Android phones and no additional technical settings are required to operate the game. The rules of the

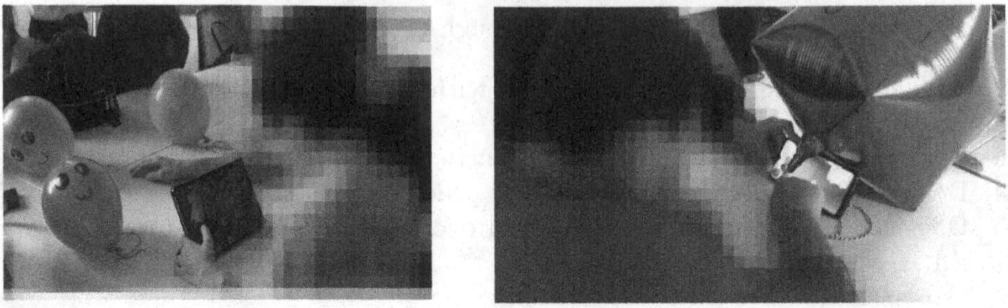

Fig. 2. User's while testing.

game were very simple and children could easily understand the game. Finally, for the usability test, the SUS score is Calculated, and the Final average score comes out to be ***88.12***, which is an excellent rating for user validation. The average score is calculated by using interpreting scores through the google form survey. Here is the radar chart shown for the usability test as can be seen from Fig. 3.

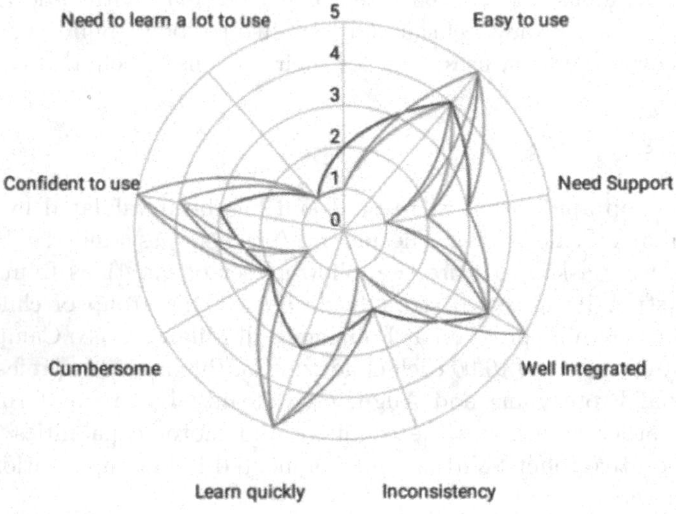

Fig. 3. User's while testing.

6 Conclusions

Throughout the paper and based on the results obtained, Augmented reality has shown a great potential towards teaching children with autism. The technology holds the promise of being effective where the traditional methods have failed since it can provide an intervention i.e. customizable to fit the needs of the learners. Since autism is a wide range of the spectrum, and behavior varies from child to child, the Balloon pop application can be customized according to the needs of the child. It can be used to improve social and language skills to communicate with the child while they are playing, by asking different questions. The game has proven to be useful for memorization and problem-solving skills, which helps them to focus on 2 tasks at the same time. Through augmented reality, the application helps to focus the children to maintain concentration and connection with the real world.

With the help of the user testing with autistic children, the application proves to be helpful for children to understand, investigate and learn the concept of shapes, colour, and emotions through just one application. The biggest benefit of the application is that augmented reality technology is proven to be able to connect abstract concepts and make them relevant to their own life. It helped in bridging the gap between traditional instruction methods and bringing abstract concepts to real life. The application holds a lot of opportunities for future work like making the application more advanced by integrating databases to store the high score, developing more advanced levels with different shapes of 3D balloons to make children understand the abstract educational topics.

References

1. American Psychiatric Association: Diagnostic and Statistical Manual of Mental Disorders, 5 edn. American Psychiatric Association (2013)
2. El-Seoud, A., Halabi, O., Geroimenko, V., et al.: Assisting individuals with autism and cognitive disorders: an augmented reality based framework (2019)
3. Autism and Developmental Disabilities Monitoring Network Surveillance Year 2008 Principal Investigator. Prevalence of autism spectrum disorders-autism and developmental disabilities monitoring network, 14 sites, United States, 2008. Morb. Mortal. Weekly Rep. Surveill. Summ. **61**(3), 1–19 (2012)
4. Christensen, D.L.: Prevalence and characteristics of autism spectrum disorder among children aged 8 years-autism and developmental disabilities monitoring network, 11 sites, united states, 2012. MMWR Surveil. Summ. **65**(3), 1 (2016)
5. Blumberg, S.J., Bramlett, M.D., Kogan, M.D., Schieve, L.A., Jones, J.R., Lu, M.C.: Changes in prevalence of parent-reported autism spectrum disorder in school-aged US children: 2007 to 2011–2012. No. 65, US Department of Health and Human Services, Centers for Disease Control and ... (2013)
6. Lim, K.C., Selamat, A., Alias, R.A., Krejcar, O., Fujita, H.: Usability measures in mobile-based augmented reality learning applications: a systematic review. Appl. Scie. **9**(13) (2019). https://doi.org/10.3390/app9132718, https://www.mdpi.com/2076-3417/9/13/2718

Making Person-Centred Health Care Beneficial for People with Mild Cognitive Impairment (MCI) or Mild Dementia – Results of Interviews with Patients and Their Informal Caregivers

Henrike Gappa[1], Yehya Mohamad[1(✉)], Martin Breidenbach[1], Pedro Abizanda[2], Wolfgang Schmidt-Barzynski[3], Antje Steinhoff[3], Timothy Robbins[4], Harpal Randeva[4], Ioannis Kyrou[4], Oana Cramariuc[5], Cristiana Ciobanu[5], Theodoros N. Arvanitis[6], Sarah N. Lim Choi Keung[6], Gokce Banu Laleci Ertürkmen[7], Mert Gencturk[7], Mustafa Yüksel[7], Jaouhar Ayadi[8], Luca Gilardi[8], Angelo Consoli[8], Lionello Ferrazzini[9], and Carlos A. Velasco[1]

[1] Fraunhofer Institute for Applied Information Technology (FIT), Sankt Augustin, Germany
{henrike.gappa,yehya.mohamad,martin.breidenbach, carlos.velasco.nunez}@fit.fraunhofer.de

[2] Facultad de Medicina de Albacete, Universidad de Castilla-La Mancha, Ciudad Real, Spain
pabizanda@sescam.jccm.es

[3] University Hospital OWL, Bielefeld, Germany
{wolfgang.schmidt-barzynski, antje.steinhoff}@klinikumbielefeld.de

[4] University Hospitals Coventry & Warwickshire NHS Trust, Coventry, UK
{timothy.robbins,harpal.randeva,ioannis.kyrou}@uhcw.nhs.uk

[5] Centrul IT pentru Stiinta si Technologie, Bucharest, Romania

[6] Institute of Digital Healthcare, WMG, University of Warwick, Coventry, UK
{t.arvanitis,s.n.lim-choi-keung}@warwick.ac.uk

[7] SRDC Software Research Development and Consultancy Corp, Ankara, Turkey
{gokce,mert,mustafa}@srdc.com.tr

[8] Eclexys Sagl, Riva San Vitale, Switzerland
{jaouhar.ayadi,luca.gilardi,angelo.consoli}@eclexys.com

[9] Octilium Sagl, Bioggio, Switzerland
lionello.ferrazzini@octilium.ch

Abstract. In the health care sector, person-centred treatment approaches have shown the potential to improve treatment outcomes and quality of life of patients. In particular, this applies where patients are living with complex conditions like multimorbid older patients with Mild Cognitive Impairment (MCI) or mild dementia. Such treatment approaches quite often include input from modern health technologies like health/home monitoring platforms which also offer services to patients for self-management of their conditions. This approach is also followed in the research project CAREPATH (An Integrated Solution for Sustainable Care for Multimorbid Patients with Dementia). To achieve acceptance of such complex health technologies, their services must be beneficial in the eyes of target end users which included in the case of CAREPATH, the patient's informal caregivers.

K. Miesenberger et al. (Eds.): ICCHP-AAATE 2022, LNCS 13341, pp. 468–474, 2022.
https://doi.org/10.1007/978-3-031-08648-9_54

Therefore, understanding the user requirements of patients and their informal caregivers is of utmost importance which was achieved in CAREPATH by interviews. These revealed that patients' preferences in regard to what services and information shall be provided to them shall be limited to what they deem necessary which is highly personal. Informal caregivers as opposed to patients, are much interested in receiving most possible information about their care-dependent's health status. Thus, provision of services and information for these user groups need to be highly customizable to their personal preferences and needs.

Keywords: Person-centred care · Health technologies · Home monitoring · Human-centred design · Usability · User requirements engineering

1 Introduction

In the health care sector, person-centred treatment is understood nowadays as a very promising approach to improve the treatment and quality of life, also for patients with complex conditions such as multimorbid older patients suffering from multiple chronic conditions as well as Mild Cognitive Impairment (MCI) or mild dementia. To reach best results, such treatment approaches quite often include input from modern health technologies such as health data collected by a health/home monitoring platform and self-reports from patients. Self-reports are most of the time gathered on platforms where patients are presented their care plan with tasks to complete in order to manage their health situation, such as measure their weight, take their medication, make an appointment with a health professional or fill out a health questionnaire - Patient-Reported Outcome Measures (PROMs). In this way, implementation of such technologies bears the potential to support patients in the self-management of their diseases. Informal caregivers may also benefit from such technologies because it will ease their care tasks, if they have access to, e.g., the care plan of their care-dependent and know about the status of tasks to-do. However, such technologies are often complex and require collaboration with the patient. Thus, to take advantage of their potential, it is of utmost importance to understand thoroughly the requirements of target end users, so they will be perceived as useful and offer a good user experience (UX) both known as key factors for acceptance.

Therefore, in the EU-funded research project CAREPATH (An Integrated Solution for Sustainable Care for Multimorbid Patients with Dementia) a process was established to elicit, document, update and follow-up on user requirements. It is the focus of CAREPATH to accomplish an ICT-based solution for optimising the clinical practice in the treatment and management of multimorbid older adults with MCI or mild dementia (see Fig. 1). In order to achieve this, CAREPATH will elaborate on a methodology for computer interpretable clinical guidelines and computationally derived best clinical practice for best suitable treatment of this patient group. Thereby, a multidisciplinary care approach is considered, with a focus on the very individual needs of patients in this group to be translated into personalized care plans. The project utilizes a health/home monitoring platform to receive health data analysed by artificial intelligence (AI) algorithms for clinical decision support and provides an integrated care platform for creating personalized care plans for the patients based on a patient's most recent context received from the health/home monitoring platform, AI algorithms as well as Electronic Healthcare Records.

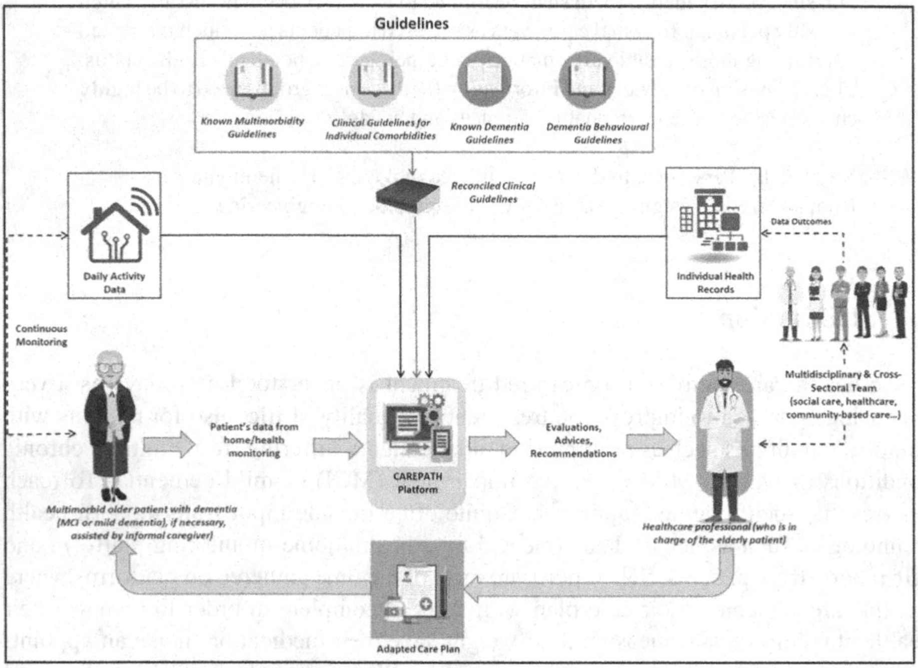

Fig. 1. The CAREPATH ecosystem

The CAREPATH approach will be validated in a clinical study with 208 multimorbid older patients with MCI or mild dementia (104 patients intervention group/104 patients control group) at pilot sites in Spain, UK, Romania, and Germany. In the project a strict human-centred design approach is followed according to ISO 9241–210:2019 [1] and thus target end user groups were involved in the design of the CAREPATH platform from the beginning of the project. As first activity user requirements were collected from in total 16 health professionals of various disciplines, 16 patients and 16 informal caregivers at the 4 pilot sites by interviews. In the course of the project, these will be updated and missing ones added by group-based expert walkthroughs with prototypes and a usability evaluation before the clinical study starts. In the following sections, the methodology for elicitation of first user requirements by interviews with patients and informal caregivers will be presented.

2 Methodology

It was considered most appropriate to involve patients and their informal caregivers in the elicitation of user requirements by conducting interviews, first, due to the pandemic situation not favouring group formats and second, because interviews are assumed to offer a situation where patients will feel most comfortable and safe. Interviews are an acknowledged method for gathering valid in-depth information suitable particularly in early design stages where issues to be considered for technical development are rather large [2]. They also offer a valuable means to gather information about opinions and attitudes of target end user towards IT-based environments such as CAREPATH and necessary pre-conditions for user acceptance. In the following a description of the test sample, the interview guidelines and interview results where user requirements were derived and documented for technical realization.

2.1 Test Sample

Since the project was at its beginning and ethics approvals and data protection agreement were not finalized yet, the interviews needed to be conducted under 'Patient and Public Involvement (PPI)' or similar regulations at each country involved which means no personal data of interviewees could be recorded. However, inclusion criteria were agreed on with pilot sites to ensure that the group of interviewees represents crucial characteristics of the CAREPATH target end user groups and that interview results are comparable. Each pilot site conducted interviews with 4 patients and 4 informal caregivers. For patients the inclusion criteria specified that they are of age 65 or older, are clinically diagnosed as living with MCI or mild dementia and are affected by at least one of the morbidities in focus of the project, e.g., diabetes, heart failure, hypertension, and chronic obstructive pulmonary disease (COPD). Beyond this, they should be using at least one electronic device such as a mobile phone. It had to be ensured that at each pilot site, two females and two males were interviewed and that two patients lived together with their informal caregivers whereas two lived alone and the informal caregiver somewhere else. Following this approach, inclusion criteria for informal caregivers determined that two are female and two are male, two live with their care-dependent and two do not live in the same household.

2.2 Interview Guidelines

As mentioned above, interviews were conducted at the 4 pilot sites of the CAREPATH project by health professionals with patients and informal caregivers they were familiar with. In order to ensure that in the interviews key themes were addressed that the project consortium aims to investigate and that interview results can be somehow related, an interview guideline was developed that included questions with a range of possible response options describing in more detail what information is sought for. For example, in case it was asked how patients are managing medication intake, possible responses included that either the informal or a professional caregiver helps them, they use a pill box, a calendar, an app etc. However, interviewers were always free on how to follow-up on a question, what issues to explore and even encouraged to elicit information not covered by the provided response options to learn best about users' requirements. In order to keep the effort for pilot sites within reasonable limits to document results of the interviews, the response options could also be used for documentation purposes and new information recorded in a dedicated section. According to the feedback from pilot sites, this approach was suitable to help them conduct and document results of the interviews. Since new preferences and needs of interviewees were recorded, it can be assumed that the structure of the interview guidelines did not seem to have narrowed down the investigation of issues.

The goal of patient interviews was to gain a better understanding of how the organization of everyday life is affected by their health conditions, what they would like help with and what specific tasks they need to fulfil in order to manage their conditions. The consortium is aware that people with cognitive impairments are a vulnerable user group and that interview question need to be very concrete and concise. Therefore, key themes to investigate were broken down into bits of information, so they are easy to answer, for instance 'Do you need help with taking your medication' was one of the questions to find out about care management at home and if the interviewee responded with 'Yes', they were asked what help is needed.

The interview guideline for patients covered the following key themes (number of questions is in parentheses): technical expertise and accessibility issues (3), care organisation at home (10), coping with cognitive impairment and management of everyday life (4), exercise and diet control (9), improvement of personal management (5). The interview guideline for informal caregivers included questions on: technical expertise and accessibility issues (3), care management (3), design of devices and sensors (1).

3 Results of Interviews

The interviews allowed the consortium to collect a plenitude of information in regard to how patients manage their health conditions, what informal caregivers seek help with and what are the preferences of both user groups. In the following some results will be highlighted. The majority of patients used a smartphone (n = 15), one a tablet. They used it mainly for making calls and chatting with the family by messaging services. Accessibility issues mentioned referred to problems with gestures such as swiping or pinching and design issues like too small buttons and cluttered screens. Fear of fraudsters and being observed were also mentioned. If asked what makes an application easy to use, main characteristic mentioned was that they are used to it. This hints at that when delivering a new application to this patient group, the first hurdle will be to support them while using it until they feel totally comfortable with handling it.

When presented with an example of a daily care plan, that could be shown to patients on a tablet to support them in achieving their daily care tasks, 6 patients responded that this could be of help to them, 10 stated that they do not think so. Reasons provided were that they do not have many tasks to do, that it is everyday routine for them and 4 patients would feel supervised. However, 8 informal caregivers were interested in receiving such a plan for them as well their care-dependent to be aware of the to-dos and their status, 5 said this could be helpful in a later stage.

About half of the patients (n = 9) measure vital parameters mainly in case they do not feel well. However, they do not document results and take this information along when visiting physicians. 7 patients admitted though that this could be useful. Along this line, in the opinion of 7 patients utilizing technology could help to receive better overview on the personal health condition by, e.g., checking results of blood pressure measurements (n = 7), weight (n = 4), sleep (n = 3) and pain (n = 3). 11 informal caregivers stated that they would be much interested in being presented results from their care-dependents' health measurements.

8 patients stated that they would like to remind themselves of doctor's appointments and the medication list. They also would like to document symptoms such as how they feel on a day, when they have health problems such as headaches, constipation issues etc. It was also mentioned by 8 patients that they need support with everyday activities such as shopping or preparation of meals. 9 patients said that they forget things they wanted to do, e.g., call a friend or a family member or listen to a concert on the radio, 5 of these patients would like to be reminded of such activities.

The majority of informal caregivers (n = 10) stated that they need help with their care tasks, 5 said that for now they can handle the situation. Main issues mentioned were keeping track of appointments with health professionals (n = 4) as well as taking to and picking up their care-dependent from appointments with therapists, friends, social activities etc. (n = 4). Furthermore, they were worried to leave the house, because they do not know what is happening when they are away (n = 4). They are mainly afraid that the care-dependent might fall, starts wandering in the house or leaves the house (n = 4) and that accidents may happen with using the kitchen and water spilling over (n = 3).

When asking informal caregivers whether they feel sometimes unsure about their care-dependent's health situation, 7 stated that they do not feel unsure, but 9 felt unsure though in regard to a risk of fall (n = 7), deterioration of cognitive status they do not notice (n = 5) and unnoticed worsening of the physical conditions (n = 3).

Finally, informal caregivers together with their care-dependent were asked about design requirements for sensors and devices used by a health/home monitoring platform. Requirements most often mentioned were the following: Be comfortable to wear (n = 11), easy to handle (n = 10) and provision of means to find the device in case it is misplaced (n = 9).

4 Conclusion

Results from the interviews revealed that the preferences and needs of patients vary in regard to what information they are interested in, what they would like to be reminded of and in their perception of health technology providing potentially a powerful tool to support them in self-management of their health conditions. The latter might be due to some reluctancy to give up established routines, even though sometimes perceived as suboptimal.

Another relevant finding of the interviews was that much care needs to be taken to avoid that patients will feel overwhelmed by too many tasks and new situations they may easily experience as obstructive. Besides this, patients aim to lead a self-determined life as much as possible and, therefore, seek support only where deemed necessary. The view of informal caregivers differed a bit sometimes in regard to where help is needed, however, a major issue for both target groups was management of appointments with health professionals.

So, from the interviews it became apparent that services and information presented on the CAREPATH platform for patients and informal caregivers need to be highly customizable to their personal needs to make them beneficial.

Acknowledgments. This work was partially funded by the European Union's Horizon 2020 research and innovation programme under grant agreement No 945169. The authors would like to acknowledge the support of the CAREPATH consortium.

References

1. ISO 9241–210:2019 Ergonomics of human-system interaction – Part 210: Human-centred design for interactive systems (2019)
2. Fricker, S.A., Thümmler, C., Gavras, A. (eds.): Requirements Engineering for Digital Health. Springer, Cham (2015). https://doi.org/10.1007/978-3-319-09798-5

Augmentative and Alternative Communication (AAC): Emerging Trends, Opportunities and Innovations

Augmentative and Alternative Communication Emerging Trends, Opportunities and Innovations

Introduction to the Special Thematic Session

E. A. Draffan[1](✉) and David Banes[2]

[1] WAIS, ECS, University of Southampton, Southampton, UK
ead@ecs.soton.ac.uk
[2] David Banes Access and Inclusion Services, Milton Keynes, UK

Abstract. Augmentative and Alternative Communication (AAC) technologies, training and support have benefitted from significant emerging trends in recent years to cope with the changing environments experienced by many users. The landscape of inclusion, whether it means different forms of digital accessibility, tele-support or more built-in assistive technology in everyday devices, has helped many more individuals with speech and language difficulties communicate effectively. There has also been an increased use of artificial intelligence, including machine learning and natural language processing with improved multilingual automatic speech recognition (ASR) and text to speech, location capturing apps and the Internet of Things being just a few of the technologies providing the world of AAC with a wealth of exciting emerging trends, opportunities and innovations. This special thematic session aims to provide an insight into some of the trends developing across Europe and the wider community.

Keywords: AAC · Augmentative and Alternative Communication · Disability · Symbols · Assistive technology · Participatory

1 Introduction

According to the International Telecommunication Union in 2019, 85% of European households had access to the internet, 77.7% had access to a computer, "with mobile cellular subscriptions far in excess of 100 subscriptions per 100 inhabitants in 38 out of 45 countries" [1]. However, these statistics do not highlight the fact that within Europe 25% of the population are disabled and half of these individuals fail to use the internet regularly [2]. This is concerning, as the majority of new technologies available to support functional limitations require online access, even if it is just to download an app or in the case of augmentative and alternative communication (AAC) speech generating devices (SGDs), chosen symbol sets or voices, vocabularies and links to support. This disparity may be due to a lack of connectivity, digital skills, knowledgeable support or a combination of all three. Its impact on those with complex communication needs (CCN) may prevent access to more affordable and adaptable technologies than have been

K. Miesenberger et al. (Eds.): ICCHP-AATE 2022, LNCS 13341, pp. 477–482, 2022.
https://doi.org/10.1007/978-3-031-08648-9_55

available in the past. Networked systems also have the potential to give AAC users a voice and independence, using increasingly socially acceptable devices and applications [3].

The fact that AAC devices have become increasingly dependent on some form of internet connection, at some stage, is often based on a need to upload data as well as to download it. An app may need to be downloaded, but it may also need to gather data from the cloud (servers accessed via the Internet). So, for example an accurate GPS tracker can provide location specific vocabularies to aid symbol selection on a communication board or when required, family members, carers or technical staff can access information about the user's device to support any issues that are arising.

Many AAC systems that provide translations, speech to text or text to speech nowadays depend on some form of artificial intelligence (AI) [4]. The machine learning with natural language processing (NLP) usually looks for patterns in the language and aims to provide as accurate an output as possible. English speakers often have an advantage in this area, due in part to large cleaned datasets with good labelling and no accents or diacritics. The range of English speech synthesizers for AAC users is more plentiful compared to some other languages, where acceptable text to speech requires an understanding of the nuances of pronunciation and the different ways diacritics are used, especially if these have been omitted in written text and context becomes important.

There can also be challenges when an AAC user interacts with a device that is using automatic speech recognition, such as a smart speaker within the home environment. The clarity and time taken to speak can have an impact, but it has been shown how these devices not only work with dysarthric speech, but also with messages on SGDs. These tools can provide chances for social engagement, feelings of independence and freedom as well as positive outcomes in terms of daily care [5].

The ideas discussed in this introduction will be presented in more detail under the following three main themes namely: Assessment and Frameworks, Participation and Collaboration and finally Independence, as a series of emerging trends, opportunities and innovations for those involved with Augmentative and Alternative Communication (AAC).

2 Assessment and Frameworks

Over the years many frameworks for the assessment of a potential user's abilities to engage with different types of Assistive Technologies (AT) and AAC have been proposed as well as the frameworks providing support for technology choices. Frameworks can provide a basic conceptional structure for any task, but they have to be adaptable over time as circumstances change. In the world of AT some lean towards a medical model, highlighting functional limitations and others such as The Human, Activities, Assistive Technology (HAAT) model "conceptualizes the consumer, their activities, environment, and assistive technology as an integrated system in which changing one element affects all other elements in the system" [5].

Although AAC users may be introduced to systems that involve the use of technology and HAAT can guide clinical decision making, there are often gaps in the assessment framework that need to be considered when working with those who have autism. The paper titled "AAC for individuals with autism: additional considerations" suggests these gaps mainly relate to the need for constant reviewing of assessed capabilities, motivation and the possibility of "disruptions in sensory processing [that] may produce cascading effects on social and communication development" [6] as well as the need to consider the communication partner's understanding of the individual's sensory needs [7]. In order to address these issues, the authors further suggest the need to adjust existing frameworks, such as the participation model [8] as well as considering the skills of those around the potential AAC user and "provision of sensory processing interventions". They conclude with a note about the need for careful selection of the AAC system itself, which provides an interesting lead into the following paper.

Sacchi et al. state that when assessing the functions available on an AAC SGD the framework developed needs to address the "communicative and linguistic functions of the communication software". Feature lists for devices are usually available, but it is rare for the information to contain in depth descriptions of the potential linguistic capabilities of the content provided. There may be mention of the voices used for various languages, different symbol sets and vocabularies available. However, a lack of more in-depth descriptions can become an issue when considering bi-lingual or multilingual situations. Future SGD communication boards may even lack certain dynamic elements in some languages because of the complexities involved resulting in poorer messaging.

As has been suggested in the introduction, many AAC systems are based on the English language, which has a very different grammatical and syntactical structure to some other languages, even those that use Latin as a base, such as Italian and Spanish. Sacchi et al. illustrate how important it is to assess the pragmatic, semantic and morpho-syntactic elements within a language and their impact on the generation of fluent messaging. Just as frameworks can be adapted to suit individual abilities, so they can be added to in order to consider spoken and written language differences. In this case it is the adaptation of the 'Graphic Symbol Utterance and Sentence Development Framework' [9] covering the progression from pragmatic symbol use to meaningful semantic levels of symbol combinations onto basic sentences and finally grammatically correct constructions that has been required.

These two papers highlight the importance of evaluating the assessment criteria presented within any framework prior to its use, in order to ensure it is fit for purpose. The components need to be sufficiently open for any adaptation to occur, so that they can support a wide range of skills, tasks, resources, environments (linguistic, social, cultural or physical), expertise and tools at the time of the assessment.

3 Participation and Collaboration

Participatory technology design can have many positives in particular when working in the field of disability but it is not without challenges [11]. It is interesting to see in the paper shared by Clastres-Babou et al. that it is the experts working with those who have complex communication needs who are drawn into the user-centered design process. They illustrate how these stakeholders are encouraged to actively demonstrate their expertise and decision making when trialing various features available on an AAC tool. The process shows how changes are made to the application and the addition of a version for the web would eventually be available. By following up with trials using prototypes, stakeholders could further shape the outcome of the software prior to its final release.

Stakeholders may come with many different views about how a product should be designed, but by ensuring decisions were made in a participatory manner with the original development team, it was clear that there was a certain degree of ownership of the outcome. This was seen in the discussions concerning enhanced features and the setting of further goals (such as the introduction of a web version). The participation of stakeholders clearly enabled a co-design process, as has been suggested by other researchers in the past [12].

The rationale behind a collaborative ecosystem for open licenced AAC, has distinct similarities to the participatory approaches already described as will be presented by Draffan and Banes. However, in this case the project design involved the planning of a "sequence of activities that not only produced a meaningful result, but also facilitate small groups working together to achieve common goals" [13]. As there was a common goal at the outset, the combining of very different types of expertise and knowledge meant that the small groups in different localities could co-create projects, technologies, training and support for AAC users.

Nevertheless, projects that involve participation and collaboration can result in task allocation challenges, time management issues and communication mishaps, but the overall impact of sharing ideas, innovating designs and providing successfully inclusive outcomes can produce life long changes for those who benefit from the results as has been demonstrated in these papers.

4 Independence

The final three papers all present users with the chance of independence, despite using very different technologies. They depend on different forms of AI but are linked through communication, whether via the use of symbols or voice. The devices used are those available to the public, such as mobile phones and smart speakers, but the innovations provide specific support for those with speech and language difficulties.

Ahn et al. have suggested a location and situation based AAC service that could offer the potential user with the symbols relevant to a place visited and commonly used circumstances, such as choosing a menu and paying. GPS tracking and map services make it possible for a user to choose locations that are then linked to a recommender system that predicts suitable symbols for secondary or sub communication boards.

One of the issues for many AAC users is not having a wide range of specific vocabularies to hand, or as subsidiary boards linked to a general core board or home board on their device. So, to have the potential to make it possible to offer automated selections based on context and frequency of use, could not only increase independence, but also be a time saver if the AAC user is a skilled user.

However, being able to control devices when AAC users have co-occurring physical disabilities is a challenge that can require assistance. So, an alternative to human help could be a positive move towards increased independence. This appears to be happening in part by the use of the Internet of Things (IoT) using sensors, the internet and smart speakers. Ryu et al. suggest that linking these systems as part of an interconnected service, allows users to listen to their favourite music, turn lights on and off, answer a phone and carry out many other tasks, thus "enhancing their quality of life and self-esteem".

Once again issues can arise, in this case with ASR systems failing to work with spoken language that is not enunciated clearly or at a regular pace. It appears that the datasets for atypical speech such as dysarthria are limited. This means that there is insufficient training data to enhance accuracy and the problem may be exacerbated when the language in not English, as discussed by Madina et al. In this case the choice for those with poor articulation is not to turn to the use of pictographs, but rather to work with speaker-adaptive systems that allow for personalization in order to achieve independence of use and take control of devices via their own spoken commands.

5 Discussion and Conclusion

The thread following through all the papers moving from assessment to participation and independence allows us to believe that we can help to provide improved strategies for AAC users and those with speech and language difficulties, by introducing technological solutions to enhance engagement with society. Nevertheless, challenges remain with the way artificial intelligence supports the process, often due to a lack of data that can be used for training algorithms. Time will tell whether different types of generative models and deep learning will produce better results for a minority population. Nevertheless, there is no doubt that over the last ten years there have been many interesting AAC trends emerging, providing increased opportunities and innovations to support users with speech, language and literacy difficulties.

References

1. International Telecommunication Union, Digital trends in Europe 2021 ICT Trends and Developments in Europe, 2017–2020 (2021)
2. Evidence Digest #6 Digital Inclusion for People with Disabilities. Medici Project, https://digitalinclusion.eu/wp-content/uploads/2021/03/Evidence-Digest-Digital-Inclusion-people-with-disabilities.pdf Accessed 28 Mar 2022
3. McNaughton, D., Light, J.: The iPad and mobile technology revolution: benefits and challenges for individuals who require augmentative and alternative communication. Augment. Altern. Commun. **29**(2), 107–116 (2013)
4. Sennott, S.C., Akagi, L., Lee, M., Rhodes, A.: AAC and artificial intelligence (AI). Top. Lang. Disord. **39**(4), 389 (2019)
5. Corso, C.L.: The Impact of Smart Home Technology on Independence for Individuals Who Use Augmentative and Alternative Communication. Ohio University (2021)
6. Cook, A.M., Polgar, J.M., Livingston, N.J.: Need-and task-based design and evaluation. In: Design and Use of Assistive Technology, pp. 41–48. Springer, New York (2011)
7. Feldman, J.I., et al.: Relations between the McGurk effect, social and communication skill, and autistic features in children with and without autism. J. Autism Dev. Disord. **52**(5), 1920–1928 (2021)
8. Beukelman, D.R., Mirenda, P.: Augmentative and Alternative Communication. Paul H. Brookes, Baltimore (1998)

9. Binger, C., Kent-Walsh, J., Harrington, N., Hollerbach, Q.C.: Tracking early sentence-building progress in graphic symbol communication. Lang. Speech Hear. Serv. Sch. **51**(2), 317–328 (2020)
10. Robb, N., Boyle, B., Politis, Y., Newbutt, N., Kuo, H.J., Sung, C.: Participatory technology design for autism and cognitive disabilities: a narrative overview of issues and techniques. Recent Advances in Technologies for Inclusive Well-Being, pp. 469–485 (2021)
11. Everitt, A., Hardiker, P., Littlewood, J., Mullender, A.: Applied Research for Better Practice. Macmillan, London (1992)
12. Calder, D.: Multimedia speech therapy tools and other disability solutions as part of a digital ecosystem framework. In: International Conference on Intelligent Information Processing, pp. 326–335. Springer, Heidelberg (2010). https://doi.org/10.1007/978-3-642-16327-2_39

Open Licensed AAC in a Collaborative Ecosystem

E. A. Draffan[1(✉)] and David Banes[2]

[1] ECS, University of Southampton, Southampton, UK
ead@ecs.soton.ac.uk

[2] David Banes Access and Inclusion Services, Milton Keynes, UK

Abstract. A collaborative ecosystem that encompasses the use of open-licensed augmentative and alternative communication (AAC) solutions and systems has the potential to provide positive outcomes for children with severe speech and language difficulties. This has been shown through a project that highlighted the willingness to provide a considerable amount of teamwork and participation of families and carers involving 124 children with complex communication needs across three Eastern European countries. Participation was based around a UNICEF hub in each capital city. The hub provided support for small groups of AAC experts sharing their knowledge with limited resources and widely varying groups of other professionals, families and carers of potential AAC users. Initial face to face training sessions provided introductory sessions to open licensed AAC solutions and systems. These sessions were backed up by 'anytime' access to an open licensed eLearning platform containing freely adaptable interactive AAC online training resources to be translated into modules by participants in each country. The level of content was based on the first three levels of the European Qualifications Framework. There followed the development of pictographic symbol sets to enhance the localization of already available sets suitable for children. Cultural, linguistic, and social settings were catered for within an open-source communication app. Feedback and formal evaluations provided by parents, carers and professionals showed that the benefits to the children were not just in AAC use, but also in their social competency levels, self-esteem and adaptability.

Keywords: Open license · AAC · Augmentative and Alternative Communication · Disability · Symbols · Assistive technology · Participatory · PIADS

1 Introduction

Open licensed Augmentative and Alternative Communication solutions and systems for those with complex speech and language difficulties, have the potential to support interventions where collaboration with localization occurs. The nature of open-licensed technologies and content also expands the options available to those living in areas where support for AAC is limited and acquiring suitable technologies can be costly [1]. However, at the time of writing, gaps still remain in the market, such as a lack of easily

K. Miesenberger et al. (Eds.): ICCHP-AAATE 2022, LNCS 13341, pp. 483–488, 2022.
https://doi.org/10.1007/978-3-031-08648-9_56

developed open licensed speech synthesis for text to speech in minority languages and not all multilingual AAC apps are available for Android tablets. Despite these barriers, open licenses can offer the chance to ensure that any choices made and decisions taken, can respect local languages, cultures, religions and social settings, because opportunities for local adaptations can be embraced with a degree of flexibility.

The collaborative model chosen for this project included 'person-focused learning' where colleagues already knowledgeable about AAC supported those wishing to learn more about AAC "to work directly with family members and individuals with disabilities in collaborative teams, using augmentative and alternative communication systems" [2]. The amount of international engagement within the model depends on the requirements gathered by local teams. As several countries were coming together to support AAC within a larger region, under the auspices of the United Nations Children's Fund (UNICEF), the model needed to be sustainable and scalable. Even at the outset, it was hoped that more countries would implement the collaborative ecosystem concept independently of the original project.

The initial scope of the project included plans to create additional AAC symbol sets to support local languages and culture, to be used alongside a more extensive previously developed open-licensed AAC pictographic symbol set. There was the provision of Android tablets with an open-source AAC app that would automatically link to the newly created symbol sets, as well as other open licensed symbol sets and newly created voices for text to speech in the relevant languages. Open licensed online and face to face training resources were developed with various feedback systems put in place for evaluation purposes.

There was a commitment to sharing knowledge throughout the process, with an understanding that any time constraints and cost implications to participants would be carefully monitored by local UNICEF teams. Finding solutions and systems for complex technical problems, such as the development of the AAC app and speech synthesis were contracted out to independent companies. The website hosting the multilingual repository of symbols and open-licensed learning platform was open to all those registering on the system. This not only allowed authors to create surveys for voting on the new symbols but also for the development of paper-based communication boards and personalized images or symbols with additional elements to denote concepts such as tense or number.

2 Methodology

Action research could best be described as the way the study was undertaken as it had at its core the aim of being able "to contribute both to the practical concerns of people in an immediate problematic situation and to the goals of social science by joint collaboration within a mutually acceptable ethical framework" [3]. However, as many local participants became involved in the project and co-created the gathering of data, shared knowledge and outcomes, the actual method used over the eighteen months would better be described as Participatory Action Research (PAR) where "communities of inquiry and action evolve and address questions and issues that are significant for those who participate as co-researchers" [4].

An implementation plan was collaboratively developed with UNICEF and experts in each country with a series of work packages or eight main steps that were designed to overlap or run concurrently depending on local situations:

1. scoping the project and finding potential stakeholders,
2. making symbol choices for complex communication needs,
3. capacity development of professionals,
4. symbol design and building with the development of localised symbol sets).
5. introduction to technical AAC devices depending on requirements and
6. the adaptation and deployment of applications to potential users
7. support for families and carers
8. development of resources

Due to the geographical distances between the three participating Eastern European countries (Croatia, Montenegro and Serbia), all those involved in the project used online methods of communication and ethics procedures were dealt with by the individual countries. A series of interactive virtual training modules were developed to back up an initial three short face to face training days. Those involved included collaborators from a university department or a government representative from each country, teachers and therapists as well as family members or carers of potential AAC users. Each country also had a UNICEF office as the hub and 50 participants took part in the face to face meetings in Croatia and Serbia. Throughout the 18-month project strategies were developed and written up as blogs, short notes on social media, presentation slides, videos with AAC users, plus instructions for use of the CBoard[1] communication app and Android tablets. The addition and creation of new symbols involved voting for acceptance by all those supporting AAC users in each of the countries. The training package modules were created with support from both experts in AAC and translators. Those critiquing the end result included experts in AAC as well as local team participants, UNICEF and those working with potential AAC users. Social media and email groups were used for dissemination purposes and AAC forums grew up around the project in the various languages.

Online analytics were set up to judge the amount of interest in the project, because much of the development of communication boards and symbols occurred via the symbol repository site. Usage statistics plus downloads and registration for the training package were designed to provide quantitative data as part of the evaluation process.

A series of app development phases were planned with localised speech synthesis for Android devices. Across the three countries over 124 children (under 10 years of age cognitively) took part in the project and were supplied with the AAC systems. Their speech and language disabilities were mainly co-occurring with cognitive and physical difficulties such as cerebral palsy, autism, Downs Syndrome and sensory impairments. A wide range of professionals from teachers, therapists and psychologists supported the children living in urban and country areas. The Psychosocial Impact of Assistive Devices Scale (PIADS) was used to evaluate progress at three-monthly intervals. This scale was translated and had already been validated in several languages for use with children [5] making it a suitable tool to provide standardized user results across the three countries.

[1] https://www.cboard.io/.

3 Findings and Discussion

The impact of the initial project resulted in the development of three new symbol sets in Croatian and Serbian (also used in Montenegro), with the latter in both Latin and Cyrillic script. The process of voting on symbols, uploading and making symbol sets public was found to be much easier to demonstrate in face to face training, rather than via the email queries or further adaptations to the online instructions and short videos. The additions occurred with subsequent symbol set developments, where there had been no face to face demonstrations. It is proposed that the development of a knowledge base using queries and feedback received during the lifetime of the project and beyond, would further help with time management. Three more symbol sets in Urdu, Bulgarian and Turkish have since been uploaded with many of the initial issues having been resolved with another project having translated symbols into Greek. From a low base of 500 users two years ago the symbol repository site had over 8000 28-day active users from across the world by the beginning of 2022.

After the initial trials with the three countries, the AAC training modules, originally based on themes for AAC, were adapted to fit the European Qualifications Framework (EQF) first three skill levels and re-created with four additional translations. At times the sharing of technological skills was essential, as content authors/translators often had differing digital skill levels. Nevertheless, because Moodle was chosen as the open-licensed elearning platform, there were numerous resources and forums available when issues arose. At the beginning of 2022, 663 users had registered and two more translations were in progress. Those countries that took part in the translations have since been maintaining their own learning resources and when issues have arisen there has been good communication to ensure materials and links are kept up to date across the site.

The impact of the Cboard app with the localized symbol sets downloaded, via a Global Symbols application programming interface onto the Android tablets was overwhelmingly positive despite the impact of the COVID-19 pandemic. The latter occurred towards the end of the project, when traditional methods for exploring the experiences of parents and experts supporting the children, such as interviews and focus groups, were impossible. The amount of Cboard use was explored through the app's analytics, although this aspect of the program had not been fully developed at the time. Across the 124 children, positive progress was also reported in all but one case via an online version of the PIADS. There were 328 entries carried out by both professionals and parents or carers, so that the majority of children had 2 assessments and some had three. The subscales for competency, self-esteem and adaptability showed a high degree of achievement, reflecting the way all those involved in the project had broken down potential barriers to the use of AAC, as well as enabling the integration of the app and other AAC resources within both home and school settings. The overall survey results (Fig. 1) reflect progress made by the children six months after intervention, where around 50% had never used any form of Assistive Technology or AAC prior to the project.

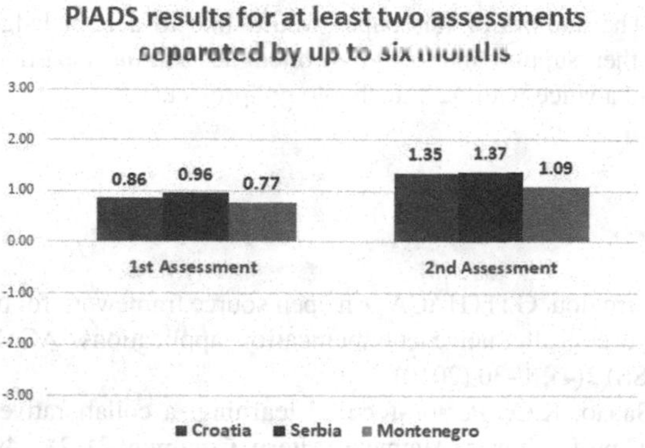

Fig. 1. "Individuals given a score of +1 or higher are more likely to continue to use their device" (Jutai, 2020 email message)

4 Conclusion and Future Recommendations

Making use of open licensed AAC in a collaborative ecosystem has the potential to offer positive outcomes when supporting children with complex communication needs. It is not often that one has the size and scale of the cohort of participants gathered together in this UNICEF project and further evaluations of the results still need to be validated and interrogated. However, it is possible that the cost-effectiveness and method of delivery could become part of a more detailed implementation plan for future open-licensed AAC projects.

Despite the major limitation to the study being the amount of face to face collaboration that was cut short with AAC users and between all the stakeholders including families and carers, due to the COVID-19 pandemic, many experts have remained directly involved with AAC user' participating teams. The collaboration has also stretched beyond the original three countries into North Macedonia, Bulgaria and Albania, that are now following through the steps discussed.

Nevertheless, there remains the need to ensure early intervention occurs for those groups of disabled children who may be hard to reach due to socio-economic and geographical isolation. Increased levels of training remain necessary in order to provide cost-effective AAC solutions and systems so that children can "develop sufficient skills to meet the functional communicative demands within real-world interactions with various partners in their natural environment. Communication is not an end goal in and of itself; rather, it is a tool to allow individuals to participate effectively and attain their goals at home, at school, at work, or in the community" [6].

This project provided training, technologies and support using open licensed AAC devices, apps and resources, that with the collaboration of those involved, resulted in increased levels of competency, self-esteem and adaptability (as part of a toolkit of skills) for a small group of AAC users. It is hoped that what has been achieved will have given participating children and others an increased chance of developing enhanced functional communication skills for social and academic inclusion, with continuing capacity building occurring in all the countries and beyond.

Acknowledgments. The authors of this paper would like to acknowledge their gratitude to UNICEF ECARO for their support and to all the colleagues and those participants involved with the "Giving every child a voice with AAC technology" project.

References

1. Pino, A., Kouroupetroglou, G.: ITHACA: An open source framework for building component-based augmentative and alternative communication applications. ACM Trans. Accessible Comput. (TACCESS) **2**(4), 1–30 (2010)
2. Robinson, N.B., Sadao, K.C.: Person-focused learning: a collaborative teaching model to prepare future AAC professionals. Augment. Altern. Commun. **21**(2), 149–163 (2005)
3. Rapoport, R.N.: Three dilemmas in action research: with special reference to the Tavistock experience. Human relations **23**(6), 499–513 (1970)
4. Reason, P., Bradbury, H.: The Sage Handbook of Action Research: Participative Inquiry and Practice. Sage, CA (2008). ISBN 978–1412920292
5. Jutai, J., Bortolussi, J.: Psychosocial impact of assistive technology: development of a measure for children. In: The 131st Annual Meeting (2003)
6. Light, J., Mcnaughton, D.: Designing AAC research and intervention to improve outcomes for individuals with complex communication needs. Augment. Altern. Commun. **31**(2), 85–96 (2015)

Development of a Location and Situation Based Augmentative and Alternative Communication Service

Seo-Yeong Ahn[1], Ki-Hyung Hong[2](✉), Kyungyang Kim[3], and Heeyeon Lee[4]

[1] Department of Future Convergence Technology Engineering, Sungshin W. University, Seoul, Korea
98_0731@honglab.org

[2] Department of Service and Design Engineering, Sungshin W. University, Seoul, Korea
khhong@sungshin.ac.kr

[3] Center of Communication Rights in Seoul for the People with Disabilities, Seoul, Korea

[4] Department of Special (Inclusive) Education, Gyeongin National University of Education, Incheon, Korea
hylee@ginue.ac.kr

Abstract. Mobile Augmentative and Alternative Communication (AAC) applications have great advantages in portability. Choosing the appropriate AAC board for a user's current location or situation is a very difficult and hard job for people with cerebral palsy, motor disabilities, or intellectual disabilities due to their limited motor skills or cognitive abilities. We developed a location and situation-based AAC service that automatically recommends a board suitable for the AAC users' current location and communication situation. Through a survey to identify places that those people with disabilities and their facilitators consider important, 20 built-in place type AAC boards were developed. The users can also create their own customized AAC boards for the specific locations where they visit frequently. The built-in and customized AAC boards for locations may consist of situation sub-boards with the order of communication contexts in the locations. We developed an algorithm to recommend the most appropriate location and situation-based AAC board from the built-in and customized boards based on the user's current location and communication context in that location. The location and situation-based AAC service is expected to improve the convenience of AAC users who have difficulties in using AAC applications due to their limited motor skills or cognitive abilities, and to facilitate the independent life of those AAC users.

Keywords: Augmentative and Alternative Communication · Location-based service · Communication · Situation · Mobile application

1 Introduction

Mobile Augmentative and Alternative Communication (AAC) applications [1–4] on smart devices have great advantage in portability. People with communication disabilities

K. Miesenberger et al. (Eds.): ICCHP-AAATE 2022, LNCS 13341, pp. 489–495, 2022.
https://doi.org/10.1007/978-3-031-08648-9_57

who are proficient in AAC use various AAC boards depending on the location or situation those people should choose the one of their AAC boards that is designated for the location or situation with their own hands. Choosing the appropriate board for the location or situation is a very difficult and hard job for people with cerebral palsy, motor disabilities, or intellectual disabilities due to their limited motor skills or cognitive abilities.

In this study, we developed a location and situation-based AAC service that automatically recommends a board suitable for the AAC users' current location and communication situation.

2 Related Work

Attempts [4–7] to automatically recommend AAC boards or symbols have persisted to improve the operating ability of people struggled with the physical operation of AAC tools.

Park [4] proposed the context-aware based smart work flow AAC system. The system uses the infrared sensor to recognize the user's current location and displays the AAC symbol suitable for the user's current location. The system can only be used in places where infrared transceivers are installed. The AAC tool proposed by Park and Kim [5] adaptively changes its layout and AAC symbols depending on location, time and click count information. It was developed especially for using only in school. The context aware AAC system proposed by Hossain [6] records history context including data about location, time-of-day, and season when user uses the system, and rearrange the AAC symbols by using that information. GeoAAC [7] recommend AAC boards based on user's location. GeoAAC only considers location information.

The location and situation based AAC service developed in this study uses location information provided by mobile devices without the need for special sensors or devices such as infrared transceivers in the place to be used. The developed service improves GeoAAC by considering the communication situations that are the topics of communication between AAC users and people around them on the location.

3 Location-Based AAC Boards

The location-based AAC service uses location-based AAC symbols and boards that are the addition of location information to general AAC symbols and boards [8] as shown in Fig. 1(a).

There are two types of location information.

- *Place type* information is the type of place such as 'coffee shop' and 'hair shop'.
- *Specific location* information includes latitude, longitude, and the name of the place.

We designed three types of location-based boards (built-in place type, customized place type, and customized specific location type) as shown in Fig. 1(b).

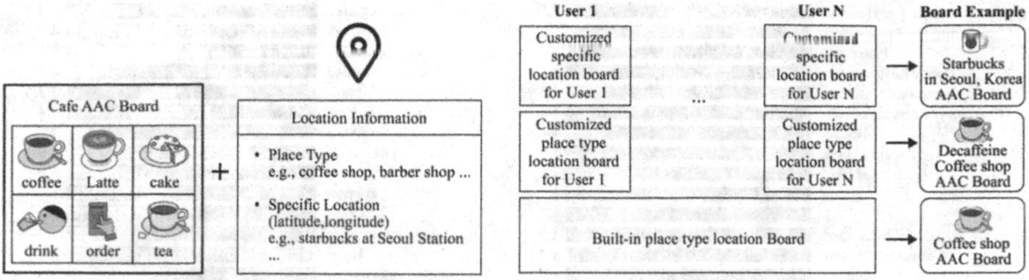

(a) Location-based AAC board (b) Location-based AAC board types

Fig. 1. Location-based AAC boards

3.1 Built-In Place Type AAC Boards

We conducted a user survey[1] to find out the types of places that people with cerebral palsy or severe multiple disabilities and their facilitators need the most. The participants of the survey were 18 people with disabilities and their facilitators through snowball sampling. The initial 50 types of places were selected from the AAC vocabulary lists for people with communication disabilities developed by Chae et al. [10]. After the 50 location categories were presented to the participants, they were asked to rate the importance of the location on a 5-point scale. For top 20 places in the preference order in the result of the survey as shown in Fig. 2, we developed the built-in place type AAC boards provided by default in the service. We will continuously add location-based AAC boards for other place types as built-in ones.

3.2 Customized Location Boards

In addition to the built-in board, the service supports facilitators for AAC user to create customized location-based boards. The process of creating customized location boards is given in Fig. 3.

There are two types of customized location-based boards.

Customized Place Type AAC Boards

Facilitators can personalize location-based boards of place types for a specific AAC user. For example, the built-in place type board for the 'coffee shop' includes common menu items provided at regular coffee shops, whereas the customized place type board for the user who drinks only de-caffeine drinks consists of only caffeine-free menu items.

Customized Specific Location AAC Boards

Customized specific location AAC boards can be made for specific places that AAC users frequently visit. It has the specific location information such as 'Starbucks at Seoul Station' as the name of the specific location and (37.554, 126.971) as its latitude and longitude. A customized specific location AAC board has the specific menu items that are served only in the user's favorite cafe.

[1] This study was approved by a university institutional review board (No. ewha-202104-0009-01) and consents obtained prior to the start of the study.

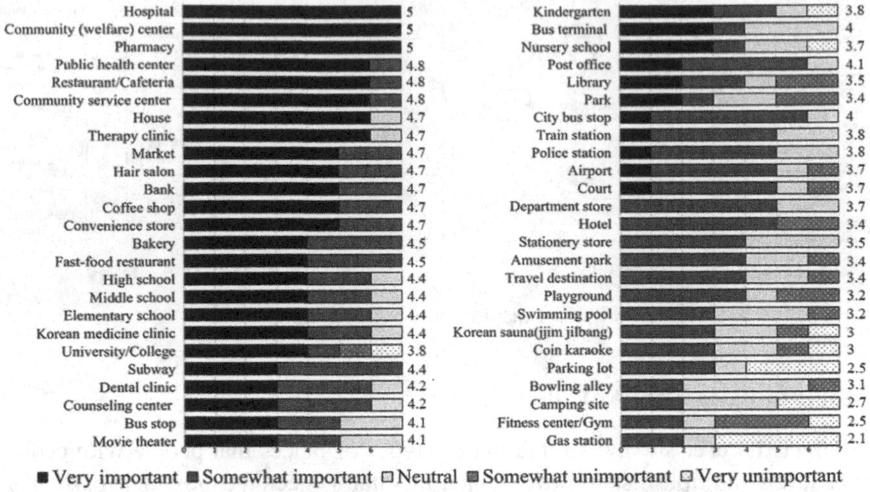

Fig. 2. The result of a user survey on the place preference

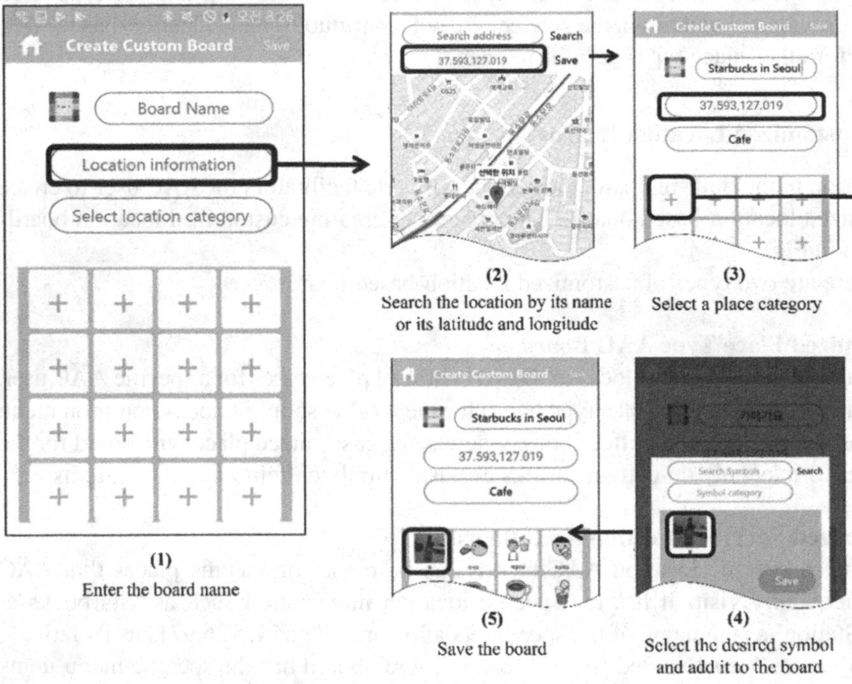

Fig. 3. The process of customizing location-based boards

4 Situation Sub-boards

Each place may have one or more communication situations. The situations refer to the contexts of communication between AAC users and people around them. A 'café' has "choosing a menu," "ordering," and "paying" situations. A situation tag can be attached to the AAC symbols that are used in the situation. Each symbol can have zero or more situation tags. Collecting symbols with the same situation tag becomes a situation sub-board that can be used in the situation.

The order of situations refers to the order of communication contexts in a location. For example, "ordering" usually occurs before "paying" When the situation sub-boards are displayed in the order of situations, user convenience is further improved as shown in Fig. 4. The 'café' place type board of Fig. 4 consists of three situation sub-boards in the order of "greeting", "ordering", and "paying". Among the symbols with the same situation tag, frequently used symbols are displayed first.

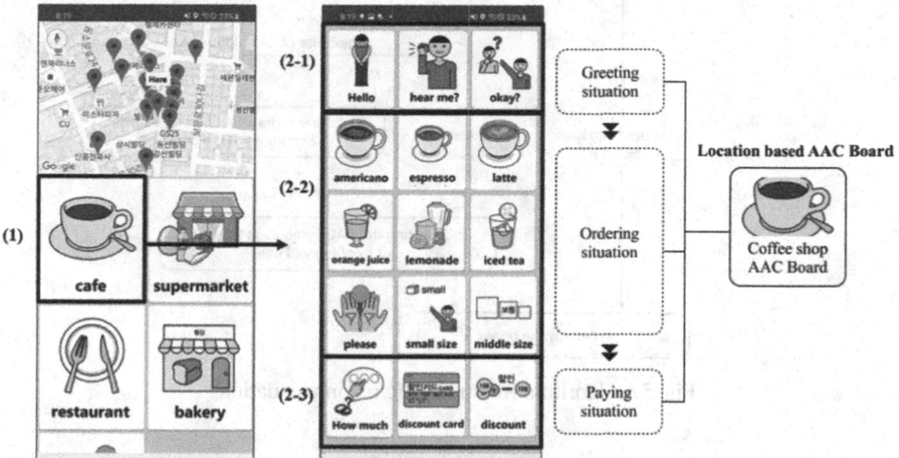

Fig. 4 Three situation sub-boards in a 'café' place type board

5 Algorithm for Automatic Recommendation

Figure 5 shows the algorithm to find the appropriate location-based AAC board based on the user's location and situation. The brief description for each step in the algorithm is as follows;

1) Searching nearby places based on the user's current location. The surrounding places are searched and collected based on the current user location information. When we get the user's current location, there is a location information error range. The error range vary depending on location determination methods. Generally, in the area such as Seoul where wireless data networks are well established, the error range is less than 3 m, but in the rural area where GPS is the only one to be used for location determination, it is about 5 m under the fine weather condition.

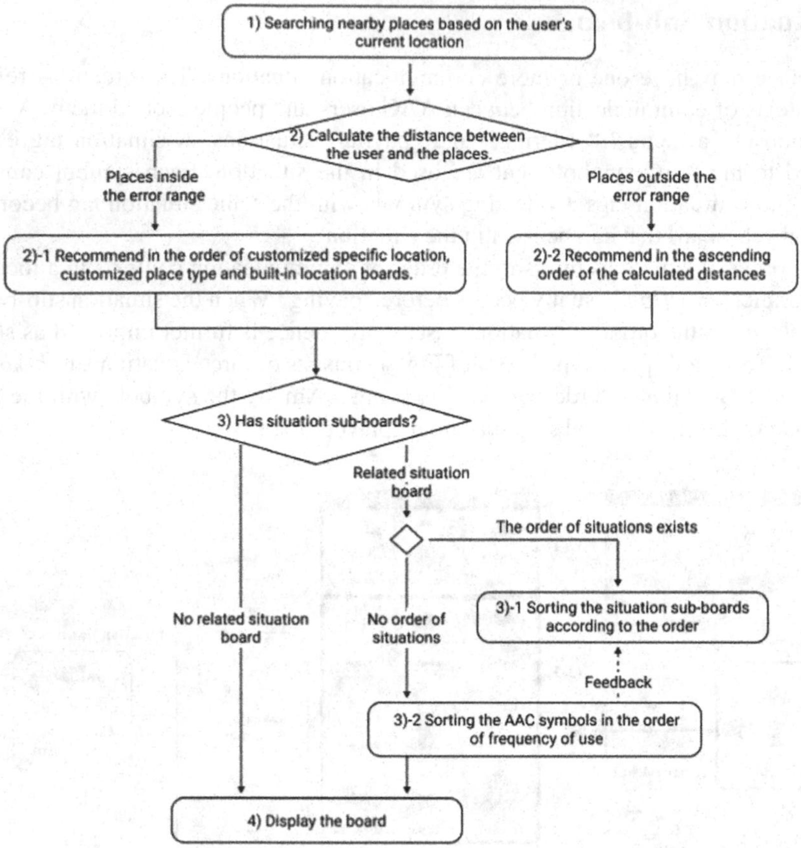

Fig. 5. Algorithm for automatic recommendation

2) Calculating the distances to the searched places and classifying places. The distances between the user and the searched places are calculated. The searched places are divided into two groups according to their distances from the user's location. The places within the error range take precedence over the places outside the error range.

2)-1 For the places within the error range, the calculated distances are meaningless information to find the most suitable location-based board. We first collect all types of location-based boards the user has for those places. Among those collected location-based boards, we recommend in the order of customized specific location boards, customized place type boards and built-in location boards. Within the error range, customized specific location boards for specific places frequently visited by users are arranged prior to other boards, and customized place type boards are placed prior to built-in place type boards.

2)-2 If the searched places are all outside of the location information error range, the board are aligned in ascending order of distance, and the first board in the order is recommended.

3) For the recommended board from step 2) consists of some situation sub-boards,

   3)-1 If there is an order of situations, the situation tagged AAC symbols are arranged in that order.

   3)-2 If there is no order of situations, the situation tagged AAC symbols are listed in the order of frequency of use.

4) Display the recommended location and situation-based AAC board from step 2 and 3.

6 Conclusion

The developed location and situation-based AAC service in this study automatically recommend an AAC board appropriate to the location and situation. The location and situation-based AAC service is expected to improve the convenience of AAC users who have difficulties in using AAC applications due to their limited motor skills or cognitive abilities, and to facilitate the independent life of those AAC users. Future study needs to be implemented to expand the built-in location boards for all of the places that AAC users generally visit.

Acknowledgments. This research was supported by the Assistive Technology R&D Project for People with Disabilities and the Elderly funded by the Ministry of Health & Welfare, Republic of Korea (grant number : HJ21C0007).

References

1. Mytalkie. http://www.mytalkie.co.kr Accessed 6 Mar 2020
2. Snap Core First. https://www.tobiidynavox.com Accessed 6 Mar 2020
3. Proloquo2Go. https://www.assistiveware.com/products/proloquo2go Accessed 6 Mar 2020
4. Quicktalk. https://digitalscribbler.com/quick-talk-aac Accessed 6 Mar 2020
5. Park, H., Kim, J.: Context-aware based smart workflow AAC (Augmentative and Alternative Communication) system. J. Digital Contents Soc, **10**(3), 469–477 (2009). (in Korean)
6. Park, D., Kim, Y.: Context-aware mobile system for augmentative and alternative communication. J. Korea Inst. Inf. Commun. Eng. **17**(7), 1740–1746 (2013). https://doi.org/10.6109/jkiice.2013.17.7.1740. (in Korean)
7. Hossain, S., Takanokura, M., Sakai, H., Katagiri, H.: Using context history and location in context-aware AAC systems for speech-language impairments. In: IMECS Proceedings of the International Multi-Conference of Engineers and Computer Scientists, pp. 128–133 (2018)
8. Cho, H., Hong, K.: A location-based augmentative and alternative communication mobile application. AAC Res. Practice **8**(1), 87–117 (2020). https://doi.org/10.14818/aac.2020.6.8.187. (in Korean)
9. Jang, Y., Hong, K.: An HTML5 based AAC board making system. KIISE Trans. Comput. Practices **21**(5), 365–372 (2015). https://doi.org/10.5626/ktcp.2015.21.5.365. (in Korean)
10. Chae, S., Lee, H., Hong, K.: Development of AAC vocabulary list for community living of people with communication disabilities – focusing on public institutions. AAC Res. Practice **9**(1), 1–26 (2021). https://doi.org/10.14818/aac.2021.8.9.1.1. (in Korean)

Augmentative and Alternative Interaction Service with AI Speakers to Access Home IoT Devices and Internet Services for People with Multiple Disabilities

Se-Hui Ryu[1], Ki-Hyung Hong[2(✉)], Soojung Chae[3], and Seok-Jeong Yeon[4]

[1] Department of Future Convergence Technology Engineering, Sungshin W. University, Seoul, Korea
rsh725@honglab.org

[2] Department of Service and Design Engineering, Sungshin W. University, Seoul, Korea
khhong@sungshin.ac.kr

[3] Department of Secondary Special Education, Jeonju University, Jeonju, Korea
sjchae7@jj.ac.kr

[4] Graduate School of Education, Inha University, Incheon, Korea
stonewell@inha.ac.kr

Abstract. With the growing demand for Internet-of-Things (IoT) and internet services for people with multiple disabilities, including communication and motor disabilities, we propose an Augmentative and Alternative Interaction (AAI) service for them. Interacting with IoT devices and internet services can be done by voice-controllable smart (or Artificial Intelligence (AI)) speakers. AI speakers are difficult to use for those people with multiple disabilities. The direct application of Augmentative and Alternative Communication (AAC) to the interaction is ineffective, since AAC mainly focuses on face-to-face communication and the sound produced by Text-to-Speech (TTS) for AAC symbols does not reflect the AI speakers' speech recognition features. Based on a user survey for AI speaker commands, we developed AAI symbols and boards to interact with home IoT devices and internet services through AI speakers. In order to improve speech recognition performance of AI speakers, we developed the TTS production format for AAI service, including wake-up words, silence intervals and commands. The AAI service allows people with multiple disabilities to control home IoT devices by themselves and to enjoy their spare time on their own by interacting with internet services such as music streaming, Over-the-Top (OTT) media services, and news searching through AI speakers.

Keywords: Augmentative and Alternative Interaction · Text-to-Speech production · Home Internet-of-Things device · Internet service · Artificial Intelligence speaker · Multiple disabilities

1 Introduction

Recently, as smart home services and various internet services such as music streaming, Over-the-Top (OTT) media services, and news searching have become popular, the desire

K. Miesenberger et al. (Eds.): ICCHP-AAATE 2022, LNCS 13341, pp. 496–502, 2022.
https://doi.org/10.1007/978-3-031-08648-9_58

of people with disabilities for internet services and Internet-of-Things (IoT) control has increased [1, 2].

Interacting with IoT devices and internet services can be done by voice-controllable Artificial Intelligence (AI) speakers (or smart speakers). The AI speakers are used to assist daily life in various ways, but not enough for people with multiple disabilities, including communication and motor disabilities [3]. In addition, there has been little research on how to use these technologies by people with multiple disabilities and their attitudes [4].

People with communication disorders use Augmentative and Alternative Communication (AAC) [5] symbols for face-to-face communication. Using the existing AAC symbols can be considered, but it is ineffective because the sound produced by Text-to-Speech (TTS) for the AAC symbols does not reflect the AI speakers' speech recognition features. In order to use home IoT devices and internet services, it is necessary to improve the AAC symbols and their TTS production method by reflecting the speech input characteristics of AI speakers.

In this study, we propose an Augmentative and Alternative Interaction (AAI) service for people with multiple disabilities, including communication and motor disabilities. The AAI service is based on AI speakers to control home automation IoT devices and to enjoy internet services.

2 Related Work

There have been many studies on the impact or effect of people with disabilities using AI speakers [2–4, 6]. In most studies, they concluded that AI speakers are needed for those people through user research, but they did not lead to practical development.

TD Snap of Tobii Dynavox [7] is one of the very popular AAC software. TD Snap has a feature that integrates AI assistants such as Google assistant [8]. With that feature, people with communication disabilities can access internet services and can control IoT devices. Since the integration of AI assistants is done in the software itself, the produced sound is for AAC users, not for AI speakers.

The proposed AAI service in this study is based on AI speakers. We developed TTS production method by reflecting the speech input characteristics of AI speakers. The users can select any kind of AI speakers they want to use. The proposed service has various settings options for AI speakers' features to configure customized home automation environment and internet services more flexibly.

3 An Augmentative and Alternative Interaction Service

Figure 1 shows the AAI service environment. AAI symbols are essential to use the AAI service because they are made up of improved TTS production method and commands for connected services to the AI speaker. For example, the AAI symbol such as 'Turn on the light,' 'Turn off the light' are needed to control a lighting, and 'Play the BTS's song,' 'Raise the volume by 3' are needed to use music streaming service.

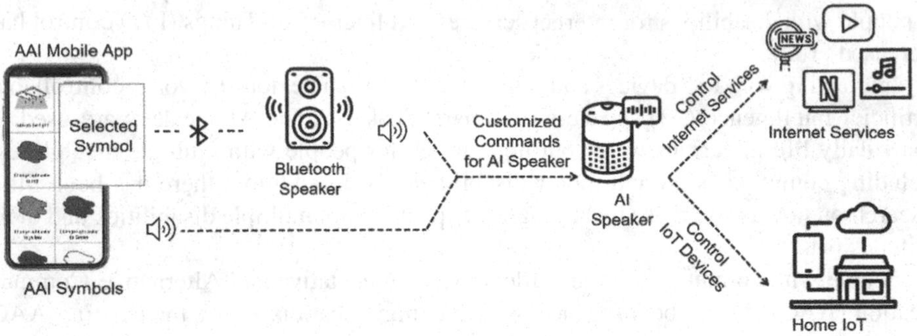

Fig. 1. AAI service environment

AI Speaker Command Survey

A Delphi survey[1] was conducted with 11 parents of children with multiple disabilities in AI speaker commands using the 5-point Likert scale (1 = strongly disagree, 2 = disagree, 3 = neutral, 4 = agree, 5 = strongly agree). As shown in Table 1, Home device control commands showed the highest demand, followed by Transportation, Diary, Search, Music, Daily life, Game, and Media.

Table 1. Results of AI speaker commands survey

	Category	Mean	(SD)
1	Home IoT	4.74	(0.41)
2	Transportation	4.52	(0.52)
3	Diary	4.46	(0.57)
4	Search	4.42	(0.50)
5	Music	4.34	(0.63)
6	Daily life	4.31	(0.64)
7	Game	4.25	(0.91)
8	Media	4.09	(0.65)
	Total	4.30	(0.60)

Development of AAI Symbols and Boards

We developed AAI symbols that users can use home IoT devices and internet services through the AI speaker. Figure 2 shows a set of AAI symbols to form an AAI board. Figure 2 is the board to control remote controllable devices, included AAI symbols such as ‘Turn on the TV,’ ‘Run the washer,’ or others. Unlike the AAC symbols for

[1] This study was approved by a university institutional review board (No. 210823-2A) and contents obtained prior to the start of the study.

communication, each AAI symbol has a control command as its name. AAI boards can be created for each home IoT device or internet service.

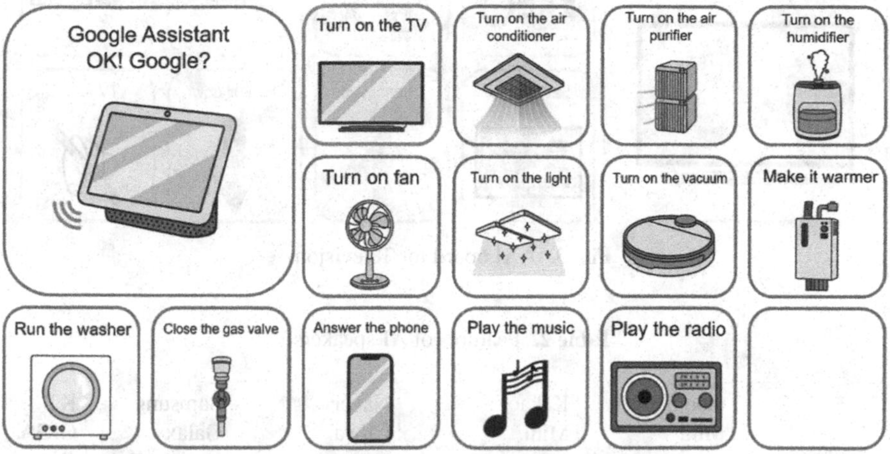

Fig. 2. AAI board for remote control

In Fig. 3 'Television' AAI board, AAI symbols such as 'Turn on the TV,' 'TV volume up' or others are included. AAI symbols such as 'What's the weather for today?', 'What's in the news?' or others are included in 'News' AAI board. Boards that are classified by services can also be organized by space, for example, if the user use lighting and searching service in his room, 'My room' board can be composed of lighting control AAI symbols and searching service AAI symbols.

Development of the TTS Production Method that Reflects AI Speaker's Features In the AAI service, AI speakers must be called and activated by their wake-up word. It takes a little time for the AI speakers to be activated after a call, but the required time varies from speaker to speaker. In order to produce improved TTS, we conducted experiments on the AI speakers of Google [9], Naver [10], Kakao [11], Samsung [12], and Korea Telecom (KT) [13]. Table 2 shows the identified features for them.

In General, the AI speakers have about 6 s of command waiting time after activation, but the AI speaker of KT (GiGA Genie) has a longer waiting time because it answers 'Yes' after activation and then it can accept commands. The speech recognition rate of AI speakers usually varies depending on wake-up words and voice colors.

It is necessary to provide suitable settings for different AI speakers according to their speech recognition characteristics.

If the user wants to use an AI speaker located farther than the distance that the sound of mobile devices can reach, using Bluetooth speakers will help increase the recognition rate. When using Bluetooth speakers, since there is some sound delay between a mobile device and its connected Bluetooth speaker, the initial-silence interval is required to prevent a command sentence from cutting off.

Figure 4 shows the TTS production format for AAI service derived from the experiment. When the user selects the AAI symbol, the sound produces as the format given

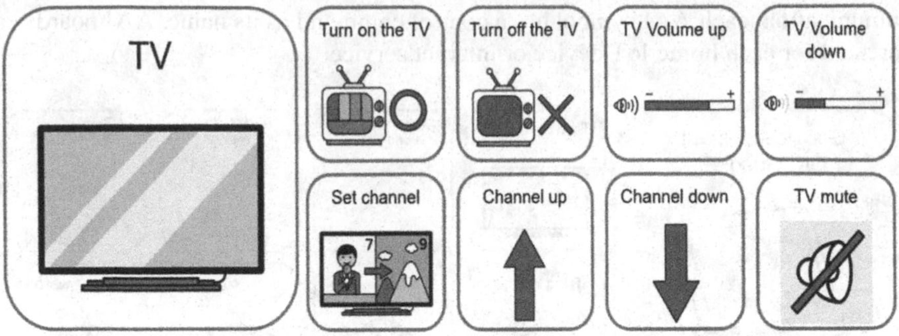

Fig. 3. AAI board for Television

Table 2. Features of AI speakers

	Google Nest Mini	Kakao Mini	Naver Clova	Samsung Galaxy Home Mini	KT GiGA Genie
Wake-up Word	"Ok Google"	"Hey Kakao"	"Clova"	"Hi Bixby"	"Giga genie"
Initial-Silence Interval (sec)	0.5	0.5	0.5	0.5	0.5
Middle-Silence Interval (sec)	0.5	0.5	1	0.5	1–2
Max. Command Waiting time (sec)	7	5	6	6	8
TTS Recognition	Recognized male voice well, but not female voice	Recognizes the sound from Bluetooth speakers well, but not from mobile devices	Speech recognition rate depends on the speech statement like "Clova", "Clova?", "Clova~" or etc.	Recognizes the sound from both Bluetooth speakers and mobile devices well	
Recognition Distance	- While playing music: recognizes well from close distance - Not playing music: recognizes well in the 1.5 m for female and 4 m for male, when using the mobile device speaker				-

in the figure. The TTS production format consists of the initial-silence, wake-up word, middle-silence and command word. The silence intervals are the initial-silence and middle-silence intervals. The initial-silence interval (0.5 s) is the silence time that precedes the wake-up word and is required when using Bluetooth speakers. Since AI speakers need some time to ready to accept control commands after listening their wake-up words, the middle-silence interval (0.5 to 2 s) is required. The AAI service provides a function that allows users to set silence intervals, wake-up word, and voice color according to their AI speakers. If users select their own AI speakers in their home using the AAI mobile application of the AAI service, it automatically sets the initial-silence interval, wake-up word and the middle-silence interval for the selected AI speaker.

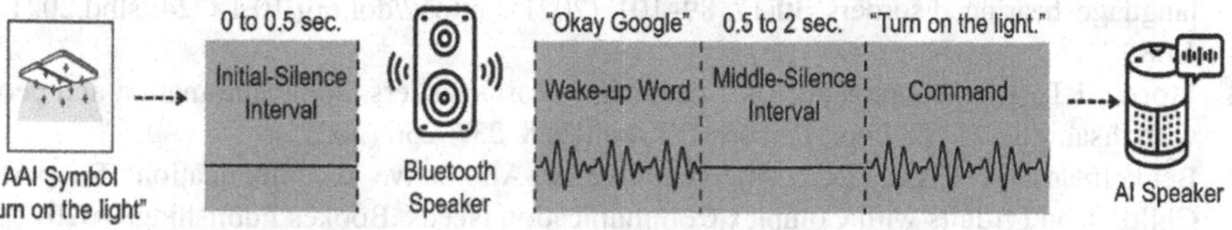

Fig. 4. TTS production format for AAI service

Selection of the Voice Color (of TTS) for AI Speakers
To increase speech recognition rate of AI speakers, we conducted an experiment to find which voices are well recognized for AI speakers, by using ReadSpeaker Korea TTS engine [14]. As shown in Table 2, Google Nest Mini recognizes the male voice better. The result shows that the AI speaker's speech recognition distance is longer when using the male voice than the female voice. Through the experiment, we found that the AI speakers usually recognize male voices better than female voices, and also the male voices have a longer recognition distance than the female voices.

4 Conclusion

It has been difficult for people with multiple disabilities to control home IoT devices or use internet services through the voice-controllable AI speakers. As a solution to this issue, we developed the AAI service, that consists of AAI symbols to control home IoT devices and to interact with internet services. With the help of the AAI service, people with multiple disabilities can create a desired home environment using home IoT devices without any help from others. Furthermore, they can receive the information that they need and spend their spare time on their own by interacting through internet services. The users can form an emotional stability and intimacy with AI speakers due to its personification characteristics [6]. Accordingly, people with multiple disabilities have a higher chance of enhancing their quality of life, self-esteem and confidence of independence.

Acknowledgements. This research was supported by the Assistive Technology R&D Project for People with Disabilities and the Elderly funded by the Ministry of Health & Welfare, Republic of Korea (grant number: HJ21C0007).

References

1. Kim, M., Yang, H., Lee, W., Lee, H.: IoT smart home adoption: the importance of proper level automation. J. Sensors (2018). https://doi.org/10.1155/2018/6464036
2. Kim, D.I., Jeong, E.H.: An effect of interaction using AI speakers on communication intensions and pragmatic characteristics of students with intellectual disabilities. Educ. Hearing-Lang. Impairments **11**(3), 91–113 (2020). https://doi.org/10.24009/ksehli.2020.11.3.005. (in Korean)
3. Kim, S.Y., Yim, D.: The effects of parents training on narrative interaction for parents with hearing loss who have children with normal hearing; a case study using AI speakers. J. speech-language hearing disorders **30**(1), 89–101 (2021). https://doi.org/10.15724/jslhd.2021.30.1.089
4. Morris, J.T., Thompson, N.A.: User personas: smart speakers, home automation and people with disabilities. J. Technol. Persons Disabilities **8**, 237–256 (2022)
5. Beukelman, D., Light, J.C.: Augmentative & Alternative Communication: Supporting Children and Adults with Complex Communication Needs. Bookes Publishing (2020)
6. Park, H., Lee, S.: A study on the factors affecting the intention to use artificial intel-ligence speakers of the people with physical disability. J. Korea Contents Association **21**(1), 572–578 (2021). https://doi.org/10.5392/JKCA.2021.21.01.572
7. Google Assistant. https://assistant.google.com/ Accessed 30 Mar 2022
8. TD Snap. https://us.tobiidynavox.com/pages/td-snap Accessed 15 Mar 2022
9. Google Nest Mini. https://store.google.com/product/google_nest_mini Accessed 24 Jan 2022
10. Naver Clova. https://clova.ai Accessed 24 Jan 2022
11. Kakao Mini. https://kakao.ai/product/kakaomini Accessed 24 Jan 2022
12. Samsung Galaxy Home Mini. https://www.samsung.com/sec/ai-speaker/galaxy-home-mini/ Accessed 24 Jan 2022
13. Korea Telecom GiGA Genie. https://gigagenie.kt.com/main.do Accessed 24 Jan 2022
14. ReadSpeaker Korea; ReadSpeakerTM. http://readspeaker.co.kr/kor/product/product1.php Accessed 24 Jan 2022

Language Accessibility for the Deaf and Hard-Of Hearing

Language Accessibility for the Deaf and Hard-of-Hearing

Introduction to the Special Thematic Session

Matjaž Debevc[1(✉)], Rosalee Wolfe[2], and Sarah Ebling[3]

[1] University of Maribor, Maribor, Slovenia
matjaz.debevc@um.si
[2] Institute of Language and Speech Processing, Athens, Greece
rosalee.wolfe@athenarc.gr
[3] University of Zurich, Zurich, Switzerland
ebling@cl.uzh.ch

Abstract. The Special Thematic Session on Language Accessibility for the Deaf and Hard-of-Hearing focuses on two separate groups of individuals – the hard-of-hearing and the deaf. Both groups have faced barriers to language access, but they have different perspectives and priorities. Those who are hard-of-hearing still use a spoken language as their preferred language even though they have experienced a hearing loss. Those who identify as deaf often do not use a spoken language but a sign language as their preferred language. This session contains a wide range of papers that illustrate different aspects of using language technologies in various environments. Studies show the possibilities for improvements in higher education, captioning, and sign language interpretation, all with the common purpose of fostering better access to language.

Keywords: Accessibility · Deaf and hard-of-hearing · Hearing systems · Captioning · Sign language avatars

1 Introduction

Studies in Europe and USA show that around 10–15% of the population is either deaf or hard-of-hearing (World Health Organization 2021). In the United States, one in eight people aged 12 years or older has hearing loss in both ears (Lin et al. 2011), and the percentage is expected to increase as the population ages (National Institute on Deafness and Other Communication Disorders 2021).

Although both deaf and hard-of-hearing people face barriers to accessing spoken language, they form separate groups with different perspectives and priorities. Those who are hard-of-hearing typically start life as hearing and experience hearing loss as they age. They use a spoken language, such as Greek or French, as their preferred, or first language.

K. Miesenberger et al. (Eds.): ICCHP-AAATE 2022, LNCS 13341, pp. 505–511, 2022.
https://doi.org/10.1007/978-3-031-08648-9_59

On the other hand, those who identify as deaf often use a sign language,[1] such as Greek Sign Language or French Sign Language, as their preferred language. Both groups require better access to the information contained in speech, but those who identify as deaf also require better access to *written* forms of spoken language.[2]

The impact of hearing loss can be profound. Communication with others is difficult and has worsened recently due to the impact of preventive measures against COVID-19, including masking and social distancing. This can lead to a feeling of social isolation (Vas 2017). The lack of communication also creates barriers to education and job opportunities, which has resulted in an estimated 60 billion dollars in lost productivity due to costs related to unemployment and premature retirement in Europe and the US (World Health Organization 2021).

Both groups could potentially benefit from specially designed information and communication technology (ICT). ICT holds great promise in supporting communication needs. Today's hearing devices and assistive listening technologies are powerful miniaturized computing systems, and increasingly offer options for coupling and connectivity with modern communication devices to expand access to audible and written forms of spoken language. This promises to contribute to better health and a better standard of living (Davis and Hoffman 2019).

However, even the most sophisticated technology may be of little use if it is not fit well to a person's individual usage requirements. ICT can support visual as well as acoustic modalities with pictures or written forms of speech on a screen allowing individuals to extend both their general knowledge and use of language without utilizing sound. ICT also has the potential to support translation from acoustic and written forms of spoken language to the preferred sign language of a deaf user. Additionally, using ICT for collaborative activities can encourage a group of persons to improve their use of language and their understanding of concepts as they plan and carry out their work.

There are a wide variety of technologies that have promising potential: smart hearing instruments, adaptive and user-controlled hearing systems, machine learning-based hearing systems for individualisation of listening experience, algorithms for improving the acoustics of sound, and other types of cutting-edge technology which can assist people with listening, speaking, reading and writing. Further, avatar-based systems have the potential for enhancing communication for those whose preferred language is signed, and for whom a spoken language is a second language.

The following sections examine the challenges discussed by researchers working to improve language accessibility for both the deaf and hard-of-hearing communities.

2 Live Captioning

Live captions as words displayed on the screen allow real-time transcription of speech into a visually perceptible representation of language. They give all viewers, including

[1] We follow the newly (re-)introduced convention of referring to deaf signers with lower-case *d* (Napier and Leeson 2016), (Kusters et al. 2017). Previously, (upper-cased) *Deaf* was used to describe members of the linguistic community of sign language users, while *deaf* was used to describe the audiological state of a hearing loss (Morgan and Woll 2002).

[2] A *spoken language* is a language that is not signed, whether it is represented as speech or text.

those who are deaf or hard-of-hearing as well as non-native speakers, a visual medium to follow audible information. Traditionally, live captions are created by a human (captioner) who manually transcribes or respeaks the content into automatic speech recognition (ASR) software. In this way, the quality of live captioning is affected by the delay of a human's response in listening and transcribing live speech, and, consequentially, has a higher error rate due to transcribing under pressure. A study by Karam et al. (2022) demonstrates that the pressure brings a higher perceived subjective mental workload to captioners, especially when live-captioning fast-paced sports, talk shows, and weather.

To help to overcome this challenge, ASR has started to be used widely. With the rise of artificial intelligence (AI) technology in the last decade, the quality of ASR has increased rapidly. A recent comparison of commercial software reported up to 94% accuracy for live conversations, however, this rate was only achieved with recordings of excellent audio quality (Piskorek et al. 2022). There is a need to achieve 98% accuracy. For this reason, manual editing of automatic captions is still necessary. Piskorek et al. (2022) present a possible solution with the help of collaboratively corrected AI-generated live captions. In their study they compared the accuracy rates of the AI-generated and user-corrected captions using the Word Error Rate (WER) metric, which showed promising results for collaborative work on captions.

The WER metric which was used in Piskorek's study is widely employed in the development of caption metrics. However, there is a question if this metric is actually appropriate for measurement of caption quality. Current research focuses on human-centered metrics, and Wells et al. (2022) conducted a user study in which they compared two caption metrics, the traditional WER and the human-centric Automated-Caption Evaluation (ACE), for their suitability in evaluating caption quality in live television. Interestingly, they found that ACE was more sensitive to large accumulations of errors than WER and penalized those errors more than human participants would. However, the difference in performance between WER and ACE was not statistically significant. Therefore, there is still a need to explore usability and optimization of human-centric captions metrics for the measurement of caption quality.

Another interesting discussion regarding captions is the question of their placement on screen. Olson et al. (2022) investigated preferences by deaf and hard-of-hearing users and found that the target audiences prefer to have captions appear to the right of a speaker's head, especially in Web Real-Time Communication (WebRTC) environments together with a texting format that allows real-time text communication in a letter-by-letter mode.

In another application of captions, Suzuki et al. (2022) investigated the use of see-through live captions as part of a guided tour in a museum as a typical environment where deaf and hard-of-hearing people need assistance. The study showed that the proposed see-through captions were well received, however, there were issues related to the design of the system itself, such as its application for sign language users, who were not fully accommodated by this text-based system. According to the researchers, it will be necessary to consider an interface using sign language, such as sign language avatars.

3 Sign Language Avatars

For their entire lives, deaf sign language users struggle with a barrier to information. The barrier is not simply one of sound but one of language. Sign languages are independent, fully qualified linguistic systems in their own right and thus are different from spoken languages. For a person using a sign language as a first, or preferred language, even the written form of a spoken language poses a barrier, because the spoken language is different from their preferred language. Reliable access to spoken language requires the services of certified sign language interpreters. Unfortunately, qualified interpreters are in very short supply, and can be difficult to find. Without professional and sufficient interpretation services, deaf sign language users' participation in education, society and general social life is severely hampered, especially if majority members are not sign-language-competent.

Avatars that display sign languages have the potential to improve accessibility for deaf sign language users when used as part of an automatic translation system. Such technology could possibly remove the necessity of finding an interpreter in situations that would be simple if both parties shared a common language. However, the use of animated avatars instead of professional human interpreters is regarded very critically from different perspectives, as noted in the study by Krausneker and Schügerl (2022). They researched opinions and perceptions and discuss possible long-term effects of using sign language avatars. The study showed that deaf and hearing participants were critical towards sign language avatars but not categorically opposed to them. In principle, having quick and easy access to information would be a welcome development, but current technology is not equal to the task.

4 Environmental Sound Recognition

Deaf and hard-of-hearing people usually cannot recognize the sounds of daily life, such as running water, door chimes, home alarms and other sudden and occasional sounds. These sounds are called environmental sounds, and deaf and hard-of-hearing people need warning signs communicated to them by their family, friends, and even hearing assistance dogs and special products which are used to support them. A study, carried out by Furukawa et al. (2022), investigates how to convert environmental sounds into visual information or vibrations and to present them to the final users. Using support vector machines, the researchers were able to achieve an average discrimination rate of 83.3% for six types of sound (from car horn to natural background noises).

5 Assistive Technology

Due to the COVID-19 pandemic it was evident that assistive, mobile, and other contemporary accessible technologies have become increasingly important in the everyday lives of deaf and hard-of-hearing people. This target group already has difficulties with access and active participation in communication, education, and social engagement. During the pandemic the shift to online communication and use of assistive technology caused additional challenges. A study by Halbach (2022) shows that deaf and hard-of-hearing people have been dependent on their hearing instruments and assistive technologies. According to the study, approximately 75% of users were satisfied or very satisfied with their assistive technologies, which primary refers to hearing aids. Other people, especially elderly, were not equally satisfied since they have difficulties using the devices in their everyday lives. The survey shows a number of technical solutions for several situations. However, the author also uncovered several areas where technology can be improved. This picture of technology as an enabler with weaknesses was confirmed by interviews.

In this way, it is important to determine which technologies are currently available for the purpose of communicating, listening to speech and audio devices, sound recognition, informing, sensing, alerting, and learning. A study by Kožuh et al. (2022) provides a comprehensive list of assistive technologies and a list of mobile technologies together with a description of new technologies, like WebRTC, ASR and Metaverse. It is evident that technologies for communication and language acquisition are among the most important assistive technologies.

6 Conclusion

The richly diverse papers in this special thematic session cover a wide range of exciting innovations and provide thoughtful analyses that lend a clear-eye perspective on the current state of the art. Although the technologies differ quite remarkably one from another, they all are designed for improved accessibility – accessibility to late-breaking broadcast news, accessibility to classroom lectures, to guided tours, to the surrounding environment and even to entirely different languages. Innovations of these sorts will make possible future gains in productivity through higher educational achievement, better health care and improved job opportunities.

Entwined and intrinsic to the theme of accessibility is the centrality of the user and user needs. Sensibility to the usability of assistive technology, as demonstrated in these papers, is essential for continued innovation and progress toward the goal of equal accessibility for all.

Acknowledgements. The study was co-funded by the European Commission, in the framework of the research project Smart Solutions for the Inclusion of Students with Disabilities in Higher Education, Grant number Ref. 2020-1-LV01-KA203-077455, and the EASIER project, Horizon 2020 Programme under grant agreement number 101016982.

References

Kožuh, I., Čakš, P., Debevc, M.: Contemporary technologies assisting students with hearing loss in higher education. In: Petz, A., Hoogerwerf, E.J., Mavrou, K. (eds.) Assistive Technology, Accessibility and Inclusion, ICCHP-AAATE 2022 Access Compendium. Johannes Kepler University, Linz (2022, accepted for publication). https://www.icchp-aaate.org

Davis, A.C., Hoffman, H.J.: Hearing loss: rising prevalence and impact. Bull. World Health Organ. **97**(10), 646 (2019)

Furukawa, M., Hanafusa, A., Mohanaddan, S., Takagi, M., Nakajima, Y.: Environmental sounds recognition system for assisting deaf and hard-of-hearing people. In: Petz, A., Hoogerwerf, E.J., Mavrou, K. (eds.) Assistive Technology, Accessibility and Inclusion, ICCHP-AAATE 2022 Access Compendium. Johannes Kepler University, Linz (2022, accepted for publication). https://www.icchp-aaate.org

Halbach, T.: Modern communication technology, assistive technology, and hearing loss: how do they go together? In: Petz, A., Hoogerwerf, E.J., Mavrou, K. (eds.) Assistive Technology, Accessibility and Inclusion, ICCHP-AAATE 2022 Access Compendium. Johannes Kepler University, Linz (2022, accepted for publication). https://www.icchp-aaate.org

Karam, M., et al.: Workload evaluations for closed captioners. In: Petz, A., Hoogerwerf, E.J., Mavrou, K. (eds.) Assistive Technology, Accessibility and Inclusion, ICCHP-AAATE 2022 Access Compendium. Johannes Kepler University, Linz (2022, accepted for publication). https://www.icchp-aaate.org

Krausneker, V., Schügerl, S.: Avatars for sign languages: best practice from the perspective of deaf users. In: Petz, A., Hoogerwerf, E.J., Mavrou, K. (eds.) Assistive Technology, Accessibility and Inclusion, ICCHP-AAATE 2022 Access Compendium. Johannes Kepler University, Linz (2022, accepted for publication). https://www.icchp-aaate.org

Kusters, A., O'Brien, D., De Meulder, M.: Innovations in Deaf Studies: Critically Mapping the Field. Oxford University Press, Oxford (2017)

Lin, F.R., Niparko, J.K., Ferrucci, L.: Hearing loss prevalence in the United States. Arch. Intern. Med. **171**(20), 1851–1853 (2011)

Morgan, G., Woll, B.: The development of complex sentences in British Sign Language. In: Morgan, G., Woll, B. (eds.) Directions in Sign Language Acquisition: Trends in Language Acquisition Research, pp. 255–276. John Benjamins, Amsterdam (2002)

Napier, J., Leeson, L.: Sign Language in Action. Palgrave Macmillian, London (2016)

National Institute on Deafness and Other Communication Disorders: Quick statistics about hearing (2021). From National Institute on Deafness and Other Communication Disorders: https://www.nidcd.nih.gov/health/statistics/quick-statistics-hearing. Accessed 23 Mar 2022

Olson, M., Sit, I., Williams, N., Vogler, C., Kushalnager, R.: Caption user interface accessibility in WebRTC. In: Petz, A., Hoogerwerf, E., Mavrou, K. (eds.) Assistive Technology, Accessibility and Inclusion, ICCHP-AAATE 2022 Access Compendium. Johannes Kepler University, Linz (2022). https://www.icchp-aaate.org

Piskorek, P., Sienel, N., Kuhn, K., Kersken, V., Zimmermann, G.: Evaluating collaborative editing of ai-generated live subtitles by non-professionals in German university lectures. In: Petz, A., Hoogerwerf, E.J., Mavrou, K. (eds.) Assistive Technology, Accessibility and Inclusion, ICCHP-AAATE 2022 Access Compendium. Johannes Kepler University, Linz (2022, accepted for publication). https://www.icchp-aaate.org

Suzuki, I., Yamamoto, K., Shitara, A., Hyakuta, R., Iijima, R.: See-through captions in a museum guided tour: exploring museum guided tour for deaf and hard-of-hearing people with real-time captioning on transparent display. In: Petz, A., Hoogerwerf, E.J., Mavrou, K. (eds.) Assistive Technology, Accessibility and Inclusion, ICCHP-AAATE 2022 Access Compendium. Johannes Kepler University, Linz (2022, accepted for publication). https://www.icchp-aaate.org

Vas, V.F.: The biopsychosocial impact of hearing loss on people with hearing loss and their communication partners. Ph.D. dissertation, University of Nottingham, Nottingham, UK (2017)

Wells, T., Christoffels, D., Kushalnager, R., Vogler, C.: Comparing the accuracy of ACE and WER caption metrics when applied to live television captioning. In: Petz, A., Hoogerwerf, E.J., Mavrou, K. (eds.) Assistive Technology, Accessibility and Inclusion, ICCHP-AAATE 2022 Access Compendium. Johannes Kepler University, Linz (2022). https://www.icchp-aaate.org

World Health Organization World report on hearing (2021). From World Health Organization: https://apps.who.int/iris/bitstream/handle/10665/339913/9789240020481-eng.pdf. Accessed 23 Mar 2022

Contemporary Assistive Technologies for Students with Hearing Loss in Higher Education

Ines Kožuh(✉), Peter Čakš, and Matjaž Debevc

Faculty of Electrical Engineering and Computer Science, University of Maribor, Maribor, Slovenia
{ines.kozuh,peter.caks,matjaz.debevc}@um.si

Abstract. The COVID-19 pandemic has brought several challenges to students with hearing loss in Higher Education. Accordingly, assistive, mobile and other contemporary accessible technologies have become more important than ever before. This study provides an overview of the needs and requirements of students with hearing loss in Higher Education. The findings, firstly, include a list of assistive technologies for the purpose of communicating, listening to speech and audio devices, sound recognition, informing, sensing, alerting and learning. Secondly, the findings provide a list of mobile technologies for the purpose of communicating, managing sound, sensing, alerting, learning sign language, learning in general and leisure activities. Thirdly, the findings encompass new dimensions of contemporary technologies, having the potential to support students with hearing loss in challenging educational settings. These findings may primarily serve students with hearing loss, practitioners in Higher Education and other relevant stakeholders.

Keywords: D/deaf · Hard of hearing · Hearing loss · Assistive technology · Higher education

1 Introduction

The current situation in society regarding the COVID-19 outbreak has brought several challenges to Higher Education (HE). The education process has either moved online, has been performed fully physically in the premises of HE institutions, or both approaches have been combined.

Such conditions have become even more challenging for students with hearing loss. They already have difficulties with access and active participation in the education process when it is held face-to-face. During the COVID-19 pandemic, the shift to online learning caused additional challenges, as teachers' support was inadequate, and the content of learning systems was in some way inaccessible [1].

Thus, The World Federation of the Deaf and its Youth Section have released a Statement and Guidelines on Best Practice for Access to Higher Education for Deaf Students during the COVID-19 pandemic. It was stressed that Deaf students must be

K. Miesenberger et al. (Eds.): ICCHP-AAATE 2022, LNCS 13341, pp. 512–521, 2022.
https://doi.org/10.1007/978-3-031-08648-9_60

considered when the change in the implementation of the education process is performed, national sign language interpretation must be provided, and all course materials must be accessible to all students at the time of release [2].

As the support of the personnel at HE institutions was found to be limited during the COVID-19 pandemic [1], it is essential that students with hearing loss and other relevant stakeholders, such as teachers and tutors, are informed about available assistive, mobile, and other contemporary technologies that may support them in various forms. The current study thus aims to review the needs and requirements of students with hearing loss in HE, and, consequently, aims to respond by providing the list of available contemporary technologies which was an output of the Erasmus+ KA2 Strategic Partnership project "Smart Solutions for Inclusion of Students with Disabilities in Higher Education" (hereinafter the project) [3].

2 Needs and Requirements of Students with Hearing Loss in Higher Education

Hearing loss pertains to a decline in the intensity of sound perception where higher frequencies are usually affected more than lower frequencies. Hearing loss can be treated from various perspectives, such as medical, cultural, culturo-linguistic, and social [4–6]. According to the medical model, hearing loss is treated as a disability where various categories of hearing loss are defined, ranging from mild to profound hearing loss. In this paper, we rely on the medical model when referring to students with hearing loss.

There is a lack of detailed statistics on how many students with hearing loss are currently included in HE. Worldwide, more than 1 billion people live with some form of disability [7], and in the student population over 10% have at least one special educational need [8]. The European figures show that the percentage of students with disabilities included in HE is even 25% or above in some national cases. A similar trend has been observed in the USA [9]. Regarding hearing loss, statistics show that, in Slovenia, 1% of deaf people had HE in 2011 [10].

The needs and requirements of students with hearing loss are very heterogeneous. Those related to communication seem to be the most important. No two students with hearing loss are the same. They either need technical adaptations at HE institutions for Assistive Technology (AT) to be used efficiently, or they rely more on visual communication approaches due to sign language use [11]. Another type of needs and requirements are related to the availability of personnel at the HE institutions who may assist students when they need certain adaptations.

3 Response to the Needs and Requirements of Students with Hearing Loss in Higher Education

3.1 Methodology

The authors selected a literature review as the basis for empirical research and remote personal interviews with four deaf and hard of hearing students. For the literature review, we chose a review in the period from 2017 to 2022, which allowed an overview of the latest technologies rather than outdated ones. For the search, we used the internal search engine of the University of Maribor UM: NIK, which provides access to large amounts of electronic resources, including Science Direct, Springer Link, IEEE Xplore, Taylor & Francis, and others. The keywords were: "Assistive Technology", "Deaf", "Hard of Hearing" and "Education". Further, the authors used the database Global Accessibility Reporting Initiative (GARI) for searching, which is a project designed to help identify accessible devices and applications. In addition, we acquired requirements and needs from four deaf and hard of hearing students, with whom we had email communication and conducted a semi-structural interview with them.

3.2 Support to Students with Hearing Loss in Higher Education

The academic performance of students with hearing loss relies heavily on the available and effective support services [12]. These can include support in terms of human resources, advice on teaching styles tailored to individual needs and technical aids [13].

Firstly, support as human resources may include sign language interpreting, as those students who use sign language as a preferred means of communication are reported to have more significant difficulties during the speech-based education process [14]. For instance, in some European countries, students have an official right to a sign language interpreter [15]. Nevertheless, there is a lack of sign language interpreters according to the needs, and not all of them have the required competencies to be able to interpret the content from various disciplines professionally, and the available number of sign language interpreter hours financed by the State does not cover the actual needs [16]. These issues are even more evident when the education process is held online, or when a combined approach is performed of online and face-to-face education processes.

Secondly, while teachers are advised to tailor their teaching styles to individual needs, they are frequently unaware of how to perform such adaptations appropriately [17]. They may follow specific guidelines in one-to-one communication and communication in a group. In one-to-one communication, the following is essential [18]:

- A person's attention needs to be gained before the speaker starts talking.
- The speaker should be seen clearly to enable lip reading.
- When wearing masks is required, it is recommended to wear a protective transparent shield instead of a mask.
- The speaker must speak clearly and at a medium speed.
- The speaker should have enough lighting on the face.
- The use of visual aids, gestures and posture to emphasise something.
- In the case of major communication difficulties, the speaker can also write down what has been said.

Likewise, the group activities involving students with hearing loss should consider the following [18]:

- The speaker should use a sound system with wireless devices (a transmitter with microphone and receivers for hearing aids, or cochlear implants)
- The sign language interpreter should be present near the speaker if needed.

- The "Raise your hand" rule, whereby a student who wants to say something raises his/her hand and only one student speaks at a time.
- Use of leaflets or collaborative online documents with the main topics of the activity.

Thirdly, in the HE process, technical aids may have a vital role for students with hearing loss. During the COVID-19 pandemic such technology has turned out to be an efficient support when the education process has been altered [1, 19]. However, it is significant that students with hearing loss and practitioners in HE are informed about available technologies that may assist them. Thus, we present a response to these needs and requirements which was examined in the project.

3.3 Assistive Technologies Supporting Students with Hearing Loss in Higher Education

Assistive Technology (AT) is "a term covering the systems and services related to the delivery of assistive products and services" [20]. According to the Assistive Technology Act of 2004 [21], AT can be defined as "any item, piece of equipment, or product system, whether acquired commercially, modified, or customised, that is used to increase, maintain or improve the functional capabilities of individuals with disabilities". Table 1 lists ATs for students with hearing loss, where the purpose of use is defined as well as found in the literature review.

Table 1. Assistive technologies supporting students with hearing loss.

Purpose	Assistive technology	Description
Communication, listening to speech and audio devices	FM system	A wireless device, with frequency modulation, helps people hear audio devices better in noisy listening situations, or to a voice at a distance. The transmitter with remote microphone and receiver is typically used, in conjunction with hearing aids or cochlear implants
	Classroom audio distribution systems	Allows amplifying the speech of the person wearing the microphone for everyone present in the room, and provides an added boost to those with hearing aids and cochlear implants

(*continued*)

Table 1. (*continued*)

Purpose	Assistive technology	Description
	Hearing loop	A hearing loop (also an audio induction loop) provides a magnetic, wireless signal that is picked up by the hearing aid when it is set to the "Telecoil" setting. The hearing loop consists of a microphone, an amplifier which sends the signal through the loop cable, and a wire placed around the perimeter of a specific area
	Personal hearing loop	A powered personal neck loop which allows connection to any external audio device (e.g. a Smartphone) that has a 3.5 mm headset socket
	Infrared systems	A wireless device, with infrared technology, is used for amplifying conversations and audio devices for use with or without a hearing aid. The sound source signal is sent by the transmitter with a remote microphone on an infrared bandwidth in line of sight. The receivers use either headphones or neck loop listening options
	Bluetooth streamer	A streamer provides a communication link between the wireless technology in the hearing aids and any Bluetooth-enabled device. The streamer can be worn around the neck, or in a pocket

(*continued*)

Table 1. (*continued*)

Purpose	Assistive technology	Description
	WiFi audio transmitter	It can be connected to any audio device, and connect a sound receiver to the same Wi-Fi network, or directly without a router. The sound receiver is further connected to a hearing aid or cochlear implant using a cable or wireless connections for audio devices
	Text-To-Speech device	A Text-To-Speech (TTS) device reads digital text aloud. The TTS can take words on a computer or other digital device and convert them into audio
Informing, alerting	Alerting devices	They include alarms and technology with flashing lights and loud sounds to alert students in an emergency. These devices are particularly important in classrooms when fast action is necessary in an emergency, such as a fire
Sound recognition, informing	Speech-To-Text interpreting	A high-quality service in which a certified provider listens to speech, either at events or remotely, and translates the speech instantaneously to text and shows it on displays. The minimum standard for a provider is 180 words per minute with 96% accuracy (word error rate). The providers use a stenotype or velotype machine with a phonetic keyboard and software

3.4 Mobile Technologies Assisting Students with Hearing Loss in Higher Education

Likewise, several mobile technologies can assist students with hearing loss. Table 2 shows their purpose of use and a description of what they allow.

Table 2. Mobile technologies assisting students with hearing loss.

Purpose	Description	Mobile applications
Speech to text transfer	Allows automatic recognition of speech and its transcription into text	Google Live Transcribe, AVA, Pedius, Rogervoice, Speech to Text, Talk to deaf, VoxSci, TextHear, Hearing Helper, Otter Voice
Leisure	Allows the possibility of subtitles for movies and TV series via a mobile phone or tablet. In addition, they allow you to organize notes and help access information	Subtitles viewer, Evernote
Notices and alerts	Allow assistance in detecting notifications and alerts with various physical signals	Braci, Flashlight Alarm
Sign language and learning sign language	Allows communication in sign language and learning sign language	Purple VRI, Signly, BuzzCards, Signing Savvy, SignSchool, Marlee Signs
Sound management	Allows adjustment of the sound	ReSound Smart 3D, Sound Amplifier, Decibel X, Chatable, Mobile Ears
Learning	Provides learning assistance	Live remote captioning, Bellman Audio Domino Pro FM
Communication	Facilitates communication (mostly text-to-speech transfer)	HelpTalk, Voiceitt, Voice4u AAC, Talk to deaf, TapSOS, P3 Mobile

3.5 Advanced Technological Dimensions on Assisting Students with Hearing Loss in Higher Education

When students were at home and not in classroom settings due to the COVID-19 pandemic, they frequently used videoconferencing applications. These do not support viewing the sign language interpreter alone in a separate window on the computer or mobile phone display easily. The possible solution is the Web-based Video Remote Interpretation (Web-VRI), based on Web Real Time Communication (WebRTC). Accordingly, the student with hearing loss can use his/her own device with a usual web browser in which (s)he uses a web-based application which further uses WebRTC, that allows peer-to-peer sharing of audio and video signals between web browsers [22].

Live captioning or speech-to-text services is another way for students with hearing loss to participate fully in the verbal communications. Live captioning provides access to spoken dialogue displayed on a screen and delivered in real-time. It may also improve the literacy and language comprehension of students with hearing loss [23]. With rapid developments in technology, the use of Automatic Speech Recognition (ASR) software has grown significantly. Unfortunately, ASR technology has limitations in the environment where dialect, low voice speakers, overlapping speakers in a group discussion and environmental noises, are included. Thus, a trained speech-to-text human professional is more accurate [24].

Metaverse, as another example of new Assistive Technology for students with hearing loss, which integrates today's Internet with Virtual Reality (VR), Augmented Reality (AR), and Blockchain technology. This is a place where students will interact virtually in an accessible way with each other, where they will gather new knowledge and experiences in simulated environments [25]. However, the development of metaverse is still at the beginning, with a need for an improvement in terms of privacy, security and social inclusion.

4 Conclusion

Our study aimed to provide a response to the needs and requirements of students with hearing loss by introducing a list of available contemporary technologies. That was also an output of the international project aimed at developing integrated digital AT system services for students with various types of disabilities.

The main contributions of this study, firstly, encompass the examination of ATs which can be used by students with hearing loss for the purpose of communicating, informing, sound recognition and alerting. Secondly, a list of mobile technologies has been provided, where students with hearing loss can benefit from assistance in communication, speech to text transfer, leisure activities, noticing and alerting, learning sign language and learning in general. Thirdly, we introduced new dimensions on assisting students with hearing loss when the education process may not be held at the premises of HE institutions. Namely, Web-VRI, live captioning or speech-to-text services and metaverse were discussed.

Our findings may serve students with hearing loss, enrolled in HE, in participating actively in lectures. The findings may also encourage those who have some hearing loss but have not enrolled in the HE process due to a lack of knowledge on which technologies may facilitate their participation. Lastly, the findings may be of significant help to practitioners at HE institutions when assisting students with hearing loss.

Acknowledgement. We would like to thank the students attending the course Human-Computer Interaction in the study years 2020/21 and 2021/22, who contributed to the content of the paper by their research. The study was funded by the European Commission, in the framework of the research project Smart Solutions for the Inclusion of Students with Disabilities in Higher Education, Grant number Ref. 2020-1-LV01-KA203-077455.

References

1. Aljedaani, W., Aljedaani, M., AlOmar, E.A., Mkaouer, M.W., Ludi, S., Khalaf, Y.B.: I cannot see you—the perspectives of deaf students to online learning during COVID-19 pandemic: Saudi Arabia case study. Educ. Sci. **712**(11) (2021)
2. World Federation of the Deaf Homepage. http://wfdeaf.org/news/resources/access-to-higher-education-for-deaf-students-during-the-covid-19-pandemic/. Accessed 03 Feb 2022
3. Smart Solutions for the Inclusion of Students with Disabilities in Higher Education Homepage. https://sssd-he.liepu.lv/. Accessed 03 Feb 2022
4. Jacobson, J.T.: Nosology of deafness. J. Am. Acad. Audiol. **6**, 15–27 (1995)
5. Torres, M.T.: A postmodern perspective on the issue of deafness as culture versus Pathology. J. Am. Deaf. Rehabil. Assoc. **29**, 1–7 (1995)
6. Ladd, P.: Understanding Deaf Culture: In Search of Deafhood. Multilingual Matters Ltd., Clevedon (2003)
7. World Health Organization Homepage. https://www.who.int/news-room/fact-sheets/detail/disability-and-health. Accessed 03 Feb 2022
8. Petretto, D.R., et al.: The use of distance learning and e-learning in students with learning disabilities: a review on the effects and some hint of analysis on the use during COVID-19 outbreak. Clin. Pract. Epidemiol. Mental Health CP EMH 17, 92 (2021)
9. McNicholl, A., Casey, H., Desmond, D., Gallagher, P.: The impact of assistive technology use for students with disabilities in higher education: a systematic review. Disabil. Rehabil. Assist. Technol. **16**(2), 130–143 (2021)
10. Slovenian press agency Homepage. https://english.sta.si/2905068/equal-opportunities-ombudsman-says-deaf-disadvantaged-in-education. Accessed 03 Feb 2022
11. Smith, D.H., Andrews, J.F.: Deaf and hard of hearing faculty in higher education: enhancing access, equity, policy, and practice. Disabil. Soc. **30**(10), 1521–1536 (2015)
12. Lang, H.G.: Higher education for deaf students: research priorities in the New Millennium. J. Deaf Stud. Deaf Educ. **7**(4), 267–280 (2002)
13. Powell, S.: Special Teaching in Higher Education. Successful Strategies for Access and Inclusion. Routledge, London (2003)
14. Richardson, J.T.E., MacLeod-Gallinger, J., McKee, B.G., Long, G.L.: Approaches to studying in deaf and hearing students in higher education. J. Deaf Stud. Deaf Educ. **5**, 156–173 (2000)
15. World Federation of the Deaf Homepage. https://wfdeaf.org/news/the-legal-recognition-of-national-sign-languages/. Accessed 03 Feb 2022
16. Vrtačič, V.: Vloga tolmača za slovenski znakovni jezik v procesu visokošolskega izobraževanja gluhih (The role of the sign language interpreter for Slovene sign language in the process of higher education of the deaf). Fakulteta za uporabne družbene študije v Novi Gorici, Nova Gorica (2014)
17. Kermit, P.S., Holiman, S.: Inclusion in Norwegian higher education: deaf students' experiences with lecturers. Soc. Incl. **6**(4), 158–167 (2018)
18. U.S. Department of Education Homepage. https://www.nationaldeafcenter.org/sites/default/files/Communicating%20with%20Deaf%20Individuals.pdf. Accessed 03 Feb 2022
19. Lazzari, M., Baroni, F.: Remote teaching for deaf pupils during the Covid-19 emergency. In: Proceedings of the 14th International Conference on e-Learning, Lisbon, 15–17 December 2020, pp. 170–174 (2020)
20. World Health Organization (2018). https://www.who.int/news-room/fact-sheets/detail/assistive-technology. Accessed 03 Feb 2022
21. American Foundation for the Blind, The Assistive Technology Act of 2004. www.afb.org. Accessed 03 Feb 2022

22. International Telecommunication Union. https://www.itu.int/dms_pub/itu-t/opb/tut/T-TUT-FSTP-2020-ACC.WEBVRI-PDF-E.pdf. Accessed 03 Feb 2022
23. Debevc, M., Milošević, D., Kožuh, I.: A comparison of comprehension processes in sign language interpreter videos with or without captions. PLoS ONE **10**(5), e0127577 (2015)
24. National Deaf Center. https://www.nationaldeafcenter.org/news/auto-captions-and-deaf-students-why-automatic-speech-recognition-technology-not-answer-yet. Accessed 03 Feb 2022
25. Sparkes, M.: What is a metaverse. New Scientist **251**(3348), 18 (2021)

Comparing the Accuracy of ACE and WER Caption Metrics When Applied to Live Television Captioning

Tian Wells[1], Dylan Christoffels[1,2], Christian Vogler[1,2], and Raja Kushalnagar[2](✉)

[1] Columbia University, New York, NY, USA
{tian.wells,dylan.christoffels,christian.vogler}@gallaudet.edu
[2] Gallaudet University, Washington, DC 2002, USA
raja.kushalnagar@gallaudet.edu

Abstract. The development of caption metrics is relatively new in the accessibility research community. However, little work has been done comparing the effectiveness of newly developed caption metrics. More specifically, in low accuracy settings such as live television, where users report the most difficulty using captions. Through a user study with fifteen participants, we compared two caption metrics systems, Word Error Rate (WER) and Automated-Caption Evaluation (ACE), for their accuracy in evaluating caption quality in live television. We compared human-perceived quality statistics with each caption metric's data. Analysis of the correlation between human statistics and each caption metric found that WER had a slightly higher correlation with participants. We found that ACE was more sensitive to errors that WER, and penalized captions more than participants. However, the difference in performance between WER and ACE was not statistically significant, and neither WER nor ACE are optimized for use with live television captioning. Future work should explore how caption metrics could be better optimized for use with live television.

Keywords: Word Error Rate (WER) · Automated-Caption Evaluation (ACE) · Deaf or Hard of Hearing (DHH) · Caption metrics · Accessibility · Live television

1 Introduction

The task of evaluating the quality of captions is not an easy one. Quality in captioning has no clear definition, but for deaf and hard of hearing (DHH) individuals that use captions, quality is often synonymous with comprehension. Real-time captioning used for news, for example, are a lifeline for DHH individuals that wish to stay up to date with current events. Additionally, live videos on social media platforms such as Facebook and Instagram are a widespread tool DHH individuals use to interact with friends. The quality of captions goes hand in hand with their ability to relay information accurately and effectively to DHH viewers.

However, a lack of resources and cost restrictions often result in mistakes during the captioning process, particularly in live captioning [1]. Because computer systems used to

K. Miesenberger et al. (Eds.): ICCHP-AAATE 2022, LNCS 13341, pp. 522–528, 2022.
https://doi.org/10.1007/978-3-031-08648-9_61

evaluate captions employ a universal dictionary, live captions also often will not include proper nouns such as names, places, and people in the broadcast [2]. Captions generated with steno captioning, a process that often requires a skilled Court Reporter to create real-time captions, leads to user-based errors [3]. Consequently, holistic assessment of the quality of stenography-generated captions will require other methods—caption metrics. To assess the quality of captions, caption metrics numerically compare what is spoken with the captions. Common metrics include Word Error Rate (WER), Weighted Word Error Rate (WWER), Automated-Caption Evaluation (ACE), and NER, which are helpful for DHH individuals in rating the quality of a captioned video [4]. Although there are many different caption metrics, there is little research exploring how these metrics compare to each other. Our aim is to compare the WER, WWER, and ACE captioning metrics and assess how well they correlate with quality.

1.1 WER

WER tests the performance of vocabulary continuous speech recognition in captions, comparing what is spoken on the TV with the captions displayed on screen [4]. WER is a metric that penalizes words that are incorrect, due to a mistake in one of the three categories: [3].

1. Substitution (S)
   Substitution errors are where an erroneous word is substituted for the correct word in the reference transcript.
2. Deletion (D)
   Deletion errors are when a word has been deleted or omitted from the transcript.
3. Insertion (I)
   Insertion errors are when one word has been inserted into the transcript that was not spoken.

These three error categories do not have weights based on error severity. The WER is calculated by the following formula (Fig. 1).

$$WER = \frac{S + D + I}{N}$$

Fig. 1. The WER formula. Where S indicates substitution, D indicates deletion, I indicate insertion, and N indicates the total number of words in the original transcript.

In the equation above, the errors are divided by N - the total number of words in the reference text [3].

1.2 WWER

WWER is based on WER, except errors are instead weighted based on severity. There are 17 error types that each have a weight. Each of the 17 types belongs to one of the 3

WER error types. The calculation for WWER takes the sum of each error type multiplied by its weight and divides the sum by N, the number of words in the reference [5] (Fig. 2).

$$WWER = \frac{\sum_{t=1}^{Error\ Types} severity_t * errors_t}{N}$$

Caption Error Types:

		Substitution	Deletion	Insertion
1	Substitute singular/plural	Yes		
2	Substitute wrong tense	Yes		
3	Substitute pronoun (nominal) for name	Yes		
4	Substitute punctuation	Yes		
5	Split compound word, contraction (Correct words, incorrect segmentation)	Yes		Yes
6	Two words from one (one wrong)	Yes		Yes
7	Duplicate word or insertion			Yes
8	Word order		Yes	Yes
9	Correction by steno			Yes
10	Dropped word - 1 or 2		Yes	
11	Dropped word(s) - 3+		Yes	
12	Homophone	Yes		
13	Substitute wrong word	Yes		
14	Not a valid word	Yes		
15	Random letters (gibberish)	Yes		
16	Word boundary error	Yes		
17	Transmission errors/garbling	Yes		

Fig. 2. The results of the 2010 WGBH NCAM study. For each error type, the number expresses the percentage of respondents that determined the error type would greatly affect their understanding of the content [5].

The 2010 WGBH National Center for Accessible Media (NCAM) study surveyed deaf, hard-of-hearing and hearing individuals to define the severity of each error type [3]. The table shows the percentage of respondents who thought that the caption error would "greatly affect" or "completely destroy my understanding" of the content [3].

1.3 ACE

The Automated-Caption Evaluation (ACE) model is an automatic caption evaluation metric that was designed for use specifically with DHH individuals and ASR-generated captions. Unlike WER, it distinguishes between harmful and less harmful errors. ACE uses a word predictability score to measure keywords in a text and a semantic distance model (between the word spoken and the word displayed in a caption text) to approximate deviation [6]. Semantic distance is calculated through a tool from Google called Word2vec [7]. Finally, the word predictability and semantic distance scores are combined using a weight of 0.65 (represented by α in the metric formula). This indicates that the ACE score depends slightly more on the word predictability score than the semantic distance score. These scores are used to calculate the impact of an error as follows (Fig. 3):

$$I(e_i) = \alpha * E(w_i) + (1 - \alpha) * D(w_i, e_i) \quad (1)$$

Fig. 3. The equation shows steps on how to calculate the error by the ACE system [6].

Where e is the error word, and w is the reference word in the caption text. α is the experimentally determined weight, 0.65, that is applied to the scores. E(wi) refers to the predictability score, and D(wi, ei) refers to the semantic distance score [6]. We will be using the ACE2 automatic evaluation tool for the purposes of this study.

2 Methodology

In order to assess how well the caption metrics assess quality in captioning, we compared each of the metrics' scores alongside participants' perceived quality scores of the captions. We used clips from live television with captions that have been generated through either ASR or steno captioning as stimuli for this study.

2.1 Stimuli

The stimuli used in this study is drawn from over 200 recordings of segments of US and British live television, ranging from 20 min to over an hour in length. Accurate transcripts of the clips were obtained from the online Rev Captioning service (Figs. 4 and 5).

Fig. 4. A screenshot of Clip 2 (ABC News - Feb 5) with error captions.

Fig. 5. A screenshot of Clip 2 (ABC News - Feb 5) with accurate captions.

2.2 Participant Recruitment

Fifteen people were tested in total. Six deaf, six hearing, and three hard-of-hearing people participated in the study. The age of participants varied but most participants were ages 18–24. The gender identities of participants were 66.7% female and 33.3% male. The common methods of communication amongst participants also varied. 66.7% of participants reported that they used spoken English most often and 33.3% reported that they primarily used American Sign Language. The instructions for the study were given in the participant's preferred language.

2.3 Procedure

We conducted each individual study through Zoom. Participants were told to watch each clip one time through with captions and to respond to questions in the order they were shown. After being shown the first clip with caption errors, participants were asked if they noticed any caption errors and to rate the quality of the captions on a scale of 1 to 7 (poor to excellent). After being shown the second clip with accurate captions, participants were asked again to rate the quality of the original error captions on a scale of 1 to 7. For the final two questions, participants were asked if they felt they were able to fully understand the content of the first clip and were asked to compare the qualities of the error and accurate captions on a scale of 1 to 7 (little difference to big difference). Participants independently repeated this process 10 times for each set of stimuli and were given support and additional instructions over Zoom if needed.

3 Results and Analysis

All data was obtained through Google forms. The data from the last two questions of each set of clips were chosen for analysis, as they best encapsulated caption quality and were asked after participants had watched both the error and accurate stimuli clips. We determined that participants would be able to best identify caption errors, and thus, caption quality, if they were able to compare the original caption errors with a correct transcript. The first question (**Q1**) chosen for analysis asks: "Do you feel you were able to fully understand the content of the error clip?". The second question (**Q2**) chosen asks: "Comparing the original captions and the accurate captions, how would you rate the difference between the two?".

4 Results and Discussion

On average, participants reported that on a scale of 1 to 7, they were able to fully understand the content of the error clip at a 5.37 rating. Additionally, respondents had an average score of 3.91 when asked to compare the difference between the original and accurate captions on a scale of 1 to 7 (little difference to big difference).

The figures below show the distribution of Q1 and Q2 scores in comparison to ACE and WER. Q1 is scored such that 1 indicates little to no understanding of the error captions, while 7 indicates complete understanding. As such, a positive relationship between responses and metric scores is expected. Q2 is scored such that 1 indicates little to no difference between the error and accurate captions, while 7 indicates a large difference. In this case a negative relationship between responses and metric scores is expected (Fig. 6).

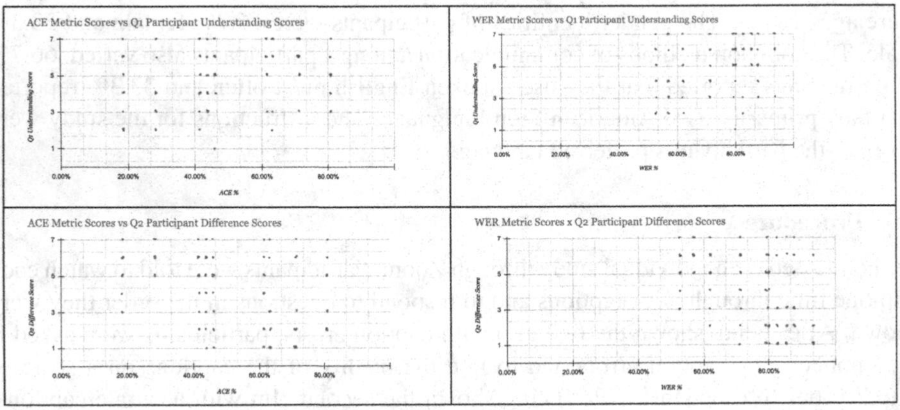

Fig. 6. From L to R: Scatter plot of all participant responses to Q1 for all stimuli with the corresponding ACE metric.

4.1 Analysis

As shown above, the ACE and WER scores differ. For ACE, Clip #5 has the greatest accuracy and Clip #7 the lowest. For WER, Clip #10 has the greatest accuracy and Clip #7 the lowest. The WER scores are noticeably higher than ACE across all stimuli. Differences in ACE and WER can be attributed to their vastly different scoring methodologies, as mentioned in Sects. 1.1 and 1.3. Primarily we suspect ACE's inclusion of word weights, and WER's lack thereof. ACE more precisely scores caption errors, which also contributes to its lower accuracy scores overall, since errors are more penalized as a result. It is also important to note that ACE was designed specifically with deaf and hard of hearing people in mind, while our study includes deaf, hard of hearing, and hearing people.

5 Conclusions and Future Work

Through a user study with fifteen participants, we compared two caption metrics systems, WER and ACE, for their accuracy in evaluating caption quality in live television. We compared human-perceived quality statistics with each caption metric's data. Analysis of the correlation between human statistics and each caption metric found that WER had a slightly higher correlation with participants. Live television may be a less suitable environment for ACE than the types of stimuli used by prior work. Data was highly varied, leading us to conclude that neither WER nor ACE are optimized for use with live television captioning. While we were able to discover much about the performance of ACE and WER in an under researched setting, there were few limitations associated with our study. The link between participants' self-reported scores and caption quality is not a direct one.

In the future, our goal is to expand this work to other metrics such as WWER and NER. Future work should also explore how caption metrics could be better optimized for use with live television. More broadly, there is also work to be done to better define caption quality in metrics research. None of the study participants involved reported having a perfect experience with captions in the past. With new analysis of caption metrics, we hope to inform future revisions of ACE and WER so that caption metrics can better assess and improve captioning for all that use it.

Acknowledgements. The contents of this paper were developed in part under a grant from the National Science Foundation, grant #1757836 (REU AICT) and under a grant from the National Institute on Disability, Independent Living, and Rehabilitation Research (NIDILRR grant number #90DPCP0002). NIDILRR is a Center within the Administration for Community Living (ACL), Department of Health and Human Services (HHS). The contents of this poster do not necessarily represent the policy of NIDILRR, ACL, HHS, and you should not assume endorsement by the Federal Government. We thank Akhter Al-Amin and Mariana Arroyo Chavez for their help with calculating the caption metrics for the videos.

References

1. Jang, P.J., Hauptmann, A.G.: Improving acoustic models with captioned multimedia speech. In: Proceedings IEEE International Conference on Multimedia Computing and Systems, vol. 2, pp. 767–771. IEEE, June 1999
2. Block, M.H., Okrand, M.: Real-time closed-captioned television as an educational tool. Am. Ann. Deaf **128**(5), 636–641 (1983)
3. Apone, T., Brooks, M., O'Connell, T.: Caption Accuracy Metrics Project. Caption Viewer Survey: Error Ranking of Real-time Captions in Live Television News Programs. Boston (2010)
4. Al Amin, A.: Audio-Visual Caption Evaluation Metric for People who are Deaf and Hard of Hearing (2020)
5. Apone, T., Botkin, B., Brooks, M., Goldberg, L.: Research into Automated Error Ranking of Real-time Captions in Live Television News Programs. The Carl and Ruth Shapiro Family National Center for Accessible Media at WGBH (NCAM) (2011)
6. Kafle, S., Huenerfauth, M.: Evaluating the usability of automatically generated captions for people who are deaf or hard of hearing. In: Proceedings of the 19th International ACM SIGACCESS Conference on Computers and Accessibility, pp. 165–174, October 2017
7. https://code.google.com/archive/p/word2vec

Workload Evaluations for Closed Captioners

Maria Karam[1], Christie Christelis[2], Evan Hibbard[3], Jenny Leung[1], Tatyana Kumarasamy[1], Margot Whitfield[1], and Deborah I. Fels[1](✉)

[1] Ryerson University, Toronto M5B2K3, Canada
{maria.karam,jenny3.leung,tkumarasamy,dfels}@ryerson.ca
[2] Technology Strategies International Inc., Oakville, Canada
christie@tsiglobalnet.com
[3] California State University at Sacramento, Sacramento, USA
evan.hibbard@csus.edu

Abstract. Live captioning in broadcasting involves the translation from spoken words in broadcasted programming to text equivalents, speaker identification and some non-speech audio information in real-time where there is little or no opportunity for editing, or correction. Some of this live content can be too fast to type, and/or read, which then can translate into difficulties and barriers for viewers. Recently, paraphrasing has been permitted in order to attempt to mitigate some of these difficulties, but different cognitive elements must be recruited compared with verbatim translation. This research presents preliminary results of live captioner's subjective mental workload (SMW) using the NASA TLX, and their experiences with paraphrasing. We hypothesize that the cognitive processes of paraphrasing increase SMW. Results indicate that live captioners experience high SMW particularly for fast-paced sports. Paraphrasing may contribute to higher perceived SMW for live captioning fast-paced sports, talk shows and weather.

Keywords: Closed captioners · Live captioning · Fast-paced captioning · NASA TLX · Subjective mental workload

1 Introduction

1.1 Live Captioners: Investigating Workload Stresses

Live closed captioning involves the translation of spoken words and some non-speech audio of live broadcasted content into verbatim text equivalents that are combined and presented as closed captions on-screen with the visual content as it plays in real-time [1]. Currently, the process involves a person, called a captioner, who listens to the broadcast content and produces the text equivalents of the spoken words using a stenographic keyboard or respeaking technique in real-time with little or no opportunity for corrections, editing or revisions [2]. Inherent in this process are various types of caption errors such as spelling, grammar and missing words, as well as delays between the spoken words and the appearance of the captions, and differences in speed of presentation [3]. There are some techniques employed to increase the efficiency or accuracy of this process such as

K. Miesenberger et al. (Eds.): ICCHP-AAATE 2022, LNCS 13341, pp. 529–535, 2022.
https://doi.org/10.1007/978-3-031-08648-9_62

employing stenographic dictionaries customized for a specific show (e.g., with proper names). Because of the real time nature of the process, the captioner is often unable to make error corrections, which cause Deaf and Hard of hearing (D/HoH) viewers to become confused, lost, or mis-informed due to the errors inherent in this kind of captioning, creating a barrier to consumption of that content. These errors usually increase as the speed or rate of speaking increases [4]. One solution to this issue has been to allow paraphrasing as an alternative to typing verbatim text, provided that the meaning of the original spoken words is not degraded [1]. While in theory, this seems to be a reasonable solution, it may change the cognitive workload requirements for captioners from a practiced and automated "typing" process to one that requires cognitive oversight and decision making when choosing which spoken word grouping should be paraphrased and what alternative wording to use. This process, coupled with the real time text input requirements, suggest that live captioners will experience a higher than normal mental workload when including the task of paraphrasing fast paced live action content. To date there has been very little research focused on the stresses that live captioners experience while producing real time captions. Our work aims to contribute to a better understanding of the workload that live captioners experience. This paper presents an initial research study focused on exploring the subjective mental workload and paraphrasing practices that live closed captioners experience from within English speaking countries, mainly Canada and the U.S.

1.2 Evaluating Workload

There are many studies focused on evaluating the mental workload for a variety of workers and tasks, including pilots [5], nurses [6] court reporters [7], language interpreters [8], medical professionals, and machine operators. Stenographers who provide live transcripts for courts experience some of the highest levels of workplace stress and cognitive load [9] due to multitasking, working memory overload, performance anxiety, and other characteristics associated with the speed and accuracy required to input, process, and produce language content in real time [9]. Live captioners have similar tasks to court stenographers and may experience similar effects [10, 11]. To the best of our knowledge, however, there have been no studies examining the mental workload specifically for live captioners or speech-to-text translators. Like the workload of simultaneous interpreters and court stenographers [11], live captioners must produce work in real-time with little or no opportunity for review or correction, which likely increases their mental workload. Many current broadcast accessibility regulations (e.g., [12]) require verbatim captioning as much as possible, regardless of the speaking speed. However, human physical and reading limitations restrict how fast a person can type, even with a stenographic keyboard [11], and how fast a Deaf/HoH person can read [4]. An often cited maximum captioning speed is 200 words per minute (wpm) [13]. Beyond that speed, it is difficult to produce and read captions, but there are live broadcasts, which exceed 220 spoken wpm, such as live sports and talk shows.

Researchers, captioners, D/HoH viewers, and regulators have introduced the acceptability of paraphrasing to address the limitations of captioning fast-paced content. However, the task of paraphrasing necessitates cognitive oversight and decision-making processes that are not required for the automatic brain processes used in highly practiced typing [10]. These cognitive processes involve identifying when paraphrasing are needed, then determining specific and appropriate revisions. Understanding the impact of paraphrasing on a captioner's mental workload is necessary in order to develop ways to mitigate the mental and physical workload involved in live captioning and reduce the errors in live captions.

One of the primary tools used to assess subjective mental workload (SMW) is the NASA TLX questionnaire [5, 14]. This tool involves a two-step process; where a respondent decides which of six workload factors is more important to them in paired comparisons between all factors, and then rates the strength of each factor for a specific task on a 20-point scale from very low to very high. The six factors are: Mental, Physical, and Temporal Demand, Performance (satisfaction with), Effort and Frustration. The end-points for the rating scale are low/high except for Performance, which are good/poor.

2 Subjective Workload for Captioners of Live Content

2.1 Study Design

To implement this research, participants were asked to complete a 55 question online survey containing the 21 paired weighting and six rating questions for the NASA TLX, four demographic questions such as gender and education, 14 questions on captioners training, and experience with live captions, and 10 questions about attitudes and preferences for paraphrasing with live captioning.

2.2 Participants

Following ethics approval, participants were recruited through our network of stakeholders, via email, web links, and social media outreach techniques. Seventeen respondents (16 female, 1 male) completed the entire survey. The participant group represented three different countries, Canada (11 of 17), United States (5 of 17), and one from Australia. Age groups ranged from 18 to more than 60 years old, with two respondents in the 18 to 29 years age range, four between 30–39 years, three between 40–49 years, three between 50–59 years, five with more than 60 years.

The majority of participants (12 of 17) had more than eight years of live captioning experience, where they captioned a variety of live programming including nine participants who captioned broadcasted fast paced sports such as ice hockey and soccer, four captioned slower sports such as golf, two captioned talk shows (day or night time), four captioned sports talk shows, 15 captioned news, weather or entertainment news, and nine captioned other types of live shows such as government or business meetings, and live religious events. Most respondents had experience captioning more than one genre. Finally, 16 of 17 respondents used stenography for live captions, and one used respeaking.

2.3 Evaluation of Data

The workload data were analyzed using the standardized NASA TLX evaluation methodology to determine the results of the workload factor evaluations. Demographic and other questions in the survey were analyzed using descriptive and crosstab analyses.

3 Results and Discussion

Regarding attitudes and practices for paraphrasing, a majority of participants (13 of 17) worked in situations where paraphrasing was permitted, one where paraphrasing was not permitted and three where paraphrasing was not permitted but was practiced regardless. Figure 1 shows the frequency of paraphrasing for different genres of live captioning.

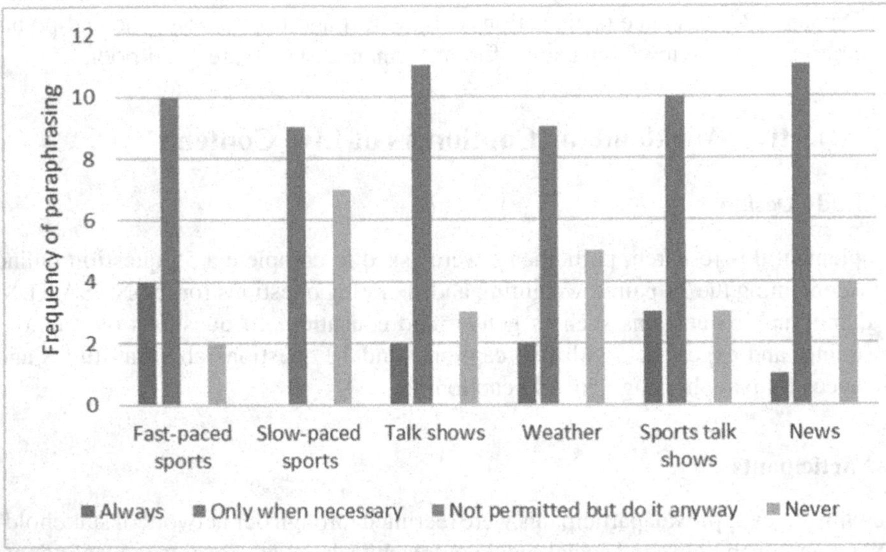

Fig. 1. Frequency of paraphrasing practice for different genres of live programming. All respondents live captioned more than one genre.

Participants were asked to rate their SMW based on the last live show they captioned. Nine captioned a fast-paced sports show, three a slower paced sports show, three a talk show and two captioned a sports talk show. In order to calculate the SMW of respondents, the NASA TLX algorithm was followed [14]. SMW was calculated to be in a range from 1 to 100 from a combination of weightings and ratings. The range of workload in these data was a low of 31.3 to a high of 99.5 ($M = 67.7$, $SD = 22.9$). As seen in Fig. 2, the SMW factor, Performance, contributed most to the SMW of live captioners, followed by Mental Demand. Frustration and Physical Demand factors contributed the least.

While there are no benchmarks for determining what SMW value is considered "high", Grier [15] divided 237 studies that used the NASA TLX into 20 different task categories (e.g., cognitive, driving, etc.). In those studies, Grier suggests that evaluation of workload using the TLX is highly dependent on the specific task type, and that the results may not be comparable across different tasks because of additional factors, such as vigilance versus complacency, determining workload. The SMW for live captioning is at or above the 75th percentile for most of the task types, including medical, reported by [15] suggesting that the SMW for live captioning is comparably high. Lowndes et al. [16] suggest that tasks with high SMW can result in reduced perceived performance in medical personnel, and modifications to tasks should be considered to reduce the contributing workload factors. In order to determine which captioning tasks to modify, and how to modify them requires further research, however, examining what is contributing to high Mental Demand ratings, and the captioner's performance is a starting point.

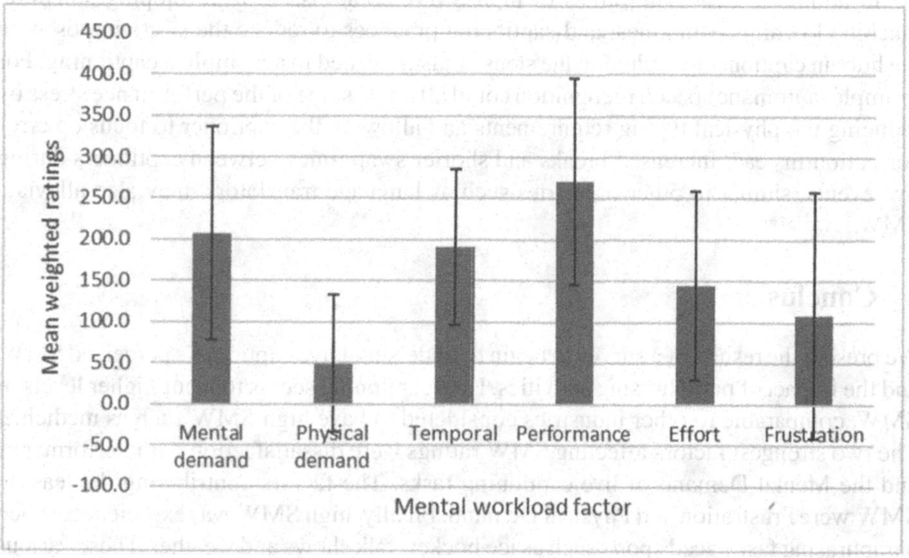

Fig. 2. Mean and standard deviation of the weighted ratings of each factor comprising the NASA TLX mental workload value. The range for individual workload factors is between 0 and 500.

The workload values for all factors and the overall SMW were segmented into high, medium and low categories, where the total possible range of values (1–100) was divided into three equal categories (1–33.3 - low, 33.4–66.7 - medium, and 66.8–100 - high). A crosstab analysis was carried out between participant's last captioned show, and mental workload factors and total SMW. There were no significant correlations, likely as there was insufficient data, but seven of nine participants whose last captioned live show was a fast-paced sports event had a total SMW in the high category.

A second crosstab analysis was carried out between SMW and reported paraphrasing practices for each genre. There were no significant correlations between any of the workload factors and paraphrasing practices for each genre, again because there was likely insufficient data or the reported paraphrasing questions had insufficient granularity to capture nuances. However, examining the total SMW distribution by paraphrasing practice, high SMW was associated with captioners who always paraphrased fast-paced sports, entertainment-type talk shows, weather, and sports talk shows. Finally, no respondents experienced low SMW in conditions where paraphrasing was always used or considered necessary for any genre. It appeared that paraphrasing tasks affected SMW in that live captioners experienced medium to high SMW compared with those who did not paraphrase. Szarkowsk et al. [17] reported that the cognitive demand on real-time foreign language translators, who may have similar cognitive demands to live captioners who paraphrase, was high, but that it was potentially influenced by many factors such as expertise levels, length of time for a translator to be working on a single task, and secondary tasks. Understanding captioner perspectives, and factors, including paraphrasing, that influence perceived workload, requires further research, observation and more in depth discussion with captioners.

In addition, identifying areas of high SMW could assist in developing software, machine learning techniques, and captioning practices to reduce the stress imposed on the human captioner by reducing the steps or tasks needed to accomplish captioning. For example, automatic speech recognition could alleviate some of the performance stress by reducing the physical typing requirements and allowing the captioner to focus on error correction instead. Increased breaks and shorter swap times between captioners during live events, similar to other industries such as language translators, may also alleviate SMW.

4 Conclusion

We present the results of a survey to begin to understand live captioner's perceived SMW, and the impact of paraphrasing activities. Live captioning seems to incur higher levels of SMW, comparable to other industries considered to have high SMW such as medicine. The two strongest factors affecting SMW ratings were dissatisfaction with Performance and the Mental Demand of live captioning tasks. The factors contributing the least to SMW were Frustration and Physical Demand. Finally, high SMW was experienced when paraphrasing fast-paced sports such as ice hockey, talk shows and weather. These various factors of SMW provide pointers for future directions and modifications for practice and research in live captioning, as well as for the development of new technology or software that can reduce the high levels SMW experienced by captioners.

Acknowledgements. Funding was generously provided by Accessibility Standards Canada. We also thank Quoc Viet Andy Nguyen for preparing the survey, and all of the respondents who persisted in completing it.

References

1. Fresno, N., Sepielak, K., Krawczyk, M.: Football for all: the quality of the live closed captioning in the Super Bowl LII. Univ. Access Inf. Soc. **20**(4), 729–740 (2020). https://doi.org/10.1007/s10209-020-00734-7
2. Psutka, J.V., Pražák, A., Psutka, J., Radová, V.: Captioning of live TV commentaries from the olympic games in Sochi: some interesting insights. In: Sojka, P., Horák, A., Kopeček, I., Pala, K. (eds.) TSD 2014. LNCS (LNAI), vol. 8655, pp. 515–522. Springer, Cham (2014). https://doi.org/10.1007/978-3-319-10816-2_62

3. Fresno, N.: Of bad hombres and nasty women; the quality of the live closed captioning in the 2016 US final presidential debate. Perspectives **27**, 350–366 (2019). https://doi.org/10.1080/0907676X.2018.1526960
4. Burnham, D., et al.: Parameters in television captioning for deaf and hard-of-hearing adults: effects of caption rate versus text reduction on comprehension. J. Deaf Stud. Deaf Educ. **13**, 391–404 (2008)
5. Alaimo, A., Esposito, A., Orlando, C., Simoncini, A.: Aircraft pilots workload analysis: heart rate variability objective measures and NASA-task load index subjective evaluation. Aerospace **7**, 137 (2020). https://doi.org/10.3390/aerospace7090137
6. Vasel, L.A.: Exploring the Invisible Work of Nursing: A Case Study of Simulated Increases in Intensity of Care on Nurses' Cognitive Load, Clinical Judgment, Stress, and Errors (2020)
7. Jones, T., Kalbfeld, J.R., Hancock, R., Clark, R.: Testifying while black: an experimental study of court reporter accuracy in transcription of African American English. Language **95**, e216–e252 (2019). https://doi.org/10.1353/lan.2019.0042
8. Chen, S.: The construct of cognitive load in interpreting and its measurement. Perspectives **25**, 640–657 (2017). https://doi.org/10.1080/0907676X.2016.1278026
9. Seeber, K.G.: Cognitive load in simultaneous interpreting: existing theories — new models. Interpreting **13**, 176–204 (2011). https://doi.org/10.1075/intp.13.2.02see
10. Christoffels, I.K., Groot, A.M.B.D.: Components of simultaneous interpreting: comparing interpreting with shadowing and paraphrasing. Bilingualism Lang. Cognit. **7**, 227–240 (2004). https://doi.org/10.1017/S1366728904001609
11. Downey, G.: Constructing "computer-compatible" stenographers: the transition to real-time transcription in courtroom reporting. Technol. Cult. **47**, 1–26 (2006)
12. 47 CFR 79.1 – Closed captioning of televised video programming. https://www.ecfr.gov/current/title-47/chapter-I/subchapter-C/part-79/subpart-A/section-79.1
13. Canadian Association of Broadcasters: Closed captioning standards and protocol for Canadian English language television programming services (2008)
14. Hart, S.G., Staveland, L.E.: Development of NASA-TLX (Task Load Index): results of empirical and theoretical research. In: Hancock, P.A., Meshkat, N. (eds.) Human Mental Workload, pp. 139–183 (1988)
15. Grier, R.A.: How high is high? A meta-analysis of NASA-TLX global workload scores. In: Proceedings of the Human Factors and Ergonomics Society Annual Meeting, pp. 1727–1731. SAGE Publications, Los Angeles (2015)
16. Lowndes, B.R., et al.: NASA-TLX assessment of surgeon workload variation across specialties. Ann. Surg. **271**, 686–692 (2020)
17. Szarkowska, A., Krejtz, K., Dutka, Ł., Pilipczuk, O.: Cognitive load in intralingual and interlingual respeaking – a preliminary study. Poznan Stud. Contemp. Linguist. **52** (2016). https://doi.org/10.1515/psicl-2016-0008

Caption User Interface Accessibility in WebRTC

Michelle Olson(✉), Ianip Sit(✉), Norman Williams(✉), Christian Vogler(✉), and Raja Kushalnagar(✉)

Gallaudet University, 800 Florida Ave NE, Washington, DC 20002, USA
{michelle.olson,ianip.sit,norman.williams,christian.vogler, raja.kushalnagar}@gallaudet.edu

Abstract. We investigate caption information and communication preferences by deaf and hard-of-hearing users of captions or subtitles, which are the text representation of language, whether spoken or written, in an open-source teleconferencing platform: WebRTC. We find that users prefer captions that are displayed next to the speaker's head and a texting setting that allows real-time text communication in a letter-by-letter format for most teleconference settings.

1 Introduction and Literature Review

WebRTC, also known as Web Real-Time Communication [1] is widely used today on many platforms, such as Google Meet, Google Duo, Zoom, WhatsApp, Facebook, Discord, and Snapchat [2, 3]. It is an open-source project that allows for real-time communication between two parties through video conferencing [4]. While around only 40% of people met virtually prior to the pandemic, this number has risen to nearly 100% over the pandemic [5]. WebRTC has proved its usefulness during the pandemic, especially as it is also used for Virtual Remote Interpreting (VRI). For instance, it was considered unsafe at one point for interpreters to show up in person at hospitals, so VRI was used as an alternative to that [6]. An impressive feature of WebRTC is its speed and ability to deliver data quickly allowing it to be used for live captions, as well as Real-Time Text (RTT) in Zoom, Google Meet, and other video conferencing platforms. As such, we are interested to know whether or not captions differ between WebRTC video conferencing and news broadcasting and entertainment, including TV shows, movies, or other media.

Captioning research shows that most people prefer when captions are positioned outside of the video rather than overlaying a portion of the video, which may block content [7]. Yet another way to implement captions in an in-person environment is through using Augmented Reality (AR). AR caption users prefer captions near the speaker, particularly to the right, rather than at the bottom of the screen [8]. In-person captioning may also be implemented by using a projector where text is displayed on a board near the speaker's head, which also found that caption users prefer to have the text appear next to the right side of the speaker's head [9].

We want to look specifically at how the types of WebRTC caption-UI affect the understanding among DHH participants in a video conference environment. For example, we can adjust the caption position or the RTT frequency to find the most optimized setting for users' understanding. From this study, we intend to identify ways to improve WebRTC UI for DHH users, and thus improve its accessibility.

K. Miesenberger et al. (Eds.): ICCHP-AATE 2022, LNCS 13341, pp. 536–541, 2022.
https://doi.org/10.1007/978-3-031-08648-9_63

2 Method

We recruited participants residing in the United States in July of 2021 through social media (e.g.: Facebook and Discord) and word of mouth. Participants were compensated $25 for their time in an hour-long study, including questionnaires during the WebRTC demonstration to gather their responses based on the Likert scale.

The data we collected include a sample size of 21 adult participants. A demographic questionnaire administered to participants asked about their gender, age, ethnicity, education level, deaf identity, hearing ability, sign language skills, lip-reading skills, and experience with using technology and captions. The last few questions ask about their experience with using WebRTC. Questions include "How well do you understand speakers in TV, videos, and other media without using captions or subtitles?" with a rating scale of 1 (Not at all) to 5 (Very well).

We evaluated the following captions-UI conditions: 1) single captions for all speakers, vs individual captions per speaker and 2) captions word-by-word and line-by-line. Once participants joined the Zoom meeting and provided consent, we introduced ourselves and explained what our research is about and our agenda for Phase One and Two. During the Zoom meeting, they were asked to share their screen to allow us to follow their progress and their response in using the WebRTC demo. Participants were directed to open the demonstration link shared via Zoom chat and asked to turn the Zoom camera off for the duration of the demonstration so the WebRTC camera would work properly.

Phase One, which was designed to show the location preference for captions, consisted of four pre-recorded videos of a hearing speaker posing a series of open-ended questions to the participant, conversation-style. The caption locations were inside the bottom of the video, outside the bottom of the video, a transcript in a new window, and dynamic captioning that changed location when the speaker moved. Participants could respond either in ASL, orally, or by typing their answers. Upon completion of all four videos and respective questionnaires, we transitioned to the second part of testing.

Phase Two looked at the type of RTT style, in a constant location, during a conversational style live interview with one of the authors. In this phase, the author typed questions to the participants which showed up on their screen in the different RTT styles. The participants were required to type their responses, while their cameras remained on for us to track their responses and eye movements. All captions were at the inside bottom of the video, but the RTT style changed from letter-by-letter to word-by-word, then to line-by-line. For the last two RTT styles, participants saw a status of "[author] is typing.." to reduce the speculation of whether the interviewer was still typing. As in Phase One, participants completed short questionnaires after completing each scenario.

Between both phases, there were seven scenarios that participants were asked to evaluate. The captioning conditions are listed in Fig. 1 below:

Video (location of captions)	RTT (style and location of captions)
Inside & bottom of the video	Letter by letter (by typing)
Outside & bottom of the video	Letter by letter (by typing)
Transcript off to the side	Letter by letter (by typing)
Next to the speaker's head	N/A style
Inside & bottom of the video	Letter by letter (by typing)
Inside & bottom of the video	Word by word (by typing)
Inside & bottom of the video	Line by line (by typing)

Fig. 1. Captioning conditions

3 Results

The data we gathered from participants for each video condition is summarized in Fig. 2 below. "Mean understanding" was the average rating provided among participants for the question "How easy was it for you to understand the caption?" Mean visibility" was the average rating that participants gave for the question "How easy was it for you to see the captions and the speaker at the same time?" "Mean favorites" was the average response to the question "Can you organize the live captions settings you've seen from most favorite to least?".

Video Conditions	Mean understanding	Mean visibility	Mean favorites
Inside the video	4.428571429	3.904761905	3.095238095
Outside the video	3.952380952	3.333333333	2.19047619
Transcript	4.095238095	2.666666667	1.476190476
Dynamic	4.714285714	4.666666667	3.238095238

Fig. 2. Responses for video conditions

The data for RTT conditions are summarized below in Fig. 3, where "Mean predictability" refers to "How often did you know what the other person was going to say before they finished?" "Mean favorites" refers to "Can you organize the texting settings you've seen from most favorite to least?".

RTT Conditions	Mean predictability	Mean favorites
letter-by-letter	3.904761905	2.571428571
word-by-word	3.666666667	2.285714286
line-by-line	2.428571429	1.142857143

Fig. 3. Responses for RTT conditions

4 Discussion and Analysis

Our data shows that the majority of participants prefer dynamic captions regardless of their main form of communication shown. This could be because the closer the captioning is to the speaker's head, the easier it is to watch facial expressions and identify emotions. There were a couple of outliers among the participants who preferred the captions on a transcript window or outside of the video instead to avoid obscuring any content. We compared the main form of communication among our participants and their preference for the RTT settings in Fig. 4 below.

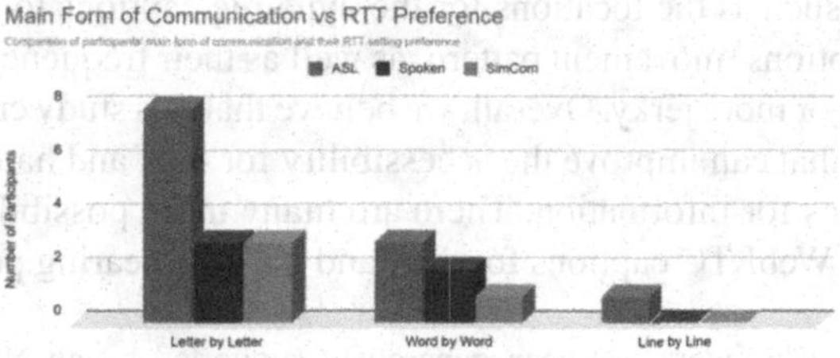

Fig. 4. Main form of communication vs RTT preference

Out of all RTT settings we tested, most participants disliked line-by-line because they were unsure if a speaker was still typing despite our typing indicator at the top of the video. They preferred the letter-by-letter format. We believe that it is because they liked the predictability of RTT with letter-by-letter which allowed them to know what the typing user may want to convey before they've finished, which gives the participant more time to think and respond.

5 Limitations

Several issues arose during the study which may have affected the accuracy of the data.

The most notable one was the Internet speed on our side as well as the participants' side. Contrary to our literature review, our study required more speed and stability in the connection in order for us both to see each other smoothly with no latency.

The live caption errors weren't consistent. For example, when the speaker says, "without them," the captions sometimes show, "without the map," while at other times completely omit a word, or on rare occasions convey the speaker's words correctly. Hence, participants saw different versions of the captions which we did not intend.

6 Conclusion and Future Work

Based on our study, we found that in one-on-one or speaker-to-audience video conference settings, the dynamic captions based on face tracking settings were preferred over outside of video captions, inside of video captions, and transcripts in another window. We believe that this is because it is easier to read captions and at the same time keep track of the speaker's facial expressions as well as their lips for understanding when the captions are close to the speaker's head as he moves. The letter-by-letter style is ranked first for RTT preference. We believe it is because it is much quicker for participants to know what the other side is about to say which allows them to respond quickly for faster communication As such, we propose that dynamic caption be one of the options in the caption setting for the WebRTC environment along with a letter-by-letter RTT setting. We did not include Internet speed as a factor to test the quality of WebRTC during sessions. Lastly, we hope the future study will increase the sample size based on some factors such as age groups, race, main language preferences, or caption reliance. Additionally, we can focus on things such as the font size, font color, or font family as some participants feel like the fonts are too big whereas other participants feel like it is too small.

Dynamic captioning is also a possibility to focus on in a future study by testing various conditions such as the locations for the dynamic captions to be placed near the speaker, and the captions' movement pattern, as well as their frequency in the movement to make it less jerky or more jerky. Overall, we believe that this study creates a foundation for future research that can improve the accessibility for deaf and hard-of-hearing users who rely on captions for information. There are many more possibilities in improving the accessibility of WebRTC captions for deaf and hard-of-hearing people.

Acknowledgements. This work has been generously supported by an NSF REU Site Grant (#1757836) awarded to Dr. Raja Kushalnagar, PI, and Dr. Christian Vogler, Co-PI. We would like to thank all of our mentors, Dr. Raja Kushalnagar, Dr. Christian Vogler, Mr. Norman Williams, and Katja Jacobs from Gallaudet University who helped and invested their time supporting our research and we would like to thank REU AICT for the opportunity to do this research.

References

1. Bergkvist, A., Burnett, D.C., Jennings, C., Narayanan, A. (eds.) WebRTC 1.0: Real-time Communication Between Browsers, 27 October 2011. https://www.w3.org/TR/2011/WD-webrtc-20111027/
2. Gross, G.: WebRTC technologies prove to be essential during pandemicGrant Gross. IETF, 8 December 2020. https://www.ietf.org/blog/webrtc-pandemic/
3. Morton, A.: Top 19 Companies in WebRTC. AT&T Developer, 31 August 2015. https://developer.att.com/blog/top-19-companies-in-webrtc
4. WebRTC (n.d.). https://webrtc.org/
5. Standaert, W., Muylle, S., Basu, A.: Business meetings in a post-pandemic world: when and how to meet virtually? Bus. Horiz. (2021). https://doi.org/10.1016/j.bushor.2021.02.047. ISSN 0007-6813
6. Henney, A.J., Tucker, W.D.: Video relay service for deaf people using WebRTC. In: 2019 Conference on Information Communications Technology and Society (ICTAS), pp. 1–6 (2019). https://doi.org/10.1109/ICTAS.2019.8703631

7. Crabb, M., Jones, R., Armstrong, M., Hughes, C.J.: Online news videos: the UX of subtitle position. In: Proceedings of the 17th International ACM SIGACCESS Conference on Computers & Accessibility (ASSETS 2015), pp. 215–222. Association for Computing Machinery, New York (2015). https://doi.org/10.1145/2700648.2809866
8. Kurahashi, T., Suemitsu, K., Zempo, K., Mizutani, K., Wakatsuki, N.: Disposition of captioning interface using the see-through head-mounted display for conversation support. In: 2017 IEEE 6th Global Conference on Consumer Electronics (GCCE), pp. 1–4 (2017). https://doi.org/10.1109/GCCE.2017.8229441
9. Behm, G.W., Kushalnagar, R.S., Stanislow, J.S., Kelstone, A.W.: Enhancing accessibility of engineering lectures for deaf & hard-of-hearing (DHH): real-time tracking text displays (RTTD) in classrooms. Paper presented at 2015 ASEE Annual Conference & Exposition, Seattle, Washington, June 2015. https://doi.org/10.18260/p.23995

See-Through Captions in a Museum Guided Tour: Exploring Museum Guided Tour for Deaf and Hard-of-Hearing People with Real-Time Captioning on Transparent Display

Ippei Suzuki(✉), Kenta Yamamoto, Akihisa Shitara, Ryosuke Hyakuta, Ryo Iijima, and Yoichi Ochiai

Research and Development Center for Digital Nature, University of Tsukuba, Tsukuba, Japan

contact@digitalnature.slis.tsukuba.ac.jp, wizard@slis.tsukuba.ac.jp

Abstract. Access to audible information for deaf and hard-of-hearing (DHH) people is an essential component as we move towards a diverse society. Real-time captioning is a technology with great potential to help the lives of DHH people, and various applications utilizing mobile devices have been developed. These technologies can improve the daily lives of DHH people and can considerably change the value of audio content provided in public facilities such as museums. We developed a real-time captioning system called See-Through Captions that displays subtitles on a transparent display and conducted a demonstration experiment to apply this system to a guided tour in a museum. Eleven DHH people participated in this demonstration experiment, and through questionnaires and interviews, we explored the possibility of utilizing the transparent subtitle system in a guided tour at the museum.

Keywords: Real-time captioning · Deaf and hard-of-hearing · Transparent display · Accessibility · Museum · Guided tour

1 Introduction

Deaf and hard-of-hearing (DHH) people have difficulty obtaining auditory information. There are several technologies that have been developed to address this problem, including hearing aids, cochlear implants, and subtitles. Furthermore, as a social issue, various efforts and technologies are becoming more common to ensure accessibility for persons with disabilities.

Automatic speech recognition (ASR) is a typical example of a technology for people with deafness. ASR has long been considered a universal access method for audio information [21]. The introduction of such technology has

I. Suzuki and K. Yamamoto—These authors contributed equally to this research.

K. Miesenberger et al. (Eds.): ICCHP-AAATE 2022, LNCS 13341, pp. 542–552, 2022.
https://doi.org/10.1007/978-3-031-08648-9_64

Fig. 1. Overview of the See-Through Captions device for use in museum guided tours. The two people on the left are visitors, and the person on the right is a guide.

been attempted in the field of education [1], and user studies have been conducted to explore how DHH people use and benefit from ASR [6,7,9]. Research has also been conducted on DHH people to freely utilize speech recognition in more varied settings than the classroom [12,22]. In recent years, research into text conversion using ASR on mobile devices has increased [5,10], and studies have been actively conducted on the use of augmented reality (AR) devices for displaying captions [4,16,17].

However, there are restrictions specific to the method of real-time captioning by ASR using such mobile and AR devices. For example, when communicating using a mobile device, the facial expressions of the conversation partner cannot be properly attended to by the DHH person because the mobile device must be viewed to see the result of speech recognition. When using an AR device, DHH people can see the speech-recognized text while looking at the other person's facial expressions. However, the speaker cannot confirm whether the system has misrecognized their words, and it may occur a discrepancy in communication.

The importance of accessibility to such speech information is being examined in areas other than educational settings, such as the museum. There has been considerable research describing the importance of improving information accessibility for sensory-impaired people in museums [8,11]. For DHH people, audible information is most difficult to access in museums. Hence, sign language-guided tours are often offered [14]. Alternatively, mobile devices have also been utilized for displaying auditory information to DHH people [2,13,18]

However, these methods have various problems. First, a guided tour with a sign language interpreter has the problem that it is difficult to recruit an interpreter. Sign language translators improve the quality of information that DHH people can receive, but at a higher social and financial cost. Second, the information presented on mobile devices is a one-way information transmission method. Although users can read the information easily when using such a system, they cannot communicate with the guide on the museum tour.

To deal with these problems, we have developed a handheld type of See-Through Captions, a real-time captioning system that utilizes a portable transparent display and allows conversational partners to confirm captions without interfering with nonverbal communication, as shown in Fig. 1. We discussed findings based on the results of a case study in which DHH people actually participated in a guided tour of a museum using See-Through Captions.

2 See-Through Captions for Guided Tours

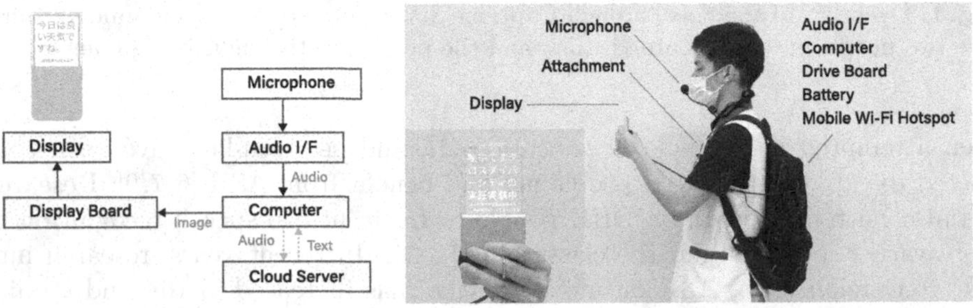

Fig. 2. System configuration of See-Through Captions.

See-Through Captions is a system that displays the results of real-time captions via ASR on a transparent display [23]. In this study, the system was downsized and made portable such that it could be used during a guided tour in a museum, as shown in Fig 2. First, we used a small, portable transparent display with a length of 8 cm and a width of 7 cm. As this prototype, Japan Display Inc.'s transparent display was used [15]. Projected images on this transparent display can be seen from both sides. The resolution of the display was 320×360 pixels. The weight of the display was approximately 130 g. Next, a headset microphone (WH20XL; Shure Inc.) was used for speech input. The computer that performed the speech recognition processing, the drive board of the display, the audio interface, the mobile Wi-Fi hotspot, and the battery were included in the backpack. The total weight of the backpack was approximately 3.3 kg. For the speech recognition process, the user inputs speech to the headset microphone, and the speech data are processed on the cloud server via the Web Speech API[1] on a web browser (Google Chrome; Google LLC).

[1] https://developer.mozilla.org/en-US/docs/Web/API/Web_Speech_API [Last access date: Apr. 1, 2022].

3 Case Study: Guided Tour in Museum

As a case study in a museum, we conducted a guided tour using See-Through Captions. We collaborated with Miraikan - The National Museum of Emerging Science and Innovation, Japan. Miraikan hosts tours for their exhibitions by science communicators. Guided tour programs using See-Through Captions were planned by discussing between authors and science communicators. Guided tours were conducted in the Japanese language.

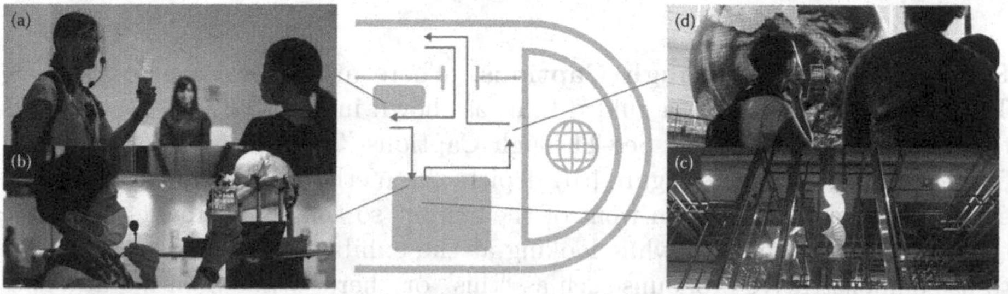

Fig. 3. Contents of the guided tour. The map depicts the third floor of Miraikan. The red arrow shows the route of the guided tour. (Color figure online)

3.1 Study Design

Tour Contents. Tour contents were designed under the following preconditions: only one group could participate in one tour, each group was required to contain at least one DHH person, a guide person used See-Through Captions when they spoke, and communication from DHH people to the guide person was through speech or writing. And the guide described the communication protocol of the tour: the guide would express "wait" in gestures of sign language if the ASR system stopped while the guide was talking, participants would raise their hand or notepad when they wanted to talk, and participants would express "applause" in gestures of sign language when someone talked one's idea. The guide described the theme of the tour and conducted some quiz games about Miraikan. After this brief introduction, they entered the exhibition area.

The tour guide explained the four exhibits. Figure 3 shows the route of the tour and the appearance of each exhibit. The theme of this tour was "The difference between humans and robots". Figure 3(a) shows an exhibition of moving androids (human-like robots). Figure 3(b) shows the exhibition of a dolphin's echolocation mechanism using sound and light. Figure 3(c) shows the exhibition of a DNA Origami's structural model. Figure 3(d) depicts the Geo-Cosmos, which is a "globe-like display" showing images of clouds. The exhibition depicted in Fig. 3(c) was excluded for some tour groups, depending on the tour's progress and other scheduled events.

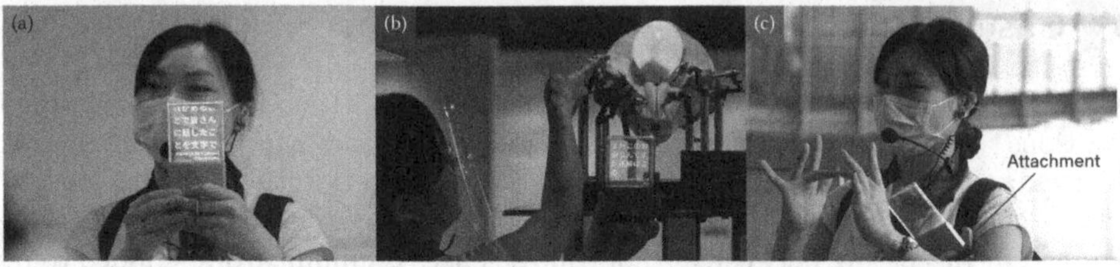

Fig. 4. Methods of See-Through Captions use in guided tour: (a) basic position, (b) overlay position, (c) hands-free position.

How to Use See-Through Captions. There are three ways to use See-Through Captions during a guided tour, as shown in Fig. 4. Figure 4(a) depicts the most basic way to use See-Through Captions. The display was placed in front of the guide's face. Figure 4(b) depicts the method in which the transparent display was overlayed in front of the exhibit so that participants could see the linguistic information while looking at the exhibit. This enabled the guide to use demonstrative pronouns such as "this" or "here" while pointing at a specific position of exhibits. Figure 4(c) depicts the method wherein the display was fixed to the chest attachment so that the guide was able to communicate hands-free. This position enabled the guide to make hand movements. For example, in Fig. 4(c), the guide describes how we can express the "International Space Station" in gestures of the Japanese sign language. Through the guided tour, the guide alternated between these three usages flexibly.

Questionnaire and Interview. We created questionnaires about the usability of See-Through Captions. The questionnaires included questions on the following: (1) the readability of the ASR results, (2) the noticeability of misrecognition of ASR, and (3) whether they wanted to continue utilizing such a device. They were rated on a 5-point Likert scale. In addition, we asked the following topics with free description questions: (4) "if you would like to continue utilizing the device, which situation in your daily life would you like to use it?", and (5) "are there any inconvenience points or improvements you think could be made to the device?".

3.2 Procedure

The study was conducted in a permanent exhibition of Miraikan. Each participant was briefly informed of the purpose of the study and told that they could exit the experiment at any time. These explanations were provided by pre-recorded videos with sign language and open captions. Participants were provided with a consent form to sign. They were then asked about the preferred position of See-Through Captions and preferred infection-prevention methods (face shield or face mask). After the completion of the guided tour, the participants were asked to fill out the questionnaires and be interviewed about the guided tour and their answers to the questionnaires. The total time required for the entire process, including one tour and interview, was approximately 60 to 90 min. This study was approved by the research ethics committee of the Faculty of Library, Information and Media Science, University of Tsukuba.

3.3 Participants

Each tour group contained at least one DHH person; some groups contained a few hearing people. We conducted nine guided tours in this study. Seven of them included one DHH person, and the others included two DHH persons. Three groups included one hearing person, and one group included two hearing persons. There are eleven DHH participants (7 females and 4 males), aged between 18 and 53 years (M = 38, SD = 10.9), four hearing participants (3 females and 1 male), aged between 36 and 56 years (M = 45.8, SD = 7.8), and one hearing participant without questionnaires. Nine DHH participants had a profound impairment, including deafness, one DHH participant had a severe impairment, and another DHH participant had not answered about one's impairment. This classification is based on the WHO's criteria for hearing impairment [3]. We recruited participants by posting on the Miraikan website and some social network services.

3.4 Qualitative Evaluation

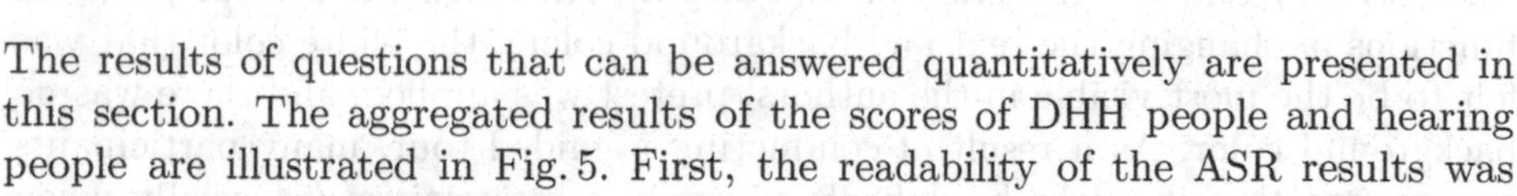

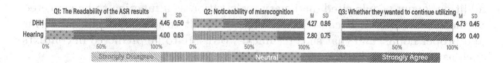

Fig. 5. Result of questionnaires (5-point Likert scale).

The results of questions that can be answered quantitatively are presented in this section. The aggregated results of the scores of DHH people and hearing people are illustrated in Fig. 5. First, the readability of the ASR results was highly evaluated by all DHH people and by all but one hearing person. Next, regarding whether it was easy to notice misrecognition in the text, some people responded that it was very easy, whereas other respondents did not find it easy. In particular, one hearing person found it difficult to notice instances of misrecognition. Finally, all participants responded positively to the question of whether they would like to continue using the device in the future. Taken together, it is interesting to note that DHH people gave higher marks to this system than hearing people did.

3.5 Quantitative Evaluation

We asked the participants to freely describe their answers to questions (4) and (5), and conducted further interviews. This section summarizes the pros/cons and issues of our method.

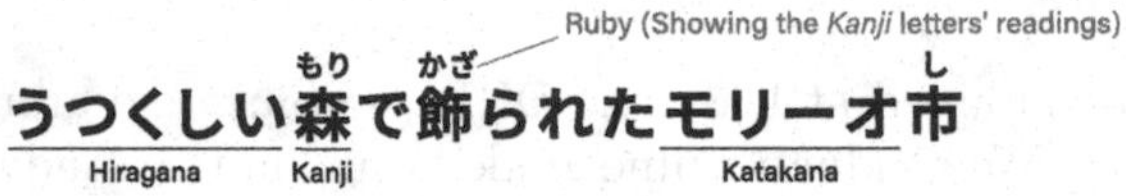

Fig. 6. Relationship between ruby, kanji, and kana in Japanese.

Automatic Speech Recognition. Because the core of this system is ASR, knowing how to interact with ASR is important. Among the functions we prepared, although ruby (giving kana above kanji to show the letters' readings, as shown in Fig. 6) was well received, many people identified that it was difficult to read when misrecognition occurred. However, such an accident is a fundamental issue of ASR, and it is difficult to completely overcome it. In the interviews, with this background in mind, participants often responded that it would be better for the speaker to acquire utterances and speaking styles that were easy for the system to recognize correctly. For example, speaking without using a double negation or writing technical terms, and proper nouns in a separate panel. In addition, many people cited dictionary registration as a function to be expected in the future. This is because it was often difficult to identify technical terms and proper nouns, and that such technical words are to be predicted in contexts such as museum-guided tours.

Readability of Captions. The readability is easily affected by the background color/scenery and the reflection on the display. Although the system provided functions of changing the text and background colors, the white color that was felt to be the most visible in the authors' pretest was applied, and there was no background color. As a result of conducting a guided tour, many participants commented that it might be difficult to see in some settings (especially when there is a strong light in the background). In addition, there was an opinion that it is important to be careful because the reflection on the display changes depending on the weather. Because these points cannot be dealt with entirely through system design, it will be important for the guide to be careful with their behavior and have a system that allows easy changes to the design.

How to Display Captions. In this experiment, the subtitle display method was basically unchanged from the initial stationary type [23], and was originally suitable for large display sizes. Therefore, in the small version, there was an opinion that the character flow was too fast and that the screen was filled with rephrasing when misrecognition occurred. There was also an opinion that the small size of the screen limited the number of subtitles that could be displayed at the same time; hence, the system should have a function to look back at the history of the conversation.

Benefits of Transparency. We were able to obtain many positive opinions from the participants that they could see the subtitles while looking at the contents of the exhibition. There was also an opinion that it was easy to communicate in both directions by being able to see the guide's face and make eye contact. Other studies have also confirmed that DHH people tend to prefer eye contact when communicating [19,20]. In addition, some participants said that transparency made it possible to see the whole without obstructing the view, and that they did not feel any gap.

Display Position. Because this was a handheld setup, it was relatively easy to change the position of the device. In addition, when starting the guided tour, we confirmed a position that was easy for the participants to see. Based on this premise, in the interview, there was an opinion that "if the display is held near the face, it is easier because there is only one place to watch."

Display Type and Size. The handheld See-Through Captions used in the guided tour have features that are not found in existing displays. Therefore, it is necessary to compare it with other methods in detail in the future. In comparison with other methods, the opinion obtained in this experiment was that although the use of AR glasses was tiring, the See-Through Captions system was easier. Alternatively, there were many opinions that the display itself was small, and there were many complaints about the number of line breaks due to the small size of the screen.

Challenges Specific to Guided Tours. See-Through Captions was originally developed as a one-to-one communication support system [23]. This experiment was the first to introduce the system to a guided tour. While there were many positive opinions, issues specific to guided tours were also found. For example, if this system is used with the guide's mouth visible, people will try to read lips and understand the presented linguistic information at the same time, which can cause confusion. When multiple people participate in the tour, it will be easier to have more fulfilling communication if the audio content of the participants is also displayed.

4 Conclusions

In this study, we conducted experiments using See-Through Captions for guided tours in a museum. While many of the evaluations of our system were well received, some issues have remained. In particular, we must carefully consider the means of information transmission from DHH people. The current system assumes that DHH people speak using voice; however, some DHH people do not tend to speak by their voice. To better accommodate communication with these people using our system, it is necessary to consider an additional input interface.

Acknowledgements. This work was supported by JST CREST Grant Number JPMJCR19F2, including the AIP Challenge Program, Japan. We would like to thank Japan Display Inc. for lending us the prototype of the transparent display, and also to thank Miraikan - The National Museum of Emerging Science and Innovation (especially Bunsuke Kawasaki, Sakiko Tanaka, and Chisa Mitsuhashi) for their unfailing support and assistance.

References

1. Bain, K., Basson, S.H., Wald, M.: Speech recognition in university classrooms: Liberated learning project. In: Proceedings of the Fifth International ACM Conference on Assistive Technologies, Assets 2002, pp. 192–196. Association for Computing Machinery, New York (2002). https://doi.org/10.1145/638249.638284
2. Constantinou, V., Loizides, F., Ioannou, A.: A personal tour of cultural heritage for deaf museum visitors. In: Ioannides, M., et al. (eds.) EuroMed 2016. LNCS, vol. 10059, pp. 214–221. Springer, Cham (2016). https://doi.org/10.1007/978-3-319-48974-2_24
3. On Prevention of Deafness, I.W.G., Hearing Impairment Programme Planning: Geneva, S., for the Prevention of Deafness, W.H.O.P., Impairment, H.: Report of the informal working group on prevention of deafness and hearing impairment programme planning, Geneva, 18–21 June 1991 (1991)
4. Jain, D., Chinh, B., Findlater, L., Kushalnagar, R., Froehlich, J.: Exploring augmented reality approaches to real-time captioning: a preliminary autoethnographic study. In: Proceedings of the 2018 ACM Conference Companion Publication on Designing Interactive Systems, DIS 2018 Companion, pp. 7–11. Association for Computing Machinery, New York (2018). https://doi.org/10.1145/3197391.3205404
5. Jain, D., Franz, R., Findlater, L., Cannon, J., Kushalnagar, R., Froehlich, J.: Towards accessible conversations in a mobile context for people who are deaf and hard of hearing. In: Proceedings of the 20th International ACM SIGACCESS Conference on Computers and Accessibility, ASSETS 2018, pp. 81–92. Association for Computing Machinery, New York (2018). https://doi.org/10.1145/3234695.3236362
6. Kawas, S., Karalis, G., Wen, T., Ladner, R.E.: Improving real-time captioning experiences for deaf and hard of hearing students. In: Proceedings of the 18th International ACM SIGACCESS Conference on Computers and Accessibility, ASSETS 2016, pp. 15–23. Association for Computing Machinery, New York (2016). https://doi.org/10.1145/2982142.2982164

7. Kheir, R., Way, T.: Inclusion of deaf students in computer science classes using real-time speech transcription. In: Proceedings of the 12th Annual SIGCSE Conference on Innovation and Technology in Computer Science Education, ITiCSE 2007, pp. 261–265. Association for Computing Machinery, New York (2007). https://doi.org/10.1145/1268784.1268860
8. Kosmas, P., et al.: Enhancing accessibility in cultural heritage environments: considerations for social computing. Univ. Access Inf. Soc. **19**(2), 471–482 (2019). https://doi.org/10.1007/s10209-019-00651-4
9. Kushalnagar, R.S., Lasecki, W.S., Bigham, J.P.: Accessibility evaluation of classroom captions. ACM Trans. Access. Comput. **5**(3) (2014). https://doi.org/10.1145/2543578
10. Loizides, F., Basson, S., Kanevsky, D., Prilepova, O., Savla, S., Zaraysky, S.: Breaking boundaries with live transcribe: expanding use cases beyond standard captioning scenarios. In: The 22nd International ACM SIGACCESS Conference on Computers and Accessibility, ASSETS 2020, Association for Computing Machinery, New York (2020). https://doi.org/10.1145/3373625.3417300
11. Majewski, J., Bunch, L.: The expanding definition of diversity: accessibility and disability culture issues in museum exhibitions. Curator: Mus. J. **41**(3), 153–160 (1998). https://doi.org/10.1111/j.2151-6952.1998.tb00829.x
12. Matthews, T., Carter, S., Pai, C., Fong, J., Mankoff, J.: Scribe4Me: evaluating a mobile sound transcription tool for the deaf. In: Dourish, P., Friday, A. (eds.) UbiComp 2006. LNCS, vol. 4206, pp. 159–176. Springer, Heidelberg (2006). https://doi.org/10.1007/11853565_10
13. Namatame, M., Kitamula, M., Wakatsuki, D., Kobayashi, M., Miyagi, M., Kato, N.: Can exhibit-explanations in sign language contribute to the accessibility of aquariums? In: Stephanidis, C. (ed.) HCII 2019. CCIS, vol. 1032, pp. 289–294. Springer, Cham (2019). https://doi.org/10.1007/978-3-030-23522-2_37
14. Namatame, M., Kitamura, M., Iwasaki, S.: The science communication tour with a sign language interpreter (2020)
15. Okuyama, K., et al.: 12.3-inch highly transparent LCD by scattering mode with direct edge light and field sequential color driving method. In: SID Symposium Digest of Technical Papers. Wiley Online Library (2021)
16. Olwal, A., et al.: Wearable subtitles: augmenting spoken communication with lightweight eyewear for all-day captioning. In: Proceedings of the 33rd Annual ACM Symposium on User Interface Software and Technology, UIST 2020, pp. 1108–1120. Association for Computing Machinery, New York (2020). https://doi.org/10.1145/3379337.3415817
17. Peng, Y.H., et al.: Speechbubbles: enhancing captioning experiences for deaf and hard-of-hearing people in group conversations. In: Proceedings of the 2018 CHI Conference on Human Factors in Computing Systems, CHI 2018, pp. 1–10. Association for Computing Machinery, New York (2018). https://doi.org/10.1145/3173574.3173867
18. Proctor, N.: Providing deaf and hard-of-hearing visitors with on-demand, independent access to museum information and interpretation through handheld computers. In: Proceedings of Museums and the Web (2005)
19. Seita, M., Andrew, S., Huenerfauth, M.: Deaf and hard-of-hearing users' preferences for hearing speakers' behavior during technology-mediated in-person and remote conversations. In: Proceedings of the 18th International Web for All Conference, W4A 2021. Association for Computing Machinery, New York (2021). https://doi.org/10.1145/3430263.3452430

20. Seita, M., Huenerfauth, M.: Deaf individuals' views on speaking behaviors of hearing peers when using an automatic captioning app. In: Extended Abstracts of the 2020 CHI Conference on Human Factors in Computing Systems, CHI EA 2020, pp. 1–8. Association for Computing Machinery, New York (2020). https://doi.org/10.1145/3334480.3383083
21. Wald, M., Bain, K.: Universal access to communication and learning: the role of automatic speech recognition. Univ. Access Inf. Soc. **6**(4), 435–447 (2008)
22. White, S.: Audiowiz: nearly real-time audio transcriptions. In: Proceedings of the 12th International ACM SIGACCESS Conference on Computers and Accessibility, ASSETS 2010, pp. 307–308. Association for Computing Machinery, New York (2010). https://doi.org/10.1145/1878803.1878885
23. Yamamoto, K., Suzuki, I., Shitara, A., Ochiai, Y.: See-through captions: real-time captioning on transparent display for deaf and hard-of-hearing people. In: The 23rd International ACM SIGACCESS Conference on Computers and Accessibility, ASSETS 2021. Association for Computing Machinery, New York (2021). https://doi.org/10.1145/3441852.3476551

Author Index

Printed in the United States
by Baker & Taylor Publisher Services

Printed in the United States
by Baker & Taylor Publisher Services